W9-BVS-980

AMERICAN POLITICS:
THE PROMISE OF DISHARMONY

By the same author:

No Easy Choice: Political Participation in Developing Countries
    (with Joan M. Nelson, 1976)

The Crisis of Democracy (with Michel Crozier and Joji Watanuki, 1975)

*Authoritarian Politics in Modern Society: The Dynamics of Established
    One-Party Systems* (coeditor with Clement H. Moore, 1970)

Political Order in Changing Societies (1968)

Political Power: USA/USSR (with Zbigniew Brzezinski, 1964)

Changing Patterns of Military Politics (editor, 1962)

The Common Defense: Strategic Programs in National Politics (1961)

*The Soldier and the State: The Theory and Politics of Civil-Military
    Relations* (1957)

American Politics: The Promise of Disharmony

Samuel P. Huntington

THE BELKNAP PRESS

OF HARVARD UNIVERSITY PRESS

Cambridge, Massachusetts, and London, England

Copyright © 1981 by Samuel P. Huntington
All rights reserved
Printed in the United States of America

This book has been digitally reprinted. The content remains
identical to that of previous printings.

Written under the auspices of the Center for International Affairs,
Harvard University

Library of Congress Cataloging in Publication Data

Huntington, Samuel P.
     American politics.

     Includes index.
     1. United States—Politics and government—
Philosophy.   2. Idealism, American.   3. Social
classes—United States.   I. Title.
JK39.H84   320.973   81–10051
ISBN 0–674–03021–4 (paper)   AACR2

For
Timothy and Nicholas
who inherit the promise

PREFACE

The ultimate origins of this book are to be found in one of my more helpless moments as a young man. At the start of my Ph.D. oral examinations in May 1949, Professor Samuel H. Beer fixed me with a steady eye and asked: "Mr. Huntington, what is the relation between political thought and political institutions?" I did not answer the question then, but I have been grappling with it ever since. This book is an effort to deal in part with this question in the American context. It was written as an extended essay and is meant to be suggestive rather than definitive. Its purpose is to set forth a way of looking at American politics that emphasizes elements that have at times tended to be neglected and to provide a perspective that in some measure explains why America has had both so much political consensus and so much political conflict.

My active work on the relation between American political ideas and political institutions began in 1973 when I was the beneficiary of a Guggenheim Fellowship and a Visiting Fellowship at All Souls College, Oxford. The results of this initial thinking were embodied in an article, "Paradigms of American Politics: Beyond the One, the Two, and the Many," *Political Science Quarterly* 89 (March 1974): 1–26, portions of which are incorporated into this book. I completed first drafts of two chapters before my entry into the government in early 1977, but the bulk of the writing was done after my return to Harvard in the fall of 1978. During this latter period my work was greatly facilitated by grants from the American Enterprise Institute for Public Policy Research and from National Affairs, Inc. Throughout, the Center for International Affairs at

Harvard helped tremendously by furnishing an intellectually and materially supportive environment for research and writing.

The refinement of the ideas in this book was forwarded by the questions and challenges to which those ideas were subjected by the students in my course on American political development. Many people provided invaluable assistance to me in my research; they include John Heine, Kenneth I. Juster, Christopher Leman, Mahmoud Mamdani, Arthur Sanders, and Steven R. Verr. Barbara Talhouni, Cynthia Knuth, and Linda Cohn patiently and expertly typed draft after draft. Aida Donald and Austin Ranney read the manuscript in toto and nicely managed to be both critical and encouraging in their comments.

To all these individuals and institutions—as well as to others not named here—I am deeply grateful for contributions that truly were indispensable to the making of this volume.

CONTENTS

AMERICAN POLITICS:
THE PROMISE OF DISHARMONY

1 THE DISHARMONIC POLITY

"Our Practice of Your Principles"

As is His wont, God did not dare. Although it had showered the night before, the morning of the second Thursday in June 1969 dawned warm and sun-drenched. Steamy vapors rose from the soaking grass and dripping chairs, carefully ordered in their rows in the Yard, promising a hot and humid day for Harvard's 318th commencement. But although the University authorities maintained their usual casual optimism about the cooperation of the Almighty, there was considerable concern that less godly creatures might dare to be less accommodating. Turmoil, protest, and violence were reaching new peaks on American campuses that spring. The previous year, Columbia University had erupted into chaos. In April 1969 had come Harvard's turn, with the seizure of University Hall, the police bust, the student strike, the disruption of classes, and the endless mass meetings and bullhorns, demonstrations and demands, caucuses and resolutions. The night before commencement, prolonged negotiations among university officials, student leaders, and SDS (Students for a Democratic Society) extremists had produced an agreement that the normal order of ceremony would be interrupted to permit one of the SDS revolutionaries to speak briefly to the throng of ten thousand. Before dawn a contingent of younger and presumably somewhat more robust faculty members had been quietly admitted through the locked gates of the Yard and had surrounded and occupied the platform—a preemptive measure to head off others with more disruptive intentions.

As it turned out, such precautions were unnecessary. Overt revolutionary challenges to civil and academic authority during the two-hour ceremony were minimal. The SDS speaker "blew it," as one student said, with a tedious, uncompromising monologue which elicited loud boos from the audience. The protest walkout from the ceremonies drew less than two hundred students. The revolutionary impulse was limited to a clenched-fist greeting to university president Nathan Pusey by the graduating seniors, serving along with the clenched fists stenciled on their academic gowns as a lingering reminder of the upheavals earlier in the spring.

The revolutionary challenge to established authority thus fizzled in Harvard Yard, as it has always fizzled in American society. But one major challenge to established authority was posed in the Yard that day, and in traditional American pattern it came not from the fringes but from the mainstream. In appropriate Harvard fashion, it was posed intellectually rather than physically. It was to be found in the English Oration delivered by Meldon E. Levine, a native of Beverly Hills, California, and a graduate student in law. "What is this protest all about?" Levine asked. Addressing himself to the alumni, faculty, and parents and presuming to speak for his fellow students, he answered this question briefly—and accurately. Our protest, he said, is not an effort "to subvert institutions or an attempt to challenge values which have been affirmed for centuries. We are NOT," he emphasized, ". . . conspiring to destroy America. We are attempting to do precisely the reverse: we are affirming the values which you have instilled in us and which you have taught us to respect. You have told us repeatedly that trust and courage were standards to emulate. You have convinced us that equality and justice were inviolable concepts. You have taught us that authority should be guided by reason and tempered by fairness. AND WE HAVE TAKEN YOU SERIOUSLY." We have tried to put into practice your principles, Levine told the older generation, and you have frustrated us and obstructed us. "You have given us our visions and then asked us to curb them." We want to do what you have taught us is right to do, but "you have made us idealists and then told us to go slowly." All we ask is that "you allow us to realize the very values which you have held forth."

Speaking on behalf of the younger generation, Levine did not contemptuously confront his elders with the claim that a youthful European Marxist or African nationalist might have made: We reject your reactionary, traditional, outworn beliefs and instead proclaim our own radical and revolutionary principles. Instead, his plea was a peculiarly American one: We of the younger generation simply want to put into practice those ideals in which you—and we—believe. It is, as he summed it up in the title of his talk, "a conflict of conscience: our practice of your principles." We question your war, your repression, your temporizing, your inaction in the name of your basic values. We do not proclaim a New Truth to challenge the old myths of earlier generations. We instead invoke the Old Truths and charge you, the older generations, with deserting those truths. You are the apostates, not we. You are, in effect, the subversives; we are the loyalists, who proudly reaffirm the principles that you ignore.

Levine's remarks were greeted with a loud, sustained, standing ovation from his classmates, while many parents and alumni, as one reporter put it, "sat stony-faced and silent."[1] As a child of the 1960s (who had been president of the Berkeley student body during the 1964 uprising there), Levine had precisely caught the spirit of that decade. By and large, the struggles of the 1960s did not involve conflicts between partisans of different principles. What the 1960s did involve was a reaffirmation of traditional American ideals and values; they were a time of comparing practice to principle, of reality to ideal, of behavior to belief. Politically the 1960s began with sit-ins, bus boycotts, and civil rights marches, focused on that area of American life where the gap between ideal and reality was most obvious and blatant. Politically this period of idealistic reaffirmation came to a climax in the end of a Presidency in which the gap between practice and principle likewise became morally and politically intolerable. The years between were filled with protests, outraged moral protests, at the failure of political institutions and leaders to perform in the way expected of them, and with escalating exposures of the breadth of the gap between political ideal and political reality. The principal struggles were between those who wanted to reshape reality to conform with the ideal—immediately—and those who were willing to tolerate the gap for varying lengths of time. Many questioned, for instance, the means and the speed with which racial inequities should be remedied, but no one articulated a systematic defense of racial discrimination. Many were reluctant to see a President driven from office, but no one systematically defended dishonesty and dissimulation by public officials. What was at issue was not a matter of principle but the way in which those principles should and could be applied in practice.

This gap between political ideal and political reality is a continuing central phenomenon of American politics in a way that is not true of any other major state. The importance of the gap stems from three distinctive characteristics of American political ideals. First is the *scope* of the agreement on these ideals. In contrast to most European societies, a broad consensus exists and has existed in the United States on basic political values and beliefs. These values and beliefs, which constitute what is often referred to as "the American Creed," have historically served as a distinctive source of American national identity. Second is the *substance* of those ideals. In contrast to the values of most other societies, the values of this Creed are liberal, individualistic, democratic, egalitarian, and hence basically antigovernment and antiauthority in character. Whereas other ideologies legitimate established authority and institutions, the American Creed serves to delegitimate any hierarchical, coercive, authoritarian structures, including American ones. Third is the changing *intensity* with which Americans believe in these basic ideals, an intensity that varies from time to time and from group to group. Historically, American society seems to evolve through periods of creedal passion and of creedal passivity.

As a result of these three characteristics, an ever-present gap exists between American political ideals and American political institutions and practice. This gap has altered during the course of American history, at times narrowing and at other times broadening. These changes reflect both changes in "objective" reality—the distribution of power in American society—and also, of course, changes in the nature of American ideals and in the intensity of commitments that Americans have to those ideals. "Witness the intensity with which" we hold to our—and your—convictions, Levine implored his commencement audience. Other decades have lacked this intensity; the rhetoric of ceremonial addresses has been the same but the passion has been absent. The age of protest of the 1960s, however, was a period of moral reaffirmation, a period in which the best as well as the worst were filled with a passionate intensity focused on the need to realize in practice the central principles and values of the American Creed.

The 1960s thus had much in common with other periods of creedal passion, when the values of the American Creed had been invoked to challenge established institutions and existing practices—periods such as the Revolutionary era of the 1760s and 1770s, the Jacksonian age of the 1820s and 1830s, and the Populist-Progressive years of the 1890s and 1900s. In a sense, the gap between ideal and institution condemns Americans to coexist with a peculiarly American form of cognitive dissonance. At times, this dissonance is latent; at other times, when creedal passion runs high, it is brutally manifest, and at such times, the promise of American politics becomes its central agony.

The One, the Two, and the Many:
Structural Paradigms of American Politics

This central characteristic of American politics has received little notice in the traditional theories or paradigms of American politics. Over the years, the prevailing images of American politics have been shaped by three such paradigms.

What is often referred to as the "Progressive" theory emphasizes the continuing conflict between the few who are rich and the many who are poor. It is, indeed, better referred to as the "class-conflict" theory of American politics, since it has been espoused by many others in addition to early-twentieth-century Progressive historians. Federalist thinkers such as John Adams assumed that "there is no special providence for Americans, and their nature is the same with that of others." Consequently, they also assumed that the social divisions that existed elsewhere would be reproduced in America. "The people, in all nations," Adams said, "are naturally divided into two sorts, the gentlemen and the simplemen . . . The great and perpetual distinction in civilized societies has been between the rich, who are few, and the poor, who are many." In similar terms, Alexander Hamilton agreed that "all communities divide themselves into the few and the many."[2] In postulating this image, Hamilton's sympathies were with the rich, while Adams was deeply and equally suspicious of both rich and poor. At the end of the nineteenth century the Progressive historians attacked Federalist politics and identified themselves with the poor, while retaining the Federalist picture of American society. The essence of the Progressive paradigm was well summed up by Vernon Parrington in notes that he wrote for but did not use in *Main Currents of American Thought*:

> From the first we have been divided into two main parties. Names and battle cries and strategies have often changed repeatedly, but the broad party division has remained. On one side has been the party of the current aristocracy—of church, of gentry, of merchant, of slave holder, or manufacturer—and on the other the party of the commonality—of farmer, villager, small tradesman, mechanic, proletariat. The one has persistently sought to check and limit the popular power, to keep the control of the government in the hands of the

few in order to serve special interests, whereas the other has sought to augment the popular power, to make government more responsive to the will of the majority, to further the democratic rather than the republican ideal—let one discover this and new light is shed on our cultural tendencies.[3]

The Progressive interpretation dominated American historical writing until after World War II, when it was displaced by the consensus theory. It was maintained, however, by Marxist analysts and radical sociologists, such as C. Wright Mills, and came back to the fore in the writings of New Left revisionist historians of the 1960s.

The key elements of the Progressive approach, as with that of the Federalists, were, first, a stress on the significance of economic interests, as distinguished from idealistic purposes, as the motive moving men in history, and, second, an emphasis on the extent to which American history (and, for the Federalists, history generally) could be interpreted in terms of the clash between two contenders for wealth and power: the popular party and the elite party. Over time, the particular groups in this conflict might change, but the struggle itself would continue. The Progressives clearly hoped that in due course the popular party would triumph, but there was nothing in their theory to specify why or when this should happen. Until that nebulous point in the distant future did arrive, American history would be an ongoing struggle between the good guys and the bad guys, and, as Louis Hartz pointed out, one of the comforting aspects of their theory was that it "always had an American hero available to match any American villain they found, a Jefferson for every Hamilton."[4]

The consensus theory of American politics posits an image of American politics that is, in many respects, the polar opposite of the Federalist-Progressive approach. According to this theory, the key to understanding American history is not the conflict between two classes but rather the overwhelming predominance of the middle class. For a variety of reasons —the absence of feudalism, the abundance of free land, the shortage of labor, the resulting opportunities for vertical and horizontal mobility, the early introduction of universal manhood suffrage, and the prevalence of a "Lockean" ethos of liberty, equality, individualism—class consciousness and class conflict never developed in the United States as it did in Europe. Instead there was the "pleasing uniformity" that had struck Crèvecoeur and the social and political equality that had so impressed Tocqueville. As a result, class-based ideologies never developed in American politics as they did in European politics. A consensus on middle-class values prevailed, and the conflicts that have existed in American politics have been over relatively narrow issues of economics and personality within the framework of the all-pervading basic consensus.

The consensus theory received its classic statement in the works of Tocqueville. It was reformulated in more nationalistic terms by the "Patriotic" historians in the latter part of the nineteenth century and then reappeared in its most self-conscious and explicit form in the two decades after World War II in the writings of Richard Hofstadter, Daniel Boorstin, Talcott Parsons, David Potter, Daniel Bell, Seymour Martin Lipset, and, most notably, Louis Hartz. The popularity of the theory at this time reflected the success of the New Deal and the failure of social revolution in the 1930s, the general prosperity and abundance of American life, and the emergence of the Cold War as the central feature of American foreign relations.

In contrast to the Progressive theorists, the consensualists tended to place their argument about the United States in a comparative context. For Hartz in particular, comparison with Europe was a central theme. Viewed from a European vantage point, he argued, the dualism that had been the focus of the Progressives shrank almost to insignificance. Unlike Europe, America lacked both feudalism and socialism. The controversies of American history were all among different varieties of liberalism. Widespread liberalism, in turn, reflected the absence of an aristocracy and of a class-conscious proletariat and the dominance of a middle class. In so arguing, Hartz used Marxist categories to arrive at Tocquevillian conclusions. Unchallenged by competing ideologies, however, American liberalism in his view lost its ideological system and rigor; it became immobile, irrational, absolute, and unthinking, at times turning in on and shadowboxing against itself.

A third theory, the pluralist paradigm, holds that the central feature of American politics is the competition among interest groups. The process version of this approach sees politics as a struggle among large numbers of relatively small interest groups. The organization version emphasizes the dominant role of a small number of large, well-organized groups in shaping public policy. Proponents of the process theory tend to be favorably disposed toward that process, seeing a rough approximation of the public interest emerge out of open, competitive struggle in the political free market, where it can be assumed that constitutional and governmental structures do not significantly discriminate among groups in terms of their access to the political process. Proponents of the organization version, on the other hand, usually emphasize the extent to which the established groups control the political process and make meaningless many of the pretensions of the democratic system premised on individual equality. At the extreme, this version of the pluralist approach can have many resemblances to the class-conflict theory.

The pluralist paradigm received its classic statement by James Madison in *The Federalist* (particularly Number 10). It was reformulated by Arthur F. Bentley in the early twentieth century, and it reemerged as the dominant interpretation of American politics among political scientists after World War II. It is, in some measure, quite compatible with the consensus paradigm, since the conflicts among interest groups over particular issues can be conceived of as occurring within the framework of a broad agreement on basic political values. In fact, one paradigm almost implies the existence of the other: they differ in that one stresses the basic agreement and the other the specific issues that are fought over within the context of this agreement.

Each of these three theories has its strengths and its weaknesses. The class-conflict theory points accurately to the existence in America of significant inequalities in wealth and income. It argues inaccurately, however, that these differences have been a principal continuing basis for political cleavage in American society. While American politics has at times been polarized, it has seldom, if ever (the New Deal was the most notable exception), been polarized between rich and poor. More generally, in attempting to sandwich American political struggle into a simple, dualistic framework, the class-conflict theory does scant justice to the complexity and variability of the struggle. For many of the class-conflict theorists, class conflict more accurately describes what they think American politics should be like rather than what it actually has been like over the course of centuries. The consensus theory, on the other hand, rightly acknowledges the absence of European class-based ideologies and the widespread agreement in the United States on liberal, democratic, individualistic, Lockean political values. Particularly in its Hartzian formulation, however, it also tended to suggest that the existence of an ideological consensus meant the absence of any form of significant social conflict. In fact, the United States has had more sociopolitical conflict and violence than many European countries. "Americans," as Hofstadter neatly put it, "do not *need* ideological conflict to shed blood on a large scale."[5] Why this should be the case is ignored by consensus theory. Finally, the pluralist paradigm—in both its process and organizational versions—clearly describes the way in which American politics functions a good part of the time. It does not, however, anymore than the consensus theory, provide for or explain the passion, upheaval, or moral intensity that at times envelopes the American political scene.

All three paradigms share one important characteristic: each explains politics in terms of social structure. The decisive influences on American politics are not the political values, institutions, and practices or the processes of change and development, but rather the nature of American society. The issue at stake among them is whether American society can best be understood in terms of one consensus, two classes, or many groups. From this structural approach flow two other implications.

First, the structural characteristics of society that shape its politics are held to be relatively permanent. Each theory, as we have seen, has had its own proponents over the years going back to the eighteenth century. The consensus theory acknowledges little or no change in the consensus. The class-conflict theory holds that the particular classes may change (that is, from landowners versus landless to capitalists versus workers), but the division of society between rich and poor—and the conflict between rich and poor—goes on. In similar fashion, the pluralist theory allows for the rise and fall of specific groups in the political process but not in the underlying pluralistic character of society or in the way groups interact in American politics. In its own way, each paradigm sets forth a picture of how American politics functions at any one point in time; none sets forth a picture of how American politics changes over time. Each is essentially static in its approach. How will American society and politics in the future differ from what they have been in the past? According to all three, the answer essentially is more of the same.

Second, all three paradigms posit the predominant role of economic and materialistic interests in politics. The upper and lower classes of the class-conflict theory are divided by their economic differences and they conflict with each other in politics over their respective efforts to maintain and enhance these differences or to reduce and perhaps even eliminate them. The interest groups of pluralist theory can include ethnic groups, but have been conceived primarily in economic terms as regional, occupational, and industrial groups. Lastly, the consensus theory does highlight the importance of political values and ideas, but argues that either the absence of such ideas or the broad agreement on them precludes serious political conflict. That agreement, in turn, rests on the overwhelming predominance of the middle class. Whereas the class-conflict and pluralist theories see American politics dominated by the scrambling of grubby materialistic interests, the consensus theory reduces it all to placid harmony and dullness.

Ideals versus Institutions

The structural paradigms of American politics are not totally wrong, but they are limited. They omit almost entirely the role that political ideas and idealism, moral causes, and creedal passions have played in American politics. Almost everyone agrees that the United States was conceived in terms of certain political ideals and inspired by the promise or dream of liberty and equality. These political ideals are central to American national identity and have played a critical role in shaping American political evolution and development. Yet the pluralist theory of American politics ignores them entirely, the class-conflict theory sees them simply as the ideological weapons of opposing economic classes promoting their own materialistic interests, and the consensus theory suggests, in effect, that because they are universally accepted they are universally irrelevant. Rich fight poor for more of the economic pie, groups squabble over their allocations of the pie, or all relax in their enjoyment of it. That the political ideals and visions which define the existence of the nation might also be central to understanding its politics and might play a crucial role in shaping its political conflicts and political development seems to be an unrecognized possibility. The structural paradigms portray an American politics without purpose, without moral conflict, without passion, without promise, and, most importantly, without guilt. Can class conflict, group process, or consensus fully explain the passions and the intensity of the 1960s, the 1890s, the 1860s, the 1830s, and, most importantly, the 1770s? The structural picture of American politics is not so much Hamlet without the Prince of Denmark as it is Deuteronomy without the vision of the promised land.

When foreigners ask, "What is American politics all about?" it cannot be explained to them simply in terms of a Namier-like struggle of faction and group, or a Marxist-like confrontation of classes, or a complacent consensus. It is, in some measure, all of these things, but it is also much more. To see American politics purely as a reflection of social structure is to miss the teleological—as distinguished from the mechanistic—dimension of that politics. The ways in which individuals, groups, and classes act in politics are decisively shaped not only by their own perceptions of their immediate interests but also by the ideological climate and the common political values and purposes that they all recognize as legitimate. The United States has lacked European-style ideological conflict, yet its politics has been infused with more moral passion than those of any European country. "America," Santayana once observed, "is all one prairie, swept by a universal tornado."[6] The consensus theory posits the uniformity of the prairie but not the fury of the tornado that the prairie's very flatness engenders. In the United States, ideological consensus is the source of political conflict, polarization occurs over moral issues rather than economic ones, and the politics of interest groups is supplemented and at times supplanted by the politics of moralistic reform. America has been spared class conflicts in order to have moral convulsions. It is precisely the central role of moral passion that distinguishes American politics from the politics of most other societies, and it is this characteristic that is most difficult for foreigners to understand.

The importance of political ideas and values in shaping the course of American development has not always been neglected in historical writing, and in part for this reason it tended to become discredited. The progressive realization of American ideals was a familiar theme among nineteenth-century "Patriotic" historians. "The unifying principle" of history for George Bancroft, as Hofstadter points out, "was progress ordained and planned by God—the advance of liberty, justice, and humanity, all of which were peculiarly exemplified in American history, where providential guidance had brought together a singularly fit people and fit institutions . . . American history could be seen as a kind of consummation of all history."[7] The same theme, viewed considerably more ambivalently, was also present in Tocqueville. Common to both was the concept of American history as a gradual but steady unfolding and realization of the ideals of liberty, equality, and democracy.

This interpretation accurately highlighted the extent to which the pursuit of these ideals was central to the American political experience. What it did not highlight, however, was the extent to which the failure to realize those ideals was equally central to that experience. The image of the triumphant realization of the American promise or ideal was an exercise in patriotic unreality at best and hypocrisy at worst. The history of American politics is the repetition of new beginnings and flawed outcomes, promise and disillusion, reform and reaction. American history is the history of the efforts of groups to promote their interests by realizing American ideals. What is important, however, is not that they succeed but that they fail, not that the dream is realized but that it is not and never can be realized completely or satisfactorily. In the American context there will always be those who say that the institutional glass is half-empty and who will spill much passion attempting to fill it to the brim from the spring of idealism. But in the nature of things, particularly in America, it can never be much more than half-full.

This gap between promise and performance creates an inherent disharmony, at times latent, at times manifest, in American society. In a harmonic society, as André Béteille has argued, the existential and normative orders are consistent with each other; in a disharmonic society they are in conflict. "In a harmonic system inequalities not only exist in fact but are also considered legitimate. In a disharmonic system inequalities are no longer invested with legitimacy although they continue to exist in fact." Traditional India with its caste system was a harmonic society because its social inequalities were considered legitimate. The United States, on the other hand, is a disharmonic society because its social and political inequalities "exist in a moral environment which is committed to equality."[8]

Social, economic, and political inequalities may well be more limited and political liberties more extensive in the United States than they are in most other societies. Yet the commitment to equality and liberty and the opposition to hierarchy and authority are so widespread and deep that the incongruity between the normative and existential orders is far greater in the United States than elsewhere. Traditional India was clearly more unequal than modern America, but modern America is clearly more disharmonic than traditional India. The extent to which a society or a political system is harmonic or disharmonic depends as much upon the values of its people as upon the structure of its institutions. Any society, moreover, necessarily involves a certain irreducible minimum of inequality and hierarchy. The variations in attitudes toward inequality, hierarchy, and authority among the peoples of different societies are likely to be at least as great as the variations in actual inequality, hierarchy, and authority among those societies, particularly in the modern world. With its unique consensus on and commitment to liberal, democratic, and egalitarian political values, the United States is the modern disharmonic polity par excellence.

2 THE AMERICAN CREED AND NATIONAL IDENTITY

Political Thought in America

The poverty of political thought in America has been a frequent source of complaint on the part of social critics and political scientists. This complaint is, by and large, justified: political theory has been relatively underdeveloped in the United States in comparison with Europe. Outstanding political philosophers and highly systematized class-based ideologies have been notably absent from the American scene. But it is a mistake to move from this truth to the assumption that political ideas have played a less significant role in the United States than they have in Europe. In fact, just the reverse may be true. In America, political ideas may have been less sophisticated in theory but they have also been more important in impact than in most other societies. They have been a critical element in the definition of national identity and in the delimitation of political authority.

People have been attempting to define American national identity or "national character" ever since national consciousness first emerged in the eighteenth century. Personality traits, social characteristics, geographic and environmental features, behavioral patterns, and historical experiences have all been invoked by one analyst or another. There is no need here to enter into or even to review this continuing debate. Our argument concerns not national character but something much more concrete, identifiable, and measurable: national political values and beliefs. We are concerned not with behavioral or cultural patterns, personality traits, or psychological makeup, but with ideas—specifically political ideas. Our argument is that:

1. Since the late eighteenth or early nineteenth century, there have existed in the United States certain basic political values and ideas that can be thought of as the "American Creed."

2. This Creed has been broadly supported by most elements in American society.

3. Although some modifications of the Creed have occurred over time, its central elements have changed relatively little in the course of two hundred years.

4. In contrast to the situation in most European societies, this Creed has played and continues to play a central role in the definition of American national identity.

Sources, Scope, and Stability of the Creed

What are the values of the American Creed? Innumerable studies have itemized them in various ways, but the same core political values appear in virtually all analyses: liberty, equality, individualism, democracy, and the rule of law under a constitution. These are different and yet related political ideas; they stemmed from several different sources and yet came together so as to reinforce one another in the American mind in the late eighteenth and early nineteenth centuries.

These core ideas are set forth succinctly in the Declaration of Independence. More broadly, they can be thought of as involving several major elements. The oldest is the constitutional strand, with its roots in medieval ideas of fundamental law as a restraint on human behavior. Law, in this sense, was conceived of as something that was beyond human control but not beyond human knowledge. Man discovered law, he did not make it, and this law, whether viewed as divine law, natural law, or customary law, provided the norms for human behavior. In Europe in the seventeenth century, these traditional ideas of law began to be supplanted by new ideas of absolute sovereignty and the power of men—be they absolute monarchs or members of supreme parliaments—to make law as they saw fit. In that same century, however, the older ideas of fundamental law as a restraint on human action were exported to and took root on the American continent.

A second major source of the ideas of the American Creed is seventeenth-century Protestantism, which contributed elements of moralism, millennialism, and individualism to the American political outlook. More particularly, Protestantism stressed the primacy of the individual conscience, the close connection between the spirit of liberty and the spirit of religion, the role of the congregation as a voluntary association, the importance of democracy within the church and its implications for the polity ("no bishop, no king"), and, in due course, the abandonment of religious establishments. The United States is the only country in the world in which a majority of the population has belonged to dissenting Protestant sects. Protestant values reinforced republican and democratic tendencies in the eighteenth century and provided the underlying ethical and moral basis for American ideas on politics and society.

To these strands, the eighteenth century added Lockean and Enlightenment ideas of natural rights, liberty, the social contract, the limited role of government, and the dependence of government upon society. Finally, the idea of equality—set forth boldly in the Declaration of Independence as the basis for organizing society—challenged accepted ideas of the legitimacy of distinctions based on rank, status, and inherited privilege. If all men are created equal, then all must count equally politically, and hence all must have an equal right to vote for their governing officials. The basis was laid for popular sovereignty and the democratization of government in the nineteenth century. The idea of equality, one aspect of the Protestant strand in the American Creed, was thus reinforced by the democratic and revolutionary currents at the end of the eighteenth century.

Ideas of constitutionalism, individualism, liberalism, democracy, and egalitarianism are no monopoly of Americans. In some societies, some people subscribe to many of these ideas and in other societies many people subscribe to some of these ideas. In no other society, however, are all of these ideas so widely adhered to by so many people as they are in the United States.

People sometimes speak of an American "ideology." But in the American mind, these ideas do not take the form of a carefully articulated, systematic ideology in the sense in which this term is used to refer to European belief systems such as traditional conservatism, liberalism, Marxism, social democracy, and Christian democracy. They constitute a complex and amorphous amalgam of goals and values, rather than a scheme for establishing priorities among values and for elaborating ways to realize values. They do not have the key characteristics that distinguish an ideology from other sets of political ideas.[1] They are, for instance, far more diffuse, incoherent, and undeveloped intellectually than Marxism. Some have described these ideas in terms of the "liberal tradition" in America. If one had to apply one adjective to them, "liberal" would be it, but even this term does not convey the full richness and complexity of the amalgam. It thus seems more accurate and appropriate to speak of American political ideas or beliefs in the plural, and in the singular to follow Gunnar Myrdal and others and simply speak of the American Creed.

The unsystematic and unideological character of this Creed is reflected in the fact that no theory exists for ordering these values in relation to one another and for resolving on a theoretical level the conflicts that inherently exist among them. Conflicts easily materialize when any one value is taken to an extreme: majority rule versus minority rights; higher law versus popular sovereignty; liberty versus equality; individualism versus democracy. In other societies, ideologies give priority to one value or the other, but in American society all these values coexist together in theory, even as they may conflict with each other when applied in practice. They coexist, indeed, not only within American society, but also within individual citizens. Though every American may have his own view of the proper balance among these conflicting values, few Americans would unhesitatingly give absolute priority to one value over another. However much one values majority rule, at some point its application is limited by the need to recognize minority rights. However much one believes in individual liberty, at some point individual aggrandizement cannot be permitted to make a mockery of political and moral equality. The checks and balances that exist among the institutions of American politics are paralleled by the checks and balances that exist among the ideas of the American Creed. This political "ideology," as Robert Mc-Closkey noted, is not "a consistent body of dogmas tending in the same direction, but a conglomerate of ideas which may be and often are logically inconsistent." It is "characteristic of the American mind . . . to hold contradictory ideas simultaneously without bothering to resolve the potential conflict between them."[2]

Nowhere is this better illustrated than in the relation between liberty and equality in the American Creed. In Europe these two values are commonly thought to be inherently opposed to each other. From Plato on, political theorists saw the extension of equality as ultimately involving the destruction of liberty, as society becomes homogenized and leveled, paving the way for the rise of the despot. In the eighteenth century, liberty was the aristocratic value and equality the bourgeois democratic value; in the nineteenth century, liberty became the bourgeois value and equality the proletarian value. The expansion of equality thus involved in the eighteenth century the suppression of the rights, liberties, and privileges of estates, orders, and corporations, and in the nineteenth century the restriction of rights of contract and private property. Tocqueville's view of equality in America reflected this European experience. Few Americans have shared his fear that the expansion of equality would signal the death-knell of liberty. The American approach is instead well summed up by Michael Walzer's argument that "liberty and equality are the two chief virtues of social institutions, and they stand best when they stand together."[3] In the United States they did historically move hand-in-hand. They developed in conjunction with, not in opposition to, each other, representing not so much the political values of opposing social classes as the opposing political values of a single middle class. The eighteenth-century value of liberty was quickly joined by the nineteenth-century value of equality. Americans generally give liberty precedence over equality, but different groups assign different weights to each, and virtually all groups give high levels of support to both values.[4] A continuing theme of American political discourse has been the effort to reconcile one with the other, most notably in the economic sphere, where ideas of equality of opportunity coexist with ideas of liberty of achievement. Those who have been concerned with the promotion of one have generally also been concerned with the promotion of the other. "In the United States," Daniel Bell observed, "the tension between liberty and equality, which framed the great philosophical debates in Europe, was dissolved by an individualism which encompassed both." As Herbert Croly put it, "the Land of Freedom became in the course of time also the Land of Equality."[5]

How broad has been the agreement on these ideas? The Americans, said Tocqueville in one of his most quoted remarks, "are unanimous upon the general principles that ought to rule human society." Some foreign and native observers before him and countless numbers after him have reiterated this point. "Americans," Gunnar Myrdal argued, echoing Tocqueville's language one hundred years later, "of all national origins, classes, regions, creeds, and colors, have something in common: a social *ethos*, a political creed."[6] In the mid-twentieth century, the validity of these impressionistic observations was underscored by the overwhelming evidence provided by public opinion poll data. Such data indicated that the key values of the American liberal-democratic Creed commanded the support of well over 75 percent of the population.[7] When the key values and principles of the American Creed are expressed in highly general terms, support for liberty, democracy, majority rule, minority rights, freedom of speech and religion, and, less clearly, equality approaches unanimity from virtually all groups in the American public.[8] As the formulation of values is made more specific and related to concrete applications of these values to particular situations, support drops off considerably and cleavage may become more pronounced than consensus. In such circumstances, those who have more education, who are more active in politics, or who occupy leadership positions in community organizations are more likely to support the values of the Creed.[9] The consensus on the values of the system, in short, is broadest among those most active in the system and who benefit the most from it. Those with higher socioeconomic status also are less likely than those of lower status to perceive major differences between the values of the system and the reality of the system. In terms of overall preferences, however, there would appear to be little doubt that, as one comprehensive analysis in the early 1970s concluded, "the United States has had a high degree of consensus on fundamental political values at the community and regime levels."[10]

The broad agreement that has existed throughout American history on these values is reflected in the fate of potential alternative political value systems. Such systems could only develop where there was some social and economic base to nurture political beliefs different from those that generally prevailed. Three such bases—regional, class, and ethnic—conceivably have existed at one time or another in American history.

The most significant effort to develop an alternative set of political values was that which occurred in the prebellum South. A society based on slavery clearly contradicted virtually all the core values of the American Creed. As a result, as the slave system came under increasing attack after 1830, Southern writers and thinkers developed a highly articulate and systematic conservative defense of the society built on that foundation. Resorting to classic conservative ideas and arguments which historically had been used to defend many other types of societies, they strove to develop an ideological alternative, and the writings of the "Reactionary Enlightenment," to use Hartz's term, constitute an outpouring of political theorizing unique in American history. Conservative ideas were, for them, a weapon to be used to defend their society against the growing economic and demographic preponderance of the North and the intensifying ideological assault of the abolitionists. Their substantive theory, however, remained ambivalent. Wishing to retain what they could of their Jeffersonian heritage, they wavered uncertainly between the philosophies of John Locke and Sir Robert Filmer.[11] In the end, when their society was destroyed in the Civil War, their efforts at alternative political theory died too and were quickly forgotten.

The rapid industrialization that followed the Civil War necessarily involved the creation of an industrial proletariat which, presumably, created the socioeconomic base for a socialist movement comparable to those that were simultaneously emerging in Europe. The failure of such a movement to develop mass political appeal is perhaps the most dramatic evidence of the preponderance of liberal-democratic values in America. The issue of "Why no socialism in the United States?" has been explored at length by a variety of social scientists beginning with Marx and Engels, and various causes have been assigned a variety of weights.[12] The absence of feudalism permitted the unchallenged spread of liberal, bourgeois values and this, in turn, prevented socialism from developing significant appeal: in effect, "no feudalism, no socialism." In addition, the nature of the original settlers (particularly those of the dissenting and separatist religious sects), the abundance of free land, and the opportunities for horizontal and then vertical mobility all promoted the dominance of the middle class. In an agricultural society the basic form of wealth is land, and in most agricultural societies the amount of land is always limited and usually fixed. The population is permanently divided between those who own land and those who do not, or between those who own more land and those who own less. In America, however, no such division of the people could last. The opportunities for land ownership were too real. The resulting failure (outside the plantation South) to develop a system of agricultural classes and the pervasiveness of a "free-farmer society" set the pattern of relative abundance and relative mobility which survived industrialization and urbanization and ensured the widespread adoption of middle-class values and standards.

Although the first working-class parties in the modern world were formed in the United States in the 1830s, industrialization failed to produce a class-conscious working-class movement committed to Marxism or some other form of socialism. This was a result of the prior achievement of universal white male suffrage, the general openness of political institutions, the continuing opportunities for vertical and horizontal mobility, the ethnic diversity and geographic dispersion of the working class, and the preexisting prevalence of the liberal-democratic norms of the American Creed. In some measure, the latter, with their stress on equality and mobility, served indeed as a surrogate form of socialism.[13]

A third possible social base for an alternative to liberal democracy was furnished by the massive influx of poor immigrants with peasant backgrounds from southern and eastern Europe at the end of the nineteenth and the beginning of the twentieth centuries. These immigrants, Hofstadter argued, brought with them an outlook that contrasted dramatically with the prevailing values and moralistic emphases based "upon the indigenous Yankee-Protestant political traditions, and upon middle-class life." This other system,

> founded upon the European backgrounds of the immigrants, upon their unfamiliarity with independent political action, their familiarity with hierarchy and authority, and upon the urgent needs that so often grew out of their migration, took for granted that the political life of the individual would arise out of family needs, interpreted political and civic relations chiefly in terms of personal obligations, and placed strong personal loyalties above allegiance to abstract codes of law or morals. It was chiefly upon this system of values that the political life of the immigrant, the boss, and the urban machine was based.[14]

The interaction between the immigrant ethic and the indigenous ethic provides one way of looking at changes in American politics during the first half of the twentieth century.

The immigrant ethic left its mark upon American political organization and practice, particularly during the New Deal years. But by the early 1960s, the most important development in urban politics was precisely the extent to which the immigrants and their children were replacing their own traditional ethos with that which had been traditional in the United States. "The immigrant lower class has been and is still being absorbed into the middle class at a rapid rate. This has profoundly affected the outlook of the electorate, for the middle class has always held to the Anglo-Saxon Protestant political ideal and those who have joined it have accepted this ideal along with others . . . Increasingly the 'new immigrant' has come to demand candidates who, whatever their origins, have the community-serving ethos and the public virtues that have long been associated with the Protestant elite."[15] The subsequent political events of the 1960s and 1970s confirmed the perspicacity of this analysis. The enhanced significance of ethnic power in American politics was paralleled by the withering of the ethnic ethic in American politics.

No lasting and significant alternatives to the liberal-democratic value system have emerged in the United States. In this respect, the basic proposition of the consensus paradigm is valid. There is, however, still the possibility that the content of the consensus, the mix of values in the liberal-democratic amalgam, may have changed over time. Are the predominant American political values of the late twentieth century basically the same as those of the late eighteenth century? By and large, the classic (that is, Tocquevillian) answer to this question has stressed the continuity in American values: "Two things are surprising in the United States: the mutability of the greater part of human actions, and the singular stability of certain principles. Men are in constant motion; the mind of man appears almost unmoved. When once an opinion has spread over the country and struck root there, it would seem that no power on earth is strong enough to eradicate it . . . Cogent reasons . . . prevent any great change from being easily effected in the principles of a democratic people."[16]

Well over a century later, the judgments of mid-twentieth-century social scientists generally confirmed Tocqueville's conclusion. "Though there were shadings through time," argued Clyde Kluckhohn in 1958, "the central and distinctive aspects of the American value system were remarkably stable from the eighteenth century until the [nineteen] thirties and, in spite of some changes that have occurred and are in process, the characteristic American values remain highly influential in the life of the United States." Five years later Seymour Martin Lipset concluded that "there is more continuity than change with respect to the main elements in the national value system." In 1967 Lloyd Free and Hadley Cantril argued that the Mayflower Compact, John Locke, and the Declaration of Independence "reflect the basic political values that have shaped the American political system for nearly three hundred and fifty years . . . The underlying personal political credos of the majority of Americans have remained substantially intact at the ideological level." An exhaustive survey in 1972 led Donald Devine to affirm in similar language that "the values of Locke, Madison, and the other liberals of the seventeenth and eighteenth centuries represent essentially the same values which comprise the American political culture at the present. Although it has changed, the remarkable phenomenon is that American political culture has survived so unchanged under substantial environmental pressure."[17]

The relative lack of change in American political values is also reflected in the way in which three distinguished European observers summarized the prevailing values at three different points in American history. From Maine to the Floridas, Tocqueville argued,

> and from the Missouri to the Atlantic Ocean, the people are held to be the source of all legitimate power. The same notions are entertained respecting liberty and equality, the liberty of the press, the right of association, the jury, and the responsibility of the agents of government.
>   . . . The Anglo-Americans acknowledge the moral authority of the reason of the community as they acknowledge the political authority of the mass of citizens; and they hold that public opinion is the surest arbiter of what is lawful or forbidden, true or false. The majority of them believe that a man by following his own interest, rightly understood, will be led to do what is just and good. They hold that every man is born in possession of the right of self-government, and that no one has the right of constraining his fellow creatures to be happy. They have all a lively faith in the perfectibility of man.[18]

A half-century after Tocqueville, James Bryce summed up the principal elements of the Creed in strikingly similar fashion: (1) the individual has sacred rights; (2) the source of political power is the people; (3) all governments are limited by law and the people; (4) local government is to be preferred to national government; (5) the majority is wiser than the minority; (6) the less government the better. A half-century after Bryce, Gunnar Myrdal argued that Americans had in common a creed of "humanistic liberalism," which developed out of the Enlightenment and which embodied the "ideals of the essential dignity of the individual human being, of the fundamental equality of all men, and of certain inalienable rights to freedom, justice, and a fair opportunity."[19]

All this suggests little change in basic American political values. In the 1950s, however, the thesis was advanced that fundamental changes were taking place in both American national character and American values. The "inner-directed" person was giving way to the "other-directed" person; the group was replacing the individual; the traditional, Puritan, moralistic style and its associated values were being supplanted by a more tolerant, more relativistic, more socially oriented and less achievement-directed style and set of values.[20] If this thesis was valid, it would suggest that substantial changes were under way in the content of the American consensus and that, at least for a time, the consensus would be disrupted along generational and perhaps class lines.

The change thesis was, however, dubious for three reasons. First, a persuasive case was made that the attitudes and values presented by the change thesis as new developments on the American scene had actually figured prominently in descriptions of America by foreign observers since the early nineteenth century.[21] What the change thesis argued was new was, in fact, actually old. Second, the 1960s saw a recrudescence of individualism and moral passion in American politics, as intense as any in American history. What the change thesis argued was passé, in fact turned out to be present a decade later. Finally, the evidence is mixed concerning the extent to which the change thesis holds valid for personal values. Looking at children's reading texts, for example, inner-directed achievement imagery increased during the nineteenth century, then decreased in the twentieth at the same time that other-directed affiliation imagery increased. Surveys of children's ideals (that is, whom they would most like to resemble) during the first six decades of the twentieth century, however, do not show any significant shift away from achievement motivation or any change in aspiration levels.[22] With respect to political values, the evidence overwhelmingly suggests a high level of continuity. Writings purporting to identify peculiarly American traits or values in four different periods of American history (pre-Civil War, 1865–1917, 1918–1933, 1933–1940) showed "no important difference between the traits mentioned by modern observers and those writing in the earlier periods of American history." Traits such as democracy, equality, and freedom were mentioned in all four periods.[23] The verbal symbols in Presidential inaugural addresses also changed little during the first one hundred fifty years of American history.[24] While clearly ideals such as liberty and equality acquire different meanings through their application in new contexts, the core meaning of the value remains. It is, indeed, reaffirmed by being continually reapplied.

Political Ideas and National Identity

For most peoples, national identity is the product of a long process of historical evolution involving common ancestors, common experiences, common ethnic background, common language, common culture, and usually common religion. National identity is thus organic in character. Such, however, is not the case in the United States. American nationalism has been defined in political rather than organic terms. The political ideas of the American Creed have been the basis of national identity.

Thirty years before the battles of Lexington and Concord, the Georgian monarchy had been threatened by another serious challenge much closer to home: in 1745 a Stuart claimant to the throne had raised a Scottish army, broken English rule in Scotland, and advanced to within one hundred twenty miles of London. Separated by only thirty years, these two crises—the '45 and the '75—could hardly have been more dramatically different. One was a traditional conflict involving family, dynasty, nationality, and religion, the other a revolutionary conflict over political principles and legitimacy. In what was truly a novel event in world history, Americans did not assert their independence because their ethnicity, language, culture, or religion differentiated them from their British brethren. The United States came into existence at a particular moment in time— July 4, 1776—and it was the product of a conscious political act based on explicit political principles. "We hold these truths to be self-evident," says the Declaration. Who holds these truths? Americans hold these truths. Who are Americans? People who adhere to these truths. National identity and political principle were inseparable. From the beginning, as Croly noted, the American past was "informed by an idea." And hence there was from the beginning the tendency, as a distinguished English historian put it, "to describe the national identity as allegiance to political principles; to equality, freedom, inalienable rights, and authority derived from the consent of the governed . . . The Americans are a political people. The Revolution, the Declaration of Independence, the constitutions of the states and the Constitution of 1787 explain their national existence." From Crèvecoeur to Tocqueville to Bryce to Brogan to Myrdal, foreign as well as domestic observers have singled out this striking phenomenon. Given all the other variety in American life and the diverse sources and times of people becoming Americans, national identity could be defined in few other ways. The Creed is, indeed, as Myrdal put it, "the cement in the structure of this great and disparate nation."[25] If it were not for the American Creed, what would Americans have in common?

Two hundred years after the Revolution, political factors were still at the heart of American national identity. In the late 1950s, for instance, national samples of the population in five countries, including the United States, were asked: "Speaking generally, what are the things about America that you are most proud of?" In response, 85 percent of Americans mentioned some aspect of the "American government or political tradition—the Constitution, political freedom, democracy, and the like."

Political factors were mentioned by only 46 percent of the British, 30 percent of the Mexicans, 7 percent of the Germans, and 3 percent of the Italians. The Americans, on the other hand, had much less pride than these others in the characteristics of their people, the physical attributes of their country, and the contributions of their country to the arts. They identified their country not with personal, social, geographical, or cultural qualities, but with political values and practices.[26] In this respect, the differences between the American and British responses are probably "indicative of the contractarian aspects of American polity by contrast with the more organic character of British life, for what most strongly joins Americans together is our consciously chosen experiment in liberal democratic politics rather than the totality of our historical culture . . . These data indicate that we *define* the nation politically; what we all have in common is a system of constitutional rights. Beyond this lies a complex cultural sphere, the vast area of private life. A more organic society like Britain does not make such a separation of the areas of life one from another."[27]

The United States thus had its origins in a conscious political act, in the assertion of certain basic political principles, and in adherence to constitutional agreements based on those principles. It is possible to speak of a body of political ideas that constitutes "Americanism" in a sense in which one can never speak of "Britishism," "Frenchism," "Germanism," or "Japanesism." Americanism in this sense is comparable to other ideologies or religions. "Americanism is to the American," Leon Samson has said, "not a tradition or a territory, not what France is to a Frenchman or England to an Englishman, but a doctrine—what socialism is to a socialist." To reject the central ideas of that doctrine is to be un-American. There is no British Creed or French Creed; the Académie Française worries about the purity of the French language, not about the purity of French political ideas. What, indeed, would be an "un-French" political idea? But pre-occupation with "un-American" political ideas and behavior has been a recurring theme in American life. "It has been our fate as a nation," Richard Hofstadter succinctly observed, "not to have ideologies but to be one."[28]

This identification of nationality with political creed or values makes the United States virtually unique. In terms of their nationality and ideological makeup, countries can generally be divided into four categories. Some countries, such as the People's Republic of China, are characterized by monism of both ideology and nationality. In some, such as France,

Germany, and Italy, several ideologies have historically coexisted within the context of a single nationality. In other countries, such as the Soviet Union and Yugoslavia, a single ideology provides the framework for bringing together several distinct nationalities. Still other countries, such as historically the United Kingdom, may be characterized by pluralism of both nationality and ideology.

The United States does not fit neatly into any of these categories. Like communist states, the United States has a single pervasive dominant political creed or ideology, but the relation between political creed and nationality in the United States differs significantly from that in communist societies. In some communist countries, like China, an ideology was superimposed on a single preexisting, well-established nationality. In similar but reverse fashion, it could be removed without destroying the basis of national identity: the Chinese could stop being communist and not stop being Chinese. In the Soviet Union, as in Yugoslavia, on the other hand, communist ideology was used to create a multinational state by superimposing the ideology on several preexisting and clearly identifiable nationalities each with its own language, culture, traditions, and territory. The existence of the Soviet Union, as well as of Yugoslavia, is thus intimately linked to the prevalence of the ideology. If the ideology and its associated political superstructure were removed the nationalities would remain and, in the absence of a new political superstructure, would provide the basis for Russian, Ukrainian, Lithuanian, Uzbekistani, and other political communities out of what had been the Soviet Union, and for Serbian, Slovenian, Croatian, and Macedonian political communities out of what had been Yugoslavia.

The United States, on the other hand, is composed, apart from the Indian tribes, not of nationalities but of ethnic groups. In America, ethnicity exists apart from nationality; ethnic groups make no claims to a separate national identity. During the early years of the Republic, British elements predominated in the population and the British heritage was central to American life. Yet even from the start, ethnic diversity also existed: as a result of the "First Immigration" of the eighteenth century, in 1790 forty percent of the American people were of non-English extraction.[29] The Second and Third Immigrations of the mid-nineteenth century and at the turn of the twentieth century dramatically multiplied the numbers and diversity of the American immigrant population. They also brought to the fore the issue of what it meant to become an American.

There were three possible answers. First, immigrants could conceivably become Americans by being fully assimilated into the culture and community of the white Anglo-Saxon Protestants, who still constituted not only the premier but the largest ethnic entity on the American scene. This, however, quickly turned out to be a result desired by neither group. Second, immigrants could become Americans by participating in a melting pot process of ethnic intermarriage and cultural interpenetration out of which would emerge a new American type reflecting the diverse origins of American immigrants. Ethnic ties and identity, reinforced paradoxically by the openness of American society, made this at best a slow process involving centuries as well as generations. Third, for the immigrants, becoming an American could mean accepting and identifying with American social, economic, and political values and institutions— whose appeal had, of course, been a principal reason for their immigration in the first place. In effect, a bargain was struck: ethnic groups retained so long as they wished their ethnic identity, but they converted to American political values, ideals, and symbols. Adherence to the latter was the test of how "American" one was, and it was perfectly compatible with the maintenance of ethnic culture and traditions. The primordial or organic ties remained in large part ethnic; the political or ideological ties were American. A hyphenated American was thus quite different from a hyphenated non-American. To say that someone is an Anglo-Italian means that he has English and Italian forebears. To say that someone is an Italian-American means that he has Italian forebears but that he has American political values and is a member of the American political community. At times, descendants of earlier immigrants could and did speak contemptuously of "hyphenated Americans," but first- and second-generation Americans were better Americans for being hyphenated. Defining and maintaining an ethnic identity was an essential building block in the process of creating an American national identity.

American political values and ideals thus had their roots primarily in British sources, but American national identity was defined in terms of the former rather than the latter. In the 1830s, Tocqueville could still inaccurately refer to Americans generally as "Anglo-Americans." A century later, the emergence of the term "WASP" marked the final phase in the demotion of the Anglo-American to the status of one ethnic group among many and the end of any effort to define American national identity in ethnic rather than political terms. As a result, in the United States, as in no other society, ideology and nationality are fused and the disappearance of the former would mean the end of the latter.

This identification of political ideas and nationality contrasts dramatically with the historical experience of western Europe. In Europe, political ideology and nationalism crossed each other. Ideologies expressed and shaped the interests of "horizontal" units (social classes), while nationalism, in its various manifestations, expressed and shaped the interests of "vertical" units (ethnic and linguistic communities). In eighteenth-century Europe, the aristocracy played an independent role in politics, and the middle class consequently had to develop a high degree of political consciousness and activity in its struggle to establish its position with respect to the aristocracy. In the course of this struggle, the two sides articulated their distinctive ideologies of liberalism and conservatism. Subsequently the development of the working-class movement produced equally systematic and highly developed socialist ideologies, the most important of which was Marxism. Thus, the high level of class development and the interaction and conflict among the classes produced the ideological trinity of conservatism, liberalism, and socialism.

Each of these ideologies tended to be articulated on a transnational basis. Conservative aristocratic doctrines, historically antinational, received their principal institutional embodiment in the Congress of Vienna in 1815. They reflected the assumption that there was more in common between two aristocrats, one of whom was a foreigner, than between two nationals, one of whom was an aristocrat. Liberal thinkers developed their own internationalism rooted in the ideas of free trade and the harmony of interests. Socialists preached the international unity of the working class. Thus, each ideology competed with nationalism as well as with other ideologies. The ideologies became more systematic and doctrinaire to counter the appeals of nationalism. Nationalism, in turn, became more romantic and mystical in order to overcome class and ideological differences—the "better Hitler than Blum" propensity which at one time or another could be found in most European social groups. Where the class struggle was more intense, as in France and Germany, so also was the nationalism; where the class struggle was more moderate, as in Great Britain, so also were the assertions of nationalism. Politically, nineteenth- and early twentieth-century Europe could be viewed as a grid of cross-cutting cleavages, divided vertically by the appeal of *patrie* and nationalism and horizontally by the appeals of class and ideology, with this two-way competition giving a peculiar stridency and intensity to each appeal.

These conflicting pulls of ideology and nationalism have been lacking in the American political experience. Ideology and nationalism reinforced each other, yet the absence of conflict between the two also meant that each in some measure diluted the other. Ideology did not have to be developed in systematic and overt form in order to articulate and justify the appeal of class against class or class against nation. Similarly, nationalism did not have to be developed in such an emotional and irrational way as to justify the appeal of fatherland over class. American "patriotism," as Bryce observed, "is in one aspect stronger than that of Frenchmen or Englishmen because it is less broken by class feeling, but it has ceased to be aggressive."[30] In comparison to European nationalism, American nationalism is in a sense more "intellectualized," since it is defined more in terms of political ideas and principles; in comparison to European ideologies, on the other hand, the American Creed is less systematic and intellectualized because it reflects a national consensus and is identified with American nationalism.

As a result of this identification of the nation with certain political ideals, the American political experience has been quite limited compared to that of other nations. Political ideas and beliefs that cannot be encompassed in the American Creed remain on the fringe of American society and the American consciousness. In western European and other societies, ideological diversity has prevailed within the context of a common national community. Don Camillo and his communist rival are both quintessentially Italian and neither would deny the Italianness of the other. In the United States, on the other hand, where the liberal-democratic ethos of the American Creed has preempted the scene, the American experience with forms of government has been similarly limited. Although significant changes have obviously occurred in American political institutions in the course of two hundred years, the United States has still had only one Constitution and one system of government based on one set of political ideas. Other nations often see constitutions come and go every generation. The Germans have had five very different political systems in this century. Between 1789 and 1979 France had five republics plus six other political systems. Even in Great Britain the constitutional system and ideological makeup were very different in the late twentieth century from what they had been in the late eighteenth century. In such societies, the nation endures while the political system changes. When the national identity and unity of these countries are endangered, it is by ethnic and subnational movements, by Basque, Breton, or Scottish nationalism, not by changes in the political system or the dominant political ideas in the society.

In the United States, in contrast, ethnic cultural identities coexist with a national identity rooted in a particular set of political ideas and institutions. "The American Constitution," Hans Kohn pointed out, "is unlike any other: it represents the lifeblood of the American nation, its supreme symbol and manifestation. It is so intimately welded with the national existence itself that the two have become inseparable."[31] For this reason, American national identity is in a sense very fragile, threatened not by ethnic separatism but by disillusionment with its political ideals or with the effectiveness of its political institutions. Destroy the political system and you destroy the basis of community, eliminating the nation and, in effect, returning its members—in accordance with the theory on which that nation was founded—back to a state of nature. In other countries, one can abrogate the constitution without abrogating the nation. The United States does not have that choice.

American identity thus involves adherence to certain substantive political ideals. "To be an American," Carl Friedrich said, "is an ideal; while to be a Frenchman is a fact."[32] American identity is defined in normative terms, French identity in existential terms. French political behavior, in this sense, is whatever Frenchmen *in fact do* in politics; American political behavior, on the other hand, is what American political ideals say Americans *ought to do* in politics. There is an external standard by which to judge what is American apart from what Americans do. Americans may think un-American thoughts, American officials may engage in un-American behavior, and American governments may fight un-American wars. The "religion of the Republic," Sidney Mead said, "is essentially prophetic," and this imposes a noble and chastening destiny because "its ideals and aspirations stand in constant judgment over the passing shenanigans of the people, reminding them of the standards by which their current practices and those of their nation are ever being judged and found wanting."[33] The "ideal national Promise," in Croly's phrase, which distinguishes the United States from other nations, is a source of anxiety and anguish. The promise of the American future is the indictment of the American present.

3 THE GAP: THE AMERICAN CREED VERSUS POLITICAL AUTHORITY

Consensus and Instability

Studies of American politics often point to the widespread consensus on the basic elements of the American Creed as evidence of the stability of the American political system. The assumption is that consensus on values translates into support for institutions. It is, indeed, frequently assumed that the stability of a democracy is particularly dependent upon the existence of a broad agreement on democratic values; democracy cannot work if a substantial portion of the public is basically opposed to it and supports authoritarian movements of the left, right, or center. Deeply felt class divisions over the proper sources of political authority, church-state relations, or the role of the state in the economy clearly can give rise to major instabilities in a democratic political system. When people think about instability, they typically have in mind this cleavage-based instability, and they tend to believe that anything that moderates the polarization, develops cross-cutting cleavages, or furnishes a basis for consensus will also contribute to greater political stability. And in a deeply polarized society, such measures may well enhance stability.

From this analysis, however, it is often implied that because dissension means instability, consensus therefore enhances stability. If people agree on democratic values, the successful functioning of democratic institutions is more or less assured. In fact, this is not necessarily the case. Just as there is an instability that follows from an excess of cleavage, so also there is an instability that follows from an excess of consensus. In comparison with Europe, the United States has had relatively little class warfare and ideological conflict. But it has had its own forms of political instability, which have in large part been rooted in the content of the American political consensus.

Whether or not a consensus on political values contributes to political stability depends on the nature of those values and the relation between them and the political institutions and practices in the society. If the prevailing political values legitimize and sanctify those institutions and practices, they enhance political stability. It is, however, quite conceivable that the core ideals and values of the consensus may provide a basis for challenging the legitimacy of the dominant political institutions and practices. This is precisely the case in the United States, and it is a phenomenon that is characteristic of politics in the United States as of that of no other major society.

The widespread consensus on liberal-democratic values provides the basis for challenging the legitimacy of American political practices and the authority of American political institutions. The consensus constitutes an external standard for judging institutions, and often for judging them harshly. Political institutions and practices never measure up to the ideals and values of the Creed, and hence can be seen as illegitimate. The extent to which this challenge manifests itself overtly depends on the way in which people perceive those institutions and practices. At times, people can look at politics as it is practiced in the United States and be blind to any divergence of this practice from the ideals of the American Creed. At other times, people may also perceive a vast gap between politics as it is in practice and politics as it should be according to the norms of the American Creed. Intense awareness of this gap becomes a driving force for reformation of the political system. These efforts to bring political reality into accord with political principle are the major source of political change in America.

Cleavage in the United States thus does not take the form of idea versus idea, as in Europe, but rather of idea versus fact. The conflict is between two groups who believe in the same political principles: those who find it in their interest to change existing institutions immediately so as to make them comply with those principles, and those who accept the validity of the principles but who perceive existing institutions as being in accord with the principles insofar as this is feasible. Other societies may be more divided than the United States along class lines and over conflicting weltanschauungs, but it is the peculiar fate of Americans that the beliefs that unite them as a nation should also divide them as a people. The same Creed that is the source of national identity is also the source of political instability. Conflict is the child of consensus, and the most passionate and traumatic controversies among Americans derive from the liberal-democratic values on which they so overwhelmingly agree.

The Antipower Ethic

The basic ideas of the American Creed—equality, liberty, individualism, constitutionalism, democracy—clearly do not constitute a systematic ideology, and they do not necessarily have any logical consistency. At some point, liberty and equality may clash, individualism may run counter to constitutionalism, and democracy or majority rule may infringe on both. Precisely because it is not an intellectualized ideology, the American Creed can live with such inconsistencies.

Logically inconsistent as they seem to philosophers, these ideas do have a single common thrust and import for the relations between society and government: all the varying elements in the American Creed unite in imposing limits on power and on the institutions of government. The essence of constitutionalism is the restraint of governmental power through fundamental law. The essence of liberalism is freedom from governmental control—the vindication of liberty against power, as Bernard Bailyn summed up the argument for the American Revolution. The essence of individualism is the right of each person to act in accordance with his own conscience and to control his own destiny free of external restraint, except insofar as such restraint is necessary to ensure comparable rights to others. The essence of egalitarianism is rejection of the idea that one person has the right to exercise power over another. The essence of democracy is popular control over government, directly or through representatives, and the responsiveness of governmental officials to public opinion. In sum, the distinctive aspect of the American Creed is its antigovernment character. Opposition to power, and suspicion of government as the most dangerous embodiment of power, are the central themes of American political thought.

When major inequalities in wealth emerged in the latter part of the nineteenth century, Americans developed a "gospel of wealth" to legitimate them. Great wealth was the reward for great effort, great merit, great risks. They continued to believe that gospel well into the twentieth century. In contrast, Americans have never developed a justification for major inequalities of power. Thus, while Americans may have a gospel of wealth, they have never had—and, in the nature of things, cannot have —a gospel of power. Instead, they have a pervasive antipower ethic.

"If there is one message I have gotten from the Pentagon Papers," Daniel Ellsberg told a cheering crowd of MIT students in the fall of 1971, "it is to distrust authority, distrust the President, distrust the men in power, because power does corrupt, even in America."[1] If there were any who did not get the message from the Pentagon Papers, they almost surely did shortly thereafter from the Watergate tapes. It is an old message, a refrain continually repeated through more than two hundred years of American history. The "first Americans," Charles Hendel argued, "still regarded authority with a jealous eye, wary and fearful of it in any guise. This general attitude became an ingrained habit of American character" and flowered into "an uncritical general philosophy unfavorable to authority in any form . . . The free, responsible, self-governing individual is thought of as self-sufficient."[2]

During the Revolutionary years, this attitude manifested itself in the contraposition of liberty and power. In Europe, as James Madison said, power granted charters to liberty; in America, liberty granted charters to power. The Jacksonians gave renewed emphasis to the dichotomy: the issue, John C. Calhoun said in 1826, was "between power and liberty." More explicitly, government itself, even democratic government, was a threat to liberty. "It is under the word *government*," declared the leading Jacksonian journal, "that the subtle danger lurks. Understood as a central consolidated power, managing and directing the various general interests of the society, all government is evil, and the parent of evil."[3]

The opposition to power and government remained characteristic of the American outlook in the twentieth century. "For as long as polls have been taken, when Americans have been asked about their attitudes toward government *in the abstract,* the attitudes expressed have been preponderantly negative." Compared to other peoples, Americans have relatively high trust in each other, but a much lower trust in government. The American tradition involves "high amounts of community and regime trust together with limited amounts of authority trust . . . The lack of trust mentioned by Dickens, and especially by Bryce, relates to the political authorities and not to the regime and community levels."[4]

Indicative of the American antipathy to power and government is the virtual absence of the concept of "the state" in American thought. In its modern form, the idea of the state originated in the fifteenth and sixteenth centuries and came to full fruition in the age of absolutism that followed. Machiavelli, Hobbes, and Bodin were its prophets, the continental absolute monarchs its creators. The idea of the state implied the concentration of sovereignty in a single, centralized, governmental authority. This concept never took hold among the English North American colonists, who had brought with them an older tradition rooted in medieval constitutionalism and the writings of Sir Thomas Smith, Richard Hooker, and Sir Edward Coke. While seventeenth-century Englishmen disputed the sovereignty of Parliament versus that of the Crown, Americans avoided both. Despite the fulminations of Blackstone that "there is and must be" in all states "a supreme, irresistible, absolute and uncontrolled power, in which the *jura summi imperii,* or rights of sovereignty reside," the Americans stubbornly held to a contrary position throughout the eighteenth century. As a result, the development of constitutional and political ideas in England separated from that in America. Jeremy Bentham and the utilitarians, with their emphasis on centralized authority, rationality, and utility (as against dispersed power, morality, and natural rights), had little impact on American thought. Bentham, indeed, denounced the Declaration of Independence as "a hodge-podge of confusion and absurdity in which the theory to be proved is all along taken for granted."[5]

Only at the end of the nineteenth century, when certain American scholars (among them Woodrow Wilson) studied in Germany, did the state make an appearance in American political thought. Its tenure was limited to a place in academic writing, and a relatively brief one at that. Even during this period, Henry James could comment that the United States had "No State, in the European sense of the word," and European visitors were impressed with the absence of any recognizable concept of the state in America. After his visit to America in 1871, the conservative Austrian aristocrat Baron von Hübner argued that "the liberty of the individual must necessarily be limited by the liberty of all represented by the State . . . You grant too much to the individual and too little to the State. The greater portion of the scandals and abuses which we see in your country arise from that source. The control of the organs of public opinion is insufficient. What is wanting, is the control of an admitted authority recognized by all the world." Two decades later, Bryce declared that the "Americans had no theory of the State and felt no need for one . . . The nation is nothing but so many individuals. The government is nothing but certain representatives and officials." A few years afterward, H. G. Wells similarly commented that "a sense of the state" was missing in the

United States, and G. K. Chesterton argued that "nowhere do they so completely despise the State, nowhere do they so utterly disunite the State, as in what we call the United States."[6] While the powers and functions of government grew tremendously in the twentieth century, they were not matched by any comparable change in the way in which people thought about the authority and autonomy of government. Government was still conceived of as the servant of society; the idea of the state as a legitimizing authoritative entity remained foreign to American thinking and, as a consequence, the European concept of *raison d'état* continued as the discredited polar opposite to American traditions of liberalism, constitutionalism, and natural rights.

The contrast between American and European attitudes toward the state is also manifest in two other areas. Early-nineteenth-century America saw the success of the movement to eliminate what remained of religious establishments and erect a wall of separation between church and state. This development is often cited as evidence of American commitment to freedom of religion. It is also evidence of the American commitment to the limitation of political authority. In Europe, state churches historically performed the function of reinforcing and legitimizing political authority. In America, political authority was stripped of this support and left alone without religious defenses to confront a suspicious liberal society. The differences in American and European attitudes toward political authority are also reflected in the nature of their extremist movements. In Europe, the nationalist or fascist Right and the socialist or communist Left have favored a strong state. In America, 'in contrast, radicals at both ends of the political spectrum have tended to be more individualistic, antistatist, libertarian, and in favor of decentralization and popular control.[7] They have shared a desire to reduce, not to enhance, political authority. Thus, in each case, what extremist movements carry to an extreme is the prevailing political disposition of their own society.

The deep-rooted American suspicion of government is also dramatically reflected in the way in which changing American views of human nature are related to American attitudes toward power and authority. "The American Government and Constitution," it has been said, "are based on the theory of Calvin and the philosophy of Hobbes."[8] In the seventeenth and eighteenth centuries, there was much truth in this observation. Puritan conceptions of sin and guilt plus Hobbesian ideas of human egotism combined to produce what can only be described as a rather unattractive view of human nature: people pursue their self-interests in wealth and power, and, at best, wise statesmanship designs institutions and processes that can produce at least a minimum of public virtue out of a superfluity of private vices. Nowhere are these basic assumptions about people and society more explicitly spelled out than in the words of the Founding Fathers in the debates of the Constitutional Convention and in the pages of *The Federalist*. One of the most striking changes in American political and social thought was that which occurred in the dominant conception of human nature during the fifty years after the Constitutional Convention. The image of man as essentially sinful, evil, and grasping, a being whose dangerous instincts and propensities had to be controlled by skillfully molded political and social institutions, gave way to an essentially benign view of human nature. Man came to be perceived as inherently good and potentially perfectible.

One might have thought that these two widely different views of human nature would give rise to two widely different views on the role of government in society. In fact, both views were used to justify limitations on government. The Founding Fathers argued that men in power would be tempted to do evil and would infringe the rights and liberties of others unless they were restrained by countervailing power. Hence, government must be weak because men are evil. Their more optimistic successors, on the other hand, started with the opposite assumption about man but arrived at a similar conclusion about government. Because men are inherently well intentioned and reasonable, strong government is not necessary to control or direct them: government should be weak because men are good.

These similar conclusions from differing premises were not necessarily dictated by pure logic. Starting from assumptions about human nature similar to those of the framers of the Constitution, Thomas Hobbes arrived at a very different concept of the role of political authority. Starting from assumptions about the inherent goodness of man similar to those of nineteenth-century democrats, Jean Jacques Rousseau arrived at very different views about the scope and role of government in society. What is striking, in short, is the way in which the American hostility to political authority led Americans, no matter what their view of human nature, to favor weak government over strong government.

In somewhat similar fashion, Americans have tended to interpret those two potentially conflicting values of the American Creed—equality and social mobility—in such a way as to be compatible with opposition to authority. In a variety of ways, Cora Du Bois has pointed out, the "American hostility to figures in authority" has operated "to play down status differences" and to produce an informality and familiarity in manners or, in Bryce's term, "equality of estimation." Success is valued, but some forms of success, particularly those that do not involve hierarchical authority relationships, are valued considerably more than others. "Upward mobility is valued as successful activity, but when it reaches a point where it outstrips the premise of equality and the focal value of conformity it borders on *hubris* . . . It is the boss, the politician, the teacher, the 'big shots' who are disvalued figures to the extent that their superordinate position implies authority. It is the movie star and the baseball hero who are valued figures since their pre-eminence connotes no authority but at the same time dramatizes the meteoric rise to fame and popularity through hard work and youthful striving."[9] Winning the race against others is good; exercising power over others is bad. Americans may praise famous men but they do not celebrate powerful ones. Similarly, the man who does achieve, the "self-made man" (itself an American term), "likes to boast of his achievement, to exaggerate the obscurity of his origin, and to point out the 'Horatio Alger' quality of his career." In Europe, on the other hand, the upwardly mobile person more "often prefers to forget his origins if they are in a lower class."[10]

Antipathy to power produces ambivalence toward wealth. "Equality" in American thinking has rarely been interpreted as economic equality in terms of wealth and income, but rather as equality of opportunity. Major social innovations such as free, universal, compulsory public education have been justified in large part by this value. Economic inequalities are legitimate insofar as they are the result of talent, work, achievement. Great wealth also becomes legitimate when it is used for socially beneficent purposes. The American tradition of philanthropy, unique in the world, is the tribute that illiberal concentrations of wealth pay to the norms of a liberal society. More generally, money becomes evil not when it is used to buy goods but when it is used to buy power. Large accumulations of wealth are acceptable until they are transformed into monopolies and trusts, which exercise economic power by dominating the marketplace. The American antitrust mania, unique among industrialized societies, focuses precisely on the point at which wealth becomes power. Similarly, economic inequalities become evil when they are translated into political inequalities. As a result, considerable effort has been invested over the years to exposing and regulating lobbying and political contributions. This outlook also manifests itself in the ambivalent American attitude toward "bigness." In objects it is good; in organizations—which involve the structuring of power—it is bad. Big buildings, big automobiles, big wealth in the sense of individual wealth, have historically been viewed favorably. Big business, big labor, and, most particularly, big government have been viewed unfavorably.

The IvI Gap

In his classic study of race relations in the United States, Gunnar Myrdal brilliantly pinpointed "an American dilemma" that existed between the deep beliefs in the concepts of liberty, equality, and individualism of the American Creed and the actual treatment of black people in American society. He probed, however, only one manifestation (albeit the most dramatic one) of the widespread gap between American political ideals and institutions—referred to here as "the IvI gap." What he termed "an" American dilemma is really "the" American dilemma, the central agony of American politics.

American liberal and democratic ideas form a standing and powerful indictment of almost all political institutions, including American ones. No government can exist without some measure of hierarchy, inequality, arbitrary power, secrecy, deception, and established patterns of superordination and subordination. The American Creed, however, challenges the legitimacy of all these characteristics of government. Its ideas run counter to the nature of government in general. They run counter to the nature of highly bureaucratized and centralized modern government. They run counter to both the original and inherited nature of American government.

Therein lies the dilemma. In the United States, government is legitimate to the extent to which it reflects the basic principles of the American Creed. Government can never, however, reflect those principles perfectly, and it is therefore illegitimate to the extent to which people take seriously the principles of the American Creed. If people try to make government more legitimate by bringing political practice more into accord with political principle, they will weaken government rather than strengthen it. Because of the inherently antigovernment character of the American Creed, government that is strong is illegitimate, government that is legitimate is weak.

In practice, in comparison with European societies, government has always been weak in America. This weakness originally was the product of the fact that no need existed in the United States to centralize power and establish a strong government in order to overthrow feudalism. In this sense, as Tocqueville pointed out, Americans "arrived at a state of democracy without having to endure a democratic revolution, and . . . are born equal instead of becoming so." The absence of feudalism thus eliminated a major negative impetus to strong government. The presence in its place of a pervasive consensus on liberal and democratic values furnished an additional, positive incentive to limit government. In the absence of a consensus, strong government would have been necessary; as Hartz pointed out, it is only because the images that the framers of the Constitution had of American society were erroneous that the system of divided and checked government that they created was able to last.[11] The fact of consensus thus made possible weak political institutions. The content of the consensus reinforced the weakness of those institutions.

Strong government has historically emerged in response to the need either to destroy a traditional society or to fight against foreign enemies. In the seventeenth-century era of state-building in Europe, absolute monarchs engaged in both activities simultaneously and unremittingly. From the start, the United States was spared the need to do the first, and shortly after its birth it was spared the need to do the second in any serious way until well into the twentieth century. The United States was able to maintain national independence and national security without having to create a strong apparatus. When this situation seemed to change in the 1940s and 1950s, many of the instrumentalities of a strong state machinery were created. This development took place, however, only because Americans at that time were relatively unconcerned about realizing their political values in their domestic political practice, however much they might have been concerned about protecting those institutions from foreign threats. In the 1960s, when Americans became concerned about the gap between their political ideals and their political institutions, they began to eviscerate the political and governmental institutions that had been developed to deal with foreign enemies.

In any society, of course, some gap exists between political ideals and political practice. In a society in which the dominant ideology is one of absolute monarchy, and in which theoretically there are no restraints whatsoever on the power of the ruler, political practice will reveal very real limits on the ruler's power. "Unofficial" reality will deviate from "official" ideology. Efforts to bridge this gap will tend to reinforce the power and authority of the existing institution; they will be efforts to make the incomplete absolutism that does exist into the more complete absolutism that should exist. Such efforts will enhance the legitimacy of the state by strengthening the state. Contrast this relationship with that which prevails in the United States. One function of an ideology in a political system is to legitimate rule, to furnish a persuasive and compelling answer to the question: Why obey? The American Creed, however, provides the rationale for restraints on rule. It is a much more fruitful source of reasons for questioning and resisting government than for obedience to government.

Political ideas do play a role in America—a purgative role that is not characteristic of other societies. In countries in which there are a variety of ideologies and belief systems, there are a variety of sources of challenge to governmental institutions, accompanied almost invariably by a variety of defenses for these institutions. Tradition and social structure furnish a basis for the legitimacy of some institutions, and particular ideologies and political theories can be used to legitimize individual institutions. Attacks on one set of institutions from the perspective of one ideology generate equally intense defenses from the perspective of other ideologies. In the United States, on the other hand, the consensus is basically antigovernment. What justification is there for government, hierarchy, discipline, secrecy, coercion, and the suppression of the claims of individuals and groups within the American context? In terms of American beliefs, government is supposed to be egalitarian, participatory, open, noncoercive, and responsive to the demands of individuals and groups. Yet no government can be all these things and still remain a government. "Credibility gaps" develop in American politics in part because the American people believe that government ought not do things it must do in order to be a government and that it ought to do things it cannot do without undermining itself as a government.

The ideological challenge to American government thus comes not from abroad but from home, not from imported Marxist doctrines but from homegrown American idealism. The stability of political institutions is threatened not by deep-rooted cleavages but by deeply felt consensus. Americans cannot be themselves unless they believe in the Creed, but they also must be against themselves if they believe in the Creed. The more intensely Americans commit themselves to their national political beliefs, the more hostile or cynical they become about their political institutions. As a result of the IvI gap, the legitimacy of American government varies inversely with belief in American political ideals.

The Gap in Comparative Perspective

A gap between political ideal and political reality exists in all societies, but the United States is unique among countries in the scope and depth of its commitment to liberal, democratic, and egalitarian values. This "atomistic, individualistic ideology," George Lodge observed, truly "constitutes a fundamental aberration from the historically typical norm."[12] Over the years, dozens of systematic studies and hundreds of impressionistic ones have compared American values, political and otherwise, with those of other countries. Almost without exception they show Americans to believe more strongly in liberal, egalitarian, democratic, and individualistic values than people in other societies.[13] The United States differs from some societies, particularly those in Europe, in the extent of its historical consensus on these values. It differs from other societies, including Asian and communist societies, in the substance of that consensus. In most other countries, not only is the political ideology supportive of the state but the formulation and articulation of that ideology is controlled by those who control the state. In the United States the gap between political ideal and political reality is a weapon always available for use by social groups against those who control the state. The dominant political creed constitutes a standing challenge to the power of government and the legitimacy of political institutions. Political authority is vulnerable in America as it is nowhere else.

European Societies

Consider the contrast between the United States and European societies. Most western European societies have inherited patterns of ideological pluralism, giving rise to interclass and interparty ideological conflict. As a result, the political institutions reflect a variety of ideological influences. The adherents of particular ideologies typically have had distinctive and continuing affinities with particular political institutions. Conservatives support the monarchy (if there is one), the executive, the aristocracy, upper houses in the legislature, the courts, and, traditionally, the bureaucracy. Liberalism and republicanism are identified with parliaments and parties. Socialists and Marxists support trade unions, working-class parties, universal suffrage, and, in some circumstances, popularly elected legislatures. As a result, when the legitimacy of an institution is challenged in terms of one ideology, it can usually be defended in terms of another that has significant appeal within the society.

In the French republics, the republicans and the Left historically challenged and the Right defended the power of the executive; their roles were reversed with respect to the power of the assembly. In Britain a Marxist attack on the Crown or Parliament will lead to liberal, democratic, socialist, or conservative defenses of these institutions. In America, on the other hand, if an institution or practice is illegitimate according to the democratic and liberal norms of the American Creed, it has no alternative defenses available in conservative, aristocratic, Marxist, or Christian democratic traditions, as there would be in most western European countries. There is only one source of legitimacy, and if it is taken seriously much of what is inherent in any government—including government in the United States—verges on illegitimacy. Political institutions and practices stand alone and defenseless before the overpowering liberal consensus.

The ideological pluralism in Europe also means that liberal, democratic, and egalitarian norms are generally weaker in European countries than they are in the United States and that nonliberal, nondemocratic norms stressing hierarchy, authority, and deference are stronger. Comparisons of political culture consistently document these differences. From Crèvecoeur and Tocqueville to the present, almost without exception, European observers have focused upon egalitarianism, openness, absence of social hierarchy, suspicion of political authority, and belief in popular sovereignty as critical characteristics distinguishing American from European politics. In the mid-twentieth century, as Max Beloff summarized it, the "United States is still essentially, in the things that make it different from Western Europe or from Britain, the United States that Tocqueville saw."[14] In comparison with major European countries such as Britain, Germany, and Italy, the United States has a "participant" political culture. The "participant orientation in the United States appears better developed than subject orientation and to some extent dominates it." This imbalance, Gabriel Almond and Sidney Verba argued, "is the result of American historical experience with governmental and bureaucratic authority—an experience that began with distrust and revolution against the British Crown, and that has been consolidated by the American tendency to subject all governmental institutions, including the judiciary and bureaucracy, to direct popular control." Similarly, a significantly lower proportion of Americans than Europeans agreed that "the individual owes his first duty to the state and only secondarily to his personal welfare."[15] (See Table 1.)

The political values and attitudes of young people reveal differences between Europe and America comparable to those found in the political

Table 1. Individual freedom versus duty to the state.[a]

	United States	United Kingdom	Germany	Italy	Mexico
Agree	25%	38%	41%	48%	92%
Disagree	68	55	45	32	5
Don't know, etc.	7	7	14	20	3

Source: Donald J. Devine, *The Political Culture of the United States* (Boston: Little, Brown, 1972), p. 193, reporting results of survey included in Almond-Verba study.

a. Statement presented to respondents: "The individual owes his first duty to the state and only secondarily to his personal welfare."

cultures generally. In a study of the attitudes toward democracy of teenagers in the United States, the United Kingdom, Germany, and Italy, the Americans were "more often highest in choosing the democratic options and lowest in choosing the anti-democratic options."[16] Similar results were obtained by Greenstein and Tarrow when they polled American, English, and French schoolchildren as to their reactions to a hypothetical situation in which a policeman stopped the head of state for speeding. The American children were almost twice as likely as the British and French children to imagine that the head of state would be punished (that is, they expected the President to be treated like any other citizen), were much more likely to imagine the head of state approving the action of the policeman (that is, they expected the President himself to adhere to egalitarian norms), and were almost twice as likely to maintain that in this situation "everyone should be equal before the law."[17] In yet another study, American, British, and German schoolchildren were asked to choose individual values and priorities that they would use in organizing a hypothetical island society. The "overall orientation" of the Americans was described as "equalitarian," combining both a commitment to the public good with a stress on "negative freedom," whereas the British were found to be oriented to private interest and the Germans were concerned with rules and obedience.[18]

With its interlocking history and its similar social, economic, political, and geographical characteristics, Canada closely resembles the United States. No other country, except possibly Australia, has political and social values so similar to those of the United States.[19] Yet significant differences exist. Canada has no counterpart to the dynamic drive "to realize the American dream of liberty and justice for all." As a result, its politics has lacked the messianic strand and the extremist movements that have existed in American politics; it has been more relaxed, tolerant, varied, and uninspiring. American political culture is utopian and pragmatic, Canadian political culture only pragmatic.[20]

Canadians have historically been more conservative, more collectivist, more pro-state and respectful of authority, and less egalitarian and individualistic than Americans. "What is clearly absent from Canadian political consciousness, though salient in the American, is the conviction that the state and its apparatus are the natural enemies of freedom."[21] Canadian national character, it has been argued, "tends to be ascriptive, anti-egalitarian, and bureaucratic; the American tends to be egalitarian, achievement-oriented, and entrepreneurial." Canadian conservatism has not been of the same individualistic, antigovernment, laissez-faire variety as American conservatism. In contrast to American politics, Canadian politics encompasses a strong corporatist strand, deferential patterns of authority, and a "quasi-participative" politics. Fundamentally, "the difference is between the American Lockean, individualistic conception of society and an organic, collective view brought initially to Canada by the Empire Loyalists who settled there following the American Revolution."[22] More generally, in contrast to the United States, English Canada is not a "one true myth culture" and the pattern of Canadian development established "the legitimacy of ideological diversity in English Canada."[23]

Bilateral comparisons between the United States and individual European countries underline even more dramatically the American commitment to egalitarian and democratic values, and the differences between ideological homogeneity and ideological pluralism. Since the eighteenth century, the contrast with Britain has been particularly striking. Even allowing for the hyperbole of which he was capable, Edmund Burke still articulated a central aspect of the attitudes of Englishmen toward authority when he declared, "We fear God; we look up with awe to kings; with affection to parliaments; with duty to magistrates; with reverence to priests; and with respect to nobility." Fear, duty, awe, reverence, respect, even affection are not words that one would ever use to describe American attitudes toward sources of authority. The American approach was equally well summed up by Burke when he said that the "fierce spirit of liberty" was stronger among the Americans, "probably, than in any other people of the earth," and that in the American character "a love of freedom is the predominating feature which marks and distinguishes the whole." The Americans "are Protestants, and of that kind which is the most averse to all implicit submission of mind and opinion . . . The dissenting interests have sprung up in direct opposition to all the ordinary powers of the world . . . All Protestantism, even the most cold and passive, is a sort of dissent. But the religion most prevalent in our northern colonies is a refinement on the principle of resistance: it is the dissidence of dissent, and the Protestantism of the Protestant religion."[24]

In the following centuries, acute observers, including Tocqueville and Bagehot, continued to stress the egalitarian and competitive elements in American political culture in contrast to the deferential and ascriptive values prevalent in Britain. Deference has historically been characteristic of both British middle-class and working-class viewpoints.[25] Writing in the mid-1960s, historian A. P. Thornton concluded that the British people were "still habituated to authority, and still—despite the satire from the flanks of the middle class—inclined to that deference to it that Bagehot had commented on a century before, although more perceptive as to its nature."[26] Similarly, a study of the personal qualities most admired by American and English insurance clerks found the Americans much more likely to admire "un-moral, environment-exploiting qualities," whereas the English were much more likely to admire "control of anti-social impulses." Young elites in England are more ideologically diverse than those in the United States, who are overwhelmingly liberal in outlook. The central theme among the Americans, moreover, "was of a failure to live up to American ideals, in matters of race, poverty and the use of national power abroad."[27]

Both the United States and Great Britain are democratic and pluralistic, but the United States is also egalitarian, individualistic, and populist, whereas Britain is hierarchical and collectivist. "Even when it is distrusted," Edward Shils observed, "the Government, instead of being looked down upon, as it often is in the United States, is, as such, the object of deference." These different attitudes toward authority produce markedly different approaches to government secrecy and individual privacy in England and America, differences that were dramatically revealed during the McCarthy years of the early 1950s and again during the years of exposure of the late 1960s. "The United States has been committed to the principle of publicity since its origin . . . Repugnance for governmental secretiveness was an offspring of the distrust of aristocracy." In contrast, "the acceptance of hierarchy in British society permits the Government to retain its secrets, with little challenge or resentment."[28]

A major contrast also exists between American attitudes and those that have historically prevailed in Germany. Authoritarianism in the family, in society, and in politics was widely perceived as characteristic of German culture. The state and its authority were central to German political practice and theory. Discipline was much more stringent, authority much more respected, and status differences much more clearly defined and valued in the German military than in the American armed forces. "For the American," Alex Inkeles and Daniel Levinson observed, "precise differences in status are a source of discomfort, since they challenge his conception of himself as an equal, as an individual who will be valued for his personal qualities and on the basis of those alone." In contrast, the Germans manifested "a strong interest in status" and were said to be "most comfortable in relations where status is precisely defined. Correspondingly, status differences are always kept unmistakably distinct in the German military . . . Authority and discipline are infinitely more demanding and rigorous in the German Army, because the American values the self and sees obedience to authority as essentially ego-humbling."[29]

Similar differences existed between German and American children. In the mid-1930s, comparing the status of children in pre-Hitler Germany with their status in the United States, Kurt Lewin observed that "to one who comes from Germany, the degree of freedom and independence of children and adolescents in the United States is very impressive. Especially the lack of servility of the young child toward adults or the student toward his professor is striking. The adults, too, treat the child much more on an equal footing, whereas in Germany it seems to be the natural right of the adult to rule and the duty of the child to obey."[30] These differences undoubtedly narrowed after 1945, but they did not disappear. In the 1966–67 four-country study, for instance, which revealed American schoolchildren most likely to choose democratic options and least likely to choose antidemocratic ones, German schoolchildren were most likely to do just the reverse. (Schoolchildren in the United Kingdom and Italy ranked in the middle.)

In similar fashion, German parents were much more likely than American parents to engage in "parenting behavior," controlling, directing, and associating with their children. For German children, this meant "a prolongation of dependency, postponement of participation in semi-autonomous peer-group activity, and delay in the development of motives for self-directed achievement." Research in the late 1960s found among German adolescents "a docile, dependent, almost childlike attitude towards government authority"—an attitude missing among their English and American peers. In yet another study of Germans and Americans in their late teens, the Americans were found to be more achievement-oriented, more insistent on their individual freedom to choose what they wanted, and more willing to adapt these free choices to group norms. The Germans, on the other hand, found their sense of self by controlling themselves in terms of an idealistic code. "The German starts with 'I must' —a sense of living up to standards expected of him, rather than an 'I want' as the American does. In fact, starting with an 'I want' seems inexcusably selfish to the Germans. 'Wants' need to be suppressed for the good of the whole. Hence the emphasis on will power: 'I must be able to do what I should.' " These differences, in turn, were reflected in the high esteem that government employment had in Germany, compared with its low esteem in the United States.[31]

In the United States, the critical question has always been whether democratic and liberal norms are sufficiently tolerant to accommodate an effective system of government. In Germany, the question has historically been whether traditional authoritarian and hierarchical norms can be sufficiently modified to accommodate a democratic system of government. The gap between political norms and political institutions was too great to permit the Weimar Republic to survive. In West Germany, political institutions have been less democratic and political values less authoritarian than they were in Weimar. Yet even in the early 1960s, the striking passivity of the Germans with respect to politics, the lack of political involvement by a large portion of the population, and their "subject orientation" toward the output-bureaucratic side rather than the input-political side of government all seemed to "indicate a political system in which firmly democratic attitudes are as yet not established." Eighteen years after World War II it could thus still be concluded that "ascriptive, elitist values are far from dead in West Germany." Other studies showed that the themes in German reading texts for children in the 1950s did not different significantly from those in texts written in the 1920s. Consequently it was wrong, at least as of the early 1960s, to think that "the Germans have fundamentally changed" and become "good democrats like the Americans"; the Germans, it was argued, "have a political but not a psychological democracy."[32]

Between the early 1960s and the late 1970s, however, important changes did occur in West German political culture and support for democratic values increased significantly. In 1953, for instance, 50 percent of the West German public favored a democratic system of government; in 1967, 74 percent thought that democracy was the best system for Germany; and in 1972 and 1976, 90 percent said they were satisfied with democracy in West Germany. Other studies and surveys support the conclusion that in the years after 1959 "democratic and participatory norms" became "widespread" in West Germany.[33] This shift in German political values and attitudes was largely a product of generational change, with the generations that emerged on the political scene after 1945 manifesting much greater commitment to democratic values than those who had matured during the Empire, the Weimar Republic, or the Third Reich. In the early 1970s, Karl Dietrich Bracher argued that there still existed within Germany "a continuation of pre-fascist and authoritarian conditions and patterns of behavior," and another scholar could claim that "the state tradition" was "still alive in the German political consciousness."[34] It seemed probable, however, that such tendencies would continue to subside as successive age cohorts were socialized into the democratic political culture of the Federal Republic.

These changes in German political culture reduced the differences between the German and American political values. At the end of the 1970s, it was, indeed, claimed that German political culture was, in some respects, closer to the ideal, democratic "civic culture" than either British or American political culture. This broadening support for democratic values in Germany was also associated, at least temporarily, with broader support for and pride in German political institutions. In 1959, for instance, only 7 percent of West Germans mentioned their political institutions as something they could be "most proud of." In 1978, 31 percent of the German public said they were especially proud of their political institutions.[35] In the 1960s and early 1970s, consequently, a mixed political culture, including both authoritarian and democratic elements, gave way to one characterized by a fairly broad consensus on democratic values. During these years, this consensus generated support for and pride in the democratic political institutions of the Federal Republic. It also, however, contained within itself the seeds of a new cleavage similar to that which traditionally existed in the United States. In the early 1950s, the emerging democratic institutions of West Germany were challenged by the significant support that still existed for authoritarian political values. In the late 1970s, the established democratic political institutions of West Germany were criticized because they deviated too far from the democratic political values that had become dominant in the country. Germans were increasingly "likely to demand that it [their political system] live up to its ideals . . . The elements most critical of German society in the late 1970s are found among the same groups, the young and the well educated, that spearheaded the growth of democratic norms during the preceding three decades."[36] Democratic consensus was generating a German version of the "American disease" of cognitive dissonance rooted in the gap between political ideals and political reality.

Perhaps the outstanding aspect of French political culture is its dual character. On the one hand, there is a tradition of elitism, hierarchy, and sharp class divisions. On the other, there is the French Revolution's legacy of liberty, equality, and fraternity. The result has been continuing cleavages and at times polarization in political values. "The ascriptive, elitist, and particularistic aspects of French values," Lipset observed, "facilitated the emergence of politics along class lines, while the emphasis on equalitarianism, universalism, and achievement has led the less privileged strata to sharply resent their position." The attitudinal consequences of this bifurcated legacy are neatly reflected in a 1960s poll of Grenoble schoolchildren on the question: "Was the Revolution of 1789 a good or an evil?" Fifty-five percent of the children said good, 30 percent evil.[37]

Interpretations of French political culture are dominated by what William Schonfeld labeled "two-France theories." At the individual level, this means that "each Frenchman has two distinct sets of dispositions toward political authority: he both fears, dislikes, distrusts, and seeks to avoid submission to authority and concurrently needs, seeks, and depends upon political authority." The reluctance of the French to resolve problems in face-to-face negotiations among equals results in both the strengthening of authority and its centralization. Yet, at the same time, authority has to be exercised within certain defined constraints and may be subject to sudden disruption. The result, as Stanley Hoffmann suggested, is neither a democratic nor an authoritarian pattern, but rather "the coexistence of *limited* authoritarianism and *potential* insurrection against authority."[38] In a sense, the authoritarian strand of the French tradition faces an ever-present potential challenge from the revolutionary strand of that tradition. The parallel and contrast with the United States are clear: in the United States the equivalent of the revolutionary tradition is the only tradition in politics, and there is no authoritarian tradition in government.

Fewer studies have been done comparing political values in the United States with those in Southern European or Latin American countries. It seems probable, however, that such comparisons would yield differences similar to those between the United States and Britain, France, and Germany. It has been observed, for instance, that North Americans most often fear tyranny, oppression, and the abuse of power, whereas Argentinians—and Latin Americans generally—fear disorder and anarchy. Americans feel uneasy when the government is too strong, Argentinians and other Latins when it is too weak. In support of this argument, one study of Mexican and American schoolchildren concerning the concept of respect found that among the Americans "there seems to be a consistent overall pattern of relatively detached give-and-take among equals." The Mexican pattern was "quite different" and tended "to be on the authoritarian mode. Most of the Mexicans think that respect involves a positive duty to obey; and a third of them, unlike most American students, feel that respect means you *have* to obey the respected person, whether you like it or not." Another study found that 94 percent of Mexican students, compared with only 59 percent of American students, agreed with the statement that "obedience and respect for authority are the most important virtues a child should learn."[39] As in other societies, attitudes in Mexico toward authority relations in politics parallel those toward authority relations in the family, the dominant authority of the father going hand-in-hand with his responsibility for the other members of the family.

Major differences have thus existed between American political values, with their stress on individualism, liberty, equality, and opposition to power and authority, and political values in other Western countries where values are more varied and more heavily weighted toward authority and hierarchy. In the 1960s and 1970s support for democracy did become more widespread in West Germany, but liberal, democratic, and anti-government values still did not have in Europe the virtual unanimity of support that they commanded in the United States. Liberty and equality have historically also been more widespread in practice in America than they have been in Europe. Yet the IvI gap has been smaller in Europe than in the United States, and hence European observers have not been sensitive to its existence in America. At least since Tocqueville, they have stressed the relative prevalence of equality and liberty in America without differentiating the normative and existential dimensions. With the notable exception of Gunnar Myrdal, they have focused on the gap that separates American ideals and institutions from European ideals and institutions, glossing over the gap between American ideals and American institutions. They have, consequently, missed the disharmony that is such a central feature of American politics.

Non-Western Societies

The Anglo-American relies upon personal interest to accomplish his ends and gives free scope to the unguided strength and common sense of the people; the Russian centers all the authority of society in a single arm. The principal instrument of the former is freedom; of the latter, servitude.   *Alexis de Tocqueville (1835)*

Their reliance upon order and hierarchy and our faith in freedom and equality are poles apart and it is hard for us to give hierarchy its just due as a possible social mechanism. Japan's confidence in hierarchy is basic in her whole notion of man's relation to his fellow man and of man's relation to the State.   *Ruth Benedict (1946)*

The American cultural perspective, of course, places strong emphasis on the importance of the individual in society, on personal responsibility, and on self-realization. The Chinese emphasis on social interrelatedness, on the basic importance of group life, and on submission of the individual to collective interests, stands out as a fundamental cultural difference.   *Richard H. Solomon (1971)*

The Soviet Union and the major societies of Asia—China, Japan, India—lack the tradition of class-based ideological pluralism that has characterized western European development. Some of them, indeed, have been characterized by a high degree of homogeneity in political values and ideology. In some measure, the Soviet Union, China, and Japan are "consensus" societies like the United States and unlike the societies of western Europe. What distinguishes these societies from the United States is the content of the consensus. In Japan, despite the import of Western democratic, socialist, and Marxist ideologies, a continuity in basic norms of social and political organizations has been maintained from the late feudal Tokugawa era into the modern, post–World War II period. In the Soviet Union, a successful revolutionary party eliminated the liberal tendencies that appeared in the late nineteenth century and imposed ideological homogeneity on a reconstructed society. In China, revolutionary upheaval produced a new political culture combining elements of both revolutionary and traditional (Confucian) political culture. In all three societies, however, as the quotations above suggest, the dominant values and norms of the political culture differ fundamentally from the liberal, democratic, egalitarian, and individualistic values that prevail in the United States. The tradition of middle-class liberalism, which preempts the scene in the Uinted States and shares the stage in western Europe, has been totally absent or has had only a marginal or aborted existence in these non-Western societies. As a result, in all three societies the dominant norms have tended to reinforce and to strengthen political authority, in contrast to the United States, where they tend to limit and weaken that authority.

The Soviet Union resembles the United States in that its identity is defined primarily in political and ideological terms. In terms of its abstract substance, Soviet ideology could also, like that of the United States, pose challenges to political authority. Marxism is, after all, the revolutionary ideology par excellence; it contains substantial humanistic elements; and it posits the withering away of the state in the postrevolutionary transition from socialism to communism. Thus, in both the United States and the Soviet Union, the political system is, in a sense, closeted alone with an ideology that is against authority and against hierarchy, while at the same time favorable to social, economic, and political equality and the dilution of government into society. Yet Marxism, as it exists in the Soviet Union, is not just Marxism, it is Marxism-Leninism, and the latter makes explicit provision for an organ—the communist party—whose functions include both ideological interpretation and political rule. The central tenet of Marxism-Leninism is the dominance of the party; the corresponding tenet of "Americanism" is the dominance of the people. In the Soviet Union, the ideology cannot be used against the system because the ideology holds that those who control the system also control the ideology. Marxism-Leninism thus becomes a tool for the maintenance of the Soviet system and a theoretical framework in terms of which leadership elites may debate political and policy choices, but it cannot become a vehicle for challenging the system.

In the United States, no single group or institution monopolizes the interpretation of American political ideas and principles. Those principles are, in many respects, even more hostile to established authority than those of Marxism, and hence they are regularly used by social forces to limit, constrain, and weaken political authority. Hence, too, the more intensely committed one becomes to American ideals, the more critical one becomes of the structure of authority in American institutions. In the Soviet Union, on the other hand, the more intensely committed one becomes to Marxism-Leninism, the more supportive one becomes of the structure of authority in Soviet institutions. The problem for Soviet leaders is caused by people losing their commitment to the ideology of the leaders and becoming indifferent, passive, and cynical. The problem for American leaders is caused by people intensifying their commitment to the ideology of the leaders and attempting to reform and change institutions, practices, and leaders. Dissidents in the United States often—and successfully—appeal to the values of American liberalism. Dissidents in the Soviet Union typically are driven to appeal against the values of Soviet Marxism-Leninism and to urge that these values be moderated or supplemented by religious, liberal, or humanistic norms.

At the more basic, if less conscious, cultural level, Soviet norms and attitudes toward authority represent a natural evolution out of the Russian past. In the sixteenth century, Ivan the Terrible said that "the rulers of Russia have not been accountable to anyone, but have been free to reward or to chastise their subjects," and this traditionally has been the case. Autocratic rule, the subordination of all to the state, the centralization of political authority, and the necessity for obedience were all continuing elements in the Russian political tradition—elements that were challenged only weakly and transitorily by the liberalism imported from the West in the late nineteenth and early twentieth centuries. "It can be said of the Russians, great or small," the Marquis de Custine observed in the 1830s, that "they are intoxicated with slavery." The "terrified reverence for authority" denoted by the Russian word *strakh* marks a holdover from peasant Russia to communist Russia. In this, as in the broader pattern of "dual Russia"—the existence of a state above and apart from the nation—the political norms and practice of the Soviet system have their roots in the autocracy of the czarist past.[40]

In Soviet Russia, "the demand for obedience" is the central element in the political creed. It is also the first imperative in the upbringing of the Soviet child, self-discipline being the second. In comparison with their American counterparts, Soviet children tend to be less hostile toward adults, less rebellious, less aggressive, and less delinquent. They have "less inclination to engage in anti-social behavior," and less autonomy, reflected in the fact that in the United States, peer group pressures on children typically conflict with adult pressures, while in the Soviet Union they reinforce such pressures.[41] More generally, Russians seem to have a long-standing need for authority and order, and a fear of too much freedom that makes them uncomfortable with a politically free-wheeling, individualistic polity. Even émigrés from the Soviet Union in the 1940s were disturbed by the extent of free speech in the United States and "seemed basically disposed as well to accept the idea of centralized and essentially autocratic determination of national policy." In the late 1970s, a keen observer of the Soviet Union used similar terms: "Deeply rooted values that have prevailed since Czarist times foster a mystical respect for central authority, a yearning for order and unanimity, a distaste for disagreement and diversity, a dread of any turmoil of ideas. From this perspective, American society looks chaotic and frightening."[42]

The dominant social and political norms in Japan also differ sharply from American values and are much more supportive of existing structures of authority. There are, indeed, many similarities between the historical development of the Japanese and Russian political cultures, including their stress on collectivism, the state, and hierarchy and their opposition to individualism, which distinguish them from the American and other Western traditions.[43] In key respects, the political cultures of the United States and Japan "are as different from one another as may well be" and represent "deviant cases, ideal-type extremes in the spectrum of world experience." American ideals of "individualism, equality, mobility, competition" have little appeal in the Japanese context. "[The Japanese] ethic is group loyalty, hierarchical subordination redeemed by human intimacy, disciplined cooperation, a furious concern with the honor of their role. Their responsibility is not to the universal god or the singular self but to the social nexus and the particular lord. Their dogged virtue is in conformity to social demands and in the hard work that fosters social harmony."[44]

Instead of the egalitarian values prevalent in the United States, "rank is the social norm on which Japanese life is based." Japanese typically organize themselves vertically into a hierarchy of unequals rather than horizontally as an association of equals. "Japanese admit the fact of inequality; it is given; it is natural." "Ranking consciousness," or what Ruth Benedict referred to as the Japanese "faith and confidence in hierarchy," is a preeminent characteristic of the Japanese approach to the relations among individuals, groups, and nations. Each unit must be located at its appropriate spot in a hierarchy of superior-subordinate relations. For a country engaged in international relations, it is a question of "taking one's proper station." As one perceptive Japanese analyst put it, "the first element" in the problems posed by Japanese psychology in viewing relations with another nation is "the Japanese tendency to view their foreign relations hierarchically, in terms of 'high' and 'low' (jō-ge kankei), just as Japanese usually view their personal relations."[45]

In contrast to the individualism of Western societies, the Japanese person tends to be much more group-oriented and to identify with a single group of heterogeneous individuals who perform a variety of diffuse or relatively unspecialized roles. Loyalty to the group is emphasized; mobility from one group to another is discouraged; overt disagreement within the group is frowned upon. Japan, as one scholar has observed, "is a collectivistic society." In such a society, the critical need is to avoid competition and disharmony, and hence elaborate consultation within the group is required before a decision can be reached. Americans, on the other hand, are comfortable with open conflict, majority votes, and a more individualistic, "lone ranger" style of leadership.[46]

The preference for hierarchy and collectivity over equality and individualism reinforces the system of authority. At the time the Jacksonian passion for equality was engulfing the United States and impressing Tocqueville, the population of Tokugawa was stratified into classes and the political roles of the lower classes—merchants, artisans, peasants— was "restricted to the provision of loyalty, obedience, and support." The historical "iconic image" in the United States has been "the revolution against power misused . . . From the foundation of the United States there has been an explicit concern for the limitation of power. The history of Japan, on the other hand, is one of anarchic struggle and civil war or authoritarian domination, with nothing between these two extremes, for almost two millennia. How should the Japanese not welcome authority?"[47] After the Meiji Restoration the old system changed, but traditional patterns of deference and respect for authority continued into the late twentieth century. As Chie Nakane described it:

> The preeminence of authority implants in the Japanese a ready submissiveness, alongside fear and hostility. They are afraid to offer open hostility to authority and instead commit themselves to it, while admonishing one another to "wrap yourself up in something long" or "stand in the shadow of a big tree." Obedience in Japan takes the form of total submission. Any criticism of or opposition to authority tends to be seen as heroism . . . And, interestingly enough, such deeds today are labelled as democratic action. Often it is merely opposition for opposition's sake; it is nearer in essence to emotional contradiction, than to the rational resistance from which further reasonable development might be expected.[48]

In the thirty years after World War II, liberal and democratic values gained support in Japan, particularly among younger people. In 1953, for instance, the statement "If a competent political leader is available, it is better to leave things to him instead of discussing them among ordinary citizens" evoked agreement from 43 percent of the Japanese public and disagreement from 38 percent. In 1973, only 23 percent agreed with this statement, while 51 percent disagreed with it. Other indicators suggest, however, that even in the late 1960s, Japanese attitudes toward democracy were ambivalent. In 1973, 43 percent of the Japanese public said that they had a good opinion of democracy, 30 percent said they had a good opinion of liberalism, and 40–50 percent in each case said that their view would depend on the circumstances.[49] Between early 1953 and 1973 the proportion of the population that would follow conscience over custom in a personal decision decreased somewhat (41 percent to 36 percent), while the proportions that would prefer a paternalistic supervisor at work (81 percent) to a nonpaternalistic one (13 percent) and "discipline" (66 percent) over "freedom" (22 percent) in the upbringing of children were virtually unchanged. In the early 1960s, Japanese were also about evenly divided as to whether politics was improved by holding elections from time to time.[50] As of the early 1960s, the dominant value pattern in Japan, it was said,

> has in it substantial elements of the old order which emphasized the family and nation over the individual; discipline, duty, and obligation over freedom; distinction in status over equality; and racial arrogance over egalitarianism. The younger generation and the better educated, however, are slowly moving toward individualism and commitment to "democracy," but the movement is uneven, with strong survivals of ethnocentric, hierarchical, and holistic attitudes.

Authoritarian views—summarized in the phrase *kanson mimpi* (the official respected, the people despised)—remained a significant component in the national outlook.[51]

These traditional values supporting group loyalty, hierarchical ranking, and submission to authority are a product of Japanese history. They have been and will be modified by the impact of imported democratic, liberal, and socialist ideas. It would be a mistake, however, as Nakane warns, to assume that such traditional values are necessarily out of place in a society shaped by modernization and industrialization. Indeed, just the reverse may be true, and here there is a striking paradox in the comparison between the United States and a society like Japan. In some measure, "equality" is a modern, democratic value. In the absence of an aristocratic, feudal, or hierarchical tradition in the United States, this value takes precedence. In Japan as well as in the societies of western Europe, ideas of equality and democracy must compete with norms of social distinction, hierarchy, and inequality. The actual functioning of modern society, particularly a large, industrialized, bureaucratized society, requires, however, some measure of distinction, hierarchy, and inequality. Hence a society like Japan, which preserves into the modern era significant elements of its "traditional" value pattern, may find that these values have new relevance and usefulness. The great strength of the Japanese vertical type of organizational structure, Nakane suggests, "lies in its effectiveness for centralized communication and its capability of efficient and swift mobilization of the collective power of its members. The importance of its contribution to the process of modernization is immeasurable . . . This structure served to underpin Japan's post-war economic growth."[52] Americans and American-influenced Japanese who look upon this structure as feudal or traditional fail to see the extent to which it operates positively rather than negatively in "the interests of modernization."

The contrast between American values and Chinese values is equally striking. As was the case with Japan, Chinese society "stands at the opposite pole from American society. It rests on a fundamentally different ordering of values and principles." Unlike Americans, Chinese traditionally did not exist apart from their group. They had no natural rights or liberties. Instead the emphasis was on the "individual's duties and responsibilities to society and its subcollectivities."[53]

The central characteristics of traditional Chinese political culture were inequality, hierarchy, and absolutism. Absent from such a culture were elections, participation, representation, separation of powers, independent religion, and outside law. Or, as another scholar put it, in Chinese culture "authority was supposed to be absolute, harsh, and even ruthless; yet it was also seen as being subtle, wise, and the source of morality. It was to be feared and distrusted, yet also to be revered and relied upon."[54] Hierarchy, is pervasive. "An equal relationship," John Fairbank argued, "has little precedent in Chinese experience . . . Their solution [to politics] began with the observation that the order of nature is not egalitarian but hierarchic." Hence as Lucian Pye said, "in politics, there are no equals, only superiors and inferiors." Government is of supreme importance in China. In traditional China, there were no significant sources of status, power, or wealth outside of government—a phenomenon that continued into republican China and exists on a reintensified scale in communist China. The contrast with the United States—where wealth and status have traditionally been achieved outside government—is particularly marked. Government itself commands respect and prestige in China on a scale that is almost unique among societies. The "Chinese never developed," Pye observed, "the concept that governmental authority should be held in check in order to respect the integrity and the logical necessity of other large-scale systems of human interrelationships." The Chinese thus place "an extreme value on political power."[55]

Within traditional Chinese society, the state was seen as above and autonomous from society, and authority was centralized. "The distinction between ruler and subject, official and citizen, was sharp in both theory and practice." The emphasis on respect for authority pervaded all human relationships. It began with "the paramount value of filial piety . . . No other culture in history has placed such a stress upon filial piety as has the Chinese." The pervasiveness of authority in the society reinforced that of the state. In traditional China, the "sense of respect for authority which Confucian family life sought to instill was seen as basic to the stability of the dynasty." Or as one eleventh-century Chinese philosopher observed: "Only recognition of the relationship between superior and subordinate, between high and low, can insure order and obedience without confusion. How can people live properly without some means of control?"[56]

The Chinese demand for strong systems of authority, it has been argued, is related to their fear of the confusion and conflict that will result from its absence. At the same time, there is the need to maintain not only respect for authority but distance from authority, in order to avoid its potentially harsh impact. "People eat people," and hence government is necessary, but "oppressive government is more terrible than tigers." The result is a traditional outlook that could best be described as a "sense of passive impotence before power." It involved "an anxiety before social authority which produces such behavior as indirection in dealings with superiors, great reluctance to criticize, and an over-willingness to please those in power."[57] The concentration of power is the desirable, appropriate, and necessary remedy to the tendencies toward divisiveness and conflict.

Traditional Chinese culture thus strongly emphasized the value of hierarchical authority, centralized power, and a strong state. During periods of dynastic breakdown, these features tended to weaken or disappear. A Chinese IvI gap would then open up, precisely the reverse of that which has typified American politics during periods of creedal passion. In due course, however, after an interlude of confusion and war, a new ruler would seize control and establish his possession of the Mandate of Heaven, and the reality of Chinese government would once more be brought back into greater accord with its underlying principles. In large measure this is what happened after 1949, when the communists reestablished a strong system of authority throughout China for the first time since the beginnings of the decay of the Ch'ing dynasty in the nineteenth century.

Communist ideology—even, and in some respect particularly, in its Maoist version—clearly differs significantly from the traditional Confucianist creed. There is, as James Townsend summarized it, a stress on collectivism as against the particularism of clan and village, on class struggle as against social harmony, on activism as against passivity, on self-reliance as against dependence, and on egalitarianism as against hierarchy.[58] The weaving of these conflicting strands into an integrated political culture is still under way. On the other hand, Maoism and Chinese traditional political culture both reject any role for political liberty and individualism; both stress the necessity for a strong state and the subordination of society to the state; and, although their ideas as to what constitutes legitimate authority obviously differ, both see the need for respect for authority.

In many societies, principally in Europe, several different ideologies have existed, and the state has therefore not confronted a monolithic challenge. In Germany, a growing consensus on democratic values in the 1960s and 1970s began to create a relation between democratic ideals and existing institutions that had some parallels to that in the United States. Even so, American political culture still differed significantly from German political culture in its individualism, egalitarianism, and antistatism. In non-Western societies, a single belief system reinforces the authority of the existing order. In Europe, the security of the "is" rests on the plurality of "oughts"; in Russia and Asia, it rests on the control of the single "ought" by the single "is." In the United States, in contrast, the single all-pervasive "ought" rampages wildly beyond the control of the "is." The result is a unique and ever-present challenge to authority posed by the gap between the ideals by which the society lives and the institutions by which it functions.

4 COPING WITH THE GAP

The American Case of Cognitive Dissonance

"Men are not corrupted by the exercise of power or debased by the habit of obedience," observed Tocqueville, "but by the exercise of power which they believe to be illegitimate, and by obedience to a rule which they consider to be usurped and oppressive."[1] But what happens when the prevailing beliefs in a society taint almost all forms of power with illegitimacy and question most governmental rules as at least potentially usurped and oppressive? Precisely because of the liberal-democratic values embodied in the American Creed, the opportunities for the corruption of leaders and the debasement of the people are far more widespread in the United States than they are elsewhere. Americans are, in effect, compelled to develop their own distinctive ways of coping with the gap between liberal ideals and political reality and thus making power legitimate and obedience acceptable.

In a less developed society, traditional institutions lose legitimacy when key elements in the elites in those societies (intellectuals, the military) abandon their traditional beliefs and absorb modern values. In ideologically complex societies, existing institutions lose legitimacy as the social groups adhering to one ideology (for example, the working class) rise in importance and as those adhering to another ideology (for example, the land-owning aristocracy) decline in importance. Established institutions lose their legitimacy because of a change in either the substance or the scope of the prevailing political beliefs and attitudes. In the United States, in contrast, established institutions confront an ever-present challenge to their legitimacy. The gap between the real and the ideal poses a distinctive national problem of cognitive dissonance.

The formal theory of cognitive dissonance was devised by Leon Festinger to explain aspects of individual behavior, but it may also help illuminate the dilemmas facing collectivities. The theory postulates that inconsistency or dissonance in a person's beliefs, attitudes, or perceptions will be "psychologically uncomfortable" and "will motivate the person to try to reduce the dissonance and achieve consonance." The person will also "actively avoid situations and information which would likely increase the dissonance."[2] Among other things, the theory predicts that when the beliefs of a person are dissonant with his own observed behavior shaped by external restraints and requirements, he is likely to attempt to reduce this dissonance by altering his beliefs so as to bring them more into accord with his behavior. This would suggest that insofar as Americans perceive the gap between principle and practice (that is, in terms of the theory, insofar as this relationship is "important" to them), there would be strong tendencies for them to reduce their collective dissonance by bringing their beliefs more into line with their behavior. They would tend to moderate, reduce, or abandon their ideals. Is this a realistic way of resolving the national problem of cognitive dissonance?

The problems posed by this question were nicely illustrated by a panel discussion of the New England Political Science Association held in Amherst, Massachusetts, in the early 1950s. The subject of the panel was national security and individual freedom. The participants included two scholars presumably representing liberal and moderate viewpoints. The star of the panel, however, was Professor Willmore Kendall of Yale, who at that time was well known as a leading and controversial political theorist, an intellectual light in the New Conservative movement, and the mentor of William Buckley. Kendall had obviously been selected to present a "conservative" viewpoint in the discussion. The audience and the panel members were braced for a strong defense of Senator Joseph McCarthy, the FBI, the House Un-American Activities Committee, and government crackdown on radicals and dissidents.

Professor Kendall was not two minutes into his speech when it became clear that his audience had totally misjudged his intentions and outlook. He began with an eloquent and learned articulation of the basic American ideals of individual rights and due process of law, of John Locke and Thomas Jefferson, of the Declaration of Independence and the

Bill of Rights, of the American tradition of freedom of conscience and speech, and of the need to protect these rights against abuses by government. Eloquently and forcefully, he then documented the extent to which these traditional principles and liberties had been violated in recent years. There had been congressional witch-hunts, senatorial inquisitions, book burnings, character assassination, blacklisting of people who exercised their constitutional privileges against self-incrimination, attacks on the freedom of the press, and a wide variety of other actions by governmental agencies, popular groups, and self-proclaimed vigilantes—all of which clearly violated the traditional American ideals of individual rights and liberties.

This situation, Professor Kendall said, is clearly intolerable. What can we do to bring our practices and beliefs into accord with each other? At this point he paused, while his audience waited in pleased expectation for the reforms that he would now propose. And then it came: clearly, Kendall said, we must get rid of our obsolete eighteenth-century ideas about individual rights and freedoms. Two hundred political scientists gasped in shock, incredulity, horror, and dismay. They sat in stunned silence throughout the remainder of his talk.

The well-meaning professors could not bring themselves to believe that Kendall believed what he said. And conceivably he did not: he was quite capable of playing games with audiences. But the shocked disbelief that his remarks engendered illustrates dramatically the extent to which Americans are incapable of solving their problem of national cognitive dissonance by substantially abandoning their values. The Kendall Choice, the alternative most generally predicted by the theory of cognitive dissonance, simply will not work in the American case. If, indeed, Americans could so easily resolve their problem by altering or abandoning their values, they would be like the people of any other nation. But they cannot do so. Their political ideals are at the very core of their national identity. Americans cannot abandon them without ceasing to be Americans in the most meaningful sense of the word—without, in short, becoming "un-American." The Kendall Choice may be a real one for quixotic political theorists, but it is not a real one for the American public and it has never played a significant role in American history.

The dissonance—and the dilemma—thus remain. Americans cannot be themselves unless they believe in their Creed, and if they believe in their Creed they must be against themselves.

Patterns of Response

What are the ways in which Americans cope with their national cognitive dissonance? Consensus and stability have generally characterized American political values, and the IvI gap is always present. Variations do occur, however, in the intensity with which groups of Americans hold to their beliefs in American political ideals—that is, the level of creedal passion in American society—and in the clarity with which Americans perceive the gap to exist. Differences in these two variables can yield the four major responses set forth in Table 2.

Table 2. American responses to the IvI gap.

Intensity of belief in ideals	Perception of gap	
	Clear	Unclear
High	Moralism (eliminate gap)	Hypocrisy (deny gap)
Low	Cynicism (tolerate gap)	Complacency (ignore gap)

1. *Moralism.* If Americans intensely believe in their ideals and clearly perceive the IvI gap, they moralistically attempt to *eliminate* the gap through reforms that will bring practice and institutions into accord with principles and beliefs.

2. *Cynicism.* If intensity of belief is low and perception of the gap is clear, Americans will resort to a cynical willingness to *tolerate* the gap's existence.

3. *Complacency.* If intensity of belief is low and their perception of the gap is unclear, Americans can attempt to *ignore* the existence of the gap by in effect reducing its cognitive importance to themselves through complacent indifference.

4. *Hypocrisy.* If they are intensely committed to American ideals and yet *deny* the existence of a gap between ideals and reality, they can alter not reality but their perceptions of reality through an immense effort at "patriotic" hypocrisy.*

---

* Some may observe that the labels I have given these four responses all carry unfavorable connotations—and this is certainly true. One could, perhaps, find euphemisms and talk about morality rather than moralism, realism rather than cynicism, satisfaction rather than complacency, and patriotism rather than hypoc-

At various times social critics, including foreign observers of the American scene, have seized upon one or another of these four responses as *the* typical American response. In fact, however, all four have been present throughout most of American history, interacting with one another in mutually reinforcing and mutually counterbalancing ways.[3] Complacency is probably the most prevalent response, but it is also the least noted and least notable one. The others have all left a definite mark on American culture.

The tolerance of the IvI gap which is the essence of the cynical response is, for instance, a major source of American humor. Comedy depends on incongruity, and the sources of incongruity vary from one society to another. It has been observed that "nearly all the greatest British comedy rests on class differences. From *The Country Wife* to *The Diary of a Nobody,* from P. G. Wodehouse to Anthony Powell, or from Chaucer to Nancy Mitford, few writers have set out to amuse their readers without going straight to the class structure."[4] In America the source of comedy is not the incongruity between classes, but, as Louis Rubin argued, "the incongruity between the ideal and the real . . . [that] lies at the heart of the American experience." This incongruity provides the central theme of most American humor, manifested most notably, perhaps, in the work of that most American of humorists, Mark Twain. "Out of the incongruity between mundane circumstance and heroic ideal," Rubin goes on to observe, "material fact and spiritual hunger. . . . theory of equality and fact of social and economic inequality, the Declaration of Independence and the Prohibition Act, the Gettysburg Address and the Gross National Product, the Battle Hymn of the Republic and Dollar Diplomacy, the Horatio Alger ideal and the New York Social Register—between what men would be and must be, as acted out in American experience, have come a great deal of pathos, no small bit of tragedy, and also a great deal of humor." This was what Robert Penn Warren identified as the "burr under the metaphysical saddle of America," the problem of living in the same house with "a big promise—a great big one: the Declaration of Independence."[5] The gap between how Americans ideally should behave and how they actually behave furnishes an inexhaustible lode for the ridicule of moral pretense. The Americans delight in being "debunked"—

risy. Yet these pleasant alternative labels obscure the critical point: that each response is, in some measure, unsatisfactory and cannot be maintained for long by substantial numbers of people. They tend to hide the problem of the gap rather than to highlight it.

"bunk" itself being an American word.[6] Humor becomes one way of coping with the national problem of cognitive dissonance. The promise of American life is transformed into "the great American joke."

Not surprisingly, foreign observers have often pointed to hypocrisy as a distinctive characteristic of American culture. Although there is no reason to assign it a predominant role, there can be little doubt that it occupies a central place in American politics. Americans want to believe that their liberal-democratic ideals are reflected in their institutions. This belief is often expressed to foreigners and engenders the view abroad that Americans are given to hypocritical moralistic cant. As Irving Kristol suggested, this public hypocrisy has its roots in the "deep emotional commitment" of Americans "to the idea that government—all government, everywhere—should be subservient to the citizen's individual life, his personal liberty, and his pursuit of happiness."[7] Americans find it congenial to believe that at least their government and political system meet this standard. In this respect, hypocrisy, defined by the dictionary as the "false pretense of moral excellence," is a product not just of practice deviating from one's principles, but also of asserting principles that cannot be practiced. Americans thus reduce their cognitive dissonance by clouding their perception of the realities of power, inequality, hierarchy, and constraints in American life.

All ruling classes must in some measure be hypocritical. This is especially true of modern liberal democracies, and the eruption of democracy in America during the Jacksonian years led writers such as Nathaniel Hawthorne to seize upon hypocrisy as the pervasive characteristic of American society. In a democracy, leaders such as Lincoln and Franklin Roosevelt are open to "endless accusations of hypocrisy" because they gave "a new vigor to flagging political principles and loyalties" and "raised the level of moral and political expectations," but were unable "to fulfill the standards they had themselves revived."[8] The most distinguished spokesmen of the American Establishment mouth the clichés of American liberalism as if they were realistic descriptions rather than pious aspirations. Ashamed of their power, their ability to wield it is constrained by their felt need to pretend that it does not exist. Yet although Americans may relish the exposure of hypocrisy, they are not comfortable when it is absent in their leaders. People demand high-mindedness in their public figures, and if "you are extraordinarily high-minded in your political pronouncements, you are bound in the nature of things to be more than ordinarily hypocritical."[9]

In the United States, indeed, public figures may be attacked for not being hypocritical enough—a point well illustrated by the reactions of some political figures to the earthy realism, vulgarity, and pathos revealed in the Nixon Watergate tapes. "There's no reference throughout the whole transcription," observed Senator Bob Packwood sanctimoniously, "to what is good for the American people. There are not even any token clichés about what is good for the people." In similar tones, Chairman Robert Strauss of the Democratic Party felt moved to complain: "It's sadder and sicker than I ever imagined. I keep looking for some mention of the American people, some concern for the nation."[10] Along with his other misdoings, Nixon was guilty of not carrying over into his private conversations with his aides the hypocritical clichés demanded of public rhetoric.

In similar fashion, moralism is also often pointed to as a peculiarly American trait. "Americans are eminently prophets," Santayana once observed. "They apply morals to public affairs; they are impatient and enthusiastic . . . They are men of principles, and fond of stating them."[11] Others have noted how this leads to a penchant, almost perverse in European eyes, for self-criticism, and have pointed to this attitude as the distinguishing characteristic of Americans. Gunnar Myrdal, indeed, defended Americans against the charge of hypocrisy and insisted upon their devotion to the moralistic exposure of evil:

> The *popular* explanation of the disparity in America between ideals and actual behavior is that Americans do not have the slightest intention of living up to the ideals which they talk about and put into their Constitution and laws. Many Americans are accustomed to talk loosely and disparagingly about adherence to the American Creed as "lip-service" and even "hypocrisy." Foreigners are even more prone to make such a characterization.
> This explanation is too superficial. To begin with, the true hypocrite sins in secret; he conceals his faults. The American, on the contrary, is strongly and sincerely "against sin," even, and not least, his own sins. He investigates his faults, puts them on record, and shouts them from the housetops, adding the most severe recriminations against himself, including the accusation of hypocrisy. If all the world is well informed about the political corruption, organized crime, and faltering system of justice in America, it is primarily not due to its malice but to American publicity about its own imperfections.[12]

Myrdal's statement about the passion of Americans for exposing their sins is perfectly true. But it is equally true that at various times some Americans may tolerate, ignore, or deny their sins. Moralism, cynicism, complacency, and hypocrisy are all familiar ways by which Americans respond to their cognitive dissonance problem. The role and importance of these responses, however, differ from time to time and from group to group.

Response Dynamics

The propensity of American society as a whole to resort to one response or another, or some combination of responses, varies. The national mood can at different times be described as predominantly one of complacency, hypocrisy, moralism, or cynicism. Experience suggests that recourse to one of these responses may generate consequences that encourage recourse to another response. No one response, however, provides a lasting satisfactory solution to the problem of cognitive dissonance. Each is tried for a while and then abandoned in a never-ending search for a way out of the national dilemma. The logical dynamics of such a cyclical pattern of response are as follows.

1. *Moralistic reform (eliminating the gap).* Since cognitive dissonance cannot be eliminated by changing fundamental principles, changes must occur in institutions and behavior. The moralistic response occurs when people feel intensely committed to American political values, clearly perceive the gap between ideals and reality, and attempt to restructure institutions and practices to reflect these ideals. The combination of intensity and perception furnishes the moral motive to reform. "The history of reform," Emerson said, "is always identical; it is the comparison of the idea with the fact."[13] Major groups in American society become obsessed with the facts of inequality, lack of freedom, arbitrary power. They dramatize those facts and force them upon the public consciousness, making it impossible for decision makers and the attentive public to ignore the extent to which the actuality of political life contradicts American beliefs. The moral indignation of the few stimulates public outrage from the many. Institutions and practices that had been accepted as part of the way things are lose their legitimacy. Demands for curtailing power and reforming the system sweep to the top of the political agenda: reality must be made to conform to the ideal. During such creedal passion periods, the latent disharmonic qualities of American society come to the surface.

2. *Cynicism (tolerating the gap).* Large bodies of people can sustain high levels of moral indignation for only limited periods of time. The un-

veiling of evil, which was first the instrument by which moralism laid bare hypocrisy, later furnishes the vindication of cynicism against moralism. The perception of the IvI gap remains, but the expectation that anything can be done to close the gap dwindles. Those who had expounded the Creed in order to change reality find themselves increasingly divorced from reality. The exposers of hypocrisy become the exemplars of hypocrisy.

Reform begins with the assumption that the elimination of evil can be achieved by the elimination of evil men-in-power. It moves on to the assumption that some restructuring of institutions is necessary. It comes to an end with the realization that neither of these will suffice. Some reformers conclude that the "system" itself must be totally changed and advocate revolution. Others let the intensity of their commitment to reform values decline and lapse into at least temporary cynical toleration of the gap. The feeling that the gap must be eliminated is replaced by the feeling that nothing can be changed. Moral indignation is replaced by moral helplessness. All politicians are crooks, all institutions corrupt. The gap must be accepted—and perhaps even enjoyed, as its role in American humor suggests.

3. *Complacency (ignoring the gap).* Cynicism is an effort to live with cognitive dissonance. But just as most people cannot maintain moral intensity indefinitely, neither can they indefinitely sustain toleration of the gap between ideal and practice. "Cognitive dissonance is a noxious state," and the "severity or the intensity of cognitive dissonance varies with the importance of the cognitions involved and the relative number of cognitions standing in dissonant relation to one another."[14] Whereas the escape from creedal passion to cynicism involves a dulling of moral sensibility, the escape from cynicism to complacency involves a dulling of perceptual clarity. The importance of the dissonant cognitions is reduced simply by turning attention to other matters. During such periods of creedal passivity and perceptual opaqueness, Americans may, if compelled to do so, admit the existence of a gap between ideal and reality— as they did for years with respect to the role of black people in American life—but then shunt it off into a back corner of their consciousness and simply not become terribly concerned about it. The dilemma, as Myrdal argued, exists but it does not trouble people nor lead them to become intensely and passionately concerned with resolving it. Cognitive dissonance lurks uneasily beneath the surface of conscience but is not sufficiently commanding to trouble people seriously. There is no intense concern

with American ideals or with the discrepancy between ideal and reality.

4. *Hypocrisy (denying the gap)*. The ideological nature of their national identity means that Americans cannot indefinitely eschew the affirmation of the basic values and principles of the national Creed. Responding to the need to articulate these values, however, they may still be reluctant to acknowledge the existence of the IvI gap. They may then view themselves through filtering lenses. American institutions are seen to be open and democratic; America is the land of opportunity; the equality of man is a fact in American life; the United States is the land of the free and the home of the brave; it is the embodiment of government of the people, by the people, and for the people. During these periods, Americans so shape their perceptions that they cannot see any gap between the unpleasant facts of political institutions and power in the United States and the values of the American Creed. Reality is hailed as the ideal. The discrepancies are strained out and avoided. The United States not only should be the land of liberty, equality, and justice for all; it actually is.

In due course, however, the intense assertion of American ideals leads to renewed perception of the IvI gap. New individuals and groups begin to use the affirmation of the ideals as a means not of glorifying the American way of life but of exposing it. The hypocritical identification of reality with ideal gives way to the moralistic denunciation of reality in terms of the ideal. The way is cleared for another wave of creedal passion directed toward reform.

This sequence of responses is designed as a model and not as a representation of empirical reality. History does not necessarily develop according to logical patterns. Some measure of psychological dissatisfaction is, however, the inevitable result of the IvI gap and some combination of moralism, cynicism, complacency, and hypocrisy is required to reduce that dissatisfaction. Particular phases in American history often tend to be colored more by one response than by the others, and one response often creates conditions favorable to the rise of another. History does not follow a logical model, but neither is the logical model irrelevant to the understanding of history.

Group Propensities

Just as different responses may predominate in different historical phases, so also different groups in society may have propensities toward

different responses. Age and socioeconomic status appear to have a significant effect upon people's choices

The American educational system, particularly at the elementary-
school level, indoctrinates its students in American ideals and minimizes
the disparity between ideal and reality. As a result, grade-school children
generally have highly positive and benign images of the political system,
the government, and particularly of the President.[15] They are, in short,
educated in the hypocritical response. These attitudes provide the basis
for their subsequent adult acceptance of the legitimacy of the political
system. Secondary-school children have more "realistic" and, in some respects, more cynical attitudes toward politics. There still remains, however, a substantial difference between their views and those of young adults
who have been out of school for several years. In addition, high-school
seniors have considerably lower levels of political cynicism than do their
parents who went to high school. Among those who leave school after
high school, increasing exposure to the unpleasant realities of political
life combines with feelings of limited political efficacy to produce a significantly more cynical approach to the political process. Among those
who go on to college, on the other hand, an increasingly clear perception
of the IvI gap encourages more of a shift toward moralism The educational system that minimizes the distinction between ideal and reality for
young children maximizes the impact of perceptions of that gap among
college-age youth. "Societies teach youth to adhere to the basic values of
the social system in absolute terms . . . Compromises which are dictated
by contradictory pressures and are justified in the eyes of many adults are
viewed by idealistic youth as violations of basic morality. Young people
tend to be committed to ideals rather than institutions. Hence, events
which point up the gap between ideals and reality often stimulate them to
action, though cynicism and withdrawal occur as well if they see no
appropriate way to act."[16] As people age, however, the intensity of belief
necessary for either hypocrisy or moralism tends to decline, and among
adults a high correlation exists between cynicism and age.[17]

Socioeconomic status plays an even more important role in shaping
response propensities. The available evidence suggests two significant
tendencies. First, almost all groups in American society favor the basic
liberal-democratic values of the American Creed. People who are better
educated, who are of higher socioeconomic status, and who occupy positions of social or political leadership are, however, more likely to support

those values than are other people. That is, the proportion of such groups affirming support for these values may be 85 percent rather than 65 percent or 70 percent.[18] This difference in breadth of support does not necessarily demonstrate anything about the relative intensity of support from these two groups, but it does suggest the probability that intensity of support will be greater among those of higher socioeconomic position. In addition, people with more education and of higher socioeconomic status are more likely to support the application of liberal-democratic values in specific instances than are other people.[19] Such evidence would clearly seem to indicate greater commitment to and intensity of belief in those liberal-democratic values. In short, there is reason to believe that higher-status people are more likely to be hypocritical or moralistic, and lower-status people cynical or complacent.

A second difference among groups according to socioeconomic status is even more clearly documented by the evidence. People who have less income and less education and who do not occupy leadership roles are more likely than others to have a critical view of the political process and to perceive a significant gap between American ideal and American reality. People of higher status, position, and education are less likely to perceive a wide gap between the two. As Table 3 indicates, Herbert McClosky found substantial differences in political cynicism between "political influentials," that is, people who had been delegates or alternates to a national party convention, and a cross-section of the general electorate. Overall, 10.1 percent of the influentials scored "high" on the cynicism scale, compared with 31.3 percent of the general population.[20] Similarly, a study of political ideology in Muskegon, Michigan, found that "the higher their income, the more people believe that the ideology of pluralism accurately describes the way the system works and, as a corollary, the lower their income, the less symmetry people see between normative and actualized aspects of the ideology . . . Higher income strata tend to equate normative and existential statements about political pluralism, while lower income strata tend to deny their symmetry and to support action to make them more congruent."[21] In similar fashion, black children and poor Appalachian children see the President as deviating significantly more from idealistic norms than do white middle-class children.[22] In short, higher-status people are more likely to be hypocritical or complacent, lower-status people to be cynical or moralistic.

These two conclusions on the relation of socioeconomic status to intensity of creedal beliefs and to clarity of perception of the IvI gap com-

Table 3. Responses to statements expressing cynicism toward government and politics.

	Percent of agreement	
Statement	Political influentials (N = 3020)	General electorate (N = 1484)
Most politicians are looking out for themselves above all else.	36.3	54.3
Both major parties in this country are controlled by the wealthy and are run for their benefit.	7.9	32.1
The people who really "run" the country do not even get known to the voters.	40.2	60.5
The laws of this country are supposed to benefit all of us equally, but the fact is that they're almost all "rich-man's laws."	8.4	33.3
Most politicians don't seem to me to really mean what they say.	24.7	55.1
There is practically no connection between what a politician says and what he will do once he gets elected.	21.4	54.0
All politics is controlled by political bosses.	15.6	45.9

Source: Herbert McClosky, "Consensus and Ideology in American Politics," *American Political Science Review* 58 (June 1964): 370.

bine to suggest one broad generalization. People of higher socioeconomic status are more likely than people of lower status to believe intensely in the values of the Creed and are less likely to perceive a major gap between those values and political reality. They consequently are likely to have a propensity toward the hypocritical response. People of lower socioeconomic status are less likely to have intense beliefs in the Creed. A large number of lower-status people probably do not concern themselves with politics and hence do not perceive a significant gap between ideal and reality. They are thus likely to have a propensity toward complacency. Insofar as lower-status people become politically aware, however, they will tend toward a cynical response.

This pattern of group propensities underlies the stability of the political system. Those who most intensely believe in the values of the system are less likely to see a gap between those values and political reality. Those who see such a gap are less likely to have the moralistic fervor to do anything about it. Upper-class and upper-middle-class hypocrisy combines with working-class and lower-class cynicism to perpetuate the status quo. At least this seems to be the predominant tendency for much of the time. To be sure, some people within the higher-status groups are ever sensitive to the gap between ideal and reality and regularly attempt to do something about it. Their success, however, is dependent upon their ability to mobilize additional support from those who are either hypocritical or cynical. Change in the system—or, if one views it unfavorably, instability —occurs when those who perceive the gap develop moralistic passion or when those who feel such passion come to perceive the gap. The latter shift, which normally involves significant changes in the perceptions of the upper middle class, has historically been the most important source of change in American political institutions and practices. Shifts in either perceptions or intensity may also affect different groups in the population differently. In the 1960s, for example, higher-status and lower-status groups both developed clearer perceptions of the gap betv en political ideals and political reality. As a result, higher-status groups became less hypocritical and more moralistic, furnishing the impetus for wide-ranging reforms of institutions and practices; at the same time, lower-status groups became less complacent and more cynical, causing a massive decline in popular trust and confidence in government, as reflected in public opinion polls.

If Americans do not blind themselves to reality, they have a choice between moralism and cynicism. If Americans do not falter in the intensity of their belief in American ideals, they have a choice between moralism and hypocrisy. Moralism is thus the one response that, in some sense, combines both realism and idealism. It involves the effort to remove the fundamental cause of American cognitive dissonance by reducing or eliminating the gap between promise and practice. In this sense it is the most positive American political response. As American history demonstrates, however, it can be not only the reformer but the destroyer of American institutions. Henry Stimson, at the end of an extraordinarily distinguished career of public service, concluded his memoirs with the words: "The only deadly sin I know is cynicism."[23] As a central figure of the American Establishment, Stimson focused on the popular sin of cynicism and did not recognize the Establishment sin of hypocrisy. More important, he also failed to note that in America the only deadly virtue is moralism.

The Gap and American Political Style

The Power Paradox

The coexistence in America of the antipower ethic with inequality in power gives rise to what may be termed the "power paradox": effective power is unnoticed power; power observed is power devalued. At times Americans have gloried in the conspicuous consumption of wealth, but never in the conspicuous employment of power. The architects of power in the United States must create a force that can be felt but not seen. Power remains strong when it remains in the dark; exposed to the sunlight it begins to evaporate.

The power paradox has manifested itself again and again in American political history and public debate. It is well illustrated by two major analyses of the power of that central institution of American politics, the Presidency.

The first, Richard Neustadt's penetrating volume, *Presidential Power,* published in 1960, was designed "to explore the power problem of the man inside the White House." This is "the classic problem of the man on top in any political system: how to be on top in fact as well as name." This is not easy for the President to achieve. *"The same conditions that promote his leadership in form preclude a guarantee of leadership in fact."* The book's basic theme was quite simple: the President does not have much power, or at least he has a lot less power than people assume. He is hemmed in by forces and groups outside his direct control, particularly Congress, the bureaucracy, and public opinion. Except in rare cases, the President does not have the power to command. His is essentially a power to persuade. He has great and diverse resources but has power only insofar as he can employ them in negotiations and bargaining. Neustadt dramatizes his point by quoting the remarks of President Truman on the frustrations awaiting his successor: "He [Eisenhower]'ll sit here, and he'll say, 'Do this! Do that!' *And nothing will happen.* Poor Ike—it won't be a bit like the Army. He'll find it very frustrating."[24] In 1960, Neustadt's picture of the limited, restrained, checked-and-balanced President was quite persuasive.

Thirteen years later, Arthur Schlesinger, Jr., painted an equally persuasive but very different picture in his work *The Imperial Presidency.*

Presidential primacy, he argued, has "turned into presidential supremacy." The "constitutional Presidency" had become the "imperial Presidency and threatens to be the revolutionary Presidency." The Presidency had appropriated the power of Congress in both foreign and domestic affairs, particularly in the former. The result was "an unprecedented concentration of power in the White House and an unprecedented attempt to transform the Presidency of the Constitution into a plebiscitary Presidency." The underlying issue confronting the country was "the expansion and abuse of presidential power."[25]

Readers of these two books would be tempted to conclude that the Presidency was weak in the late 1950s and early 1960s, and, following a decade of steady accretion of presidential power, became overwhelmingly strong in the early 1970s. But this conclusion would in many respects be wide of the mark. Due to the power paradox, something close to the opposite is true. The late 1950s and early 1960s represented a peaking of presidential power; by the early 1970s, it had been checked and reduced to its lowest point in at least forty years. Eisenhower and Kennedy represented the zenith.[26] The decline began with Lyndon Johnson and snowballed during the administration of Richard Nixon, reaching a nadir when he became the first American President to be driven from office.

The process of and the reasons for the decline of the Presidency have been set forth elsewhere. What is relevant here is the extent to which these two seminal books on the Presidency reflect the change in its power. Power revealed is power reduced; power concealed is power enhanced. Neustadt's concern over the "power problem" of the President in 1960 reflects the pervasiveness of presidential power. Schlesinger's equally deep concern over the imperial quality of presidential power in 1973 testifies to the waning of that power. In general, if it becomes widely accepted that the Presidency lacks extensive power and that its occupant is readily checked by other officials and groups, this fact in itself is evidence of *support for* presidential power and hence *the existence of* presidential power. If, on the other hand, people believe that the President is extremely powerful, this in itself is evidence (since great power is viewed as wrong) that the President is not so powerful or that his power is declining. When presidential power is really great, public opinion never considers it to be too great; when presidential power is fading, public opinion considers it inordinate.

The Presidency is not the only example of this phenomenon. In 1961, for instance, as he left office Eisenhower issued his famous warning about the "potential for the disastrous rise of misplaced power" and "unwarranted influence" stemming from the existence of the "military-industrial complex." Apart from a few pro forma nods, these words provoked little immediate reaction. But they could not have been more apposite and timely. The power, well placed or misplaced, of the military-industrial complex peaked in the early 1960s. Three days after Eisenhower issued his warning, John F. Kennedy assumed office and almost immediately launched a major increase in military spending which involved a 45 percent increase in the number of army divisions, a 50 percent increase in Polaris submarine construction, a 100 percent increase in Minuteman missile production capability, and a 100 percent increase in the number of nuclear weapons in strategic alert forces. The early 1960s were the high point of the post–World War II investment in major new military weapons systems. A President of the United States warned of the dangers that could arise from this power complex, yet neither Congress, nor the media, nor public opinion, nor scholars were motivated to act.

Ten years later, the situation was totally reversed. The power of the military-industrial complex was clearly on the decline; public priorities had shifted elsewhere; Congress closely scrutinized and at times rejected new weapons proposals; a variety of antimilitary interest groups and lobbies attacked the defense budget; military spending in real dollars, and particularly spending for hardware, declined year after year in the late 1960s and early 1970s; Lockheed teetered on the brink of bankruptcy. At the same time, and as a part of this decline in the power of the military-industrial complex, warnings about its power and attacks on its power escalated through the media and public debate. Eisenhower's remarks, which had been apposite and ignored in 1961, became inapposite and constantly quoted in 1971. In the course of a few years, a flood of volumes issued forth with titles such as *The Economy of Death, Pentagon Capitalism, American Militarism 1970, How to Control the Military, The Weapons Culture, The War Business, Militarism USA.* No issue of a popular journal was complete without an exposé of the machinations and power of the arms-manufacturing companies and their uniformed allies in the Pentagon. All this furor over the supposedly outrageous power of the military-industrial complex was, however, evidence of the very successful effort to reduce that power.

In some measure, this has always been the American pattern. Even as it achieved independence the nation was denouncing George III as a repressive tyrant and at the same time demonstrating how completely ineffective he was in that role. Throughout American history, the exposés of power, whether by the Muckrakers in the 1900s or their descendants in the 1960s, have been part and parcel of the reduction of power. This is not to say that all people and institutions who are identified, and hence criticized, as powerful are necessarily ineffectual. This clearly is not the case. But it does mean that individuals, groups, and institutions whose power is widely recognized and discussed are less powerful than if this were not the case. In other societies, individuals and groups may go to great lengths to call attention to their power. Awareness of power induces respect, obeisance, fear, awe: power breeds power. In the United States, however, awareness of power induces suspicion, hostility, and outrage. Because of the prevalence of the antipower ethic, awareness of power breeds its own reduction and hidden power is more effective. Because power is less legitimate in the United States than in other cultures, greater efforts have to be made to obscure it. It becomes necessary to deny the facts of power in order to preserve those facts. Yet the opportunities and the pressures to expose and publicize power pervade American public life. Consequently, because its visibility is its greatest vulnerability, the most effective exercise of power is the concealment of power; to cover up power becomes the first imperative of power.

The Cover-Up Imperative and Conspiracy Theories

In the American context, the cover-up of power is no easy task. A distinguishing characteristic of American politics is its open, public quality compared with the politics of other democratic (much less authoritarian) societies. Government is supposed to be open and aboveboard; secrecy implies evil. The American tradition, Edward Shils said, is one of "luxuriating publicity." The idea of *raison d'état,* of secrets of state, never took hold in America, any more than did the idea of "the state" itself. The United States is distinguished by "its passion for publicity and the weakness of traditions which would sustain the conventions of governmental privacy that are common in the democracies of western Europe." As a result, the principal institution of publicity, the press, has a status in the United States that is unequaled in Europe. In the United States, in contrast to Britain, one would never speak of "the awe of the press before the majesty of Government" because "the balance of power between Government and the press favors the Government in Great Britain and the press in the United States."[27] Open government is an American ideal

that has not been fully achieved in reality but it is also an American reality
that has never been approximated by other societies.

Not only is publicity more pervasive, it is also more erosive of power
in the United States than in any other society. Hence, greater efforts are
required to hide power in order to preserve its reality and its legitimacy.
A vicious circle develops: because power is abhorrent, it must be concealed, and because it is concealed, it becomes even more abhorrent. The
pervasive threat of publicity to power produces the pervasive need for
secrecy and deception about power. Because exposure is more devastating
in its consequences in the United States, secrecy becomes more necessary
and more difficult to achieve. There is thus, as Shils pointed out many
years ago, a close and natural affinity between publicity and secrecy that
works to the detriment of privacy. In Great Britain there has historically
been some sort of an equilibrium among these three; in the United States
the mania for publicity undermines privacy and creates a hypnotic fascination with secrecy. "Secrecy is less fascinating in Great Britain because
privacy is better maintained and publicity less rampant." The United
States, on the other hand, is characterized by "the preponderance of publicity and its attendant stress on salvationary secrecy over privacy."[28]

In an environment in which secrecy is salvationary, conspiracy theories
are heuristically indispensable. Three circumstances affect the prevalence
of conspiracy theories concerning the existence of secret power.

First, if power is clearly concentrated in an absolute monarch, a
charismatic leader, or a politburo—if, in other words, there is a single
open source of power—little incentive exists to develop a conspiracy
theory positing a single hidden source of power. If, however, power appears to be widely dispersed among a number of individuals, institutions,
and groups, then many people will find reason to believe that this cannot
really be the case, that some hidden locus of power must exist behind the
apparent dispersion, and that a small group of all-powerful leaders must
be manipulating the actions of others.

Second, conspiracy theories are less likely to be prevalent in societies
where politics is viewed simply as the struggle for benefits among self-
interested individuals and groups. They are much more likely to take
root in societies in which it is viewed as having a major moral dimension,
involving the conflict between the forces of good and the forces of evil.
Conspiracy theory is the logical extension of political moralism, "for if
historical movement at every stage is almost exclusively a matter of good

will or ill will, freely chosen, those who make a mistake are not just wrong; they are evil. And all our social and political pathologies are the result of deliberate evil-doing. Given the moralistic premise, how else could we account for them? Senator Joseph McCarthy asked: 'How can we account for our present situation unless we believe that men high in this government are concerting to deliver us to disaster?' "[29]

Third, conspiracy theories are less likely to be prevalent in societies in which power is positively valued. On the other hand, in societies with a strong antipower ethic, hostility to power is likely to generate fear and suspicion concerning the existence of concealed power. In addition, in such societies power that is secret is likely to be more "powerful" than power that is public. Hence, there is good reason to be concerned about the possible existence of secret power.

The dispersion of power in America, the moralistic component of American politics, and the pervasive hostility toward power all conspire to make the United States particularly receptive to conspiracy theories. And, in fact, this has been the case, as many native and foreign observers have noted. "In the history of American political controversy," Richard Hofstadter commented, "there is a tradition of conspiratorial accusations which seem to have been sincerely believed."[30] Conspiracy theories were the midwife at the birth of the American republic: the "fear of a comprehensive conspiracy against liberty throughout the English-speaking world —a conspiracy believed to have been nourished in corruption, and of which, it was felt, oppression in America was only the most immediately visible part—lay at the heart of the Revolutionary movement." The fear of conspiracy had deep roots in the political traditions of eighteenth-century Britain and America, encouraged by both the theory of mixed government and the tendency to dichotomize liberty and power. Whereas Americans and English Whigs saw the threat in a ministerial conspiracy —a view "almost universally shared by sympathizers of the American cause"—George III saw the actions of the rebellious colonists as "a seditious and unwarrantable combination" and a "desperate conspiracy."[31] After independence, every generation and almost every decade saw the existence of a secret conspiratorial power, in one form or another—Illuminati, Masons, Catholics, Mormons, bankers, Jews, communists—threatening the vitals of the Republic. The idea that secret power exists comes most naturally to those distant from power. The conspiratorial interpretation is hence peculiarly characteristic of populist movements and of movements infused with creedal passion for exposure and reform. "There was something about the Populist imagination that loved the secret plot and the conspiratorial meeting."[32] Concern over conspiracy did not die with the Populists, however, and Shils could easily observe in the mid-1950s that "worry about conspiracy has been a constant feature of American life for half a century at least."[33]

This tendency to be obsessed with conspiracy has a realistic basis in the prevailing American attitude toward power. If power is of dubious legitimacy, it must be concealed to be effective. Not only this, but the act of concealment itself must also be concealed. The rewards of conspiratorial power are thus much greater in the American context than they are in societies in which public power is not devalued power, and one should assume that those who wish to wield power will also conspire to keep that fact secret. In sum, there are more incentives to develop conspiracies of power in the United States than in other societies, and hence conspiracy theories about power which appear to be more prevalent in the United States than in other societies may also be more justifiable. Indeed, if the effective exercise of power involves the cover-up of its existence, then it is only a small logical jump to the ultimate conclusion, the *reductio ad absurdum* of conspiracy theory, that the most persuasive evidence for the existence of secret power is the total absence of any such evidence.

The Sincerity Test

Secrecy is thus necessary to hide the facts of power, and deception is necessary to make those facts appear different from what they are. The latter is the natural extension of the former: secrecy is the shield of power and deception the cloak of secrecy. Deception becomes an inherent aspect of the relationship between government and the public, between political leaders and followers. The hypocrisy that seizes all of the people some of the time is common coin for some of the people—their leaders—all the time. Governmental institutions are made to appear more open and more responsive to public opinion than they are. Political leaders also must appear to reflect the will of the people more than is actually the case. They have no choice but to kowtow to the appearances of democracy, however much they have attempted to avoid the reality of democracy. The increasing demands, beginning in the early nineteenth century, that government be made more democratic did in fact increase democracy, but they also multiplied the institutions and practices by which government could be made to appear more democratic than it actually was. The demands for democracy in government produced both more democracy and more deception. Because people in the United States expect government to be more democratic than it can be, the government must make itself appear more democratic than it is.

These consequences of the IvI gap help explain the central role that the problem of sincerity plays in American politics. Sincerity can only be an important issue when ideals are taken seriously. In a very different way, as Rubashov illustrated, it can also play a critical role in the politics of communist systems. In them, as in the United States, political figures may feel an overwhelming need to assert and to demonstrate their sincere commitment to the political values and goals of their society. The difficulty of doing this, of course, gives rise to cynicism, hypocrisy, and deception. Implicit recognition of their prevalence enhances the concern with and the value of sincerity.

The meaning of sincerity differs from one culture to another. In Asian cultures, sincerity means almost the opposite of what it means in the United States. In Japan, the emphasis is on the anticipation of the interests of a superior. In China, sincerity involves following a general external code: "One demonstrates 'sincerity' by commitment to one's interpersonal obligations, to society, and not to one's inner feelings. Indeed, one is perhaps most sincere when doing the socially correct thing at precisely the time that inner feelings are urging a different course of action."[34] In both China and Japan, the stress is on the relation of the individual to his associates, to his peers, to his superiors, to his group. Sincerity, in a sense, is almost a group characteristic.

In the United States, on the other hand, sincerity involves the relation of the individual to himself and to his beliefs. It has two dimensions. It involves frankness, truthfulness, and openness about oneself and one's feelings—"telling the truth about oneself to oneself and to others," as Lionel Trilling summarized its meaning in French literature. But in the American context, it means something more. A person might wholeheartedly espouse the view that people are universally devious, narrow-minded, and mean, but Americans would not normally call such a person sincere. They would call him a cynic, and a "sincere cynic" would, in their view, be a contradiction in terms. Nor would they describe as sincere a politician who said that he loved power for its own sake and for the opportunity it gave him to manipulate and dominate others. The concept of sincerity in American culture (and probably, as Trilling suggested, in English culture as well) simply does not encompass the possibility of being sincerely evil. Sincerity involves a "single-minded commitment" to "dutiful enterprise."[35] It involves a substantive, moral dimension, a dedication to right beliefs. Americans cannot conceive of Hitler or Stalin as sincere men. In the American context, in short, sincerity means commitment to the liberal-democratic, individualistic ideals of the American Creed. Only in a society in which the incentives to hypocrisy are so numerous could the concern with sincerity as a moral virtue be so deep.

The American definition of sincerity often makes it difficult for Americans to understand foreigners. In foreign cultures sincerity may not only be defined differently, but in the American sense it may also be irrelevant. As Margaret Mead pointed out, to the Bolshevik "all acts commanded by the Party are ethical," and hence "the essential virtue consists in being so goal-oriented (*tseleustremenyi*) that no contradiction can arise between behavior demanded by changes in the Line and the individual behavior— in a diplomat or officer on a border—needed to implement the Line." The more flexible Soviet officials are in implementing the Line, the greater their integrity in terms of their ethic. To Americans, however, such behavior is proof of insincerity. "As consistency and sincerity are regarded by Americans as essential to integrity, and as both are lacking in the behavior of the Soviet leadership, there is temptation to continue to apply American standards of judgment and to regard Soviet behavior as insincere, cynical in the American sense, and so without integrity."[36]

In America, political leaders, both foreign and indigenous, must undergo a sincerity test: Do they really believe what they say? Americans ask this question with mixed hope, incredulity, and skepticism, all of which reflects how difficult it is to be sincere in American public life. Supporting in 1978 the admission to the United States of the white Rhodesian leader, Ian Smith, Senator S. I. Hayakawa argued, "I think the American people deserve to see Smith first-hand. If he's patently a fraud, let's find that out. If he's a sincere man, let's find that out, too."[37] The possibility that Smith might sincerely hold views on race relations that would be abhorrent to a vast majority of Americans was not admitted. Sincerity means a real belief in American ideals. For American public figures, the problem is how to square this belief with the knowledge of how imperfectly those ideals are realized in American institutions and practices. Not sincerity but its opposite, hypocrisy, seems almost unavoidable. Only those who become passionate reformers, clearly and unchallengeably committed to bringing institutions and practices into accord with American ideals, are able to escape having their sincerity questioned. No one asked "Is he sincere?" of William Lloyd Garrison. But for others, the sincerity question—How does he reconcile his belief in American values with his perception of American reality?—is inescapable.

5 THE POLITICS OF CREEDAL PASSION

Creedal Passion Periods in American History

The responses of cynicism, complacency, and hypocrisy to the national problem of cognitive dissonance do not have major direct consequences for the stability and continuity of the political system—although obviously they may have important long-term effects on how it operates. None of these responses challenges the continued existence of the IvI gap. The fourth possible choice, moralism, does attempt to eliminate the gap by bringing reality into accord with the values and ideals of the American Creed. It thus has direct behavioral and institutional consequences for the operation of the political system and involves major efforts to alter institutions and practices. The impetus for these reforms comes from combining the perception that a major gap does exist with the intense belief that it should not exist.

In various periods of American history, the level of creedal passion has increased generally throughout the body politic. New generations deeply concerned with the gap between ideal and practice supplant earlier generations that were less deeply concerned. Those who were previously relatively unconcerned manifest a new passion to bring reality into accord with principle. The values of the Creed come to play a more central role in people's lives; people become aroused, agitated, politicized.

Although the intensity of this concern cannot be shown to vary regularly over time, four periods of creedal passion stand out in American history: the Revolutionary, Jacksonian, and Progressive eras and the years of protest, exposure, and reform of the 1960s and early 1970s.

These periods differ from other times in American history in the extent to which traditional American ideals were articulated and efforts made to bring institutions and practices into accord with those ideals, in the way in which social conflicts cut across the usual lines of class and region, and in the degree to which major realignments occurred between social forces and governmental institutions.

These periods, of course, have not been the only years of change in American politics. They are distinguished by institutional realignment and reform. At other times in American history, significant shifts have taken place in the relative power of social and economic groups. Such changes, indeed, seem to alternate with the changes of creedal passion periods. The early 1800s, for instance, saw the agrarian interests of the South and West displace the Federalist mercantile and commercial groups as the controlling force behind the national government. The 1860s saw the virtual elimination from power in the central government of Southern agrarian interests and the rise to power of Northern business and industrial interests. In the 1930s recent immigrant groups, organized labor, and the urban working class gained enormous political influence. The focus of change in these periods concerns the role and power of social forces; the focus of change during creedal passion periods concerns the structure and character of political institutions and practices.

The four creedal passion periods share a number of specific characteristics that distinguish them from other periods in American history:

1. Discontent was widespread; authority, hierarchy, specialization, and expertise were widely questioned or rejected.
2. Political ideas were taken seriously and played an important role in the controversies of the time.
3. Traditional American values of liberty, individualism, equality, popular control of government, and the openness of government were stressed in public discussion.
4. Moral indignation over the IvI gap was widespread.
5. Politics was characterized by agitation, excitement, commotion, even upheaval—far beyond the usual routine of interest-group conflict.
6. Hostility toward power (the antipower ethic) was intense, with the central issue of politics often being defined as "liberty versus power."
7. The exposure or muckraking of the IvI gap was a central feature of politics.

8. Movements flourished devoted to specific reforms or "causes" (women, minorities, criminal justice, temperance, peace).
9. New media forms appeared, significantly increasing the influence of the media in politics.
10. Political participation expanded, often assuming new forms and often expressed through hitherto unusual channels.
11. The principal political cleavages of the period tended to cut across economic class lines, with some combination of middle- and working-class groups promoting change.
12. Major reforms were attempted in political institutions in order to limit power and reshape institutions in terms of American ideals (some of which were successful and some of which were lasting).
13. A basic realignment occurred in the relations between social forces and political institutions, often including but not limited to the political party system.
14. The prevailing ethos promoting reform in the name of traditional ideals was, in a sense, both forward-looking and backward-looking, progressive and conservative.

The remainder of this chapter elaborates these general aspects of creedal passion periods. First, however, it may be desirable to say a few words as to why one major political event, the American Revolution, can usefully be analyzed as a creedal passion period, and then why another major political event, the New Deal, does not fit into this pattern.

The American Revolution has always posed peculiar problems for historical interpretation. Was it a "real" social revolution, comparable to the English, French, and Russian Revolutions? Was it simply a national war of independence or liberation? Or was it a unique uprising not classifiable into any of the common broader categories of revolution or international conflict—perhaps even essentially conservative in nature? Each of these interpretations may be useful for some analytical purposes. But the Revolution can also be thought of not as a somewhat suspect member of the broader class of social revolutions or as simply a unique historical event, but rather as one—and the first on a national level—of a class of events that have recurred throughout and are unique to American history. The Revolutionary era was the prototypical period of creedal passion. The three later periods represented a rearticulation of the themes of the Revolutionary years and a replay of the features and patterns of Revolutionary politics.

The Revolution was the most dramatic, most sweeping, and most successful of the efforts to articulate and to realize in practice American
political values and ideals. This aspect of the Revolution was neatly
caught by Benjamin Rush, in his Fourth of July address in Philadelphia
in 1787: "There is nothing more common than to confound the terms
American Revolution with those of the late American War. The American War is over, but this is far from being the case with the American
Revolution. On the contrary but the first act of the great drama is
closed."[1] In comparison with other major revolutions, the American
Revolution does appear to have a conservative cast. It clearly did not
involve a class struggle along Marxist or French Revolutionary lines; no
particular social group was destroyed. But it did set loose a radical and
revolutionary ideology—that government derived its legitimacy from the
consent of the governed—which defined the basis of political legitimacy
in America and set forth a new standard of legitimacy for the world. In
this sense, the Revolution was "the most creative period in the history of
American political thought. Everything that followed assumed and built
upon its results."[2] In the context of American history, the Revolution was
indeed a revolutionary event and an event of decisive importance not only
in terms of its own immediate consequences, but because it was "the first
act" of a drama whose subsequent acts would reiterate in a variety of
ways its initial themes and plot. In the later creedal passion periods,
Americans attempted to reenact with new targets their successful overthrow of the British monarchy in the 1700s.

The Revolutionary era thus saw the first formulation on a national
basis of American political ideas and the first effort to reshape political
institutions in their image. The purpose of the Revolution, Irving Kristol
said, was "to bring our political institutions into a more perfect correspondence with an actual 'American way of life' which no one ever
dreamed of challenging." The effect of the Revolution, in turn, was to
reshape "political institutions in such a way as to make them more responsive to popular opinion and less capable of encroaching upon the personal
liberties of the citizen."[3] In later creedal passion periods, this purpose was
reaffirmed, and the effect was, even if in weakening degree, to make
political institutions more responsive, more liberal, more democratic. In
each of these four periods, people were agitated over the gap between
political ideal and political reality, and in each they attempted to reshape
their institutions and practices so as to reduce or to eliminate that gap. As
a result, in each of these periods politics has been more intense, more

"idealistic," more infused with moral passion than it has been at other times when the pragmatic bargaining among interest groups dominates the scene. There are thus two American politics: the politics of movements and causes, of creedal passion and reform, and the politics of interests and groups, of pragmatic bargaining and compromise. In this respect, too, a contrast existed between late-eighteenth-century politics in England and America: the former embodied a politics of family, faction, and interest, whereas "the Namier denigration of ideas and principles is inapplicable for American politics because the American social situation in which ideas operated was very different from that of eighteenth-century England."[4]

Viewing the American Revolution as the first of a series of periods of upheaval and change peculiar to American history helps explain the striking difference in the appeal of the *ideals* of the Revolution and the *experience* of the Revolution. However much it may have differed from other revolutions, the American Revolution "resembled every other major revolution in western history" in that it possessed "comprehensive and utopian revolutionary ideology" which was "just as much a system of ideas for fundamentally reshaping the character of the society as were the ideologies of those other revolutions."[5] This ideology was republicanism. Its ideals, articulated in the Revolution, are universal in their formulation and in their appeal; they have inspired revolutionaries elsewhere; they have been quoted by radicals and reformers across the globe. The experience of the American Revolution—that is, the usefulness of the Revolution as a historical model—has been much more limited. It was, as Hannah Arendt observed, "from the course of the French Revolution, and not from the course of events in America or from the acts of the Founding Fathers, that our present use of the word 'revolution' received its connotations and overtones everywhere, this country not excluded. . . The sad truth of the matter is that the French Revolution, which ended in disaster, made world history, while the American Revolution, so triumphantly successful, has remained an event of little more than local importance."[6] Epitomizing republican and liberal ideals, the American revolutionary ideology has had a wide appeal, even though no other society has been conceived in its image. As a historical model, however, the American revolutionary experience has been ignored. The concepts, phases, and semantics of the revolution, and, most important, the lessons of how to behave in revolutionary situations, have been drawn first from the French and then from the Bolshevik Revolution.

The moralistic intensity of the creedal passion periods clearly has distinguished them from other times of change in American politics, as well as from eras of stalemate and stagnation. There has been, however, at least one period of American history that has often been thought of as a period of major reform and yet did not fit the pattern of a creedal passion period. This was the New Deal. In fact, the New Deal was a very different sort of phenomenon.

First, the primary concern of the New Deal was not the reform of politics but the restoration of prosperity. Unlike most creedal passion periods, the 1930s was a period of economic depression. The overwhelming issue was how to deal with the country's economic problems. As a result, political reform was a distant second to economic recovery as a New Deal goal.

Second, the need to deal with economic problems meant that the emphasis was on how to use governmental power, not how to break it up. Although New Deal rhetoric incorporated Jacksonian and populist criticism of the malefactors of great wealth, the principal imperatives of the New Deal were directed toward the solution of immediate and pressing economic problems, through governmental action if necessary, rather than the reshaping of political and economic institutions to bring them into accord with the ideals of the American Creed. The opposition to "bigness," so characteristic of creedal passion periods, was evident during the New Deal, but it was a subordinate strand. Governmental interventionism and even collectivism rather than traditional individualism set the dominant tone. As Hofstadter pointed out, the New Deal never manifested any sustained and consistent hostility to the two great ogres of the Progressive era, the machines and the trusts.[7]

Third, almost totally absent from the New Deal were the moralism and Puritanism characteristic of creedal passion periods. The hallmark of the New Deal was pragmatism, opportunism, "bold, persistent experimentation," rather than the passionate reaffirmation of moral values. Progressivism had been characterized by "its traffic in moral absolutes, its exalted moral tone. While something akin to this was by no means entirely absent from the New Deal, the later movement showed a strong and candid awareness that what was happening was not so much moral reformation as economic experimentation."[8] Moral indignation, indeed, was more characteristic of its conservative critics than it was of the New Deal itself. The traditional moral virtues of politics did not rate high in the New Deal pantheon. Leading intellectual figures such as Max Lerner and Thurman

Arnold stressed the importance of means, technique, expertise, and organization over individualism, honesty, integrity, and morality. The New Deal outlook was almost entirely future-oriented, in contrast to the Janus-faced moods prevailing during creedal passion periods.

Fourth, during the New Deal, probably more than at any other time in American politics, political cleavages tended to be along economic class lines. Although the alignment was never perfect, the have-nots were gathered into the Roosevelt coalition in the Democratic Party, while the haves, including many former Democrats, rallied to the Republican Party. The basic political cleavage tended to be horizontal, as opposed to the more vertical cleavage characteristic of creedal passion periods.

Finally, in terms of its results, the New Deal produced major new economic policies and programs—a new relation between the government and the economy—without the efforts to cleanse and purify government, to open up government, and to make government more democratic which had been characteristic of the creedal passion periods. The New Deal resulted in a proliferation of governmental activity and an increase in presidential power. Not the reform of government but the expansion of government was the New Deal's legacy to the next generation.

In contrast to the New Deal years, the Revolutionary, Jacksonian, and Progressive eras and the 1960s and 1970s all were characterized by strikingly similar political climates, patterns of conflict and reform, and realignments of social forces and political institutions.

The Climate of Creedal Passion

The political climate of creedal passion periods is distinguished by widespread and intense moral indignation. Political passions are high, existing structures of authority are called into question, democratic and egalitarian impulses are renewed, and political change—anticipated and unanticipated—occurs. In each of America's four creedal passion periods, similar ideas and methods were employed by comparable constellations of social forces to reshape political institutions and practices in terms of the values of the American Creed.

The atmosphere of discontent. All four periods were characterized by a pervasive unhappiness with things as they were. Discontent was the prevailing disposition, manifested in the widespread questioning and rejection of authority, hierarchy, specialization, and expertise. Actions by governmental officials, which earlier would have been accepted without notice or complaint, were noticed, highlighted, and denounced. Americans came to hate themselves because they were not themselves. All four periods were thus in some measure "revolutionary situations," in R. R. Palmer's sense of the word—times "in which confidence in the justice or reasonableness of existing authority is undermined; where old loyalties fade, obligations are felt as impositions, law seems arbitrary, and respect for superiors is felt as a form of humiliation; where existing sources of prestige seem undeserved, hitherto accepted forms of wealth and income seem ill-gained, and government is sensed as distant, apart from the governed and not really 'representing' them." These words, Palmer and Bailyn agree, aptly describe the temper of the 1760s and early 1770s.[9] They are almost equally applicable to the 1830s, and 1900s, and the 1960s.

Emerson's description of the 1830s could also apply to the other periods: "In politics . . . it is easy to see the progress of dissent. The country is full of rebellion; the country is full of kings. Hands off! let there be no control and no interference in the administration of this kingdom of me." Nor was the individualistic rejection of external authority limited to politics. "The same disposition to scrutiny and dissent appears in civil, festive, neighborly, and domestic society. A restless, prying conscientious criticism broke out in unexpected quarters. Who gave me the money with which I bought my coat? Why should professional labor and that of the counting-house be paid so disproportionately to the labor of the porter and woodsawyer?" All established institutions were under challenge: "Christianity, the laws, commerce, schools, the farm, the laboratory; and not a kingdom, town, statute, rite, calling, man, or woman, but is threatened by the new spirit."[10] The "predominant characteristics" of the Revolutionary period, historian Gordon Wood argued, were "fear and frenzy, the exaggerations and the enthusiasm, the general sense of social corruption and disorder out of which would be born a new world of benevolence and harmony where Americans would become the 'eminent examples of every divine and social virtue.' " In similar fashion, Daniel Webster observed that in the 1820s "society is full of excitement," and Theodore Roosevelt spoke of "a condition of excitement and irritation in the public mind" as characteristic of his times.[11]

Each period was a period of agitation, dominated by the questioning of prevailing institutions and authority. Each gave rise, in some sense, to a crisis of legitimacy which people attempted to resolve by reshaping American political institutions and practices to be more in accord with the values of the American Creed. Because of the nature of American society and the widespread consensus on these liberal values, revolution in the familiar European class-oriented sense of the word did not occur. Instead, the very forces that gave rise to the revolutionary situation produced a nonrevolutionary outcome.

Political ideas and moral passion. In all four periods, political ideas—and ideals—were taken seriously. The years immediately before the American Revolution saw the first significant articulation throughout a society of the ideas of equality, liberty, and popular sovereignty. Among the striking features of these years, Bailyn observed, was "the seriousness with which colonial and revolutionary leaders took ideas and the deliberateness of their efforts during the Revolution to reshape institutions in their pattern." The Revolution, in John Adams' words, was effected between 1760 and 1775 in the minds of the people. *"This radical change in the principles, opinions, sentiments, and affections of the people was the real American revolution."* For the first time, authority was challenged and overthrown in the name of universal democratic principles. Each subsequent period of creedal passion witnessed a manifestation of "a new consciousness" (to use Emerson's phrase) of these old principles.[12]

The meanings of liberty, equality, and democracy and the ways to realize them through institutional reform became a focus of public debate, but no great systematic political theories were articulated. The level of political theory during the four periods failed to rise much above that of a Thomas Paine or a Herbert Croly: neither was an original political thinker but each brilliantly reformulated familiar ideas to meet the needs of his times. Although Paine did not set forth new political ideas, he did create the "secular language of revolution, a language in which timeless discontents, millennial aspirations, and popular traditions were expressed in a strikingly new vocabulary."[13] One talks not about the political theory of these periods but about their political ideas, which were in each period rearticulations and reformulations of ideas that were already well known.

Americans have been variously held to be both a highly idealistic people and a highly pragmatic one. During the periods of creedal passion, the idealistic strain became the dominant one. An intense concern with values, principles, rights, and morality pervaded the public arena. Political ideas became important not primarily for intellectual reasons but for moral ones, and moral indignation generated creedal passion and political controversy. There was a rush to moral judgment on the rights and wrongs of politics. The minds of the American revolutionaries were gripped by an "aroused moral passion" and "meliorative, optimistic, and idealist impulses . . . that led them to condemn as corrupt and oppressive the whole system by which their world was governed."[14] In a similar manner, the Jacksonian years were characterized by the prevalence of a "matched set of attitudes, beliefs, projected actions: a half-formulated moral perspective involving emotional commitment. The community shares many values; at a given social moment some of these acquire a compelling importance." All the Jacksonians seemed to be "moralizers." The Jacksonian persuasion was "always more a decalogue of moral prohibitions than an articulate set of social ends and means." So also, the Progressives tended to talk in "moral rather than economic terms"; they "set impossible standards"; they were "victimized, in brief, by a form of moral absolutism." Theodore Roosevelt always thought of himself as a moralist, believing that the central issue in American politics was "the fundamental fight for morality."[15] And morality, moralism, and moral absolutism were surely the hallmark of the 1960s, which, among other things, saw the emergence of what was labeled the "new political morality."

The affirmation of moral values during creedal passion periods is Janus-faced. The values and ideals that are invoked are traditional ones; they derive their legitimacy and their appeal from their earlier presence in American history. At the same time, the affirmation holds out the promise, the hope, the dream of realizing these values in the not-too-distant future. The intellectual temper of the age is both backward-looking and forward-looking, traditional and radical. During the American Revolution, the colonists used the language of Locke and the early-eighteenth-century Whigs to invoke the traditional rights of Englishmen. As Hartz said, the remarkable thing about the "spirit of 1776" was "not that it looked forward to the future but that it worshipped the past as well."[16] The American mission for the future was to realize the values of the American past. The ideas of the Jacksonians, the Progressives, and the protesters of the 1960s were similarly ambivalent, although a widening gulf opened between the inherited ideals they hoped to realize and the institutional reality produced by industrialization and global involvement that they confronted. Like revitalization movements in other societies, those of American creedal passion periods have thus, in varying degrees, been both archaistic and futuristic.[17]

The attack on power and hierarchy. In all four periods, democratic ideals were reaffirmed: liberty, equality, individualism, and popular control of government, and opposition to hierarchy, specialization, bureaucracy, and especially power. The antipower theme was a critical aspect of public discourse in all these eras, and the central issue of the time was often defined as "liberty versus power." The Americans of the 1770s were preoccupied, even obsessed, with the problem of power. Power was inherently evil and corrupting. For them the essential characteristic of power was its aggressiveness: "its endlessly propulsive tendency to expand itself beyond legitimate boundaries." Along with the opposition to privilege, opposition to power was the major theme of the American Revolution. The revolutionaries believed

> that power is evil, a necessity perhaps but an evil necessity; that it is infinitely corrupting; and that it must be controlled, limited, restricted in every way compatible with a minimum of civil order. Written constitutions; the separation of powers; bills of rights; limitations on executives, on legislatures, and courts; restrictions on the right to coerce and to wage war—all express the profound distrust of power that lies at the ideological heart of the American Revolution and that has remained with us as a permanent legacy ever after.[18]

The same dichotomy between liberty and power came to the fore again in the Jacksonian years. "Money power," for instance, was "damned precisely as a *power*, a user of ill-gotten gains to corrupt and dominate the plain republican order." The Jacksonian onslaught on power, however, did not last. "Between the Jacksonian war on the bank in the 1830s and the Populist-Progressive agitation of the 1880s and 1890s, few political leaders or movements questioned the concentration of private economic power."[19] In the 1890s this questioning was vigorously resumed. It remained an active theme until the country entered into World War I and then subsided, to reappear with equal intensity in the 1960s. In all four eras, institutions of power were summoned to judgment before the ideals of liberty, and the antipower ethic reinvigorated as a guide to political action.

In each period, the power that was perceived as the threat to liberty took a different specific form. In the 1760s and 1770s it was the imperial power of the British Parliament and Crown. In the 1830s the threat came from monopoly, the Bank of the United States, chartered corporations, and the caucus system. At the turn of the century, the attacks were directed against the machines and the trusts. For the Muckrakers, the enemy included "the 'interests,' 'the System,' high or frenzied finance, plutocracy, the industrial aristocracy, the trusts and monopoly . . . The specific agent in the national orgy of corruption was the corporation."[20] In the 1960s the target was executive power, the Presidency, and the military-industrial complex. In all four periods, the focus was on some combination of economic and political power: imperial power, money power, slave power, corporate power, executive power. The common enemy in all was large-scale organization. At the extremes, the concern over power and organization became a paranoia about conspiracies that threatened to undermine free society and government. The "paranoiac obsession with a diabolical Crown conspiracy" which existed during the Revolution was matched in the 1820s and 1830s by the fantasies and the fervor of the Anti-Masons, who saw their target as "a conspiratorial order of evil, immoral men who sought to control politics and community life," and by the rhetoric and imagery of the Populists in the 1890s.[21]

The common goal in all four periods was the break-up or reduction of organized power, its reform and control, the opening up of the processes of decision making to public participation. The Jacksonians, it has been said, engaged in "a dismantling operation: an effort to pull down the menacing constructions of federal and corporate power, and restore the wholesome rule of 'public opinion and the interests of trade.' "[22] And "dismantling operations" were precisely what all four periods engendered: major efforts to tear down the perceived structures of political and economic power. The Jacksonians "directed popular resentment of closed political corporations against the caucus system, which they branded as a flagrant usurpation of the rights of the people, and spread the conviction that politics and administration must be taken from the hands of a social elite or a body of bureaucratic specialists and opened to mass participation."[23] Earlier, the American revolutionaries had dismantled the existing structures of British imperialism; subsequently, Populists and Progressives energetically attempted to dismantle political machines by introducing primaries, city managers, civil service, and other institutional reforms, and to break up corporate monopolies through antitrust laws and other forms of government regulation. In the 1960s, similar efforts were made to bring to heel the military-industrial complex, the CIA, and presidential power in foreign affairs.

In addition to attacks on what were perceived to be the central institutions of power, each period also witnessed a more general challenge to authority, hierarchy, and specialization. The themes of one period reappeared in the next. In each there was a stress on the abilities of the amateur, the common man, the citizen, against those of the specialist or expert. Each was in some measure a period in which distinctions—

whether based on status, occupation, knowledge, or position—were denigrated, in which there was a stress on homogenization, on "the great principle" (in the words of the Jacksonians) "of amalgamating all orders of society." Specialized learning and specialized institutions of learning were attacked. The military profession in particular usually became a target, and the existence of the military academies was called into question. Whereas power was challenged in the name of liberty, other social, economic, and institutional distinctions were attacked in the name of equality. The Jacksonian goals—"political democracy, equality of economic opportunity, and opposition to monopoly and special privilege"— were equally prevalent and intensely held in the other three periods.[24]

Political participation and organization. The promotion of a cause requires participation and organization. Creedal passion periods thus tend to be characterized by intense and widespread political activity. People are mobilized for action in new ways. New forms of voluntary association appear: committees of correspondence, interest associations, new political parties, farmers' and workers' organizations, cause organizations of various types. The peculiar American contribution to achieving the common good, the public-spirited voluntary association, had its roots in the dissenting Protestant sects that gave New England its being, spread throughout the colonies during the Revolutionary years in the form of committees of correspondence, Sons of Liberty, and Minutemen units, and came truly into its own in the multifarious organizations to promote various causes which proliferated in the Jacksonian period. Tocqueville was indeed right in his oft-quoted remark that when something has to be done in France, the government does it; in England, a local magnate or aristocrat does it; while in America, "you are sure to find an association. . . . The Americans make associations to give entertainments, to found seminaries, to build inns, to construct churches, to diffuse books, to send missionaries to the antipodes; in this manner they found hospitals, prisons, and schools."[25] The number and diversity of associations that Tocqueville marveled at was in fact a major way in which Americans attempted to bring their institutions and practices into line with their beliefs and values. The formation of associations during the Jacksonian years was also accompanied by a substantial expansion of voting participation.

In the Progressive period, too, new movements and associations materialized in great number. This represented a second major wave of voluntary association founding, particularly noticeable in the first years of the twentieth century. It was not accompanied by a parallel increase in voting participation rates—which would have been difficult in any event, given the high levels of voting participation in the 1880s—but it was accompanied by a movement for women's suffrage. In the 1960s there was an increase in voting participation among blacks and the young, and a dramatic surge in other forms of political activity, including demonstrations, protests, associations, propagandizing, and lobbying by conscience and so-called public interest groups. This creedal passion period, like earlier ones, saw the proliferation of new forms of social organization, including utopian communities that attracted enthusiastic adherents. In the 1830s, as James Russell Lowell said, "communities were established where everything was to be common but common-sense."[26]

Modern techniques of creating associations date from the Jacksonian period. As one observer then sardonically commented:

> Whatever is started, a national society must at once be got up, which is imposing in its very name; a list of respectable names must be obtained, as members and patrons, which is also imposing and influential; a secretary and an adequate corps of assistants must be appointed and provided for from the first-fruits of collections; a band of popular lecturers must be commissioned, and sent forth as agents on the wide public; the press, with its many-winged messengers, is put in operation; certificates fitted for the purpose are made out, submitted, subscribed, and sworn to; the entire machinery is put in operation; subsidiary societies are multiplied over the length and breadth of the land; the end proposed is manifestly a good one; and how can the community resist the sway of such an influence?[27]

The tactics of the freedom-riders and other reformers of the twentieth century were not dissimilar from those of the abolitionists of the nineteenth; in talents and behavior, William Lloyd Garrison was the forerunner of Ralph Nader. "So thoroughly did these [Jacksonian] crusaders work out the pattern of reform organization and propaganda a hundred years ago," Arthur Schlesinger, Sr., observed in 1950, "that later generations have found little to add beyond taking advantage of new communication devices such as the movies and radio."[28]

The formation of organizations—both evidence of political participation and a means of channeling such participation—is linked with efforts to reduce the IvI gap. Generalizing from the experience of the Jacksonian and Progressive eras, James Q. Wilson suggested:

> Periods of rapid and intense organizational formation are periods in which the salience of purposive incentives has sharply increased.

Organizations become more numerous when ideas become more important. The most obvious fact in support of such a view is that widespread organizing seems always to be accompanied by numerous social movements. During the era of the 1830s and 1840s, for example, both the Antimasonic party and the abolitionist organizations were formed at the same time, and out of many of the same impulses, as the Great Revival of religious fervor. In 1895–1910, there was similarly an outburst of new gospels, many of them this time secular in nature though still evangelical in tone: free silver, prohibition, nativism, suffragism, the social gospel, Marxism, Taylorism, the settlement-house movement, and countless others.[29]

Veterans of the 1960s will attest to the continued validity of the proposition that organizational activity is a function of creedal commitment.

The media and political communications. The dismantling of power requires the exposure of power. In each of the four creedal passion periods, reform efforts were fueled by the uncovering of and publicity given to the facts of privilege hierarchy, inequality, and corruption. Each period also saw the emergence of new forms of the media, which enhanced the ability of the reformers to communicate their facts and their indignation to the public.

During the Revolutionary years, for the first time in Europe and America "a public opinion, as such, took form, and indeed, the very expression, 'public opinion,' dates in several languages from this time." This public opinion consisted of "groups of people habitually interested in public events, subscribing as individuals or in clubs to newspapers and magazines, incipiently political in their outlook . . . in the sense that they were aware of the importance of government and political institutions, and believed that there was something called the public welfare, which depended on the policies of governments and on the enlightened behavior of citizens." These people were concerned about political affairs at both the local and national levels. Their concern was made possible by and fueled by "the phenomenal growth of the press, both of books and of newspapers and magazines." These improvements in communication constituted "one of the fundamental preconditions to the whole revolutionary era" in America and in Europe.[30] In America the increased circulation of petitions and remonstrances, sermons and orations, almanacs, broadsides, and newspapers contributed to the development of revolutionary consciousness. Most characteristic of and central to the new intensity of communication was the pamphlet, "the most effective weapon of political argument" in the colonies and in Britain. The flexible length, timeliness, and *ex parte* quality of the pamphlet made it the ideal vehicle for the polemical argument of revolution. More than four hundred pamphlets relating to the struggle with Britain were published in the colonies between 1750 and 1776, and more than fifteen hundred had appeared by 1783. "Explanatory as well as declarative, and expressive of the beliefs, attitudes, and motivations as well as the professed goals of those who led and supported the Revolution, the pamphlets are the distinctive literature of the Revolution."[31]

The Jacksonian years saw another jump in the scope and intensity of political communication. Public schools, library companies, bookstores, and adult education movements all played their role. Of striking importance was the growth in newspaper circulation. In 1800 there had been two hundred forty-two newspapers in the United States with a circulation of two hundred thousand. By 1829, there were over one thousand newspapers with a circulation of over one million, a rate of increase in circulation more than double that of population.[32] The growth of the press was intimately related to the emergence of political parties (it was, in large part, an overtly partisan press) and, more generally, to the growth of political and civil associations. As Tocqueville recognized, in a democratic society with a widely dispersed pattern of governmental decision making, the newspaper plays an indispensable role in bringing together those who wish to work toward common public goals. There is "a necessary connection between public associations and newspapers: newspapers make associations, and associations make newspapers." Of all countries in the 1830s, the United States had "at the same time the greatest number of associations and of newspapers . . . The power of the newspaper press must therefore increase as the social conditions of men become more equal."[33]

Mass media developments during the Progressive years were comparable to those that occurred during the Revolutionary and Jacksonian eras. If the pamphlet was the distinctive medium of the Revolution, and the penny press of the Jacksonians, the mass popular press and the cheap magazine were the vehicles of Progressive reform. William Randolph Hearst, Joseph Pulitzer, and Edward Scripps developed the large-circulation daily, directed to the needs of the urban populace. They promoted human-interest appeals, relished scandal, exposed corruption, created news where it had to be created, and elevated "events, hitherto considered beneath reportorial attention, to the level of news occurrences by clever, emotionally colored reporting." The magazine world, too, changed dramatically. A "magazine revolution" occurred in the last years of the century, with genteel, limited-circulation periodicals such as *The Atlantic Monthly* and *Harper's* being overtaken by mass-circulation, cheap magazines created by businessmen rather than literary men.[34] These magazines took on many of the characteristics of newspapers in developing their circulations and hit the circulation jackpot when, as with *McClure's* and *The American*, they created the muckraking exposé as a distinctive stock in trade. The average monthly circulation of the muckraking magazines was over three million copies. If *The Saturday Evening Post* and *The Ladies Home Journal* are added, their combined circulation came to over five million copies, at a time when there were only twenty million families in the United States. Similarly, the circulation of daily newspapers increased tremendously, reaching 24.2 million in 1909.[35] Without the development of the newspapers and magazines, political reform and, indeed, the Progressive movement generally would hardly have been possible.

In a somewhat similar manner, in the 1960s television emerged as a major political force, reflecting and shaping a new public conscience and extending still further the political impact of the media through the body politic. A new national press also took shape, in which individual newspapers like *The New York Times* and *The Washington Post,* as well as newsmagazines like *Time* and *Newsweek,* became the dominant outlets for the national political community and organs of opinion capable, as in the Pentagon Papers and Watergate, of challenging and defeating the elected leadership of the national government. Coincidentally, earlier norms of "objective" or "impartial" journalism gave way to those of "advocatory" and "adversary" journalism.

Each of the creedal passion periods has thus seen the emergence of new forms of mass media, which serve as the means through which those who challenge the IvI gap bring their case before an ever-widening public. The press in America has a political role different from that of the press in most other societies. As Tocqueville suggested, there is a relationship between the prevalence of associations and the power of the press. There is also a relationship between the existence of a widespread consensus on basic political values and the power and role of the press. In a consensual society, one function of the press is to embody the consensus and to bring individuals and institutions to judgment. In the United States, the press is almost never governmental and rarely overtly partisan; instead, it is or aspires to be societal. The unique power of the press in American society is in part a product of the American liberal consensus. The media are, in effect, the clergy of the liberal society: they act as custodians of its ultimate values; they expose and denounce deviations from those values; they bestow legitimacy on individuals and institutions who reflect those values. In creedal passion periods, the media have no recourse but to challenge and expose the inequities of power.

Muckraking and the politics of exposure. Long before Theodore Roosevelt gave it a label, muckraking had become a distinctive American style of politics. Only in a society with a consensus on basic values can the simple exposure of facts that run counter to those values trigger political change. Muckraking is effective only when there is agreement on what is muck and what is not. Reform, consequently, involves the exposure of facts rather than argument over values. In this respect, the efforts at change in the United States in the early twentieth century, for instance, stand at an opposite extreme from contemporary Russian efforts. "The difference in the two environments is reflected in the differences between Lenin and Steffens and between the contents of *Iskra* and those of *McClure's*. The Bolshevik attacked with the revolutionary manifesto, the American reformer with the Brandeis brief."[36] From Samuel Adams' publication in 1773 of Governor Hutchinson's private letters, which " 'proved' to an outraged public that purpose, not ignorance, neglect, or miscalculation, lay behind the actions of the British government,"[37] to the *New York Times* publication of the Pentagon Papers two hundred years later, American politics, particularly in creedal passion periods, has been a politics of exposure, and the media as the means of exposure have played a far more influential role in American politics than in the politics of any other society. But exposure is effective only where there is a conscience to be outraged.

Each creedal passion period was distinguished not by the elaboration of new political theory, but by the disclosure of new political facts that ran counter to the central tenets of old political theory. At no time was this better illustrated than during the American Revolution. Then, as later, it was not necessary to argue ideas; it was simply necessary to state them and to demonstrate the extent to which the existing situation departed from them. The revolutionaries believed their truths to be "self-evident," and hence all that was required was that the "facts be submitted to a candid world." In a similar vein, the activities of the Jacksonian reformers inspired Emerson's observation that reform stems from the comparison of the idea with the fact. At the turn of the century, the phenomenon surfaced again with the Populists and Progressives and was duly christened by Theodore Roosevelt. The journalistic exposé, so successfully developed by Ida Tarbell, Lincoln Steffens, Upton Sinclair, David Graham Phillips, Ray Stannard Baker, and their associates, furnished the rationale and the impetus for legislative reforms just as the Brandeis brief, arguing from the facts, became the means of promoting social reform through judicial action. The 1960s and 1970s, in turn, saw the appearance of "the new muckrakers" and a new politics of exposure.

During creedal passion periods, the process of exposure and dismantling tends to expand both horizontally and vertically. In the beginning, outrage may focus on a particular individual, institution, or practice, but it rapidly tends to broaden and to affect widening circles of people and organizations. Walter Lippmann observed that in the early 1900s, "as muckraking developed, it began to apply the standards of public life to certain parts of the business world." In somewhat similar fashion, although it was "originally a fight against political privilege," the Jacksonian movement soon "broadened into a fight against economic privilege."[38] What starts as a drive to expose the evils of politics may soon spread to a concern with the evils of corporation, church, school, and association.

The vertical escalation of moral standards obfuscates the distinction between the serious violation of commonly accepted norms and the minor, seeming, or potential violation of such norms. If bribery cannot be proved against a public official, let it be shown that he accepted a gift; if there is no clear evidence that a public official used his position to advance his own private interest, let it be shown that there exists a potential conflict of interest between his public duty and his private gain. "If the facts will not make out a case of moral deficiency by accepted standards, the standards must be escalated to the point where facts can be found that *will* make out a deficiency; and the public must be educated to be horrified by the resulting new sins in substantially the same degree that they were horrified by the old."[39] The higher the actual level of honesty, the greater the push given to the moral escalator.

In the end, intensifying moral indignation gives way to moral exhaustion and cynicism. This process has been commented upon in each of the three most recent creedal passion periods. "The criticism and attack on institutions which we have witnessed," observed Emerson of the Jacksonian reformers, "has made one thing plain, that society gains nothing whilst a man, not himself renovated, attempts to renovate things around him: he has become tediously good in some particular, but negligent or narrow in the rest; and hypocrisy and vanity are often the disgusting result . . . The wave of evil washes all our institutions alike." In a very similar manner, Hubert Humphrey in 1975 commented on one aspect of a decade of moralistic exposure: "Accountability is the cry of the day. A kind of consumerism is in the air, and neither the Congress nor the public is taking the President's or anybody's word for anything. But there comes a time when suspicion can go too far. There comes a time when you have to trust someone."[40]

The most dramatic description of the political consequences of the politics of exposure and of moralistic reform was supplied by Theodore Roosevelt. It is necessary, he said, "that we should not flinch from seeing what is vile and debasing." There are times and places when the muckraker serves a useful purpose. Nonetheless, "the man who never does anything else, who never thinks or speaks or writes save in his feats with the muckrake, speedily becomes, not a help to society, not an incitement to good, but one of the most potent forces for evil." In elaborating this theme, Roosevelt argued that "there are, in the body politic, economic, and social, many and grave evils, and there is urgent necessity for the sternest war upon them. There should be relentless exposure of and attack upon every evil man, whether politician or business man, every evil practice, whether in politics, in business, or in social life." But it is also necessary to avoid "an epidemic of indiscriminate assault" upon the characters of public men. A balance must be maintained. "Expose the crime, and hunt down the criminal; but remember that even in the case of crime, if it is attacked in sensational, lurid, and untruthful fashion, the attack may do more damage to the public mind than the crime itself." The unlicensed exposure of wrong may lead to the corruption of the public conscience and an obliteration of the distinction between right and wrong. "To assail the great and admitted evils of our political and industrial life with such crude and sweeping generalizations as to include decent men in the general condemnation means the searing of the public conscience. There results a general attitude either of cynical belief in and indifference to public corruption or else of a distrustful inability to discriminate between the good and the bad."[41]

In due course, the climate of creedal passion produces a climate of political cynicism.

Creedal Conflict: The Movement and the Establishment

In its day-to-day functioning, conflict in American politics approximates the Madisonian model posited by pluralist theory. Interest-group politics accounts for most of American politics most of the time, but it does not describe all of American politics all of the time. Consensus theory errs in postulating a low level of conflict in American society; Progressive theory errs in focusing on class polarization as the central cleavage; pluralist theory is inadequate in its description of the sources of American political conflict. Conflicts occur over political ideas as well as over economic and communal interests. Opinion polarizes in great debates and constitutional controversies over the ways in which the principles and values of American politics should be realized in political institutions and practices. The actors in American politics include social movements and crusaders as well as pressure groups and lobbyists. Interest-group politics is thus at times supplemented, and even supplanted, by creedal politics. In contrast to interest-group politics, creedal politics tends to be intermittent rather than continuous, passionate rather than pragmatic, idealistic rather than materialistic, reform-minded rather than status-quo oriented, and formulated in terms of right and wrong rather than more or less. The actors in creedal politics are no less self-interested than the actors in interest-group politics, but their interests are set forth in different terms. Interest-group politics gives way to creedal politics when the groups involved (1) define their goals in terms of basic American values and principles, thereby articulating their appeal in universal terms, (2) make demands for structural change and reform of political institutions and practices, and (3) pursue these demands with moral passion and fervor.

The conflicts of the 1770s, 1830s, 1900s, and 1960s involved interest groups, but the depth of the cleavages, the significance of the issues at stake, and the passions of the participants transcended what is normally meant by the term "interest-group politics." At the same time, although economic issues played a role in these conflicts, the principal cleavages were not primarily along economic class lines. As a result, the nature and causes of cleavage in each of these periods have been subject to extensive debate among historians. Just what was the structure of political battle in the Revolutionary, Jacksonian, and Progressive eras? Efforts to explain these cleavages simply in terms of interest groups or economic classes do not wash. During the Revolution, rich and poor, planters and merchants, small farmers and tradesmen were found among both loyalists and revolutionaries. In some cases, of which the Franklins were the most notable, families divided down the middle. During the Jacksonian period, the lines of cleavage cut across class divisions, with farmers, workers, and entrepreneurs on both sides of the battles over party and issues. The well-to-do were as often on the side of reform as they were in opposition to it. During the Progressive period, major elements of the urban middle classes, the working class, and the farmers were both for and against political and economic reform. And in the 1960s middle-class professionals, intellectuals, and students joined with lower-class blacks to oppose other middle-class professionals and businessmen who were allied with major elements of the working class. In all of these periods, the principal lines of cleavage involving the major issues of the day, although not perfectly vertical, were far from being primarily horizontal.

In each of these periods, the impetus for change sprang from the coming together in a parallelism of interest of elements from both the middle class and the less well-off farmers or working class. The common factor that brought together these diverse social and economic groups appears to be the extent to which they were divorced from and felt threatened by the existing political and economic establishment. During the Revolution, insofar as any one factor differentiated revolutionaries and loyalists, it was the extent to which individuals and groups either were involved with, and saw their interests connected to, the British imperial establishment or saw themselves actually or potentially threatened by the future growth in power of that establishment. Some less well-off groups in colonial society, for instance, viewed the British presence as a counterweight to the economically dominant groups in colonial society and hence had good reason to support British power. In the Jacksonian period, group alignments can in large part be explained by the relation of the groups to existing political and economic institutions, such as the Bank of the United States, which the Jacksonians were attempting either to destroy or to open up and penetrate. Similarly, insofar as there was one characteristic that seemed to distinguish Progressives from their opponents, it was the extent to which the Progressives were recruited from groups outside the local political-economic establishment. Since control of the local establishment rested with different groups in different places, the social-economic background of the Progressives also varied from one place to another.[42] Similar criteria would go far toward explaining the cross-cutting vertical cleavages of the 1960s. In each period, the primary cleavage was between

those of whatever economic class who see their interests intimately connected with the existing political and economic structures, whatever their
nature, and those of whatever economic class who see their interests
connected to the opening up or dismantling of those structures. Polarization during creedal passion periods can divide and has divided economic
classes, social strata, interest groups, and even families. As a result, the
goals of those spearheading change are invariably defined in the liberal,
democratic, and antipower terms of the American Creed.

The assertion of these "traditional" values serves two purposes. It
provides the unifying goals, arguments, and rhetoric for the diverse
middle-class and lower-class groups divorced from the existing establishment. It also defines the limits within which change is possible without
disrupting the reforming coalition. Those with more income, wealth, and
education typically have broader and deeper commitment than others to
the liberal and individualistic values of the American Creed. Those with
economically less commitment to the existing order have ideologically
less commitment to the Creed. During a creedal passion period, the values
of the Creed are largely articulated by middle-class groups. Middle-class
hypocrites become moralists and, by articulating those values, attempt to
mobilize lower-class indifferents and cynics. This articulation reinvigorates lower-class acceptance of the Creed. Yet the Creed is the only
ideological weapon that can be used to challenge the established order.
Here, clearly, is the reason why change and reform in America can go
only so far and no further. Middle and upper strata may have an ideological commitment to political reform, but they also have an economic
interest in not permitting reform to alter significantly the existing distribution of income and wealth. The poorer classes, on the other hand, may
have an interest in substantial economic change, but they lack the ideological motivation to make that change a reality, and, indeed, they are
mobilized for political action by appeals to values which guarantee that
major economic change will not become a reality.

The articulation of the values of the Creed not only unifies reformers
but, second, it places their opponents on the ideological defensive. They
are, as Bailyn described the loyalists of the Revolution, ideologically
disarmed. There are no alternative creeds readily available to counter
the demands for change formulated in terms of the liberal-democratic
values on which almost everyone agrees. The argument thus often
becomes one over the relative desirability of specific means of change and
over the speed and timing of change. The basic cleavage in American

politics can often be defined "as a matter of tempo. It is a division, essentially, between those who want to move rapidly toward their vision of a good society, even at the risk of errors of commission, and those who would minimize that risk—but in turn risk errors of omission—by moving too slowly."[43] In a creedal passion period, those who want rapid change increase in both numbers and in the intensity with which they put forward their demands. The controversy is between those who want liberal ideals realized immediately and those who are more willing to adopt an incremental, gradualist strategy for dealing with the IvI gap. "Immediatism" was the label aptly applied to the approach of the man who was, perhaps more than anyone else, the prototypical American radical, William Lloyd Garrison, "the most forceful reformer in our history"—and in some respects the most dramatically successful. "Gradualism in theory," in his words, "is perpetuity in practice." Or, as Garrison's contemporaneous reformer on the peace front, William Ladd, expressed it: "It is an incontrovertible axiom, that *everything of a moral nature which ought to be done, can be done.*"[44] No excuse, in short, exists for a gap between ideal and reality. The opposite approach was represented by William Ellery Channing, no less opposed to slavery than Garrison, but firmly against reliance on "excitement and vehemence" to bring it to an end. It "is not true," as he put it, "that God has committed the great work of reforming the world to passion."[45]

In creedal passion periods, politics tends to become polarized between those who are in favor of reform and change and those who are willing to accept existing institutions as they are. The recurring division is thus not between upper class and lower class, or between elite and mass, but rather between reformers and standpatters, between the "Movement" or movements and the "Establishment" or establishments. The latter always exist; the former are more evanescent, and the intensity of the conflict varies with their rise and fall. In creedal passion periods, more people become intensely involved, committed to the realization of ideals, more agitated, more participant. In the language and meaning of the 1960s, they become "radicalized"—that is, alienated from and intensely critical of the existing structures of power and demanding their reform in terms of American liberal and democratic ideals. In such times, the "conscience community" becomes larger, more active, more focused on particular issues. Not the radical right or the radical left, but the radical center emerges as a major force on the political scene. The dichotomy that Progressive historians claim exists in American politics does not exist continuously between upper and lower classes, but rather intermittently between the Movement and the Establishment.

The Movement is a multifaceted thing. Each creedal passion period sees an eruption and proliferation of particular reform causes and social movements. The causes of women, racial minorities, including particularly blacks and Indians, the ill, the mentally retarded, criminals, and consumers became, in one form or another, the subject of intense political action. Crusades also surface on behalf of moral issues, such as temperance and peace. During the Jacksonian years, as James Russell Lowell observed, "every possible form of intellectual and physical dyspepsia brought forth its gospel. Bran has its prophets . . . Plainness of speech was carried to a pitch that would have taken away the breath of George Fox . . . Everybody had a mission (with a capital M) to attend to everybody-else's business . . . All stood ready at a moment's notice to reform everything but themselves."[46] In the 1830s, as in the 1960s, there was The Movement, all encompassing, in favor of all good things, and there were lesser, component movements (for peace, women, civil rights) in favor of particular good things. The movement on behalf of women's rights crested in the 1830s, the early 1900s, and again in the 1960s. The abolitionist movement got underway in the 1830s; the rights of blacks were a subordinate theme in the 1900s; but the civil rights movement and black consciousness dominated the scene in the 1960s. The belief that various social ills could be solved through particular institutions, what David Rothman termed "the discovery of the asylum," manifested itself in the 1820s and 1830s with the introduction of insane asylums, prisons, hospitals, and orphanages. In the 1900s there was a new wave of enthusiasm for other types of reform institutions, such as the settlement house. The "peace movement" in the United States had its real origins in 1828 with the founding of the American Peace Society; it came to the fore again in the anti-imperialist surge against the acquisition of colonies following the Spanish-American War; and it reappeared in dramatic and successful fashion in the opposition to the Vietnam War in the 1960s. Consumer activism, which played a minor role in the 1830s, emerged as a major focus in the 1900s, then disappeared from sight, to resurface prominently and successfully in Naderism and related movements in the 1960s.

There is thus considerable *repetition* from one creedal passion period to another: the favorite causes of one era tend to reappear in the next. There is also, within any one period, a high degree of *affinity* between causes: those who are active on behalf of one cause are also likely to become active on behalf of other causes. "In these movements," Emerson observed, "nothing was more remarkble than the discontent they begot in the movers." Some, like Thomas Paine, Wendell Phillips, Upton Sinclair, and Ralph Nader, seemed to be active in everything. Phillips in addition to abolition, "stood for a multitude of causes, demanding equal rights for women, temperance, freedom for Ireland, justice for the American Indian, abolition of capital punishment, kinder treatment of the mentally ill."[47] Sinclair was active on behalf of consumers, women, labor, economic equality, and public ownership of utilities. Other reformers concentrated their energies on one particular cause while expressing their sympathy for others, as Garrison did in connection with equal rights for women.

The relation of one particular movement to other movements is well illustrated by Alan Grimes' discussion of woman suffrage. Before the Civil War, a close connection existed between this movement and the anti-slavery and temperance crusades. "The feminist movement of the nine-teenth century, like the civil rights movement today, sponsored not only immediate reforms benefiting its own group such as the right of women to enter the universities and the professions, to hold property, and to have custody of their children in divorce cases, but also a host of broader reforms such as peace, temperance, abolition of slavery, and the begin-nings of social welfare legislation." This pattern of relationships during the Jacksonian years reappeared during the Progressive period. "The social ethic of woman suffrage conveniently corresponded to the broader social ethic of progressivism itself. Woman suffrage was, like the direct primary, the direct election of the Senate, the initiative, the referendum, and the recall, not only a reform in itself but an instrument for further reform within the prevailing conception of social goals."[48] The 1960s saw similar close relations between the women's movement and the civil rights and antiwar movements. In sum, an individual or group that has a specific concern with one particular reform also usually has a general reformist weltanschauung which induces the individual or group to be favorably disposed to all reforms.

In the American experience, consensus is not an alternative to political conflict but is, rather, a source of political conflict. Interest-group politics is compatible with consensus; creedal politics is a product of consensus. Conflict occurs not when the consensus breaks down but when the con-sensus is activated, when the consensus couchant becomes the consensus rampant, and when efforts are made to embody the values of the con-sensus in the structure and practice of institutions. The conflicts of creedal politics are not simply over how to promote particular interests that divide people, but also over how and to what extent to realize general ideals that unite people. A consensus on basic values can be a very disquieting and unsettling phenomenon, serving as both an incentive to challenge existing institutions and as a weapon that one coalition of groups can use against another. The most significant upheavals in American politics have arisen not from the absence of consensus but from the assertion of consensus, from efforts to return to first principles, from what in China would be called "purification campaigns" to eliminate arbitrary power and special privilege, economic oligarchs and corrupt politicians. Americans become polarized less over the substance of their beliefs than over how seriously to take those beliefs. At times, they disagree fundamentally on how to apply their ideals and principles to their political institutions and structures. Americans divide most sharply over what brings them together.

In the United States, political change and conflict are associated not with the introduction of new ideas but with renewed commitment to old ones. The appearance of new ideologies, such as Marxism, has had only marginal impact on American politics. Conflict and change derive from creedal passion; they stem from efforts to realize the prevailing values rather than from efforts to challenge them. The reaffirmation of these values can achieve a compelling intensity precisely because of what it is: the invocation of old, accepted, familiar, legitimate, widely supported political beliefs. As Hartz pointed out with respect to the abolitionists, "Ironically, the greatest moral crusade in American history produced practically no original political thought. Garrison is not a creator of political ideas; neither is Phillips. Even Channing is not." The abolitionists saw a need for passion but not for philosophy, and hence "they unite with their very passion a strange and uncritical complacency." As Garrison asked, "Argument is demanded—to prove what?"[49] The self-evident truth that all men are created equal? That slavery is therefore wrong?

Political change in the United States, in contrast to change in western Europe, is normally associated with the appearance of new social movements rather than by the rise to power of new political parties. This contrast is particularly sharp with respect to Canada, which, despite many social, political, and geographic similarities, has largely lacked American-style messianic movements of the left and right because it has also lacked a national Creed.[50] Particular reform efforts in the United States often take on a distinctive moralistic quality not present to the same degree in comparable efforts elsewhere. Comparing American and European anti-slavery movements, for instance, Stanley Elkins observed that "the simple harsh moral purity of our own antislavery movement, from the 1830s on, gave it a quality which set it apart from the others." For the American abolitionists, far more than for the others, the end of slavery "was a problem of conscience"; they displayed "that peculiar quality of abstraction which was, and has remained, uniquely American. For them, the question was all *moral*."[51]

The struggle between the activist and the standpatter in American politics has its parallels in the consensus politics of the Soviet Union. In Soviet politics, too, some are committed to realizing the goals of the Party and its ideology while others are indifferent, masking this indifference behind the meaningless reiteration of official rhetoric. In outlook, the indifferent Soviet citizen may not seem to differ much from the indifferent American citizen. But the Soviet arrives at his similar posture from the opposite direction. Their alternatives to indifference have little in common. The American is indifferent to the reform of government, the Russian to the demands of government. In the Soviet Union, the ideological activist is the insider; in the United States he is the outsider. He crusades not for the system but against the system. When the Soviet citizen loses his indifference, he becomes mobilized in support of the government; when the American citizen loses his indifference, he becomes mobilized in opposition to the government. Most important, in the Soviet Union the capacity to mobilize people politically is monopolized by the Communist Party. The ability of the party activists to mobilize people on behalf of the Soviet system, however, appears to decline over time, as the revolution recedes into history. In the United States, on the other hand, social change regularly produces incentives for different social groups to mobilize people politically to change the system. As a result, the relatively inchoate American liberal ideals have a recurring political vitality—they are put to use— while the much more systematic Marxist-Leninist ideology of the Soviet Union becomes formal, ritualized, and sterile.

Reform and Its Limits

Two major types of political change occur during creedal passion periods. *Reform* is the conscious attempt to bring political institutions and practices more into accord with liberal-democratic values and principles. *Realignment* is a general change in the pattern of relationships between social forces and political institutions; it is not the product of conscious design but the result of the rise of some social forces, the decline of others, and changes in the structure and composition of particular political institutions. The processes of reform and realignment are closely intertwined. The changes in the relations between political institutions and political ideals that are reform interact with the changes in the relations between political institutions and social forces that are realignment.

In the way in which they manifest themselves, both these processes are peculiar to the United States. Neither reform nor realignment is typical of an ideologically divided society. The classic European pattern of political change, for instance, can be seen as involving a distinct series of steps. A new self-conscious social force emerges as a result of social and economic change. This new social force articulates a new ideology reflecting its interests in opposition to those of established social forces. The new social force becomes the base of a new political party and identifies itself with particular governmental institutions that "belong" to the old social forces. A period of political struggle and upheaval leads to the conquest of power (or the substantial sharing of power) by the new social force with its distinctive ideology and its particular political institutions. The rise of the middle class, for instance, led to the emergence of liberalism as an ideology, the development of liberal parties, the rise in the power of the governmental institution (the lower house of parliament) associated with middle-class interests, and the decline in power of those parties and governmental institutions (monarchy, upper house) associated with aristocratic interests. The pattern has been one of ideological conflict and change and the displacement of one institution by another.

In the American process of political change, a new social force similarly emerges and becomes self-conscious as a result of social and economic change. This new social force, however, does not advance a new ideology but articulates with heightened intensity the ideals and principles of the old, prevailing ideology. Instead of developing and promoting new political institutions, it demands that existing institutions be reshaped in the light of the core values of that ideology. This is the distinctive American meaning attached to the word "reform." In some measure, of course, every particular "reform" proposal serves the interest of some particular group and is most ardently advanced by that group. But the proposal, if it is to be considered seriously, must also be couched in terms of the universal values and beliefs of the American Creed. It cannot be seen as simply embodying the exclusive interests of a particular class or group.

To campaign for "Black Power" is to go down a dead-end street; to crusade for "equal rights" is to open up—however slowly and creakingly —doors to new opportunities. The legitimacy and persuasiveness of reform depend upon the extent to which its goals can be formulated in terms of the broadly appealing values of the American Creed.

In America, as in Europe, ideas are weapons, and ideology is the handmaiden of political change. Without the articulation of political ideas and the commitment to ideology, political change does not occur. In Europe, however, the ideology that leads to change in the twentieth century is very different from that which led to change in the eighteenth century. In the United States, in contrast, the themes, slogans, and concerns of one creedal passion period strongly resemble those of another. The arguments for reform, reflected in these themes, also are similar, and the values appealed to by one social force in one reform period are reasserted by a different social force in the next.

At the same time that the rising social force seeks to identify its interests with the values of the American Creed, it also seeks to identify its interests with and to further those interests by securing access to established political institutions. It can, of course, attempt to create a new political party or to develop new governmental institutions. Such efforts may briefly contribute to the furtherance of change. But the success of the new social force depends generally on the extent to which it is able to embody its interests in the existing political parties and existing government institutions. This struggle for access typically leads to a shift in the relations between social forces and political institutions, a political realignment, in which institutional constituencies and functions change. This orientation toward existing institutions is encouraged by the distinctive institutional characteristics of American government: federalism, the separation of power, and loosely structured, decentralized political parties. In America, ideological monism and institutional pluralism thus combine to produce a process of political change fundamentally different from that which has historically prevailed in the ideologically divided societies of Europe.

Political change in the United States has usually meant reform—that is, efforts to bring political institutions and practices into line with previously accepted political ideas and values. Reform is possible only within the context of ideological agreement. Its origins as a concept lie deep in the history of the Judeo-Christian tradition, in the ideas of redemption, renewal, resurrection, reformation, and rebirth. It has even been argued that the idea of reform itself is "essentially Christian in origin and early development" and that there was "no true equivalent in pre-Christian times." Within early Christianity the idea focused on the reform of the individual, but it was not limited to that. Its essence was "the idea of free, intentional and ever perfectible, multiple, prolonged and ever repeated efforts by man to reassert and augment values pre-existent in the spiritual-material compound of the world."[52] The reform impetus within the Christian church had its ups and downs over the years, but reemerged in its full glory in that greatest of all efforts at reform in the sixteenth and seventeenth centuries. At this time, the idea of reform acquired broader and more radical connotations as the Puritans worked to create a new heaven and new earth. Its essence, however, continued to involve the ideas of purification and a return to first principles. Reform, as Croly defined it several centuries later for American politics, is "a moral protest and awakening, which seeks to enforce the violated laws and to restore the American political and economic system to its pristine purity and vigor . . . Reform means at bottom no more than moral and political purification."[53]

The impetus to reform has peaked at recurring intervals in American history, coinciding with creedal passion periods. Party reform, for instance, has occurred in three major waves: the Jacksonian reforms of 1820–1840, the Progressive reforms of 1890–1920, and the reforms of the 1960s and 1970s.[54] Together with the Revolution, however, these creedal periods are characterized not just by party reform, but by the widespread efforts to reform a variety of political institutions and practices. With the notable exception of the abolition of slavery, virtually all the major political reforms in American history occurred in the context of these periods. Reforms "tend to cluster in highly concentrated and usually quite brief periods of time."[55]

The Revolutionary era was the first, the greatest, and in many respects the most successful period of political reform in America history. It set the political and ideological pattern for subsequent creedal passion periods. The revolutionaries loosed the spirit of reform on the American waters. The "Republic's designers launched a new faith in political engineering that has persisted strongly in American culture ever since. The main articles of that faith still hold that for every problem there is a solution. That it is better to do something about a problem than to do nothing even though that something may be less than perfect. That, above all, if we can figure out and establish the right *institutions,* the right policies are bound to follow." It is precisely this faith that has "animated our history's most powerful political movements," including those of the Jacksonian and Progressive eras.[56]

The Revolution itself, of course, produced major political reforms. The most sweeping and important involved the break with the British Crown and the establishment of a republican government with legitimacy derived from the consent of the governed. In the context of the eighteenth century this was a totally unprecedented and, in one sense, revolutionary step. But it was also a limited step; it did not involve the social and economic upheaval associated with subsequent class-based revolutions. It involved a change in government, not a change in society; it was a political reform, albeit a most far-reaching and innovative one. In the course of bringing about this reform, the "revolutionaries" introduced other and related changes: the abolition of primogeniture, entail, quit-rents, and other vestiges of feudalism; the separation of church and state; the abolition of slavery in northern states; the enactment of bills of rights; some extensions of the suffrage; reform of the penal codes; removal of some restrictions on business enterprise; and, most important and all encompassing, the passionate, eloquent, and learned articulation of the political ideas—and ideals—that would inspire, guide, and serve subsequent generations of political reformers.

The second major cluster of reforms occurred during the Jacksonian decades of 1820s and 1830s. In politics and government these years witnessed: the introduction of universal white male suffrage and a major expansion of political participation; the fading of the congressional caucus, and the formation of national political parties and the first national political party conventions; popular election of presidential electors and the emergence of the President as the "tribune of the people"; the development of lobbyists and lobbies as an additional means of influencing government; high levels of turnover in elected office, particularly marked in the House of Representatives; the partial democratization of the selection of senators as a result of statewide canvasses in connection with legislative elections; a stress on rotation in office and the spoils system in appointments to government; and a proliferation of the number of elected officials, including judges, at the state and local level. Paralleling these changes in political institutions were equally significant ones in the social and economic spheres: the disestablishment of the Bank of the United States and the opening up of state banking systems; the passage of general incorporation laws that changed incorporation from a special privilege into a routine right; the reform and expansion of public elementary education; and the construction for the first time of institutions—penitentiaries, insane asylums, orphanages, reformatories—as the "places of first resort, the preferred solution to the problems of poverty, crime, delinquency, and insanity." The approach of the reformers was well summed up in Rothman's comment: "The asylum was to fulfill a dual purpose for its innovators. It would rehabilitate inmates and then, by virtue of its success, set an example of right action for the larger society. There was a utopian flavor to this first venture, one that looked to reform the deviant and dependent and to serve as a model for others."[57]

The principal reform targets of the Progressive period were the trusts and the machines. The efforts to correct the evils associated with the big corporation and concentrated economic power included the first antitrust laws, regulatory commissions, consumer legislation, and other laws restricting and imposing standards on the ways in which businesses could conduct their business. In a similar vein, the direct primary, the initiative, referendum and recall, direct election of United States senators, and further extension of the electoral principle to state and local offices were designed to limit the machine by expanding the means of popular control. In addition, civil service, scientific management, and business methods were designed to limit the concentrated political power of the machine by expanding the scope of nonpolitical, technical, and merit considerations in government. In the social sphere, the asylum was rediscovered. "Poverty, squalor, and disease," Lawrence Cremin pointed out, "were hardly new in the nineties." What was new was "an awakening of social conscience, a growing belief that this incredible suffering was neither the fault nor the inevitable lot of the sufferers, that it certainly could be alleviated." The result was a proliferation of new institutions—"civic commissions, charity associations, church leagues, and reform societies galore"—of which perhaps the most notable and distinctive was the social settlement. In education, the progressive movement emerged as "one part of a vast humanitarian effort to apply the promise of American life— the ideal of government by, of, and for the people—to the puzzling new urban-industrial civilization that came into being during the latter half of the nineteenth century."[58] What Horace Mann had been to educational reform in the Jacksonian years, John Dewey was in the Progressive era. In the 1960s and early 1970s, the major institutions of American life were again subjected to a plenitude of reforms similar in goals to those of the three earlier creedal passion periods, although less notably in the extent to which they were realized.

The introduction of reforms does not guarantee their success in producing the consequences their proponents desire. "The perpetual bane of the reformer's existence," Lowi observed of the New York City experience, "is the ease with which the party leaders adapt new structures to old purposes."[59] The point is a familiar one. The institutions and procedures that reformers create are seldom disestablished. Their existence is secure but their purposes and functions change. With rare exceptions, the accomplishments of the reformers over time seem to be "twisted," "perverted," "corrupted," to serve ends very different from those of their creators. There seems to be a certain inevitability and universality to the process.

The ways in which the workings of reforms may frustrate the intentions of reformers are well illustrated by the direct primary. Primaries were a favorite party reform both in the Progressive period and in the 1960s and 1970s. In the Progressive period, primaries were introduced in order to take control over nominations away from the party bosses. Yet the bosses were better able than anyone else to mobilize their lower-class, immigrant supporters to the polls in the low turnout primary elections, and hence used the primary to sustain their power against the middle-class reformers who were attempting to displace them. In the1960s, primaries again became a popular reform, this time designed to take power away from upper-middle-class WASPS and broaden the participation in the system of the lower classes and ethnic minorities. Yet little change occurred in the usual pattern: those who vote in primaries "are richer and better educated . . . more interested in politics . . . and more likely to have strong opinions on the issues and personalities of the day."[60] The introduction of primaries did not enhance the power of the middle classes in the first decade of the twentieth century and did not enhance the power of the lower classes in the seventh decade. The same reform in two different periods was designed to achieve two different results and failed to achieve either.

How can these seemingly perverse results be explained? The answer relates to the determinants of voter turnout. Few people vote in primaries. Voter turnout is a function of organization and socioeconomic status. In the Progressive period, the strong party machines turned out the low-income voters and frustrated the wishes of middle-class reformers. In the

1960s and 1970s, the party machines were gone. Hence primary participation tended to reflect socioeconomic status. Hence the reform that was designed to enhance the influence of the lower classes instead benefited the middle classes. In each case, the reform failed because it did not affect the underlying realities of political organization and social class. When this is the case, the "actual consequences of party reform are, in the future as in the past, likely often to disappoint their advocates, relieve their opponents, and surprise a lot of commentators."[61]

Other instances of this phenomenon abound. The principal beneficiaries of the campaign finance legislation of the 1970s, designed to curb the influence of money in elections, turned out to be millionaire and incumbent candidates. Sunset laws, designed to curb bureaucratic agencies, assigned them new functions and provided them with new incentives to develop strong constituencies. Sunshine laws, designed to open up governmental proceedings, forced the real decisions further back into the recesses of informal, off-the-record caucuses and conversations. In the economic arena, regulatory agencies designed originally to protect the interests of consumers and the general public were captured by the industries they were created to regulate, a process well described in Richard Olney's famous advice to the railroad president who asked him to help abolish the Interstate Commerce Commission. "Looking at the matter from a railroad point of view exclusively," said Olney, this "would not be a wise thing to undertake . . . The Commission . . . is, or can be made, of great use to the railroads. It satisfies the popular clamor for a government supervision of railroads, at the same time that that supervision is almost entirely nominal. Further, the older such a Commission gets, the more inclined it will be found to take the business and railroad view of things. It thus becomes a sort of barrier between the railroad corporations and the people and a sort of protection against hasty and crude legislation hostile to railroad interests . . . The part of wisdom is not to destroy the Commission, but to utilize it."[62] In similar fashion, in the social field, the asylums created to "reform" the indigent, the sick, and the criminal soon adapted to the achievement of other goals. "The promise of reform had built up the asylums; the functionalism of custody perpetuated them. . . . Proposals that promise the most grandiose consequences often legitimate the most unsatisfactory developments. And one also grows wary about taking reform programs at face value; arrangements designed for the best of motives may have disastrous results."[63] The reforms of one generation often produce the vested interests of the next.

Why this should be the case is reasonably clear. The intense moral fervor that gives reformers and the reform movement their political clout cannot be sustained for any length of time. It is one way of attempting to bridge the gap between political ideals and political reality; in due course it exhausts itself and is superseded by some combination of cynicism, complacency, and hypocrisy. Lowi's analysis of reform in New York City describes a general pattern. "The onset of reform is the beginning of a temporary rejection of the system, the establishment of a channel for making innovations in the established order of things." The reformers' rejection of the system "takes the form of direct participation." The "most outstanding feature of the reform movement in New York," however, "has been its short life." It has not lasted; instead, it followed a cyclical pattern. "Each time its onset was widespread, energetic, irresistible." But each time, the components of the movement dispersed, the energy behind it drained, and the reform system itself was never institutionalized.[64] Such is the pattern of reform generally, a direct result of the nature of reform as an effort to bridge the gap between political ideals and political institutions.

In most other countries, periods of change, particularly social and economic innovation, are associated with the centralization of power in the political system. In America, too, there have been some tendencies in this direction. During periods of creedal passion, however, the prevailing thrust in politics has been toward the opening up of the system, the expansion of political participation, the diffusion and popularization of power. In part this is because the stress during creedal passion periods is not just on social and economic changes, but on political reform as well.

The relative openness and permeability of the American political system make reform possible. Groups previously outside the system can mobilize, organize, participate, and inaugurate structural changes in the system. The goals of reform usually involve enhancing these qualities of openness, permeability, "responsiveness." In the longer term, however, the very success of the reformers in achieving these goals helps to defeat reform. The same features of the American political system that make reform possible and that are strengthened by reform also ensure that its victory will be temporary. The changes that reform produces are the product of a temporary mobilization and coalition of groups. The institutions that reformers create reflect one constellation of political interests and purposes. When this constellation fades in significance, those institutions then respond to the changes in the political environment. The political system, open to reform and further opened by reform, is also open to counter-reform.

The reform process, moreover, contains its own paradox. Those reforms most easily adopted are presumably those that have the broadest appeal, that is, those where the gap between existing practice and accepted ideal adversely affects the largest groups in the population. These reforms are most clearly seen to be "in the public interest." In a creedal passion period, public sentiment, consequently, can be quickly aroused and directed toward their enactment. Once enacted, however, these reforms are also most likely to lack a well-organized constituency to sustain and protect them and to ensure that they are administered and applied so as to achieve the intended results. Beneficial to everyone, they are guarded by no one, and hence they are highly vulnerable to efforts of special-interest groups to twist them to serve their purposes. Those reforms, on the other hand, that, while legitimized in terms of the values of the American Creed, also primarily benefit particular interest groups may be more difficult to enact precisely for that reason. Their consequences for the balance of power among groups are easily seen. At the same time, the existence of an ongoing organized constituency means that such reforms are more likely to be applied over a longer period of time in a way more congruent with their original purposes. In short, those reforms that are most easily introduced to serve the general interest are also most easily corrupted to serve special interests.

The frustrations of the Burkean conservative in America have been graphically described by Louis Hartz. Lacking a feudal tradition, monarchy, aristocracy, an established church, and significant status differences, the American conservative can only find liberal institutions to conserve. The frustrations of the progressive reformer, on the other hand, have similar roots in the liberal consensus but assume a different form. The conservative in America is frustrated by the fact that American political institutions are modeled on the liberal ideal; the reformer is frustrated because, despite his best efforts, those institutions always fall short of the ideal. Creedal passion periods are periods of progressive reform. Yet the dragons of inequality and concentrated power that are slain by one band of reformers in one period rise up again to challenge another band in another period. The British Crown is eliminated but is replaced by a commercial oligarchy centered in a national bank. The oligarchy is displaced but a slave-owning aristocracy becomes even more powerful. The plantation aristocracy is broken in a civil war which heralds the rise of an industrial plutocracy with wealth and power far transcending that which existed previously. In due course, corporate power is tamed, in part by the expansion of executive power, which then becomes the source of new threats to liberty, equality, and popular control of government. Ralph Nader, Bob Woodward, and Carl Bernstein have to redo in one generation what Upton Sinclair and Lincoln Steffens did in an earlier one. For the reformer, it is, as Michels said, at best a spectacle "simultaneously encouraging and depressing."[65] Through two hundred years and four major periods of reform fervor, the history of progressive reform is, apparently, the history of much reform but modest progress. Reform seems ephemeral, privilege reincarnate, and the realization of the democratic ideal only marginally closer in 1976 than it was in 1776.

Political Earthquakes and Realignment

Creedal passion periods are characterized by an impetus to reform because social forces invoke traditional political ideals in order to advance their own interests by bringing political institutions more into accord with those ideals. Specific institutional reforms may, however, produce unanticipated or contrary consequences. The most sweeping and lasting impact of a creedal passion period is found not in the progressive reforms that it produces, but in the political realignment that accompanies it: the cry is reform, the result is realignment. This realignment involves a fundamental restructuring of the relations between the principal social forces in society and the principal institutions in the political system. It involves changes in the powers, functions, and constituencies of governmental institutions, usually including but certainly not limited to political parties.

A political realignment in this sense is a much more all-encompassing phenomenon than simply a party realignment or what Walter Dean Burnham has termed a "critical realignment"—that is, "a major change rooted in the behavior of critically large minorities of American voters which durably alters electoral coalitions, the shape of election outcomes, and the flow of public policy."[66] Party or critical realignments have occurred at fairly regular intervals in American history, typically culminating in "critical elections" every twenty-eight to thirty-six years: 1800, 1828, 1860, 1896, 1932. These elections signal major and lasting shifts in party power and in the link between particular parties and particular social forces. In some of these instances, however, the focus of the realignment was the rise of a new social force: 1800 marked the ascendancy of the agrarian Republicans over the mercantile Federalists, 1860 the ascendancy of the industrializing North over the plantation South, and 1932 the ascendancy of the urban working class over the previously dominant business groups. These elections signaled major shifts in power among social groups and between the parties that represented them. They did not, however, involve the profound upheaval in the overall relations between social forces and political institutions that occurred during the Revolutionary, Jacksonian, and Progressive eras and in the 1960s and 1970s. The realignments of 1828 and 1896, for instance, involved shifts not only among and between political parties and social forces but also more general changes in the structure, power, and functioning of governmental institutions. In these cases, party realignment was only one aspect of a broader political realignment.

Viewing party realignments in this broader context helps explain something that perplexed political analysts of the 1960s. According to the view that party realignments occur every twenty-eight to thirty-six years, a party realignment should have occurred between 1960 and 1968. Many of the familiar prerequisites and correlates of such a realignment were present: increased political participation, a rise of new issues (civil rights, Vietnam) that cut across the New Deal party division inherited from the past, third-party movements, and a loosening of party ties among many groups in the population, particularly the young. Yet no significant party realignment occurred; it was, as Burnham said, "a kind of waiting for Godot" on the part of political analysts.[67] The dynamics that had previously operated with such regularity in American politics for over a century and a half seemed to have failed. How can this be explained?

One possible explanation is that what was supposed to happen in the 1960s was not a simple party realignment but a more complex political realignment—which did in fact occur. What distinguished this political realignment from those of the Progressive and Jacksonian periods was that political parties were less important in the overall political system in the 1960s than they had been previously. Consequently the changes in roles, power, and constituencies that occurred did not have a major impact on political parties. The political realignment of the 1960s did not involve a major party realignment because parties were weak, just as the political realignment of the Revolution did not involve a party realignment because parties, in a modern organized sense, simply did not then exist. The frustrated political analysts of the 1960s were, in short, simply waiting for the wrong Godot.

Political realignments can occur in creedal passion periods because of two principles that govern the links between social forces and political institutions. These principles were reflected in the frame of government that the Founding Fathers created in the eighteenth century, and were reinforced by the way in which that frame evolved in subsequent centuries. These are the principles of *constituent plurality* and *constituent mutability*. Both represented major innovations in the theory of government. In the eighteenth century, preoccupation with the goal of balanced government usually manifested itself in the concept of mixed government. According to this theory, each branch of government, as in Great Britain, should represent or embody the interests of a particular estate of the realm. This theory was a not a completely inaccurate description of the British Constitution: the crown represented the royal family, the House of Lords the aristocracy, and the House of Commons the gentlemen, burghers, and other property owners qualified to participate in parliamentary elections. Mixed government assumed a more-or-less immutable and exclusive relation between a social force and a political institution. The number and character of the political institutions in government were to reflect the number and character of the social forces in society. A balance among social orders would be reflected in a balance among political organs.

If this were the case, however, what justification would there be for a multiplicity of political institutions in government in the United States? Charles Pinckney raised precisely this question in the discussion of the Senate in the Constitutional Convention. England, he said, had three orders in society and hence three institutions in government. The United States, however, "contains but one order that can be assimilated to the British nation—this is the order of the Commons. They will not surely then attempt to form a Government consisting of three branches, two of which shall have nothing to represent . . . We must . . . suit our Government to the people it is to direct."[68] For a society composed of "one order" and yet also of many interests, a one-on-one theory of representation would have required either a single central governing body or a large number of such bodies to reflect the diverse factions identified by Madison in Number 10 of *The Federalist*.

The framers of the Constitution, however, did not base their structure of government on a theory of representation. With a few exceptions like Gouverneur Morris and John Adams (who did not participate in the Constitutional Convention), they held little brief for the theory of mixed government. Both in the Convention debates and in *The Federalist,* as well as elsewhere, they paid relatively little explicit attention to the relations between the social forces in American society and the political institutions they were creating. They occasionally referred to the Senate in terms suggesting that they thought it would be more reflective of the interests of small states and that it would be the more conservative and restrained of the two houses of the national legislature. This was almost always in the context of their view that the House of Representatives, directly elected by the people, would be more likely to be swept by popular passions. Although they referred at times to the various interests and groups which at that time made up American society, nowhere did they elaborate a systematic theory of what groups would be represented in what way in which institutions of government. They talked a great deal about the *powers* of the different branches of government, but they said little about the *constituencies* of those branches. The stress of the framers was on "the interior structure of the government," not on its external relations to society. And this interior structure was designed to ensure that "its several constituent parts may, by their mutual relations, be the means of keeping each other in their proper places."[69]

In Europe, Latin America, and elsewhere, governmental institutions and political parties tend to be attached indissolubly and often exclusively to particular social forces; when those social forces decline, they carry "their" political institutions with them. In western Europe, each institution has also tended to be associated with a particular sociopolitical ideology. In the United States, however, in a major political innovation matched in modern history only by the creation of the Leninist party, the framers of the Constitution created a system of government that was responsible to society yet also autonomous from it. Each institution of government was not necessarily linked exclusively to a particular social force, nor was it necessarily linked permanently to any combination of social forces. Pluralism and mutability were provided for in the relations between society and government. They ensured the stability of the latter and the access of the former. In the United States, political institutions have become adept in shifting constituencies to reflect the changing power and influence of emerging and declining social forces. Social forces in turn have confronted multiple potential channels of access to government, and if they have not been able to promote their interests effectively through one institution, they have almost always been able to establish links with another.

During the course of American political development, the constituencies of most formal institutions and of the major political parties have changed dramatically. The principal interest groups in American society —agrarian, commercial, industrial, and labor; religious, regional, and ethnic; liberal and conservative—have at one time or another been on each side of the arguments concerning states rights versus national power, Congress versus the President, the power of the judiciary, Republicans versus Democrats. Governmental institutions have been almost entirely free of sustained association with any particular point of view; they are not thought of as being inherently or irremediably liberal or conservative. Institutional ideologies or briefs advanced by one interest group in one generation on behalf of "its" political institution are taken over by another, often competing, interest group in the next generation. The case for presidential leadership, or judicial review, or states rights may be a conservative argument at one time and a liberal argument at another.

This relationship between social forces and political institutions has two consequences for public debate. First, the arguments between social forces over their respective claims on the polity become transmuted into debates over the respective roles of political institutions within the polity. The head-on clash of social force against social force is thus filtered through institutional channels and in part transformed into a struggle of one institution against another. Second, the advocates in the debate over institutional roles are necessarily to some degree restrained by their unconscious knowledge, if not conscious awareness, that the brief they are arguing one day may be the one they challenge on a later day. How many people active in American public life for several decades have consistently favored either presidential power or congressional power, national authority or states rights, judicial activism or judicial quietism?

A high degree of institutional continuity seems to characterize American government. The relations between the Ninety-fourth Congress and the thirty-eighth President in 1976 did not seem to be fundamentally different from those between most of their predecessors. In this sense, the Founding Fathers designed well: their system of checks and balances has provided for the sustained division of power among the different branches and levels of government. The fact that the balance of power they valued has been largely maintained over the years is, however, to a great extent a product of that aspect of the political system to which they devoted relatively little attention—that is, the relations between political institutions and social forces. The balance of power they valued has been maintained because of the ability of political institutions to adapt to changes in the influence and interests of social forces. No major governmental institution and only one early rudimentary political party (the Federalists) has suffered the fate of the Crown, the House of Lords, or the Liberal Party. Institutional continuity has been the product of institutional adaptability. The interests of a group are not connected indefinitely or exclusively with the interests of any particular political institution. The connection between them, which may be intense and politically important while it lasts, is nonetheless a marriage of convenience, a product of the existing political environment, without deep social or ideological roots. When common interests are no longer served, divorce and remarriage to other partners invariably follow.

The framers' concern for maintaining a balance of power within government led them away from the ideas of both mixed government and the separation of processes, and toward the idea of checks and balances. The concept of mixed government assumed a more or less one-to-one relationship between a social force and a political institution. Far from presupposing the autonomy of governmental institutions, it in effect presupposed "captive" institutions, much as Marxist theory sees the state as the captive of the bourgeoisie. The lack of institutional autonomy means that the power of the governmental institutions varies with the power and importance of the social forces to which they are attached. In the eighteenth century in Britain, a rough equilibrium existed among the monarchy, the aristocracy, and the middle class as social forces, which was reflected in the relations among the Crown, Lords, and Commons as institutions. The balance of power in government was the temporary consequence of a balance of power in society. The onset of democracy, however, upset the societal balance, and during the course of the next century the decline of the monarchy and aristocracy transformed the Crown and the House of Lords into dignified institutions and resulted in the supremacy of the Commons. Neither the Crown nor the House of Lords was able to adapt effectively to changes in society.

In different fashion, the separation of processes produces a similar result. Assigning the legislative, executive, and judicial powers to distinct institutions leads to the supremacy of the legislature, since the legislative or law-making power is clearly superior to the law-executing and law-interpreting powers. If all legislative power is concentrated in one institution, that body will clearly be superior to the executive and judicial branches. In order to moderate this tendency, the theory of the separation of processes, as, for instance, it was developed by Jefferson, often postulated the division of the legislature into two branches that could check each other. This represented a first step away from a pure separation of processes toward checks and balances, in which the executive and even the judiciary would have some share in the legislative power.

The checks and balances theory, which was uppermost in the minds of the framers, alone of the three theories of balanced government ensured the maintenance of a balance of power in government. This was done in part by allowing each branch of government to share in the powers of the other branches. More fundamentally, if implicitly, this result was also achieved by allowing for flexibility in the relations between governmental institutions and social forces. On the one hand, no governmental institution was linked indissolubly and exclusively to any single social force (as would have been the case in the theory of mixed government). On the other hand, no governmental institution monopolized the law-making power which would have enabled it to dominate the other institutions of government (as would have been the case with separation of processes). Instead, the checks and balances system provided for competition among governmental institutions and permitted mutability in the relations between governmental institutions and social forces.

Changes in the linkages between social forces and political institutions are always taking places. They are not limited to creedal passion periods. Indeed, realignments between social forces and political parties seem to take place not only as part of more general reconstitutions of the political system during creedal passion periods, but also at regular intervals between creedal passion periods. In less regular fashion, governmental institutions may shift constituencies through extended periods of time, as the Supreme Court did in the shift from the Hughes Court to the Warren Court. Changes in constituency linkages between social forces and political institutions do, however, tend to be more numerous, more rapid, and more significant during creedal passion periods than at other times in American history. During these periods, the clumping of linkage changes produces a reconstitution of the political system. The system that emerged out of the Revolution was significantly different from that which had existed previously; the Jacksonian system embodied additional basic changes in the powers, functions, and constituency linkages of political institutions; the reconstitution of the system that occurred during the Progressive period, often labeled by political scientists as "the system of 1896," likewise marked a new pattern of politics and institutional relationships which lasted until the 1960s, when a "new American political system" again emerged.

The peculiar genius of the American system is that, more than other major political systems, it allows for this periodic reconstitution of its principal institutional components. This reconstitution is clearly related to changes in the roles of social forces—classes, interest groups, regions—in the society. The external institutional façade remains, so that the reality of change is obscured in appearance and the fundamental principle of autonomous institutions competing with each other is not challenged. Yet major changes do take place in the powers, functions, interrelations, and constituencies of political institutions. This is the way in which a new balance is struck between the political system and society. Stresses and strains develop along the major political fault line between the plate of social forces on the one hand and that of political institutions on the other, until a political earthquake accurs, releases the tension, and produces a new equilibrium between the societal plate and the political one. These periodic realignments are, as Walter Dean Burnham suggested, "America's surrogate for revolution."[70]

In sum, creedal passion periods involve intense efforts by large numbers of Americans to return to first principles. They are characterized by a distinctive type of political cleavage, major efforts at reform, and significant shifts in alignments between political institutions and social forces. Without the absence of moral intensity that characterizes the "normal" pattern of American politics, the American political system could not long endure. Without the moral intensity of creedal passion periods, it could not change and hence avoid stagnation and decay. From time to time the long-term stability of the system requires a moralistic drive to narrow the gap between ideal and reality. In this sense, a creedal passion period is American politics' finest—and most dangerous—hour.

6 THE SOURCES OF CREEDAL PASSION

Why Creedal Passion Periods?

The place of creedal passion in American politics must be explained at two levels. At the most general level, what causes this overall pattern of political continuity and equilibrium, occasionally interrupted by the intrusion of passion, moralism, intensified conflict, reform, and realignment? Why is interest-group politics from time to time displaced by creedal politics? The general causes of this pattern are to be found in the extent and nature of the American liberal consensus. The pattern is distinctive but not unique to American politics, and it remains to be shown how this general American pattern both resembles and differs from similar patterns in other societies characterized by ideological consensus.

At the more specific level, why do particular manifestations of creedal passion appear at particular moments in American history? Does each outburst of creedal passion have its own specific causes? Or are there some recurring factors that can be identified as the common precipitants of creedal passion periods?

In the end, an exploration of the sources of creedal passion, both general and specific, cannot help but lead the analysis back to the historical origins of it all, to the initial causes of both the general pattern and the specific manifestations of that pattern, which are to be found in seventeenth-century England.

General Sources: Comparable Phenomena in Other Societies

Political change in the United States is distinctive in that: (1) it is episodic, tending to be concentrated in periods of creedal passion occurring roughly at sixty-year intervals; (2) it is associated not with a change in ideologies but rather with a reinvocation and reaffirmation of traditional American liberal values and beliefs; and (3) the overriding purpose of reform during periods of change is to bring American political institutions and practices into accord with these values and beliefs. This pattern of change could only occur in a society with an overwhelming consensus on liberal and democratic values. It could not occur and has not occurred in societies with traditions of ideological pluralism, such as most of those of western Europe.

In societies characterized by a nonliberal ideological monism, phenomena comparable, if not similar, to creedal passion periods may occur when efforts are made to reduce the gap between prevailing political reality and the basic values of the ideology. In most cases, this will mean strengthening governmental authority in order to make it correspond more closely to an autocratic or totalitarian ideal. In a political system produced by a major revolution, however, efforts may be made from time to time to renew or to reaffirm revolutionary values. Such values usually involve elements of purification, puritanism, mass participation, egalitarianism, and a renewal of moralistic devotion and commitment to revolutionary principles. In the Soviet Union since the suppression of the Kronshtadt revolt in 1921, such revolutionary values have been subordinated to the goals of bureaucratic centralism and party supremacy. In Communist China, on the other hand, at least in its first quarter-century, periodic efforts were made to give renewed meaning to revolutionary values, of which the most notable was the Great Proletarian Cultural Revolution.

Despite their basic differences, striking similarities exist between the Cultural Revolution in China and the simultaneous outburst of creedal passion in the United States in the 1960s. In one form or another, virtually all of the fourteen characteristics of creedal passion periods set forth in the opening pages of Chapter 5 can be found in Chinese politics during the Cultural Revolution. The purpose of the Cultural Revolution was "not to replace existing authority but to purify it," and the ideology of the revolution hence "may have more in common with restoration or revitalization movements than with rebellion."[1] This pattern had its roots, in many respects, in Confucianism, in which there was an uneasy gap between principle and practice and which consequently provoked periodic demands for reform in the name of the fundamental values of the system.

> Confucian ideology had this potential—to purify the system as well as to justify it. Confucianism coexisted uneasily with imperial and bureaucratic institutions. The high standards of virtue to which Confucius failed to convert even the petty princes of his day were still less reachable for the rulers of a vast empire. What made the ideology vital and the system viable was the ability of the former to hold a critical mirror to the latter. Periodically throughout Chinese history one discovers a kind of Protestant fundamentalism—the mobilization of the ideas of officialdom against established institutions and practices. One finds echos of this in Maoist fundamentalism which, like its Confucian parallels, is based on a highly selective version of the Sacred Canon.[2]

"Protestant fundamentalism," here used to describe a phenomenon in the Chinese tradition, could not be a more apt phrase for American creedal passion periods. During the Cultural Revolution, too, the effort was made to move forward in practice by turning backward in theory, to cleanse existing practice and rectify evils by a reassertion of "traditional" (that is, Maoist or revolutionary) values. "Purification" in Communist China is the functional equivalent of "reform" in liberal America. In a one-ideology society, change cannot be mediated by a shift in the prevailing ideology: instead, there has to be a reinvocation of the underlying or fundamental values of that ideology. This occurred in Confucian China; it has occurred in Communist China; it recurs in liberal America. It could not occur and did not occur in those brief years in the early part of the twentieth century when ideological pluralism prevailed in China and traditional Confucian, republican, regional, and revolutionary movements vied for control.

Anthropologists have analyzed societies in terms of the differences between "shame cultures" and "guilt cultures." It has been argued that shame, as an external sanction, has been the principal means of social control in Asian societies, including both Japan and China. In Western societies, there has been a greater reliance "on a sense of guilt or 'conscience' as an internal sanction."[3] Although some scholars have claimed that guilt has played a significant role in both traditional and modern Chinese society, the weight of scholarly authority has stressed the importance of shame in shaping behavior in China.[4] In some sense, indeed,

American society may be the guilt culture par excellence, whereas Chinese society is the shame culture par excellence. And it is precisely the strength of these two forms of social control that makes these societies similar. In many societies shame and guilt will both be very weak, but in the United States and China at least one of these two forms of social control is strong. Shame or guilt can be an effective means of social control only in societies with explicit and generally agreed-upon standards of morality. China and the United States meet this criterion. More important than the fact that one may rely on guilt and the other on shame is the common intensity with which they are applied in Chinese and American societies. This shared characteristic makes possible creedal passion periods in one and a· Cultural Revolution in the other.

"The widening dissonance between Maoist ideology and Party practice in 1962–66," one scholar argued, "led to the Cultural Revolution," and another social scientist explicitly analyzed the Cultural Revolution in terms of the theory of cognitive dissonance.[5] In the United States, perceptions of the Ivl gap and of its immorality and intolerability have tended to surface first in society among social forces and interest groups seeking to preserve or to expand their access to government. In China, on the other hand, the central leadership in the government provided the initiative; the affirmation of "traditional" values and the attack on existing institutions first came from the top down rather than from the bottom up. Mao Tse-tung, as one Red Guard officer put it, "changed his demands" and began to condemn officials "who were doing what they always had done." In the Cultural Revolution, however, as in American creedal passion periods, the more radical members of the protest movement were those who had previously been least connected with the existing establishment.[6] Both the creedal passion of the 1960s and the Cultural Revolution also involved expansion of political participation and diversification in its forms. In China this was, at least initially, a calculated and controlled process designed to serve the ends of the central leadership. Hence, unlike American creedal passion periods, the Cultural Revolution had a fairly well-defined beginning (in November 1965, with Yao Wen-yuan's attack on Wu Han) and an officially announced end almost three years later (in September 1968).

In the United States, the politics of creedal passion has supplemented and supplanted the normal patterns of interest-group politics. In China, too, the politics of the Cultural Revolution differed significantly from the normal pattern. It was not simply a struggle for power between individuals and factions. As Paul Hiniker asked, "If the Cultural Revolution is to be explained solely as a power struggle, how does one account for the passionate displays of ideological ferver?" Similarly, Lowell Dittmer argued that the Cultural Revolution, particularly with respect to the attack on Liu Shao-ch'i, was not a power struggle disguised as a revolution but rather a revolution disguised as a power struggle, in which the attack on Liu was a means to educate the masses and to produce revolutionary upheaval.[7] During the Cultural Revolution, muckraking became a central form of politics. There was an emphasis on willingness to "wash dirty linen in public" and "an almost obsessive Red Guard concern with exposure," this mass criticism serving the functions of both rectification and mass mobilization.[8] The forms and intensity of mass communication multiplied. There was also, as in the America of the 1960s, an intensification of verbal aggression and of symbolic as well as physical violence. "One outstanding phenomenon of the Cultural Revolution was the prevalence of incivil words and deeds on the part of both the elite groups and the masses."[9]

Much of the other activity in the Cultural Revolution will be familiar to Americans who experienced the passion of the 1960s in the United States. As the Cultural Revolution came to its peak, students at Peking's two major universities "took the initiative to press charges against the university faculties, administration, and the party committees." At Peking University, students denounced "the university president and two other officials for enforcing bourgeois ideology in education, which discriminated against proletarian students and at the same time exalted curriculum and academic learning over policy and ideology." Shortly thereafter, the student movement was expanded into the Red Guards. "Ruthlessly attacking power centers and hysterically demanding mass action, the Red Guards were told to disrupt and paralyze the establishment."[10] The goal of the leaders of the revolution involved "rejuvenating the revolutionary spirit by smashing revisionism and of unifying huge masses of people by recapturing power." The central thrust was against bureaucracy, hierarchy, and specialization. The ideas of "populism, anti-bureaucratism, and rebellion" were used to attack officialdom and bureaucratic authority, but not ideological authority. The ideology of the revolution, indeed, emanated from Mao and those about him. The slogans of the revolution included: "Good men and simple government!" "To rebel is justified!" "Down with officials!"—rallying cries that would have been right at home in the American protest movements of the 1960s.[11]

In China, as in other communist states, the Communist Party was the principal institutional source of legitimacy. During the Cultural Revolution, however, the central position of the party was challenged and undermined. "The whole thrust of the Cultural Revolution," as Benjamin Schwartz said, was "to devalue and diminish its significance." The dictatorship of the proletariat was no longer identified with the dictatorship of the party. Following the Cultural Revolution, efforts were made with some difficulty to rebuild the party.

> The crux of the matter is not whether the Party survives in some form but whether it can ever recover its central sacred charter . . . the Cultural Revolution has unmasked many truths which will not be easily forgotten, particularly by the young who have participated in recent events. The Party may not have engaged in all the heinous bureaucratic crimes attributed to it in Red Guard newspapers but its profane nature as simply another bureaucratic organization devoid of any inbuilt proletarian grace or powers of self-redemption now stands revealed. The institutional charisma will not easily be restored.[12]

No institution has occupied a role in American politics comparable to that of the Communist Party in Chinese politics. But the Presidency clearly has come close to performing such a role, and the "whole thrust" of the democratic surge of the 1960s was, in many ways, "to devalue and diminish" presidential authority. Striking parallels exist between the impact of the Cultural Revolution on the Communist Party and the impact of the passion of the 1960s on the Presidency.

Both the Cultural Revolution and the American upheaval of the 1960s manifested a marked hostility toward norms, such as expertise, specialization, and efficiency, that were associated with economic and bureaucratic development. Mao Tse-tung's thought emphasized the predominance of the social-ethical over the economic-technocratic, the victory of Rousseau over Saint-Simon, as Schwartz summarized it. In the Cultural Revolution, Mao demonstrated that he was "bent on achieving the reign of virtue as he understands virtue and remains unprepared to accept any progress of the 'arts and sciences' which is not based on virtue."[13]

The institutional changes or "reforms" of the Cultural Revolution were, in many respects, the Chinese equivalents of the types of reforms introduced in American creedal passion periods. Mao's approach was "hostile toward increased differentiation and specialization in political structure." The Cultural Revolution "reduced the number of central ministries and simplified the central party apparatus; combined state and party functions at the subnational level in the unified structure of the revolutionary committees; dissolved, suspended, or curtailed parts of the political infrastructure (communications media, the old mass organizations, and the democratic parties); and cut back on the overall size of bureaucracy thereby restricting the possibilities for specialization."[14] In similar fashion, it has been argued that many particular reforms advanced during the Cultural Revolution, such as "the open-door rectification process, the transformation of China's educational system, the establishment of May 7 cadre schools, and the extension of direct class representation in China's revolutionary committees" suggested that the Chinese Communists were trying "to build greater responsiveness and accountability into the system." But the Chinese, like the Americans, could not escape the irony of reform. Particularly with respect to their efforts to eliminate the vestiges of capitalism and to expand mass participation, Lucian Pye argued, "the extraordinary paradox appears to be that Maoists will have produced out of the Cultural Revolution the very results that they have been denouncing."[15]

Scholars of political development in Communist China almost invariably speak in terms of cyclical oscillations between phases of "mobilization" and "consolidation." As Michel Oksenberg put it, "They alternate between periods of mobilization, with an emphasis upon social change, unleashed advance, and conflict and periods of consolidation, with an emphasis upon developing institutions, planned advance, and reconciliation." Mobilization phases, another author observed, "have followed the style of the mass movement, relying on political organization and ideological incentives. Consolidation phases have relied more on administrative organs, bureaucratic procedures, and material incentives."[16] In China, the phases themselves are generally brief and the shift from one to the other quite rapid. The principal mobilization periods are often identified as the phase of socialist consolidation (1955–56), the Great Leap Forward (1958–59), and the Cultural Revolution (1965–68).[17] The aftermath of the Cultural Revolution also resembled the aftermath of America's 1960s: a reemphasis on education, specialization, economic goals, and the reconstituting of institutions that had been disrupted during the years of passion.

The rapidity of the oscillations in China contrasts markedly with the longer-term alternation of creedal passion periods in the United States, this contrast being a dramatic consequence of the different sources of power and initiative in the two societies. The rapid oscillation in China is the product of control from the top; the central leadership in the society has the power to define goals and to change them as well as to mobilize the population and then to demobilize and redirect it. In the United States, on the other hand, oscillations in the intensity of creedal passion depend upon changes in the social structure, the shift in generations, the rise and fall of social groups, and the gradual shifts in perceptions by social groups.

The same considerations that made possible frequent changes between mobilization and consolidation in the first decades of communist rule may make them less frequent subsequently. If the initiative must come from the top, the exercise of that initiative depends upon the attitudes and interests of those who are at the top. Chairman Mao placed great value on the periodic renewal of revolutionary ideals and goals: he "stated more than once that new cultural revolutions would be needed every fifteen or twenty years, i.e., every new generation, to rekindle the sinking flames of enthusiasm."[18] Mao was continuously suspicious of the bureaucratic establishment and rejected a simple identification of the interests of the revolution with the interests of the party. Whether his successors— particularly those of postrevolutionary generations who are not products of the Long March and Yenan—will have the same commitment to the renewal of those values appears dubious. In the United States, basic liberal values remain alive and efforts to realize them are a recurring phenomenon in politics because they can be articulated and used by any social force which finds that to its advantage. In China the top leadership controls the articulation of revolutionary values, and it seems likely that as years pass the leadership may find it less and less in its interest to articulate those values. The revolutionary impulse slackens; consolidation triumphs over mobilization; the interests of the party, state, and military bureaucracies dominate the political scene.

This change in China from a pattern involving regular alternation of moralism and instrumentalism to one in which instrumental values and approaches predominate will dramatically lessen a major source of ambiguity and tension in the political system. The leaders of communist states necessarily have an ambivalent attitude toward the process of modernization. "On the one hand, modernization is positively valued as a social goal, for modernization means economic development and economic development means national power. On the other hand, however, modernization entails bureaucracy, instrumentalism, and the consequent

attenuation and ritual sterilization of ideological principles." Soviet leaders, for a variety of reasons, early gave priority to "the goal of professionalism, to the creation of a rational, highly differentiated bureaucratic
apparatus, and to a degree of operational autonomy for 'expert' hierarchies, particularly in the industrial, state-administrative, and military
spheres."[19] In contrast, the Chinese placed greater emphasis on populism
than on professionalism, an emphasis that manifested itself most dramatically in the Cultural Revolution, a phenomenon unknown to and
impossible in the Soviet system. This Cultural Revolution was thus, in
some sense, "a revolution against history—that is, against what appears
to be the inevitable development of a privileged stratum in the process of
economic development, or, even more boldly, against modernization
itself."[20] The Cultural Revolution is, for example, widely held to have set
Chinese higher education back by more than a decade. In a fundamental
sense, once the revolution is in power, revolutionary values work against
social development.

In the aftermath of other major revolutions, revolutionary values and
goals gradually disappeared from the scene. In China, at least until the
1970s, periodic efforts were made to keep them alive. With the passing
of Mao, these efforts are likely to become less frequent, less important,
and less successful. After two hundred years, the American political system still retains its capacity for ideological renewal. The Chinese system
could well lose its capacity after a quarter of a century. In losing the
capacity to reassert revolutionary values, however, it will also lose the
impetus to rebel against history.

Specific Sources: The Timing of Creedal Passion Periods

The reasons why an overall pattern of political change through creedal
passion exists in the United States are general and clear. The reasons why
creedal passion should come to the fore at particular times in American
history are not necessarily so evident. Each major manifestation of creedal
passion could conceivably have its own particular cause. Undoubtedly, in
each creedal passion period, unique factors were at work that gave the
period its own distinctive momentum and character. Yet the periods also
have much in common in terms of their political moralism, themes, passion, reforms, and consequences. Were common causes in some way at
work in the 1770s, the 1830s, the 1900s, and the 1960s to produce these
similar results? Why did American politics in these decades share so

many distinctive characteristics? Why should major changes and upheavals—in terms of both political reforms and political realignments—
be concentrated at these particular times in American history?

This chapter will not try to provide definitive answers to these questions, but will discuss three types of explanation that could plausibly
account for the appearance of particular creedal passion periods. These
periods can be explained as: (1) a rational response to objective changes
in the concentration and abuse of power; (2) the product of exogenous
events—social, economic, demographic, or cultural—that arouse people
to passionate political action; and (3) a phase in a recurring generational
or cyclical process of change in which events in one phase in the cycle
generate the conditions leading to the next phase. No one of these explanations is probably sufficient and all three may be necessary to account
for the eruptions of creedal passion at particular points in American
history.

Rational Response

A central characteristic of creedal passion periods is the scope and
intensity of concern with the concentration and abuse of power. That
underlying uneasiness which Americans always have about power comes
to the fore and shapes the definition of political issues and the patterns
of political development. What must be explained, consequently, is a
change in public consciousness, social mood, and ethos.

One obvious explanation—not necessarily wrong for being obvious—
is that this change in public mood and concern is a rational response to
"objective" changes in the distribution and utilization of power. The targets of creedal passion are, in this sense, also its causes. New structures
of power and authority develop; those in power eventually abuse their
power; the gap between liberal ideal and institutional practice broadens;
and the moralism characteristic of creedal passion periods surfaces as an
effort to reform institutions and reduce the IvI gap. The years before the
American Revolution saw the rationalization and extension of British
power in America and new efforts to impose on the colonists some of the
costs of empire. In this sense, the American Revolution was a rational
response, as the Whigs argued, to the usurpation and abuse of authority
by the Crown and its agents. Similarly, the Jacksonians attacked not
only the undemocratic aspects of the existing political system but also,
and most vehemently, the new centers of economic and political power
that had emerged and that seemed to portend monopoly of the economic

future of the country. The Bank of the United States "was a giant, immensely powerful even on the political side, where it was most exposed. Economically, it was the greatest corporation in the country, by far the leading single domestic agency in the currency and credit system, and accordingly in business affairs. Upon its conduct depended the fiscal routine of the national government and, potentially, the national credit." In its symbolic relations to the country, the bank more closely resembled "that of the powerful king to his state than that of the flag to the sentiment of loyalty."[21] The 1890s saw the emergence of national industrial corporations, trusts, and monopolies, and of urban political machines and bosses, on a scale that had not existed previously. In the 1950s and 1960s, the military-industrial complex and the imperial Presidency were undeniable facts that had developed in the aftermath of World War II and in the context of the Cold War and that clearly concentrated unprecedented power in the national executive. Major abuses of authority did, in fact, occur in the late 1960s and early 1970s.

Prior to each creedal passion period there thus existed "objective" tendencies toward the concentration of power and away from the political values of the American Creed. It seems reasonable that each of these developments should produce a response that exposed the concentration of power, denounced its abuse as a deviation from American political values, and promoted political action and reform to instigate remedies. Such "objective" circumstances may be a necessary condition for the emergence of creedal passion, but the question remains as to whether they are a sufficient condition. Can one conclude that a one-to-one cause-and-effect relationship exists between the concentration of power and abuse of authority, and creedal passion movements to limit power and constrain authority?

The answer is no for three reasons.

First, such a conclusion rests on the assumption that variations in outrage about the abuse of power accurately reflect variations in the actual abuse of power. This may be true, but there is no way in which this can be proved, and there are some good reasons to think that it may not be true. Documented exposure of abuses at one point in time simply sets the minimum for that point in time. The abuses exposed vary from period to period, and conceivably the level of abuse varies in the same way. But this is not necessarily the case. There are two other possibilities. The level of exposure and the level of actual abuse could vary quite independently of each other. The only limitation is that presumably the former can never be higher than the latter, although widespread charges and smears may create the impression of more abuse than there actually is. Alternatively, the level of exposure of abuse could vary inversely with the level of actual abuse. Widespread exposures of the abuse of power, as we have seen, demonstrate extensive public concern about the abuse of power and hence may help reduce those abuses. The principal "objective" variation in the abuse of power may be not an increase above the norm before a period of creedal passion, but rather a decrease below the norm during and after such a period. Or, conceivably, public moralism about the abuse of power could in itself be evidence of an already existing low level of actual abuse. Low levels of public immorality might well coincide with high levels of public concern about public immorality.

The problem here, in more generalized form, is the classic one concerning corruption and other forms of illegitimate behavior. Do multiple exposures of the existence of corrupt behavior indicate the greater prevalence of such behavior or greater antagonism toward such behavior? It has been suggested, for instance, that "crime waves" are as likely to be the product of waves of public concern about crime or variations in media attention to crime as they are likely to be the product of variations in the incidence of criminal behavior.[22] "Corruption," Theodore Lowi similarly noted, "is an index of the level of public morality, but *awareness* of corruption may well be the sign of a healthy system." Well-organized competitive party politics is likely to produce more exposures of corruption than loosely structured personal and factional politics. Hence, over the years, New York City may have appeared to be more corrupt than Alabama, while in fact there may have been relatively little difference in the absolute levels.[23] In comparable fashion, variations in a political system, such as a shift from interest-group politics to creedal politics, may lead to more exposures of corruption with little variations in absolute levels. Theories from both sociology and social psychology suggest that variations in people's perceptions of the IvI gap and in the intensity of their feelings about the gap are likely to vary more frequently than the behavior of political leaders, groups, and institutions. In an established consensual system, the facts of power do change, albeit slowly; the intensity of concern about power also changes, often rapidly.

The second reason why the concentration and abuse of power cannot alone account for periods of creedal passion is that such changes in power have dramatically occurred at times in American history without generating full-scale moral outrage. Consider, for example, the conservative commercial-oligarchical reaction that purportedly manifested itself in the Constitutional Convention and the 1790s; the wild corruption and abuse of power with the onslaught of industrial and transportation predators in the 1870s; and the Palmer raids, Teapot Dome, and Wall Street–dominated normalcy of the 1920s. These apparent deviations from the Creed did not go entirely unnoticed or entirely unprotested, but they clearly did not produce outbursts of moralism comparable to those of the creedal passion periods. As Herbert Croly accurately observed of the reaction to the political and economic evils of the 1870s and 1880s, "The average good American refused to take these evils seriously. He was possessed by the idea that American life was a stream, which purified itself in the running, and that reformers and critics were merely men who prevented the stream from running free. He looked upon the first spasmodic and ineffective protests with something like contempt. Reformers he appraised as busy-bodies, who were protesting against the conditions of success in business and politics. He nicknamed them 'mugwumps' and continued to vote the regular tickets of his party."[24] It was not until a quarter of a century later that the passion for reform blossomed forth in full bloom.

The third reason is that moral outrage has erupted in American history without any clearly observable intensification of the abuses toward whose elimination it is directed. Here, surely, the most puzzling case is "the mystery of the 1830s." Why did reform, including but certainly not limited to abolitionism, erupt in that decade, although it failed to manifest itself in the 1790s, the 1880s, or the 1920s? "American antislavery sentiment," Ronald Walters argued, "took a very different turn after 1831. Where early abolitionism accepted a gradual end to slavery, after 1831 immediate emancipation became the goal and abolitionism became a passion driving men and women into life-long reform careers. Yet slavery was not new in 1831—it had been present for nearly two centuries. And slavery did not suddenly become evil in 1831; by abolitionist logic it had been sinful all along."[25] As David Donald put it, "Were there more men of integrity, were there more women of sensitive conscience in the 1830s than in any previous decade? A generation of giants these reformers were indeed, but why was there such a concentration of genius in those ten years from 1830 to 1840? . . . We need to know why so many Americans in the 1830s were predisposed toward a certain kind of reform movement."[26] Clearly, neither the evil of slavery nor the existence of the Puritan conscience nor both together are sufficient to explain what happened.

In somewhat similar fashion in the Progressive era, Walter Lippmann found that the popular appeal of muckraking was not a result of higher levels of corruption and abuse of power, but rather of a shift in public opinion in which a people "notorious for its worship of success" turned "savagely upon those who had achieved it": "The muckrakers spoke to a public willing to recognize as corrupt an incredibly varied assortment of conventional acts." Why did conventional behavior become corrupt behavior? The reasons, Lippmann said, must be sought in broader social changes that produced unhappiness in the public, "new necessities and new expectations," and hence "a distinct prejudice in favor of those who make the accusations." The level of corruption did not go up; public tolerance of corruption simply went down. "A happy husband will endure almost anything, but an unhappy one is capable of flying into a rage if his carpet-slippers are not in the right place."[27]

So also, in the 1970s, "post-Watergate morality" imposed new, more stringent standards on the behavior of public officials than had existed previously. The question is whether the Watergate-type behavior of public officials in the late 1960s and early 1970s differed more significantly from the pre-Watergate behavior of public officials than the post-Watergate criteria for official morality differed from pre-Watergate criteria. In the initial phases of exposure, the assumption was that the Watergate acts differed significantly not only from the model of what the behavior of public officials should be, but also from the normal pattern of what the behavior of public officials actually had been. As the dynamic of exposure worked itself out, however, this assumption gradually faded. Revelations of the Johnson, Kennedy, and Roosevelt administrations showed that no individual or party monopolized the misuse of power. "It Didn't Start with Watergate" was not just the title of a polemical tract; it also stated a historical truth. As a result, public indignation over the immorality of a few politicians was gradually transformed into public cynicism at the immorality of all politicians.

Exogenous Events

Creedal passion, although aimed at the reduction of excessive power, is thus not caused simply by the existence of excessive power. A high level of the abuse of power may exist with little or no protest. A high level of protest may develop with little or no significant increase in the abuse of power. Moral outrage is impossible without some abuse of power, but some abuse of power is always occurring. Other, exogenous factors must consequently play a role in precipitating outbursts of creedal passion. To pursue Lippmann's metaphor, what happens at work to cause the husband to fly into a rage because his slippers are in the wrong place?

Social scientists have found the causes of social unrest and protest movements in societal strains, relative deprivation, the authoritarian personality, the group structure of society, the contradictions of capitalism, and elsewhere.[28] Almost all of these theories attempt to explain the origins of particular social movements composed of particular people; they are not directed toward the general condition of society as a whole. Although certain groups in society have a greater propensity than others toward moralistic reform, in a creedal passion period this propensity pervades society. What distinguishes such a period is not the existence of social movements, utopian communities, or reform organizations, but rather the extent to which the activities and concerns of these groups set the dominant themes for the entire society. Thus, the exogenous events responsible for creedal passion periods will have to be broader and more pervasive than those that explain the rise of particular social protest movements. The question is not why reform causes and protest organizations exist, but why they "catch on" with so many different groups. Why do large numbers of husbands simultaneously fly into rages over the misplacement of their slippers?

At least four types of exogenous developments may cause people in various social groups to become incensed about the concentration and abuse of power.

First, creedal passion periods have normally occurred during times of generally rising prices and relative prosperity. People were able to focus their attention on political and moral issues rather than on bread-and-butter ones. Conceivably, of course, unrest produced by economic hardship could be displaced onto questions concerning the IvI gap, but in the American context economic concerns are normally articulated in fairly explicit and direct fashion. Consequently, a sense of relative economic optimism and well-being would appear to be a necessary condition for moral and political concerns to come to the fore. In addition, the principal actors during creedal passion periods are social movements that, while primarily middle class in makeup, appeal across class lines, so that both the well-off and the poor are caught up in the passion for reform.

Second, although overall economic development may provide the necessary background for widespread manifestations of creedal passion, asymmetries or imbalances in the process of development could provide the more immediate impetus to such outbreaks. Relative deprivation has been widely identified by social scientists as a source of protest, insurrection, and revolution. Such deprivation occurs when a group's perceptions of the way in which it is or will be treated fall short of its aspirations as to how it should be treated. This is likely to occur during periods of rapid social and economic change, when established relationships among groups are disrupted. Some form of political action or social protest is likely when increases in social mobilization—literacy, education, media consumption, urbanization—outpace increases in the economic wherewithal to meet the escalating aspirations produced by this mobilization.[29] In this sense, the new forms of the media and of political organization that are associated with creedal passion periods may, in part, themselves be exogenous events contributing to the characteristic politics of such periods. In the history of most societies, rapid economic and social change enhances the role of ideology in politics. In European politics, this historically meant the sharpening of class-based ideologies; in American politics, it means renewed commitment to traditional consensual values.

Third, changes in the relative social and economic status of particular groups may motivate those groups to focus on the IvI gap and to attempt to bring about reforms in political institutions and practices. For reasons elaborated by Tocqueville, increased prosperity for all may become intolerable to those who share less fully in it than others. The American Creed, moreover, is an effective and legitimate weapon for a group to use in attempting to promote its entry into the existing establishment. A group would, presumably, be particularly likely to use this weapon if it had improved itself socially and economically but still felt excluded from important centers of decision making. It might also resort to creedal passion under exactly the opposite circumstances—that is, if it felt that it was on the verge of suffering a relative decline in its position in the power structure. This possibility is the central theme of the "status anxiety" interpretations which David Donald applied to the abolitionists of the 1830s and Richard Hofstadter to the Progressives.[30] A creedal passion period may result when social change is so intense and pervasive that some established social groups have reason to fear an imminent "changed pattern in the distribution of deference and power" *and* when other social groups have reason to think they can and should bring about such a change. In these circumstances, "status politics"—or, better, "cultural politics"—may provide an explanation for "a wide range of behavior for which the economic interpretation of politics seems to be inadequate or misleading or altogether irrelevant."[31]

Fourth, young people appear to have a relatively high group propensity toward moralistic behavior. The extent to which society as a whole seems to become consumed in creedal passion could thus vary with the number of and political influence of youth in the society, which in turn are affected by exogenous events such as wars and economic crises. Much historical evidence suggests that young people have, throughout history, played leading roles in revolutionary movements and political upheavals, and that the appearance of these movements and upheavals may be related to rapid increases in the population between the ages of about fifteen and thirty.[32] The 1960s were distinguished by just such an increase. In 1960, young men between fifteen and twenty-nine made up 19.5 percent of the total male population; in 1970 they made up 24.4 percent of the total, an increase unprecedented in demographic records. The absolute increase— 13.8 million—in the youthful population (ages fourteen to twenty-four) during the 1960s was greater than the total increase in the youthful population—12.5 million—during the seventy years prior to 1960.

The available statistics also suggest that the youthful proportion of the population increased significantly, although not nearly as dramatically, between 1880 and 1910. This period, too, was characterized by relatively high levels of protest among college students.[33] The critical demographic factors relating youth to politics could be the absolute size of the youth cohort, its size relative to the rest of the population, or, more likely, its size relative to the immediately preceding cohort. An increase in the number of youth, for instance, is likely to increase interactions within that age cohort and reduce the participation of youth in age-heterogeneous groups. Hence, "societal conditions that intensify age-grading (such as a sudden increase in the size of one age stratum or the prolongation of education with a consequent delay in labor force entry) can thus contribute to potential polarization of the age strata." In a similar vein, James Kurth argued that a significant increase in the size of one cohort relative to that of its predecessor is likely to create a "near-peer bottleneck," in which institutions accustomed to handling a certain number of young people are overwhelmed by dramatic increases in those numbers. The inability of these institutions to deal with this flow could, in turn, encourage youth to turn to social and political protest.[34]

Consciousness Cycle

A cycle is a set of regularly recurring patterns of interactions among variables, in which the interaction pattern at time t_1 is necessary and sufficient to produce the interaction pattern at time t_2, and in which the interaction pattern at time t_n is necessary and sufficient to reproduce the pattern that prevailed at time t_1. A cycle thus involves both regular recurrence and internal self-sufficiency. Major manifestations of creedal passion in American history have occurred at fairly regular intervals of sixty to seventy years. At about the midpoint of these intervals, other significant changes have occurred in political power among major economic interests. The instances are limited but the suggestion of periodicity is strong, and the pattern may well antedate the American Revolution.

No one of the four possible responses to the IvI gap can long be sustained by substantial numbers of people. Recourse to one response tends to generate psychological conditions favorable to the emergence of a different response: moralism eventually elicits cynicism, cynicism produces complacency, complacency leads to hypocrisy, and hypocrisy in due course reinvigorates moralism. Given the regularity in the major manifestations of creedal passion plus the logic of a changing response pattern, one can hypothesize that these manifestations may be a result, at least in part, of a cycle in the workings of American public consciousness.

Although it has not been demonstrated that the *logical* sequence of response describes any *historical* sequence of response, the possible validity of such a hypothesis is reinforced by the frequency with which cycles seem to occur in American politics. Cycles have not generally been characteristic of the ideologically pluralistic, class-based politics of western Europe. In the modern world, they are more likely to be observed in postrevolutionary societies characterized by high levels of ideological consensus. This fundamental consensus defines the limits of change, and the search for change within those basic limits swings from one pole to the other. Post-1949 China, as we noted, was marked by swings back and forth between mobilization and efficiency, the Red Guard and the expert. Somewhat similarly, postrevolutionary Mexican politics since the 1930s has been marked by a very conscious and deliberate alternation of more economically conservative and more socially radical presidencies.

As the consensual society par excellence, American society and its politics have been particularly prone to cyclical interpretations. The American party battle has been interpreted as involving the regular cycle

of a critical election, party realignment, the emergence of new majority
("sun") and minority ("moon") parties, establishment of an equilibrium,
the gradual undermining of that equilibrium by the emergence of new
issues inadequately dealt with by the existing party system, a weakening
of established party ties among individuals and groups, and a critical or
realigning election that starts the process over again. "American political
development in general and political party development in particular," as
William Chambers summed it up, "have tended to follow a roughly cyclic
pattern."[35] Various observers have also noted the existence of a different,
but not necessarily entirely unrelated, reform cycle in American politics at
both the local and national level, as well as a cycle in Supreme Court
behavior between judicial activism and judicial quietism.[36] Somewhat
similarly, Arthur Schlesinger, Sr., perceived "tides" in American politics
involving the alternation of liberal and conservative eras, averaging about
sixteen years each, while another scholar portrayed a twelve-year cycle of
conflict, conscience, and conciliation in the politics of presidential elections.[37] The case has also been made that in America "the history of value
change is neither progressive nor regressive, but basically cyclical," with
shifts occurring in both long-term cycles of one hundred forty-eight years
and short-term cycles of forty-eight years. In another notable study, Frank
L. Klingberg persuasively demonstrated the existence of a cycle of intro-
version and extroversion in American foreign policy.[38] It has also been
argued that no significant long-term secular trends exist toward either the
opening or the closing of avenues of vertical mobility in the United States,
but that instead there have been "substantial, relatively short-term, largely
cyclical changes in recruitment" to top leadership positions. Incorporating
both foreign and domestic politics, David McClelland suggested that a
cycle of reform and war is produced by recurring shifts in the American
public's psychological need for Power and the need for Affiliation.[39]

To cite these theories is not necessarily to subscribe to them. What is
striking about them, however, is not only that they often seem to have a
high degree of "fit" in terms of past historical development but that they
may produce reasonably accurate forecasts of the future of American
politics. Writing in 1939, for instance, Arthur Schlesinger, Sr., predicted
that the post–World War II "recession from liberalism" would end about
1962 "with a possible margin of a year or two in either direction." He
also predicted that the "next conservative epoch" in American politics
would begin in 1978. Written in 1973, Namenwirth's analysis of his
forty-eight-year cycle pointed to the peaking of a parochial value concern

with wealth and economic problems in 1980. Writing in 1952, Frank Klingberg confidently and accurately pooh-poohed contemporary fears that the United States would withdraw into isolation in that decade. He also predicted that the twenty-seven-year extroversion phase that had begun in 1940 would come to an end in the mid-1960s, which indeed it did, right on schedule.[40] Not even Lyndon Johnson could break the Klingberg cycle.

Political change in the United States can thus often be usefully and accurately interpreted in cyclical terms, and the existence of a moralism-cynicism-complacency-hypocrisy cycle in American public consciousness would be quite in keeping with these other cyclical patterns found in American politics.

Original Sources:
The Roots of It All in the English Revolution

The Revolutionary experience of the 1770s was the first large-scale, organized assertion of American political principles on a national basis. Sixty to seventy years earlier, however, in the last years of the seventeenth and the first years of the eighteenth century, there had been widespread upheaval and unrest in the British settlements in America. These were the years when English colonies were transformed into American provinces. Underlying this transition was a marked increase in social instability deriving from social mobility and status anxiety—"the downright anxiety of all colonials, regardless of the social and economic position they had attained, as they faced an unsettled present and a thoroughly unpredictable future."[41] The situation was characterized by the emergence of new sources of wealth and power, a new flood of immigrants, efforts by the British government to rationalize and strengthen its control over the North American settlements, and the reactions of the colonists to those efforts. In the north, for instance, the effect of the British attempt to create the Dominion of New England and then of its overthrow "was shattering." In its wake the "vast inclusive framework of the New England mind," which had given order to the seventeenth century, "disintegrated speedily after 1690, and by 1730 was virtually dead."[42]

The shift from colony to province "placed a serious strain upon peoples and institutions. On occasion the strain was great enough to bring about rebellions—in most cases short-lived—and nonviolent but dramatic changes that bordered on revolution."[43] Thirteen of eighteen major uprisings during the colonial period, all of them examples of a "pervasive antiauthoritarianism in colonial America," occurred during the last decades of the seventeenth century "among them the crucial Bacon's, Culpeper's, Leisler's, anti-Andros, and Coode's rebellions." This was an age "when men were not content to let sleeping dogs lie. Fears and suspicions were easily aroused; hatred and anger cut deep into men's souls; and trifling incidents were sufficient to arouse doubt and mistrust. Colonial society at this time was in a ferment and quick to respond to outside forces. . . . During the years from 1676 to 1690 insurrections broke out in nearly all the colonies."[44]

Several of the rebellions were associated with the Glorious Revolution of 1688, but others stemmed from a variety of causes. Most produced or reflected changes in the distribution of power in the colonies, either between the Crown and a colonial elite or from one elite to another. Their aim was "to alter the tight distribution of power and profit from what it had been under the arbitrary claims of the oligarchies during the reigns of Charles and James." As in subsequent creedal passion periods, there were at least two objects of attack: "popery" (the threat of Catholic conspiracy) and "slavery" (the abuses of "arbitrary government"), which ran counter to the inherited rights and liberties of Englishmen. The rebellions of 1688–89 involved the well-off as well as the poor and, as in subsequent periods, the revolutionaries were looking both backward and forward.[45] Underlying the instability and the efforts at reform was the realization of second- and third-generation Americans that the English social structure from which they were detached was not to be replicated in the New World. All in all, the reconstitution of the colonial societies that took place at the end of the seventeenth century bears many striking resemblances to the realignments of social forces and political institutions that took place in subsequent creedal passion periods. The last years of the seventeenth century were, as Richard Maxwell Brown said, "the first American revolutionary period."[46]

They were not, however, the first revolutionary period. Pursuing the sixty-to-seventy-year periodicity thesis back from the end of the seventeenth century brings us, interestingly enough, precisely to the beginning of the first true revolution of modern times. As Michael Walzer argued, the politics of "power, faction, intrigue" is universal in history, even as the politics of interest groups is ubiquitous in American history. With the rise of Calvinism, however, there appeared for the first time a "politics of party organization and methodical activity, opposition and reform, radical ideology and revolution."[47] At this point the history of reform and revolution begins. The desire to reconstitute political and social institutions, to remake society in the image of the ideal, appears on the scene.

In more extreme, dramatic, and revolutionary form, the English Revolution furnished the model for the subsequent manifestations of creedal passion in American politics. The immediate causes of that revolution are found in the efforts of the Crown between 1629 and 1640 to reestablish its power and that of the Church. The issues that were at stake between Crown and Parliament, Episcopacy and Puritans, William Laud and John Pym were not primarily economic and social but rather political, ideological, constitutional, and religious. "The fiscal policies of the 1630s caused formidable opposition, not because royal taxation was particularly oppressive to any class of society—indeed it was quite certainly lighter than anywhere else in Europe—but because the money was levied in an unconstitutional and arbitrary manner, and was used for purposes which many taxpayers regarded as immoral."[48]

In the 1630s, as in creedal passion periods in America, efforts were made to centralize and rationalize authority and to increase the efficiency of government and its ability to penetrate and direct society. The gentry and peers who had exercised influence under the Tudors and even during the reign of James I found their access to power increasingly curtailed. As in the subsequent periods, these developments provoked a reaction. The components for this reaction had, in turn, been produced by and strengthened by previous processes of economic development and social change; the general growth in discrepancies in access to status, power, and wealth; the expansion of literacy and of higher education; the availability of the Bible in English; and the overproduction of educated men in relation to available jobs.[49]

The English Revolution was thus in some measure both a rational response to the attempt by Charles I and Archbishop Laud to strengthen the Crown and the Church and also a product of exogenous economic, social, and cultural developments. It had many other characteristics of a creedal passion period. Since the primary issues at stake were basically political and religious, not social and economic, the lines of cleavage did not divide society along economic class lines, but rather along lines of religion, age, and political access. "Every order of society, every kind of occupation, was represented in considerable numbers on both sides," noted Austin Woolrych. "Puritanism was not just a religion of townsmen, for it ramified through every order of society. It enjoyed wide support among the landed gentry, from affluent knights down to depressed squireens, and its converts were certainly not restricted to the minority of landowners who shared in the entrepreneurial activities of the merchants. At least a fifth of the peers were Puritan in 1640, and so, at the other end of the scale, were thousands of small craftsmen and work-people who were not so much the exploiters of rising capitalism as its victims."[50] When it came to arms, the English Revolution, like the American, "did not merely fissure the landed classes right down the middle, it also split families apart, father against son and brother against brother: one in every seven peerage families was fragmented by war."[51] As in later creedal passion periods, the moral onslaught was directed at twin targets: first the bishops, and then the court and the Crown. The vision of the reformer was also Janus-faced—looking forward, in apocalyptic terms, to "the planting," in Stephen Marshall's words, "of a new heaven and new earth among us" and also to the reconstitution of traditional rights and privileges.

Of central importance to the revolution was the word and the passion behind the word. This derived from the Puritan emphasis on the primacy of the individual conscience and hence on the need to communicate to and guide that conscience on the road to salvation. Puritanism was a preaching religion; the Puritan divines "conceived of themselves as a ministry dedicated to preaching the Word of God, rather than as a priesthood whose prime function was to celebrate the sacraments."[52] As in subsequent creedal passion periods, the reach of the media expanded immensely and took new forms, most notably the widespread circulation of the English Bible, the delivery of sermons and their circulation along with other statements in pamphlet form, and the appearance of weekly newsletters produced by "the first professional journalists." Puritanism was, as Lawrence Stone suggested, something of a cultural revolution and a revolution in which the ideas and doctrines were pressed with passion. Intense moralism was the essence of Puritanism. "The quintessential quality of a Puritan was not the acceptance of any given body of doctrine, but a driving enthusiasm for moral improvement in every aspect of life, 'a holy violence in the performing of all duties.' "[53] The theological and political ideas of the Puritans were not necessarily either terribly sophisticated or terribly original, but although they "may (or may not) be second-hand," as Christopher Hill put it, "the passion behind them is not." When creedal passion reached its peak in the late 1640s, there was a great overturning, questioning, revaluing, of everything in England. Old institutions, old beliefs, old values came in question. Men moved easily from one critical group to another, and a Quaker of the early 1650s had far more in common with a Leveller, a Digger or a Ranter than with a modern member of the Society of Friends.

. . . There was a period of glorious flux and intellectual excitement, when, as Gerrard Winstanley put it, 'the old world . . . is running up like parchment in the fire.' Literally everything seemed possible; not only were the values of the old hierarchical society called in question but also the new values, the protestant ethic itself.

. . . What was new in the seventeenth century was the idea that the world might be *permanently* turned upside down.[54]

The English Revolution ended with a restoration. The king, Crown, Lords, court, bishops, and Anglicanism reappeared in full splendor on English soil. "Milton's nation of prophets became a nation of shopkeepers."[55] Puritanism, which had appealed to people in all strata of society before the revolution, came to have a restricted appeal to a much narrower segment of society after the revolution. The nonconformist strand of the English political-religious tradition went through various Methodist, Radical, and Labour reincarnations in the following centuries, but the radicalism it inherited from the English Revolution was bottled up, contained, limited to particular classes, regions, and sects. In America, on the other hand, Puritan radicalism spread and diffused to become the core of a credo for a new society. England had a Puritan revolution without creating a Puritan society; America created a Puritan society without enduring a Puritan revolution. England became a society of stable cleavage; America one of unstable consensus, where the gap between the "city upon a hill" and the city in the valley recreated the conditions for further efforts to realize the Puritan goals of the English Revolution.

The Puritan Revolution was a unique event in English history, but it was also a prototypical event for American history. The anguish, the moralism, the passion, the reform conscience, and the exhilaration of that revolution were manifested again and again on American soil in the upheavals in the colonies at the end of the seventeenth century, in the American Revolution, and in the subsequent creedal passion periods of American history. In 1641, for instance, a Puritan minister, Thomas Case, preaching before the Commons articulated the reform spirit as follows:

Reformation must be universal . . . Reform all places, all persons and callings; reform the benches of judgment, the inferior magistrates . . . Reform the universities, reform the cities, reform the countries, reform inferior schools of learning, reform the Sabbath, reform the ordinances, the worship of God . . . You have more work to do than I can speak . . . Every plant which my heavenly father hath not planted shall be rooted up.[56]

Compare this with Emerson's summary precisely two hundred years later of the reform spirit sweeping America in 1841:

> In the history of the world the doctrine of Reform had never such scope as at the present hour. Lutherans, Hernhutters, Jesuits, Monks, Quakers, Knox, Wesley, Swedenborg, Bentham, in their accusations of society, all respected something—church or state, literature or history, domestic usages, the market town, the dinnertable, coined money. But now all these and all things else hear the trumpet, and must rush to judgment,—Christianity, the laws, commerce, schools, the farm, the laboratory; and not a kingdom, town, statute, rite, calling, man, or woman, but is threatened by the new spirit.[57]

The spirit of Thomas Case, the Puritan legacy of the English Revolution, is permanently lodged deep in the American consciousness. Periodically, once every second generation, it reemerges to implant its mark of conscience on the otherwise placid and materialistic surface of American politics. At these times, the American nation of shopkeepers again becomes a nation of prophets. The origins of American politics are to be found in the English Puritan Revolution. That revolution is, in fact, the single most important formative event of American political history.

The Protestantism of American Politics

The Intermingling of Religion and Politics

As the decisive religious and political event of the early seventeenth century, the Puritan Revolution was the original source both of the close intermingling of religion and politics that characterized subsequent American history and of the moral passion that has powered the engines of political change in America. Not only was America born equal and hence did not have to become so, but it was also born Protestant and hence did not have to become so. In America, wrote the German theologian Philip Schaff in 1853, "everything had a Protestant beginning."[58] American Protestantism consequently was "constructive Protestantism," in the sense that it was devoted not to the dismantling of Catholicism but to the construction of a new, unspoiled, Protestant society in a virgin land, which, Puritans believed, God had saved from European discovery until they were ready to use it for His purposes.[59]

These origins also explain both the pluralism of religious bodies and the pervasiveness of religious beliefs in America. In the early colonies, church and state were often closely linked. The multiplication of colonies and of churches, however, precluded the creation of a national religious establishment; eventually the identity between church and state broke down, even in the Massachusetts Bay Puritan theocracy. By the nineteenth century, established churches had given way to the separation of church and state and to the continuing proliferation of churches, sects, denominations, and other religious bodies. This proliferation was the product of the nature of Protestantism as a movement. American Protestantism produced no significant theologian between Jonathan Edwards and Reinhold Niebuhr, but it renewed itself continually. America is unique in the world in the number of religious bodies to which it has given birth since the early seventeenth century. This religious fecundity is a product of the extent to which American society has been overwhelmingly Protestant. New churches and movements were founded to dissent from or to protest against those that had been founded earlier. "Protestantism in its many varieties is not the product or carrier of a single protest against one order of religious and political life; it represents rather a whole series of protests directed against many successive orders of Christian faith and against their political guarantors."[60] Each generation saw the formation of new groups and a reordering of groups according to their size. In this context, the Catholic church was not an established presence that Protestants challenged, but rather came "in afterwards as one sect among others, and has always remained subordinate."[61]

The multiplicity of religious groups has been matched by the pervasiveness of religious beliefs among Americans. The widespread practice of religion and of adherence to religious beliefs has been noted by foreign observers since the eighteenth century and is also attested to by the available figures on church membership and attendance. "There is no country in the world," Tocqueville observed, "where the Christian religion retains a greater influence over the souls of men than in America."[62] In the late twentieth century, this judgment still held true. Although figures suggest that the level of religious involvement and the extent of religious practice (such as church attendance) may vary from time to time, until the late twentieth century they did not show any long-term decline in religious commitment among the American public. Americans generally manifested a significantly higher level of religious commitment than did other peoples. Members of religious bodies in America appeared to attend church more frequently than members of the same bodies elsewhere. Twice as many Americans said that their religious beliefs were very important to them as did people in most other industrialized societies. Ninety-four percent of Americans said that they believed in God—a considerably higher proportion than in other societies. (See Table 4.)

Table 4. Religious commitment in the 1970s.

	Religious beliefs very important[a]	*Believe in God*[b]	*Believe in life after death*[c]
United States	58%	94%	71%
Canada	36	89	54
Italy	36	88	46
Benelux	26	78	48
Australia	25	80	48
United Kingdom	23	76	43
France	22	72	39
West Germany	17	72	33
Scandinavia	17	65	35
Japan	14	44	18

Source: Surveys in 1974–75 by Gallup International Research Institute for non-U.S. countries and in 1978 by the American Institute of Public Opinion (Gallup), Princeton Religion Research Center, and the Gallup Organization, Inc., for the United States. Reported in *Public Opinion* 2 (March/May 1979): 38–39.

a. Question asked: "How important are your religious beliefs—very important, fairly important, not too important, or not at all important?"

b. Question asked: "Do you believe in God or a universal spirit?"

c. Question asked: "Do you believe in life after death? Do you believe that there is life after death?"

A substantial consensus thus exists among Americans on a few core religious beliefs comparable to that which exists among Americans on the core political ideas of the American Creed. Why should Americans, almost uniquely among modern peoples, manifest such a commitment to religion? The sources lie, in large part, in the nature of the original Protestant religious inheritance. The plurality of sects and the resulting separation of state and church significantly weakened the state but strengthened religion. As a voluntary association, each church and sect had no alternative but to enlist all the energies of its members in its development and expansion. Most of the Protestant sects were committed to active preaching and proselytizing. They had a missionary mission aimed at conversion and regeneration. "Free and powerful in its own sphere, satisfied with the place reserved for it, religion never more surely establishes its empire than when it reigns in the hearts of men unsupported by aught besides its native strength."[63] The ease with which new sects could be founded, moreover, meant that church organization, doctrine, ritual, and functions could be almost infinitely varied to meet the needs of particular ethnic, social, economic, and geographic groups. Each sect thus tended to have its own constituency, and hence the vigorous *pursuit of* members did not translate into equally intense *competition for* members. Instead, almost all sects shared a general commitment to basic Protestant moral values and good works and emphasized the central role of morality in their preaching, causing Tocqueville to marvel at the extent to which ministers of one church often preached in other churches. The explanation, he found, was that in Protestant churches, "you will hear morality preached, of dogma not a word . . . The different preachers, treating only the common ground of morality, cannot do each other any harm."[64] The Protestant emphasis on morality and good works rather than on theology and doctrine made it easier for people to adhere to a generalized religious code, without necessarily, if they did not wish to, becoming committed to the deeper and more esoteric doctrines and practices of particular creeds.

The plurality of religious organizations and the pervasiveness of religious beliefs led to a distinctive relation between religion and politics. In Europe, a single universal church historically coexisted with a plurality of nations. During the Reformation, many of these nations established their own national churches. In America, however, a single universal nation has coexisted with a plurality of churches. From the start, the religious aims of the churches overlapped with and reinforced the political aims of the emerging nation. American revolutionaries of 1776 did not have to react against and challenge an established church supporting the established political order. Hence, unlike the French revolutionaries of 1789, they did not need a secular religion. All could adhere to a generalized religious religion, to the extent that "even the atheists in America speak in a religious key."[65]

The plurality of religious organizations and the pervasiveness of religious belief produced three forms of intermingling between religion and politics.

First, seventeenth-century Protestantism was the source of many of the ideas in the Creed, particularly those related to the central role of the individual conscience. The generalized religious values that were shared first by the Protestant sects, then by Catholic and Protestant churches, and still later by Jewish and Orthodox churches, easily fused with the national political beliefs. In the nineteenth century, "secular life was suffused with a pan-Protestant ideology that claimed to be civic and universal. Pledged to leave private beliefs undisturbed, it was vague enough so that increasing numbers of Jews and Catholics could embrace it. But it infused a generalized piety in school textbooks and civic oratory."[66] The congruence of religious and political values was most notable in the extent to which both reinforced the commitment to democracy and the primacy of the individual conscience. Protestantism in America was "a democratic and republican religion," and this contributed powerfully to "the establishment of a republic and democracy in public affairs." Religious influences have played key roles in shaping the ideas and the semantics of American politics, as shown by the prevalence of such terms as "dirty politics," "the good man," "the moral issue," the "change of heart," and "the crusade."[67]

Second, the absence of any particular established state or national religion opened the way for the direct incorporation of many of the ideas and symbols of generalized religion into American political behavior. Just as the national flag is a symbol found in almost all American churches, so is God found in almost all American national rites and ceremonies. The declaration of their birth assures Americans that they are endowed by their Creator with unalienable rights; Americans pledge their allegiance to one nation "under God"; they proclaim their trust in God on their currency; they are told by their Supreme Court justices that their institutions presuppose a Supreme Being; their public ceremonies invariably begin with an invocation by a clergyman from one religion and end with a benediction by a clergyman from another. Nowhere else in the world are church and state more firmly separated institutionally and religious and political ideas and symbols more closely interwoven in national beliefs.

Third, because national identity is defined in terms of a set of political ideals, the national Creed and the political practices related to it also perform some religious functions. The plurality of sects ensured that all sects would be particularistic and that none could plausibly serve as the instrument for realizing God's purposes on earth. In the absence of a national church, the nation and its political Creed came to serve as a civil religion. Americans bestowed on the nation "a catholicity of destiny similar to that which theology attributes to the universal church" and came to view it as "the primary agent of God's meaningful activity in history."[68]

The result was to give the nation many of the attributes and functions of a church. The United States is, indeed, as G. K. Chesterton said, "a nation with the soul of a church." Fifty years later another European observer could also observe, "You don't have a country over there, you have a huge church."[69] The point is well taken. Just as Americanism as an ideology is a substitute for socialism, at the same time that it incorporates some socialist values, so Americanism as a creed constitutes a national civil religion. The United States, Chesterton said, "is founded on a creed" that "is set forth with dogmatic and theological lucidity in the Declaration of Independence." The Declaration and the Constitution constitute the holy scripture of the American civil religion. Their basic messages have been elaborated and extended in the addresses and sayings of American leaders. The essence of the Creed was succinctly summarized in the "American's Creed" in obvious imitation of that of the Apostles:

> I believe in the United States of America as a Government of the people, by the people, for the people; whose just powers are derived from the consent of the governed; a democracy in a republic; a sovereign Nation of many sovereign States; a perfect union, one and inseparable; established upon those principles of freedom, equality, justice, and humanity for which American patriots sacrificed their lives and fortunes. I therefore believe it is my duty to my country to love it; to support its Constitution; to obey its laws; to respect its flag, and to defend it against all enemies.

Little wonder that D. W. Brogan should comment wonderingly on the use of this Creed in the schools in early-twentieth-century America: "Little boys and girls, in a school from which religion in the old sense is barred, solemnly rising each morning and reciting together the 'American's Creed' are performing a religious exercise as truly as if they began the day with 'I believe in God the Father Almighty' or asserted that 'There is no God but God.' "[70] Like other religions, the American civil religion has its hymns and its sacred ceremonies, its prophets and its martyrs. It also has its mission: to create "a city on a hill," "the last best hope of earth," and to bring about a "new heaven and new earth" through its "errand in the wilderness" of the world. The "religion of the Republic," Sidney Mead said, "is essentially prophetic,"[71] and it is this Protestant sense of mission that has furnished the dynamic motive force of American politics.

Great Awakenings and Creedal Passion

The Puritan Revolution bequeathed to the American people the belief that they were engaged in a righteous effort to ensure the triumph of good over evil and thus to realize God's will on earth. "No truth is more patent in American history than the fact that this nation is an Old Testament people."[72] Religion was the source of the morality that required the saving of souls on the one hand and the regeneration of society on the other. Each was possible; both were necessary. Passive acceptance of the gap between what should be and what is is intolerable for both the individual and the community. The gap is evil; to condone it is sinful; duty demands moral action to eliminate it. Throughout American history, the principal efforts to achieve these goals have taken the form of religious and political revivals—great awakenings and creedal passion periods.

In the Puritan Revolution, religion and politics were inseparable. In subsequent American history, the religious and political manifestations of the Puritan passion took distinct forms. Yet it surely cannot be a coincidence that the four major creedal passion periods in American political history have been matched by what historians of religion have identified as the four great awakenings of the religious spirit. In addition, while great awakenings are no more subject to precise dating than creedal passion periods, it does appear that each great awakening began a decade or more before the flame-up of creedal passion and then often overlapped with it. The First Great Awakening swept through the colonies in the 1730s and 1740s; the second began in the first years of the nineteenth century and lasted until about 1830; the third began about 1890 and continued into the first decade of the twentieth century; the fourth originated in the late 1950s.[73] Distinct though they may be, the expressions of religious fervor and of creedal passion share similar characteristics and stem from similar sources. As the chronology suggests, they may also be linked to one another in a causal pattern, in which the passion for reform is first directed to the conversion of the individual and then to the reformation of society.

The parallels between great awakenings and creedal passion periods are striking and have not gone unnoted. An awakening or major religious revival can only occur in situations where large numbers of people have previously committed themselves to religious beliefs and in which "backsliding" from those beliefs has become evident. Awakenings are "a *revitalizing* of religion, a repeat performance . . . They do not introduce religon into a region . . . It is simply impossible to have a revival unless there is some institutional and ideational framework that has provided a meaningful context for the revival in the first place."[74] The great awakenings, as a leading scholar put it, occurred when "by the standards of our culture core and the experiences of daily life, our society deviated too far from the moral and religious understandings that legitimized authority in church and state." They were ways "to overcome jarring disjunctions between norms and experience, old beliefs and new realities, dying patterns and emerging patterns of behavior." The awakenings resulted in drastic "restructuring" of "social, political, and economic institutions" and propelled Americans into wars "to speed up the fulfillment of their manifest destiny."[75] The dynamics of the First Great Awakening involved "a public rhetoric able to exploit subconscious feelings of guilt and dependency that were weakly defended against by a hedonistic indifference in the young, or that were easily reactivated in older persons who had externally committed themselves to the evangelical framework but had grown conventional in their piety." The awakening thus required a society in which a gap existed between "religious norms and authority" that had been internalized and "ordinary behavior" that "did not match the accepted injunctions."[76] Revivals were thus one way of dealing with cognitive dissonance at the individual level, securing the forgiveness of past sins, and recommitting errant wanderers to the way of the Lord.

In this respect, awakenings served the same function for Americans individually that creedal passion periods did for Americans collectively. Efforts to reform masses of individuals and efforts to reform society as a whole have similar effects. The American Revolution "was not so much the result of reasoned thought as an emotional outburst similar to a religious revival." It involved an "evangelical Revolutionary impulse, like that of the Great Awakening."[77] In attempting to portray its true significance in American history, one historian has described the Great Awakening of the 1740s as resembling "the civil rights demonstrations, the campus disturbances, and the urban riots of the 1960s combined. All together these may approach, though certainly not surpass, the Awakening in their impact on national life." This was seconded by another religious historian who, in reverse direction, characterized the 1960s "as another Great Awakening which also left the human landscape profoundly changed. In the realm where values, hopes, fears, and cosmological attitudes are shaped, the period was profoundly disturbing."[78]

The immediate sources of great awakenings are similar to and as diverse as those of creedal passion periods. At least five major explanations have been advanced for the First Great Awakening—rapid social change, ideological polarization, western expansion, increased British influence, and class conflict—all of which can, in some sense, be subsumed under the general heading of "changing structures of authority and power."[79] Areas of rapid economic change were often centers of religious revival. During almost half a century of rapid economic development in eastern Connecticut, for instance, land and money were avidly pursued. This generated high levels of "personal instability" and guilt, which then made the area a major center of the First Great Awakening. That awakening was the response of the evangelical mind "to the emergence in colonial America of disparities of wealth, as well as ways of life unknown to earlier, and presumably purer, generations."[80]

In somewhat similar fashion, the intense manifestation of the Second Great Awakening in the "burned-over" district of western New York has been attributed to the broad-gauged economic development of that region, the central feature of which was the building of the Erie Canal. Religious enthusiasm was most intense in those areas of the district in which economic growth had leveled off and stabilized and which had reached "a stage of economy either of full or of closely approaching agrarian maturity."[81] More generally, the Second Great Awakening has been interpreted as a result of the intensification of social strains and dislocations caused by economic development and geographic expansion. The "explosion of religious energy in 1800 was an overt expression of social discontent and political aspiration."[82] The Third and Fourth Great Awakenings, too, followed periods of intense economic development which produced social strains, status insecurity among many groups, and new perceptions of massive deviations in individual behavior from the straight and narrow path.

The awakenings furnished the means of relieving psychological stresses and strains through the experience of conversion. Just as the moralism of creedal passion periods derived from the desire to return to the basic ideals of the American Creed, so the religious fervor of the awakenings derived from the desire to return to the basic teachings of the Bible. People who had internalized highly demanding religious norms came to bear an increasing burden of guilt as their behavior deviated from those norms. The preachers of the awakenings forced people to confront their sinfulness and inevitable damnation. "This confrontation of guilt, the first part of conversion, drove men to despair," as one account of the First

Great Awakening described it, "but the revivalists did not leave their hearers there to suffer. By publicly identifying the sources of guilt and condemning them, the preachers also helped to heal the wounds they first inflicted. Converts were persuaded that by acknowledging and repudiating their old sins, they were no longer culpable. The reborn man was as joyful and loving when the process was completed as he was miserable at its start."[83] Young people were, the revivalists argued, particularly susceptible to the appeals of this process and hence played disproportionate roles in the First Great Awakening as well as in its successors.[84] The "political radicalization" of creedal passion periods is the secular equivalent of the conversion experience that people go through in the awakenings.

Each great awakening witnessed the polarization between those who had seen the light and those who had not. The division in the First Great Awakening between New Side and Old Side Presbyterians and between New Light and Old Light Congregationalists was repeated in later awakenings, paralleling the division in creedal passion periods between "the Movement" and "the Establishment." As in creedal passion periods, those within each denomination who experienced the religious awakening were drawn from diverse sources. In the First Great Awakening "people from all ranks of society, of all ages, and from every section underwent the new birth. In New England virtually every congregation was touched."[85] The division cut across the usual lines of class and status. "The parties and debates of eighteenth-century American religion simply will not yield to the categories of Marx and Beard, for the reason that the fundamental post-Awakening division was an intellectual one—one more aesthetic, in fact, than economic or social . . . What distinguished Americans, so far as the 'great debate' of the eighteenth century was concerned, were differences not of income but, in substance, of taste."[86] And differences in taste corresponded sociologically only with differences in age. Just as the success of reform has often been dependent upon reformers with powerful personalities, so has conversion been the product of powerful revivalists: George Whitefield, Charles Grandison Finney, Billy Sunday, and Billy Graham, to mention only the most outstanding preacher of each awakening.

Each great awakening involved mass proselytizing, often, as in creedal passion periods, accompanied by widespread reliance on new forms of mass communication and persuasion. The great evangelists were also great innovators in the techniques of mass mobilization. Before the mid-eighteenth century, religion was a local phenomenon, rooted in the small community of minister, church, congregation, and parish. The First Great Awakening, however, was marked by the key role played by itinerant preachers, who made religion more universal and more individualistic and less of a community phenomenon.[87] The oral techniques and rhetorical styles of the awakening were then adapted to extend to the masses the revolutionary appeals of the 1770s.[88] In the Second Great Awakening, Finney and others expanded and refined the techniques of the camp meeting and the use of "vigorous advertising methods" to arouse interest and participation. At the end of the century, Dwight Moody became the first revivalist to make extensive use of newspapers and billboards, to organize and train "ushers, choir, counselors, and prayer meeting leaders," and to develop the methods of mass solicitation necessary to fund these efforts. These techniques were more fully developed and expanded in the Fourth Great Awakening, but the decisive factor in that awakening, reaching tens of millions of Americans, was skillful exploitation, most notably by Billy Graham, of the new medium of television. The awakening and television developed simultaneously during the 1950s.[89]

The awakenings were also characterized by mass organizing. Between 1740 and 1760, one hundred fifty new churches were founded in New England and between thirty thousand and forty thousand new church members were added to the rolls. In the Second Great Awakening, the success of the Methodists and Baptists were due primarily not to their theology or doctrine but to the means they developed and employed for mobilizing and organizing people. The legacy of the Second Great Awakening in Oneida County, New York, for instance, consisted of the "Mormon Church, several Adventist denominations, two species of Methodism, and a sprinkling of spiritualist groups."[90] Each awakening gave a new impulse to the proliferation of religious organizations. New sects were formed. Old ones divided and became stronger as a result of the division. As H. Richard Niebuhr suggested, the development of American Protestantism can be interpreted in terms of successive waves of protest against the existing establishment—waves that make church history "one of many reformations" and that reach their peak in the formation of new churches during the years of the awakenings. These waves of "reformation, regeneration, awakening, and renewal" are directed "not against the authority of the old, but against its acceptance and establishment of a mediocre form of men's moral and religious existence."[91]

In theory, success in the reform of the individual could remove any need for the collective, purposeful reform of society, and several great evangelists opposed social and political reforms precisely on the ground that they were not directed to the regeneration of the individual soul.[92] In fact, however, the great awakenings did not just resemble creedal passion periods; they also preceded them, overlapped with them, and, particularly in the earlier years, contributed to them ideas, techniques, people, and passion. In the eighteenth and nineteenth centuries, the religious enthusiasm of the awakenings was easily converted into the political enthusiasm for reform. The ideological and political roots of the American Revolution lay at least as much in the evangelical Calvinism of the First Great Awakening as in the liberal rationalism of the Enlightenment. "What the colonies had awakened to in 1740," Alan Heimert said, "was none other than independence and rebellion." Another scholar wrote that "the roots of the Revolution as a political movement were so deeply imbedded in the soil of the First Great Awakening forty years earlier that it can be truly said that the Revolution was the natural outgrowth of that profound and widespread religious movement."[93] The Second Great Awakening has been called the American "Revolution at work in religion" and the "second American revolution, inward and spiritual . . . evangelical and revivalist."[94] The great reform surges of the Jacksonian years, most notably the temperance and abolitionist movements, were, in turn, religion at work in politics. Throughout the nineteenth century, revivalism was a major source of social reform.[95] By the end of the century, however, the connection between the Third Great Awakening and the reform drives of the Progressive era had become more tenuous than it had been in previous outbreaks of religious and political passion. The Puritan ethic was a significant factor in the movements for woman suffrage and prohibition, but neither of these reforms reflected the interests of the growing masses of urban workers.[96] The roads to individual salvation and societal reform began to diverge.

This divergence became even clearer in the 1950s and 1960s. Many similarities exist between the religious revival of the 1950s and 1960s and the creedal passion of the 1960s and 1970s, and religious leaders and religious groups—most notably in Martin Luther King and the Southern Christian Leadership Conference—played a central role in the development and the success of the civil rights movement. Yet clearly the main thrust of the fourth awakening was not in the direction of the social and political reforms that came to the top of the political agenda. The similarities between Billy Graham and Ralph Nader are clear; the direct connection between them is not. They do nonetheless have common roots in the same Protestant moral passion, which will not tolerate a gap between the ideals of what ought to be and the realities that are.

In America, the ideas of liberty and equality are compatible in a way that contrasts with their stormy opposition in European history. So also in America, religion and politics, religious campaigns and political crusades, have historically reinforced each other despite, and perhaps in part because of, the constitutional and institutional separation of church and state. The passion of the Puritan Revolution has reappeared in periodic religious and political surges that interact with one another, stemming from the same sources, taking comparable forms, mobilizing similar groups, and producing parallel consequences. People aroused about the need to reform themselves are also easily aroused about the need to reform society. And during the periods of great awakening and creedal passion, neither the individual nor the institution that falls short of the prescribed norms can expect to escape their holy terror. In America, the common sources of religious and political belief give political relevance to religion and add religious passion to politics.

7 THE S&S YEARS, 1960–1975

From the Fifties to the Seventies:
The Changing Pattern of Response

The high points of historical eras are usually clearly visible. Any historian will feel relatively comfortable in identifying the years when the Renaissance was at its peak, or the Age of Absolutism, or the Victorian era. The starting and ending points of eras, however, are often lost in the complexity, ambiguity, and incrementalism of history. So is it also with the "era of sixes and sevens," or the "S&S Years," which constitute America's fourth major creedal passion period since independence.* The high point of that era was clearly between 1968 and 1971. But when did

---

* The problem of what to call this period is a difficult one. People often refer to "the sixties," but the era also extended well into the seventies. One could speak of "the early sixties to the mid-seventies," but that is unusably cumbersome. Alternatively, we could call it the age of protest, or of outrage, or of exposure, but each of these catches only one aspect of the period and each aspect was also characteristic of other creedal passion periods. If one accepts the argument of this book, one could label 1960–1975 simply "the Fourth Period." That, however, suggests the closing moments of an athletic contest, and, more importantly, it denies these years an independent label and identity of their own (comparable to the labels "Revolutionary," "Jacksonian," and "Progressive") apart from their being one in a series of similar phases. In an effort to come up with a succinct name that will accommodate these various considerations, I have opted for "the era of sixes and sevens" or, more briefly, "the S&S Years," for both numerological and characterological reasons. First, this name does suggest the sixties and seventies. Second, according to *The Oxford English Dictionary*, "sixes and sevens" refers to "the creation or existence of, or neglect to remove, confusion, disorder or disagreement"—a not unreasonable summary of what happened during these years.

it begin and when did it end? Sometime in the late fifties or early sixties? Sometime in the middle or late seventies? Any particular starting and terminal points can serve only symbolic purposes. Yet it is also useful and potentially enlightening for such purposes to be served, and appropriate symbolic starting and ending points for the fourth creedal passion period can be identified with some precision.

The S&S Years began February 1, 1960, when four black college freshmen entered a Woolworth's in Greensboro, North Carolina, sat down at the lunch counter, asked for coffee, were refused service, and stayed seated. The Fourth Period ended almost exactly sixteen years later on January 29, 1976, when the House of Representatives voted 246 to 124 not to release the report of its Select Committee on Intelligence until that report had been cleared by the White House. The Greensboro sit-in began the politics of protest that constituted the first part of the S&S Years; the House vote marked the end of the politics of exposure that dominated the last part. The period began in that area of American life where the gap between democratic ideals and behavioral reality was most marked, and it achieved its most dramatic public policy result in effectively ending government sponsorship and toleration of racial discrimination in America. The dominant tone of the period was set in the late sixties and early seventies in the pervasive, unrelenting questioning of and opposition to authority in almost any form, reaching a peak in August 1974 with the "killing of the king"—the deposition of the central authority figure in American politics, who had been elected to office less than two years earlier by an overwhelming popular vote. It concluded many months later with the exposure of the workings of the country's intelligence agencies, where the contrast between American values of openness and democratic control and the requirements of secrecy and deception was most marked. The desegregation of a society, the resignation of a President, and the dismantling of an intelligence system stand as eloquent testimony to the at least partial effectiveness of the period's assault on inequality, authority, hierarchy, and secrecy.

Between 1960 and 1976 American politics was characterized by an intensity and emotionalism found only in earlier phases of creedal passion. During these years most of the major actors on the political scene were largely, if not entirely, moralistically responding to the dissonance produced by the IvI gap in American politics. Yet complacency, hypocrisy, and cynicism also had their roles to play. The relative importance of each of these responses changed over time, due to changes in people's perceptions of the extent of the IvI gap and to changes in the intensity of their commitment to American ideals. From the mid-1950s to the late-1970s, American responses to the IvI gap moved through the cycle that we earlier identified as the logical pattern for them to follow. This progression can also be related to changing dominant attitudes toward governmental authority and toward governmental action to solve problems. (See Table 5.) The S&S Years thus began in complacency and ended in cynicism. In

Table 5. The sequence of responses in the S&S Years.

| | Prevalent attitude toward governmental authority | |
Prevalent attitude toward governmental action	Con	Pro
Pro	Mid-sixties to mid-seventies moralism	Early sixties hypocrisy
Con	Late seventies cynicism	Mid-late fifties complacency

between they were dominated by intense moralism. Almost all of the characteristic features found in American creedal passion periods manifested themselves, leaving consequences for the operation of the American political system that would be felt for years into the future.

Complacency and the End (?) of Ideology

The middle and late 1950s were predominantly years of complacency. After the bitter divisions over McCarthyism and the Korean War in the early 1950s, Eisenhower achieved in actuality what he said he wanted to achieve: "an atmosphere of greater serenity and mutual confidence."[1] Americans at that time were generally supportive of governmental authority and also saw little or no reason for either more government or more active government. The prevailing atmosphere was one of contentment and satisfaction. Until the very end of the decade, the gap between ideals and institutions was not clearly perceived and people did not feel intensely committed to the realization of American political values. Those values were, as Daniel Boorstin put it in the mid-1950s, "*given* by certain facts of geography or history peculiar to us." Americans historically tended "to confound the 'ought' and the 'is,' " and American values were implicit in American institutions. "What one *could* build on this continent tended to become the criterion of what one ought to build here."[2] In Boorstin's view, environment, institutions, and values were all part of one seamless web: a dramatic and violent contrast between institutions and ideals was precisely what American history lacked.

Concerns about the concentration and abuse of power were at the far margins of American consciousness during these years of creedal passivity in the 1950s. The prevailing image of American politics combined the consensus and organizational pluralism paradigms. Consensus existed and was good. Power existed in a plurality of large organizations—veto groups —that at times made governmental action difficult but also made the serious abuse of governmental power extremely unlikely. What is more, in a brief but notable inversion of the traditional American approach, thinkers in the 1950s became intrigued with the idea that large organization in itself could be good. Big business was more responsible, more enlightened, more likely to act in the public interest than small business. Small businessmen, indeed, were much more likely than big businessmen to be narrow-minded, prejudiced, avaricious, and supporters of Senator Joseph McCarthy. Large-scale organization was not merely accepted; it was defended and justified, and many of its most significant apologists were veterans of the New Deal. "The growth of large organizations," Seymour Martin Lipset suggested, may "actually have the more important consequences of providing new sources of continued freedom and more opportunity to innovate."[3] Opposition to large-scale organization, big corporations, concentrated power, and militarism was relegated to the extreme left and right of the political spectrum. A scholar like C. Wright Mills could publish an eloquent and passionate exposé titled *The Power Elite,* but it would have to wait for another decade before it found its audience. In the meantime, Americans believed in consensus and pluralism as both facts and values.

Reflecting this complacency, political alienation in America reached a low point in the 1950s. The responses of the public with respect to three key questions designed to measure alienation showed significantly less alienation in 1956 than in 1952 and less in 1960 than in 1956. From 1960 on, however, the trend reversed itself, with alienation increasing steadily during the 1960s and early 1970s.[4] The end of the fifties, in short, witnessed the peak of Americans' satisfaction with and identification of their political system. It is hardly surprising that when asked in 1960 of what aspects of their country they felt proud, some 85 percent of the American public mentioned their governmental and political institutions.

The atmosphere of the 1950s prompted intellectuals to argue that the decline or end of ideology was occurring. This idea, stimulated originally by post–World War II developments in Western Europe, became the conventional wisdom of the Western intellectual world following a major conference in 1955 of intellectual and political figures from democratic countries. The outstanding discovery of the conference was that the differences between the left and the right had narrowed and that the two had much in common, particularly when confronted by the challenge posed by Soviet communism. Ideology and ideological combat were seen to be disappearing from democratic politics as a result of "the fact that the fundamental political problems of the industrial revolution have been solved: the workers have achieved industrial and political citizenship; the conservatives have accepted the welfare state; and the democratic left has recognized that an increase in over-all state power carries with it more dangers to freedom than solutions for economic problems."[5] More specifically, the phrase "the end—or decline—of ideology" was used to refer to: (1) the elimination of both fascism (through defeat in war) and, less conclusively, communism (by its identification with the Soviet Union) as viable options in a democratic society; (2) the general decline in intellectual and public discussion of broad ideological alternatives, political theories, far-reaching goals, and utopias; (3) the narrowing of the political distance—in terms of policies and programs—between the major parties in democratic societies; and (4) the weakening of the correlation between socioeconomic class and voting behavior.

For the end-of-ideology theorists, the basic cause for these developments was the steadily expanding economic prosperity of Western society. This clearly proved Marx wrong, made it easier for the industrial working class to be incorporated as full participants into the economic, social, and political system, greatly expanded the middle class, and made possible the state provision of social security and welfare benefits that competitive democratic politics demanded. As a result, politics would be reduced, in John Kennedy's words, from "basic clashes of philosophy and ideology ... to ways and means of reaching common goals."[6]

Given the seeming success of the mixed economy, democratic politics, and the welfare state, end-of-ideology proponents implicitly and at times explicitly suggested that the trend they described was both *universal* in its applicability to advanced industrial societies and *irreversible* in that it reflected the needs of a new stage of economic development. As so stated, however, the end-of-ideology thesis was not to be borne out by events.

In the first place, it did not take sufficient account of the basic differences in historical development between American and European societies. The thesis was propounded at the same time that Louis Hartz and others were emphasizing the differences between the liberal consensual politics of the United States and the class-based ideological politics typical of Europe. Given these differences, the same phenomenon—sustained economic growth and prosperity—could and did have different consequences. In Europe, affluence created the base for the moderation of class conflict, the reduction in the policy differences between major parties, and the at least temporary cooling of grand ideological debate. Affluence in the United States, on the other hand, produced not the end of ideology (which had never existed in a European sense anyway) but the economic precondition for the rebirth of American moralism. What was taken to be the same thing in Europe and America was, in fact, two quite different things: the long-term easing of class conflict in Europe and short-term prevalence of creedal complacency in America.

Second, in 1962 John Kennedy suggested that as a result of the economic and social changes that had occurred in the United States, there would be no further need for "the great sort of 'passionate movements' which have stirred this country so often in the past."[7] He could not have been more wrong. Equally wrong, however, were those European intellectuals who subsequently saw the failure of the end-of-ideology thesis as proof of the end of American consensus and "the beginning of political doctrine" and conflict among those doctrines: "Ex unibus plures!"[8] What was erroneously interpreted as the beginning of ideological conflict and political doctrines was only the renaissance of political moralism produced by the American consensus. In the 1960s, the American consensus on basic values did not come apart; it came alive.

This awakening produced a politics from the mid-sixties to the mid-seventies that makes those years a clearly identifiable period in American political history. The agenda of politics, the tone of politics, the issues, the intensity, the cleavages, the actors, the forms of political activity—all took on distinctive characteristics. The politics of the S&S Years thus differed significantly from that of the late 1950s and from that of the late 1970s. The distinctive profile of politics from 1960 to 1976 is dramatically revealed in the horseshoe bulge that recurs during these years in a variety of important quantitative indicators of political activity. Predominant were forms of political action—protest, exposure, and reform—that are common in creedal passion periods but of secondary importance in the more normal years of American politics. As a result of what happened during these years, the politics of the late 1970s also differed significantly from that of the late 1950s. More specifically, during the S&S Years major changes occurred in the substance of political attitudes and in the structure and power of political institutions. These changes represent the lasting legacy of creedal passion for American politics during the final quarter of the twentieth century.

Interlude of Hypocrisy, Surge of Moralism

Complacency began to deteriorate at the end of the fifties, particularly in the wake of the successful Soviet launching of the first sputnik in 1958 and the concerns that aroused. There was a renewed feeling of the need to rededicate the nation to American values, reflected in President Eisenhower's creation of a Commission on National Goals. The increasing concern with and commitment to American liberal values was eloquently epitomized in the Kennedy candidacy and the Kennedy Presidency. During the 1960 campaign, Kennedy caught the mood of the times perfectly in stressing the importance of asserting those values in the face of the Soviet threat and the need "to get this country moving again." The dominant views of the times remained highly supportive of governmental authority and strongly in favor of vigorous governmental action in the international field. The largest peacetime increase in military spending up to that time occurred in the Kennedy administration. The prevailing response was perfectly articulated in Kennedy's inaugural address, devoted as it was almost entirely to the projection of American values abroad rather than to their realization within American society. Apart from the slowly growing civil rights movement, Americans paid relatively little attention to the gap between American ideals and institutions at home. One could hardly rally Americans to defend freedom abroad while at the same time pointing to either its absence or the threats to it at home. Consequently, for some people the shift from complacency to moralism was mediated by a brief and partial engagement with hypocrisy. At the same time, others were making the shift from passivity to intense commitment to reform directly, without the foreign detour: the antiwar demonstrations of the late 1960s included veterans of both the Peace Corps and the civil rights marches of the early sixties. While the Kennedys were clearly the master practitioners of cool pragmatic politics, they also, perhaps for that very reason, articulated and capitalized upon the desire of Americans to feel intensely committed to some higher purposes. As John Steinbeck observed in 1960, there existed in the country "a nervous restlessness, a thirst, a yearning for something unknown—perhaps morality."[9]

The willingness to "pay any price, bear any burden" to defend freedom throughout the world did not remain the dominant theme for long. At first, Kennedy had consciously subordinated domestic policy and had gone along with the civil rights movement only to the extent that it was politically necessary, but in 1963 he began to listen to the voices of outrage. The moralistic passion that the struggle for civil rights engendered among both black and white activists spread to other areas, most notably in the opposition to U.S. involvement in the war in Vietnam. Outward-directed patriotic fervor was replaced by inward-directed moralistic indignation. The images that elites and public opinion generally had of American political institutions changed drastically; American politics began to seem radically different from what they thought it ought to be. Respect for authority declined precipitously at the same time that demands increased for governmental action to remedy the IvI gap. Intense moralism surged to the fore among significant politically active groups.

Intensity of commitment cannot be measured easily by any quantitative yardstick. But the fact that commitment increased in the 1960s is surely unquestionable. These were the years, as I have argued elsewhere, that

> witnessed a dramatic renewal of the democratic spirit in America
> ... The spirit of protest, the spirit of equality, the impulse to expose
> and correct inequities were abroad in the land. The themes of the
> 1960s were those of the Jacksonian Democracy and the muckraking
> Progressives; they embodied ideas and beliefs which were deep in
> the American tradition but which usually do not command the pas-
> sionate intensity of commitment that they did in the 1960s. That
> decade bore testimony to the vitality of the democratic idea. It was
> a decade of democratic surge, of the reassertion of democratic
> egalitarianism.[10]

The classic values of the American Creed—equality, democracy, liberty, individual rights, the limitation of power—were rearticulated with an intensity and fervor fully equal to that of any previous outbreak of creedal passion.

The shift from complacency to commitment was paralleled and, to some extent, followed by changes in the images that Americans had of their political system. These changes are quantitatively visible in public opinion polls. The public's perception of government shifted dramatically between the early 1960s and the early 1970s. The trends in response to five key questions are set forth in Figure 1. In 1964, 64 percent of the public thought the government was run for the benefit of all the people, and 29 percent thought it was run by a few big interests looking out for themselves. By 1974, opinion was almost exactly reversed: 66 percent thought that government was run for a few big interests; 25 percent thought it was run for the benefit of all. Similar shifts occurred in the extent to which people thought government could be trusted to do what is right, wasted tax money, and was run by smart people or crooks. Major changes also occurred in the degree to which people perceived government to be responsive to their views. In 1960, for instance, 73 percent of the public disagreed with the statement that public officials did not "care much what people like me think," while 25 percent agreed with it. By 1974, a quarter of the public had changed its mind: 50 percent believed that officials did not care what they thought, while 46 percent believed that they did.[11]

Changes in public perceptions were not limited to perceptions of government. During the late 1960s and early 1970s, the public's confidence in many other institutions in American society plummeted. Between 1966 and 1976, the proportion of the public that had "a great deal of confidence" in the leadership of the executive branch of the federal government went from 41 percent to 11 percent, of Congress from 42 percent to 9 percent, and of the Supreme Court from 51 percent to 22 percent. During the same ten-year period, drastic reductions also occurred in the proportion of the public that had great confidence in the leaders of medicine (73 percent to 42 percent), higher education (61 percent to 31 percent), the military (62 percent to 23 percent), major companies (55 percent to 16 percent), organized religion (41 percent to 24 percent), and organized labor (22 percent to 10 percent). Among the major institutions of American society, the only one whose leaders commanded greater confidence in 1976 (28 percent) than in 1966 (25 percent) was television news.[12]

Increased commitment to liberal, democratic values, combined with increasingly unfavorable perceptions of governmental and other institutions, necessarily made moralism and opposition to authority the dominant theme of politics. Outrage and protest, together with their sometime children, invective and violence, set the tone for the politics of the late sixties and early seventies. The issues of politics concerned not questions of more or less or of competence versus incompetence, but rather ques-

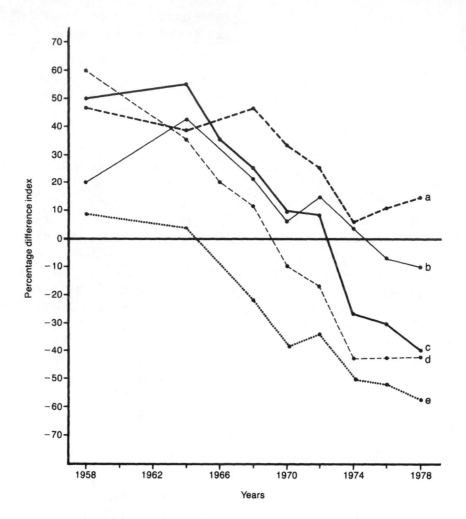

Figure 1. Percentage Difference Index (PDI) for five measures of trust in government. The PDI is the difference obtained by subtracting that portion of the population expressing less trust in government from that portion expressing greater trust in government. (*Source:* Based on data in Warren E. Miller, Arthur H. Miller, and Edward J. Schneider, *American National Election Studies Sourcebook, 1952–1978* [Cambridge, Mass.: Harvard University Press, 1980], pp. 257–259.)

a. "Do you think that quite a few of the people running the government are a little crooked, not very many are, or do you think hardly any of them are crooked at all?" PDI = "hardly any" and "not many" minus "quite a lot."

b. "Do you feel that almost all of the people running the government are smart people who usually know what they are doing, or do you think that quite a few of them don't seem to know what they're doing?" PDI = "know what they're doing" minus "don't know what they're doing."

(Figure 1 continued)

c. "How much of the time do you think you can trust the government in Washington to do what is right—just about always, most of the time, or only some of the time?" PDI = "always" and "most of the time" minus "some or none of the time."

d. "Would you say the government is pretty much run by a few big interests looking out for themselves or that it is run for the benefit of all the people?" PDI = "benefit of all" minus "a few big interests." (Note: In 1958 the question was worded differently from the way it was worded in other years.)

e. "Do you think that people in government waste a lot of money we pay in taxes, waste some of it, or don't waste very much of it?" PDI = "not much" and "some" minus "a lot."

tions of right and wrong. The heart of the S&S Years is, indeed, very neatly defined by the disappearance of economic issues from the top of the political agenda. From 1950 through 1959, an average of 23.6 percent of the American public rated an economic issue as "most important question confronting the country"; in 1971–72, an average of 21.5 percent of the American public singled out economic issues as of critical importance; and from 1973 to 1979, the percentage skyrocketed to 71.7 percent. Between 1960 and 1970, however, only a bare 11.1 percent of the public identified an economic question as the most important problem facing the country: civil rights, foreign policy, the Vietnam War, crime and disorder, and honesty in government supplanted economics in the public's concerns.[13]

The difference between creedal politics and "normal" politics generally was reflected more specifically in the differences between the New Left and the Old Left. The Old Left had been shaped by the economic trauma of the 1930s—the classic struggles for labor union recognition, collective bargaining, jobs, pay, social security, and related benefits. During the 1930s the major issues were economic issues and people divided along class lines with respect to those issues.[14] The Old Left was clearly identified with the working class and the labor union movement and shaped its thinking in Marxist or semi-Marxist terms. In the 1960s, on the other hand, the New Left eschewed the working class and stressed moralism rather than ideology. As the first president of Students for a Democratic Society explained in the early 1960s, "Revolution and the crude Marxian dynamics of the class struggle are rejected or highly modified"; the New Left "begins from moral values which are held as absolute." Similarly, other early New Left activists argued that the movement had to stress "moral issues in place of ideology" or that "the trademark of the new radicals is a primitive moral ideology."[15] Even more explicitly, the purpose of the New Left was concretely defined as the realization in practice of fundamental American political values. "The origins of the New Left," as one SDS statement put it in the mid-1960s, "are not based on ideological (class) confrontation but, on the contrary, emanate from a serious commitment to certain features of the dominant American ideology. The denial of civil rights to the black population was the first issue that led to the emergence of the New Left. The exposure of this denial directly contradicted the dominant rhetoric of equal opportunity and democratic rights."[16]

The difference between the Old Left and the New Left was thus the difference between class politics and economic concerns on the one hand, and creedal politics and moralistic concerns on the other. In somewhat comparable fashion, the mainstream manifestation of the political spirit of the times, the New Politics, differed from the Old Politics because it wished to reform existing institutions to embody more fully American values rather than simply to work within those institutions to achieve materialistic benefits.

The shift in political attitudes was also more broadly reflected in "the way in which the public conceptualized politics." During the central years of the Fourth Period the public was both "more likely to evaluate candidates and parties in terms of issue positions and ideology" and also more likely to develop consistent and coherent positions on political issues. As a result, the proportion of the public that evaluated presidential candidates in ideological terms was much higher in the 1964, 1968, and 1972 elections than it was in the preceding elections or in the 1976 election.[17] (See Figure 2.)

When asked in the early 1970s about the state of morality in America, Alexander Bickel is reported to have replied, "It threatens to engulf us."[18] He was guilty of understatement; it did. But the moralism of the S&S Years was also peculiarly public in nature. With respect to individual personal behavior in a private setting, the old standards of morality were challenged, discredited, and often thrown away with purposeful abandon. With respect to public behavior, however, the old standards of morality were reinvigorated, reasserted, and often applied with relentless conscientiousness. The target of this moralism was almost invariably some form of established authority. The arrogance of power was superseded by the arrogance of morality, and for more than a decade authority—in

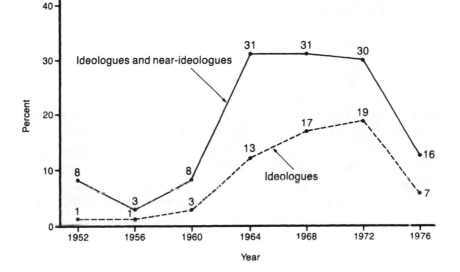

Figure 2. Ideological evaluation of presidential candidates, 1952–1976. (*Source:* Norman H. Nie, Sidney Verba, and John R. Petrocik, *The Changing American Voter,* enl. ed. [Cambridge, Mass.: Harvard University Press, 1980], p. 367.)

government, business, education, religion, the family, and elsewhere— was called into question and often effectively undermined. Politics focused on the evils of hierarchy and officialdom: arbitrary power, unresponsiveness, secrecy, deception.[19] As a result, people no longer felt obligated to obey those whom they had previously considered superior to themselves in age, rank, status, expertise, character, or talents. Within most organizations, discipline eased and differences in status became blurred. Each group claimed its right to participate equally—and perhaps more than equally—in the decisions that affected it.

In American society, authority had commonly been based on organizational position, economic wealth, specialized expertise, legal competence, and electoral representativeness. Authority based on hierarchy, expertise, and wealth all obviously ran counter to the democratic and egalitarian temper of the times, and during the 1960s all three came under heavy attack. In universities, students, who lacked expertise, came to participate in the decision-making process on many important issues. In government, organizational hierarchy weakened, and organizational subordinates acted more readily to ignore, criticize, or defeat the wishes of their superiors. In politics generally, the authority of wealth was challenged and reforms were introduced to expose and limit its influence. Authority derived from legal and electoral sources did not necessarily run counter to the spirit of the times, but when it did, it too was challenged and restricted. The decisions of judges and the actions of legislatures were legitimate to the extent that they promoted, as they often did, egalitarian and participatory goals. "Civil disobedience," after all, was the claim to be morally right in disobeying a law that was morally wrong. It implied that the moral value of law-abiding behavior in a society depended upon the content of the laws, not on the process by which they were enacted. Electoral legitimacy was, obviously, most congruent with the democratic surge, but even so, it too at times was questioned, as the value of "categorical" representativeness was elevated to challenge the principle of electoral representativeness.

The legitimacy of institutions in America derives from liberal, democratic, individualistic values. If institutions are seen, as they were in the Fourth Period, to deviate from those values, they are to that extent illegitimate.[20] This perception, in turn, then releases the constraints on a wide variety of behavior not normally a part of conventional politics. "Take but degree away, Untune that string, And hark! what discord follows," succinctly summarizes the course of American politics during the sixties and seventies. Or, as Daniel Patrick Moynihan warned President-Elect Nixon in 1968, "The sense of institutions being legitimate—especially the institutions of government—is the glue that holds society together. When it weakens, things come unstuck."[21] In the late 1960s, much of America came unstuck.

The Mobilization of Protest

The politics of the S&S Years, like that of other creedal passion periods, was characterized by protest and exposure on behalf of reform. These three forms of politics do not appear only during creedal passion periods, but they do tend to dominate the politics of such periods, while other forms of politics, such as party, electoral, and interest group politics, tend to decline in significance. Moralistic indignation generates passionate drives to expose evil, to protest evil, and to reform evil.

The early years of the Fourth Period were marked by significant changes in political participation and by the mobilization of protest focused largely on civil rights and the Vietnam War. In the United States, much more so than in most other industrialized democracies, political participation rates tend to correlate with socioeconomic status. This overall correlation was not reversed during the S&S Years. Yet the composition of those most active in politics did change significantly. Before 1960, blacks and youth were among the least participant groups in American society. These groups were, however, far more sensitive than others to the gap between American ideals and the realities of racial discrimination and foreign war. During the 1960s, consequently, the participation of these groups in politics increased dramatically; they became, indeed, among the most politically active groups—the political shock troops, as it were, of the American conscience constituency

For the three presidential elections between 1952 and 1960, the electoral participation index for the American public averaged 13.3; for the four elections between 1964 and 1976, it averaged 17.3. This increase was entirely accounted for by the rise in black electoral participation. The index for whites was 18.7 for the first three elections and 19.3 for the succeeding four. The black electoral participation index, in contrast, zoomed upward from a level of −35.7 for the earlier elections to 7.5 for the four later ones.[22] The increase in political participation among blacks was clearly greater than that which might have been predicted by their slowly improving socioeconomic status. In the 1952 and 1956 elections, black campaign activity was significantly below that which would have been expected on the basis of their educational status. Between 1960 and the 1970s, black campaign acts significantly exceeded the level predicted by education. White campaign acts, in contrast, continued at a relatively constant level slightly above that predicted by education. By the late 1960s, overall political participation rates for blacks were much more equal to those of whites than they had been previously, and blacks were usually more active in politics than whites of similar socioeconomic status. It seems reasonable to conclude that this increased participation by blacks was the result of heightened group consciousness related to the salience of civil rights issues.[23]

As people age, they usually become more politically active, until they reach their fifties when their activity begins to decline; if socioeconomic status is held constant, the decline sets in when people are in their late sixties. Those under age 26 participate less than any other age group.[24] In the late 1960s and early 1970s, however, this generally prevailing pattern did not hold. Young people who were roughly 18 years old in 1965 engaged in an average of 2.1 political activities between 1965 and

1973, compared to an average of 1.7 for their parents. Young adults (21–29 years old) were significantly more active in the 1968 and 1972 elections than those a generation older (44–64 years old). In sum, "young adults in the late 1960s and early 1970s were indeed exceptional in their political participation. The young participated at higher rates than did the young in other years, and they were more active than mature adults during this period. Both patterns were unusual and unexpected."[25] In addition, during these years, liberals of any age tended to be more politically active than conservatives of the same age. The young also tended to be much more liberal than those who were more elderly, and this reinforced their propensity for political action.

The 1960s and the early 1970s are generally thought to be a period of great political controversy and activity in which large masses of citizens became passionately involved in politics in a variety of ways. Yet this impression contrasts rather markedly with the extent to which people engaged in the most widespread form of political participation: voting in elections. Voting participation rates increased significantly during the 1950s, peaked in 1960, and then declined steadily thereafter through 1980, with the sharpest drop coming between 1968 and 1972. If the 1960s were the decade of political action, how can this seeming anomaly be explained?

The answer lies in the purposes of political action in the 1960s. In a creedal passion period, the primary purpose of politics is protest. Political protest is the expression through collective action of opposition to particular conditions, policies, or officials. It can be legal or illegal, peaceful or violent, diffuse or focused. It can take the form of direct action and civil disobedience; it can include meetings, demonstrations, teach-ins, riots, picketing, marches, sit-ins, strikes. In some circumstances, voting itself can be a means of protest, but so also can not-voting. In addition, there are many other more effective and more satisfying ways of registering protest. During the 1960s, all age groups increasingly disagreed with the statement: "Voting is the only way that people like me can have any say about how the government runs things." In 1952, however, virtually the same proportions of those in their twenties and those over sixty agreed with this statement. In 1960, a small generational gap appeared, with 69 percent of those in their twenties and 78 percent of those over sixty agreeing with the statement. By 1968, a wide chasm had opened up, with 37 percent of the younger and 62 percent of the older group agreeing with the statement.[26] Young people, blacks, and other constituencies became disillusioned with voting and ready to engage in a variety of other forms of political action.

As a result, as in previous creedal passion periods, the tactics and arenas of political participation multiplied outside conventional channels. New organizations designed to make political practice conform to political principle proliferated in number and intensified in activity. These included radical and protest organizations, as well as more moderate, reform organizations. A survey of some eighty-three "public interest" organizations in 1972–73, for instance, found that fifty-two (63 percent) had been formed after 1959.[27] People also became mobilized to new levels of activity within the confines of more specialized, supposedly "nonpolitical" institutions: students participated in decision making within universities; stockholders challenged corporation managements; soldiers asserted the right to unionize and bargain collectively; government lawyers organized to protest decisions by the attorney general; priests asserted their claims against bishops. Stimulated in part by the success of the civil rights movement but also in larger part by the ethos of the times, many other sectors of American society—women, Indians, Chicanos, homosexuals, white ethnic groups—developed new levels of group consciousness and engaged in much more intense forms of political activity. In addition, as in previous creedal passion periods, organizations became active on behalf of those unable to help themselves: children, the handicapped, the insane, prisoners, animals.

Americans are known throughout the world as a litigious people. During creedal passion periods this propensity increases markedly. Between 1970 and 1976, for instance, the number of civil rights employment cases initiated in federal courts increased from 344 to 5,321; the number of private antitrust cases rose from 877 to 1,504. In increasing numbers, Americans attempted to use judicial processes to right perceived social wrongs. As one so-called public interest group urged citizens: "Sue them! Sue the IRS! Sue Congress! Take federal agencies to court! Even sue the President himself! You can, you know."[28] During the S&S Years to use Emerson's phrase, a "restless, prying, conscientious criticism" prevailed throughout the land, as people actively asserted and attempted to realize rights that they had previously disregarded.

Even as political participation expanded in a horizontal sense, to new forms and channels, it also escalated in a vertical sense, with a marked increase in the intensity of the protests mounted by the Movement or movements against the established order. Particular expressions of protest, although individually limited in time, occur in clumps, particularly in creedal passion periods. In a liberal environment, moreover, protest can be used to generate protest, by provoking the authorities to react by coercion or violence that in itself is perceived to violate the Creed and serves to mobilize new participants unmoved by the original issue. In the politics of exposure, the most appealing issue is the effort by authority to cover up evil; in the politics of protest, the most appealing issue is the effort by authority coercively to suppress protest against evil. In each case, the creedal immorality of the counteraction by authority provides the basis for a broader appeal. In a liberal society, particular issues appeal to particular groups, but opposition to the misuse of authority appeals to almost all groups.

During the 1960s, protest was of crucial importance in mobilizing public opinion concerning racial discrimination and the Vietnam War. Sit-ins, freedom rides, civil rights marches, and the responses of Southern authorities to them, particularly as revealed through the mass media, helped generate the public support necessary for the enactment of the mid-1960s civil rights legislation. The tactics of protest were perfectly suited for exploitation by the media. Similar tactics were used in the teach-ins, peace marches, and demonstrations that played a key role in mobilizing opposition to the war in Vietnam. The very fact that protest tactics were used commanded the attention of both public and leaders and underlined the intensity of the commitment of those who were marching. Without recourse to the tactics of protest, neither opposition to discrimination nor opposition to the war would have achieved its goals.

Those who became more active politically in the S&S Years also tended to resort to the more intense forms of protest. Eighteen-year-olds in 1965 were six times as likely as their parents to engage in protests or demonstrations during the following eight years, with one out of every six in the younger group participating in such action. Blacks, too, were more willing than other groups in the population to endorse demonstrations as a form of political action, with those blacks who were young and middle class more inclined to do so than other blacks.[29] The role of protest as the characteristic form of political participation in the S&S Years is graphically revealed in the relative frequency of protest demonstrations and riots from the 1950s to the 1970s. (See Figure 3.) From 1948 to 1959, the United States averaged 5 major protest demonstrations annually; from 1960 to 1972, the annual average was 144. In 1973 the number of demonstrations dropped precipitously, averaging 57 annually during

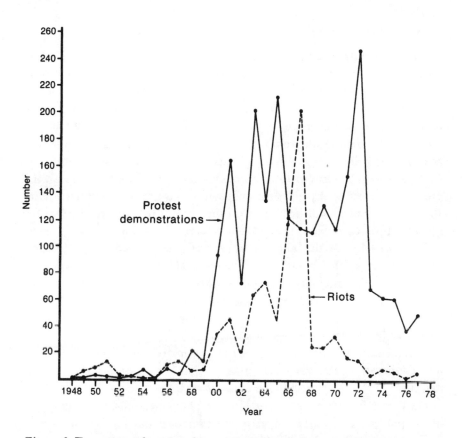

Figure 3. Frequency of protest demonstrations and riots, 1948–1977. (*Source:* Based on data in Charles Lewis Taylor and Michael C. Hudson, *World Handbook of Political and Social Indicators,* 2nd ed. [New Haven: Yale University Press, 1972], pp. 88–89, 94–95, and Charles Lewis Taylor and David A. Jodice, *World Handbook of Political and Social Indicators III* [New Haven: Yale University Press, forthcoming, 1981].)

the next 5 years. The distribution of riots followed a similar pattern: very few in the 1950s, a sharp increase in 1960 that continued to 1967, a tremendous drop-off to an average of 22 for the next five years, followed by a still further drop to single-digit figures in 1973. The curves portrayed by this data dramatically highlight the silhouette of the age of protest.

Many Americans engage in protest during creedal passion periods. The more intense forms of protest are, however, the characteristic political tactic of radicalism. Reform involves efforts to make American political institutions and practices conform to American ideals and values. Revolution is the effort to overthrow both political ideals and political institutions and to replace them with different (for example, Marxist) ideals and institutions. What, then, is radicalism? In the American context, is it reform or is it revolution? These two categories do not seem to leave much room between them. In fact, the essence of American radicalism is precisely its ambivalence on this issue. In the United States, radicals on the Left are those who respond to the question "Are you a liberal or a Marxist?" by answering "both" or "neither." For various reasons (see Chapter 8), radicalism in America is able to encompass both those who are trying to improve the system and those who are trying to destroy it. In terms of tactics, both can agree on the central role of protest. On the one hand, protest eschews violence as a preferred instrument and violence for its own sake. On the other hand, protest goes beyond the pallid confines of conventional politics. It involves moving out of the committee room, legislative chamber, and voting booth "into the streets" for mass action, which may not in itself be illegal but which contains the potential of illegality, and which if illegal may not be violent but which could easily spawn violence.

Liberal reformer and Marxist revolutionary can thus blend together and cooperate in the mobilization and organization of protest. As the data in Figure 3 suggest, however, the more intense forms of protest do not last long. Protest has an ever-decreasing half-life. Substantial numbers of people cannot maintain high levels of moral outrage for sustained periods of time and hence must seek new ways of coping with their dissonance. They may come to feel that their protest has been substantially successful and subside into a more complacent outlook and reliance on more conventional forms of political action to achieve particular legislative goals. They may feel that their protest has been unsuccessful, conclude that no effort of theirs can succeed, and hence lapse into cynicism. Or they may come to reject the entire system—both ideals and institutions —and turn to revolutionary activities to destroy and replace it.

In the late 1950s and early 1960s both New Left organizations—most notably SDS—and black organizations—most notably CORE (Congress of Racial Equality) and SNCC (Student Nonviolent Coordinating Committee)—pursued reformist goals with radical tactics. SDS, like other radical coalitions, stretched "from moderates to Maoists"; the Port Huron statement of 1962 was a statement of general radical reform goals, well within the broad limits of the American radical tradition. "Until 1964," one historian said, "the New Left, in fact, was decidedly reformist and convinced that American institutions could be made to reflect proclaimed ideals."[30] After 1964, however, the appeal of reformism began to subside. In 1965, SDS dropped the anticommunist clause from its constitution and opened its membership to all those on the Left.[31] Parallel changes occurred in its organization, as the needs of central bureaucratic control eclipsed the values of participatory democracy. Marxism, which had been rejected a few years earlier as the out-of-date ideology of the Old Left, was now embraced. Following the 1968 election, SDS was drained still further by factional conflict and began to reject the tactics of protest for those of violence. In 1969, the Weathermen made SDS into a revolutionary organization which, after the failure of the Chicago "Days of Rage" of violent protest in October, went underground at the end of the year. In March 1970, the symbolic end of the transition from protest to revolution came when three Weathermen accidentally blew themselves up making bombs in a house on New York's West Eleventh Street. SDS had always been radical, but the sense in which it was radical changed drastically between Port Huron and Eleventh Street. In its early years it was a radical reform organization because it wanted to realize American liberal values; at the end it was a radical revolutionary organization because it wanted to destroy American liberal institutions. But as a radical protest organization, it could not last: Inevitably, its leaders were driven either to making bombs (like Kathy Boudin) or running for Congress (like Tom Hayden).

The leading protest organizations in the civil rights movement went through a similar metamorphosis. In 1960–61, tens of thousands of people participated in hundreds of sit-ins to desegregate lunch-counters and other commercial facilities; blacks and whites cooperated together in the Student Nonviolent Coordinating Committee and in the Southern Christian Leadership Conference; a quarter of a million people participated in the civil rights march on Washington in 1963. The successful mobilization of support, made easier by the seemingly ruthless opposition to desegregation by some elements in the South, created the political environment for the passage of the Civil Rights Acts of 1964 and 1965. In achieving this, some black leaders became absorbed into the electoral and bureaucratic politics of the Establishment, shifting "from protest to politics."[32] Others, however, felt that the civil rights organizations should move in a more radical direction. In 1965–66, SNCC shifted course, substituted the slogan "black power" for "freedom," segregated and then expelled its white workers, and came out against the Vietnam War and in favor of resistance to the draft. At the same time, CORE broke with its nonviolent tradition and endorsed black power and a community organizing strategy in the North.[33]

The general pattern in these organizations involved a shift from protest to violence, from a broad base to a narrow one, and from ideals derived from the American Creed to ones rooted in Marxist or other revolutionary ideology. Perhaps most notable was the shift from shared goals to particularistic goals, reflected most clearly in demands for "black power," "student power," and "workers' power." In American politics, when a group makes the acquisition of power its explicitly articulated goal, it is confessing its inability to achieve that goal. A slogan like "black power" embodies two negative symbols. First, power in general is distrusted and any group that proclaims power as its goal is immediately suspect. Second, "black power" implies power for one group at the expense of others. By so defining its goal, the group sharply limits its appeal. Whites feel compelled by the American Creed to support civil rights for blacks; they are under no such compulsion to support black power. In the American context, the former is in the end irresistible; the latter is from the start self-defeating.

The Dynamics of Exposure

Government in the United States has always been more open than government in other societies, including democratic societies. This has been one result of the absence in America of a "state" in the European sense. The business of government is the business of the public, and consequently it should be conducted in public. This proposition, totally foreign to most cultures, is a basic component of the American Creed. It is reflected in the constitutional guarantees of freedom of speech and of the press, in the penetration of journalists into governmental precincts and processes, in the absence of an Official Secrets Act on the British model, and in the looseness of libel laws. As a result, government in America is subject to much more constant and pervasive exposure to its people than is government in other societies.

Exposure takes two forms. Investigatory exposure is designed to reveal wrongdoing; it is normally the product of particular efforts by investigatory agencies—journalists, congressional committees, law enforcement agencies—aimed at particular targets. Regulatory exposure, on the other hand, is designed primarily to prevent wrongdoing by requiring publicity or permitting publicity for certain types of action. Often the product of exposés produced by investigatory exposure, it takes the form of sunshine laws, the Freedom of Information Act, and legislation requiring reports of lobbying expenditures and campaign contributions. Both investigatory and regulatory exposure are far more prevalent in the United States than in other societies.

Publicity is always present, but it tends to peak during periods of creedal passion. The exposure to which political authority in the United States was subjected in the late 1960s and the early 1970s was unique in modern history, aside from the investigations by revolutionary regimes of their predecessors. During the 1960s various liberal and radical groups and publications intensified their efforts to expose the operations of those in authority, particularly with respect to foreign policy and the Vietnam War. The great age of exposure did not begin, however, until 1971, when Daniel Ellsberg found a newspaper outlet for the Pentagon Papers. This was followed by further revelations concerning the conduct of the war and, in the summer of 1972, by the beginnings of Watergate, which slowly gained momentum and dominated the national media for the next two years. (Watergate was a front-page story in *The New York Times* every day except three during May, June, and July of 1973.)[34] The expanding revelations of the web of involvement in Watergate provided what seemed to be an irresistible lure and a promising career for scores of journalists. In due course, also, the gradual release of the Nixon tapes dramatically revealed the casualness and banality, meanness of motive and narrowness of purpose, that may characterize political leaders at work.

In the fall of 1973, Watergate was supplemented by the revelations and prosecution that led to the resignation of Vice-President Agnew. The resignation of President Nixon the following summer substantially closed down the Watergate exposures, but throughout the fall of 1974 the media were able to continue in the same vein and strip away much of the mystery that had surrounded the wealth, lifestyle, and political operations of Nelson Rockefeller, who had been nominated for vice-president. In December 1974, *The New York Times* broke the story of the domestic intelligence operations of the CIA; during the following year, the press, three governmental investigatory bodies, and sundry individuals competed and cooperated in revelations concerning U.S. intelligence and internal security agencies. Surveillance activities; assassination plans; interception of mail and cable traffic; use of missionaries, businessmen, and journalists as agents; support and financing of political parties, media, and political leaders in other countries; disinformation operations; the names of agents; efforts to overthrow or weaken foreign governments—all these were laid bare in what could only be viewed and was viewed by incredulous foreign officials and publics as a peculiarly virulent form of American madness. In the spring of 1976, the exposure momentum slackened, but for roughly five years the American public was provided with unprecedented revelations of the inner workings of government and the behind-the-scenes actions of public officials.

The great exposés were thus concentrated in the latter part of the S&S Years. On the surface, this seems puzzling. One might think that during a creedal passion period, exposure of injustice and wrongdoing would come first. The veils of rhetoric and official cover-ups would be ripped away, exposing the brutal—and un-American—reality of American politics. This, in turn, would lead to a swelling mass of protest, which would generate reforms to eliminate the evils. The comparison of the ideal and the fact is normally the indispensable prerequisite to reform. How can this apparently perverse appearance of exposure at the end of the process be explained? Two factors are relevant.

First, both protest and reform could precede exposure because the principal evils to which protest and reform were directed—racial discrimination and foreign war—were obvious and blatant. Little or no exposure efforts were necessary to uncover them. What was necessary was to communicate these facts to the public, and this the national media —particularly television—did, with tremendous impact on American politics. As was the case during other creedal passion periods, the media played a central role in the politics of the S&S Years. In the 1960s, that role was played largely by television, which transmitted instantly and vividly to the people images of what was happening in the American South and in South Vietnam. In the 1970s, the critical role was played by the print media, which revealed the malfeasance and misfeasance of public officials in Washington. The electronic media had its impact through the communication of public events, the print media through the revelation of secret events. As a result of the former, protest and reform could and did occur on a major scale before the process of exposure reached its peak.

Second, exposure could not occur until the authority of the executive branch—that is, the plausible targets of exposure—had been weakened, and it could not occur until the power of the press and Congress—that is, the necessary agents of exposure—had been enhanced. The exposure of governmental evil requires the weakening of governmental authority because of the nature of the exposure process. Protest requires the mobilization of outsiders against political authority; exposure requires the disaffection of insiders from political authority. It becomes possible when the lines of authority and control in government and other institutions begin to break down and people within those institutions lose their sense of loyalty to and their belief in the legitimacy of their leaders. A major exposé requires a Daniel Ellsberg or a Deep Throat, and the appearance of such informants in the early 1970s testified to the breakdown of authority in the Pentagon, the White House, and the Department of Justice. Those who are exposed in American politics are not those who are evil and powerful but those who are evil and weak. Exposure produces evidence of villainy; it is itself evidence of weakness, and in turn contributes to this weakness.

On occasion in American history, congressional committees and newspapers have undertaken to investigate military defeats, intelligence failures, and other gross deficiencies or breakdowns in the process of government that are the product of poor judgment, bad communications, insufficient foresight, sloppy administration, or simple stupidity. Such exposures, however, rarely occur during creedal passion periods, because the target at such times is not the incompetence of leadership but its villainy. Exposure is directed toward corruption, bribery, deception, lying, obstruction of justice, nepotism, cronyism, extortion—actions that clearly violate legal or ethical standards. In a different atmosphere, for instance, congressional committees investigating the CIA might have been curious as to why the agency failed so miserably in its efforts to assassinate Lumumba and Castro. But in 1975 no one was interested in the inability of the agency to do what it was told to do, but only in the immorality of what it was told to do. For this type of exposure to occur, there must be a broader climate of opinion which makes people willing to believe evil of their leaders and passionately eager to find such evil.

The weakening of governmental authority was a preeminent characteristic of the politics of the 1960s and the necessary prerequisite to the exposures of the 1970s. Few Presidents came into office with more important enemies and potential enemies than did Richard Nixon. Congress, the national media, the eastern Establishment, the federal bureaucracy, and the aroused protest and reform organizations of the 1960s were all seen—correctly—as enemies of the new administration. In connection with the media, for instance, commentator John Chancellor accurately observed that "other Administrations have had a love-hate relationship with the press. The Nixon Administration has a hate-hate relationship."[35]

In similar terms, Nixon and other members of his administration spoke feelingly and accurately about their isolated and vulnerable position at the peak of power in the federal executive. The weakness of the Nixon administration was revealed in the readiness of informants in the executive branch to cooperate with journalists and congressmen. This erosion of its authority also stimulated the administration to misuse its authority, thereby providing more behavior to be exposed.

A somewhat similar process also made the CIA and FBI into attractive targets. Public unhappiness with the Vietnam War did not become widespread until 1969, whereupon the way was prepared for the revelation of the Pentagon Papers in 1971 and for the subsequent investigations of the CIA in 1975. When the United States was finally driven out of Vietnam in the spring of 1975, congressional committees did not investigate why the United States had lost the war and did not attempt to apportion responsibility among civilian and military officials for this outcome. Congress wanted to pursue evil rather than failure, and to do this it had to find a weak target. The opposition to foreign involvement, going back to the early 1960s, made conditions favorable for an assault on U.S. intelligence agencies. Again, the question of timing was crucial. In early 1967, for instance, a radical employee of the National Student Association learned of the long-standing CIA funding of certain NSA international activities. Three articles detailing these revelations were published in a radical San Francisco magazine, and *The New York Times* and other newspapers wrote stories of possible CIA funding of other programs through foundation channels. The national media, did not, however, rush to exploit this information for their own purposes, and congressional leaders moved not to exploit but to support the actions of the CIA. President Johnson appointed a cabinet-level committee to review quietly CIA covert funding practices; no major congressional investigation was launched.[36] In 1974–75, on the other hand, the initial revelations about the CIA came not from *Ramparts* but from *The New York Times;* Congress and the media rushed in to follow up on these leads; and President Ford's appointment of a commission to investigate alleged CIA misbehavior stimulated the House and Senate to launch their own parallel and competing probes. Investigative reporters and congressional staff members kept the stream of revelations going for an entire year.

Once a favorable climate exists for exposure of the abuses of authority, the process of exposure develops its own characteristics and dynamics. First, the agents of exposure multiply. In the American system, exposure typically requires the participation of three types of people: informants, journalists, and congressmen and their staffs. At the beginning, the informant in the executive decides that the public or his personal interest requires him to bring into the open some information so as to affect either the substance of policy or the identity of the policy makers. Since the informant normally does not wish to reveal his own role in the exposure process, he seeks out someone in the media or in Congress to whom he can in confidence transmit the information and who then assumes responsibility for making it public. As in the case of Ellsberg and the Pentagon Papers, this process may take a while. In terms of securing the timely revelation of his information, Ellsberg undoubtedly made a mistake in going first to the chairman of the Senate Foreign Relations Committee. Newsmen are likely to have fewer inhibitions and greater interest in quick action than congressmen. The informant will, in most cases, wish to transmit the information to a journalist in the national media, where its exposure will receive the attention of those involved in the making of national policy. Once the information is out in the media, appropriate congressmen then move to investigate the charges or revelations. Once a congressional investigation is launched, congressional committee staff members normally establish a symbiotic relationship with the journalists covering the revelations, feeding one another information and tips and promoting their joint interests in continuing the process as long as possible.

An informant who successfully leaks to the press or to Congress evidence of the abuse of authority both encourages others who wish to expose the same target and provokes other informants to retaliate against other targets. Consequently, as the history of both the Pentagon Papers and Watergate exposés illustrates, a scoop by one journalist promotes vigorous competition from others: a "muck race" develops as newsmen pursue old clues and scurry after new leads, in an intense competition to see whose revelation will dominate the next day's headlines. Congressional committees, normally at least one in each house, compete in comparable fashion.

Second, the targets of exposure multiply. Initially, the focus is usually on the presumed wrongdoing of a few officials. The process of exposing those officials, however, uncovers wrongdoing by other officials. In addition, as Watergate again illustrates, the process of exposure may lead officials to take counteractions to coverup their wrongdoing, which in turn provide additional behavior to expose. There is, moreover, a finite limit on the amount of wrongdoing any one official can undertake, and consequently once the machinery of exposure gets moving, it will, in due course, exhaust one target and move on to others. Journalists made every effort to duplicate Watergate in a succession of follow-on "gates": Koreagate, Lancegate, Billygate. The exposure of some targets stimulates counterexposure efforts of other targets. Thus, the revelations of the abuse of authority by President Nixon generated revelations of seemingly comparable abuses of authority by Presidents Johnson, Kennedy, and Roosevelt. Exposure agents who have scored successfully with one target will attempt to duplicate their success with other targets; the scourgers of the Nixon White House became the purveyors of petty gossip concerning the Burger Supreme Court.

Third, as this last example suggests, the process of exposure very quickly begins to produce decreasing marginal returns, which, however, are as likely to increase as to decrease the intensity of the efforts of the exposure agents. The impact of Watergate, and particularly the final exposure in July 1974 of the tapes that precipitated the President's resignation, gave additional appeal to what Michael Kinsley and Arthur Lubow called "the smoking-gun fallacy"—that is, the belief that "important truths will emerge from this process of sending reporters out to dig up little clues, which will lead to big clues, which will lead to THE TRUTH."[37] This proclivity is rooted in American conspiracy theories that contend that something important is hidden beneath the surface of politics, and that great efforts are necessary to strip away the various layers of deception and reveal the rotten reality of official behavior. In fact, however, just the reverse is true. The longer investigations go on, the less likely they are to uncover major new scandals. The significance of what is exposed varies inversely with the effort required to expose it. The major violations of the American Creed—concentrations of power and wealth, abuses of authority, denials of equal justice and individual rights, discrimination and inequalities—are not easily hidden. The evidence is there for those who wish to see it, appropriate it, and use it. Once started, however, the exposure process, in the effort to uncover major new evils, moves from the momentous to the trivial. It is, consequently, hardly surprising that the wave of exposures in the early 1970s, which had focused on the conduct of a major foreign war, ended in the later 1970s with a focus on the sexual peccadillos of live congressmen and dead presidents.

Fourth, the exposure process requires the multiplication of exposable activity—that is, the multiplication of secrets. To some degree, the credibility of a fact becomes dependent upon how secret it is. An action viewed as evil in itself becomes more evil if it is done in secrecy. Consequently, facts that are not secret often have to be portrayed as secret in order to increase the public's indignation and to enhance the informants' contributions: they become not merely the communicators of the knowledge of evil, but the exposers of the existence of evil. Perhaps the most notable example of the manufacture of a secret concerned the Nixon administration's bombing of Cambodia in 1969 and 1970. The President made the decision to do so on March 16, 1969; the first bombing attack occurred two days later. To avoid embarrassing Prince Sihanouk and complicating peace negotiations with the North Vietnamese, no public announcement was made. On May 9, *The New York Times* ran a long front-page article describing the bombing, which the news magazines and other media followed up in the subsequent weeks. The bombing, which continued for another year, was public knowledge for over ninety percent of the time it was conducted. In subsequent years, however, the "secret" bombing of Cambodia became one of the most frequent and passionately invoked counts in the indictment of the Nixon administration. A "secret" that almost immediately became an "unsecret" continued to be described as a secret for years afterward.* What this incident demonstrates, however, is, first, the inability of the American government to keep a secret, and second, the need for the exposers of secrets to label as "secret" things that are in fact very public.

The multiplication of exposure agents and targets was not limited to the national level of the U.S. government. The success of exposures at

* Typical of these efforts to manufacture a secret was that of *New Republic* columnist TRB in 1974: "Two months after Nixon took office, in March 1969, he started the bombing of the neutral country. He didn't tell Congress or the public. He kept it up for four years. The alleged justification of protecting Prince Sihanouk from embarrassment clearly ceased when Sihanouk was overthrown in March 1970. Nixon kept up the bombing as Commander-in-Chief, orchestrating the conspiracy of silence to keep the lid on the antiwar movement. The Pentagon knew it, the Cambodians knew it, the enemy knew it, the Americans didn't know it" (*The New Republic*, September 7, 1974, p. 2). If Americans read their newspapers, however, they obviously knew about the bombing. In this instance, it should be noted, the critics of President Nixon ate their cake and had it, too. The administration reacted to the rash of news stories about the bombing by tapping the phones of several newsmen and subordinate officials in an (unsuccessful) effort to find the source of the leak. Critics vehemently denounced the administration for doing this, while at the same time continuing to denounce the administration for carrying on a secret bombing which could have been secret only if the leak had not occurred.

that level stimulated new waves of "investigative reporting" at the state and local levels, as local and regional media attempted to duplicate on their level the success of *The New York Times* and *The Washington Post* at the national level. In some instances, this occurred very directly, as when U.S. congressional investigating committees uncovered evidence of corrupt relations between American corporations and officials of foreign governments. The unveiling and purifying effect of American creedal passion led to the exposure and disgrace of the prime minister of Japan, the premier of Italy, and the prince of the Netherlands. In an age of economic interdependence, efforts to reform American political practice thus produced effects in the politics of other countries that would never, in all likelihood, have been produced by the indigenous political processes of those countries.

Pressures for publicity are continuingly present in the American system, but during a creedal passion period they take new and more intense forms. The process of exposure acquires its own momentum, which gives it an existence quite apart from the dynamics of protest and reform. During the S&S Years, exposure peaked in the early 1970s as the momentum of protest began rapidly to fade away. Exposure, in turn, produced extraordinary revelations of the use and abuse of authority in the presidency, intelligence and security agencies, foreign policy establishment, Congress, regulatory agencies, and elsewhere. It also contributed marginally to reform, primarily through the removal of some people from office and their replacement by others. The escalating exposure also, however, hastened and made more pervasive the shift from outraged moralism to jaundiced cynicism in the prevailing public mood. In that way it sounded the death knell of reform and of the S&S Years.

The Legacies

The politics of creedal passion—of moralism and protest, outrage and exposure, ideals and reform—came to an end in the mid-1970s. Like the English in the 1650s, a nation of prophets again became a nation of shopkeepers. A phase in U.S. political life had come and passed, and the politics of the late 1970s did not, at least on the surface, appear to differ that much from the politics of the late 1950s. Indeed, as Russell Baker perceptively suggested, a Rip Van Winkle who had gone to sleep in 1957 and awakened in 1977 would find it hard to believe that the country had been through more than a decade "of assassination and Asian war, of bizarre political plots and impeachment, of men walking on the moon, of snapshots taken of Mars, of burning cities and massive demonstrations." During this period, Baker observed, the American people had passed "through an extraordinary cycle of public emotion" that "began with elation (the New Frontier), changed abruptly to horror (assassination), then to rage (Vietnam), then to shock (Watergate) which turned into disgust as the age of investigation revealed a depth and span of political corruption inconceivable in 1957." Yet, in the end, public life seemed about back where it had been twenty years before, with President Carter delivering homilies on virtue more correct in syntax but little different in substance from those President Eisenhower had delivered twenty years before. "If the streets once swarmed with a citizenry passionately engaged in great political controversies and campuses once catered to miniature revolutions,," wrote Baker in 1977, "the citizenry today, as in 1957, yawns at the smallest suggestion of politics, and campus debates, as in 1957, center on which career may lead to the most comfortable retirement."[38]

History does not, however, return to its starting point. The politics of the late 1970s differed greatly from that of the late 1960s, but it also had to differ significantly from that of the late 1950s if only because the S&S Years had intervened. The political attitudes, practices, and institutions of the late 1970s were inevitably shaped by what happened during that period of creedal passion. The issue is: What were the consequences of creedal passion and how profoundly and permanently did they change American politics?

The most significant legacies of the S&S Years can be seen in: the different impact of reform in narrowing the IvI gap; the realignment of political institutions; the depletion of political authority; and the changes in public attitudes.

Reform and the IvI Gap

As is typical of creedal passion periods, reform efforts during the S&S Years were directed at a wide variety of institutions and practices—political, social, economic, cultural. These included areas of public policy such as consumer and environmental affairs. The principal foci of reform during the S&S Years, however, were civil rights, foreign-military policy, and the political process. To what extent did the reform efforts in these areas achieve their goals?

No meaningful and precise balance sheet can be compiled. Yet even an impressionistic assessment can yield the conclusion that, in terms of the goals of the reformers, the reforms were usually incomplete, often temporary, and at times self-defeating. The degree of success of the reforms was influenced by: (1) the saliency of the evils to be corrected and of the changes proposed to the basic values of the American Creed; (2) the extent to which reforms could be put into effect by essentially one-shot, readily implemented, and hence irreversible decisions; (3) where this condition did not prevail, the extent to which implementation of the reforms was supported by politically effective, permanently organized interest groups; and (4) the extent to which the behavior to be changed by the reforms was rooted in institutions and practices subject to political control within the context of the American Creed, rather than in factors outside such control such as the international environment, the fundamentals of the private enterprise economic system, or the unchangeable irrascibility of human nature. These factors produced a differential pattern of success among the three areas of greatest concern to the reformers.

The most dramatic and far-reaching reform of the S&S Years clearly was sweeping away the structure of legally sanctioned racial segregation and discrimination in the South. By any standard for judging social change, this was no mean achievement. It required the combination of authoritative action from above by the federal courts, Congress, and the federal bureaucracy, plus widespread mobilization and intense activity on the part of blacks and white civil rights workers from below. In hardly more than a decade, basic and essentially irreversible changes occurred in southern politics, government, and education. Prior to the passage of the Voting Rights Act of 1965, 29 percent of eligible blacks in seven southern states were registered to vote, compared with 73 percent of eligible whites. By 1972 one million blacks had been added to the voting rolls: 56 percent of blacks registered, compared with 67 percent of whites. On a national basis, in 1956 the percentage of whites who said they voted was forty-two percentage points higher than that of blacks who said they voted (77 percent versus 35 percent). By 1976 this difference had been reduced to eight percentage points (73 percent versus 65 percent). In the mid-1950s perhaps 100 to 200 blacks held elective office nationwide; by 1979 about 4,500 blacks—including 17 congressmen and the mayors of Detroit, Los Angeles, Atlanta, and New Orleans—held elective office, although this still constituted only about 1 percent of all elected officials.[39]

In somewhat comparable fashion, levels of education achieved by blacks and whites narrowed significantly. The results on school desegregation, on the other hand, were not as impressive. In the South, dramatic changes occurred once the federal government began vigorous enforcement of the Supreme Court's decision in *Brown* v. *Board of Education:* in 1964, ten years after *Brown,* 98.2 percent of southern black schoolchildren still attended all-black schools; by 1972, the number had declined to 8.7 percent. In the North, on the other hand, school desegregation moved more slowly and spottily, reflecting residential patterns, white flight to the suburbs, increasingly active local resistance to busing, and the less than vigorous support of school desegregation by the Nixon administration. Finally, with respect to more strictly economic issues, shifts in previous patterns were least marked. The median family income of blacks increased from about 54 percent of white family income in the early 1960s to 62 percent in 1975, and more blacks moved into higher-status and better-paying types of jobs. At the end of the 1970s, however, substantial economic differences still existed, particularly in unemployment rates, and residential desegregation had made little progress.[40] One careful observer summed up the situation in 1978: "black inequality" still remained a "major problem in American society," yet the gains of the previous two decades had "placed blacks in general much closer to equality—however defined—than ever before in our history." More important, because blacks were a self-conscious, well-organized group with a special interest in preventing backsliding, the reforms that had been made would not be easily reversed. The United States, it was argued in 1978, "cannot return to the conditions which prevailed before the 1960s: blacks are too conscious, civil rights legislation barring overt discrimination is too much a part of our practice, and blacks have achieved enough of a political foothold to prevent a return to a not terribly benign neglect."[41] The S&S Years reduced substantially and permanently the IvI gap with respect to Myrdal's American dilemma.

The efforts in the S&S Years to secure more equal rights for other groups of Americans—Indians, Asians, women, homosexuals—were less clearcut in their results. This resulted in part from the fact that the violations of the civil rights of these groups did not appear to be as blatant as those suffered by blacks in the South, and in part from the fact that efforts to promote civil rights for these groups in considerable measure followed in the train of the campaign for black civil rights. As a result, less time existed to produce comparable results before the moralistic passion for reform began to subside and countercurrents to develop. In the most obvious case, the Equal Rights Amendment almost became part of the Constitution in the mid-1970s, having been approved by Congress and ratified by thirty-five states. At that point, however, the opposition mobilized and it became stalemated.

Reform efforts in the area of foreign and military policy took three forms. First and most immediately successful were the efforts to compel the United States to reduce and then end its participation in the Vietnam War. Opposition to the war was gradually fueled by increasingly massive protests between 1965 and 1968; the war clearly played a major role in the election of Nixon; and by 1969 a majority of the American public opposed U.S. involvement. The new administration almost immediately began the gradual reduction of U.S. troops in Vietnam. The invasion of Cambodia in 1970, however, reactivated massive opposition, and in due course resulted in U.S. agreement to an armistice and disengagement from the conflict. In 1973 it also produced an act of Congress prohibiting U.S. involvement in military action in the Indochinese peninsula, thereby removing the sanction underpinning the armistice agreement completed the previous January. Second, reformers moved to reduce the resources, autonomy, and influence of the major U.S. agencies—the military and intelligence services—involved in overseas operations. For the first time after World War II, Congress refused to approve and drastically reduced funds for major weapons programs. In real terms, military spending declined every year from 1969 through 1975. The personnel strength of the armed forces was reduced to a level significantly below that which existed before the Vietnam buildup. Intelligence budgets were similarly slashed. Covert operations for purposes other than intelligence-gathering were prohibited except with the express approval of the President reported to congressional foreign relations committees. Finally, congressional reformers also moved to rectify what they saw as the excessive power of the President in foreign relations. A War Powers Act attempted to limit his ability to commit the armed forces to military action. Many other actions also contributed to a significant reallocation of authority over foreign affairs between the executive and legislative branches.

The actions designed to produce U.S. withdrawal from the Vietnam War were clearly successful. Whether designed to have that effect or not, they made it much easier for North Vietnam to establish its control over the entire country in 1975. The actions reducing and weakening the military and intelligence services had a major impact that lasted at least through the following decade. By the end of the 1970s, however, people's perceptions of the nature of the threats to national security, coupled with their perceptions of the relative decline of American power, drastically changed public and congressional attitudes on these matters. Military spending became highly popular; restrictions on intelligence and military operations were loosened; the so-called "intelligence charter" originally designed to prevent abuses of power by intelligence agencies became stalemated in Congress, joining the ERA as one of the unconsummated reforms of the S&S Years. Finally, the balance of authority between legislature and executive slowly began to shift back toward the the latter.

The third major set of reforms was directed at the political processes through which public officials were selected and government decisions were made. The major targets at both state and national levels were political parties and elections, legislatures, and the bureaucracy. In all these areas, many reforms were proposed and a considerable number were made. These included the removal or relaxation of restrictions on voting (poll taxes, literacy tests, age requirements, residency requirements); expanded use of the initiative and referendum; the campaign finance laws of 1971 and 1974; and changes in internal party processes to promote greater representativeness of party leaders and, most notably, to expand the use of presidential primaries from seventeen states in 1968 to thirty-seven states in 1980. Reforms in Congress were directed toward weakening the seniority system, expanding congressional staff, multiplying leadership opportunities within Congress, enhancing congressional control over the budget process, opening up committee hearings and meetings to the public, and enacting "ethics" codes designed to minimize potential conflicts of interest. With respect to the bureaucracy, "sunshine laws"—the most notable of which were the Freedom of Information Acts of 1966 and 1974—attempted to open bureaucratic proceedings and records to public scrutiny, while "sunset laws" attempted to place terminal dates on the existence of bureaucratic agencies. In general these reforms in the electoral, party, legislative, and executive processes were designed to make political decision making more public, less susceptible to the influence of money and "special interests," and more open to popular participation and control, and to make decision makers more representative of the people to whom they were presumably responsible.

The extent to which individual reforms achieved the goals of their proponents varied greatly. The overall record of process reforms is mixed at best, and in some cases downright perverse. The removal of restrictions on voting was accompanied by a steady decline from 1960 to 1980 in the proportion of the population exercising the suffrage. The initiative and referendum that had been proposed primarily by populist and liberal advocates in the 1960s became, in the 1970s, the great weapon of conservatives who wanted to cut back taxes and governmental spending. As interpreted by the Supreme Court, the campaign finance laws strengthened the positions of incumbents and millionaires, while at the same time very likely contributing to the decline in voting participation. The proliferation of presidential primaries gave major advantages to out-of-office candidates and to the voters of Iowa and New Hampshire. The efforts to secure more representative national conventions in terms of sociological composition produced national conventions unrepresentative of party voters in terms of political outlook. The diffusion of power in Congress made it increasingly difficult to enact any major legislative program, including one directed toward the goals of reform. The limits on outside earned income enhanced the importance of outside unearned income and, as the Abscam investigation suggested, may have made congressmen more rather than less susceptible to bribery. The growth in congressional staffs created new sources of power no more likely than executive staffs to be responsible to the public. The requirements for publicity drove real decision making back into more informal and unrecorded channels. The Freedom of Information Acts produced a significant expansion in bureaucratic personnel to respond to requests, the bulk of which came from business corporations and lobbyists rather than from the media, public interest groups, or the general public. Sunset laws imposed new responsibilities on bureaucratic agencies and provided them with additional incentives to develop supportive political constituencies to ensure their continued existence.

In the other two major areas of reforms, reformers could point to major accomplishments in racial desegregation and U.S. withdrawal from Vietnam. In the political process area, however, no such dramatic achievements were clearly visible, and the consequences of reform were often quite contrary to the intentions of the reformers. Even the overall record of lasting reform achievements in all three areas was, apart from desegregation, a rather limited one at best, testifying to the resiliency of the gap between ideal and practice and justifying Tom Hayden's perplexed query from the vantage point of the late 1970s: "We ended a war, toppled two Presidents, desegregated the South, broke other barriers of discrimination. How could we accomplish so much and have so little in the end?"[42]

Institutional Realignment

The realignment of political institutions during the 1960s and early 1970s involved shifts in the structures, functions, power, and constituencies of major political institutions similar to those that occurred during the Revolutionary, Jacksonian, and Progressive eras. By the late 1970s, as Anthony King and his colleagues argued, "a substantially new political system" had emerged compared to that which existed in 1960. In key respects, such as presidential nominations, the system that existed in 1960 bore closer resemblance to that of 1932 or even 1912 than it did to that of 1976.[43] The scope and depth of the institutional changes that occurred during the S&S Years have been explored elsewhere and cannot be elaborated here.[44]

Four major changes in institutional roles do, however, warrant mention, both because they involved the central political institutions of society and because they were representative of the type of changes that occurred during the S&S Years. These were the increase in the functions and power of the media and Congress and the decline in the power and functions of the political parties and the Presidency. These changes were not simply a zero-sum reallocation of power. The new importance of the media contributed to the decline of political parties, but this decline had causes that went considerably beyond the rise of television. Similarly, the assertiveness of Congress was only one key factor among many that contributed to the decline of the Presidency.

These shifts were peculiarly significant in their overall implications for the workings of the political system. Historically, the Presidency and the political parties were the two major institutions primarily concerned with integrating diverse interests into effectively functioning electoral and governing coalitions. Congress and the media are ill-equipped to play such integrating roles and are much more capable of playing critical, investigatory, checking, and controlling roles. As we have seen, the relative increase in their power was a prerequisite for the emergence of exposure politics in the early 1970s. As a result of these changes in institutional power, the American political system of the 1970s was less well-equipped to integrate interests into coalitions and to combine policy preferences into legislative programs than the political system that existed prior to 1960.

Technological developments, social trends, and political needs produced four major changes in the position of the press in American politics. First, there was the emergence in the 1950s and 1960s of a truly national printed press, the major elements of which were the national weekly newsmagazines and the major newspapers with a national reach, such as *The New York Times, The Washington Post* and, in due course, *The Wall Street Journal*. These media, together with others, formed the core of a national press establishment that carved out a relationship for itself with the President and other agents of national authority comparable to that which local newspapers had long held with mayors and local authorities in major American cities. To a substantial degree, the journalists associated with these national media determined what was news and set the model for how it should be covered and interpreted. Second, the emergence of television had tremendous impact on how people got their news and, perhaps even more important, on who got the news. The nightly network newsbroadcasts reached an audience far larger than that which had followed printed sources of news. In addition, the television camera affected what was considered news and the making of news. In the beginning, television covered the news; soon, news was produced for television. Third, the increased size and the changed role of the press had its impact on recruitment into journalism. Careers in the media came to attract larger numbers of college graduates, particularly graduates of the better and more prestigious liberal arts colleges. This produced more confident and more vigorous reporters, and more penetrating and extensive news stories. Finally, the combination of these three developments laid the basis for a redefinition of the role of the press, from that of the passive observer and recorder of events to that of the "adversary" of government. Appropriately enough, the highest function of the press came to be defined as "investigative reporting," a multisyllabic label for what a previous creedal passion period had termed "muckraking."

These developments gave the press more power during the S&S Years than it had in the 1950s. Professional students of politics have two principal ways of judging power. One is the reputational technique, which involves asking a cross-section of the relevant public who they think has power. The second is through the analysis of contested decisions to see whose side won. By both these measures, the press did well in the S&S Years. In annual polls from 1974 to 1980, for instance, several hundred leading Americans ranked television on the average as second only to the White House in influence on national policy; in 1974 they ranked it the most influential institution in the country, markedly ahead of the White House. In these polls newspapers always ranked among the dozen most influential institutions, also achieving their top position in 1974 in fourth place behind television, the White House, and the Supreme Court.[45] General public confidence in the leadership of most institutions declined by 15–30 percent between 1966 and 1973; in contrast, confidence in television rose by 16 percent and in the press by 1 percent during these years.[46]

The media, and particularly television, also played major roles in disseminating the images that mobilized public opinion to bring about the passage of civil rights legislation in 1964 and 1965 and U.S. withdrawal from Vietnam at the end of the decade. Television's images of the civil rights struggle in the South were, as Michael Robinson argued, "unusually vivid" and were to a significant degree responsible for the change over a few months in 1963 from 4 percent to 52 percent in that proportion of the American public believing civil rights to be the most important problem confronting the country.[47] With respect to Vietnam, "the greatest emotional force against the war was television news film coverage. As we cannot forget, television showed endless film clips of American troops being killed and injured . . . The contrasts in the treatment of American defeats and alleged defeats (Bataan, Kasserine Pass, the Bulge, compared with *Tet*) or of atrocities (which went essentially unreported in World War II) should stimulate thoughtful people to ask searching questions."[48] Or, as the dean of American newspapermen observed on the last day of the war: "Maybe the historians will agree that the reporters and the cameras were decisive in the end. They brought the issue of the war to the people, before the Congress or the courts, and forced the withdrawal of American power from Vietnam."[49] In the most dramatic institutional confrontations of the Nixon administration, *The New York Times* and Daniel Ellsberg defeated the administration in the Pentagon Papers cases, and *The Washington Post* successfully exposed and eventually brought down the administration in the contretemps sparked by the Watergate burglary. As the *Post*'s executive editor succinctly put it: "The press won in Watergate."[50] In other battles over institutional privileges—the confidentiality of sources, access to judicial proceedings, the law of libel— the press also scored notable victories.

The decline of political parties was an oft-noted phenomenon of the 1960s and 1970s, with many informed observers agreeing with Austin Ranney that the United States was approaching a "no-party system."[51] The decline in party could be seen in the extent to which functions traditionally performed by political parties were increasingly discharged through other means and by other institutions. With the expansion of the primary system, the central function of *nominating candidates for public office* was less and less subject to the control of party organizations and party leaders. The *conduct of political campaigns,* including the raising of funds, was increasingly taken over by the personal organizations of candidates and by professional campaign managers, polling organizations, and political consultants (who could work for a Democratic candidate in one state and a Republican candidate in a neighboring one). Direct mail organizations moved into key positions in fund-raising. In presidential contests, public finance also came to play a role. The central role of television in reaching the voters meant that much less effort was devoted to mobilizing local campaign workers and attempting to reach voters through personal contact.

A third function of political parties had been to *provide a guide to people for voting.* During the 1960s, however, straight-ticket voting in any one election and consistency in party voting from one election to the next both declined precipitously. In the 1940s and 1950s independents made up 20–23 percent of the electorates; in the early 1960s, this proportion began to rise, leveling off at about 37–38 percent in the late 1960s, with 45–50 percent of the new age cohorts entering the electorate in the late 1960s and 1970s refusing to identify themselves with either major party. People no longer relied primarily on party as their guide to a choice among candidates. Issue voting increased in salience as party voting declined. In the 1976 presidential election, issue voting declined somewhat and party staged a modest comeback.[52] The significance of party still remained, however, far below what it had been in the 1950s, with the personal qualities of the candidates and their positions on issues being most important in shaping the average American's vote.

A fourth function of party historically was to provide the channels and means for *recruiting appointed officials in government.* In some measure, parties continued to play this role in the late 1970s. A change in administration in either a state capital or in Washington normally involved a significant change in the higher levels of the executive branch of government. This relationship, however, had already been eroded by the extension of civil service earlier in the century, and it was further reduced in mid-century by the rise of "issue networks" of experts concerned with particular issues and from whose ranks appointments to key positions in the executive branch and on legislative staffs were increasingly made.[53]

Finally, political parties have played a role in the *formulation and implementation of public policy.* Historically this role has been less important in the United States than in other societies, apart from certain exceptional periods such as Woodrow Wilson's first term. In the 1960s, those most active in the two political parties increasingly came to embody two polarized views with respect to public policy. This development made it difficult for the political party to play an integrating function, in terms of creating an electoral coalition, while at the same time the diffusion of authority within both the executive branch and Congress inhibited its ability to decide upon and put through a coherent legislative program. In some respects, as in modifications of the seniority rule by the party caucus, party did become more important in shaping public policy. But these developments did not effectively counterbalance the impact of the major trends toward the further weakening of party.

A variety of different factors contributed to the decline of political parties. Higher levels of education and affluence among voters enhanced the tendencies toward issue voting and toward the development of overall ideological positions on issues. The ease with which candidates (who had the money) could reach voters through television reduced the importance of party organizations and party workers. Many of the reforms introduced during the 1960s and 1970s had the effect (if not the intent) of further undermining the role of party. And, finally, the increasing complexity of issues required increasing expertise and professionalization, which party organizations were generally ill-equipped to provide.

The increase in the power of Congress during the S&S Years had its roots in a natural reaction against the long period of presidential dominance, beginning with the New Deal and reinforced during World War II and the Cold War. It also derived from the changing make-up of Congress —with the influx of younger, more liberal, better educated, and more policy-oriented representatives and senators in the late 1950s and early 1960s. For most of the twentieth century, liberals viewed the Presidency as the principal source of enlightened leadership and progressive legislation and Congress as a bastion of conservatism dominated by southern Democrats and Republicans. In the 1960s and 1970s, both the image and the reality changed. Liberals became fearful of presidential power and entranced with the opportunities for progressive reform through Congress. In the S&S Years, Congress became the institutional channel through which liberal forces attempted to promote changes in American government, American society, and, most notably, American foreign policy.

The shift of power toward Congress was also encouraged by reforms within Congress that reduced reliance on seniority, opened up choice committee assignments to younger members, and multiplied subcommittee chairmanships. The resulting diffusion of power *within* Congress enhanced the power *of* Congress, reducing the ability of any single leader or small group of leaders to "deliver" Congress in negotiations with the President or other outside officials. The ability of Congress to play a more active and positive role in shaping public policy was also significantly strengthened by the growth in congressional staff support during the S&S Years. Two new staff support agencies, the Office of Technology Assessment and the Congressional Budget Office, were created in 1972 and 1974 respectively, and the staffs of the existing agencies, the Congressional Research Service and the General Accounting Office, were significantly expanded. Committee staffs almost tripled in size between 1957 and 1975, and the personal staffs of congressmen more than doubled.[54]

The reforms that groups powerful in Congress wanted to make in foreign-military policy required, as we have noted, a reallocation of power between President and Congress and the extension of congressional control over executive branch activities. In foreign policy, Congress moved to curtail presidential discretion and to compel the executive to be more accountable to Congress. In the 1950s Senator Richard Russell had remarked, "God help the American people if Congress starts legislating military strategy." In the 1970s Congress did just exactly that. In 1970 it imposed deadlines on the withdrawal of U.S. ground forces from Cambodia. In 1973 it prohibited all U.S. "combat activities in or over or off the shores of Cambodia, Laos, North Vietnam, or South Vietnam." The same year it passed the War Powers Resolution prescribing the circumstances under which the President could commit U.S. forces to combat, requiring the prompt reporting to Congress of any such commitment, and limiting the duration of such commitment without express congressional approval. In 1975 Congress prohibited covert U.S. aid to the insurgent forces in Angola opposing the Cuban-supported MPLA. In 1974 and 1975 congressional action seriously affected U.S. relations with the Soviet Union and Turkey by imposing conditions for the granting of "most favored nation" status to the former and the continuation of military assistance to the latter. Throughout the late 1960s and early 1970s Congress displayed a new assertiveness in considering military programs and the defense budget, not hesitating to arrive at its own judgments concerning the merits of the former or to cut significantly the latter.

In 1974 Congress also passed the Budget Control and Impoundment

Act, which restricted the control of the President over the expenditure of appropriated funds and which strengthened the ability of Congress, through new budget committees and the Congressional Budget Office, to exercise overall control over the scope and purposes of government spending. In the same year, Congress required that the director of the Office of Management and Budget and his deputies in the Executive Office of the President be subject to senatorial confirmation. During the S&S Years, Congress also greatly multiplied its use of the legislative veto as a device for controlling executive action. A 1976 survey identified thirty-seven laws, ranging from the Amtrack Improvement Act to the Foreign Military Sales Act, that provided for the use of the veto, the overwhelming majority of which had been passed during the previous decade.[55] Other legislative provisions greatly expanded the range of reports that the executive was required to submit to Congress. At the same time, Congress further asserted its control over the executive branch through its investigations of Watergate, intelligence activities, and other matters.

During the S&S Years, Congress thus enacted a rash of "Presidency-curbing legislation."[56] The overall waning of Presidential power during these years was, however, also rooted in other factors. The reaction against an active role for the United States in the world scene implied a diminished role for the President in the U.S. political scene. The decline of the political parties reduced the importance of the President as party leader and, as a consequence, reduced the certainty that he could secure renomination.[57] Four-year presidential terms became the mean between 1961 and 1981, with one President assassinated, one forced to resign, one induced not to run for reelection, and two defeated at the polls when they did run. In any political system, longevity breeds power, and the contrast between the brief term of Presidents and the Washington durability of senators, representatives, Supreme Court justices, bureaucrats, lobbyists, and journalists necessarily redounded to the disadvantage of the President. In addition, as we have also pointed out, presidential weakness was marked in relation to the press and to the bureaucracy. Every President during the S&S Years expressed his frustration over his inability to secure prompt, active, and responsive compliance with his directives from the bureaucracy.

More generally, during the S&S Years it became clear that a person could become President by creating an effective electoral coalition, but that did not give him the means to govern the country. Election conferred legitimacy but not power, and both were necessary for the exercise of authority. Creating power required the creation of a governing coalition, which became increasingly difficult if not impossible to do as power itself became diffused throughout society. As a result, Presidents increasingly felt a sense of helplessness, an inability to find the levers to be pulled by which to produce the results they felt they had been mandated to achieve. Lyndon Johnson, elected by one of the largest majorities in American history, ruminated as to how essential it was for him to get "the support of the media . . . the Easterners . . . the intellectuals," because "without that support I would have had absolutely no chance of governing the country." He lost much of that support. His successor had almost none; four months after also winning election by one of the largest majorities in American history, he concluded in exasperation, "Nobody is a friend of ours. Let's face it." Neatly expressing the siege mentality of the White House, a senior White House aide advised a young recruit, "One thing you should realize early on, we are practically an island here;" the highest calling was to "protect the President" against the hostile forces surrounding the island. At the end of the 1970s, Gerald Ford could with some legitimacy argue that far from having an imperial Presidency, the United States in fact had "an imperiled presidency."[58]

The four shifts in institutional power that have been noted as major features of the new American political system seem to peak toward the end of the S&S Years. In the later 1970s the public standing of the media declined somewhat, with perhaps some slight moderation of its political clout. With the expenditure of great time and effort, President Carter was able to secure narrow congressional approval for his major foreign policy initiatives, although he was notably less successful in domestic policy. At the beginning of the 1980s, both the capability and will of Congress to challenge the President were less than they had been a decade earlier. The decline of political parties, on the other hand, seemed to continue through the seventies although the Republican Party made something of an organizational comeback, using the federal funds available to the national parties to play an active role in congressional elections. At the beginning of the 1980s, the modest ebbing of the trends that had prevailed earlier was still very far from erasing the basic changes that occurred in American politics after 1960. The Presidency was significantly weaker than it had been then; the parties were shadows of their former selves; Congress was institutionalizing its new power; and the media, particularly the national press and television, played central roles in shaping both elite and popular political attitudes and behavior.

The Misuse and Erosion of Authority

Political authority—that is, the legitimate exercise of power by public officials—can become deficient in two ways. The misuse of authority involves the exercise of power by public officials in ways other than those which have been thought legitimate by the prevailing opinion in society: the realm of power expands beyond the realm of legitimacy. The erosion of authority, on the other hand, involves the shrinkage of the realm of legitimacy within the realm of power. Ways of exercising power previously accepted as legitimate cease to be so considered. The misuse of authority entails a change in the behavior of officials; the erosion of authority entails a change in the substance of or the commitment to the norms of society. Through different means, each produces a disjunction between legitimacy and power in which the exercise of the latter falls outside the sanction of the former. In complex ways, too, each can feed on the other. In some measure, each is unavoidable in any society, and each, carried to an extreme, can disrupt the functioning of society. In the United States, the misuse of authority is more blatant but also more curable; the erosion of authority is less obvious and also less tractable.

During the S&S Years political authority became deficient in both ways. The misuse of authority by officials of the national government was dramatically revealed in 1973 and 1974. Conspiracy to obstruct justice, kickbacks, illegal campaign contributions, burglary, bribery, violation of the civil rights of citizens—the list of alleged crimes by those in high office was a lengthy one. The list of those accused or convicted of those crimes was even more impressive: the President, the Vice-President, three cabinet secretaries, almost a dozen White House staff members, and a variety of other federal officials. The record reveals the misuse and abuse of authority in incredible richness, and strongly suggests the extent to which one abuse of authority breeds another.

The record also demonstrates something else. It is persuasive evidence of the relative effectiveness of the American political system in dealing with the misuse of authority. A primary motive of the framers of the Constitution was to create a system of government that would prevent the abuse of authority and, if that failed, one that would expose abuse, provide the means of ending it, and ensure the bringing to justice those who were guilty of that abuse. To provide security against the concentration of power, as Madison put it, "ambition must be made to counteract ambition. The interest of the man must be connected with the constitutional rights of the place." Hence, the system of checks and balances. Hence also "dependence on the people," which is "the primary control on the government." In the years since 1787, the constitutional checks have multiplied and been institutionalized; government has become more dependent on the people, at least in the sense of being more dependent on choice through popular elections; and other extraconstitutional checks, such as a vigorous and independent press, have served the constitutional purposes of preventing and curbing the abuse of authority. In the history of the world, the government of no other major state is or has been subjected to such an extensive network of controls and checks. In exposing the abuses of authority in the early 1970s, the constitutional system and the political system functioned effectively and precisely in the way in which the framers wanted them to function.

During the 1960s and 1970s, however, authority was not only abused, it was also eroded, and, in some respects and at times, almost eliminated. The range of activity by governmental officials accepted as legitimate by predominant opinion shrank significantly in the S&S Years. Behavior of public officials that had previously induced acquiescence now provoked outrage. The authority of government declined as people ceased to see it as dedicated to the public interest. This erosion was, of course, dramatically reflected in the declining trust and confidence that people had in governmental institutions and leadership. These changes in public attitudes were only one index of a deeper challenge to governmental authority which manifested itself in a variety of other ways.

It would, undoubtedly, be comforting if one could believe that this erosion of authority were simply a product of the misuse of authority. In some respects, the decline of public confidence in government did speed up in the late 1960s and early 1970s, and this phenomenon was undoubtedly in part the result of the revelations of wrongdoing in high places. But it would be totally erroneous to believe that this was the principal causal sequence. The erosion of authority went on independently of the abuse of authority and was not primarily a product of that abuse. As we have seen, in many respects the erosion of authority antedated the misuse of authority, or, more exactly, it antedated the principal revelations of the misuse of authority. The former first manifested itself significantly in the early 1960s; the latter did not appear until the late 1960s and early 1970s. In addition, the questioning of authority was not limited to politics and government, but was part of a much broader challenging of authority in almost all areas of society: the family, schools, universities, churches, businesses, private associations, the military. The erosion of authority, in short, stemmed from both earlier and more general causes than the misuse of authority.

The misuse of authority, on the other hand, may have been in part a product of the erosion of authority. First, the decline in the authority of public officials and, in particular, changes in their own perceptions of their power and legitimacy can stimulate officials to abuse their authority in an effort to restore their authority. The White House under both Johnson and Nixon became pervaded by a sense of political paranoia, as the President and his men confronted an increasingly critical Congress, hostile press, and resistant bureaucracy. In some instances, as with the leaks of the Pentagon Papers and the Cambodian bombing stories, a cause-and-effect relationship between the attack on authority and the abuse of authority was clearly evident. Second, and more important, is the extent to which the erosion of authority leads not simply to an increase in the actual abuses of authority, but rather a change in the public's attitude toward those abuses. In the American context, as we have suggested, increased exposures of official misbehavior are as likely to be a product of increased public concern about such misbehavior as a product of increased misbehavior. There are, indeed, good psychological grounds alone for thinking that variations in the intensity of public attitudes are likely to occur more frequently than variations in the behavior of public officials. Hence, behavior that went quite unremarked at one point in time may well a few years later become the subject of intense indignation and criticism. In 1969, for instance, to take a minor but representative example, various organs of the national press reported at some length on the public expenditures being made to create a "Western White House" at San Clemente. The overwhelming reaction was one of approbation: nothing was too much to ensure the safety and well-being of the President. Five years later the media rediscovered these expenditures and "exposed" them as the improper use of public funds for private purposes. And everyone waxed indignant over such a gross abuse of power. What had changed, however, was not the behavior of the public official but the perception of that behavior by public opinion. Outrage was not a product of changed behavior; the changed perception of the behavior was a product of outrage. People turn against political authority; they challenge and question authority; and this, in turn, produces revelations of the abuse of authority. Indignation is not the consequence of the exposure of wrongdoing; rather, indignation is the motive for exposure, and, in due course, cynicism is the consequence. Indignation, in short, colors the perception, and the perception then legitimates the indignation. In this way, public knowledge of the abuse of authority is a product of the. breakdown of authority.

There was significant erosion of authority in the 1960s, and, partly as a result of this erosion, evidence became available in the late 1960s and early 1970s of the existence of significant abuses of authority. But were these abuses of authority more or less horrendous than the abuses that occurred prior to the 1970s? The opportunities and incentives to abuse authority change over time, but they are not likely to fluctuate widely. Some individuals may be more prone to misbehavior than others. But all public officials violate moral and legal norms at some point in their career. Why are some pursued, exposed, and prosecuted for actions that are ignored when they are done by other politicians? The answer for the S&S Years, as for other creedal passion periods, lies not so much in the behavior of officials as in the temper of their times and the extent to which the American psyche becomes possessed by moralistic demons outraged at the gap between ideal and practice. In these circumstances, authority drains away before the flood of moralism. The American political system, which is so superbly designed to prevent and to rectify abuses of authority, is very poorly equipped to reverse the erosion of authority.

Cynicism and the Restoration of Authority

In the early 1960s the rise of moralistic outrage generated protests at the gap between American ideals and American practices. These protests led to some reforms in those practices and they were accompanied by significant changes in the power and functions of key political institutions. These shifts, in turn, facilitated a politics of exposure, which produced ever-widening revelations of further gaps between ideal and practice. In the end, rampant exposure helped undermine the impetus to reform and caused people to adapt to the pervasiveness and inevitability of the existing patterns of behavior. In the dynamics of the S&S Years, in short, moralism produced protest, protest against obvious evils yielded to exposure of hidden evils, and exposure produced cynicism which eliminated the motivation for both protest and exposure. The forces it generated brought the creedal passion period to an end.

In the mid-1960s the American people developed highly unfavorable views of the responsiveness and trustworthiness of their government. At the end of the 1970s these attitudes were as strong as or stronger than they had ever been before. In early 1980, 84 percent of the American public felt that special interests obtained more from the government than the people did, 78 percent that the rich were getting richer and the poor poorer, 70 percent that the people in Washington were out of touch with the rest of the country, 64 percent that what they thought didn't count very much anymore, and 50 percent that the people running the country did not really care what happened to them.[59]

In the 1960s, attitudes such as these were accompanied by feelings of outrage, and efforts were made to correct these perceived deficiencies in government. In the late 1970s, the unfavorable perceptions of government remained, but the impulse to take corrective action had disappeared. Like other creedal passion periods, the S&S Years left a stratum of organizations—public interest lobbies, environmental groups, women's groups, minority organizations, and the like—that in some measure institutionalized higher levels of political consciousness and activity than had existed before the 1960s. In the 1970s, however, the intensity and breadth of appeal of these organizations declined from the peaks they had reached a few years earlier. Indignation exhausted itself. The impetus for exposure and reform waned. Political participation and interest in politics subsided. Illustrative of the shift was the fact that whereas 58 percent of college freshmen in 1966 said that "keeping up to date with political affairs" was "essential" or "very important" to them, in 1978 only 37 percent responded similarly.[60] The political efficacy of the American people—that is, their confidence in their ability to influence the political process—went down. Alienation plus apathy yielded cynicism.

By the late 1970s people were disillusioned with the possibility of society reforming government. They had also become disillusioned about the possibility of government improving society. The shift in the mood of the country in 1976 was caught by Jimmy Carter in his campaign with his emphasis on morality, honesty, and integrity on the one hand (which appealed to the lingering elements of moralism in the public mood) and his emphasis on the limits of governmental action on the other (which reflected the rising currents of cynicism and indifference). This country deserves, Carter said, "a government as good as its people" (and, implicitly, as good as its people think it *ought* to be), yet at the same time he foresaw a government that would not and could not do much good for the people. "Lowered expectations" were the keynote of the times.

The political climate of the late 1970s was distinguished by the increasing ascendancy of conservative, antigovernment attitudes among the public at large and of conservative, antigovernment ideas among the intellectual elite. This shift to the right was first marked in the 1976 election results, as Carter defeated his liberal opponents for the Democratic nomination and Ronald Reagan almost unseated an incumbent Republican President. It was marked again in 1978 by the defeat of liberal candidates for state and local office and the victory of conservative, antitaxation referenda in several states. It continued in 1980 with the primary victories of Carter and Reagan, the defeat of Carter in the November election, and the unseating of a number of liberal Democratic senators. Americans were not only distrustful of governmental authority, they were also hostile to governmental activity. In 1959, for instance, when asked to identify which was "the biggest threat to the country in the future," only 14 percent of the public picked "big government," compared to 41 percent who picked "big labor" and 15 percent who chose "big business." In 1978, in contrast, 47 percent of the public picked big government for this honor, compared to 19 percent each for big business and big labor. Similarly, in 1964 only 43 percent of the American public thought the government in Washington was "too big"; by 1976 over 58 percent of the public believed this, and in both 1972 and 1976, 50 percent or more of those identifying themselves as liberals, moderates, and conservatives held this view.[61] During the S&S Years, in sum, the latent antigovernmentalism of the American Creed surged to the forefront of public consciousness.

The immediate legacy of the S&S Years with respect to public attitudes was thus high levels of distrust in government and relatively deep beliefs that little could be done to correct that situation. So long as Americans perceived their government to have deviated far from their ideals as to what government should be, they were, perforce, driven to either a moralistic or cynical response. So long as they remained morally exhausted by the passions of the S&S Years, they were, perforce, inclined to cynicism.

Yet human beings also want leadership, direction, and authority, and in the last years of the 1970s this desire began to emerge. Political commentators and social critics began to criticize the operation of the separation of powers and other constitutional mechanisms for dividing and limiting power. There was a growing feeling that the President then in office had failed them in not providing such a lead. Jimmy Carter had been elected President in 1976 in part because he appealed to the need of

Americans at that point for someone who was personally irreproachable and who was divorced from what had been going on in Washington. He was defeated for reelection in 1980 in part because people then wanted a President who not only was virtuous but also forceful and decisive. We have been "gasping for a lead," as one young congressman said in 1980, but the "hungry sheep looked up and were not fed."[62]

The diminished power of the Presidency became a major cause of concern. In some cases, the shift was remarkably quick. On March 13, 1975, for instance, Joseph Kraft published a column titled "Meddling by Congress in Foreign Affairs Works after All"—a headline that perfectly reflected the fear of presidential power that had prevailed during the previous half-decade. Eighteen months later, he published another column under the heading "It's Time to End 'Congressional Foreign Policy,' " which neatly mirrored the shift in informed public opinion that occurred in the course of a few brief months.[63] In 1978 and 1979 expressions of concern multiplied about the weakness of the Presidency and the need for presidential leadership. Less than a decade after the outpourings of outrage over the "imperial Presidency," Washington analysts were making the case for presidential "majesty."[64] As I argued earlier, these arguments as to the weakness of presidential power were, in fact, evidence of the revival of presidential power.

These signs suggested the possibility of continued movement in the cycle of public responses to the gap between ideal and reality in American politics: from cynicism coupled with distrust of governmental authority and hostility to governmental activity, to complacency marked by acceptance of both governmental authority and existing levels of governmental activity. A shift in public attitudes toward authority cannot in itself, however, bring about the restoration of authority. The latter requires not only a subjective yearning for leadership but also the objective conditions that make leadership possible. These include, first, a change in either the role or the influence of those institutions and groups that most strenuously resist authority, and, second, a reconstitution of the fragmented structures of authority below the national level.

During the S&S Years the media were the institution whose power expanded most significantly and that posed the most serious challenges to governmental authority. The national press was more hostile to political authority than the local press, and national television seemed more critical of such authority than the national press. In part this reflected the attitudes of the people involved in the national media, who, in addition to being liberal on policy issues, also tended to be antigovernment on institutional issues. "Most newsmen," Walter Cronkite said, ". . . come to feel very little allegiance to the established order. I think they are inclined to side with humanity rather than with authority and institutions."[65] The antiauthority attitude of the media also reflected their choice of an adversarial relationship with government. "The media have become the nation's critics," Roger Mudd commented. "As critics, no political administration, regardless of how hard it tries, will satisfy them." A leading print journalist came to the same conclusion: "The national media," said Theodore H. White, "have put themselves into the role of permanent critical opposition to any government which does not instantly clean up the unfinished business of our time." Hence, "no government will satisfy them."[66] The negative impact of the media on the legitimacy of political institutions led one analyst to formulate an "iron law" to the effect that "in nations where news is produced commercially and independently, the level (or branch) of government which receives the greatest emphasis will, in the long run, also experience the greatest public disdain."[67]

With its stress on what was sensational, simple, and controversial, television played a particularly strong role in undermining authority. "Although it has been only recently and partially documented, network journalism tends to be more 'anti-establishment' than print journalism, especially compared to the non-prestige newspapers."[68] In 1963, early in the S&S era, the major networks inaugurated half-hour nightly news broadcasts, which greatly increased popular dependence on television as a source of news and greatly expanded the size of the audience for news. In the late 1960s, greater reliance on television for news was associated with low political efficacy, social distrust, cynicism, weak party loyalty, and low political efficacy. By the mid-1970s, these characteristics had become so widespread among the electorate that the correlation with reliance on television had virtually disappeared.[69] During the S&S Years the overall impact of the media, particularly of television, was to undermine the legitimacy of government. "The messages received by ordinary people during the past fifteen years," Stanley Rothman observed in 1979, "have tended to give the impression that the country's institutions are corrupt and that modern technology is leading us into a cul-de-sac."[70]

"How can we rebuild confidence in the credibility of our institutions?" asked a *Washington Post* editor in the midst of the Watergate tumult.[71]

One way presumably would be for media giants like *The Washington Post* to stop undermining the credibility of American institutions. That is, the media could again redefine their role, this time from an adversarial one to a supportive one. The alternative means of changing the media's impact on governmental authority would be to reduce their influence on public attitudes and behavior. At the end of the 1970s some evidence existed that this might be underway. One significant indication was the extent to which the power of the press itself became a subject of debate, with 40 percent of the American public in 1979 thinking that the existing curbs on the press were "not enough."[72] The courts shifted toward a more restrictive position concerning press powers, rejecting claims that First Amendment rights took automatic precedence over other rights, denying arguments as to the special "protected position" of the press under that amendment, and broadening the applicability of the law of libel. By the end of the 1970s the power of the media seemed to be subsiding somewhat from the peaks it had reached at the beginning of the decade.

The broadest, most pervasive, and most fundamental consequence of the turmoil of the S&S Years was its impact on authority structures throughout American society. The surge of participatory democracy and egalitarianism gravely weakened, where it did not demolish, the likelihood that anyone in any institution could give an order to someone else and have it promptly obeyed. In this situation, support for a stronger Presidency could not automatically translate into the fact of a stronger Presidency. In practice, a stronger Presidency could emerge only with the restoration of authority within other institutions and by the reconstitution of the complex matrices of personal relations and obligations among leaders. A President can exercise leadership at the national level only if there are institutional, bureaucratic, associational, and local leaders with whom he can deal at the subnational level. It is through such a system rather than through broad appeals to public opinion that Presidents achieve the policy results they desire. Vigorous and responsible national leadership requires a network of petty tyrants. The protests, exposure, reforms, and realignment of the S&S Years substantially shredded that network. Creating another such network is a complex and drawn-out process. Until that happens, the gap between the leadership that people desire and the leadership that the system permits will further discredit those in leadership positions and, in a vicious circle, make it still more difficult for them to act.

The S&S Years thus left the United States with a more equitable society, a more open politics, a more cynical public, and a less authoritative and effective government. They left the American people confronting foreign and domestic challenges that required the exercise of power, yet still unwilling to legitimize power.

8 THE VIABILITY OF AMERICAN IDEALS AND INSTITUTIONS

The Future of the Gap

American political ideals and values—the core of American national identity—have been continuously and overwhelmingly liberal, individualistic, democratic. American political institutions have reflected these values but have always fallen short of realizing them in a satisfactory manner. The resulting IvI gap has been a persistent source of tension and cognitive dissonance, which Americans have attempted to relieve through various combinations of moralism, cynicism, complacency, and hypocrisy. The "burr under the saddle," as Robert Penn Warren called it, and the efforts to remove that burr have been central features of American politics, defining its dynamics and shape, since at least the eighteenth century and perhaps before. The question now is: Will the IvI gap and the responses to it continue to play the same role in American politics in the future that they have in the past? Or are there changes taking place or likely to take place in American political ideals, political institutions, and the relation between them that will make their future significantly different from their past?

Three possibilities exist. The relation between ideals and institutions, first, could continue essentially unchanged; second, it could be altered by developments within American society; and, third, it could be altered by developments outside American society and by American foreign involvements. Domestic developments within American society or changes in the international environment could alter the relation between American political ideals and institutions in four ways: the content of the ideals could change; the scope of agreement on the ideals could change; the nature of American political institutions could more closely approximate American ideals, thereby reducing the gap between them; and American political institutions could be significantly altered in an illiberal, undemocratic, anti-individualistic direction; or some combination of these developments could take place.

History versus Progress?

Americans have historically attempted to eliminate or reduce the IvI gap by moralistic efforts to reform institutions and practices in creedal passion periods. These periods have had much in common, and almost always the proponents of reform have failed to realize their goals completely. The relative success of reform however, has varied significantly: in particular, the goals of reform have tended to be more widely achieved in the early periods than in the later ones. In the earlier periods, the affirmation of the goals of liberty, equality, democracy, and popular sovereignty was directed at the destruction or modification of traditional political and economic institutions; in the later periods, it was directed at the elimination or modification of modern political and economic institutions that had emerged in the course of historical development. In the earlier periods, in short, history and progress (in the sense of realizing American ideals) went hand in hand; in the later periods, the achievement of American ideals involved more the restoration of the past than the realization of the future, and progress and history worked increasingly at cross purposes.

The revolutionaries of the 1770s were the first to articulate the American Creed on a national basis and were generally successful in effecting major changes in American institutions: the overthrow of British imperial power, the end of monarchy, the widespread acceptance of government based on popular consent, some extensions of the suffrage, an end to what remained of feudal practices and privileges, and the substitution of a politics of opinion for a politics of status. In part, the articulation of their goals was conservative; the rights asserted were justified by reference to common law and the rights of Englishmen. But the formulation and public proclamation of those rights was also a revolutionary event in terms of political theory and political debate.

In the Jacksonian years, the American ideology was still new, fresh, and directed toward the elimination of the political restrictions on democracy, the broadening of popular participation in government, the abolition of status and the weakening of specialization—that is, of both ascriptive and achievement norms—in the public service, and the destruction of the Bank of the United States and other manifestations of the "money power," so as to open wide the doors of economic opportunity. "Originally a fight against political privilege, the Jacksonian movement . . . broadened into a fight against economic privilege, rallying to its support a host of 'rural capitalists and village entrepreneurs.' "[1] Except for the South and the role of blacks in American society, the Jacksonian reforms did complete the virtual elimination of traditional institutions and practices, inherited from a colonial past or concocted by the Federalist commercial oligarchy, which deviated from liberal-democratic values. All this was progressive in the broad sense, but it too carried with it elements of conservatism. The paradox of the Jacksonians was that even as they cleared away obstacles to the development of laissez-faire capitalism, they also looked back politically to ideals of rural republican simplicity.[2] Restoration, not revolution, was their message.

The institutional changes of the Jacksonian years did not, of course, bring political reality fully into accord with Jacksonian principle. Neither property nor power was equally distributed. In the major cities a small number of very wealthy people, most of whom had inherited their position, controlled large amounts of property.[3] As is generally the case, however, income was much more equally distributed than wealth, and both wealth and income were far more evenly distributed in the rural areas, where 90 percent of the population lived, than in the urban areas. In addition, there were high levels of social and political equality, which never failed to impress European visitors, whether critical or sympathetic. All in all, money, status, and power were probably more equally distributed among white males in Jacksonian America than at any other time before or since. The other central values of the American Creed—liberty, individualism, democracy—were in many respects even more markedly embodied in American institutions at that time.

For these reasons, Gordon Wood argued, the Jacksonian generation "has often seemed to be the most 'American' of all generations." This "Middle Period" in American history has been appropriately labeled because

many of the developments of the first two centuries of our history seem to be anticipations of this period, while many of the subsequent developments taking us to the present seem to be recessions from it. In the traditional sense of what it has meant to be distinctly American, this Middle Period of 1820–1860 marks the apogee in the overall trajectory of American history. Americans in that era of individualism, institutional weakness, and boundlessness experienced "freedom" as they rarely have since; power, whether expressed economically, socially, or politically, was as fragmented and diffused as at any time in our history.[4]

After the democratization of government and before the development of industry, the Middle Period is the time when the United States could least well be characterized as a disharmonic society. It was a period when Americans themselves believed that they had "fulfilled the main principles of liberty" and hence were exempt from "further epochal change."[5] All that was needed was to remain true to the achievements of the past.

In the Middle Period, in short, American dream and American reality came close to joining hands even though they were shortly to be parted. The gap between American ideals and institutions was clearly present in Jacksonian America but, outside the South, probably less so than at any other time in American history. The inequality of social hierarchy and political aristocracy had faded; the inequality of industrial wealth and organizational hierarchy had yet to emerge. Primogeniture was gone; universal (white male) suffrage had arrived; the Standard Oil trust was still in the future.

In the Middle Period and the years following, the only major institutional legacy that was grossly contradictory to the American Creed was slavery and the heritage of slavery, the remnants of which were still being removed a hundred years after the Civil War. With respect to the role of blacks, the Creed played a continuingly progressive role, furnishing the basis for challenging the patterns of racial discrimination and segregation that ran so blatantly against the proposition that "all men are created equal." Hence, in analyzing the American dilemma in the 1930s, Gunnar Myrdal could take an essentially optimistic attitude toward its eventual resolution. He could see hope in America because his attention was focused on the one area of inequality in American life that was clearly an anachronistic holdover from the past.

More generally, the Middle Period marked a turning point in the nature of progress in America. Prior to that time, "progress" in terms of the realization of American ideals of liberty and equality did not conflict with "historical development" in terms of the improvement of economic well-being and security. After the Middle Period, however, progress and history began to diverge. Progress in terms of the "realization of the democratic ideal," in Croly's phrase, often ran counter to historical trends toward large-scale organization, hierarchy, specialization, and inequality in power and wealth that seemed essential to material improvement. Political progress involves a return to first principles; politically Americans move forward by looking backward, reconsecrating themselves to the ideals of the past as guidelines for the future. Historical development involves pragmatic responses to the increasing scale and complexity of society and economy, and demands increasing interaction, both cooperative and competitive, with other societies.

This distinctive character of the Middle Period and its inappropriateness as a foretaste of things to come are well reflected in the observations of the most celebrated foreign observer of the Jacksonian scene. Tocqueville was, in a sense, half right and half wrong in the two overarching empirical propositions (one static, one dynamic) that he advanced about equality in America. The most distinctive aspect of American society, he argued, is "the general equality of condition among the people." This "is the fundamental fact from which all others seem to be derived and the central point at which all my observations constantly terminated." Second, the tendency toward equality in American and European society constitutes an "irresistible revolution"; the "gradual development of the principle of equality" is a "providential fact"; it is "lasting, it constantly eludes all human interference, and all events as well as all men contribute to its progress."[6] Like other European observers before and since, Tocqueville tended to confuse the values and ideals of Americans with social and political reality. His descriptive hypothesis, nonetheless, still rings true. By and large, American society of the Middle Period was characterized by a widespread equality of condition, particularly in comparison to conditions in Europe. Tocqueville's historical projection, in contrast, clearly does not hold up in terms of the distribution of wealth and only in limited respects in terms of the distribution of political power.

In attempting to sum up the diversity and yet common purpose of the Jacksonian age, Joseph L. Blau employs a striking metaphor: "As one drives out of any large city on a major highway, he is bound to see a large signpost, with arrows pointing him to many possible destinations. These arrows have but one thing in common; all alike point away from the city he has just left. Let this stand as a symbol of Jacksonians. Though they pointed to many different possible American futures, all alike pointed away from an America of privilege and monopoly."[7] The Jacksonians were, however, more accurate in pointing to where America should go in terms of its democratic values and ideals than they were in pointing to the actual direction of economic and political development. Industrialization following the Civil War brought into existence new inequalities in wealth, more blatant corruptions of the political process, and new forms of "privilege and monopoly" undreamed of in the Jacksonian years. This divorce of history from progress had two consequences for the reaffirmation of American political values in the Progressive period.

First, during both the Revolutionary and Jacksonian years, the articulation of American political ideals was 'couched to some degree in conservative and backward-looking terms, as a reaffirmation of rights which had previously existed and as an effort to reorder political life in terms of principles whose legitimacy had been previously established. During the Progressive era, the backward-looking characteristics of the ideals and vision that were invoked stood out much more sharply. As Hofstadter suggested, the Founding Fathers "dreamed of and planned for a long-term future," the Middle Period generations were absorbed with the present, and the Progressives consciously and explicitly looked to the past: "Beginning with the time of Bryan, the dominant American ideal has been steadily fixed on bygone institutions and conditions. In early twentieth-century progressivism this backward-looking vision reached the dimensions of a major paradox. Such heroes of the progressive revival as Bryan, La Follette, and Wilson proclaimed that they were trying to undo the mischief of the past forty years and re-create the old nation of limited and decentralized power, genuine competition, democratic opportunity, and enterprise."[8] The Progressives were reaffirming the old ideals in opposition to large-scale new organizations—economic and political—which were organizing and giving shape to the twentieth century. This was most manifest in William Jennings Bryan, who was, as Croly said, basically "a Democrat of the Middle Period." Bryan, according to Walter Lippmann, "thought he was fighting the plutocracy" but in actuality "was fighting something much deeper than that; he was fighting the larger scale of human life." Bryan was thus a "genuine conservative" who stood for "the popular tradition of America," whereas his enemies were trying to destroy that tradition.[9] But he was also a radical attempting to apply and to realize the ideals of the American Revolution. Bryan was, in fact, just as radical as Garrison, but Garrison was moving with history and Bryan against it. In a similar vein, Woodrow Wilson also reacted to the growth of large-scale economic organization with the call to "restore" American politics to their former pristine, individualistic strength and vigor. To achieve this goal Wilson was willing to employ governmental power, thereby, as Lippmann pointed out, creating the inner contradiction that was at the heart of the Progressive outlook. Among the Progressives, Theodore Roosevelt was most explicit in arguing that large-scale economic organizations had to be accepted; nonetheless he, too, held to much of the older ideal; his argument was couched in pragmatic rather than ideological terms: "This is the age of combination, and any effort to prevent all combination will be not only useless, but in the end vicious, because of the contempt for the law which the failure to enforce law inevitably produces."[10]

Second, the reaffirmation of American ideals at the turn of the century could not be as effective as the Revolutionary and Jacksonian affirmations in realizing those ideals in practice. At the extreme, Bryan became the Don Quixote of American politics, battling for a vision of American society that could never be realized again. In the Revolutionary and Jacksonian periods, the institutional reforms had been substantial and effective. In the Progressive period, both economic and political reforms could, at best, be described as only partly successful. The antitrust laws and other efforts to curb the power of big business made a difference in the development of American business—as any comparison with Europe will demonstrate—but they clearly did not stop or reverse the tendencies toward combination and oligopoly. In the political sphere, the introduction of primaries did not bring an end to political machines and bossism, and, according to some, may even have strengthened them. In Congress, the attack on "Czar" Joseph Cannon established the dominance of the seniority system; paternalistic autocracy, in effect, gave way to gerontocratic oligarchy. The efforts to make government more responsible encouraged the growth of presidential power. That institutional changes were made is indisputable, but so is the fact that, by and large, they were substantially less successful than the changes of the Revolutionary and Jacksonian years in realizing the hopes and goals of their proponents.

The passion of the 1960s and 1970s was, in some respects, ideologically purer than the theories of the Progressives. Perhaps for this reason, it was also somewhat more effective in eroding political authority. Yet outside of race relations, its more specific reforms were little more successful than those of the Progressives. Economic power was assaulted but remained concentrated. Presidential authority was weakened but rebounded. The military and intelligence agencies declined in money, matériel, and morale in the 1970s but were reestablishing themselves on all three fronts by the early 1980s. It seemed likely that the institutional structure and the distribution of power in American society and politics in 1985 would not differ greatly from what they had been in 1960. With the important exception of race relations, the IvI gap of the early eighties duplicated that of the early sixties.

This changing record of success from one creedal passion period to the next reflected the changing nature of reform. In the earlier periods, reform generally involved the "dismantling" of social, political, and economic institutions responsible for the IvI gap. The disharmony of American politics was thought to be—and in considerable measure was—man-made. Remove the artificial restraints, and society and politics would naturally move in the direction in which they morally should move. In later creedal passion periods, beginning with the Progressive era, this assumption of *natural* congruence of ideal and reality was displaced by the idea of *contrived* congruence. Consciously designed governmental policy and action was necessary to reduce the gap. In the post–World War II period, for instance, "for the first time in American history, equality became a major object of governmental policy."[11] The Progressives created antitrust offices and regulatory commissions to combat monopoly power and promote competition. The reformers of the 1960s brought into existence an "imperial judiciary" in order to eliminate racial segregation and inequalities. To a much greater degree than in the earlier periods, in order to realize American values the reformers of the later periods had to create institutional mechanisms that threatened those values.

In a broader context, the actual course of institutional development is the product of the complex interaction of social, political, economic, and ideological forces. In the United States, any centralization of power produced by the expansion of governmental bureaucracy is mitigated by pluralistic forces that disperse power among bureaucratic agencies, congressional committees, and interest groups and that undermine efforts to subordinate lower-ranking executive officials to higher-ranking ones. Yet an increasingly sophisticated economy and active involvement in world affairs seem likely to create stronger needs for hierarchy, bureaucracy, centralization of power, expertise, big government specifically, and big organizations generally. In some way or another, society will respond to these needs, while still attempting to realize the values of the American Creed to which they are so contradictory. If history is against progress, for how long will progress resist history?

Acute tension between the requisites of development and the norms of ideology played a central role in the evolution of communist China during its first quarter century. China can avoid this conflict for as long as its leaders agree on the priority of development over revolution. In the United States, in contrast, no group of leaders can suppress by fiat the liberal values that have defined the nation's identity. The conflict between developmental need and ideological norm that characterized Mao's China in the 1960s and 1970s is likely to be duplicated in the American future unless other forces change, dilute, or eliminate the central ideals of the American Creed.

What is the probability of this happening? Do such forces exist? Several possibilities suggest themselves.

First, the core values of the Creed are products of the seventeenth and eighteenth centuries. Their roots lie in the English and American revolutionary experiences, in seventeenth-century Protestant moralism and eighteenth-century liberal rationalism. The historical dynamism and appeal of these ideals could naturally begin to fade after two centuries, particularly as those ideals come to be seen as increasingly irrelevant in a complex modern economy and a threatening international environment. In addition, to the extent that those ideals derive from Protestant sources, they must also be weakened by secular trends toward secularism that exist even in the United States. The four great awakenings that preceded and were associated with outbursts of creedal passion successively played less central roles in American society, that of the 1950s being very marginal in its impact compared to that of the 1740s. As religious passion weakens, how likely is the United States to sustain a firm commitment to its traditional values? Would an America without its Protestant core still be America?

Second, the social, economic, and cultural changes associated with the transition from industrial to postindustrial society could also give rise to new political values that would displace the traditional liberal values associated with bourgeois society and the rise of industrialism. In the 1960s and 1970s in both Europe and America, social scientists found evidence of the increasing prevalence of "postbourgeois" or "postmaterialist" values, particularly among younger cohorts. In somewhat similar vein, George

Lodge foresaw the displacement of Lockean, individualistic ideology in the United States by a "communitarian" ideology, resembling in many aspects the traditional Japanese collectivist approach.[12]

Third, as Hofstadter and others argued, the early twentieth-century immigration of Catholics, Orthodox, and Jews from central, eastern, and southern Europe introduced a different "ethic" into American cities. In the late twentieth century, the United States experienced its third major wave of postindependence immigration, composed largely of Puerto Ricans, Mexicans, Cubans, and others from Latin America and the Caribbean. Like their predecessors, the more recent immigrants could well introduce into American society political and social values markedly in contrast with those of Lockean liberalism. In these circumstances, the consensus on the latter could very likely be either disrupted or diluted.

Fourth, the historical function of the Creed in defining national identity could conceivably become less significant, and widespread belief in that Creed could consequently become less essential to the continued existence of the United States as a nation. Having been in existence as a functioning national society and political entity for over two hundred years, the United States may have less need of these ideals to define its national identity in the future. History, tradition, custom, culture, and a sense of shared experience such as other major nations have developed over the centuries could also come to define American identity, and the role of abstract ideals and values might be reduced. The *ideational* basis of national identity would be replaced by an *organic* one. "American exceptionalism" would wither. The United States would cease to be "a nation with the soul of a church" and would become a nation with the soul of a nation.

Some or all of these four factors could alter American political values so as to reduce the gap between these values and the reality of American institutional practice. Yet the likelihood of this occurring does not seem very high. Despite their seventeenth- and eighteenth-century origins, American values and ideals have demonstrated tremendous persistence and resiliency in the twentieth century. Defined vaguely and abstractly, these ideals have been relatively easily adapted to the needs of successive generations. The constant social change in the United States, indeed, underlies their permanence. Rising social, economic, and ethnic groups need to reinvoke and to reinvigorate those values in order to promote their own access to the rewards of American society. The shift in emphasis among values manifested by younger cohorts in the 1960s and 1970s does not necessarily mean the end of the traditional pattern. In many respects, the articulation of these values was, as it had been in the past, a protest against the perceived emergence of new centers of power. The yearning for "belonging and intellectual and esthetic self-fulfillment" found to exist among the younger cohorts of the 1960s and 1970s,[13] could, in fact, be interpreted as "a romantic, Luddite reaction against the bureaucratic and technological tendencies of postindustrialism." This confrontation between ideology and institutions easily fits into the well-established American pattern. Indeed, insofar as "the postindustrial society is more highly educated and more participant than American society in the past and insofar as American political institutions will be more bureaucratic and hierarchical than before, the conflict between ideology and institutions could be more intense than it has ever been."[14]

Similarly, the broader and longer-term impact of the Latin immigration of the 1950s, 1960s, and 1970s could reinforce the central role of the American Creed both as a way of legitimizing claims to political, economic, and social equality and also as the indispensable element in defining national identity. The children and grandchildren of the European immigrants of the early twentieth century in due course became ardent adherents to traditional American middle-class values. In addition, the more culturally pluralistic the nation becomes, particularly if cultural pluralism encompasses linguistic pluralism, the more essential the political values of the Creed become in defining what it is that Americans have in common. At some point, traditional American ideals—liberty, equality, individualism, democracy—may lose their appeal and join the ideas of racial inequality, the divine right of kings, and the dictatorship of the proletariat on the ideological scrap heap of history. There is, however, little to suggest that this will be a twentieth-century happening.

If the IvI gap remains a central feature of American politics, the question then becomes: What changes, if any, may occur in the traditional pattern of responses to this gap? Three broad possibilities exist.

First, the previous pattern of response could continue. If the periodicity of the past prevails, a major sustained creedal passion period will occur in the second and third decades of the twenty-first century. In the interim, moralism, cynicism, complacency, and hypocrisy will all be invoked by different Americans in different ways in their efforts to live with the gap. The tensions resulting from the gap will remain and perhaps increase in intensity, but their consequences will not be significantly more serious than they have been in the past.

Second, the cycle of response could stabilize to a greater degree than it has in the past. Americans could acquire a greater understanding of their case of cognitive dissonance and through this understanding come to live with their dilemma on somewhat easier terms than they have in the past, in due course evolving a more complex but also more coherent and constant response to this problem.

Third, the oscillations among the responses could intensify in such a way as to threaten to destroy both ideals and institutions.

In terms of the future stability of the American political system, the first possibility may be the most likely and the second the most hopeful, but the third is clearly the most dangerous. Let us focus on the third.

Lacking any concept of the state, lacking for most of its history both the centralized authority and the bureaucratic apparatus of the European state, the American polity has historically been a weak polity. It was designed to be so, and traditional inheritance and social environment combined for years to support the framers' intentions. In the twentieth century, foreign threats and domestic economic and social needs have generated pressures to develop stronger, more authoritative decision-making and decision-implementing institutions. Yet the continued presence of deeply felt moralistic sentiments among major groups in American society could continue to ensure weak and divided government, devoid of authority and unable to deal satisfactorily with the economic, social, and foreign challenges confronting the nation. Intensification of this conflict between history and progress could give rise to increasing frustration and increasingly violent oscillations between moralism and cynicism. American moralism ensures that government will never be truly efficacious; the realities of power ensure that government will never be truly democratic.

This situation could lead to a two-phase dialectic involving intensified efforts to reform government, followed by intensified frustration when those efforts produce not progress in a liberal-democratic direction, but obstacles to meeting perceived functional needs. The weakening of government in an effort to reform it could lead eventually to strong demands for the replacement of the weakened and ineffective institutions by more authoritarian structures more effectively designed to meet historical needs. Given the perversity of reform, moralistic extremism in the pursuit of liberal democracy could generate a strong tide toward authoritarian efficiency. "The truth is that," as Plato observed, "in the constitution of society . . . any excess brings about an equally violent reaction. So the only outcome of too much freedom is likely to be excessive subjection, in the state or in the individual; which means that the culmination of liberty in democracy is precisely what prepares the way for the cruelest extreme of servitude under a despot."[15]

American political ideals are a useful instrument not only for those who wish to improve American political institutions but also for those who wish to destroy them. Liberal reformers, because they believe in the ideals, attempt to change institutions to approximate those ideals more closely. The enemies of liberalism, because they oppose both liberal ideals and liberal institutions, attempt to use the former to undermine the latter. For them, the IvI gap is a made-to-order opportunity. The effectiveness of liberal-democratic institutions can be discredited by highlighting their shortcomings compared to the ideals on which they are supposedly modeled. This is a common response of critical foreigners to the American polity, but this approach is not limited to liberalism's foreign enemies. The leading theorists of the Southern Enlightenment, for instance, took great delight in describing the inequality and repression of the Northern "wage slave" system not because they believed in equality and liberty for all workers but because they wished to discredit the economy that was threatening the future of Southern slavery. "Their obvious purpose [was] to belabor the North rather than to redeem it."[16]

Those who have battered liberal institutions with the stick of liberal ideals have, however, more often been on the Left than on the Right. There is a reason for this, which is well illustrated by the attitudes of conservatives, liberals, and revolutionaries toward political equality. The traditional conservative opposes equality. He may perceive American political institutions as embodying more equality than he thinks desirable. In this case, he normally opts out of American society in favor of either internal or external emigration. The traditional conservative may also perceive and take comfort in the realities of power and inequality that exist in the United States behind the façade and rhetoric of equality. The liberal defender of American institutions embraces the hypocritical response: he believes that inequality doesn't exist and that it shouldn't exist. Both the perceptive conservative and the liberal hypocrite are thus, in some sense, standpatters, satisfied with the status quo, but only because they have very different perceptions of what that status quo is and very different views as to whether equality is good or bad. The ability of the traditional conservative and the liberal hypocrite to cooperate in defense of the status quo is hence very limited: neither will buy the other's arguments. In addition, articulate traditional conservatives have been few and far between on the American political landscape, in large part because their values are so contrary to those of the American Creed. (See Table 6.)

Table 6. Political beliefs and political equality.

	Traditional conservative	Liberal		Marxist revolutionary
		Hypocrite	Moralist	
Perception of political equality	Doesn't exist	Does exist	Doesn't exist	Doesn't exist
Judgment on political equality	Bad	Good	Good	Good
		Standpatters	Radicals	

On the other side of the political spectrum, a very different situation exists. Like the hypocritical liberal, the moralist liberal believes that inequality is bad. Unlike the hypocrite, however, he perceives that inequality exists in American institutions and hence he vigorously devotes himself to reform in an effort to eliminate it. To his left, however, the Marxist revolutionary has views and beliefs that, on the surface at least, coincide with those of the moralistic liberal. The Marxist revolutionary holds inequality to be bad, sees it as pervasively present in existing institutions, and attacks it and them vigorously. At a deeper and more philosophical level, the Marxist revolutionary may believe in the necessity of the violent overthrow of the capitalist order, the dictatorship of the proletariat, and a disciplined Leninist party as the revolutionary vanguard. If he blatantly articulates these beliefs, he is relegated to the outermost fringes of American politics and foreswears any meaningful ideological or political influence. It is, moreover, in the best Leninist tradition to see reform as the potential catalyst of revolution.[17] Consequently, major incentives exist for the Marxist revolutionary to emphasize not what divides him from the liberal consensus but what unites him with liberal reformers, that is, his perception of inequality and his belief in equality. With this common commitment to reform, liberal moralist and Marxist revolutionary can cooperate in their attack on existing institutions, even though in the long run one wants to make them work better and the other wants to overthrow them.

The role of Marxism in the consensus society of America thus differs significantly from its role in the ideologically pluralistic societies of western Europe. There the differences between liberal and Marxist goals and appeals are sharply delineated, the two philosophies are embraced by different constituencies and parties, and the conflict between them is unceasing. In the United States, the prevalence of liberalism means a consensus on the standards by which the institutions of society should be judged, and Marxism has no choice but to employ those standards in its own cause. Philosophical differences are blurred as reform liberalism and revolutionary Marxism blend into a nondescript but politically relevant radicalism that serves the immediate interests of both. This convergence, moreover, exists at the individual as well as the societal level: particular individuals bring together in their own minds elements of both liberal re-formism and revolutionary Marxism. American radicals easily perceive the gap between American ideals and American institutions; they do not easily perceive the conflict between reform liberalism and revolutionary Marxism. With shared immediate goals, these two sets of philosophically distinct ideas often coexist in the same mind.

This common ground of liberal reformer and revolutionary Marxist in favor of radical change contrasts with the distance between the liberal hypocrite and the traditional conservative. The hypocrite can defend American institutions only by claiming they are something that they are not. The conservative can defend them only by articulating values that most Americans abhore. The Marxist subscribes to the liberal consensus in order to subvert liberal institutions; the conservative rejects the liberal consensus in order to defend those institutions. The combined effect of both is to strengthen the attack on the established order. For, paradoxi-cally, the conservative who defends American institutions with conserv-ative arguments (that they are good because they institutionalize political inequality) weakens those institutions at least as much as the radical who attacks them for the same reason. The net impact of the difficulties and divisions among the standpatters and the converging unity of the liberal and Marxist radicals is to enhance the threat to American political insti-tutions posed by those political ideas whose continued vitality is indispen-sable to their survival.

Two things are thus clear. American political institutions are more open, liberal, and democratic than those of any other major society now or in the past. If Americans ever abandon or destroy these institutions, they are likely to do so in the name of their liberal democratic ideals. Innoculated against the appeal of foreign ideas, America has only to fear her own.

America versus the World?

The IvI gap poses two significant issues with respect to the relations between the United States and the rest of the world. First, what are the implications of the gap for American institutions and processes concerned with foreign relations and national security? To what extent should those institutions and processes conform to American liberal, individualistic, democratic values? Second, what are the implications of the gap for American policy toward other societies? To what extent should the United States attempt to make the institutions and policies of other societies conform to American values? For much of its history when it was relatively isolated from the rest of the world, as it was between 1815 and 1914, the United States did not have to grapple seriously with these problems. In the mid-twentieth century, however, the United States became deeply, complexly, and seemingly inextricably involved with the other countries of the world. That involvement brought to the fore and gave new significance and urgency to these two long-standing and closely related issues. These issues are closely related because efforts to reduce the IvI gap in the institutions and processes of American foreign relations reduce the ability of the United States to exercise power in international affairs, including its ability to reduce that gap between American values and foreign institutions and policies. Conversely, efforts to encourage foreign institutions and practices to conform to American ideals require the expansion of American power and thus make it more difficult for American institutions and policies to conform to those ideals.

Foreign-Policy Institutions

The relation of its institutions and processes concerned with foreign relations to the ideals and values of its political ideology is a more serious problem for the United States than for most other societies. The differences between the United States and western Europe in this respect are particularly marked. First, the ideological pluralism of western European societies does not provide a single set of political principles by which to judge foreign-policy institutions and practices. Those, as well as other institutions and practices, benefit in terms of legitimacy as a result of the varied strands of conservative, liberal, Christian Democratic, and Marxist political thought that have existed in western European societies. Second, and more important, in most European societies at least an embryonic national community and, in large measure, a national state existed before the emergence of ideologies. So also did the need to conduct foreign relations and to protect the security of the national community and the state. National security bureaucracies, military forces, foreign offices, intelligence services, internal security and police systems were all givens when ideologies emerged in the eighteenth and nineteenth centuries. Although the ideologies undoubtedly had some implications for and posed some demands on these institutions, their proponents tended to recognize the prior claims of these institutions reflecting the needs of the national community in a world of competing national communities. European democratic regimes thus accept a security apparatus that exists, in large part, outside the normal processes of democratic politics, and that represents and defends the continuing interests of the community and the state irrespective of the ideologies that may from one time to another dominate its politics.

In Europe ideology—or rather, ideologies—thus followed upon and developed within the context of a previously existing national community and state. In America, ideology in the form of the principles of the American Creed existed before the formation of a national community and political system. These principles defined the identity of the community when there were no institutions for dealing with the other countries of the world. It was assumed that the foreign-policy institutions, like other political institutions, would reflect the basic values of the preexisting and overwhelmingly preponderant ideology. Yet precisely these institutions— foreign and intelligence services, military and police forces—have functional imperatives that conflict most sharply and dramatically with the liberal-democratic values of the American Creed. The essence of the Creed is opposition to power and to concentrated authority. This leads to efforts to minimize the resources of power, such as arms, to restrict the effectiveness of specialized bureaucratic hierarchies, and to limit the authority of the executive over foreign policy. This conflict manifests itself dramatically in the perennial issue concerning the role of standing armies and professional military forces in a liberal society. For much of its history, the United States was able to avoid the full implications of this conflict because its geographic position permitted it to follow a policy of "extirpation"—that is, almost abolishing military forces and relegating those that did exist to the distant social and geographic extremities of society.[18] Similarly, the United States did not seem to need and did not have an intelligence service, a professional foreign service, or a national police force.

In the twentieth century the impossibility of sustained isolation led the United States to develop all these institutions. Much more so than those in western Europe, however, these institutions have existed in uneasy and fundamentally incompatible coexistence with the values of the prevailing ideology. This incompatibility became acute after World War II when the country's global role and responsibilities made it necessary for the government to develop and to maintain such institutions on a large scale and to accord them a central role in its foreign policy. During the 1950s and early 1960s Americans tended to be blissfully complacent and to ignore the broad IvI gap that this created in the foreign-policy and defense sectors of their national life. At the same time, various theories—such as Kennan's ideal of the detached professional diplomat and Huntington's concept of "objective civilian control"—were developed to justify the insulation of these institutions from the political demands of a liberal society.[19] In the end, however, the liberal imperatives could not be avoided, and the late 1960s and 1970s saw overwhelming political pressure to make foreign-policy and security institutions conform to the requirements of the liberal ideology. In a powerful outburst of creedal passion, Americans embarked on crusades against the CIA and FBI, defense spending, the use of military force abroad, the military-industrial complex, and the imperial Presidency, attempting to expose, weaken, dismantle, or abolish the institutions that protected their liberal society against foreign threats. They reacted with outraged moralistic self-criticism to their government engaging in the type of activities—deception, violence, abuse of individual rights—to protect their society that other countries accept as a matter of course.

This penchant of Americans for challenging and undermining the authority of their political institutions, including those concerned with the foreign relations and security of the country, produces mixed and confused reactions on the part of Europeans and other non-Americans. Their initial reaction to a Pentagon Papers case, Watergate, or investigation of CIA is often one of surprise, amazement, bewilderment. "What are you Americans up to and why are you doing this to yourselves?" A second reaction, which often follows the first, is grudging admiration for a society that takes its principles so seriously and has such effective procedures for attempting to realize them. This is often accompanied by somewhat envious and wistful comments on the contrast between this situation and the paramountcy of state authority in their own country. Finally, a third reaction often follows, expressing deep concern about the impact that the creedal upheaval will have on the ability of the United States to conduct its foreign policy and to protect its friends and allies.

This last concern over whether its liberal values will permit the United States to maintain the material resources, governmental institutions, and political will to defend its interests in the world becomes more relevant, not just as a result of the inextricable involvement of the United States in world affairs but also because of the changes in the countries with which the United States will be primarily involved. During the first part of the twentieth century, American external relations were largely focused on western Europe, where in most countries significant political groups held political values similar to American values. Even more important, lodged deeply in the consciousness of western European statesmen and intellectuals was the thought, impregnated there by Tocqueville if by no one else, that American political values in some measure embodied the wave of the future, that what America believed in would at some point be what the entire civilized world would believe in. This sympathy, partial or latent as it may have been, nonetheless gave the United States a diplomatic resource of some significance. European societies might resent American moral or moralistic loftiness, but they knew and the Americans knew that the moral values Americans set forth (sincerely or hypocritically) would have a resonance in their own societies and could at times be linked up with social and political movements in their societies that would be impossible for them to ignore.

In the mid-twentieth century the widespread belief in democratic values among younger Germans and, to a lesser degree, younger Japanese provided some support for the convergence thesis. At a more general level, however, the sense that America was the future of Europe weakened considerably. More important, in the late twentieth century, the countries with which the United States was having increasing interactions, both competitive and cooperative, were the Soviet Union, China, and Japan. The partial sense of identification and of future convergence that existed between the United States and Europe are absent in American relations with these three countries. Like the United States, these countries have a substantial degree of consensus or homogeneity in social and political values and ideology. The contents of their consensuses, however, differ significantly from that of the United States. In all three societies, the stress, in one form or another, is on the pervasiveness of inequality in human relationships, the "sanctity of authority,"[20] the subordination of the individual to the group and the state, the dubious legitimacy of dissent or challenges to the powers that be. Japan, to be sure, developed a working democracy after World War II, but its long-standing values stressing hierarchy, vertical ranking, and submissiveness leave some degree of "disharmony" that has resemblances to, but is just the reverse of, what prevails in American society. The dominant ideas in all three countries stand in dramatic contrast to American ideas of openness, liberalism, equality, individual rights, and freedom to dissent. In the Soviet Union, China, and Japan, the prevailing political values and social norms reinforce the authority of the central political institutions of society and enhance their ability to compete with other societies. In the United States the prevailing norms, insofar as Americans take them seriously, undermine and weaken the power and authority of government and detract, at times seriously, from its ability to compete internationally. In the small world of the West, Americans were beguiling cousins; in the larger world that includes the East, Americans often seem naïve strangers. Given the "disharmonic" element in the American political system—the continuing challenge, latent or overt, which lies in the American mind to the authority of American government—how well will the United States be able to conduct its affairs in this league of powers to whose historical traditions basic American values are almost entirely alien?

Foreign-Policy Goals

In the eyes of Americans, not only should their foreign-policy institutions be structured and function so as to reflect liberal values, but American foreign policy should also be substantively directed to the promotion of those values in the external environment. This gives a distinctive cast to the American role in the world. In a famous phrase, Viscount Palmerston once said that Britain did not have permanent friends or enemies, it only had permanent interests. Like Britain and other countries, the United States also has interests, defined in terms of power, wealth, and security, some of which are sufficiently enduring as to be thought of as permanent. As a founded society, however, the United States also has distinctive political principles and values that define its national identity. These principles provide a second set of goals and a second set of standards—in addition to those of national interest—by which to shape the goals and judge the success of American foreign policy.

This heritage, this transposition of the IvI gap into foreign policy, again distinguishes the United States from other societies. Western European states clearly do not reject the relevance of morality and political ideology to the conduct of foreign policy. They do, however, see the goal of foreign policy as the advancement of the major and continuing security and economic interests of their state. Political principles provide limits and parameters to foreign policy but not its goals. As a result, European public debate over morality versus power in foreign policy has, except in rare instances, not played the role that it has in the United States. That issue does come up with the foreign policy of communist states and has been discussed at length, in terms of the conflict of ideology and national interest, in analyses of Soviet foreign policy. The conflict has been less significant there than in the United States for three reasons. First, an authoritarian political system precludes public discussion of the issue. Since the 1920s debate of Trotsky versus Stalin over permanent revolution, there has been no overt domestic criticism of Soviet foreign policy as at one time being too power-oriented or at another time being too ideologically oriented. Second, Marxist-Leninist ideology distinguishes between basic doctrine, on the one hand, and strategy and tactics, on the other. The former does not change; the latter is adapted to specific historical circumstances. The twists and turns in the party line can always be justified as ideologically necessary at that particular point in time to achieve the long-run goals of communism, even though they may in fact be motivated primarily by national interests. American political values, on the other hand, are usually thought of as universally valid, and pragmatism is seen not as a means of implementing them in particular circumstances but rather as a means of abandoning them. Third, Soviet leaders and the leaders of other communist states that pursue their own foreign policies can and do, when they wish, simply ignore ideology when they desire to pursue particular national interest goals.

For Americans, however, foreign-policy goals should reflect not only the security interests of the nation and the economic interests of key groups within the nation but also the political values and principles that define American identity. If these values do define foreign-policy goals, then that policy is morally justified, the opponents of that policy at home and abroad are morally illegitimate, and all efforts must be directed toward overcoming the opponents and achieving the goals. The prevailing American approach to foreign policy thus has not been that of Stephen Decatur ("Our country, right or wrong!") but that of Carl Schurz ("Our country, right or wrong! When right, to be kept right; when wrong, to be put right!"). To Americans, achieving this convergence between self-interest and morality has appeared as no easy task. Hence, the recurring tendencies in American history either to retreat to minimum relations with the rest of the world and thus avoid the problem of reconciling the pursuit of self-interest with the adherence to principle in a corrupt and hostile environment, or the opposite solution, to set forth on a "crusade" to purify the world, to bring it into accordance with American principles and, in the process, to expand American power and thus protect the national interest.

This practice of judging the behavior of one's country and one's government by external standards of right and wrong has been responsible for the often substantial opposition to the wars in which the United States has engaged. The United States will only respond with unanimity to a war in which both national security and political principle are clearly at stake. In the two hundred years after the Revolution, only one war, World War II, met this criterion, and this was the only war to which there was no significant domestic opposition articulated in terms of the extent to which the goals of the war and the way in which it was conducted deviated from the basic principles of the American Creed. In this sense, World War II was, for the United States, the "perfect war"; every other war has been an imperfect war in that elements of the American people have objected to it because it did not seem to accord with American principles. As strange as it may seem to people of other societies, Americans have had no trouble conceiving of their government fighting an "un-American" war.

The extent to which the American liberal creed prevails over power considerations can lead to hypocritical and rather absolutist positions on policy. As Seymour Martin Lipset pointed out, if wars should only be fought for moral purposes, then the opponents against which they are fought must be morally evil and hence total war must be waged against them and unconditional surrender exacted from them. If a war is not morally legitimate, then the leaders conducting it must be morally evil and opposition to it, in virtually any form, is not only morally justified but morally obligatory. It is no coincidence that the country that has most tended to think of wars as crusades is also the country with the strongest record of conscientious objection to war.[21]

The effort to use American foreign policy to promote American values abroad raises a central issue. There is a clear difference between political action to make American political practices conform to American political values, and political action to make *foreign* political practices conform to American values. Americans can legitimately attempt to reduce the gap between American institutions and American values, but in terms of their values can they legitimately attempt to reduce the gap between other people's institutions and American values? The answer is not self-evident.

The argument for a negative response to this question can be made on at least four grounds. First, it is morally wrong for the United States to attempt to shape the institutions of other societies. Those institutions should reflect the values and behavior of the people in those societies. To intrude from outside is imperialism or colonialism, which also violates American values. Second, it is practically difficult and in most cases impossible for the United States to influence significantly the institutional development of other societies. The task is simply beyond American knowledge, skill, and resources. To attempt to do so will often be counterproductive. Third, any effort to shape the domestic institutions of other societies needlessly irritates and antagonizes other governments and hence will complicate and often endanger the achievement of other, more important foreign-policy goals, particularly in the areas of national security and economic well-being. Fourth, to influence the political development of other societies would require an enormous expansion of the military power and economic resources of the American government. This, in turn, would pose dangers to the operation of democratic government within the United States.

A "yes" answer to this question can, on the other hand, also be justified on four grounds. First, if other people's institutions pose direct threats to the viability of American institutions and values in the United States, an American effort to change those institutions would be justifiable in terms of self-defense. Whether or not foreign institutions do pose such a direct threat in any given circumstance is, however, no easy question to answer. Even in the case of Nazi Germany in 1940, there were widely differing opinions in the United States. After World War II opinion was also divided as to whether Soviet institutions, as distinct from Soviet policies, threatened the United States.

Second, the direct-threat argument can be generalized to the proposition that authoritarian regimes in any form and on any continent pose a potential threat to the viability of liberal institutions and values in the United States. A liberal-democratic system, it can be argued, can only be secure in a world system of similarly constituted states. In the past this argument did not play a central role because of the extent to which the United States was geographically isolated from differently constituted states. The world is, however, becoming smaller. Given the increasing interactions among societies and the emergence of transnational institutions operating in many societies, the pressures toward convergence among political systems are likely to become more intense. Interdependence may be incompatible with coexistence. In this case, the world, like the United States in the nineteenth century or western Europe in the twentieth century, will not be able to exist half-slave and half-free. Hence, the survival of democratic institutions and values at home will depend upon their adoption abroad.

Third, American efforts to make other people's institutions conform to American values would be justified to the extent that the other people supported those values. Such support has historically been much more prevalent in western Europe and Latin America than it has in Asia and Africa, but some support undoubtedly exists in almost every society for liberty, equality, democracy, and the rights of the individual. Americans could well feel justified in supporting and helping those individuals, groups, and institutions in other societies who share their belief in these values. At the same time, it would also be appropriate for them to be aware that those values could be realized in other societies through institutions significantly different from those that exist in the United States.

Fourth, American efforts to make other people's institutions conform to American values could be justified on the grounds that those values are universally valid and universally applicable, whether or not most people in other societies believe in them. For Americans not to believe in the universal validity of American values could, indeed, lead to a moral relativism: liberty and democracy are not inherently better than any other political values; they just happen to be those that for historical and cultural reasons prevail in America. This relativistic position runs counter to the strong elements of moral absolutism and messianism that are part of American history and culture, and hence the argument for moral relativism may not wash in the United States for relativistic reasons. In addition, the argument can be made that some element of belief in the universal validity of a set of political ideals is necessary to arouse the energy, support, and passion to defend those ideals and the institutions modeled on them in American society.

Historically, Americans have generally believed in the universal validity of their values. At the end of World War II, when Americans forced Germany and Japan to be free, they did not stop to ask if liberty and democracy were what the German and Japanese people wanted. Americans implicitly assumed that their values were valid and applicable and that they would, at the very least, be morally negligent if they did not insist that Germany and Japan adopt political institutions reflecting those values. Belief in the universal validity of those values obviously reinforces and reflects those hypocritical elements of the American tradition that stress its role as a redeemer nation and lead it to attempt to impose its values and, often, its institutions on other societies. These tendencies may, however, be constrained by a recognition that although American values may be universally valid, they need not be universally and totally applicable at all times and in all places.

Americans expect their institutions and policies devoted to external relations to reflect liberal standards and principles. So also, in large measure, do non-Americans. Both American citizens and others hold the United States to standards that they do not generally apply to other countries. People expect France, for instance, to pursue its national self-interests, economic, military, and political, with cold disregard for ideologies and values. But their expectations with respect to the United States are very different: people accept with a shrug behavior on the part of France that would generate surprise, consternation, and outrage if perpetrated by the United States. "Europe accepts the idea that America is a country with a difference, from whom it is reasonable to demand an exceptionally altruistic standard of behaviour; it feels perfectly justified in pouring obloquy on shortcomings from this ideal; and also, perhaps inevitably, it seems to enjoy every example of a fall from grace which contemporary America provides."[22]

This double standard is implicit acknowledgment of the seriousness with which Americans attempt to translate their principles into practice. It also provides a ready weapon to foreign critics of the United States just as it does to domestic ones. For much of its history, racial injustice, economic inequality, and political and religious intolerance were familiar elements in the American landscape, and the contrast between them and the articulated ideals of the American Creed furnished abundant ammunition to generations of European critics. "Anti-Americanism is in this form a protest, not against Americanism, but against its apparent failure."[23] This may be true on the surface. But it is also possible that failure —that is, the persistence of the IvI gap in American institutions and policies—furnishes the excuse and the opportunity for hostile foreign protest, and that the true target of the protest is Americanism itself.

Power and Liberty: The Myth of American Repression

The pattern of American involvement in the world has often been interpreted as the outcome of these conflicting pulls of national interest and power on the one hand, and political morality and principles on the other. Various scholars have phrased the dichotomy in various ways: self-interest versus ideals, power versus morality, realism versus utopianism, pragmatism versus principle, historical realism versus rationalist idealism, Washington versus Wilson.[24] Almost all, however, have assumed the dichotomy to be real and have traced the relative importance over the years of national interest and morality in shaping American foreign policy. It is, for instance, argued that during the Federalist years, realism or power considerations were generally preponderant, whereas during the first four decades of the twentieth century moral considerations and principles came to be uppermost in the minds of American policy makers. After World War II, a significant group of writers and thinkers on foreign policy—including Reinhold Niebuhr, George Kennan, Hans Morgenthau, Walter Lippmann, and Robert Osgood—expounded a "new realism" and criticized the moralistic, legalistic, "utopian," Wilsonian approaches, which they claimed had previously prevailed in the conduct of American foreign relations. The new realism reached its apotheosis in the central role played by the balance of power in the theory and practice of Henry Kissinger. Foreign policy, he said, "should be directed toward affecting the foreign policy" of other societies; it should not be "the principal goal of American foreign policy to transform the domestic structures of societies with which we deal."[25]

In the 1970s, however, the new realism of the 1950s and 1960s was challenged by a "new moralism." The pendulum that had swung in one direction after World War II swung far over to the other side. This shift was one of the most significant consequences of Vietnam, Watergate, and the democratic surge and creedal passion of the 1960s. It represented the displacement onto the external world of the moralism that had been earlier directed inward against American institutions. It thus represented the first signs of a return to the hypocritical response to the gap between American values and American institutions. The new moralism manifested itself first in congressional action, with the addition to the foreign assistance act of Title IX in 1966 and human rights conditions in the early 1970s. In 1976 Jimmy Carter vigorously criticized President Ford for believing "that there is little room for morality in foreign affairs, and that we must put self-interest above principle."[26] As President, Carter moved human rights to a central position in American foreign relations.

The lines between the moralists and the realists were thus clearly drawn but on one point they were agreed: they both believed that the conflict between morality and self-interest, or ideals and realism, was a real one. In some respects it was. In other respects, particularly when it was formulated in terms of a conflict between liberty and power, it was not. As so defined, the dichotomy was false. It did not reflect an accurate understanding of the real choices confronting American policy makers in dealing with the external world. It derived rather from the transposition of the assumptions of the antipower ethic to American relations with the rest of the world. From the earliest years of their society, Americans have perceived a conflict between imperatives of governmental power and the liberty and rights of the individual. Because power and liberty are antithetical at home, they are also assumed to be antithetical abroad. Hence, the pursuit of power by the American government abroad must threaten liberty abroad even as a similar pursuit of power at home would threaten liberty there. The contradiction in American society between American power and American liberty at home is projected into a contradiction between American power and foreign liberty abroad.

During the 1960s and 1970s this belief led many intellectuals to propagate what can perhaps best be termed "the myth of American repression" —that is, the view that American involvement in the politics of other societies is almost invariably hostile to liberty and supportive of repression in those societies. The United States, as Hans Morgenthau put it, is "repression's friend": "With unfailing consistency, we have since the end of the Second World War intervened on behalf of conservative and fascist repression against revolution and radical reform. In an age when societies are in a revolutionary or prerevolutionary stage, we have become the foremost counterrevolutionary status quo power on earth. Such a policy can only lead to moral and political disaster."[27] This statement, like the arguments generally of those intellectuals supporting the myth of American repression, suffers from two basic deficiencies.

First, it confuses support for the left with opposition to repression. In this respect, it represents another manifestation of the extent to which similarity in immediate objectives can blur the line between liberals and revolutionaries. Yet those who support "revolution and radical reform" in other countries seldom have any greater concern for liberty and human dignity than those who support "conservative and fascist repression." In fact, if it is a choice between rightist and communist dictatorships, there are at least three good reasons in terms of liberty to prefer the former to the latter. (1) The suppression of liberty in right-wing authoritarian regimes is almost always less pervasive than it is in left-wing totalitarian ones. In the 1960s and 1970s, for instance, infringements of human rights in South Korea received extensive coverage in the American media, in part because there were in South Korea journalists, church groups, intellectuals, and opposition political leaders who could call attention to those infringements. The absence of comparable reports about the infringements of human rights in North Korea was evidence not of the absence of repression in that country but of its totality. (2) Right-wing dictatorships are, the record shows, less permanent than left-wing dictatorships; Portugal, Spain, and Greece are but three examples of right-wing dictatorships that were replaced by democratic regimes. As of 1980, however, no communist system had been replaced by a democratic regime. (3) As a result of the global competition between the United States and the Soviet Union, right-wing regimes are normally more susceptible to American and other Western influence than left-wing dictatorships, and such influence is overwhelmingly on the side of liberty.

This latter point goes to the other central fallacy of the myth of American repression as elaborated by Morgenthau and others. Their picture of the world of the 1960s and 1970s was dominated by the image of an America that was overwhelmingly powerful and overwhelmingly repressive. In effect, they held an updated belief in the "illusion of American omnipotence" that attributed the evil in other societies to the machinations of the Pentagon, the CIA, and American business. Their image of America was, however, defective in both dimensions. During the 1960s and 1970s American power relative to that of other governments and societies declined significantly. By the mid-seventies the ability of the United States to influence what was going on in other societies was but a pale shadow of what it had been a quarter-century earlier. When it had an effect, however, the overall effect of American power on other societies was to further liberty, pluralism, and democracy. The conflict between American power and American principles virtually disappears when it is applied to the American impact on other societies. In that case, the very factors that give rise to the consciousness of a gap between ideal and reality also limit in practice the extent of that gap. The United States is, in practice, the freest, most liberal, most democratic country in the world with far better institutionalized protections for the rights of its citizens than any other society. As a consequence, any increase in the power or influence of the United States in world affairs generally results—not inevitably, but far more often than not—in the promotion of liberty and human rights in the world. The expansion of American power is not synonymous with the expansion of liberty, but a significant correlation exists between the rise and fall of American power in the world and the rise and fall of liberty and democracy in the world.

The single biggest extension of democratic liberties in the history of the world came at the end of World War II, when stable democratic regimes were inaugurated in defeated Axis countries: Germany, Japan, Italy, and, as a former part of Germany, Austria. In the early 1980s these countries had a population of over two hundred million, and included the third and fourth largest economies in the world. The imposition of democracy on these countries was almost entirely the work of the United States. In Germany and Japan, in particular, the United States government played a major role in designing democratic institutions. As a result of American determination and power, the former Axis countries were "forced to be free."[28] Conversely, the modest steps taken toward democracy and liberty in Poland, Czechoslovakia, and Hungary were quickly reversed and Stalinist repression instituted, once it became clear that the United States was not able to project its power into eastern Europe. If World War II had ended in something less than total victory, or if the United States had played a less significant role in bringing about that victory (as was, indeed, the case east of the Elbe) these transitions to democracy in central Europe and eastern Asia would not have occurred. But—with the partial exception of South Korea—where American armies marched, democracy followed in their train.

The stability of democracy in these countries during the quarter-century after World War II reflected, in large part, the extent to which the institutions and practices imposed by the United States found a favorable social and political climate in which to take root. The continued American political, economic, and military presence in western Europe and eastern Asia was, however, also indispensable to this democratic success. At any time after World War II the withdrawal of American military guarantees and military forces from these areas would have had a most unsettling and perhaps devastating effect on the future of democracy in central Europe and Japan.

In the early years of the Cold War, American influence was employed to ensure the continuation of democratic government in Italy and to promote free elections in Greece. In both cases, the United States had twin interests in the domestic politics of these countries: to create a system of stable democratic government and to ensure the exclusion of communist parties from power. Since in both cases the communist parties did not have the support of anything remotely resembling a majority of the population, the problem of what to do if a party committed to abolishing democracy gains power through democratic means was happily avoided. With American support, democracy survived in Italy and was sustained for a time in Greece. In addition, the American victory in World War II provided the stimulus in Turkey for one of the rarest events in political history: the peaceful self-transformation of an authoritarian, one-party system into a democratic, competitive party system.

In Latin America, the rise and fall of democratic regimes also coincided with the rise and fall of American influence. In the second and third decades of this century, American intervention in Nicaragua, Haiti, and the Dominican Republic produced the freest elections and the most open political competition in the history of those countries. In these countries, as in others in Central America and the Caribbean, American influence in support of free elections was usually exerted in response to the protests of opposition groups against the repressive actions of their own governments and as a result of American fears that revolution or civil war would occur if significant political and social forces were denied equal opportunity to participate in the political process. The American aim, as Theodore Wright made clear in his comprehensive study, was to "promote political stability by supporting free elections" rather than strengthening military dictatorships. In its interventions in eight Caribbean and Central American countries between 1900 and 1933, the United States acted on the assumption that "the only way both to prevent revolutions and to determine whether they are justified if they do break out, is to guarantee free elections."[29] In Cuba, the effect of the Platt Amendment and American interventions was "to pluralize the Cuban political system" by fostering "the rise and entrenchment of opposition groups" and by multiplying "the sources of political power so that no single group, not even the government, could impose its will on society or the economy for very long . . . The spirit and practices of liberalism—competitive and unregulated political, economic, religious, and social life—overwhelmed a pluralized Cuba."[30] The interventions by United States Marines in Haiti, Nicaragua, the Dominican Republic, and elsewhere in these years often bore striking resemblances to the interventions by Federal marshals in the conduct of elections in the American South in the 1960s: registering voters, protecting against electoral violence, ensuring a free vote and an honest count.

Direct intervention by the American government in Central America and the Caribbean came to at least a temporary end in the early 1930s. Without exception, the result was a shift in the direction of more dictatorial regimes. It had taken American power to impose even the most modest aspects of democracy in these societies. When American intervention ended, democracy ended. For the Caribbean and Central America, the era of the Good Neighbor was also the era of the bad tyrant. The efforts of the United States to be the former give a variety of unsavory local characters—Trujillo, Somoza, Batista—the opportunity to be the latter.

In the years after World War II, American attention and activity were primarily directed toward Europe and Asia. Latin America was, by and large, neglected. This situation began to change toward the late 1950s, and it dramatically shifted after Castro's seizure of power in Cuba. In the early 1960s Latin America became the focus of large-scale economic aid programs, military training and assistance programs, propaganda efforts, and repeated attention by the President and other high-level American officials. Under the Alliance for Progress, American power was to be used to promote and sustain democratic government and greater social equity in the rest of the Western Hemisphere. This high point in the exercise of United States power in Latin America coincided with the high point of democracy in Latin America. This period witnessed "the Twilight of the Tyrants": it was the age in which at one point all but one of the ten South American countries (Paraguay) had some semblance of democratic government.[31]

Obviously, the greater prevalence of democratic regimes during these years was not exclusively a product of United States policy and power. Yet the latter certainly played a role. The democratic governments that had emerged in Colombia and Venezuela in the late 1950s were carefully nurtured with money and praise. Strenuous efforts were made to head off the attempts of both left-wing guerrillas and right-wing military officers to overthrow Betancourt in Venezuela and to ensure the orderly transition to an elected successor for the first time in the history of that country. After thirty years in which "the U.S. government was less interested and involved in Dominican affairs" than at any other time in history—a period coinciding with Trujillo's domination of the Dominican Republic—American opposition to that dictator slowly mounted in the late 1950s. After his assassination in 1961, "the United States engaged in the most massive intervention in the internal affairs of a Latin American state since the inauguration of the Good Neighbor Policy."[32] The United States prevented a comeback by Trujillo family members, launched programs to promote economic and social welfare, and acted to ensure democratic liberties and competitive elections. The latter, held in December 1962, resulted in the election of Juan Bosch as president. When the military moved against Bosch the following year, American officials first tried to head off the coup, and then, after its success, attempted to induce the junta to return quickly to constitutional procedures. But, by that point, American "leverage and influence [with the new government] were severely limited," and the only concession the United States was able to exact in return for recognition was a promise to hold elections in 1965.[33]

Following the military coup in Peru in July 1962, the United States was able to use its power more effectively to bring about a return to democratic government. The American ambassador was recalled; diplomatic relations were suspended; and 81 million dollars in aid was cancelled. Nine other Latin American countries were induced to break relations with the military junta—an achievement that could only have occurred at a time when the United States seemed to be poised on the brink of dispensing billions of dollars of largesse about the continent.[34] The result was that new elections were held the following year, and Belaunde was freely chosen President. Six years later, however, when Belaunde was overthrown by a coup, the United States was in no position to reverse the coup or even to prevent the military government that came to power from nationalizing major property holdings of American nationals. The power and the will that had been there in the early 1960s had evaporated by the late 1960s, and with it the possibility of holding Peru to a democratic path. Through a somewhat more complex process, a decline in the American role also helped produce similar results in Chile. In the 1964 Chilean elections, the United States exerted all the influence it could on behalf of Eduardo Frei and made a significant and possibly decisive contribution to his defeat of Salvador Allende. In the 1970 election the American government did not make any comparable effort to defeat Allende, who won the popular election by a narrow margin. At that point, the United States tried to induce the Chilean congress to refuse to confirm his victory and to promote a military coup to prevent him from taking office. Both these efforts violated the norms of Chilean politics and American morality, and both were unsuccessful. If, on the other hand, the United States had been as active in the popular election of 1970 as it had been in that of 1964, the destruction of Chilean democracy in 1973 might have been avoided.

All in all, the decline in the role of the United States in Latin America in the late 1960s and early 1970s coincided with the spread of authoritarian regimes in that area. With this decline went a decline in the standards of democratic morality and human rights which the United States could attempt to apply to the governments of the region. In the early 1960s in Latin America (as in the 1910s and 1920s in the Caribbean and Central America), the goal of the United States was democratic competition and free elections. By the mid-1970s, that goal had been lowered from the fostering of democratic government to attempting to induce authoritarian governments not to infringe too blatantly the rights of their citizens.

A similar relationship between American power and democratic government prevailed in Asia. There, too, the peak of American power was reached in the early and mid-1960s, and there, too, the decline in this power was followed by a decline in democracy and liberty. American influence had been most pervasive in the Philippines, which, for a quarter-century after World War II, had the most open, democratic system, apart from Japan, in east and southeast Asia. After the admittedly fraudulent election of 1949 and in the face of the rising threat to the Philippine government posed by the Huk insurgency, American military and economic assistance was greatly increased. Direct American intervention in Philippine politics then played a decisive role not only in promoting Ramon Magsaysay into the presidency but also in assuring that the 1951 congressional elections and 1953 presidential election were open elections "free from fraud and intimidation."[35] In the next three elections the Philippines met the sternest test of democracy: incumbent presidents were defeated for reelection. In subsequent years, however, the American presence and American influence in the Philippines declined, and with it one support for Philippine democracy. When President Marcos instituted his martial law regime in 1972, American influence in southeast Asia was clearly on the wane, and the United States held few effective levers with which to affect the course of Philippine politics. In perhaps even more direct fashion, the high point of democracy and political liberty in Vietnam also coincided with the high point of American influence there. The only free national election in the history of that country took place in 1967, when the American military intervention was at its peak. In Vietnam, as in Latin America, American intervention had a pluralizing effect on politics, limiting the government and encouraging and strengthening its political opposition. The defeat of the United States in Vietnam and the exclusion of American power from Indochina were followed in three countries by the imposition of regimes of almost total repression.

The American relationship with South Korea took a similar course. In the late 1940s, under the sponsorship of the United States, U.N.-observed elections inaugurated the government of the Republic of Korea and brought Syngman Rhee to power. During the Korean War (1950–1953) and then in the mid-1950s, when American economic assistance was at its peak, a moderately democratic system was maintained, despite the fact that South Korea was almost literally in a state of siege. In 1956, Rhee won reelection by only a close margin and the opposition party won the Vice-Presidency and swept the urban centers.

In the late 1950s, however, as American economic assistance to Korea declined, the Rhee regime swung in an increasingly authoritarian direction. The 1960 vice-presidential election was blatantly fraudulent; students and others protested vigorously; and, as the army sat on the sidelines, Syngman Rhee was forced out of power. A democratic regime under John M. Chang came into office, but found it difficult to exercise authority and to maintain order. In May 1961, this regime was overthrown by a military coup, despite the strong endorsement of the Chang government by the American Embassy and military command. During the next two years, the United States exerted sustained pressure on the military government to hold elections and return power to a civilian regime. A bitter struggle took place within the military over this issue; in the end, President Park, with American backing and support, overcame the opposition within the military junta, and reasonably open elections were held in October 1963, in which Park was elected President with a 43 percent plurality of the vote. In the struggle with the hard-line groups in the military, one reporter observed, "the prestige and word of the United States have been put to a grinding test"; by insisting on the holding of elections, however, the United States "emerged from this stage of the crisis with a sort of stunned respect from South Koreans for its determination—from those who eagerly backed United States pressures on the military regime and even from officers who were vehemently opposed to it."[36] Thirteen years later, however, the United States was no longer in a position to have the same impact on Korean politics. "You can't talk pure Jefferson to these guys," one American official said. "You've got to have a threat of some kind or they won't listen . . . There aren't many levers left to pull around here. We just try to keep the civil rights issue before the eyes of Korean authorities on all levels and hope it has some effect."[37] By 1980, American power in Korea had been reduced to the point where there was no question, as there was in 1961 and 1962, of pressuring a new military leadership to hold prompt and fair elections. The issue was simply whether the United States had enough influence to induce the Korean government not to execute Korea's leading opposition political figure, Kim Dae Jung, and even with respect to that, one Korean official observed, "the United States has no leverage."[38] Over the years, as American influence in Korea went down, repression in Korea went up.

The positive impact of American power on liberty in other societies is in part the result of the conscious choices by Presidents such as Kennedy and Carter to give high priority to the promotion of democracy and human rights. Even without such conscious choice, however, the presence or exercise of American power in a foreign area usually has a similar thrust. The new moralists of the 1970s maintained that the United States has "no alternative" but to act in terms of the moral and political values that define the essence of its being. The new moralists clearly intended this claim to have at least a normative meaning. But in fact, it also describes a historical necessity. Despite the reluctance or inability of those imbued with the myth of American repression to recognize it, the impact of the United States on the world has, in large part, been what the new moralists say it has to be. The nature of the United States has left it little or no choice but to stand out among nations as the proponent of liberty and democracy. Clearly, the impact of no other country in world affairs has been as heavily weighted in favor of liberty and democracy as has that of the United States.

Power tends to corrupt, and absolute power corrupts absolutely. American power is no exception; clearly it has been used for good purposes and bad in terms of liberty, democracy, and human rights. But also in terms of these values, American power is far less likely to be misused or corrupted than the power of any other major government. This is so for two reasons. First, because American leaders and decision makers are, inevitably, the products of their culture, they are themselves generally committed to liberal and democratic values. This does not mean that some leaders may not at times take actions that run counter to those values. Obviously, this happens: sensibilities are dulled, perceived security needs may dictate other actions, expediency prevails, the immediate end justifies setting aside the larger purpose. But American policy makers are more likely than those of any other country to be sensitive to these trade-offs and to be more reluctant to sacrifice liberal-democratic values. Second, the institutional pluralism and dispersion of power in the American political system impose constraints—unmatched in any other society —on the ability of officials to abuse power, and also ensure that those transgressions that do occur will almost inevitably become public knowledge. The American press is extraordinarily free, strong, and vigorous in its exposure of bad policies and corrupt officials. The American Congress has powers of investigation, legislation, and financial control unequaled by any other national legislature. The ability of American officials to violate the values of their society is therefore highly limited, and the extent to which the press is filled with accounts of how officials have violated those values is evidence not that such behavior is more widespread than it is in other societies but that it is less tolerated than in other societies. The belief that the United States can do no wrong in terms of the values of liberty and democracy is clearly as erroneous abroad as it is at home. But so also is the belief—far more prevalent in American intellectual circles in the 1970s—that the United States could never do right in terms of those values. American power is far more likely to be used to support those values than to counter them, and it is far more likely to be employed on behalf of those values than the power of any other major country.

The point is often made that there is a direct relation between the health of liberty in the United States and the health of liberty in other societies. Disease in one is likely to infect the other. Thus, on the one hand, Richard Ullman argued that "the quality of political life in the United States is indeed affected by the quality of political life in other societies. The extinction of political liberties in Chile, or their extension in Portugal or Czechoslovakia, has a subtle but nonetheless important effect on political liberties within the United States." Conversely, he also goes on to say: "just as the level of political freedom in other societies affects our own society, so the quality of our own political life has an important impact abroad."[39] This particular point is often elaborated into what is sometimes referred to as the "clean hands" doctrine—that the United States cannot effectively promote liberty in other countries so long as there are significant violations of liberty within its borders. Let the United States rely on the power of example and "first put our house in order," as Hoffmann phrased it. "Like charity, well-ordered crusades begin at home."[40]

Both these arguments—that of the corrupting environment and that of the shining example—are partial truths. By any observable measure, the state of liberty in countries like Chile or Czechoslovakia has, in itself, no impact on the state of liberty in the United States. Similarly, foreigners usually recognize what Americans tend to forget—that the United States is the most open, free, and democratic society in the world. Hence, any particular improvement in the state of liberty in the United States is unlikely to be seen as having much relevance to their societies. Yet these arguments do have an element of truth in them, when one additional variable is added to the equation. This element is power.

The impact that the state of liberty in other societies has on liberty in the United States depends upon the power of those other societies and their ability to exercise that power with respect to the United States. What happens in Chile or even Czechoslovakia does not affect the state of liberty in the United States because those are small, weak, and distant countries. But the disappearance of liberty in Britain or France or Japan would have consequences for the health of liberty in the United States, because they are large and important countries intimately involved with the United States. Conversely, the impact of the state of liberty in the United States on other societies depends not upon changes in American liberty (which foreigners will, inevitably, view as marginal), but rather upon the power and immediacy of the United States to the country in question. The power of example works only when it is an example of power. If the United States plays a strong, confident, preeminent role on the world stage, other nations will be impressed by its power and will attempt to emulate its liberty in the belief that liberty may be the source of power. This point was made quite persuasively in 1946 by Turkey's future premier, Adnan Menderes, in explaining why his country had to shift to democracy:

> The difficulties encountered during the war years uncovered and showed the weak points created by the one-party system in the structure of the country. The hope in the miracles of [the] one-party system vanished, as the one-party system countries were defeated everywhere. Thus, the one-party mentality was destroyed in the turmoil of blood and fire of the second World War. No country can remain unaffected by the great international events and the contemporary dominating ideological currents. This influence was felt in our country too.[41]

In short, no one copies a loser.

The future of liberty in the world is thus intimately linked to the future of American power. Yet the double thrust of the new moralism was, paradoxically, to advocate the expansion of global liberty, and, simultaneously, to effect a reduction in American power. The relative decline in American power in the 1970s has many sources. One of them assuredly was the democratic surge (of which the new moralism was one element) in the United States in the 1960s and early 1970s. The strong recommitment to democratic, liberal, and populist values that occurred during these years eventually generated efforts to limit, constrain, and reduce American military, political, and economic power abroad. The intense and sustained attacks by the media, by intellectuals, and by congressmen on the military establishment, intelligence agencies, diplomatic officials, and political leadership of the United States inevitably had that effect. The decline in American power abroad weakened the support for liberty and democracy abroad. American democracy and foreign democracy may be inversely related. Due to the mediating effects of power, their relationship appears to be just the opposite of that hypothesized by Ullman.

The promotion of liberty abroad thus requires the expansion of American power; the operation of liberty at home involves the limitation of American power. The need in attempting to achieve democratic goals both abroad and at home is to recognize the existence of this contradiction and to assess the trade-offs between these two goals. There is, for instance, an inherent contradiction between welcoming the end of American hegemony in the Western Hemisphere and, at the same time, deploring the intensification of repression in Latin America. It is also paradoxical that in the 1970s those congressmen who were most insistent on the need to promote human rights abroad were often most active in reducing the American power that could help achieve that result. In key votes in the 94th Congress, for instance, 132 congressmen consistently voted in favor of human rights amendments to foreign aid legislation. Seventy-eight of those 132 representatives also consistently voted against a larger military establishment, and another 28 consistent supporters of human rights split their votes on the military establishment. Only 26 of the 132 congressmen consistently voted in favor of both human rights and the military power whose development could help make those rights a reality.

The new realism of the 1940s and 1950s coincided with the expansion of American power in the world and the resulting expansion of American-sponsored liberty and democracy in the world. The new moralism of the 1970s coincided with the relative decline in American power and the concomitant erosion of liberty and democracy around the globe. By limiting American power, the new moralism promoted that decline. In some measure, too, the new moralism was a consequence of the decline. The new moralism's concern with human rights throughout the world clearly reflected the erosion in global liberty and democratic values. Paradoxically, the United States thus became more preoccupied with ways of defending human rights as its power to defend human rights diminished. Enactment of Title IX to the foreign assistance act in 1966, a major congressional effort to promote democratic values abroad, came at the midpoint in the steady decline in American foreign economic assistance. Similarly, the various restrictions that Congress wrote into the foreign assistance acts in the 1970s coincided with the general replacement of military aid by military sales. When American power was clearly predominant, such legislative provisions and caveats were superfluous: no Harkin amendment was necessary to convey the message of the superiority of liberty. The message was there for all to see in the troop deployments, carrier task forces, foreign aid missions, and intelligence operatives. When these faded from the scene, in order to promote liberty and human rights Congress found it necessary to write more and more explicit conditions and requirements into legislation. These legislative provisions were, in effect, an effort to compensate for the decline of American power. In terms of narrowing the IvI gap abroad, they were no substitute for the presence of American power.

Contrary to the views of both "realists" and "moralists," the contradiction arising from America's role in the world is not primarily that of power and self-interest versus liberty and morality in American foreign policy. It is, rather, the contradiction between enhancing liberty at home by curbing the power of the American government and enhancing liberty abroad by expanding that power.

The Promise of Disappointment

The term "American exceptionalism" has been used to refer to a variety of characteristics that have historically distinguished the United States from European societies—characteristics such as its relative lack of economic suffering, social conflict, political trauma, and military defeat. "The standing armies, the monarchies, the aristocracies, the huge debts, the crushing taxation, the old inveterate abuses, which flourish in Europe," William Clarke argued in 1881, "can take no root in the

New World. The continent of America is consecrated to simple humanity, and its institutions exist for the progress and happiness of the whole people." Yet, as Henry Fairlie pointed out in 1975, "there now *are* standing armies of America; there now *is* something that, from time to time, looks very like a monarchy; there now *is* a permitted degree of inherited wealth that is creating some of the elements of an aristocracy; there now *is* taxation that is crushing."[42] In the same year, Daniel Bell came to a similar conclusion by a different path. The "end of American exceptionalism," he argued, is to be seen in "the end of empire, the weakening of power, the loss of faith in the nation's future . . . Internal tensions have multiplied and there are deep structural crises, political and cultural, that may prove more intractable to solution than the domestic economic problems."[43]

In the late twentieth century, the United States surely seemed to confront many evils and problems that were common to other societies but that it had previously avoided. These developments, however, affected only the incidental elements of American exceptionalism, those of power, wealth, and security. They did not change American political values and they only intensified the gap between political ideals and political institutions that is crucial to American national identity. They thus did not affect the historically most exceptional aspect of the United States, an aspect eloquently summed up and defended by a Yugoslav dissident in the following words:

> The United States is not a state like France, China, England, etc., and it would be a great tragedy if someday the United States became such a state. What is the difference? First of all, the United States is not a national state, but a multinational state. Second, the United States was founded by people who valued individual freedom more highly than their own country.
>
> And so the United States is primarily a state of freedom. And this is what is most important. Whole peoples from other countries can say, Our homeland is Germany, Russia, or whatever; only Americans can say, My homeland is freedom.[44]

Americans have said this throughout their history and have lived throughout their history in the inescapable presence of liberal ideals, semiliberal institutions, and the gap between the two. The United States has no meaning, no identity, no political culture or even history apart from its ideals of liberty and democracy and the continuing efforts of Americans to realize those ideals. Every society has its own distinctive form of tension that characterizes its existence as a society. The tension between liberal ideal and institutional reality is America's distinguishing cleavage. It defines both the agony and the promise of American politics. If that tension disappears, the United States of America, as we have known it, will no longer exist.

The continued existence of the United States means that Americans will continue to suffer from cognitive dissonance. They will continue to attempt to come to terms with that dissonance through some combination of moralism, cynicism, complacency, and hypocrisy. The greatest danger to the IvI gap would come when any substantial portion of the American population carried to an extreme any one of these responses. An excess of moralism, hypocrisy, cynicism, or complacency could do in the American system. A totally complacent toleration of the IvI gap could lead to the corruption and decay of American liberal-democratic institutions. Uncritical hypocrisy, blind to the existence of the gap and fervent in its commitment to American principles, could lead to imperialistic expansion, ending in either military or political disaster abroad or the undermining of democracy at home. Cynical acceptance of the gap could lead to a gradual abandonment of American ideals and their replacement either by a Thrasymachusian might-makes-right morality or by some other set of political beliefs. Finally, intense moralism could lead Americans to destroy the freest institutions on earth because they believed they deserved something better.

To maintain their ideals and institutions, Americans have no recourse but to temper and balance their responses to the IvI gap. The threats to the future of the American condition can be reduced to the extent that Americans:

—continue to believe in their liberal, democratic, and individualistic ideals and also recognize the extent to which their institutions and behavior fall short of these ideals;

—feel guilty about the existence of the gap but take comfort from the fact that American political institutions are more liberal and democratic than those of any other human society past or present;

—attempt to reduce the gap between institutions and ideals but accept the fact that the imperfections of human nature mean the gap can never be eliminated;

—believe in the universal validity of American ideals but also understand their limited applicability to other societies; and

—support the maintenance of American power necessary to protect and promote liberal ideals and institutions in the world arena, but recognize the dangers such power could pose to liberal ideals and institutions at home.

Critics say that America is a lie because its reality falls so far short of its ideals. They are wrong. America is not a lie; it is a disappointment. But it can be a disappointment only because it is also a hope.

NOTES

INDEX

NOTES

1. The Disharmonic Polity

1. *New York Times,* June 13, 1969, p. 30.

2. John Adams, *Works,* ed. Charles Francis Adams (Boston: Little, Brown, 1850–56), 4:401, 6:185, 9:570. Alexander Hamilton, in Max Farrand, ed., *The Records of the Federal Convention* (New Haven: Yale University Press, 1911), 1:299.

3. Quoted in Richard Hofstadter, *The Progressive Historians: Turner, Beard, Parrington* (New York: Knopf, 1968), p. 438.

4. Louis Hartz, *The Liberal Tradition in America* (New York: Harcourt, Brace, 1955), p. 31.

5. Hofstadter, *Progressive Historians,* p. 461.

6. George Santayana, *Character and Opinion in the United States* (Garden City, N.Y.: Doubleday Anchor, 1956), p. 129.

7. Hofstadter, *Progressive Historians,* p. 16.

8. André Béteille, *Inequality and Social Change* (Delhi: Oxford University Press, 1972), p. 15.

2. The American Creed and National Identity

1. See Zbigniew Brzezinski and Samuel P. Huntington, *Political Power: USA/USSR* (New York: Viking, 1964), pp. 17–24.

2. Robert G. McCloskey, "The American Ideology," in Marian D. Irish, ed., *Continuing Crisis in American Politics* (Englewood Cliffs, N.J.: Prentice-Hall, 1963), p. 14. See also John Higham, "Hanging Together: Divergent Unities in American History," *Journal of American History* 61 (June 1974): 16–17. On the unity of and conflicts among American values, see the systematic survey by Kaspar D. Naegele, "From De Tocqueville to Myrdal: A Research Memorandum on Selected Studies of American Values," Com-

parative Study of Values, Working Paper no. 1, October 1949, Laboratory of Social Relations, Harvard University. I am grateful to Daniel Bell for making this study available to me.

3. M. Walzer, "In Defense of Equality," *Dissent* 20 (Fall 1973): 408.

4. See, for example, Milton Rokeach, *The Nature of Human Values* (New York: Free Press, 1973), pp. 191–193.

5. Daniel Bell, "The End of American Exceptionalism," in Nathan Glazer and Irving Kristol, eds., *The American Commonwealth 1976* (New York: Basic Books, 1976), p. 209. Herbert Croly, *The Promise of American Life* (New York: Macmillan, 1909), p. 11.

6. Alexis de Tocqueville, *Democracy in America,* ed. Phillips Bradley (New York: Vintage Books, 1954), 1:409. Gunnar Myrdal, *An American Dilemma* (New York: Harper & Bros , 1944), 1:3.

7. Donald J. Devine, *The Political Culture of the United States* (Boston: Little, Brown, 1972), pp. 33, 116, 151, 362.

8. See James W. Prothro and Charles M. Grigg, "Fundamental Principles of Democracy: Bases of Agreement and Disagreement," *Journal of Politics* 22 (February 1960): 282–286. Herbert McClosky, "Consensus and Ideology in American Politics," *American Political Science Review* 58 (June 1964): 365–368. Devine, *Political Culture,* pp. 179–230. Frank R. Westie, "The American Dilemma: An Empirical Test," *American Sociological Review* 30 (August 1965): 531–532.

9. Prothro and Grigg, "Fundamental Principles," pp. 285–291. Westie, "The American Dilemma," pp. 530–535. McClosky, "Consensus and Ideology," pp. 364–373. Samuel Stouffer, *Communism, Conformity, and Civil Liberties* (Gloucester, Mass.: Peter Smith, 1963), pp. 26–57. Devine, *Political Culture,* pp. 260–265. For testimony verifying the impact of the McClosky and Prothro-Grigg studies, plus a fairly unpersuasive effort to challenge them, see Joseph V. Femia, "Elites, Participation, and the Democratic Creed," *Political Studies* 27 (March 1979): 1–20.

10. Devine, *Political Culture,* p. 33.

11. See Louis Hartz, *The Liberal Tradition in America* (New York: Harcourt, Brace, 1955), ch. 6.

12. For a comprehensive review of the literature on this question, see Seymour Martin Lipset, "Why No Socialism in the United States?" in Seweryn Bialer and Sophia Sluzar, eds., *Sources of Contemporary Radicalism* (Boulder, Colo.: Westview Press, 1977), pp. 31–149.

13. Leon Samson, "Americanism as Surrogate Socialism," in John H. M. Laslett and Seymour Martin Lipset, eds., *Failure of a Dream?* (Garden City: Doubleday Anchor, 1974), pp. 426–442, originally published in *Toward a United Front* (New York: Farrar & Rinehart, 1935).

14. Richard Hofstadter, *The Age of Reform* (New York: Knopf, 1956), p. 9.

15. Edward C. Banfield and James Q. Wilson, *City Politics* (New York: Vintage Books, 1963), pp. 329–330.

16. Tocqueville, *Democracy in America*, 2:271, 275.

17. Clyde Kluckhohn, "Have There Been Discernible Shifts in American Values during the Past Generation?" in Elting E. Morison, ed., *The American Style* (New York: Harper & Bros., 1958), p. 152. Seymour Martin Lipset, *The First New Nation* (New York: Basic Books, 1963), p. 103. Lloyd A. Free and Hadley Cantril, *The Political Beliefs of Americans* (New Brunswick: Rutgers University Press, 1967), pp. 175–177. Devine, *Political Culture*, p. 65.

18. Tocqueville, *Democracy in America*, 1:409.

19. James Bryce, *The American Commonwealth* (London: Macmillan, 1891), 2:417–418. Myrdal, *American Dilemma*, 1:4, 8.

20. David Riesman, *The Lonely Crowd* (New Haven: Yale University Press, 1950), and William F. Whyte, *The Organization Man* (New York: Simon & Schuster, 1956).

21. Lipset, *First New Nation*, pp. 101–139. Carl N. Degler, "The Sociologist as Historian: Riesman's *The Lonely Crowd*," *American Quarterly* 15 (Winter 1963): 483–497.

22. Richard deCharms and Gerald H. Moeller, "Values Expressed in Children's Readers: 1800–1950," *Journal of Abnormal and Social Psychology* 64 (February 1962): 136–142. Fred I. Greenstein, "New Light on Changing American Values: A Forgotten Body of Survey Data," *Social Forces* 42 (May 1964): 441–450.

23. Lee Coleman, "What Is American? A Study of Alleged American Traits," *Social Forces* 19 (May 1941): 492–499.

24. John McDiarmid, "Presidential Inaugural Addresses—A Study in Verbal Symbols," *Public Opinion Quarterly* 1 (July 1937): 79–82.

25. Croly, *Promise of American Life*, p. 3. William R. Brock, "Americanism," in Dennis Welland, ed., *The United States* (London: Methuen, 1974), pp. 59, 68. Myrdal, *American Dilemma*, 1:3.

26. Gabriel A. Almond and Sidney Verba, *The Civic Culture* (Boston: Little, Brown, 1965), pp. 64–65.

27. William T. Bluhm, *Ideologies and Attitudes: Modern Political Culture* (Englewood Cliffs, N.J.: Prentice-Hall, 1974), p. 100.

28. Samson, "Americanism as Surrogate Socialism," p. 426. Richard Hofstadter, quoted in Hans Kohn, *American Nationalism: An Interpretive Essay* (New York: Macmillan, 1957), p. 13.

29. John Higham, "Immigration," and C. Vann Woodward, "The Test of Comparison," in Woodward, ed., *The Comparative Approach to American History* (New York: Basic Books, 1968), pp. 98–99, 93, 351.

30. Bryce, *American Commonwealth*, 2:652.

31. Kohn, *American Nationalism*, p. 8.

32. Carl J. Friedrich et al., *Problems of the American Public Service* (New York: McGraw-Hill, 1935), p. 12.

33. Sidney E. Mead, "The Nation with the Soul of a Church," *Church History* 36 (September 1967): 275.

3. The Gap: The American Creed versus Political Authority

1. *Boston Globe,* October 14, 1971, p. 8.

2. Charles H. Hendel, "An Exploration of the Nature of Authority," in Carl J. Friedrich, ed., *Authority* (Cambridge, Mass.: Harvard University Press, 1958), pp. 4–5.

3. Quoted in Rush Welter, *The Mind of America: 1820–1860* (New York: Columbia University Press, 1975), pp. 165–166, 172.

4. William Schneider, "Public Opinion," *Politics Today* 5 (September-October 1978): 10. Donald J. Devine, *The Political Culture of the United States* (Boston: Little, Brown, 1972), p. 102.

5. William Blackstone, *Commentaries on the Laws of England,* 10th ed. (London: A. Strahan, 1787), 1:48–49. John Bowring, *The Works of Jeremy Bentham* (Edinburgh: n.p., 1843), 1:154n, 10:63, quoted in Chilton Williamson, "Bentham Looks at America," *Political Science Quarterly* 70 (December 1955): 549. On the perpetuation in America of older dispersed forms of government displaced in Europe by the rise of the modern nation-state in the seventeenth century, see Samuel P. Huntington, *Political Order in Changing Societies* (New Haven: Yale University Press, 1968), ch. 2.

6. Henry James, *Hawthorne* (Ithaca, N.Y.: Cornell University Press, 1956; originally published 1879), p. 34. Baron J. A. Graf von Hübner, in Richard L. Rapson, ed., *Individualism and Conformity in the American Character* (Lexington, Mass.: D. C. Heath, 1967), p. 24. James Bryce, *The American Commonwealth* (London: Macmillan, 1891), 2:417–418. H. G. Wells, quoted in Esmond Wright, "The End of Innocence," *Political Quarterly* 43 (January 1972): 35. G. K. Chesterton, *New York Times Magazine,* July 12, 1931, quoted in Leon Samson, *The American Mind* (New York: Jonathan Cape & Harrison Smith, 1932), p. 345n.

7. Seymour Martin Lipset, "Why No Socialism in the United States?" in Seweryn Bialer and Sophia Sluzar, eds., *Sources of Contemporary Radicalism* (Boulder, Colo.: Westview Press, 1977), pp. 94–97. See also Erwin C. Hargrove, "On Canadian and American Political Culture," *Canadian Journal of Economics and Political Science* 33 (February, 1967): 107, and, for a general elaboration of this theme, David DeLeon, *The American as Anarchist: Reflections on Indigenous Radicalism* (Baltimore: Johns Hopkins, 1978).

8. Bryce, *American Commonwealth,* 1:299.

9. Cora Du Bois, "The Dominant Value Profile of American Culture," *American Anthropologist* 57 (December 1955): 1238.

10. John George Cawelti, *Apostles of the Self-Made Man* (Chicago: University of Chicago Press, 1965), p. 2.

11. Alexis de Tocqueville, *Democracy in America,* ed. Phillips Bradley (New York: Vintage Books, 1954), 2:108. Louis Hartz, *The Liberal Tradition in America* (New York: Harcourt, Brace, 1955), pp. 85–86. Huntington, *Political Order,* p. 125.

12. George C. Lodge, *The New American Ideology* (New York: Knopf, 1975), p. 15.

13. The one notable exception to this rule is Judith V. Torney, A. N. Oppenheim, and Russell F. Farnen, *Civic Education in Ten Countries: An Empirical Study* (New York: John Wiley, 1975), which showed teenagers in America to have less commitment to democratic values than those in West Germany, Finland, Ireland, Netherlands, Sweden, Italy, and New Zealand. Only fourteen-year-olds in Israel were more undemocratic in their outlook than their American counterparts. In these comparisons, a Support for Democratic Values score was calculated by averaging scores for Anti-Authoritarianism, Tolerance and Civil Liberties, Support for Women's Rights, and Support for Equality.

14. Max Beloff, *The Great Powers* (New York: Macmillan, 1959), p. 137.

15. Gabriel A. Almond and Sidney Verba, *The Civic Culture* (Boston: Little, Brown, 1965), pp. 314-315. Devine, *Political Culture,* p. 193.

16. Jack Dennis, Leon Lindberg, Donald McCrone, and Rodney Stiefbold, "Political Socialization to Democratic Orientations in Four Western Systems," *Comparative Political Studies* 1 (April 1968): 94.

17. Fred I. Greenstein and Sidney Tarrow, *Political Orientations of Children: The Use of a Semi-Projective Technique in Three Nations* (Beverly Hills: Sage Publications, 1970), pp. 520-529.

18. Judith Gallatin and Joseph Adelson, "Individual Rights and the Public Good: A Cross-National Study of Adolescents," *Comparative Political Studies* 3 (July 1970): 240-241.

19. See Seymour Martin Lipset, *The First New Nation* (New York: Basic Books, 1963), ch. 7, and Tom Truman, "A Critique of Seymour M. Lipset's Article, "Value Differences, Absolute or Relative: The English-Speaking Democracies,'" *Canadian Journal of Political Science* 4 (December 1971): 497-525. Truman argues (contra Lipset) that Canadian and American values are closer than Australian and American values, but he also stresses the major differences separating American values from Australian, British, and Canadian values.

20. Hargrove, "On Canadian and American Political Culture," p. 107.

21. Edgar Z. Friedenberg, *Deference to Authority: The Case of Canada* (White Plains, N.Y.: M. E. Sharpe, 1980), p. 17.

22. Robert Presthus, *Elites in the Policy Process* (London: Cambridge University Press, 1974), pp. 4-15, 30-39. Lipset, *First New Nation,* pp. 86-89, 250-252.

23. Gad Horowitz, "Conservatism, Liberalism and Socialism in Canada," *Canadian Journal of Economics and Political Science* 32 (May 1966): 150.

24. Edmund Burke, *Reflections on the Revolution in France* (Chicago: Regnery, 1955), pp. 125-126, and idem, "Speech on Moving Resolutions for Conciliation with the Colonies," in Ross J.S. Hoffman and Paul Levack, eds., *Burke's Politics* (New York: Knopf, 1949), pp. 69-71.

25. Lipset, *First New Nation,* pp. 213-234. Eric A. Nordlinger, *The Working-Class Tories* (London: MacGibbon & Kee, 1967), ch. 1. R. D.

Jessop, "Civility and Traditionalism in English Political Culture," *British Journal of Political Science* 1 (January 1971): 1–24.

26. A. P. Thornton, *The Habit of Authority: Paternalism in British History* (London: Allen & Unwin, 1966), p. 386.

27. Maurice L. Farber, "English and Americans: A Study in National Character," *Journal of Psychology* 32 (October 1951): 241–250. Erwin C. Hargrove, "Values and Change: A Comparison of Young *Elites* in England and America," *Political Studies* 17 (September 1969): esp. 343.

28. Edward A. Shils, *The Torment of Secrecy* (Glencoe: Free Press, 1956), pp. 37, 48–49.

29. Alex Inkeles and Daniel Levinson, "National Character: The Study of Modal Personality and Sociocultural Systems," in Gardner Lindzey, ed., *Handbook of Social Psychology* (Cambridge, Mass: Addison-Wesley, 1954), p. 475.

30. Kurt Lewin, "Some Social-Psychological Differences between the United States and Germany," *Character and Personality* 4 (June 1936): 269.

31. Dennis et al., "Political Socialization," p. 95. Edward C. Devereux, Jr., Urie Bronfenbrenner, and George J. Suci, "Patterns of Parent Behavior in the USA and the Federal Republic of Germany: A Cross-National Comparison," *International Social Science Bulletin* 14 (Fall 1962): 488–506. Gallatin and Adelson, "Individual Rights," p. 241. David McClelland, J. F. Sturr, R. H. Knapp, and H. W. Wendt, "Obligations to the Self and Society in the United States and Germany," *Journal of Abnormal and Social Psychology* 56 (March 1958): 245–255.

32. "Subject orientation" and "firmly democratic attitudes": Sidney Verba, "Germany: The Remaking of Political Culture," in Lucian W. Pye and Sidney Verba, eds., *Political Culture and Political Development* (Princeton: Princeton University Press, 1966), p. 169. "Ascriptive elitist values": Lipset, *First New Nation*, p. 238. "Germans fundamentally changed" and "political but not psychological democracy": David C. McClelland, *The Roots of Consciousness* (Princeton, N.J.: Van Nostrand, 1964), p. 89.

33. Kendall L. Baker, Russell J. Dalton, and Kai Hildebrandt, *Germany Transformed: Political Culture and the New Politics* (Cambridge, Mass.: Harvard University Press, 1981), pp. 24–25, 287. David P. Conradt, "Changing German Political Culture," in Gabriel A. Almond and Sidney Verba, eds., *The Civic Culture Revisited* (Boston: Little, Brown, 1980), p. 234.

34. Kurt Sontheimer, *The Government and Politics of West Germany* (London: Hutchinson University Library, 1972), pp. 76, 68–69.

35. Conradt, "Changing German Political Culture," pp. 221, 230. Baker et al., *Germany Transformed*, p. 273.

36. Baker et al., *Germany Transformed*, pp. 69, 288.

37. Lipset, *First New Nation*, p. 228. Fred I. Greenstein and Sidney G. Tarrow, "The Study of French Political Socialization: Toward the Revocation of Paradox," *World Politics* 22 (October 1969): 108.

38. William R. Schonfeld, *Obedience and Revolt: French Behavior toward Authority* (Beverly Hills: Sage Publications, 1976), pp. 137–142.

Stanley Hoffmann, "Paradoxes of the French Political Community," in Hoffmann et al., *In Search of France* (Cambridge, Mass.: Harvard University Press, 1963), p. 8.

39. Mariano Grondona quoted in Peter Krogh and Wenceslao Bunge, eds., *Argentine-American Forum* (Washington, D.C.: Georgetown University School of Foreign Service, 1980), pp. 9–10. Robert F. Peck, "A Comparison of the Value Systems of Mexican and American Youth," *Revista Interamericana de Psicologia* 1 (March 1967): 46–47. Noel McGinn et al., "Dependency Relations with Parents and Affiliative Responses in Michigan and Guadalajara," *Sociometry* 28 (September 1965): 313. See generally Calman Jay Cohen, "Relations to the Polity: A Study of Mexican Fathers and Sons" (diss., Harvard University, 1976), ch. 2.

40. Ivan the Terrible is quoted in B. H. Sumner, *Survey of Russian History*, 2nd ed. (London: Duckworth, 1947), p. 67. Marquis de Custine, *Journey of Our Time,* ed. and tr. Phyllis Penn Kohler (New York: Pellegrini & Cudahy, 1951), p. 73. Henry V. Dicks, "Some Notes on Russian National Character," in Cyril E. Black, ed., *The Transformation of Russian Society* (Cambridge, Mass.: Harvard University Press, 1960), pp. 641–642. Robert C. Tucker, "The Image of Dual Russia," in Black, *The Transformation of Russian Society,* pp. 587–605.

41. Frederick C. Barghoorn, *Politics in the USSR* (Boston: Little, Brown, 1966), pp. 22ff. Urie Bronfenbrenner, *Two Worlds of Childhood* (New York: Russell Sage, 1970), pp. 9–11, 90–91, and "Response to Pressure from Peers versus Adults among Soviet and American School Children," *International Journal of Psychology* 2 (1967): 199–207.

42. Alex Inkeles and Raymond A. Bauer, *The Soviet Citizen* (Cambridge, Mass.: Harvard University Press, 1959), pp. 247–249, 279–280, 392. David K. Shipler, *New York Times,* June 14, 1979, p. 1.

43. See Cyril E. Black et al., *The Modernization of Japan and Russia: A Comparative Study* (New York: Free Press, 1975), passim, esp. pp. 53, 55, 95, 117, 147ff, 154–155, 159, 264–265, 268, 276, 318–319.

44. Lewis Austin, *Saints and Samurai: The Political Culture of the American and Japanese Elites* (New Haven: Yale University Press, 1975), pp. 1, 6, 147.

45. "The social norm": Chie Nakane, *Japanese Society* (Berkeley: University of California Press, 1970), p. 31. "The fact of inequality": Masatake Ushiro and George C. Lodge, "On the Japanese Ideology," in Lodge, *New American Ideology,* p. 344. Ruth Benedict, *The Chrysanthemum and the Sword* (Boston: Houghton Mifflin, 1946), p. 43. "The first element": Hiroshi Kitamura *Psychological Dimensions of U.S.-Japanese Relations,* Harvard University Center for International Affairs, Occasional Paper no. 28 (Cambridge, Mass.: 1971), pp. 10–11.

46. Frank Langdon, *Politics in Japan* (Boston: Little, Brown, 1967), p. 74. Austin, *Saints and Samurai,* pp. 129–130, 139–142.

47. Robert E. Ward, "Japan: The Continuity of Modernization," in Pye and Verba, *Political Culture,* p. 34. Austin, *Saints and Samurai,* p. 59.

48. Nakane, *Japanese Society*, p. 103.

49. Tatsuzo Suzuki, *A Study of Japanese National Character, Part IV* (Tokyo: Institute of Statistical Mathematics, Research Committee on the Study of Japanese National Character, 1969), p. 22. Research Committee on the Study of the Japanese National Character, *A Study of the Japanese National Character: The Fifth Nation-Wide Survey, 1973* (Tokyo: Institute of Statistical Economics, 1974), pp. 80–82. Joji Watanuki, "Japan," in Michel Crozier, Samuel P. Huntington and Joji Watanuki, *The Crisis of Democracy* (New York: New York University Press, 1975), p. 141.

50. Suzuki, *Japanese National Character*, pp. 6–7. Research Committee, *Japanese National Character: Fifth Survey*, pp. 22, 41, 55. Bradley M. Richardson, *The Political Culture of Japan* (Berkeley: University of California Press, 1974), pp. 69–70.

51. Warren M. Tsuneishi, *Japanese Political Style* (New York: Harper & Row, 1966), pp. 17–21.

52. Nakane, *Japanese Society*, p. 63.

53. Tang Tsou, "The Values of the Chinese Revolution," in Michel Oksenberg, ed., *China's Developmental Experience* (New York: Praeger, 1973), pp. 27, 30. Richard W. Wilson, *Learning To Be Chinese: The Political Socialization of Children in Taiwan* (Cambridge, Mass.: MIT Press, 1970), pp. 19, 30, 51.

54. George P. Jan, "Government and Politics of the People's Republic of China" (unpublished manuscript), ch. 1. Lucian W. Pye, *The Spirit of Chinese Politics* (Cambridge, Mass.: MIT Press, 1968), p. 86.

55. John K. Fairbank, quoted in Wilson, *Learning To Be Chinese*, p. 53. Pye, *Spirit of Chinese Politics*, pp. 25–26, 77. Francis L. K. Hsu, *Americans and Chinese* (Garden City, N.Y.: Doubleday Natural History Press, 1972), pp. 177–180.

56. James R. Townsend, *Politics in China* (Boston: Little, Brown, 1974), pp. 30ff. Pye, *Spirit of Chinese Politics*, p. 91. Ch'eng I, quoted in Richard H. Solomon, *Mao's Revolution and the Chinese Political Culture* (Berkeley: University of California Press, 1971), p. 108.

57. Solomon, *Mao's Revolution*, pp. 112–113.

58. Townsend, *Politics in China*, pp. 179–188.

4. Coping with the Gap

1. Alexis de Tocqueville, *Democracy in America*, ed. Phillips Bradley (New York: Vintage Books, 1954), 1:9.

2. Leon Festinger, *A Theory of Cognitive Dissonance* (Evanston, Ill.: Row, Peterson & Co., 1957), p. 3.

3. This has been recognized in passing by some commentators on the American scene, for example, Robin Williams, *American Society* (New York: Knopf, 1951), p. 425. Ethel M. Albert, "Conflict and Change in American Values: A Culture-Historical Approach," *Ethics* 74 (October 1963): 30–31.

4. Ronald Blythe, introduction to *Emma,* by Jane Austen (Harmondsworth: Penguin Books, 1966), p. 16.

5. Louis D. Rubin, Jr., "The Great American Joke," *South Atlantic Quarterly* 72 (Winter 1973), pp. 83–87, where the Robert Penn Warren quote appears. Harold J. Laski, *The American Democracy* (New York: Viking Press, 1948), p. 740. See generally Walter Blair and Hamlin Hill, *America's Humor: From Poor Richard to Doonesbury* (New York: Oxford University Press, 1979).

6. Leon Samson, *The American Mind* (New York: Jonathan Cape and Harrison Smith, 1932), p. 13.

7. Irving Kristol, *On the Democratic Idea in America* (New York: Harper & Row, 1972), p. 130.

8. Judith Shklar, "Let Us Not Be Hypocritical," *Daedalus* 108 (Summer 1979): 11, 14–16, 24.

9. Kristol, *Democratic Idea,* p. 130.

10. *New York Times,* May 4, 1974, p. 1, 24.

11. George Santayana, *Character and Opinion in the United States* (Garden City, N.Y.: Doubleday Anchor, 1956), p. 3.

12. Gunnar Myrdal, *An American Dilemma* (New York: Harper & Bros., 1944), 1:21.

13. Ralph Waldo Emerson, "Lecture on the Times," in Emerson, *Prose Works* (Boston: Fields, Osgood & Co., 1870), 1:149.

14. Robert B. Zajonc, "Thinking: Cognitive Organization and Processes," in David L. Sills, ed., *International Encyclopedia of the Social Sciences* (New York: Macmillan Co. and Free Press, 1968), 15:618.

15. For analyses supporting the conclusions summarized in this paragraph, see: Fred I. Greenstein, *Children and Politics* (New Haven: Yale University Press, 1965), esp. pp. 31–45; David Easton and Jack Dennis, *Children in the Political System* (New York: McGraw-Hill, 1969), esp. pp. 111–143; M. Kent Jennings and Richard G. Niemi, "Patterns of Political Learning," *Harvard Educational Review* 38 (Summer 1968): 463–465; and idem, "The Transmission of Political Values from Parent to Child," *American Political Science Review* 62 (March 1968): 169–184. For the effects of Watergate on children's attitudes toward politics, see F. Christopher Arterton, "Watergate and Children's Attitudes toward Political Authority Revisited," *Political Science Quarterly* 90 (Fall 1975): 477ff.

16. Seymour Martin Lipset, "Youth and Politics," in Robert K. Merton and Robert Nisbet, eds., *Contemporary Social Problems,* 3rd ed. (New York: Harcourt Brace Jovanovich, 1971), pp. 744–745.

17. See, for example, Robert E. Agger, Marshall N. Goldstein, and Stanley A. Pearl, "Political Cynicism: Measurement and Meaning," *Journal of Politics* 23 (August 1961): 487–492, and the data on trust in government for the years 1958–78 collected by the University of Michigan Center for Political Studies, in Warren E. Miller, Arthur H. Miller, and Edward J. Schneider, *American National Election Studies Data Sourcebook, 1952–1978* (Cambridge, Mass.: Harvard University Press, 1980), p. 269.

18. See Donald J. Devine, *The Political Culture of the United States* (Boston: Little, Brown, 1972), pp. 260–265.

19. See James W. Prothro and Charles M. Grigg, "Fundamental Principles of Democracy: Bases of Agreement and Disagreement," *Journal of Politics* 22 (February 1960): 284–291. Samuel A. Stouffer, *Communism, Conformity, and Civil Liberties* (Garden City, N.Y.: Doubleday, 1955), ch. 2.

20. Herbert McClosky, "Consensus and Ideology in American Politics," *American Political Science Review* 58 (June 1964): 371. See also Agger, Goldstein, and Pearl, "Political Cynicism," pp. 477–506.

21. Joan Huber and William H. Form, *Income and Ideology* (New York: Free Press, 1973), pp. 132–133.

22. See Edward S. Greenberg, "Children and the Political Community," *Canadian Journal of Political Science* 2 (December 1969): 471–492, and "Orientations of Black and White Children to Political Authority Figures," *Social Science Quarterly* 51 (December 1970): 561–571. Dean Jarros, Herbert Hirsch, and Frederick J. Fleron, Jr., "The Malevolent Leader: Political Socialization in an American Subculture," *American Political Science Review* 62 (June 1968): 564–575.

23. Henry L. Stimson and McGeorge Bundy, *On Active Service in Peace and War* (New York: Harper & Bros., 1947), p. 672.

24. Richard E. Neustadt, *Presidential Power: The Politics of Leadership* (New York: John Wiley, 1960), pp. vii, 7, 9, 35.

25. Arthur M. Schlesinger, Jr., *The Imperial Presidency* (Boston: Houghton Mifflin, 1973), pp. viii, 377.

26. For the ways in which Eisenhower did in fact use presidential power, see the revisionist analyses of Fred I. Greenstein, "Eisenhower as an Activist President: A Look at New Evidence," *Political Science Quarterly* 94 (Winter 1979–80): 575–599, and George H. Quester, "Was Eisenhower a Genius?" *International Security* 4 (Fall 1979): 159–179.

27. "Passion for publicity": Francis Rourke, *Secrecy and Publicity* (Baltimore: Johns Hopkins Press, 1961), p. ix. "The awe of the press": Edward A. Shils, *The Torment of Secrecy* (Glencoe, Ill.: Free Press, 1956), pp. 51–52.

28. Shils, *Torment of Secrecy*, pp. 53, 57.

29. Seymour Martin Lipset and Earl Raab, *The Politics of Unreason* (New York: Harper & Row, 1970), pp. 13–14.

30. Richard Hofstadter, *The Age of Reform* (New York: Knopf, 1956), p. 72.

31. Bernard Bailyn, *The Ideological Origins of the American Revolution* (Cambridge, Mass.: Harvard University Press, 1967), pp. ix, 153. See also Bernard Bailyn, *The Origins of American Politics* (New York: Vintage Books, 1968), pp. 136–148.

32. Richard Hofstadter, *The Paranoid Style in American Politics and Other Essays* (New York: Vintage Books, 1967), pp. 3–40, and *Age of Reform*, pp. 70–72.

33. Shils, *Torment of Secrecy*, p. 45.

34. Frederick S. Hulse, "Convention and Reality in Japanese Culture," in Bernard S. Silberman, ed., *Japanese Character and Culture* (Tucson: University of Arizona Press, 1962), p. 304. Richard Solomon, *Mao's Revolution and the Chinese Political Culture* (Berkeley: University of California Press, 1971), pp. 110–111. See also Lucian W. Pye, *The Spirit of Chinese Politics* (Cambridge, Mass.: MIT Press, 1968), p. 15.

35. Lionel Trilling, *Sincerity and Authenticity* (Cambridge, Mass.: Harvard University Press, 1972), pp. 57–58.

36. Margaret Mead, *Soviet Attitudes toward Authority* (New York: McGraw-Hill, 1951), pp. 38–39.

37. *Boston Herald-American*, October 7, 1978, p. 14.

5. The Politics of Creedal Passion

1. Benjamin Rush, address delivered July 4, 1787, in Philadelphia, in Richard B. Morris, *The American Revolution Reconsidered* (New York: Harper & Row, 1967), pp. 84–85.

2. Bernard Bailyn, *The Ideological Origins of the American Revolution* (Cambridge, Mass.: Harvard University Press, 1976), p. 21.

3. Irving Kristol, *The American Revolution as a Successful Revolution* (Washington, D.C.: American Enterprise Institute for Public Policy Research, 1973), p. 12.

4. Gordon S. Wood, "Rhetoric and Reality in the American Revolution," in J. R. Howe, Jr., ed., *The Role of Ideology in the American Revolution* (New York: Holt, Rinehart & Winston, 1970), p. 116.

5. Gordon S. Wood, "Republicanism as a Revolutionary Ideology," in Howe, *The Role of Ideology*, p. 83.

6. Hannah Arendt, *On Revolution* (New York: Viking Press, 1963), p. 49.

7. Richard Hofstadter, *The Age of Reform* (New York: Knopf, 1956), pp. 308–312.

8. Ibid., pp. 315–318.

9. R. R. Palmer, *The Age of Democratic Revolution* (Princeton: Princeton University Press, 1959), 1:21. Bernard Bailyn, "Political Experience and Enlightenment Ideas in Eighteenth-Century America," *American Historical Review* 67 (January 1962): 348.

10. Ralph Waldo Emerson, "Man the Reformer" and "New England Reformers," in Emerson, *Prose Works* (Boston: Fields, Osgood & Co., 1870), 1:126, 551.

11. Wood, "Rhetoric and Reality," p. 117. Daniel Webster, quoted in Richard Hofstadter, *The American Political Tradition* (New York: Knopf, 1951), p. 65; Theodore Roosevelt, quoted in Eric Goldman, *Rendezvous with Destiny* (New York: Knopf, 1952), p. 187, from Henry F. Pringle, *Theodore Roosevelt* (New York: Harcourt, Brace, 1931), p. 413.

12. Bailyn, "Political Experience," p. 343. John Adams, letter to H. Niles, February 13, 1818, in *The Works of John Adams* (New York: AMS

Press, 1971), 10:283. Emerson, quoted in Charles A. Madison, *Critics and Crusaders* (New York: Henry Holt, 1947–48), p. 16.

13. Eric Foner, *Tom Paine and Revolutionary America* (New York: Oxford University Press, 1976), p. xv.

14. Bernard Bailyn, "The Central Themes of the Revolution," in Stephen G. Kurtz and James H. Hutson, eds., *Essays on the American Revolution* (Chapel Hill, N.C.: University of North Carolina Press, and New York: W. W. Norton, 1973), p. 17.

15. Marvin Meyers, *The Jacksonian Persuasion* (Stanford: Stanford University Press, 1957), pp. 6, 158. George E. Mowry, *The Era of Theodore Roosevelt, 1900–1912* (New York, Harper & Row, 1958), pp. 100–101, quoted in David Mark Chalmers, ed., *The Social and Political Ideas of the Muckrakers* (New York: Arno Press, 1964), p. 112. Hofstadter, *Age of Reform*, pp. 15–16. Theodore Roosevelt, quoted in Hofstadter, *American Political Tradition*, p. 226.

16. Louis Hartz, *The Liberal Tradition in America* (New York: Harcourt, Brace, 1955), pp. 50–51. See also Clinton Rossiter, *The Political Thought of the American Revolution* (New York: Harcourt, Brace & World, 1963), pp. 42–51.

17. Walter Dean Burnham, "Revitalization and Decay: Looking toward the Third Century of American Electoral Politics," *Journal of Politics* 38 (August 1976): 146–172. On revitalization movements generally, see Anthony F. C. Wallace, *Culture and Personality*, 2nd ed. (New York: Random House, 1970), pp. 178–199.

18. Bailyn, "Central Themes of the Revolution," pp. 26–27, and *Ideological Origins*, p. 56. See also Gordon S. Wood, *The Creation of the American Republic, 1776–1787* (Chapel Hill: University of North Carolina Press, 1969), pp. 18–28.

19. Meyers, *Jacksonian Persuasion*, pp. 16–17. John G. Cawelti, *Apostles of the Self-Made Man* (Chicago: University of Chicago Press, 1965), pp. 44–45.

20. Chalmers, *Muckrakers*, p. 106.

21. Wood, "Rhetoric and Reality," p. 117. Seymour Martin Lipset and Earl Raab, *The Politics of Unreason* (New York: Harper & Row, 1970), p. 41. Hofstadter, *Age of Reform*, pp. 70–81. See generally Richard Hofstadter, *The Paranoid Style in American Politics* (New York, Vintage Books, 1967).

22. Meyers, *Jacksonian Persuasion*, pp. 18–19.

23. Hofstadter, *American Political Tradition*, p. 49.

24. Arthur M. Schlesinger, *New Viewpoints in American History* (New York: Macmillan, 1922), p. 202.

25. Alexis de Tocqueville, *Democracy in America*, ed. Phillips Bradley (New York: Vintage Books, 1955), 2:114.

26. James Russell Lowell, "Thoreau," in *The Writings of James Russell Lowell* (Boston: Houghton Mifflin, 1890), 1:362.

27. Calvin Colton, *Protestant Jesuitism* (New York: Harper and Bros., 1836), pp. 52–53.

28. Arthur M. Schlesinger, *The American as Reformer* (Cambridge, Mass.: Harvard University Press, 1950), p. 52. Howard Zinn, "Abolitionists, Freedom-Riders, and the Tactics of Agitation," in Martin Duberman, ed., *The Anti-Slavery Vanguard* (Princeton: Princeton University Press, 1965), pp. 417–451. James Q. Wilson, *Political Organizations* (New York: Basic Books, 1973), pp. 322–323.

29. Wilson, *Political Organizations*, p. 201.

30. Palmer, *Democratic Revolution*, 1:243.

31. Rossiter, *Political Thought of the American Revolution*, p. 10. Bailyn, *Ideological Origins*, pp. 1–3, 8.

32. Sidney H. Aronson, *Status and Kinship in the Higher Civil Service* (Cambridge, Mass.: Harvard University Press, 1964), pp. 20–21.

33. Tocqueville, *Democracy in America*, 2:119–122.

34. Morton Keller, *Affairs of State: Public Life in Late Nineteenth Century America* (Cambridge, Mass.: Harvard University Press, 1977), p. 566.

35. Chalmers, *Muckrakers*, pp. 10–12. Hofstadter, *Age of Reform*, p. 187.

36. Zbigniew Brzezinski and Samuel P. Huntington, *Political Power: USA/USSR* (New York: Viking Press, 1964), p. 32.

37. Bailyn, "Central Themes," pp. 13–14.

38. Walter Lippmann, *Drift and Mastery* (Englewood Cliffs, N.J.: Prentice-Hall, 1961), p. 31. Hofstadter, *American Political Thought*, p. 66.

39. Bayless Manning, "The Purity Potlatch: Conflict of Interests and Moral Escalation," in Arnold J. Heidenheimer, ed., *Political Corruption: Readings in Comparative Analysis* (New York: Holt, Rinehart & Winston, 1970), pp. 311–313.

40. Ralph Waldo Emerson, "New England Reformers," in Emerson, *Prose Works*, 1:554. Hubert H. Humphrey, statement in 1975.

41. Theodore Roosevelt, "The Man with the Muck-Rake," *Putnam's Monthly* 1 (October 1906): 42–47.

42. Martin Shefter, "Party, Bureaucracy, and Political Change in the United States," in Louis Maisel and Joseph Cooper, eds., *Political Parties: Development and Decay* (Beverly Hills: Sage Publications, 1978), pp. 230ff.

43. James L. Sundquist, *Politics and Policy* (Washington, D.C.: Brookings Institution, 1968), p. 500.

44. Madison, *Critics and Crusaders*, p. 14. Garrison quoted in Schlesinger, *American as Reformer*, p. 109. Ladd quoted in Rush Welter, *The Mind of America: 1820–1860* (New York: Columbia University Press, 1975), p. 334.

45. Schlesinger, *American as Reformer*, pp. 32–33.

46. James Russell Lowell, *The Writings of James Russell Lowell*, 1:362–363. For an excellent brief summary of Jacksonian reform movements and their mutual interaction, see Walter Hugins, *The Reform Impulse 1825–1850* (Columbia: University of South Carolina Press, 1972), pp. 1–22.

47. Emerson, "New England Reformers," p. 549. Hofstadter, *American Political Tradition*, p. 141.

48. Alan P. Grimes, *The Puritan Ethic and Women's Suffrage* (New York: Oxford University Press, 1967), pp. 4–5, 100.

49. Hartz, *Liberal Tradition*, pp. 156–157.

50. Lipset and Raab, *Politics of Unreason*, pp. 20–24. Erwin C. Hargrove, "On Canadian and American Political Culture," *Canadian Journal of Economics and Political Science* 33 (February 1967): 107–108.

51. Stanley Elkins, *Slavery: A Problem in American Institutional and Intellectual Life*, 2nd ed. (Chicago: University of Chicago Press, 1968), p. 27.

52. Gerhart B. Ladner, *The Idea of Reform: Its Impact on Christian Thought and Action in the Age of the Fathers* (Cambridge, Mass.: Harvard University Press, 1959), pp. 2, 9, 35.

53. Ibid., pp. 33–34. Michael Walzer, *The Revolution of the Saints* (Cambridge, Mass.: Harvard University Press, 1965), pp. 11–12. Herbert Croly, *The Promise of American Life* (New York: Macmillan, 1909), p. 144.

54. Austin Ranney, *Curing the Mischiefs of Faction: Party Reform in America* (Berkeley: University of California Press, 1975), ch. 1.

55. William J. Crotty, *Political Reform and the American Experiment* (New York: Thomas Y. Crowell, 1977), p. 267.

56. Austin Ranney, "'The Divine Science': Political Engineering in American Culture," *American Political Science Review* 70 (March 1976): 147.

57. David J. Rothman, *The Discovery of the Asylum* (Boston: Little, Brown, 1971), pp. xiii–xiv, xix.

58. Lawrence Cremin, *The Transformation of the School* (New York: Knopf, 1961), pp. viii, 58–59. See generally David J. Rothman, *Conscience and Convenience: The Asylum and Its Alternatives in Progressive America* (Boston: Little, Brown, 1980).

59. Theodore J. Lowi, *At the Pleasure of the Mayor* (Glencoe, Ill: Free Press, 1964), p. 201.

60. Ranney, *Curing the Mischiefs of Faction*, p. 128.

61. Ibid., p. 191.

62. Richard Olney, letter to Charles E. Perkins, December 28, 1892, quoted in Matthew Josephson, *The Politicos* (New York: Harcourt, Brace, 1938), p. 526. On how accurate Olney's predictions turned out to be, see Samuel P. Huntington, "The 'Marasmus' of the ICC: The Commission, the Railroads, and the Public Interest," *Yale Law Journal* 61 (April 1952): 467–509, and, more generally, Huntington, "Clientelism: A Study in Administrative Politics" (diss., Harvard University, 1951).

63. Rothman, *Discovery of the Asylum*, pp. 240, 295.

64. Lowi, *Pleasure of the Mayor*, pp. 184–186. See also Crotty, *Political Reform*, pp. 267ff.

65. Robert Michels, *Political Parties* (New York: Dover, 1959), p. 408.

66. Walter Dean Burnham, "American Politics in the 1970s: Beyond Party?" in William Nisbet Chambers and Burnham, eds., *The American Party*

Systems: Stages of Political Development, 2nd ed. (New York: Oxford University Press, 1975), pp. 316–317.

67. Walter Dean Burnham, "Revitalization and Decay: Looking toward the Third Century of American Electoral Politics," *Journal of Politics* 38 (August 1976): 147.

68. Charles Pinckney, in Max Farrand, ed., *The Records of the Federal Convention* (New Haven: Yale University Press, 1911), 1:402ff.

69. James Madison, in Alexander Hamilton, John Jay, and Madison, *The Federalist*, no. 51 (New York: Modern Library, 1937), p. 336.

70. Burnham, "Revitalization and Decay," p. 149.

6. The Sources of Creedal Passion

1. John Israel, "Continuities and Discontinuities in the Ideology of the Great Proletarian Cultural Revolution," in Chalmers Johnson, ed., *Ideology and Politics in Contemporary China* (Seattle: University of Washington Press, 1973), p. 25.

2. Ibid.

3. Milton B. Singer, "Shame Cultures and Guilt Cultures," in Gerhart Piers and Milton B. Singer, *Shame and Guilt: A Psychoanalytic and a Cultural Study* (Springfield, Ill.: Charles C. Thomas, 1953), p. 45.

4. See Richard W. Wilson, *The Moral State: A Study of the Political Socialization of Chinese and American Children* (New York: Free Press, 1973), pp. 20ff. Lowell Dittmer, "Thought Reform and Cultural Revolution: An Analysis of the Symbolism of Chinese Politics," *American Political Science Review* 71 (March 1977): 78–79. Lucian W. Pye, *The Spirit of Chinese Politics* (Cambridge, Mass.: MIT Press, 1968), p. 96.

5. Byung-joon Ahn, "The Cultural Revolution and China's Search for Political Order," *China Quarterly* 58 (April-May 1974): 257. Paul J. Hiniker, *Revolutionary Ideology and Chinese Realty: Dissonance under Mao* (Beverly Hills: Sage Publications, 1977).

6. Dai Hsiao-ai, quoted in Lowell Dittmer, *Liu Shao-ch'i and the Chinese Cultural Revolution* (Berkeley: University of California Press, 1974), p. 305. Hong Yung Lee, *The Politics of the Chinese Cultural Revolution* (Berkeley: University of California Press, 1978), pp. 326–328, 340–343.

7. Hiniker, *Revolutionary Ideology*, p. 17. Dittmer, *Liu Shao-ch'i*, pp. 305, 314.

8. Dittmer, "Thought Reform," pp. 75–78, and *Liu Shao-Ch'i*, p. 297.

9. Alan P. L. Liu, *Political Culture and Group Conflict in Communist China* (Santa Barbara: Clio Press, 1976), pp. 24ff.

10. George P. Jan, "Government and Politics of the People's Republic of China" (unpublished manuscript), ch. 9, pp. 26, 29.

11. See Israel, in Johnson, *Ideology and Politics*, pp. 14–15, 22–24.

12. Benjamin Schwartz, "The Reign of Virtue: Some Broad Perspectives on Leader and Party in the Cultural Revolution," in John W. Lewis, ed.,

Party Leadership and Revolutionary Power in China (Cambridge: Cambridge University Press, 1970), pp. 155–156.

13. Ibid., p. 165.

14. James R. Townsend, *Politics in China* (Boston: Little, Brown, 1973), pp. 335–336.

15. Richard M. Pfeffer, "Leaders and Masses," in Michel Oksenberg, ed., *China's Developmental Experience* (New York: Columbia University Academy of Political Science, vol. 31, March 1973), p. 165. Lucian W. Pye, "Mass Participation in Communist China: Its Limitations and the Continuity of Culture," in John M. H. Lindbeck, ed., *China: Management of a Revolutionary Society* (Seattle: University of Washington Press, 1971), p. 30.

16. Michel Oksenberg, "On Learning from China," in Oksenberg, ed., *China's Developmental Experience,* p. 8. Townsend, *Politics in China,* p. 145.

17. For an intricate analysis of political cycles in China, see G. William Skinner and Edwin A. Winckler, "Compliance Succession in Rural Communist China: A Cyclical Theory," in Amitai Etzioni, ed., *Complex Organization: A Sociological Reader,* 2nd ed. (New York: Holt, Rinehart and Winston, 1969), pp. 410–438. They identify eight two-to-three-year cycles between 1949 and 1969.

18. C. P. FitzGerald, "Mao's Tse-Tung's Cultural Revolution," *American Political Science Review* 68 (June 1974): 800.

19. Richard Baum, "Ideology Redivivus," in Baum, ed., *China in Ferment: Perspectives on the Cultural Revolution* (Englewood Cliffs, N.J.: Prentice-Hall, 1971), pp. 70–71. See also Ahn, "The Cultural Revolution," pp. 252–253.

20. Richard M. Pfeffer, "The Pursuit of Purity: Mao's Cultural Revolution," in Baum, ed., *China in Ferment,* p. 207.

21. Marvin Meyers, *The Jacksonian Persuasion* (Stanford: Stanford University Press, 1957), p. 78.

22. See Ted R. Gurr, *Rogues, Rebels, and Reformers: A Political History of Urban Crime and Conflict* (Beverly Hills: Sage Publications, 1976), pp. 171–172, and, for a classic account of how reporters made a crime wave and how Theodore Roosevelt stopped it, Lincoln Steffens, *Autobiography* (New York: Harcourt, Brace, 1931), pt. 2, ch. 14.

23. Theodore J. Lowi, *At the Pleasure of the Mayor* (Glencoe, Ill.: Free Press, 1964), pp. 182–183.

24. Herbert Croly, *The Promise of American Life* (New York: Macmillan, 1909), p. 141.

25. Ronald G. Walters, "The Erotic South: Civilization and Sexuality in American Abolitionism," *American Quarterly* 25 (May 1973): 177.

26. David Donald, *Lincoln Reconsidered: Essays on the Civil War Era* (New York: Knopf, 1959), pp. 22–23.

27. Walter Lippmann, *Drift and Mastery* (Englewood Cliffs, N.J.: Prentice-Hall, 1961), pp. 23–27.

28. For leads into this literature, see John Wilson, *Introduction to Social Movements* (New York: Basic Books, 1973). Michael Useem, *Protest Move-*

ments in America (Indianapolis: Bobbs-Merrill, 1975). Joseph R. Gusfield, ed., *Protest, Reform, and Revolt: A Reader in Social Movements* (New York: John Wiley, 1970).

29. See Ted R. Gurr, *Why Men Rebel* (Princeton University Press, 1970), and Samuel P. Huntington, *Political Order in Changing Societies* (New Haven: Yale University Press, 1968), pp. 32–59.

30. See Donald, *Lincoln Reconsidered,* pp. 19–36, and Richard Hofstadter, *The Age of Reform* (New York: Knopf, 1956), pp. 134ff. For critiques of these interpretations, see: Robert A. Skotheim, "A Note on Historical Method: David Donald's 'Toward a Reconsideration of Abolitionists,' " *Journal of Southern History* 25 (August 1959): 356–365; Richard B. Sherman, "The Status Revolution and Massachusetts Progressive Leadership," *Political Science Quarterly* 78 (March 1963): 59–65; Jack Tager, "Progressives, Conservatives, and the Theory of the Status Revolution," *Mid-America* 48 (July 1966): 162–175; and Robert W. Doherty, "Status Anxiety and American Reform: Some Alternatives," *American Quarterly* 19 (Summer 1967): 329–337. Hofstadter and other scholars also analyzed McCarthyism and other rightist movements of the 1950s and early 1960s in terms of status politics. See Daniel Bell, ed., *The Radical Right* (Garden City, N.Y.: Doubleday, 1963). For a stimulating and insightful effort to synthesize several theories on the origins of social upheaval in terms of a cognitive dissonance approach, see James A. Geschwender, "Explorations in the Theory of Social Movements and Revolutions," *Social Forces* 47 (December 1968): 127–135.

31. Hofstadter, in Bell, *Radical Right,* pp. 98–99.

32. See Herbert Moller, "Youth as a Force in the Modern World," *Comparative Studies in Society and History* 10 (April 1968): 237–260.

33. See Seymour Martin Lipset, "Youth and Politics," in Robert K. Merton and Robert Nisbet, eds., *Contemporary Social Problems,* 3rd ed. (New York: Harcourt, Brace, Jovanovich, 1971), pp. 754ff, and Lipset, in Lipset and Gerald M. Schaflander, *Passion and Politics* (Boston: Little, Brown, 1971), pp. 125, 133–139, 142–149.

34. Anne Foner, "The Polity," in Matilda White Riley, Marilyn Johnson, and Anne Foner, *Aging and Society* (New York: Russell Sage Foundation, 1972), 3:148.

35. William N. Chambers, "Party Development and the American Mainstream," in William Chambers and Walter Dean Burnham, eds., *The American Party Systems,* 2nd ed. (New York: Oxford University Press, 1975), pp. 29–30. The cyclical evolution of American party systems has been noted and analyzed in the work of Arthur N. Holcombe, Samuel Lubell, V. O. Key, Jr., Philip Converse, Charles Sellers, and Walter Dean Burnham.

36. Hofstadter, *Age of Reform,* pp. 16ff. Lowi, *At the Pleasure of the Mayor,* ch. 8, "The Reform Cycle." William J. Crotty, *Political Reform and the American Experiment* (New York: Thomas Y. Crowell, 1977), ch. 9, "The Reform Cycle." Arthur M. Schlesinger, *The American as Reformer* (Cambridge, Mass.: Harvard University Press, 1950), p. 4. Nathan Glazer, "Towards an Imperial Judiciary," in Nathan Glazer and Irving Kristol, eds.,

The American Commonwealth 1976 (New York: Basic Books, 1976), pp. 104–106. Glazer argued that the historical activism-quietism cycle was giving way to a lasting expansion of the judiciary's role.

37. Arthur M. Schlesinger, Sr., *Paths to the Present* (Boston: Houghton Mifflin, 1964), pp. 89–103. James David Barber, *The Pulse of Politics: Electing Presidents in the Media Age* (New York: W. W. Norton, 1980).

38. J. Zvi Namenwirth, "Wheels of Time and the Interdependence of Value Change in America," *Journal of Interdisciplinary History* 3 (Spring 1973): 649–683, and Namenwirth and Richard C. Bibbee, "Change within or of the System: An Example from the History of American Values," *Quality and Quantity* 10 (June 1976): 145–164. Frank L. Klingberg, "The Historical Alternation of Moods in American Foreign Policy," *World Politics* 4 (January 1952): 239–273, and "Cyclical Trends in American Foreign Policy Moods and their Policy Implications," in Charles W. Kegley and Patrick J. McGowan, eds., *Challenges to America: U.S. Foreign Policy in the 1980s* (Sage International Yearbook of Foreign Policy Studies, vol. 4, 1979), pp. 37–55.

39. P. M. G. Harris, "The Social Origins of American Leaders: The Demographic Foundations," in Donald Fleming and Bernard Bailyn, eds., *Perspectives in American History* (Cambridge, Mass.: Warren Center for Studies in American History, 1969) 3: 159–346. David McClelland, *Power: The Inner Experience* (New York: Irvington Press, 1975), pp. 330–359.

40. Schlesinger, *Paths to the Present,* pp. 96–97. Namenwirth, "Wheels of Time," p. 679. Klingberg, "Historical Alternation," pp. 271–273.

41. Clarence L. Ver Steeg, *The Formative Years: 1607–1763* (New York: Hill and Wang, 1964), pp. 129–130.

42. Perry Miller, *The New England Mind: From Colony to Province* (Cambridge, Mass.: Harvard University Press, 1953), pp. 151, 172.

43. Ver Steeg, *Formative Years,* p. 149.

44. Richard Maxwell Brown, "Violence and the American Revolution," in Stephen G. Kurtz and James H. Hutson, eds., *Essays on the American Revolution* (Chapel Hill: University of North Carolina Press, 1973), pp. 86–87. Charles M. Andrews, "General Introduction," in Andrews, ed., *Narratives of the Insurrections, 1675–1690* (New York: Charles Scribner's Sons, 1915), p. 4.

45. David S. Lovejoy, *The Glorious Revolution in America* (New York: Harper and Row, 1972), ch. 16.

46. Brown, "Violence and the American Revolution," p. 87.

47. Michael Walzer, *The Revolution of the Saints* (Cambridge, Mass.: Harvard University Press, 1965), p. 1.

48. Lawrence Stone, *The Causes of the English Revolution, 1529–1642* (London: Routledge & Kegan Paul, 1972), p. 123.

49. Ibid., pp. 110ff.

50. Austin Woolrych, "The English Revolution: An Introduction," and "Puritanism, Politics and Society," in E. W. Ives, ed., *The English Revolution, 1600–1660* (London: Edward Arnold, 1968), pp. 20, 89.

51. Stone, *Causes of the English Revolution,* p. 144.

52. Woolrych, "The English Revolution," p. 87.

53. Stone, *Causes of the English Revolution,* pp. 91, 99.

54. Christopher Hill, *The World Turned Upside Down* (New York: Viking Press, 1972), pp. 12, 14, 294.

55. Ibid., p. 306.

56. Thomas Case, quoted in Walzer, *Revolution of the Saints,* pp. 10–11.

57. Ralph Waldo Emerson, "Man the Reformer," in Emerson, *Prose Works,* rev. ed. (Boston: Fields, Osgood, 1870) 1: 125–126.

58. William Lee Miller, "American Religion and American Political Attitudes," in James Ward Smith and A. Leland Jamison, eds., *Religious Perspectives in American Culture* (Princeton: Princeton University Press, 1961), pp. 84–85. Philip Schaff, *America: A Sketch of Its Political, Social, and Religious Character* (Cambridge, Mass.: Belknap Press of Harvard University Press, 1961), p. 72. Charles L. Sanford, *The Quest for Paradise: Europe and the American Moral Imagination* (Urbana: University of Illinois Press, 1961), p. 74.

59. H. Richard Niebuhr, *The Kingdom of God in America* (Hamden, Conn.: Shoe String Press, 1956), pp. 17ff. Sanford, *Quest for Paradise,* pp. 54–55.

60. H. Richard Niebuhr, "The Protestant Movement and Democracy in the United States," in James Ward Smith and A. Leland Jamison, eds., *The Shaping of American Religion* (Princeton: Princeton University Press, 1961), p. 27.

61. Schaff, *America,* p. 72.

62. Alexis de Tocqueville, *Democracy in America,* ed. Phillips Bradley (New York: Vintage Books, 1954) 1: 314. Seymour Martin Lipset, *The First New Nation* (New York: Basic Books, 1963), pp. 140–150.

63. Tocqueville, *Democracy in America,* 1:46.

64. Quoted in Lipset, *First New Nation,* p. 155.

65. Cushing Strout, *The New Heavens and New Earth: Political Religion in America* (New York: Harper & Row, 1974), pp. 51–52. Krister Stendhal, quoted in William G. McLoughlin and Robert N. Bellah, eds., *Religion in America* (Boston: Houghton Mifflin, 1968), p. xv.

66. John Higham, "Hanging Together: Divergent Unities in American History," *Journal of American History* 61 (June 1974): 13. See also Conrad Cherry, "Two American Sacred Ceremonies: Their Implications for the Study of Religion in America," *American Quarterly* 21 (Winter 1969): 754. Sidney E. Mead, *The Lively Experiment* (New York: Harper & Row, 1963).

67. Tocqueville, *Democracy in America,* 1:311. Miller, in Smith and Jamison, *Religious Perspectives,* pp. 105–113.

68. John Edwin Smylie, "National Ethos and the Church," *Theology Today,* October 1963, pp. 313–318, quoted in Cherry, "Two American Sacred Ceremonies," p. 750. On civil religion in America, see also: Robert N. Bellah, "Civil Religion in America," in McLoughlin and Bellah, *Religion in America,* pp. 3–23; Russell E. Richey and Donald G. Jones, eds,. *American Civil Religion* (New York: Harper & Row, 1974), passim; Sidney E. Mead, "The

'Nation with the Soul of a Church,' " *Church History* 36 (September 1967): 262–283; and Mead, *Lively Experiment,* pp. 134ff.

69. G. K. Chesterton, *What I Saw in America* (New York: Dodd, Mead, 1923), pp. 11–12. *New York Times,* January 12, 1975, p. 1.

70. D. W. Brogan, *The American Character* (New York: Vintage Books, 1959), p. 164.

71. Mead, "The 'Nation with the Soul of a Church,' " p. 275.

72. Edward M. Burns, *The American Idea of Mission* (New Brunswick, N.J.: Rutgers University Press, 1957), p. 11. On American millennialism, see also Sanford, *Quest for Paradise;* Niebuhr, *Kingdom of God in America;* Strout, *New Heavens and New Earth;* Ernest Lee Tuveson, *Redeemer Nation: The Idea of America's Millennial Role* (Chicago: University of Chicago Press, 1968); Russel B. Nye, *This Almost Chosen People* (Lansing: Michigan State University Press, 1966); and Conrad Cherry, ed., *God's New Israel: Religious Interpretations of American Destiny* (Englewood Cliffs, N.J.: Prentice-Hall, 1971).

73. This dating generally follows that of William G. McLoughlin in *Revivals, Awakenings, and Reform: An Essay on Religion and Social Change in America, 1607–1977* (Chicago: University of Chicago Press, 1978). For slightly different dates, see his earlier writings: *Modern Revivalism: From Charles Grandison Finney to Billy Graham* (New York: Ronald Press, 1959), pp. 7–11, and *Billy Graham: Revivalist in a Secular Age* (New York: Ronald Press, 1960), pp. 7–11.

74. Donald G. Matthews, "The Second Great Awakening as an Organizing Process, 1780–1830: An Hypothesis," *American Quarterly* 21 (Spring 1969): 25.

75. McLoughlin, *Revivals, Awakenings, and Reform,* pp. 2, 10–11, 23.

76. Strout, *New Heavens and New Earth,* pp. 42–43.

77. Alan Heimert, *Religion and the American Mind* (Cambridge, Mass.: Harvard University Press, 1966), pp. 21, 481. William G. McLoughlin, "The American Revolution as a Religious Revival: 'The Millennium in One Country,' " *New England Quarterly* 40 (March 1967): 99ff.

78. Richard L. Bushman, ed., *The Great Awakening* (New York: Atheneum, 1970), p. xi. Sidney E. Ahlstrom, "National Trauma and Changing Religious Values," *Daedalus* 107 (Winter 1978): 19–20.

79. McLoughlin, *Revivals, Awakenings, and Reform,* pp. 52–53.

80. Richard L. Bushman, *From Puritan to Yankee* (Cambridge, Mass.: Harvard University Press, 1967), pp. 189–192. Heimert, *Religion and the American Mind,* p. 32.

81. Whitney R. Cross, *The Burned-Over District* (Ithaca, N.Y.: Cornell University Press, 1950), pp. 75–76. For a detailed study of the causes of the awakening in Rochester, see Paul E. Johnson, *A Shopkeeper's Millennium* (New York: Hill and Wang, 1978).

82. Matthews, "The Second Great Awakening," pp. 27, 32, 34. Heimert, *Religion and the American Mind,* p. 534.

83. Bushman, *From Puritan to Yankee,* p. 192.

84. Strout, *New Heavens and New Earth*, pp. 38–43.

85. Bushman, *Great Awakening*, p. xii. Mead, *Lively Experiment*, pp. 31–34.

86. Heimert, *Religion and the American Mind*, p. 10.

87. William G. McLoughlin, " 'Enthusiasm for Liberty': The Great Awakening as the Key to the Revolution," in Jack P. Greene and William McLoughlin, *Preachers and Politicians* (Worcester, Mass.: American Antiquarian Society, 1977), pp. 65–70.

88. Harry S. Stout, "Religion, Communications, and the Ideological Origins of the American Revolution," *William and Mary Quarterly* 34 (October 1977): 519–541.

89. William G. McLoughlin, Jr., *Billy Graham: Revivalist in a Secular Age* (New York: Ronald Press, 1960), pp. 15–18, and *Modern Revivalism: Charles Grandison Finney to Billy Graham* (New York: Ronald Press, 1959), passim.

90. William Warren Sweet, *Revivalism in America: Its Origin, Growth, and Decline* (New York: Scribners, 1944), p. 31. Matthews, "The Second Great Awakening," pp. 36–37. Cross, *Burned-Over District*, p. 356.

91. Niebuhr, "The Protestant Movement," pp. 24, 31–32.

92. McLoughlin, *Modern Revivalism*, p. 526.

93. Alan Heimert, quoted in McLoughlin, "The American Revolution as a Religious Revival," p. 99. McLoughlin, " 'Enthusiasm for Liberty,' " p. 48. See also Strout, *New Heavens and New Earth*, ch. 4, and Mead, *Lively Experiment*, pp. 34–35, 52, 61–62.

94. Matthews, "The Second Great Awakening," p. 35. Robert N. Bellah, *The Broken Covenant* (New York: Seabury Press, 1975), p. 44.

95. Sweet, *Revivalism in America*, pp. 152ff. Timothy L. Smith, *Revivalism and Social Reform in Mid-Nineteenth-Century America* (New York: Abingdon Press, 1957). Gilbert Hobbs Barnes, *The Anti-Slavery Impulse, 1830–1844* (New York: D. Appleton Century Co., 1933). John L. Hammond, *The Politics of Benevolence: Revival Religion and American Voting Behavior* (Norwood, N.J.: Ablex, 1979). McClelland also explores the relations among religious revivals, reform, and war in *Power: The Inner Experience*, pp. 346–359.

96. See Alan P. Grimes, *The Puritan Ethic and Woman Suffrage* (New York: Oxford University Press, 1967), esp. p. 71, and, more generally, Paul Boyer, *Urban Masses and Moral Order in America, 1820–1920* (Cambridge, Mass.: Harvard University Press, 1978).

7. The S&S Years, 1960–1975

1. "Eisenhower on the Presidency," interview with Walter Cronkite on CBS television, October 12, 1961, quoted in Emmett John Hughes, *The Ordeal of Power* (New York: Atheneum, 1963), p. 331n.

2. Daniel J. Boorstin, *The Genius of American Politics* (Chicago: University of Chicago Press, 1953), pp. 9, 161.

3. Seymour Martin Lipset, *Political Man* (New York: Doubleday & Co., 1960), p. 414. For representative works rationalizing bigness, see: David E. Lilienthal, *Big Business: A New Era* (New York: Harper & Row, 1953); Adolf A. Berle, *The Twentieth Century Capitalist Revolution* (New York: Harcourt Brace, 1954); and John Kenneth Galbraith, *American Capitalism: The Concept of Countervailing Power* (Boston: Houghton Mifflin, 1952). For the roots of this line of thought in the New Deal, see Richard Hofstadter, *The Age of Reform* (New York: Knopf, 1956), pp. 310ff.

4. Philip Converse, "Change in the American Electorate," in Angus Campbell and Converse, eds., *The Human Meaning of Social Change* (New York: Russell Sage Foundation, 1972), pp. 327ff. James S. House and William M. Mason, "Political Alienation in America, 1952–1968," *American Sociological Review* 40 (April 1975): 123ff. See also James D. Wright, *The Dissent of the Governed: Alienation and Democracy in America* (New York: Academic Press, 1976), ch. 7.

5. Lipset, *Political Man*, p. 406. See also Daniel Bell, *The End of Ideology* (Glencoe, Ill.: Free Press, 1960), esp. pp. 369–375.

6. Address, June 1962, Yale University, quoted in Seymour Martin Lipset, "Ideology and No End," *Encounter* 39 (December 1972): 19.

7. Address, May 1962, New York, N.Y., quoted in Lipset, "Ideology and No End," p. 19.

8. Bernard Crick, "The Strange Death of the American Theory of Consensus," *Political Quarterly* 43 (January–March 1972): 59.

9. Henry Fairlie, *The Kennedy Promise* (Garden City, N.Y.: Doubleday & Co., 1973), p. 19.

10. Samuel P. Huntington, "The United States," in Michel Crozier, Samuel P. Huntington, and Joji Watanuki, *The Crisis of Democracy* (New York: New York University Press, 1975), pp. 59–60.

11. Warren E. Miller, Arthur H. Miller, and Edward J. Schneider, *American National Election Studies Data Sourcebook, 1952–1978* (Cambridge, Mass.: Harvard University Press, 1980), pp. 256–260.

12. Louis Harris, "Confidence in Leadership Down Again," press release, Harris Survey, March 22, 1976.

13. These averages are computed from sixty-six Gallup surveys reported in *The Gallup Opinion Index*, 1950–1979, and distributed as follows: 1950–1959, twenty surveys; 1960–1970, nineteen surveys; 1971–1972, seven surveys; 1973–1979, twenty surveys. The question asked was: "What do you think is the most important problem facing this country today?"

14. Everett Carll Ladd, Jr., and Seymour Martin Lipset, "Public Opinion and Public Policy," in Peter Duignan and Alvin Rabushka, eds., *The United States in the 1980s* (Stanford: Hoover Institution, 1980), pp. 72–74.

15. "Revolution": Al Haber, quoted in Edward J. Bacciocco, Jr., *The New Left in America* (Stanford: Hoover Institution Press, 1974), pp. 228–229. "Moral issues": David Horowitz and Michael Rossman, quoted in Lawrence Lader, *Power on the Left* (New York: Norton, 1979), p. 169.

16. "Toward a Theory of Social Change in America, or the Port Au-

thority Statement," position paper released at SDS–REP conference, Princeton University, February 1967, quoted in Bacciocco, *New Left*, p. 229.

17. Norman H. Nie, Sidney Verba, and John R. Petrocik, *The Changing American Voter*, rev. ed. (Cambridge, Mass.: Harvard University Press, 1980), pp. 365–369. The authors of this study attribute these changes largely to the nature and political appeals of the candidates. It seems not unreasonable to assume, however, that the candidates were themselves responding to the temper of the times with the sort of appeal they thought would mobilize support.

18. Quoted in Paul Seabury, "The Moral Purposes and Philosophical Bases of American Foreign Policy," *Orbis* 20 (Spring 1976): 13.

19. The following two paragraphs are from my essay, "The United States," in Crozier, Huntington, and Watanuki, *Crisis of Democracy*, pp. 75–76.

20. See Ladd and Lipset in Duignan and Rabushka, *United States in the 1980s*, pp. 65–67, for a summary of the evidence on public confidence in institutional leadership.

21. Daniel Patrick Moynihan, letter to Richard Nixon, *New York Times*, March 11, 1970, p. 30, quoted in Lawrence Stone, *The Causes of the English Revolution, 1529–1642* (London: Routledge and Kegan Paul, 1972), p. 79.

22. Miller, Miller, and Schneider, *Election Studies Data Sourcebook*, pp. 310, 323. This electoral participation index is a percentage difference index calculated by subtracting the percentage of respondents who neither voted nor engaged in any of five campaign-related activities (talking to people, attending meetings, working for a candidate or party, displaying a bumper sticker or wearing a button, or contributing money) from the percentage of respondents who both voted and engaged in one or more of these activities.

23. Sidney Verba and Norman H. Nie, *Participation in America: Political Democracy and Social Equality* (New York: Harper & Row, 1972), pp. 151–160, 254–255. Anthony M. Orum, "A Reappraisal of the Social and Political Participation of Negroes," *American Journal of Sociology* 72 (July 1966): 32–46. Marvin E. Olsen, "Social and Political Participation of Blacks," *American Sociological Review* 35 (August 1970): 682–697.

24. Verba and Nie, *Participation in America*, ch. 9.

25. Paul Allen Beck and M. Kent Jennings, "Political Periods and Political Participation," *American Political Science Review* 73 (September 1979): 748.

26. Data adapted from Thomas Agnello by Anne Foner, "Age Stratification and Age Conflict in Political Life," *American Sociological Review* 39 (April 1974): 190.

27. Jeffrey M. Berry, *Lobbying for the People* (Princeton: Princeton University Press, 1977), p. 34.

28. *New York Times*, May 18, 1977, pp. A1, B9; Common Cause, 1978 mailing, signed by David Cohen.

29. Beck and Jennings, "Political Periods and Political Participation," p. 739; Miller, Miller, and Schneider, *Election Studies Data Sourcebook,* p. 299.

30. Lader, *Power on the Left,* p. 172.

31. Irwin Unger, *The Movement: A History of the American New Left, 1959–1972* (New York: Dodd, Mead & Co., 1974), p. 88.

32. Frances Fox Piven and Richard A. Cloward, *Poor People's Movements* (New York: Pantheon, 1977), pp. 32–33.

33. Milton Viorst, *Fire in the Streets* (New York: Simon and Schuster, 1979), pp. 347ff, 369, 375–379. James Q. Wilson, *Political Organizations* (New York: Basic Books, 1973), p. 183.

34. Theodore H. White, *Breach of Faith* (New York: Atheneum–Reader's Digest Press, 1975), p. 234.

35. John Chancellor, quoted in *Newsweek* 81 (January 15, 1973): 42.

36. Cord Meyer, *Facing Reality* (New York: Harper & Row, 1980), pp. 86–90.

37. Michael Kinsey and Arthur Lubow, "Alger Hiss and the Smoking Gun Fallacy," *Washington Monthly* 7 (October 1975): 52.

38. Russell Baker, "Ready for Sleep," *New York Times,* February 1, 1977, p. 29.

39. Elliot Zashin, "The Progress of Black Americans in Civil Rights: The Past Two Decades Assessed," *Daedalus* 107 (Winter 1978): 247–250. Miller, Miller, and Schneider, *Election Studies Data Sourcebook, 1952–1978,* p. 317. "Blacks in America: 25 Years of Radical Change," *U.S. News and World Report* 86 (May 14, 1979): 59.

40. Zashin, "The Progress of Black Americans," pp. 250–255, 260. Richard Freeman, "Black Economic Progress since 1964," *The Public Interest* 52 (Summer 1978): 52–68. *Washington Post,* April 2, 1978, pp. A1, A18.

41. Zashin, "The Progress of Black Americans," p. 260.

42. *Time* 110 (August 15, 1977): 67.

43. Anthony King, "Introduction" and "The American Polity in the Late 1970s: Building Coalitions in the Sand," in King, ed., *The New American Political System* (Washington, D.C.: American Enterprise Institute for Public Policy Research, 1978), pp. 2, 388.

44. See: King, *New American Political System;* Nie, Verba, and Petrocik, *Changing American Voter;* Seymour Martin Lipset, ed., *The Third Century* (Chicago: University of Chicago Press, 1979); Huntington, "The United States," in Crozier, Huntington, Watanuki, *Crisis of Democracy;* Nathan Glazer and Irving Kristol, eds., *The American Commonwealth 1976* (New York: Basic Books, 1976); and Everett C. Ladd, Jr., with Charles D. Hadley, *Transformations of the American Party System,* 2nd ed., (New York: Norton, 1978).

45. See *U.S. News and World Report* 76 (April 22, 1974): 34; 78 (April 21, 1975): 34; 80 (April 19, 1976): 30; 82 (April 18, 1977): 36; 84 (April 17, 1978): 38; 86 (April 16, 1979): 40; 88 (April 14, 1980): 41.

46. Louis Harris, "Confidence Climbing," press release, Harris Survey, March 14, 1977.

47. Michael Robinson, "Television and American Politics: 1956-1976," *The Public Interest* 48 (Summer 1977): 12-13.

48. Peter B. Clark, "The Opinion Machine: Intellectuals, the Mass Media, and American Government," in Harry Clor, ed., *Mass Media and Modern Democracy* (Chicago: Rand-McNally, 1974), p. 69.

49. James Reston, quoted in Max Kampelman, "The Media," in Harvey C. Mansfield, Jr., ed., *Congress against the President,* Proceedings of the Academy of Political Science, vol. 32, no. 1 (New York, 1975), p. 95.

50. Benjamin Bradlee, quoted in Kampelman, "The Media," p. 89; and, in general, Max M. Kampelman, "The Power of the Press: A Problem for Our Democracy," *Policy Review* 6 (Fall 1978): 7-39.

51. Austin Ranney, "The Political Parties: Reform and Decline," in King, *New American Political System,* p. 213.

52. Ladd and Hadley, *Transformations,* pp. 320-333. Nie, Verba, and Petrocik, *Changing American Voter,* passim, but esp. chs. 4, 7-10, and Epilogue.

53. Hugh Heclo, "Issues Networks and the Executive Establishment," in King, *New American Political System,* pp. 87ff; and idem, *A Government of Strangers: Executive Politics in Washington* (Washington, D.C.: Brookings Institution, 1977).

54. Harrison W. Fox, Jr., and Susan Webb Hammond, "The Growth of Congressional Staffs," in Mansfield, *Congress against the President,* pp. 112-124.

55. See "When Congress Has the Veto," *National Journal* 8 (May 29, 1976): 745.

56. Fred I. Greenstein, "Change and Continuity in the Modern Presidency," in King, *New American Political System,* pp. 80-82.

57. King, "American Polity," pp. 374-375.

58. Lyndon B. Johnson, quoted in Doris Kearns, *Lyndon Johnson and the American Dream* (New York: Harper & Row, 1976), pp. 177-178. Richard M. Nixon, March 13, 1973, quoted in *New York Times,* May 5, 1974, p. 40. Dwight Chapin, quoted in *New York Times,* August 5, 1973, p. 40. Gerald R. Ford, "Imperiled, Not Imperial," *Time* 116 (November 10, 1980): 30.

59. ABC News-Harris Survey, vol. 2, no. 67 (June 2, 1980).

60. "Opinion Roundup," *Public Opinion* 2 (June-July 1979): 32.

61. "Opinion Roundup," *Public Opinion* 1 (November-December 1978): 29. Nie, Verba, and Petrocik, *Changing American Voter,* pp. 370-371.

62. Quoted in John Cole, "Lament for a Faded Dream," *The Observer,* August 31, 1980, p. 11.

63. Joseph Kraft, *Boston Globe,* March 13, 1975, p. 33, and *Washington Post,* October 25, 1977, p. A19.

64. George F. Will, *Newsweek* 91 (March 6, 1978): 108. High Sidey, *Time* 116 (December 1, 1980): 18.

65. Walter Cronkite, interview, *Playboy*, June 1973, p. 76, quoted in Michael Robinson, "American Political Legitimacy in an Era of Electronic Journalism: Reflections on the Evening News," in Richard Adler, ed., *Television as a Social Force: New Approaches to TV Criticism* (Aspen: Praeger, 1975), p. 123.

66. Roger Mudd, quoted in Kampelman, "The Media," p. 94. Theodore H. White, "America's Two Cultures," *Columbia Journalism Review* 8 (Winter 1969–70):8.

67. Robinson, "American Political Legitimacy," p. 117.

68. Robinson, "Television and American Politics," pp. 18–19, 35.

69. Ibid., p. 35.

70. Stanley Rothman, "The Mass Media in Post-Industrial Society," in Lipset, *Third Century*, p. 383. Samuel P. Huntington, "Postindustrial Politics: How Benign Will It Be?" *Comparative Politics* 6 (January 1974): 182–186.

71. Harry Rosenfeld, metropolitan editor of *The Washington Post*, on BBC television, May 7, 1973.

72. *New York Times*, January 18, 1980, p. A10.

8. The Viability of American Ideals and Institutions

1. Richard Hofstadter, *The American Political Tradition* (New York: Knopf, 1951), pp. 65–66.

2. Marvin Meyers, *The Jacksonian Persuasion: Politics and Belief* (Stanford: Stanford University Press, 1957), p. 8.

3. See Edward Pessen, "The Egalitarian Myth and the American Social Reality: Wealth, Mobility, and Equality in the 'Era of the Common Man,' " *American Historical Review* 76 (October 1971): 989–1034, and *Riches, Class, and Power before the Civil War* (Lexington, Mass.: D. C. Heath, 1973), passim. For critical discussions of Pessen's evidence and argument, see Whitman Ridgway, "Measuring Wealth and Power in Ante-Bellum America: A Review Essay," *Historical Methods Newsletter* 8 (March 1975): 74–78, and Robert E. Gallman, "Professor Pessen on the 'Egalitarian Myth,' " *Social Science History* 2 (Winter 1978): 194–207. For Pessen's response, see his "On a Recent Cliometric Attempt to Resurrect the Myth of Antebellum Egalitarianism," *Social Science History* 3 (Winter 1979): 208–227.

4. Gordon S. Wood, *History Book Club Review*, June 1955, pp. 16–17, commenting on Rush Welter's *The Mind of America: 1820–1860*.

5. Rush Welter, *The Mind of America: 1820–1860* (New York: Columbia University Press, 1975), pp. 7–10.

6. Alexis de Tocqueville, *Democracy in America*, ed. Phillips Bradley (New York: Vintage Books, 1954), 1:6–17.

7. Joseph L. Blau, ed., *Social Theories of Jacksonian Democracy* (New York: Liberal Arts Press, 1954), pp. xxvii–xxviii.

8. Hofstadter, *American Political Tradition*, p. vi.

9. Herbert Croly, *The Promise of American Life* (New York: Mac-

millan, 1909), p. 156. Walter Lippmann, *Drift and Mastery* (Englewood Cliffs, N.J.: Prentice-Hall, 1961), pp. 81–82.

10. Hofstadter, *American Political Tradition*, pp. 223.

11. J. R. Pole, *The Pursuit of Equality in American History* (Berkeley: University of California Press, 1978), p. 326.

12. See Ronald Inglehart, *The Silent Revolution: Changing Values and Political Styles among Western Publics* (Princeton: Princeton University Press, 1977), and George C. Lodge, *The New American Ideology* (New York: Knopf, 1975).

13. Ronald Inglehart, "The Silent Revolution in Europe: Intergenerational Change in Post-Industrial Societies," *American Political Science Review* 65 (December 1971): 991–1017.

14. Samuel P. Huntington, "Postindustrial Politics: How Benign Will It Be?" *Comparative Politics* 6 (January 1974): 188–189.

15. Plato, *The Republic*, tr. Francis MacDonald Cornford (New York: Oxford University Press, 1945), p. 290.

16. Louis Hartz, *The Liberal Tradition in America* (New York: Harcourt, Brace, 1955), p. 181.

17. Samuel P. Huntington, *Political Order in Changing Societies* (New Haven: Yale University Press, 1968), pp. 362–369.

18. See Samuel P. Huntington, *The Soldier and the State: The Theory and Politics of Civil Military Relations* (Cambridge, Mass.: Harvard University Press, 1957), esp. pp. 143–157.

19. George F. Kennan, *American Diplomacy 1900–1950* (Chicago: University of Chicago Press, 1951), pp. 93–94. Huntington, *The Soldier and the State*, pp. 80–97.

20. Lucian W. Pye, *The Spirit of Chinese Politics* (Cambridge, Mass.: MIT Press, 1968), p. 91.

21. Seymour Martin Lipset, "The Banality of Revolt," *Saturday Review* 53 (July 18, 1970): 26.

22. Peregrine Worsthorne, "America—Conscience or Shield?" *Encounter*, no. 14 (November 1954): 15.

23. Henry Fairlie, "Anti-Americanism at Home and Abroad," *Commentary* 60 (December 1975): 35.

24. See, for example, Hans J. Morgenthau, *In Defense of the National Interest* (New York: Knopf, 1951), and "Another 'Great Debate': The National Interest of the United States," *American Political Science Review* 46 (December 1952): 961–988; Reinhold Niebuhr, *Christian Realism and Political Problems* (New York: Charles Scribner's Sons, 1953), and *The Irony of American History* (New York: Charles Scribners Sons, 1952); Kennan, *American Diplomacy 1900–1950;* Robert E. Osgood, *Ideals and Self-Interest in America's Foreign Relations* (Chicago: University of Chicago Press, 1953); Richard H. Ullman, "Washington versus Wilson," *Foreign Policy*, no. 21 (Winter 1975–76): 97–124.

25. Henry A. Kissinger, quoted in Raymond Gastil, "Affirming Ameri-

can Ideals in Foreign Policy," *Freedom at Issue,* no. 38 (November-December 1976): 12.

26. Jimmy Carter, address, B'nai B'rith convention, Washington, D.C., September 8, 1976.

27. Hans J. Morgenthau, "Repression's Friend," *New York Times,* October 10, 1974, p. 46.

28. See John D. Montgomery, *Forced to be Free: The Artificial Revolution in Germany and Japan* (Chicago: University of Chicago Press, 1957).

29. Theodore P. Wright, *American Support of Free Elections Abroad* (Washington, D.C.: Public Affairs Press, 1964), pp. 137–138.

30. Jorge I. Dominguez, *Cuba: Order and Revolution* (Cambridge, Mass.: Harvard University Press, 1978), p. 13.

31. See Tad Szulc, *The Twilight of the Tyrants* (New York: Henry Holt, 1959).

32. Jerome Slater, *Intervention and Negotiation* (New York: Harper & Row, 1970), p. 7.

33. Abraham F. Lowenthal, *The Dominican Intervention* (Cambridge, Mass.: Harvard University Press, 1972), p. 16.

34. Jerome Levinson and Juan de Onis, *The Alliance that Lost Its Way* (Chicago: Quadrangle Books, 1970), pp. 81–82.

35. H. Bradford Westerfield, *The Instruments of America's Foreign Policy* (New York: Thomas Y. Crowell, 1963), p. 416.

36. A. M. Rosenthal, *New York Times,* April 8, 1963, p. 14.

37. Quoted by Andrew H. Malcolm, *New York Times,* June 11, 1976, p. A2.

38. *The Economist* 275 (August 30, 1980), pp. 27–28.

39. Ullman, "Washington versus Wilson," pp. 117, 123.

40. Stanley Hoffmann, "No Choice, No Illusions," *Foreign Policy,* no. 25 (Winter, 1976–77), p. 127.

41. Adnan Menderes, *Cumhuriyet,* July 18, 1946, quoted in Kemal H. Karpat, *Turkey's Politics* (Princeton: Princeton University Press, 1959), p. 140, n. 10.

42. Fairlie, "Anti-Americanism at Home and Abroad," p. 34, quoting William Clarke, 1881.

43. Daniel Bell, "The End of American Exceptionalism," in Nathan Glazer and Irving Kristol, eds., *The American Commonwealth 1976* (New York: Basic Books, 1976), p. 197.

44. Mihajlo Mihajlov, "Prospects for the Post-Tito Era," *New America* 17 (January 1980): 7.

INDEX

Adams, John, 5, 93, 125

Adams, Samuel, 102

Age: and response to cognitive dissonance, 71; and periods of creedal passion, 146; and political participation, 181–182; and voting behavior, 182–183; and forms of protest, 184

Agnew, Spiro, 189

Alienation, political, in the 1950s, 170

Allende, Salvador, 252–253

Alliance for Progress, 251

Almond, Gabriel, 43

American, The, 101

American Creed, 4, 13–14; sources of, 14–16; conflicts inherent in, 16–18; alternatives to, 18–21; stability of, 21–23; as basis of national identity, 23–30; relation to political institutions, 32; antigovernmental aspects of, 33–38, 216; and socioeconomic status, 73–74; periods of passion over, 85–91; climate of passion over, 91; reformers united by, 107; and reform, 113–114; and Protestantism, 157; in S&S Years, 174; possible lessening of reliance on, 229–231. *See also* Creedal passion

American politics: ideals of, 3–4; structural paradigms of, 5–10; ideals vs. institutions in, 10–12; and IvI gap, 39–41, 51; cycles in, 147–148; relation of religion to, 165–166. *See*

also Political institutions; Political parties

"American's Creed," 159

Angola, 208

Antipower ethic, 38–39, 75; and conspiracy theory, 80; and sincerity, 81–83

Antislavery movement, and creedal passion, 111–112

Antitrust reform, 117

Antiwar movement, and woman suffrage, 110. *See also* Vietnam War

Arendt, Hannah, 89

Argentina, 50–51

Arnold, Thurman, 90–91

Asylums: as symbols of reform, 117; perversion of, 119

Atlantic Monthly, 101

Austria, 249

Authority: American attitude toward, 46, 179; German attitude toward, 47; French attitude toward, 50; Russian attitude toward, 54; Japanese attitude toward, 55; emphasis on, in China, 59–60; reaction to misuse of, 184; misuse vs. erosion of, 211, 213; during S&S Years, 211–220 cynicism and restoration of, 214–220

Bagehot, Walter, 46

Bailyn, Bernard, 33, 92, 93, 107

Baker, Ray Stannard, 103

American Archaeology
Past and Future

A Celebration of the
Society for American Archaeology
1935–1985

David J. Meltzer, Don D. Fowler, and
Jeremy A. Sabloff, editors

Published for the
Society for American Archaeology
by the
Smithsonian Institution Press
Washington and London
1986

CC
101
.U6
A46
1986

© 1986 by Society for American Archaeology. All rights reserved.

Library of Congress Cataloging-in-Publication Data
Main entry under title:

American archaeology past and future.

Includes bibliographies.
Supt. of Docs. no.: SI 1.2:Ar2/2/935–85
1. Archaeology—United States—History—Addresses, essays, lectures. 2. United States—Antiquities—Addresses, essays, lectures. 3. Indians of North America—Antiquities—Addresses, essays, lectures. 4. Society for American Archaeology. I. Meltzer, David J., 1955– II. Fowler, Don D., 1936–   . III. Sabloff, Jeremy A., 1944–   . IV. Society for American Archaeology.
CC101.U6A46 1986   973.01   85-600308
ISBN 0–87474–692–2
ISBN 0–87474–693–0 (pbk.)

Printed in the United States of America

∞

The paper in this book meets the guidelines for permanence and durability of the Committee on Production Guidelines for Book Longevity of the Council on Library Resources.

Cover photograph: "Starting a 50-foot trench in a mound," taken by Warren Moorehead, recording the 1891 World's Columbian Exposition field work at the Hopewell site. Reproduced by permission of the Ohio Historical Society.

Book design by Carol Beehler.

Contents

New Looks at Past Problems

Current Trends and Future Prospects

Editors' Introduction

A Celebration of the Society

On December 28, 1934, at the Hotel Roosevelt, Pittsburgh, Pennsylvania, 31 individuals signed the constitution for the Society for American Archaeology (Griffin 1985). This was the culmination of activities that began in the summer of 1933, aimed at creating a society "by which professional and non-professional students of American archaeology can express themselves" (Guthe 1935:142).

The initial volume of *American Antiquity* appeared in July 1935 under the editorship of Will C. McKern (see Sabloff 1985). At the end of that same year, the first annual meeting of the SAA was held at Andover, Massachusetts, in conjunction with the American Anthropological Association and the American Folklore Society. Eight papers were delivered at that meeting to an assembly of 75 (Guthe 1936:310).

Over the years the SAA membership, its journal, and its annual meetings have grown considerably. Now, five decades later, it is indeed reasonable to claim, as did one self-professed "rank outsider," that "the Society for American Archaeology is in a very real sense the premier archaeological society in the world" (Renfrew 1983:3). Certainly the Society for American Archaeology is an important organization in archaeology today, and the occasion of its 50th anniversary in 1985 warrants notice, if not celebration.

And celebrate the SAA did, with a fine Golden Anniversary issue of *American Antiquity* edited by Patty Jo Watson (April 1985), and a series of special programs and events at the Society's 50th annual meeting in May of 1985 in Denver, Colorado. The celebration at the 50th annual meeting, the largest (nearly 2000 attendees) and longest meeting in the Society's history, involved 59 sessions comprising 634 presentations.

The celebration included a series of activities organized by the 50th Anniversary Committee to commemorate the Society's founding. There were two evening plenary sessions and one day-long symposium, each focused on the broad theme "American Archaeology Past and Future." Golden Marshalltown trowels were presented to the surviving signers of the constitution of the Society: James B. Griffin, Wilton M. Krogman, and Dorothy L. Schulte (William A. Ritchie and Sallie Wagner, also signers of the constitution, were unable to attend the meeting). A luncheon was held in honor of 89 senior archaeologists who received special 50th Anniversary Award plaques from the Society (Smith 1985).

In order to record at least some of these special anniversary proceedings, we have drawn together in this volume the papers from the day-long symposium on "The History and State of the Art of American Archaeology," and from the Plenary session "Views of the Development of American Archaeology." Albert C. Spaulding gave the lead paper ("Archaeological Interpretation 1935") in the symposium and helped get the session off to a very successful start. However, he felt that many of his remarks had already appeared in print (Spaulding 1985), and therefore declined to include his paper in this volume. In addition, transcripts and an audiovisual recording from the plenary panel discussion, "American Archaeology in the Early Years of the Society" (whose participants included Frederika de Laguna, James B. Griffin, Emil W. Haury, Frederick Johnson, George I. Quimby, Albert C. Spaulding, Waldo R. Wedel and H. Marie Wormington), are not included in this volume, but have been placed in the National Anthropological Archives, Smithsonian Institution.

American Archaeology Past and Future

The Society for American Archaeology was organized in 1935, in a period when massive amounts of federal money and labor were being poured into archaeology, creating a demand for trained, professional archaeologists then coming out of newly formed university anthropology programs. It was a time when the discipline of American archaeology was embarking on an ambitious and ultimately highly successful program to write the culture history of North America. The Folsom finds of the previous decade had opened a chasm in American prehistory: though a deep human antiquity had long been suspected for the Americas, the Folsom discoveries quite suddenly expanded human prehistory on this continent many millenia. Archaeologists, armed with sophisticated new methodologies for inferring chronology (seriation and stratigraphy), were challenged with the task of filling in the details of culture history on the continent (Kidder 1936; Meltzer 1985). Not coincidentally the first major outlines of culture history appeared shortly thereafter (Ford and Willey 1941; Griffin 1946), and subsequent years saw a steady refinement of the methods and techniques of culture history.

The structure of culture-historical inquiry, its aims and intent, are touched upon by Robert C. Dunnell in the opening chapter in this volume. After a historical review of the rise and later rejection of culture history, Dunnell critically examines the tenets and goals of the new archaeology. He voices the opinion—echoed in other contributions (see Jennings, Thomas, Binford, this volume)—that the initial optimism and enthusiasm for the new archaeology has waned considerably, in the face of an inability to implement the ambitious theoretical program outlined in the 1960s. The destruction of culture history produced no coherent product. The result is that American archaeology has entered a period of extreme diversity of approach. Such diversity is not altogether negative: in diversity there is variability and criticism, and from these a better product can be formed. But as Dunnell concludes, strong choices must be made.

Over the last 50 years much has changed in American archaeology: our substantive knowledge of prehistory has increased thousand-fold. The discipline has witnessed the evolution of archaeological conservation from the first faltering steps of the Antiquities Act of 1906, through the lean years of salvage archaeology, into the world of corporate Cultural Resource Management of the 1980s. Precisely defined lines—some would say "trenches"—have been drawn within various classes of American archaeology: those within and without academia, between amateurs and avocational archaeologists, and between various theoretical schools and programs. The years of the Society have even witnessed the award of the first, arguably archaeological Nobel Prize, to Willard F. Libby for the development of radiocarbon dating. And, of course, the discipline has seen tremendous theoretical fermentation, as archaeologists began a critical process of self-reflection in the 1960s that continues to this day.

But then much has stayed the same. Throughout the last 50 years of American archaeology—indeed, throughout the last 100 years of American archaeology—one can see threads of continuity in archaeological inquiry. As shown by a number of authors in this volume many of the essential elements of our own archaeological baggage—epistemological, theoretical and methodological—have direct roots in our deep collective past.

The second part of this volume, "Themes in the History of Archaeology," presents contributions on change and continuity in the history of archaeology. This attention to the history of archaeology is not motivated by nostalgia for, as Binford (1981) has cogently argued, historical study plays an important role in the theory building process. Yet writing the history of our discipline (for that matter, of any scientific discipline) is not the straightforward matter it may at first appear. Sir Edmund Leach expresses the problem well when he writes (in reference to the history of British social anthropology, though the point applies equally well here):

> history . . . as viewed by participant observers is quite different from the same history as viewed by nonparticipant observers, and further, that even among participant observers there are several different categories. The "insiders" and the "outsiders" participate in quite different ways [Leach 1984:7].

For this reason, included in this volume are papers written from a variety of perspectives. Jesse D. Jennings and William G. Haag provide personal observations on the history of the field. Jennings' chapter is a more frankly personal history of his own 55 years in American archaeology. The contemporary reader will benefit from this account, as Jennings was a front-line participant (and, at times, catalyst) in many of the major events of the last five decades. Haag, too, has had long experience in American archaeology (particularly in the Southeast) and his experience reaches back to massive TVA excavations, the likes of which are only rarely seen today. His commentary on field methods is a valuable chronicle of the advances in this important arena of archaeological research.

The papers by Donald K. Grayson, Don D. Fowler, Jacob W. Gruber, and Bruce G. Trigger are histories of a different sort. Unlike participant histories, these chapters take an analytical approach to critical issues in the history of archaeology. These four papers share a theme as well. Each illustrates continuity and change in the development of some of the major theoretical underpinnings of the field, and each highlights the manner in which contemporary archaeology has been, and continues to be, influenced by the discipline's historical, social, and political context.

Donald K. Grayson deals with the history of "middle-range" research, an issue that has received a fair amount of attention in recent years (see also Thomas, this volume), yet one that has demonstrable precedent in the earliest stirrings of archaeology as a discipline. Grayson's intent is not only to document the extended pedigree of such research, but also to analyze the archaeological situations that prompt actualistic studies. By providing a diachronic study of "middle-range" research, Grayson adds an important dimension to our understanding of the structure of contemporary scientific inquiry.

Don D. Fowler addresses the rise and role of a conservation ethic in American archaeology. American archaeology took on its particular character in the 19th century, through an institutional and theoretical alliance with sociocultural anthropology that had as its centerpiece the study of Native Americans. Unlike contemporary European Archaeology, guided by history and geology, American archaeology adopted an anthropological frame. American archaeology was anthropology, or it was nothing. Yet, the same force responsible for the development of anthropological archaeology has retarded the development of a conservation ethic. As Fowler observes the roots of the majority of Americans do not lie in the Native American past. As a result, there is not a strong sense to preserve and conserve that past. American archaeologists are faced with the irony that what makes their study different—what makes it anthropological—also will be ultimately responsible for what makes their study obsolete.

In a valuable essay that also complements the one by Fowler, Jacob W. Gruber examines the development and use of the concept of culture in American archaeology. He notes the role of culture and material culture in the stratigraphic archaeology of the early and mid-19th century: as a means of categorizing and chronologically ordering collections of material things. It was Franz Boas who, Gruber observes, made remarkable inroads to a systemic concept of culture (a "cultural archaeology") whose product would appear consonant with the concept as used in archaeology today. Yet it was a view Boas himself ignored in his subsequent work and one that was largely absent in the archaeology of those who followed, for reasons carefully explored in Gruber's essay.

Bruce G. Trigger addresses a theme that sits squarely in the study of the "external history" (Kuhn 1977) of American archaeology: the impact of contemporary social and economic values and prejudices on the evolution of American archaeology. His essential position, that American archaeology is a product of a dialectical relationship between external social and political context and internal developmental processes, is well documented in careful argument. Yet Trigger's analysis has implications that go beyond understanding the roots of American archaeology; his analysis includes contemporary archaeology and, particularly, the role of Native Americans in that archaeology. His is a provocative analysis, and one whose conclusions are supported by the long sweep of history.

The final paper in this section is by Curtis M. Hinsley, Jr., an historian by trade. As an historian, he can bring to the study of the history of archaeology not only different scholarly tools and training, but also a perspective and sympathy for individuals and events unburdened by the prejudices of those with a stake in the outcome. His treatment of Edgar Lee Hewett and the founding of the School of American Research provides a dispassionate view of a highly controversial but important figure in American archaeology.

The explosion of the "new archaeology" was met with consternation, derision, exuberance, and, in some cases, relief. Many concerns that were either avoided, ignored, or unknown in previous decades became prime targets of inquiry beginning in the 1960s. In a remarkable release of pent-up energy, archaeological research burst into a variety of theoretical, methodological, and technical endeavors, including catastrophe theory, central place theory, foraging theory, information theory, modern material culture studies, philosophy of science, spatial analysis, simulation studies, and systems theory. One immediate result was the proliferation of a series of "archaeologies": behavioral archaeology, cognitive archaeology, contextual archaeology, ethnoarchaeology, evolutionary archaeology, experimental archaeology, geoarchaeology, individual archaeology, social archaeology, symbolic archaeology, structural-Marxist archaeology, and paleopsychology. Not all of these efforts met with stunning success. Indeed, in some significant ways the bulk of our knowledge of prehistory today is still the product of the culture historians and of traditional archaeology.

In three areas of perennial concern, the archaeology of the last 20 years has made important contributions to our knowledge of the past. Owing in part to the rise of ethnoarchaeology and actualistic studies, technical developments in archaeological chemistry and physics, and such simple improvements as the shift from site-specific to regional approaches, such long-standing concerns as the study of hunter-gatherer archaeology, the process of domestication and food production, and the evolution of civilization and complex society have increased in scope and sophistication. The papers in the third section, "New Looks at Past Problems" focus on those three perennial concerns in archaeology.

David Hurst Thomas opens this section with a commentary on hunter-gatherer archaeology. Historically, hunter-gatherer archaeology has always bobbed along in the anthropological and ecological currents; models from these disciplines have, and will continue to have, an influence on archaeology. This is not unhealthy. What presents a problem, as Thomas argues, is the uncritical acceptance of the theoretical and methodological flotsam and jetsam that accompanies the use of such models, and their attraction to archaeologists looking to beach on the Elysium island of archaeological theory. The archaeological theory-building process, as Thomas cogently argues, is not so easy to construct. Attention must be paid to issues of theory and mid-range theory: we must teach ourselves, as archaeologists, to make sense of the archaeological record on its own terms.

Charles Darwin once remarked that "we probably owe our knowledge of the uses of almost all plants to man having originally existed in a barbarous state, and having often been compelled by severe want to try as food almost everything which he could chew and swallow" (Darwin 1868:325). Barbara L. Stark takes a more contemporary look at the origins of food production, particularly plant use, in the New World. She provides a comprehensive review of the evidence for domestication from both an archaeological and botanical perspective; new methods and techniques used to procure new data; and the status of various explanations to account for the changes leading to food production.

In a paper described as "one of the great essays in the long publishing history of the *American Anthropologist* (Murphy 1976:10), Julian Steward (1949) attempted to tie together the disparate, worldwide data on state formation in an effort to understand general "cultural regularities." From the vantage point of an additional 35 years of data and information, much of which he is familiar with on a first hand basis, Henry T. Wright summarizes the current state of knowledge on the origin and evolution of cultural complexity in four major regions of the world. He addresses three issues that have garnered much attention in the last decade: sociopolitical control hierarchies, population change, and conflict. State formation, he concludes, is a relatively rapid process, and to understand that process archaeologists must focus their attention on constructing the critical linkages between the archaeological "facts" and the theory used to explain them.

These three papers provide critical reviews of where we stand in addressing these issues, and the ways in which recent developments in method and theory—particularly the former—have helped advance substantive knowledge and understanding. Importantly, these papers are more than a stocktaking of traditional concerns of prehistory; they are equally concerned with the larger question of where we go from here.

In recent years, there has been a growing chorus of discontent within archaeology, fueled by the relative lack of substantive accomplishment of the new archaeology. This dissatisfaction must be partly attributed to the heady promises made in the heyday of the new archaeology, and partly to the fact that archaeologists—neophytes in many important matters— placed a greater reliance on certain venues of salvation than, in hindsight, was appropriate.

A prime example of this dissatisfaction was the heralding of a quantitative revolution in archaeology. Though not without a role in the ultimate development of an archaeological science, quantitative methods are clearly not a panacea. In the fourth and final section of the volume, "Current Trends and Future Prospects," George L. Cowgill opens discussion with a detailed examination of the past, present, and potential role of formal and mathematical methods in archaeology. Cowgill offers his views on some of the more pernicious myths and popular fantasies surrounding certain methods and techniques in use today. He identifies, as well, some of the trends that may be as real as they are apparent. His conclusion, that what is needed more than further elaboration of elegant quantitative methods and techniques is the development of theory worthy of those methods and techniques, is a challenge to contemporary archaeology.

Like quantitative methods, Cultural Resource Management (CRM) has been both bane and blessing to archaeology in the last few decades. Certainly the level of funding has reached a point where more professional archaeologists are in the field than at any time in the discipline's history. Data recovery is proceeding apace. But the structure of CRM is an uncomfortable and awkward mix containing components of both new and traditional archaeology. Measured tension is frequently the result, as the legal requirements of resource management abruptly collide with the interests of "pure" archaeological research. Ruthann Knudson provides an assessment of the state of CRM research in contemporary archaeology, and an optimistic view of the role CRM can play in research-oriented archaeology.

There have been, in recent years, diverse reactions to the "failure" of the new archaeology. Those reactions have run the gamut from philosophic ventures into critical theory (characteristic of certain schools here and abroad), to claims to get on to the business of "doing" archaeology, ignoring concerns that prompted the theoretical debates of the last few decades. The final three papers in the volume, by Mark P. Leone, Patty Jo Watson, and Lewis R. Binford, provide ample illustration and discussion of this wide reaction, but little consensus on the value of the different approaches that have been advocated to solve problems in the modern archaeological enterprise. The chapters are a provocative but not wholly consonant view of the state of archaeological epistemology. As such they well symbolize the variability in American archaeology today.

Mark P. Leone firmly allies himself with the position that archaeologists must recognize the entanglement of history and ideology. However, while stressing the social and ideological uses of a past reconstructed, he does not take the position that the past is completely a function of the present or that the past is in some epistemological sense completely unknowable. Rather, he and certain like-minded archaeologists, particularly British archaeologists, wish to highlight the role critical theory and self-reflection can play in understanding the social uses of a past, of archaeology in the modern world: whether it be a scientific archaeology or not.

Patty Jo Watson frankly and critically reviews the state of archaeological interpretation. She observes that, with the exception of certain minority viewpoints, the diversity in archaeology is more apparent than real. She argues that underlying the diversity in contemporary archaeology is a unity and optimism about archaeology borne of a deep and abiding faith in the archaeological record as a guide to the real past. She cautions, however, that it is a faith that must be vigorously pursued at a time when archaeological site destruction is proceeding at alarming rates.

Lewis R. Binford, in the final chapter of this book, presents an epistemological statement and challenge: he outlines his views on scientific explanation and contemporary archaeology, and points the way toward achieving his program of scientific knowledge. He takes the position, similar to Popper's (1972), that while the study of objective knowledge is a past reality and can throw light on subjective knowledge and the thought processes of scientists, the converse is not true. Rather, it is the interaction and confrontation between archaeological knowledge (ignorance) and the past reality that leads to the growth of science. Binford's advocacy of a scientific understanding of the archaeological record includes the identification of obstacles to achieving that goal. The discussion is both provocative and illuminating, for like many of the authors in this volume he has strong opinions on where archaeology should be heading.

In 1935 American archaeology was remarkably uniform: research and explanation coalesced around a very specific set of goals, using a corpus of agreed upon methods and techniques. Ignorance, as Binford observes (this volume), was readily identified as sites unexcavated, regions unexplored, and time periods unfilled. In 1985, American archaeology is remarkably diverse: there is no single paradigm to guide research, theory, or explanation. It is difficult to specify the boundaries of our ignorance, since there is no unanimity on the boundaries of our field of inquiry. In 1985, American archaeology is at a crossroads, with many paths but no clear directions. As the specter of site destructions looms ever larger, the luxury of making unfettered choices decreases. In this volume we have tried to examine some of the paths of archaeological diversity, both to record their form, and use it as a forum on which to build archaeological theory.

Moreover, we have tried to emphasize in this "Editors' Introduction," as have many of the contributors to this volume, that the primary problem facing the field today is a methodological one: our ways and means of knowing the past are weak. Scientific explanation is a product of a dialectical interchange between the observational/empirical and the rational/theoretical realms. Our methods (the means of obtaining knowledge about the past) provide the critical linkage across the abyss separating the observational and rational realms. Until the unsolved methodological problems are squarely faced and resolved, the construction of archaeological theory will remain a dream.

The critical issue of methodological growth, as noted by several contributors (particularly in the third and fourth sections), is not one that seems to be fully understood. Although much polemic in the 1960s was focused on theoretical issues, there was an apparent failure on the part of the discipline as a whole to appreciate the necessity and importance of methodological development. Innovations of this sort were, and are, needed in order to realize the program introduced by the new archaeologists. Part of the feeling of frustration at the lack of accomplishment by the new archaeology is attributable to the misunderstandings generated by the polemic of the past two decades. The new archaeology was not offering a new theoretical perspective. Rather, it argued that a new materialistic view of the past would prove more productive than the old idealistic one. It was stressed then, and is worth repeating here, that such productivity would never be realized without related methodological change.

The current diversity in the discipline is a theme that runs through many of the chapters that follow. We believe that this diversity is a direct result of the confusion generated by many of the writings of the 1960s and 1970s. As several authors point out, such diversity is a double-edged sword. If it leads to new attention to the methodological question of "how" archaeologists can employ different viewpoints so that they can eventually be evaluated, then the future of archaeology is certain to be a bright one. If the diversity leads, however, to intellectual shouting matches about the efficacy of varied approaches to the past, without close attention to methodological issues, then the great promise of the last 50 years of archaeological development—so well documented in parts one and two (below)—will remain unfulfilled.

In closing, it is fitting to recall Robert C. Dunnell's remarks as he appeared on stage at the 50th annual meeting to deliver his address, following the papers by Jesse D. Jennings and Lewis R. Binford. He asked the rhetorical question, "How do you follow someone who has done everything, and someone who has said everything?" In a larger sense, American archaeology faces a similar quandry: in the last fifty years much has been done and much has been said. How can we follow that act? Perhaps the chapters in this volume, singly or *in toto,* will begin to provide an answer to that question.

Acknowledgments

A celebration of this sort would not have been possible without substantial financial support. For their help in this regard, we would like to thank the Eli Lilly Foundation, the Marshalltown Trowel Company, the National Geographic Society, the National Science Foundation, the Texas Archeological Society, and Mr. Steven Spielberg.

In addition, many individuals gave freely of their time and advice in the planning and execution of the meetings and this volume. We would like to express our gratitude to: Robert C. Dunnell, George C. Frison, Donald K. Grayson, Dee F. Green, George T. Jones, Robert D. Leonard, Jerome A. Miller, Suzanne L. Siegel, and fellow members of the 50th Anniversary Committee, Linda S. Cordell, Patty Jo Watson, Gordon R.

Willey, and Nathalie F. S. Woodbury. David C. Crass, Shelly Outlaw, and Rosanna Ridings provided important editorial assistance.

In a very real sense, this volume is a festschrift: it was conceived and assembled for the purpose of honoring the 50th anniversary of the Society for American Archaeology. In that spirit, the editors and authors have agreed that all royalties accrued from its sales will go to the Society for American Archaeology publication fund, that the Society may continue to provide a medium through which archaeologists can "express themselves."

David J. Meltzer
Southern Methodist University

Don D. Fowler
University of Nevada

Jeremy A. Sabloff
University of New Mexico

Literature Cited

Binford, Lewis R.
 1981 *Bones: Ancient Men and Modern Myths.* Academic Press, New York.
Darwin, C.
 1868 *The Variation of Animals and Plants under Domestication.* Two volumes. John Murray, London.
Ford, James A., and Gordon R. Willey
 1941 An Interpretation of the Prehistory of the Eastern United States. *American Anthropologist* 43:325–363.
Griffin, James B.
 1946 Culture Change and Continuity in Eastern United States. In *Man in Northeastern North America,* edited by F. Johnson, pages 37–95. Phillips Academy, Andover.
 1985 The Formation of the Society for American Archaeology. *American Antiquity* 50(2):261–271.
Guthe, Carl E.
 1935 The Society for American Archaeology Organization Meeting. *American Antiquity* 1(2):141–146.
 1936 Report, Society for American Archaeology. *American Antiquity* 1(4):310–316.
Kidder, Alfred V.
 1936 Speculations on New World Prehistory. In *Essays in Anthropology,* edited by R. Lowie, pages 143–151. University of California Press, Berkeley.

Kuhn, Thomas S.
1977   *The Essential Tension*. University of Chicago Press, Chicago.

Leach, Edmund R.
1984   Glimpses of the Unmentionable in the History of British Social Anthropology. *Annual Review of Anthropology* 13:1–23.

Meltzer, David J.
1985   North American Archaeology and Archaeologists, 1879–1934. *American Antiquity* 50(2):249–260.

Murphy, Robert F.
1976   Introduction: A Quarter Century of American Anthropology. In *Selected Papers from the American Anthropologist*, edited by R. Murphy, pages 1–22. American Anthropological Association, Washington, D. C.

Popper, Karl R.
1972   Epistemology Without a Knowing Subject. In *Objective Knowledge: An Evolutionary Approach*, by K. R. Popper, pages 106–152. Oxford University Press, Oxford.

Renfrew, A. Colin
1983   Divided We Stand: Aspects of Archaeology and Information. *American Antiquity* 48(1):3–16.

Sabloff, Jeremy A.
1985   American Antiquity's First Fifty Years: An Introductory Comment. *American Antiquity* 50(2):228–236.

Smith, Bruce D.
1985   SAA Honors Outstanding Senior Archaeologists. *Bulletin of the Society for American Archaeology* 3(4):5.

Spaulding, Albert C.
1985   Fifty Years of Theory. *American Antiquity* 50(2):301–308.

Steward, Julian H.
1949   Cultural Causality and Law: A Trial Formulation of the Development of Early Civilizations. *American Anthropologist* 51(1):1–27.

Overview

Five Decades of American Archaeology

Introduction

American archaeology in 1935 was very different than it is today. Some of those differences are obvious, at least to those among us who have participated in the discipline for more than a decade or two. In 1935 the number of professional archaeologists was so small that most knew each other first hand. Only a handful of major institutions offered serious training in archaeology. While both numbers increased over the entire period, save during World War II, the expansion reached explosive proportions in the late 1960s and 1970s.

In 1935, all archaeologists had essentially the same kind of jobs. They were affiliated with universities or they worked in museums, both today considered "academic" archaeology. Even though the Works Progress Administration (WPA) and the Civilian Conservation Corps (CCC) provided CRM kinds of situations (Quimby 1979; Setzler 1943; Setzler and Strong 1936), the people involved were still basically academically oriented. Major William S. Webb who simultaneously managed both the TVA program in the Tennessee Valley and the WPA program in Kentucky, also taught at the University of Kentucky and chaired the departments of Anthropology and Physics. Clearly times were simpler then. In the 1960s, when the National Park Service became heavily involved in archaeology through the Reservoir Salvage Act, a small number of administrative archaeological positions was created; but again it was the 1970s that saw a major expansion of the kinds of jobs that an archaeologist might hold. Today a large proportion of the archaeological fraternity holds jobs in non-academic settings. Basic research funding no longer dominates field work.

To cope with these kinds of changes, the structure of the profession has become more complex. In 1935 there were regional associations of archaeologists, many with a strong amateur component, and national and international specialized journals and topically focused associations of archaeologists did not exist. As the kind of employment for archaeologists diversified, niches developed for professional organizations such as Society of Professional Archaeologists, niches that simply did not exist before. Overall, the increasing sense of professionalism saw the role of amateurs shift from one of active participation to that of an interested lay public.

Technical changes in archaeology are responsible in part for the lessening role of the amateur, but they also had major impacts on the profession as well. Radiocarbon dating not only revised our notions of how old things were, it also altered research priorities. By the 1960s, the larger potential of physics, chemistry, and the life sciences was appreciated. Interdisciplinary and regional studies began to replace strictly archaeological site-oriented research, a process that continues today. Access to cheap computing also wrought a major change in archaeology. The potential of quantitative analyses was recognized early enough (e.g., Kroeber 1940; cf. Driver and Kroeber 1932), but the nature of archaeological data and archaeological problems relegated quantitative analysis to rather limited roles until computers made the manipulation of large bodies of data feasible.

These sociological and technical changes are symptoms or proximate causes of much more fundamental changes in the intellectual structure of archaeology. Such changes are marked by names such as "new archaeology" (e.g., Binford 1962; Binford and Binford 1968; Caldwell 1959; Longacre 1964) and "symbolic" and "structural" archaeology (e.g., Hodder 1982; Leone 1982), as well as the changing relationship with sociocultural anthropology (e.g., Butzer 1982; Raab 1981; Schoenwetter 1981; Taylor 1948; Wiseman 1983). In terms of methodology, the contrast between 1935 and 1985 is as much a change in the number of different kinds of archaeology as it is in goals and direction.

These sociological and technical changes are easily recognized today, and they were, by and large, appreciated at the times they were taking place. The intellectual changes, on the other hand, are a little harder to appreciate. Of course, the fact of intellectual change was perceived at the time. The famous debates that bracket the emergence of the new archaeology bear witness to such recognition (Bayard 1969; Binford 1968a; Erasmus 1968; Flannery 1967; Ford 1954a, 1954b; Sabloff and Willey 1967; Spaulding 1953a, 1954); but the precise content and implications of the changes were not always recognized. The major intellectual shifts in archaeology were not accomplished in wholesale fashion, one paradigm introduced traumatically at the expense of another. Rather, they were accomplished in bits and pieces, often focusing on particular issues and problems instead of archaeology as a whole. "New archaeologies" thus tend to be synthesized after the fact (Ford 1936; Rouse 1939; Watson et al. 1971, 1984; Willey and Phillips 1958). Even the principal architects were not always aware of the full implications. Polemics, essential to the process of change, built caricatures that obscured the essential commonalities between competing approaches and the continuity of thought that links old and new.

My own predilections lead me to believe that these more or less obscure intellectual changes are both the most interesting and most important aspects of our history and it is on them that I wish to focus. Specifically, there are three "events" that strike me as being of singular significance in our history: (1) the establishment of American archaeology as a discipline, an event I take to be roughly coincident with the founding of the Society whose 50th anniversary we celebrated in 1985; (2) the emergence of the new archaeology as the dominant force in American archaeology; and (3) the appearance of anti-new archaeologies in the last few years. In such speculative endeavors as attempting to explain why these events took place when and how they did and in the form they did, I assume that "objectivity" increases with the age of the event. Accordingly, I have given more attention to, and place greater faith in, the analysis of the first two of these events than the last, but I do so without the intention of implying that the last is any less significant to archaeology.

The Emergence of Culture History and the Founding of the Society for American Archaeology

Archaeological activities and interest in the archaeological record predate the founding of the Society for American Archaeology by 250 years

(Willey and Sabloff 1980:17–32). Institutional involvement in archaeology is nearly 150 years old in the Americas (Willey and Sabloff 1980). Major studies of lasting significance have an equally long and not unrelated history, including the work of Squier and Davis (1848), Holmes (1886a), and Thomas (1894) in the eastern United States; Cushing (1886), Holmes (1886b), and Bandelier (1892) in the western United States, and that of Stephens and Catherwood (in Stephens 1841, 1843), Holmes (1895–1897), and Squier (1877) in Latin America. Important theoretical tracts began to appear before the turn of the century (Holmes 1886c). All of these pioneers were basically exploring and reporting those explorations without any common or distinctively archaeological methodology. In fact, many of these studies were adjuncts to more general scientific and exploratory expeditions. Nonetheless, they served to awaken serious interest in archaeological remains all over the Americas and laid the foundations for an archaeological discipline. Two things seem to have been critical in forging a discipline from the natural history interest in the American archaeological record: a general and archaeological means to assess the age of archaeological remains and an established body of field technique that insured a minimal level of comparability and information content in archaeological data. The first of these was clearly paramount both in the minds of the participants and in retrospect. Although field technique was much less discussed, its importance should not be underestimated.

Solving the Chronological Problem

Some 19th century scholars made fairly accurate guesses about chronology (e.g., Bandelier 1892; Holmes 1886b) and some even recognized that chronology posed the most serious challenge in interpreting archaeological material. Until the early years of the 20th century, however, little progress was made. Association with other dated phenomena (e.g., European artifacts, Pleistocene faunas or deposits) and stratigraphy, useful as they were and are, were neither generally applicable nor archaeological. Stratigraphy, however, did provide a starting point for a general solution. Uhle, working in Peru (1903) and California (1907), and Gamio (1913) working in Mexico, followed shortly by Kroeber (1916), Nelson (1916), and Spier (1917) in the American Southwest, began to notice that whenever the relative order of archaeological deposits was known, the artifacts contained in them, if described in a certain way, later termed styles (Collins 1927; Kroeber 1919), displayed a regular and distinctive distribution. The potential of these observations for developing a general method was almost immediately recognized (Nelson 1916). Kidder's (1924) work at Pecos and Valliant's (e.g., 1930) work in the Valley of Mexico corroborated these initial findings. Within a decade and a half, similar results had been obtained from the Arctic (Collins 1937) to the Southeast (e.g., Ford 1936, 1938) to South America (e.g., W. C. Bennett 1934). The generalizations about the temporal distribution of style, now known as the occurrence and frequency laws (Dunnell 1970), led to the establishment of a standard procedure for the definition of type (Krieger 1944).

The actual chronological methods employed varied from area to area. In regions where there were other means for establishing chronological control, such as provided by dendrochronology in the Southwest after 1930, types tended to be narrowly defined and were employed in an index fossil approach. In areas where such additional chronological information was lacking, as in the Southeast, types tended to be defined so that they had lengthy temporal distributions and seriation was used to construct chronologies. The critical point is, however, that by the early 1930s, archaeologists had repeatedly demonstrated that it was possible to chronologically order archaeological materials in most parts of the New World in which archaeologists were active. Further, the means of so doing were entirely archaeological.

Field Techniques

The acquisition of archaeological data was a rather haphazard business in the 19th century. Natural stratigraphic units had been used for some excavations in the 19th century (Willey and Sabloff 1980:84). However, their use was limited by a paucity of stratified deposits in many areas, a lack of sophistication in soft-rock stratigraphy, and a general belief that no long period of time was involved in the American record (Meltzer 1983; Trigger 1980; cf. Willey and Sabloff 1980:84). The horizontal dimension was even less well controlled.

The first important ingredient in a body of field technique was the use of arbitrary levels or "metric stratigraphy" in deposits without obvious natural stratification (and unfortunately in some cases with it). Because arbitrary levels played a critical role in the chronological work of Gamio, Nelson, and Kidder, it spread widely, based on its utility in that context. The underlying assumption, that the age of artifact manufacture (or deposition) is a simple though not linear function of depth, is faulty as a general principle (as is the corresponding assumption that permits the use of natural stratigraphy in most applications), but it is approximated frequently enough in the real world to sustain its use. Nonetheless, the use of arbitrary levels signified a new interest in rigorous data acquisition, the specifics of which came to be shared by many archaeologists about the same time that the chronological methods were being developed.

Of course, we all know that the way to tell an archaeologist from a pothunter is by the shape of their respective excavations. Square holes, the mark of rigorous technique in areas lacking cultural features, such as architecture, to guide excavation horizontally, also appear during the early 20th century. Sporadic use of arbitrary Cartesian grids is present by at least 1903 when Peabody and Moorehead (1904), borrowing directly on European techniques of cave excavation, investigated Jacob's Cavern in Missouri. Photographs show that some mound excavations at Cahokia in the 1920s utilized grids (J. B. Griffin, personal communication). It was not until the 1930s, however, that this approach became standard, and then only for excavations. It was not used in surface work until the 1960s.

A general statement on field techniques was published by Guthe in 1930 based on a National Research Council study (National Research Council 1930; see also Guthe 1931). However, the most important vehicle for establishing a consistent set of field procedures were the WPA and CCC excavations of the late 1930s and early 1940s. Because large numbers of untrained people were involved, standardized procedures were essential. Fay-Cooper Cole and the University of Chicago probably played the most important role in this regard. Cole's work in southern Illinois incorporated most of the innovations in field techniques and students from that program were a principal source of WPA field supervisors. The other major innovation, use of forms to standardize field observations and measurements, was a clear adaptation to the personnel situation presented by the large scale archaeology of the Depression era. This general approach was codified in the several editions of the Heizer manual on field technique (Heizer, editor 1949, 1950; Heizer 1958; Heizer and Graham 1967; Hester, Heizer, and Graham 1975; cf. Colton 1950).

The Culture History Paradigm

None of these facts are new. What is important is that by the early 1930s an active, but intellectually diffuse, natural history interest in the archaeological record coalesced around a particular problem, chronology, for which a general methodology or research strategy had been created. This research strategy was accompanied by a visibly more rigorous set of techniques for data acquisition. It is this coherence that I take to mark the inception of the discipline. Scholars who were archaeologists shared a number of things in common, which at the same time served to distinguish them from others interested in relics and monuments (e.g., Griffin 1985; Guthe 1967). The founding of the Society for American Archaeology and of *American Antiquity* is the most obvious symptom of this consensus.

Culture history, as this approach has come to be denominated, was consensual. It was not the product of a single theoretical flash or expository synthesis. Even the early efforts to explicate the approach, such as Rouse's "Prehistory in Haiti" (1939) or Ford's introductory remarks in his "Analysis of Indian Village Site Collections from Louisiana and Mississippi" (1936), are clearly *post hoc* syntheses that integrate and make more rigorous the advances of the previous two decades.

The interesting question is *why* did a consensus on the goals and methods of archaeology emerge around chronology out of the plethora of interests that had preceded this period? I think the answer to the question lies in one simple observation. For the first time since scholars had taken a serious interest in the archaeological record, they could make empirically testable statements as archaeologists. An archaeological chronology made empirical claims that could be independently tested whenever other data on age were available. In short, for the first time it was possible to do archaeology and be wrong! This jerked archaeology out of the business of speculative natural history and placed it firmly in the realm of science. There were some things that archaeologists could say that other scientists, employing their criteria of truth, could believe. This observation not only informs on the nature of culture history, but it is also essential to understanding why it eventually gave way to the new archaeology when and how it did.

The net effects of this methodological revolution are three. First, there was a dramatic reduction in the diversity of American archaeology in both how it was done and why it was done. Second, the discipline entered a highly productive, "normal science" (Kuhn 1962) phase. And, third, at least *inter alia,* archaeologists embraced empirical testing as *the* criterion by which the correctness of conclusions was to be gauged.

The reduction in diversity came about through the concentration on chronology, the only field of interest for which a coherent methodology had developed. There were, of course, complaints. Some, like those that appeared coincident with the new archaeology, were simply resistence to change and a desire to retain the kind of intellectual independence of the earlier period (e.g., Tozzer 1937). Others, such as Steward and Setzler's "Function and Configuration in Archaeology," (1938) were positive pleas for the development of methodologies treating interests other than chronology (cf. J. W. Bennett 1943). In retrospect, both kinds of critiques failed to carry the day simply because of the empirical success of the culture history program. Culture history worked; other proposals, however attractive, were not operational.

This situation is not without parallel in other fields. Biology provides a fine example. Evolutionary theory had languished throughout most of the early 20th century and certainly had not established itself as *the* guiding principle in biology. In the late 1930s and early 1940s, a "new synthesis" of evolutionary theory and genetics was forged, with the result that both were far more effective (e.g., Mayr 1982). Evolution quickly narrowed to genetic transmission alone, a linkage that was not seriously challenged until quite recently (e.g., Gould 1980). Visible success in one area of endeavor led to the atrophy of other interests and directions.

The result of this loss of diversity in archaeology was a productive normal science phase. The existence of a coherent, widely shared methodology produced comparable products that could be integrated with one another, not only over time and space, but conceptually. Archaeology was building something; it was producing cumulative knowledge. Certainly culture historical chronologies were refined, elaborated, and, on occasion, corrected, but each of the pieces contributed by various workers could be fitted into the larger testable picture.

Adopting empirical testing as the ultimate arbiter of correctness is part and parcel of the chronological methodology. It allied archaeology with science and it provided a relatively clear means of evaluating archaeological statements. While no doubt important in shifting emphasis away from chronology as the dominant archaeological goal (Willey and Sabloff 1980:155), the advent of radiocarbon dating had its first, and perhaps most lasting, impact in confirming the essential correctness of the culture historical approach and reinforcing the empirical standard.

Radiocarbon dating showed, at least in general, that culture historians had been right in matters of chronology.

In contrast to contemporary archaeology, culture historians spent relatively little time discussing how to do archaeology and relatively greater amounts of time doing it. This is a direct result of its consensual basis. There was only one way to do archaeology, culture history. This feature of culture history tends to obscure its conceptual structure, but some of the key characteristics of its methodological core can be identified.

As I have elaborated elsewhere (Dunnell 1978, 1982, in press), culture historians took a decidedly materialistic view of the significance of variability in their chronological work. Variability was not regarded as noise obscuring a finite number of essential kinds; rather, it was a record of change. Variability allowed culture historians to tell time, though the degree to which this particular characteristic is evident varies areally with the particular methods used to construct chronologies.

I have already noted that the archaeological record was described in terms of styles. This, coupled with a second feature of culture historical description, pattern or configurational descriptions, gives culture history products their distinctive character. The stylistic nature of culture historical descriptions began with the definition of types; the test of historical significance, first voiced explicitly by Krieger (1944), insured that types were dominantly stylistic. Not only were the types used to construct chronologies stylistic, but the larger units, such as phases and foci, displayed the same characteristics because they were defined in part or in whole by these types. This procedure insured that phases and foci had contiguous distributions in time and space. Style, of course, records homologous similarities. Since the basic culture historical framework was dominantly stylistic, explanations of the record called upon processes that explained homologous similarities: diffusion, trade, persistence, migration. Because these kinds of explanations later came under criticism, it is crucial to recognize that these processes were the only ones that could explain the archaeological record as it had been described. On these grounds, culture history is a tight, thoroughly consistent, and coherent methodological package.

The second characteristic, the use of pattern discriptions, may be a little less obvious. By pattern description, I mean to call attention to the nature of culture historical units as defined by *ad hoc* sets of attributes (or types in the case of larger units) that bear no functional relation to one another; they are simply associated. As a consequence, culture historical units do not interact with other kinds of units. The pattern format of description is quite pervasive. For example, the contrasting manners in which analogy was conceived by culture history (e.g., Ascher 1961) and the new archaeology (e.g., Binford 1967) illustrates the differences between pattern descriptions and systemic ones (cf. Wylie 1982). Although the dichotomy between normative and systemic notions of culture conflates several issues, the pattern/system contrast is a major component.

The limitations of such descriptive terms seem obvious now; however, what must be recognized is that pattern descriptions were the only kind required to achieve the goals of culture history. The nonsystemic approach taken by the culture historians was not a defect; it was consistent with the overall methodology that distinguished the paradigm.

Finally, the general lack of interest in theory construction should be noted. As I have emphasized, culture history was a well-integrated methodology, but this methodology was not explicitly rationalized in theoretical terms. The key empirical generalizations that ran the culture historical program remained empirical generalizations, themselves often unstated, throughout the culture historical period. No effort was made to explain why stylistic types displayed the distributions in time and space that proved so useful. That they did was enough.

In this interpretation, many of the caricatures of culture history built by the new archaeology during its early polemical phase are simply inaccurate. Culture history was not inductive. It was decidedly deductive. What gave it its inductive appearance was its consensual, normal science nature. The premises it used were widely shared, largely uncontroversial and therefore largely invisible. They were not written down or debated, because in the absence of competition neither was required. Emphatically, culture history was not an aimless description. To an extent that is not true today, it was problem-oriented, so much so that only one problem received analytic attention. Culture history was clearly anthropological as well, a point that is elaborated shortly. While I view the latter-day caricatures as impairing our understanding of culture history, they did have a basis in fact as is shown in the succeeding section.

Up to this point I have talked about culture history exclusively in terms of its methodological core, chronology. Culture history was much more, of course, but in nonchronological matters it was a different kind of enterprise that fully merited many of the unkind characterizations it attracted. Ultimately, this duality played a major role in its undoing.

The Rise of the New Archaeology

As the application of chronological methods began to yield chronologies in many parts of the New World, interest gradually returned to the kinds of questions that had been asked of the record in earlier times. These interests were expressed commonly as sociological reconstructions.

The general strategy employed by culture historians in fleshing out the time-space frameworks involved describing the archaeological record in English, or where that was judged inappropriate, with ethnographic terms. Then common sense, or anthropology, or both, would explain the descriptions in a matter of fact way. To effect this strategy, the materialist conception of variability that characterized chronological work was replaced by an essentialist view congruent with the structure of common sense and ethnography. This shift is well expressed in many elements of the culture historical approach including their treatment of both micro- and macrospace (e.g., the lack of interest in sampling). It is most dramatically evident, however, in the periodization of chronological sequences for description. To a greater or lesser extent, depending upon the particular methods used, archaeological chronologies were ordinal sequences of data points, usually assemblages. To "interpret" such sequences, however, the continuously variable sequences had to be reduced to a set of bounded units which could be treated as internally homogeneous and externally contrastive. The products of this periodization, phases and foci, could be reconstructed, but this had the effect of eliminating change. Methodologically, temporal variability was equated with spatial variability. Sequential phases or periods differed from each other, much as contemporary phases in different places differed. As Plog (1974) noted later, periodization relegated all significant change to the lines separating phases and foci in time-space charts. Occasionally, the problem was noted. Additional phases were defined to acccommodate "transitions," but this kind of solution quickly begins to take on the appearance of Ptolemaic epicircles.

The groundwork for actual reconstruction was laid in the very earliest syntheses of the culture historical approach when types and modes were conceptualized as "standards of behavior" or "customs." This kind of equation was extended, with appropriate cautions, to the larger units by regarding them as "peoples" or "cultures" analogous to ethnographic units of similar name. In the early formulations, the equation of descriptive units with "customs" or "standards of behavior" was advanced as a tentative correlation that might obtain in some cases (e.g., Rouse 1939:18). As interest in reconstruction advanced, however, the interpretive notion of archaeological units came to dominate archaeological systematics and everything that stemmed from it. The practical importance of the equation varied from place to place. In areas where construction of chronologies was problematic because of complexities in the record, reconstruction was less important; in areas where chronology was brought under control more quickly, the interpretive aspect emerged more rapidly. Thus, for example, Ford (1936, 1954b) stuck closely to the definitional basis of his units throughout his work in the Southeast, whereas Gifford (1960), working in the Mayan area, constructed an elaborate scheme for the cultural interpretation of archaeological units.

The critical feature of this development is that reconstructive interpretations lacked an empirical warrant in the culture historical methodology. The criteria used to define archaeological units were selected for chronological purposes. There was no procedure that insured that a type was a "standard of behavior." The cultural statements were *post hoc* interpretations, not definitionally entailed meanings. Further, the pattern nature of the descriptive units precluded talking about the archaeological record in interactive and empirical terms simultaneously. In short, all of the features of culture historical methodology that worked so well to develop chronologies simultaneously insured that nonchronological interests would not be well served. Culture historians were caught in a trap of their own making. In becoming a scientifically respectable discipline, culture historians had accepted empirical testing as the ultimate criterion for judging the acceptability of archaeological conclusions. Reconstructions, increasingly central to archaeology, could not meet this criterion. To an objective observer the reconstructions appeared as unwarranted speculations. This is precisely the niche in which the new archaeology developed. The new archaeology is an effort to develop a methodology capable of delivering conclusions of comparable certainty to those which the culture historians had in chronology (homologous similarities), but for nonchronological interests (analogous similarities).

Archaeology and Anthropology

The relationship between archaeology and anthropology is often given a considerable role in the emergence of the new archaeology. Consequently, this relationship deserves some attention. It is generally appreciated that American archaeology, like archaeologies that developed in other parts of the world where there was an obvious connection between ethnographic peoples and the archaeological record (Mulvaney 1977), has always had a close relation to ethnography and ethnology (Leone 1972; Trigger 1978).

American cultural anthropology was acquiring its distinctive form at roughly the same time that culture history was developing. American ethnographers, although they underestimated the magnitude, were keenly aware that Native Americans had undergone dramatic change as a consequence of contact. Most Native American societies had become extinct; the few that remained were patently altered by the European presence. In the late 19th and early 20th centuries, anthropologists were not interested in studying Native Americans as they were found but rather as they were at the time of, or just prior to, contact. To accommodate this interest, they invented a fictive "ethnographic present," constructed from the memories of living people. While contact had everywhere produced systemic discontinuity, isolated traits persisted across this boundary. Consequently, culture became a pattern or configuration of traits that could be obtained through contemporary interviews. Thus, for historical reasons, American cultural anthropology did not have strong behavioral or functional components.

British social anthropology developed along rather different lines. In studying the peoples of the Empire, social anthropologists confronted on-going, functioning systems. It was the investigator, not the investigatee, who died from contact. As a consequence, social anthropology took a much stronger behavioral approach that was clearly systemic rather than configurational. The two kinds of anthropology remained largely independent until after World War II when British social anthropology began to have a significant influence on American anthropology (cf. G. Watson 1984).

This simplified sketch emphasizes some fundamental methodological commonalities that link American archaeology and contemporary anthropology. Early on, the approach taken by the culture historians was closely similar to that employed by their anthropological colleagues. Both took a strongly cultural view and, in retrospect, for the same reason. Neither had direct access to the behavior of the subject populations. For both, culture was a particular configuration of traits. Both saw cultural variation in essentialist terms. So while culture historians and cultural anthropologists might have talked about somewhat different things, they talked about them in fundamentally similar ways. Indeed, it was common during this period for particular individuals to do research in both fields.

As American anthropology moved toward the sociocultural mode, culture history found itself at greater and greater variance with current anthropology. This was not a result of archaeological conservativism *per se* (cf. Leone 1972). The expansion of American anthropology into a more behavioral mode drew heavily upon an increase in overseas research after World War II and was facilitated by a new interest in studying contemporary Native Americans. Neither of these options was open to archaeologists. Thus the post-war charges that archaeology was not anthropological stemmed from the fact that American anthropology had changed, not that culture historians had somehow lost interest in an anthropological approach.

Further, as long as the anthropological model was cultural, there was little hope of grounding archaeological reconstruction empirically. How could inferences about "standards" and ideas be subjected to empirical tests (cf. Osgood 1951)? In the archaeological record, much of the evidence available to anthropologists was missing as well. A behavioral model, however, had possibilities in this direction. All that was lacking, or so it seemed, was a methodology to connect the two kinds of phenomena: behavior and things.

Walter W. Taylor's "A Study of Archaeology" (1948) is often accorded a seminal role in the creation of the new archaeology. Even though this study served to make archaeologists aware of the growing disparity between archaeology and current anthropology and the narrowness of interest that characterized culture history, it had virtually no positive impact at the time (P. J. Watson 1983:x). A variety of reasons, from turgidity to offensiveness, have been offered for this lack of success. In the present view, however, more intellectual reasons may be adduced. Taylor's proposal was strongly cultural rather than social or behavioral in orientation. Further, it did not present a methodology to effect its clearly enunciated goals in a manner acceptable to empirically oriented culture historians. Both elements precluded a major impact. In retrospect, its principal importance lies in legitimizing the efforts of others who began to hammer out a new archaeology founded in a behavioral perspective in subsequent decades. Even so, "A Study in Archaeology" stands as a symbol of the difficulties that culture history was beginning to experience.

Forging a New Approach

Culture history's interpretive failures, combined with the shift in anthropology to a social orientation, set the stage for the new archaeology. The problem archaeology faced was simple enough. How could archaeologists draw conclusions about the archaeological record in nonchronological matters with the same empirical certainty that they were able to do for chronology? While we are accustomed to think of the first tangible steps in solving this problem as happening in the early 1960s (Binford 1962; Longacre 1964), the foundations of the new approach were laid a decade earlier by Albert C. Spaulding (1953a).

In "Statistical Techniques for the Discovery of Artifact Types," Spaulding laid out an inductive strategy for empirically grounding archaeological units in past behavior. Spaulding conceived artifact "types" as nonrandom associations of attributes and provided a technique whereby nonrandom associations could be detected. The technique was applicable only to single sites or components of sites (Spaulding 1953a:305), a marked contrast with the culture historical approach to unit construction. Spaulding's proposal attracted immediate negative attention from culture historians (e.g., Ford 1954a, 1954b). Predictably, the main thrust of the criticism was that Spaulding's type could not be used to construct chronologies and therefore was of no value. Spaulding's response was to assert that his types were "real," culturally meaningful units. In fact, this was guaranteed by his technique. His units were emic in Harris' (1968) sense of the term. Spaulding's position on the significance of variability fell squarely within the essentialist metaphysic. Because cultural historical types were etic and derived from a materialist conception of reality, Spaulding's approach was much more than a new technique; it represented a wholly new way of treating the archaeological record. Perhaps because it focuses on types rather than the larger issues in reconstruction, Spaulding's paper does not often receive the kind of credit due it in creating the new archaeology. Even so, it established a strategy that underlies all of the new archaeology.

The new archaeology emerged as a potent force in the 1960s, largely because of the programmatic efforts of Lewis Binford (1962, 1964, 1965, 1967, 1968b) and case studies that explored the interpretive potential of the new view (Binford and Binford 1968; Deetz 1965; Hill 1966, 1970; Longacre 1964, 1970). Early on, Watson, LeBlanc, and Redman (1971) synthesized major elements of the approach. This synthesis highlights the contrast between the emergence of culture history from the natural history interest and development of the new archaeology from culture history. The new archaeology was not built on a widely shared prior consensus. *Explanation in Archeology* was not simply a summary of things already agreed upon. It explored new ground and was an obvious effort to attract a following for the new approach, accounting for its liturgical character. The new archaeology was not founded on a new product; it was explicitly theoretical in origin.

The Structure of the New Archaeology

The core of the new archaeology is an assertion that the archaeological record should be viewed as the product of human interaction, both among people and between people and their environment, and that the resulting behavioral patterning is, to some degree, retained by the archaeological record. Thus, with the development of appropriate methods, the archaeological record gives us access to the original systems beyond the actual objects that have survived (Binford 1968b:21; Watson et al. 1971:21). From the 1960s forward this proposition identified the main task of archaeology as methodological. It did not, however, provide a methodology. It suggested only that one was possible, but it did so in a way that made the general strategy appealing to empirically inclined archaeologists.

There is much variability within this general framework. Sometimes the "original system" is understood in a behavioral sense; other times it is interpreted in a cultural sense; frequently it is vaguely both. The relationship between such systems, however construed, and the archaeological record has been elaborated most notably as a consequence of Schiffer's (1972, 1976) site formation processes. Some investigators choose to emphasize reconstruction; others choose to focus on the epistemological questions. But to a greater or lesser extent, all of the new archaeology subscribes to the core assertion.

The most obvious element is the change in the form of description from configurational, or normative as it was called, to systemic. Less obvious, but no less important, is that in shifting interest from chronology to rigorous sociocultural reconstruction, the new archaeology focused attention on analogous, rather than homologous, similarities. This had a profound influence on almost all aspects of the new archaeology.

Archaeologists were compelled to view the record in terms of the functions of its components. At another level, a wholly new tack on explanation and a new meaning to process were mandated. Explanations of analogous similarities have to be sought in laws that account for the appearance of particular forms under specifiable conditions rather than in the history of the data. This explanatory approach required systemic descriptions because interactions were the crux of explanation. Predictably, the new archaeology took a dim view of diffusion and other processes that explain homologous similarities.

The significance of variability was viewed differently as well. Culture historians took a materialist view in relation to the temporal dimension. Chronological variability could be described quantitatively; space, however, was treated in an essentialist mode. This situation is nearly reversed in the new archaeology. The whole notion of reconstruction requires having some thing to reconstruct; this is accomplished by treating the temporal dimension as a sequence of things, albeit in much thinner segments than phases or foci implied. Some took this ontological position seriously (e.g., Spaulding 1958, 1982), while others seemingly regarded it as a methodological convenience and treated time much as culture historians did. Spatial variability, on the other hand, attracted new attention. At the most general level, spatial variation was treated materialistically. One consequence was the emphasis on sampling at both inter- and intrasite scales. Culture historians had been interested in sampling, to be sure, but in sampling the temporal variation, not spatial variation. At the practical level, however, an essentialist view prevailed, because the use of inductive statistical methods and establishing behavioral correlates for interpretative reconstruction require it.

I have suggested that the new archaeology is united in terms of a set of goals and in terms of a general strategy for reaching those goals. Sociocultural accounts of the archaeological record were to be given the same empirical certainty as culture historians had obtained for chronology. The patterns of the archaeological record were to provide the empirical basis for those accounts. Over time, interest in reconstruction has tended to dominate, giving rise to the appellation "anthropological archaeology." Probably because the investigation of analogous similarities was conceived by many as literal reconstitution of past sociocultural systems, much of the new archaeology has an emic flavor to it, reinforced by inductive statistical methods. But many other new archaeologists, generally those concerned with epistemological questions and thus in a "scientific" or "processual" tradition, have taken an ostensibly deductive approach. The search for laws, or at least empirical generalizations, has occupied many scholars. Laws have proved decidedly elusive and there is a variety of opinion on why this is the case.

It is impossible to even scratch the surface of this issue here. Importantly, to the extent to which archaeological conclusions are credible, their credibility rests on the techniques by which they were derived, much in the fashion of Spaulding's original proposal; hence the emphasis on method in the new archaeology. The means to test reconstructions empirically and independent of the means by which they were made have not yet come into being. The objectives of the new archaeology are clear; the kinds of data required to achieve them have been identified. But no new methodology comparable in power to that which ran culture history has been created to link the two. As a result, the new archaeology, despite much wishful thinking and very considerable advances on lesser issues, has never entered into a normal science phase. Its product is largely isolated case studies, not cumulative knowledge. The clearest evidence of this condition comes from our own literature. In the culture history era, most debate centered on archaeological conclusions; throughout the tenure of the new archaeology, not just in the initial phases, debate centers on how to reach conclusions.

The Acceptance of the New Archaeology

Given the lack of a coherent methodology, how has the new archaeology come to dominate modern archaeology? A number of factors have contributed. First, and perhaps most important, the polemic mounted against culture history damaged its credibility beyond repair. Regardless of the virtues of the criticisms of it, culture history simply is not a respectable position to hold. Second, the general strategy proposed is intuitively plausible and, indeed, may eventually prove do-able. Schiffer (1979) has, however, identified the proximate cause when he points out that most practicing archaeologists received their degrees after culture history ceased to be a respectable paradigm. The concurrent expansion of CRM has played a major role. The character of modern CRM has given practical expression to many elements stressed by the new archaeology, such as a regional orientation, sampling, and explicit "research" designs. It has encouraged standardization as did the WPA and CCC programs, though not to the same extent. The division of the field that occurred with the separation of academic and CRM jobs has enhanced the symbolic value of identifying with a particular archaeology. Whatever the reason for the broad appeal of the new archaeology, it is clearly based on the promise of the new approach, not its products.

Current Americanist Archaeology

From an academic perspective, the failure of the new archaeology to develop a methodology capable of explaining analogous similarities and differences in an empirically testable fashion might be considered simply a function of time and the inherent difficulty of the problem. Certainly, this is my view (Dunnell 1982). However, the failure to solve the central methodological issues and the consequent lack of a substantive product is coupled to the effective destruction of culture history as a guiding paradigm. This combination has brought the whole of the new archaeology into serious question. We are entering a new phase of our history, one marked by an extreme diversity of approach. The anthropologist in most of us might view this as a neutral or even positive sign. From a scientific perspective, however, the situation is anathema. Further, to the extent that CRM is committed to a theory-laden (problem-oriented) approach (cf. Tainter and Lucas 1983), the situation is even more disturbing because it promises to have a lasting effect on the kind of archaeology that will be possible in the future.

Many archaeologists continue to pursue the general program laid out by the new archaeology and strive to solve the key methodological issues (Binford 1977, 1978, 1981a, 1981b, 1983; Dunnell 1978, 1980, 1982, in press; Watson et al. 1984), but this is not the modal reaction. A large number seem to have tired of the effort and avoid methodological issues in favor of "doing archaeology" (Flannery 1982). "Doing archaeology" under these conditions means almost anything, from thinly disguised culture history and outdated elements of the new archaeology to the bold new ventures into symbolic and structural archaeology (Deetz 1977; Handsman 1983; Hodder 1979; Hodder, editor 1982; Leone 1982). This diversity is possible because there is no way, apart from simple subjective appeal, to choose among the growing number of alternatives. One is reminded of Spaulding's (1953b:590) critique of culture history: "truth is to be determined by some sort of polling of archaeologists, that productivity is doing whatever other archaeologists do, and that the only purpose of archaeology is to make archaeologists happy."

The contemporary situation is not total anarchy. Some gross patterns, arising from the dual goals of the new archaeology, may be detected. The desire to "do archaeology" in the absence of a methodology for doing it has driven many of those most strongly committed to the reconstructive aspect to eschew science as a goal, denying either its practicability or desirability or both (Leone 1982). The same conditions have pushed many of those most deeply committed to science to pursue their investigations in tightly circumscribed "specialties," where some guiding principles, usually taken from non-archaeological fields, are available. Both tendencies have clear, though not American, roots in the 1960s (Leroi-Gourhan 1967; Brothwell and Higgs 1963). Thus both strains can claim to be in the tradition of the new archaeology without making a substantial contribution to it.

It is impossible to divine what course American archaeology will take in the next 50 years. I do think, much as we might like to believe otherwise, that real choices are involved and that we are at a major crossroads in our discipline's history (Trigger 1984). Whatever choices are made, the next 50 years are going to be very different from the last 50 years.

Acknowledgments

Elements of this paper were developed in papers presented at the Philosophy of Science Association 1984 Biennial Meeting and at the University of Tennessee. Comments on those papers, especially those of Merrilee Salmon, materially aided in the preparation of the manuscript. I have also benefited, sometimes surreptitiously, from conversations with J. B. Griffin, G. I. Quimby, and A. C. Spaulding on the history of American archaeology and from the reminiscences of W. S. Webb. M. D. Dunnell made valuable editorial suggestions. B. May typed the manuscript and its several predecessors. To all of these, and any inadvertantly omitted, I owe my sincere thanks.

Literature Cited

Ascher, R.
   1961   Analogy in Archaeological Interpretation. *Southwestern Journal of Anthropology* 17:317–325.

Bandelier, A. F.
  1892 Final Report of Investigations among the Indians of the Southwestern
        United States. *Paper of the Archaeological Institute of America* 4:1–
        591.

Bayard, D. T.
  1969 Science, Theory, and Reality in the "New Archaeology." *American An-
        tiquity* 34:376–384.

Bennett, J. W.
  1943 Recent Developments in the Functional Interpretation of Archaeologi-
        cal Data. *American Antiquity* 9:208–219.

Bennett, W. C.
  1934 Excavations at Tiahuanaco. *Anthropological Papers of the American
        Museum of Natural History* 34(3):359–494.

Binford, L. R.
  1962 Archeology as Anthropology. *American Antiquity* 28:217–225.
  1964 A Consideration of Archaeological Research Design. *American An-
        tiquity* 29:425–441.
  1965 Archaeological Systematics and the Study of Cultural Process. *Ameri-
        can Antiquity* 31:203–210.
  1967 Smudge Pits and Hide Smoking: The Use of Analogy in Archaeological
        Reasoning. *American Antiquity* 32:1–12.
  1968a Some Comments of Historical Versus Processual Archaeology. *South-
        western Journal of Anthropology* 24:267–275.
  1968b Archeological Perspectives. In *New Perspectives in Archeology,* edited
        by S. R. and L. R. Binford, pages 5–32. Aldine, Chicago.
  1977 General Introduction. In *For Theory Building in Archaeology,* edited by
        L. R. Binford, pages 1–10. Academic Press, New York.
  1978 *Nunamiut Ethnoarchaeology.* Academic Press, New York.
  1981a Behavioral Archaeology and the Pompeii Premise. *Journal of Anthro-
        pological Research* 37:195–208.
  1981b *Bones: Ancient Men and Modern Myths.* Academic Press, New York.
  1983 *In Pursuit of the Past: Decoding the Archaeological Record.* Thames
        and Hudson, London.

Binford, L. R., and S. R. Binford (editors)
  1968 *New Perspectives in Archeology.* Aldine, Chicago.

Brothwell, D., and E. Higgs (editors)
  1963 *Science in Archaeology: A Comprehensive Survey of Progress and Re-
        search.* Thames and Hudson, London.

Butzer, K. W.
  1982 *Archaeology as Human Ecology.* Cambridge University Press, Cam-
        bridge.

Caldwell, J. R.
  1959 The New American Archaeology. *Science* 129:303–307.

Collins, H. B., Jr.
  1927 Potsherds from Choctaw Village Sites in Mississippi. *Journal of the
        Washington Academy of Sciences* 17:259–263.
  1937 Archaeology of St. Lawrence Island, Alaska. *Smithsonian Miscella-
        neous Collections* 96(1). Washington, D. C.

Colton, H. S.
  1950 Field Methods in Archaeology. *Museum of North Arizona Technical Series* 1. Flagstaff.

Cushing, F. H.
  1886 A Study of Pueblo Pottery as Illustrative of Zuni Culture Growth. In *Fourth Annual Report of the Bureau of Ethnology*, pages 467–521. Washington, D. C.

Deetz, J.
  1965 The Dynamics of Stylistic Change in Arikara Ceramics. *Illinois Studies in Anthropology* 4. University of Illinois Press, Urbana.
  1977 *In Small Things Forgotten: The Archaeology of Early American Life.* Anchor/Doubleday, New York.

Driver, H. E., and A. L. Kroeber
  1932 Quantitative Expression of Cultural Relationships. *University of California Publications in American Archaeology and Ethnology* 31:211–256.

Dunnell, R. C.
  1970 Seriation Method and Its Evaluation. *American Antiquity* 35:305–319.
  1978 Style and Function: A Fundamental Dichotomy. *American Antiquity* 43:192–202.
  1980 Evolutionary Theory in Archaeology. *Advances in Archaeological Method and Theory* 3:35–99
  1982 Science, Social Science, and Common Sense: The Agonizing Dilemma of Modern Archaeology. *Journal of Anthropological Research* 38:1–25.
  In press Methodological Issues in Contemporary Archaeology. *PSA 1984*, edited by P. D. Asquith and P. Kitcher, volume 2. Philosophy of Science Association, East Lansing, Michigan.

Erasmus, C.
  1968 Thoughts on Upward Collapse: An Essay on Explanation in Anthropology. *Southwestern Journal of Anthropology* 24:170–194.

Flannery, K. V.
  1967 Culture History vs. Culture Process: A Debate in American Archaeology. *Scientific American* 217:119–122.
  1982 The Golden Marshalltown: A Parable for the Archaeology of the 1980s. *American Anthropologist* 84:265–278.

Ford, J. A.
  1936 Analysis of Indian Village Site Collections from Louisiana and Mississippi. *Department of Conservation, Louisiana State Geological Survey, Anthropological Study*, 2. New Orleans.
  1938 A Chronological Method Applicable to the Southeast. *American Antiquity* 3:260–264.
  1954a Comment on A. C. Spaulding, "Statistical Techniques for the Discovery of Artifact Types." *American Antiquity* 19:390–391.
  1954b The Type Concept Revisited. *American Anthropologist* 56:42–54.

Gamio, M.
  1913 Arquelogia de Atzcapotzalco, D. F., Mexico. In *Proceedings of the Eighteenth International Congress of Americanists*, pages 180–187. London.

Gifford, J. C.
   1960 The Type-Variety Method of Ceramic Classification as an Indicator of
         Cultural Phenomena. *American Antiquity* 25:341–347.

Gould, S. J.
   1980 The Promise of Paleobiology as a Nomothetic, Evolutionary Discipline.
         Paleobiology 6:96–118.

Griffin, J. B.
   1985 The Formation of the Society for American Archaeology. *American An-
         tiquity* 50:261–271.

Guthe, C. E.
   1931 Archaeological Surveys. *Colorado Magazine,* July [unpaginated].
   1967 Reflections on the Founding of the Society for American Archaeology.
         American Antiquity 32:433–440.

Handsman, R. G.
   1983 Historical Archaeology and Capitalism, Subscriptions, and Separa-
         tions: The Production of Individualism. *North American Archaeologist*
         4:63–79.

Harris, M.
   1968 *The Rise of Anthropological Theory.* T. Y. Crowell, New York.

Heizer, R. F.
   1958 *A Guide to Archaeological Field Methods.* National Press, Palo Alto,
         CA.

Heizer, R. F. (editor)
   1949 *A Manual of Archaeological Field Methods.* National Press, Palo Alto,
         CA.
   1950 *A Manual of Archaeological Field Methods.* 2nd revised edition. Na-
         tional Press, Palo Alto, CA.

Heizer, R. F., and J. A. Graham
   1967 *A Guide to Archaeological Field Methods: Approaches to the Anthro-
         pology of the Dead.* National Press, Palo Alto, CA.

Hester, T. R., R. F. Heizer, and J. A. Graham
   1975 *Field Methods in Archaeology.* Mayfield Press, Palo Alto, CA.

Hill, J. N.
   1966 A Prehistoric Community in Eastern Arizona. *Southwestern Journal of
         Anthropology* 22:9–30
   1970 Broken K Pueblo: Prehistoric Social Organization in the American
         Southwest. *Anthropological Papers of the University of Arizona* 18.
         Tucson.

Hodder, I.
   1979 Economic and Social Stress and Material Cultural Patterning. *American
         Antiquity* 44:446–454.

Hodder, I. (editor)
   1982 *Symbolic and Structural Archaeology.* University of Cambridge Press,
         Cambridge.

Holmes, W. H.
   1886a Pottery of the Ancient Pueblos. In *Fourth Annual Report of the Bureau
         of Ethnology,* pages 257–360. Washington, D. C.

1886b Ancient Pottery of the Mississippi Valley. In *Fourth Annual Report of the Bureau of Ethnology,* pages 361–436. Washington, D. C.

1886c Origin and Development of Form and Ornamentation in Ceramic Art. In *Fourth Annual Report of the Bureau of Ethnology,* pages 437–465. Washington, D. C.

1895–1897 Archaeological Studies among the Ancient Cities of Mexico. *Field Columbian Museum Anthropological Series* 1(1). Chicago.

Kidder, A. V.

1924 An Introduction to the Study of Southwestern Archaeology, with a Preliminary Account of the Excavations at Pecos. *Papers of the Southwestern Expedition, Phillips Academy* 1. Yale University Press, New Haven.

Krieger, A. D.

1944 The Typological Concept. *American Antiquity* 9:271–288.

Kroeber, A. L.

1916 Zuni Potsherds. *Anthropological Papers of the American Museum of Natural History* 18(1):7–21.

1919 On the Principles of Order in Civilization as Exemplified by Changes of Fashion. *American Anthropologist* 21:235–263.

1940 Statistical Classification. *American Antiquity* 6:29–44.

Kuhn, T. S.

1962 *The Structure of Scientific Revolutions.* University of Chicago Press, Chicago.

Leone, M. P.

1972 Issues in Anthropological Archaeology. In *Contemporary Archaeology: A Guide to Theory and Contributions,* edited by M. P. Leone, pages 14–27. Feffer and Sons, London.

1982 Some Opinions about Recovering Mind. *American Antiquity* 47:742–760.

Leroi-Gourhan, A.

1967 *The Art of Prehistoric Man in Western Europe.* Thames and Hudson, London.

Longacre, W. A.

1964 Archaeology as Anthropology. *Science* 144:1454–1455.

1970 Archaeology as Anthropology: A Case Study. *University of Arizona Papers in Anthropology* 17. Tucson.

Mayr, E.

1982 *The Growth of Biological Thought.* Harvard University Press, Cambridge, MA.

Meltzer, D. J.

1983 The Antiquity of Man and the Development of American Archaeology. *Advances in Archaeological Method and Theory* 6:1–51.

Mulvaney, D. J.

1977 Classification and Typology in Australia. In *Stone Tools as Cultural Markers: Change, Evolution, and Complexity,* edited by R. V. S. Wright, pages 263–268. Australian Institute of Aboriginal Studies, Canberra.

National Research Council [C. Guthe]
  1930 Guide Leaflet for Amateur Archaeologists. *Reprint and Circular Series of the National Research Council 93*. Washington, D. C.

Nelson, N. C.
  1916 Chronology of the Tano Ruins, New Mexico. *American Anthropologist* 18:159–180.

Osgood, C.
  1951 Culture: Its Empirical and Non-Empirical Character. *Southwestern Journal of Anthropology* 7:202–214.

Peabody, C., and W. K. Moorehead
  1904 The Exploration of Jacob's Cavern McDonald County, Missouri. *Bulletin of the Department of Archaeology, Phillips Academy* 1. Andover, MA.

Plog, F. T.
  1974 *The Study of Prehistoric Change*. Academic Press, New York.

Quimby, G. I.
  1979 A Brief History of WPA Archaeology. In *The Uses of Anthropology*, edited by W. Goldschmidt, pages 110–123. American Anthropological Association, Washington, D. C.

Raab, L. M.
  1981 Do Cultural Explanations of the Past Have a Future? *North American Archaeologist* 2:331–344.

Rouse, I. B.
  1939 Prehistory in Haiti: A Study in Method. *Yale University Publications in Anthropology* 21. New Haven.

Sabloff, J. A., and G. R. Willey
  1967 The Collapse of Maya Civilization in the Maya Lowlands: A Consideration of History and Process. *Southwestern Journal of Anthropology* 23:311–336.

Schiffer, M. B.
  1972 Archaeological Context and Systemic Context. *American Antiquity* 37:156–165.
  1976 *Behavioral Archaeology*. Academic Press, New York.
  1979 Some Impacts of Cultural Resource Management on American Archaeology. In *Archaeological Resource Management in Australia and Oceania*, edited by J. McKinlay and K. Jones, pages 1–11. New Zealand Historic Trust, Auckland.

Schoenwetter, J.
  1981 Prologue to a Contextual Archaeology. *Journal of Archaeological Science* 8:367–379.

Setzler, F. M.
  1943 Archaeological Explorations in the United States, 1930–1942. *Acta Americana* 1:206–220.

Setzler, F. M., and W. D. Strong
  1936 Archaeology and Relief. *American Antiquity* 1:301–309.

Spaulding, A. C.
1953a Statistical Techniques for the Discovery of Artifact Types. *American Antiquity* 18:305–314.
1953b Review of "Measurements of Some Prehistoric Design Developments in the Southeastern States." *American Anthropologist* 55:588–591.
1954 Reply. *American Anthropologist* 56:112–114.
1958 [Letter to G. R. Willey and P. Phillips]. In *Method and Theory in American Archaeology,* by G. R. Willey and P. Phillips, pages 15–16. University of Chicago Press, Chicago.
1982 Structure in Archaeological Data: Nominal Variables. In *Essays on Archaeological Typology,* edited by R. Whallon and James A. Brown, pages 1–20. Center for American Archaeology Press, Evanston, IL.

Spier, L.
1917 An Outline for a Chronology of Zuni Ruins. *Anthropological Papers of the American Museum of Natural History* 18(3).

Squier, E. G.
1877 *Peru: Incidents of Travel and Exploration in the Land of the Incas.* Harper, New York.

Squier, E. G., and E. H. Davis
1848 Ancient Monuments of the Mississippi Valley. *Smithsonian Contributions to Knowledge* 1. Washington, D. C.

Stephens, J. L.
1841 *Incidents of Travel in Central America, Chiapas and Yucatan.* 2 volumes. New York.
1843 *Incidents of Travel in Yucatan.* 2 volumes. New York.

Steward, J. H., and F. M. Setzler
1938 Function and Configuration in Archaeology. *American Antiquity* 4:4–10.

Tainter, J. A., and G. J. Lucas
1983 Epistemology of the Significance Concept. *American Antiquity* 48:707–719.

Taylor, W. W.
1948 A Study of Archaeology. *Memoir of the American Anthropological Association* 69. Menasha, WI.

Thomas, C.
1894 Report of the Mount Explorations of the Bureau of Ethnology. In *Twelfth Annual Report of the Bureau of Ethnology, 1890–91.* Washington, D. C.

Tozzer, A. M.
1937 Review of Valliant's Work in the Valley of Mexico. *American Anthropologist* 39:338–340.

Trigger, B. G.
1978 *Time and Traditions.* Columbia University Press, New York.
1980 Archaeology and the Image of the American Indian. *American Antiquity* 45:662–676.
1984 Archaeology at the Crossroads: What's New? *Annual Review of Anthropology* 13:275–300.

Uhle, M.
  1903 *Pachacamac.* University of Pennsylvania Press, Philadelphia.
  1907 The Emeryville Shellmound. *University of California Publications in American Archaeology and Ethnology* 7(1).

Valliant, G. C.
  1930 Excavations at Zacatenco. *Anthropological Papers of the American Museum of Natural History* 32(1).

Watson, G.
  1984 The Social Construction of Boundaries between Social and Cultural Anthropology in Britain and North America. *Journal of Anthropological Research* 40:351–366.

Watson, P. J.
  1983 Foreward. In *A Study of Archeology,* by W. W. Taylor, pages ix–xvi. Center for Archaeological Investigations, Southern Illinois University, Carbondale, Il.

Watson, P. J., S. A. LeBlanc, and C. L. Redman
  1971 *Explanation in Archeology: An Explicitly Scientific Approach.* Columbia University Press, New York.
  1984 *Archeological Explanation: The Scientific Method in Archeology.* Columbia University Press, New York.

Willey, G. R., and P. Phillips
  1958 *Method and Theory in American Archaeology.* University of Chicago Press, Chicago.

Willey, G. R., and J. A. Sabloff
  1980 *A History of American Archaeology.* 2nd edition. W. H. Freeman, San Francisco.

Wiseman, J.
  1983 Conflicts in Archaeology: Education and Practice. *Journal of Field Archaeology* 10:1–9.

Wylie, A.
  1982 An Analogy by Any Other Name is Just as Analogical: A Commentary on the Gould-Watson Dialogue. *Journal of Anthropological Archaeology* 1:382–401.

Themes in the History of Archaeology

American Archaeology, 1930–1985

Since 1930–1931 my major activities have been directed toward archaeological study. I have been privileged to do research in Illinois, North Carolina, Florida, Tennessee, Mississippi, New Mexico, Utah, Nevada, Georgia, the Plains states, Guatemala, and lately in Western Samoa. It is a point of great satisfaction that I have no project unfinished or unreported; every piece of research for which I was personally responsible, no matter how trivial, has been reported, mistakes and all.

Perhaps because of that wide experience, or much more likely because of longevity, I have been asked to offer "a personal, informal perspective on the development of American archaeology since the founding of the SAA" a half century ago. It has been particularly pleasant to remember the excitement as new ideas and events changed the shape of the discipline from 1930 to 1985.

My adventures in archaeology began quite accidentally as a part of graduate work at the University of Chicago. There I heard of the work in Fulton County, Illinois, and felt no spark of interest. At that time I aspired to a career in either linguistics or cultural anthropology, because of exciting classes from Edward Sapir and Robert Redfield. Departmental policy demanded, however, that each able-bodied graduate student sacrifice one summer of his/her life to furthering the understanding of Illinois archaeology as it was preserved in Fulton County. Remember, that at that time, only the archaeological knowledge of the Southwest was in any degree ordered or controlled by a reliable chronology just arrived at through tree rings. In the Midwest and elsewhere, there was no time control. The scattered archaeological remains, e.g., the Red Paint People, the Hopewellian sites, the Effigy mounds, and Cahokia, were known but were merely dated as "old"; there was no time perspective nor culture history.

The primary concern, it seemed to me, in my first field experience, was with technique, not with time nor history nor science nor adaptation nor other lofty goals. The aim was to record the phenomena and their relationships and the truth would be revealed—to someone. To this end, there were mandatory, rote, and often mindless procedures to be observed during excavation. But I profited greatly from this experience because, being new and unwilling at the job, I was perhaps overcritical. I attempted to assess the validity of each procedure at any given time; my conception of technique derives from this experience in that I learned to apply any given procedure *only* as it was appropriate, not because it appeared in a sequence of ritual acts to be performed. There I developed many of my professional stances (including a respect for detail), such supervisory/administrative skills as I have, and a flexible arsenal of field techniques.

In none of my learnings was I hampered by classes in American archaeology. During my seven years (1929–1936) as intermittently a graduate student, there was offered one class in European prehistory (I remember the instructor's disdain for L.S.B. Leakey and his extravagant claims of the early 1930s!!), and one sketchy seminar in field techniques. A few BAE annual reports and the lavish works of C. B. Moore gave me the limited insights into American archaeology I acquired during my graduate work. Then, as today, we learned by reading. My own reading was guided by curiosity or by whatever my field work required for comprehension of the data I was uncovering. In all my research, except the Southwest, I was extremely fortunate in that most of the projects were located in blank spots on the archaeological map. Of course, most of the map was blank in the 1930s. That meant that any reported data were new and therefore comprised slight increments or contributions to knowledge. But archaeologists were then few in number. One was alone; the stimuli of discussion, pooling of ideas, debate and argument were never available. Except for rare, informal meetings and correspondence with colleagues, there were no exchanges. Thus, I largely made my own mistakes and reached my own conclusions, with little blame attaching to others.

What was it like to develop along with a discipline? It was, and remains, a continuous learning and unlearning process. By unlearning I mean the necessity of mentally replacing incomplete, even false, data learned earlier, with this year's more complete or corrected findings. The shape of the reconstructed prehistoric landscape was forever changing. Thanks to the Society and its bulletin, *American Antiquity*, there became available a series of once-manageable annual meetings and a flow of current data and interpretation. *American Antiquity* was read avidly. Then, as now, some of its content was trivial, but through its pages one began to perceive a patterning of American prehistory that all of you here today can learn with much less effort than I did.

Perhaps the most efficient way to give a personal "perspective on the development of American archaeology" is to list the events that, so far as I recall, expanded and enriched the discipline for me. I have taken my assignment seriously and have sadly suppressed the invidious comments I could make about my colleagues, or all the libelous and terribly funny anecdotes with which I could have filled this piece.

The first step toward understanding the Eastern Culture Sequence was through the McKern (1939) classificatory system. Devoid of chronological intent, its aim was Linnean; it was to establish prehistoric cultural relationships by comparing attributes (traits), and thus group, in ever larger clusters, the chaotic but numerous archaeological data of the East and Midwest. While the groupings accumulated, excavations continued, so that a relative chronology was established for many clusters of sites as these were grouped or separated by traits alone. Soon regional cultures and subcultures and sequences were recognized. Once that occurred, the usefulness of the McKern system ended and its use largely discontinued. Introduced about 1933, it helped order the data of half a continent and disappeared within a few years. Few ideas succeed so well. Its use was flawed because many did not fully understand its goals.

The 1930s were marked by other methodological matters. Trait lists dominated reports and the resultant cultural ascriptions. Comparisons were paramount; they remain in use today and are evidently a basic tool in doing culture history. And pottery types dominated thinking. Both trait lists and ceramic types were and are, useful in many ways. They are important aids in cultural classification but they tended in the 1930s, to become ends in themselves and thus stultified thought. Their interpretive limitations still haunt us; many reports of that day are well-nigh useless for other than ceramic study.

During those years dendrochronology was much refined in the Southwest. The technique was also introduced into Southeast studies and showed great promise in several areas. Its abandonment there was lamentable, in that a valuable tool was denied to Eastern archaeologists.

At this same time excavations in the Great Basin and Plains brought many new claims of association of extinct Pleistocene fauna with distinctive flint artifacts. All over the west small bands of men sought the oldest and finest of these objects. The basic scaffolding of the Early Man (or Paleoindian) chronology and content was erected during this decade; in fact, the Clovis site had provided a complete stratigraphic yardstick by 1933. Those terminal Pleistocene remains of the Plains forced the discarding of the constricting 3000 to 4000 years Holmes, Hrdlička, Kidder, and others had allowed for human occupancy of the New World. Before 1940 Luther Cressman in Oregon had discovered, and correctly interpreted, an early level of what came to be called the Western Archaic. His claim of an ancient era of habitation of the Great Basin was dismissed, flatly rejected, by Smithsonian scholars.

And in considering the 1930s, one must emphasize the tremendous impact of the Works Progress Administration (WPA) and Tennessee Valley Authority (TVA) dragnet, those vast archaeological programs that revealed the variety, richness, and depth of Southeastern prehistory. But the true time depth of the sequence was not realized because there was still the straitjacket of the Southwestern calendar. At that time the Southwest's high cultures were acknowledged to be precedent and ancestral to all other North American cultural developments. There were also extensive WPA programs in the Plains during these years.

As one involved at three separate times in WPA-TVA excavation programs, where large crews, unskilled assistants, and bureaucratic obstructionism created an optimal atmosphere for frustration, I look back on those years affectionately but somewhat sadly. I survived only because of my legendary patience and optimism. Many WPA excavations, no doubt including my own, were criminally inept. Many deeply stratified sites were dug and reported as if they were the debris of only a moment in time. Many more were not reported at all, or in some cases years later, when the skimpy notes were cold and the excavator no longer available. I will not dwell on this aspect of WPA research because it has been dealt with before. But one is compelled to mention Major William S. Webb, physicist *cum* archaeologist, who, acting in response to pressure from the Smithsonian (SI) and later this Society, was the prime visible force in creating government awareness of its responsibility for preservation of cultural resources as he directed the TVA program.

One would be even more remiss in failing to mention that the era ended with a masterly synthesis by James Ford and Gordon Willey (1941) of the decade of Southeastern WPA-TVA research. That study, spectacularly wrong in some ways but enduringly correct in most things, is truly a benchmark in establishing a regional cultural sequence where there had been but a vacuum. Even earlier Duncan Strong (1935) produced a synthesis of the scattered data of the Plains so brilliantly that Plains scholars stood in his shadow for 20 years.

After World War II the tempo of archaeological life was permanently changed. There came the River Basin Surveys. The Missouri River Basin and many other river basins were soon populated by archaeologists; my involvement was first with the Missouri River Basin and was relatively early and richly rewarding. I was assigned to the Midwest Region of the National Park Service (NPS) in Omaha, but no one knew what I was expected to do. Because the NPS took the lead in the basin program, justifying and defending the budget for the operation, and then transferring the funds to the SI which reluctantly undertook the research, I was assigned as liaison between the SI, NPS, and all institutions of higher learning in the Missouri River Basin. I worked as closely as possible with the administrative hierarchy of the SI (F.H.H. Roberts, W. Wedel, and P. S. Cooper) as consultant, gadfly, and co-conspirator. (Wedel once took written notice of my efforts as "helpful and stimulating," a most charitable description.) But my most useful activity was persuading the archaeologists of the Missouri Basin to divert their research funds, field schools, etc., to sites jeopardized by the dam/reservoir construction. That kind of cooperation of course was built into the River Basin Surveys design from the beginning. The cooperative program I helped establish soon evolved into the NPS contract system, a system still operating. The River Basin Surveys ultimately involved some 200 reservoirs. The research resulted in extraordinary gains in knowledge, the ordering of the major cultures in all major river valleys from Washington State to North Florida. Serendipitously, the salvage operation crystallized the conservation ethic as a governmental obligation so far as archaeological data are concerned.

In 1948, before my stint on the Plains was over, two major events led to almost catastrophic changes in the already unstable landscape of archaeological fact. First was Antevs' (1948) reconstruction of Holocene climate of the continent westward from the Mississippi River. He provided an environmental framework that both stimulated and restricted research. The reasoning went thus: if the archaeological record of the region was apparently locally blank, from 5000 to 3000 B.C., the explanation was ready at hand. That period was the height of the Antevs Altithermal and humans had left the region in order to survive. It offered instant explanation and was invoked daily in the Great Basin, the Southwest, and the Plains. Very soon, the Antevs sequence of environments became dogma and served to delay the acceptance of any data that ran counter to Antev's scheme. Interestingly, Antevs himself did not postulate anything but climate! It was the archaeologists who created the equation: Altithermal = too hot for humans = abandonment. Most of the problems that grew out of Antevs' contribution have been survived; his findings are still valid and are still used but with more restraint.

Then, again in 1947, the results of Libby's experiments with C-14 on dated organic artifacts (whose ages were already known by other means) were available by word of mouth. Long before the publication of his famous paper (Libby 1949) the revisions of chronological perspective had begun. Suddenly, the true time depth of the Southeast was known, outmoding all previous wisdom; the true relationship of Adena to Hopewell became apparent; the extreme age of the Tennessee River shell mounds was established. Cressman's insistence that the desert cultures of the West were ancient was instantly confirmed. There are scores of other examples of changes in then-current belief because of the availability of C-14 dates. The importance of C-14 to the discipline today need not be examined, being universally recognized. A third event, ignored by many and therefore largely futile, was W.W. Taylor's (1948) essay in which a somewhat new view of the nature of archaeology was proposed. Although ignored for a time, its essence was reissued serially by many authors in the 1960s as the "new archaeology."

In retrospect, the 1950s were no more tranquil than the last half of the 1940s, because other methodological breakthroughs occurred. That decade was one of consolidation of data, expansion of field research, and the quiet reintroduction of at least one idea—human ecology—that was highly attractive to many of us. (The step to systems, made by Clarke in the 1960s, intensified the concern with ecology). Several Paleoindian sites were excavated and lucidly reported. The most outstanding events, however, were a series of seminal publications that gave new vitality to field archaeology by opening new avenues of interpretation. One was Willey's Viru Valley study and its use of settlement patterns to gain new perspectives on prehistoric cultures; another was Spaulding's first article on statistics, which was not the first by any means but had the greatest impact; the Willey and Phillips (1958) volume on method and theory brought a pseudotheoretical base, a classificatory scheme, and the phrase "archaeology is anthropology or it is nothing" thus expanding the scope of archaeological interpretations. And, diffidently, I mention Danger Cave (Jennings 1957) which suggested a different interpretation of Great Basin prehistory. The study of American prehistory has not yet outgrown the concepts of that decade. Salvage projects—I prefer to say "emergency archaeology"—have continued. One long-term project, the Glen Canyon program under my direction, marks the first explicit and continual use of multidiscipline research teams. Soon thereafter the much more tightly organized and widely reported Tehuacan Project firmly established the value of such field teams and their ecological findings in expanding the scope of archaeological understanding.

The stimulation of the 1950s was shattered in the 1960s by an effort, by a few vocal zealots (who had read and varyingly understood, Binford's 1962 seminal article, "Archeology as Anthropology") to confine archaeological endeavor within the sterile boundaries established by the logical positivists and the philosophers of science. Having discovered, studied, and discarded the philosophers of science at least a decade earlier, I was dismayed, but relatively untouched and unscarred by the storm of preachment and polemic that confused and polarized the then-younger students of prehistory. Many have since recovered. To characterize the decade of the 1960s and into the 1970s, I paraphrase the felicitous words of the prominent British scholar, and see it as a time of polemic, the decline of literacy, and the denigration of field work. There also arose a temporary contempt for culture history as being intellectually barren and wasteful, or as being a humanistic interest for which there was no room in the science archaeology was to become. Throughout this phase the dominant theme was a demand for theory and the discovering of laws. Of more lasting value was the concern with culture change and its causes. If the causes are indeed discoverable, the search is taking far longer than was predicted.

When the stifling polemic dust subsided and polarization diminished, a series of important, useful, if not powerful, ideas from geography, ecology, statistics, and biology, among others, can be identified as having survived. Archaeologists of the 1980s routinely invoke a series of conceptual tools, most of which can be subsumed under the single rubric of human ecology. I refer, of course, to concerns (from different conceptual spheres) with such things as paleo-environments, subsistence, paleobotany (which involves both macrofossils and palynology), faunal analysis, ethno-archaeology, central place theory and trade/exchange networks, settlement pattern and locational analysis and other concepts that enrich and refine our interpretations of prehistoric human behavior. All these concepts can best be recognized as powerful technical and methodological refinements in both data collection and manipulation.

Even while I recognize the value of these new ways of looking at archaeological data, I truly deplore the trend toward the narrowing of scholarly focus. Careers can now be built on flint technology or use-wear studies, what happens to an archaeological deposit after abandonment, the uses and abuses of sampling in archaeological research, taphonomy, bone tool industries, and the like. With such narrow interests I see many archaeologists becoming terribly parochial, losing the holistic view that has made archaeological synthesis the life blood of the discipline. Here I mention with pleasure that there has been a call of late by some young scholars for a "return to basics." There is no problem for those of us who tried never to leave them.

I mention the last convulsive event merely in passing, because all of you know much about it. It is the traumatic refocusing or unfocusing of archaeological effort in the early 1970s on what is called Cultural Resource Management. This I can conservatively label as a mixed blessing, which has often led to grave mistakes and has had costs far beyond its scientific rewards; while there are a few bright spots in the record, on balance CRM has generally harmed our discipline.

One important last positive continuing force in shaping our discipline must be identified. I have already mentioned those times in the past when huge quantities of new data were being generated but were not always understood by isolated researchers new to the region. Here the regional working conference has time and again been a powerful force in the consolidation and synthesis of those newly discovered regional data. I have been privileged to have been active in three such conferences: the Southeastern Archaeological Conference in the 1930s, the Plains Conference in the 1940s and 1950s, and the Great Basin Conference in the 1950s. All three have broadened to become Anthropological Conferences; two sponsor journals. The importance of these informal, lightly structured voluntary associations of scholars in facilitating the early ordering of widely divergent data cannot be overstressed even today.

An encouraging trend that began in the late 1970s continues today. That was the appearance of several summaries of regional culture sequences: volumes dealing with New England, the Great Lakes area, Florida, the Southeast, the Southwest, and California by regional authorities are some examples. As might be expected, they vary in excellence. Their very existence is an important comment upon the increasingly complete knowledge of regional culture histories now available, and the continuing need for the careful building of such histories.

As for the 20 years effects of the "revolution" of the 1960s, I still see, along with Dunnell (1984), (1) a lack of any comprehensive theory; (2) the continuing conflicts in CRM archaeology; (3) parochialism characterizing the discipline; and (4) loss of faith in the new archaeology.

Although this account is an undocumented highly personal one, I think I have identified most of the breakthroughs and some of the residual constraints of our discipline, in what has been a progression from gathering data to attempts at explanations. Certainly I have listed the events that required me to continuously rearrange and replace ideas and data, and, therefore, have contributed to my own ever-broadening conception of what archaeology is and is not, and to the changing pattern of American culture history over the years.

In order to terminate these nostalgic ramblings, I recapitulate. I have been both a participant and observer as the Society grew from a few dozen forlorn, but courageous, souls to several thousand members. To the corpus of data and concepts that comprise American archaeology today I have contributed energy, mistakes, and a few scattered ideas. So, perforce, I have been *in seriatum* involved in gathering, classifying, ordering, sequencing, and synthesizing data; proselyting, sympathizing, and even agonizing as I learned and passed on to students and others what I know about American prehistory. And in recent decades I witnessed wrangling and jangling, and division, prostitution, and even moral destitution of some segments of our profession. More lately, I have seen the healing of psychic wounds and a return to field work.

Those who know me best know that throughout 50 of the 55 years of my professional life I have enjoyed the moral support of my wife, Jane. Therefore, this year brought me another anniversary of a more personal and valued kind. As Jane and I shared those years, the love and respect we hold for each other grows ever stronger.

Thus, I have experienced more than 50 years of excitement, spent much time with collections, journals, and books, and have enjoyed great intellectual and emotional satisfaction. As I always have, I see archaeology as rooted in anthropology, the humanities, and in certain aspects of science. Further, I see culture history as the core of the discipline, a core much enriched by today's concern with human ecology and culture as a system. Despite some pessimism in the remarks above, I feel that archaeology is today in ferment and therefore healthy. It is much more interesting than ever before.

Literature Cited

Antevs, Ernst
　1948　Climatic Changes and Pre-White Man in the Great Basin with Emphasis on Glacial and Postglacial Times. *The Bulletin of the University of Utah* 38(20), *Biological Series* 10(7):168–191.

Binford, Louis R.
　1962　Archeology as Anthropology. *American Antiquity* 28(2):217–225.

Dunnell, R. C.
　1984　The Americanist Literature for 1983: A Year of Contrasts and Challenges. *American Journal of Archaeology* 88:489–513.

Ford, James A., and Gordon R. Willey
　1941　An Interpretation of the Prehistory of the Eastern United States. *American Anthropologist* 43(3):325–363.

Jennings, Jesse D.
　1957　Danger Cave. *Memoirs of the Society for American Archaeology* 14.

Libby, W. F., D. C. Anderson, and J. R. Arnold
　1949　Age Determination by Radiocarbon Content: World-wide Assay of Natural Radiocarbon. *Science* 109:227–228.

McKern, William C.
　1939　The Midwestern Taxonomic Method as an Aide to Archeological Culture Study. *American Antiquity* 4(4):301–313.

Strong, Duncan
　1935　An Introduction to Nebraska Archeology. *Smithsonian Miscellaneous Collections* 93(10).

Taylor, Walter W.
　1948　A Study of Archeology. *American Anthropological Association Memoir* 69.

Willey, Gordon R., and Philip Phillips
　1958　*Method and Theory in American Archeology.* University of Chicago Press.

Field Methods in Archaeology

Introduction

Fifty years ago the aims of American archaeology were little different from those of today. The means to these ends, however, have changed markedly. Fifty years ago we had left behind our antiquarian image and we were striving to enter the scientific world. Today we try to excavate sites so carefully that we could rebuild them exactly. Each decade has seen advances in field and laboratory techniques that more nearly enable us to grasp that goal. A half century ago we were on the brink of great change.

The archaeologists of 50 years ago had few mentors to whom to turn for guidance. These teachers often had their field experience with Europeans and most recognized their obligations to such training. For example, Fay-Cooper Cole spent 1906 at the University of Berlin. J. W. Fewkes was at Leipzig from 1878 to 1880. Dorothy Cross worked in the Near East in 1931 and 1932. There were several others in this category, but all profited from this experience with Classical and other European prehistorians. The first archaeological area course taught at the University of Chicago in 1931–1932 by Harry Hoijer was on European prehistory, although instruction and training in field methods had been begun earlier.

Many Southwesternists were trained in eastern schools and of these few can be more notable than A. V. Kidder. Carl Guthe had a close association with Kidder at Pecos and only a distinguished career in administration took him afield. J. O. Brew with extensive training in Europe and Africa did his most lasting work in the Southwest. And the dean of them all, Emil Haury, came from the Midwest by way of Harvard to become the most influential figure in Southwest archaeology. Field schools had their beginnings about a decade earlier in the Southwest than in the East and not a few students went west in the summer. The National Park Service (NPS) was early involved in field work in the Southwest and several archaeologists received their basic field training in this manner. Other names could be added here, but this all suggests a cross-fertilization and close relationship between East and West so that new developments in field work were quickly shared.

A few of the most respected archaeologists of the 1920s and the 1930s were almost wholly self-taught. Americanists have always had a body of amateurs who could rival any professional in stature. Witness our two Webbs—William S. and Clarence H. They began as amateurs but made great and enduring contributions to the discipline.

Early Concepts and Field Work

In America there was not the cultural continuity that characterized history to prehistory in Europe. The American settlers were recently arrived Europeans whose antecedents were rooted in the "Old Country," whereas the panoply of archaeological remains—mounds, earthworks, middens, and other ancient ruins—were left by unknowns. It was a long time before we generally agreed that they were all the works of Indians, not necessarily like the historic survivors but Indians nonetheless.

This concept influenced ideas of procedure in studying these remains and all notions of classical and biblical origins were soon abandoned. Perhaps we had no widely held model of New World prehistory but we did have a shared commitment to a number of basic tenets that guided our field work. Despite a constant search for chronology, for the erection of a time scale to render order out of the jumble of different cultural manifestations that ranged through the Americas, there was no framework to serve as a guideline. Yet, there were firmly held convictions that were embraced by all. James B. Griffin (1976:35), speaking of 1925, stated it thusly:

> Our conceptual tools when I began working in archaeology were ones developed in the past with an emphasis on the definition and description of a culture area, the identification of its center and of marginal groups. The age-area hypothesis was sometimes employed to obtain a temporal framework. We worked with diffusion, independent invention, cultural borrowing and acculturation. The

"psychic unity of mankind" was employed as an explanation for similar behavior.

In addition, archaeologists were involved in working with the complexity of stratigraphy, typological dating, patination, varves, tree rings, and eventually radiocarbon dating. There were associations to be found of human materials with fossil beaches, river terraces or channels, extinct fauna and bog or lake bottoms where a pollen profile could be obtained. We worked with trait distribution and seriation of different cultural features.

Another fact of our life was the small number of professionals 50 years ago. Only a few universities offered graduate programs in anthropology and of these even fewer specialized in archaeology. In 1934 there was a demand for archaeologists to supervise the large-scale excavations that were required by the numerous hydroelectric and flood control projects on some of the major eastern streams. There simply were not enough trained men available. The University of Chicago was one of the few schools that had an organized training program in field archaeology and had been producing graduates for several years. Fay-Cooper Cole came to the faculty of the Anthropology Department in 1924. In 1926 the first field training in archaeology was initiated and an archaeological survey of Illinois was begun with Paul Martin and John Blackburn serving as the field crew. Some students of Cole's had previously worked with the Ohio State Historical and Archaeological Society, but after 1925 there was a continuous offering of field training each summer. In 1926, Paul Martin, then a graduate student, began training other students, and in 1927 Wilton Krogman, who had worked with Henry Shetrone in Ohio, served in that capacity. J. B. Griffin and W. C. McKern aided in the analysis of the field data that began to accumulate. The earliest field work in Illinois was concentrated in Jo Daviess County, northwestern Illinois (Bennett 1945), but activity moved to Fulton County in the central part of the state and continued there during the summers of 1930, 1931, and 1932 (Cole and Deuel 1937). Graduate students active in Fulton County included Richard Morgan, Fred Eggan, Alden Stephens, J. C. Harrington, Georg Neumann, and Jesse D. Jennings.

In 1934 Cole was introduced to the Kincaid site in southern Illinois, which promised to give a basis for study and description of what he then called "the Middle phase of the Mississippian cultural pattern" (Cole 1951:v). The site was acquired by the University that year and for the succeeding seven years it served as the training ground for a large number of American archaeologists. Thorne Deuel was the principal director of these sessions, but other persons were brought in from time to time: Edward Spicer in 1939 and Frank Setzler in 1940. Cole felt this assured a variety of ideas and techniques to be presented. I have been personally told that it was the experienced graduate students—J. D. Jennings, R. S. MacNeish, H. M. Minor, J. H. Caldwell, and J. C. Harrington—who really ran the training program. Both graduate and undergraduate courses were offered. Sundays were devoted to seminars on the current progress of the digging.

Because I worked closely with and learned much from such notables as Ralph Brown, David DeJarnette, James B. Griffin, Stuart Neitzel, and Charles Wilder I feel I am almost a Kincaid by-product myself (Haag 1985).

Although the above list of names is small, no other university can match it, and in 1934 the roster of available field archaeologists was minuscular. There were a few men trained at other universities, as George Quimby at Michigan, A. R. Kelley, Phil Phillips, and Bob Wauchope, and others, from Harvard. James Ford, who may seem to many to have just walked in out of the blue was, of course, a pupil of a thorough teacher, Henry B. Collins, to whom Ford was first exposed as a high school student at Deasonville in Mississippi. Later Collins invited him to join in some Alaskan field work (Haag 1961).

Meanwhile, the Southwest was producing its own especially qualified men as was the Far West. Interest in Southwestern archaeology by both amateur and professional began so early as to merit a history of its own. University departments at Arizona and at New Mexico produced field schools in archaeological methods years before eastern universities felt the need for such training. Actually, many eastern schools (e.g, Harvard and Yale) sent their archaeology majors to be trained by Haury and others. Ralph Brown, later a Kincaid graduate, sharpened his field acumen with experience at Betatakin under Frank Roberts. This is only one example, but a comprehensive history of the development of field work in the Southwest would demand a more competent treatment than I can give. Now a few archaeologists who ultimately became successful in the East had their field training in the Southwest.

Because there were not enough trained archaeologists to fill the needs of the early 1930s other disciplines were called upon to furnish the necessary staff. When Works Progress Administration (WPA) and Tennessee Valley Authority (TVA) excavation programs began in 1934 there were trained archaeologists with every crew. Later, however, they trained others who were drawn from several scientific endeavors, such as zoology, geology, museology, and even photography. Fortunately, their individual commitment to the sciences was sufficient to assure that competent results would accrue.

The body of professional archaeologists remained small even in the late 1930s. In 1938 it was possible that the founding fathers of the Southeastern Archaeological Conference (SEAC) could gather around a single table in the office of James B. Griffin in Ann Arbor. The 15 archaeologists, plus a few unable to attend, remained for some years the core of professionals who contributed so much to developing southeastern archaeology. Although that initial meeting of the SEAC was entirely devoted to ceramics, interests soon broadened. The 1951 session of the organization, with John Goggin hosting at Gainesville, saw all the participating members around one large table in his laboratory.

The conference had its beginning in 1925 when a group of archaeologists met in St. Louis to discuss some common problems of prehistory. The first Pecos conference was held only two years later. At first glance a conference is nothing new or earth-shaking (even the Pecos conference had its precedents), but they did have a profound effect on field work in America because techniques became generally the same within any given sphere. Also, innovations in techniques, methods, or ideas were shared and, without much fanfare, became the standing operating procedure. After WPA archaeology became widespread the SEAC became an annual clearinghouse, not only in the development of new chronologies but in refinement and improvement of field methods (Woodbury 1985). It is significant that the SEAC was looked upon as a band of mavericks by the few Old School archaeologists. Even A. R. Kelley was considered a Young Turk.

The Search for Chronology

We may look at the discovery of radiocarbon dating in the 1950s as revolutionary, but it had little effect on field work. Daniel (1967:266) felt that "it is no exaggeration to say that the discovery of radiocarbon dating is the most important development in archaeology since the discovery of the antiquity of man and the acceptance of a system of three technological ages." Only the collecting of appropriate specimens became more specific and meticulous. In the field today we are much more careful to delineate what is actually being dated.

Stratigraphy.—Turning to the subject of stratigraphy we can see that a change has taken place here. The original concepts have been refined and we approach excavations with new views about stratigraphy. In the first quarter of this century the time was obviously right for the development of stratigraphic employment in excavations. Several archaeologists, quite independent of one another, used the stratigraphic technique for deriving chronology. This development has been amply explored by a number of authors (Willey and Sabloff 1974; Woodbury 1960). Certainly by 1930 nearly all archaeologists excavated in "layers" but most used arbitrary levels of 6 inches or 15 centimeters. A few sought to dig in natural layers or to use "onion skin peeling." Some sought to do both.

All this concern with careful stratigraphic excavation was to enhance our chronology and to render more precise a model of the lifeway of the culture with which we were concerned.

One outgrowth of the preoccupation with stratigraphy was the development of the "block" technique. This merely meant that a column of block of the site (most useful in middens) was isolated by trenching on all four sides then carefully removing the block by layers, either arbitrary or natural. In the TVA excavations we were motivated to use this technique for an additional reason, namely, to prevent contamination of our records.

The North Alabama shell middens were so large that we usually sampled them by trenches, 5 or 10 feet (1.5 or 3.0 m) wide. During cold winter nights the profile faces of these trenches would freeze then thaw by midmorning. This thawing caused a few centimeters of the faces to slough off and fall into the trench bottom where active digging was taking place. Occasionally artifacts from a higher level fell into the lower diggings and "fogged the record" in the words of Major W. S. Webb. To prevent this contamination we regularly adopted the block technique (Webb and DeJarnette 1942:95).

Kidder (1924:19) had done much the same thing two decades before at Pecos, again with the thought of getting an unadulterated collection from each stratum.

> Most important results [of the 1915 season] were of course stratigraphic. . . . In various parts of the digging columns of earth had been isolated, marked out in horizontal sections and carefully excavated. . . . It was possible to establish eight major pottery types and to determine their exact chronological sequence, thus confirming and in many ways amplifying similar results then being obtained by Nelson at the ruins of the Galisteo basin a few miles to the west.

Seriation.—Another concern in the WPA-TVA excavations, particularly earth mounds, was with burials or tombs and burial pits. The Adena sites, especially, had examples of tombs constructed on top of other partially collapsed tombs or atop of one another, so that the uppermost tomb and its burials had to be dug away first. This meant that reading the profile was of utmost importance. We spent an inordinate amount of time developing and cleaning the profile of each cut to give us guidance about the next trench's content. This complicated archaeological technique was a test for the field man. The example of Elliott's results at the Robbins Mound in North Kentucky shows how fruitful this could be (Webb and Elliott 1942).

The increased concern with stratigraphy also sharpened interest in seriation, but the latter did not materially affect field methods except as it concerned surface collecting and excavations in unstratified sites. Nevertheless, the constant search for chronology led to misuses and abuses of seriation as some practitioners did not understand the limitations of seriation based on artifact types alone. A seriation chart derived from typology only could be arrived at with ranking the rarest artifact the youngest or the oldest. Without stratigraphic proof of their chronologies, the sequence between Adena and Hopewell cultures might have remained inverted for other generations to unravel (Webb and Snow 1945; Haag 1974). The use of seriation and its relation to field work are well illustrated by Ford's (1962) educational pamphlet "A Quantitative Method for Deriving Cultural Chronology." He prepared this pamphlet in 1961 for teaching seminars in methods of establishing chronological sequences in Pre-Columbian cultures in the Americas. The seminars were sponsored by the Pan American Union in Barranquilla. However, because seriation cannot reveal hiatuses in the stratigraphy nor can it readily disclose the length of time intervals, it has been viewed with caution by many. In the Lower Mississippi alluvial valley survey Phillips and Griffin were not nearly so enthusiastic about the seriational results as was Ford, who wrote that section of the volume (Phillips et al. 1951).

Although a major concern of archaeological field work has always been with three-dimensional accuracy in recording, the influences that were brought into WPA-TVA archaeological operations made us all acutely aware of the necessity for clarity as well. Others than the field supervising archaeologists were probably going to write the final reports. Photography was a major recording device and note taking was highly systematized. For the first time since Flinders Petrie could we do such large scale operations with results almost immediately realized. New techniques could be tried on a grand scale and shared or rejected. In the associated laboratories the effects were more visible and probably longer lasting. In North America archaeology was everywhere transformed to more nearly an exact science.

One of the WPA-TVA activities that seemed to hold great prospects was dendrochronology. In many of the Small-log or Large-log town-houses, butts of wall posts still remained as thoroughly charred sections, which we preserved by repeated applications of paraffin dissolved in gasoline (Hawley 1938). One living cedar gave a 600-year continuous ring record. Elsewhere in the East studies looked even more promising (Bell 1951, 1952), but little has been done in this area in recent decades. A surprisingly optimistic overview of dendrochronology in the East recently appeared (Stahle and Wolfman 1985). Those several thousand beautifully hydrocarbon-saturated specimens we collected may finally become the nucleus of revitalizing dendrochronological research.

In some of our excavations in the 1930s we were surrounded by heavy machinery. Giant earth-movers called Euclids wheeled away or deposited many cubic meters of earth per load. This machinery inspired the use of a pair of mules with an old hand-operated slip scoop to remove spoil material (Webb and DeJarnette 1942 pl. 129). Because we were not required to fill-in our excavations nor in any way restore them, the removal of spoil was only to facilitate more excavations or enable better photographs. The use of heavy machinery, however, was contrary to the WPA philosophy of putting men to work.

In my own experience at the Poverty Point site, a backhoe was used with success to develop a long profile from one earthworks ridge to another. In another instance, the Monte Sano site, two mounds were to be removed from the premises of a large chemical plant in Baton Rouge. Because of a limited amount of time available and labor disagreements the company furnished a front-loader complete with 9-foot blade to do the excavation. When asked to remove one inch from the trench floor the masterful operator removed one inch. Incidentally, this was the last piece of field work in which James Ford was involved.

Sampling.—If one were to identify the single most important innovation that has influenced, even altered, field techniques in the last 50 years it would have to be the adoption of sampling theory. Nothing else has so modified our surface collecting habits and our site excavation programs as has probability theory. It would seem that most archaeologists have come to the realization that results arrived at without appropriate sampling and statistical treatment are mere science fiction.

Perhaps the first statistical treatment of data to appear in archaeological reports was percentage comparisons. Cultural correlations that were based on similar percentages (how similar?) of artifact types, particularly ceramics, gave the researcher a more comfortable "feeling" about his reconstructions. Despite the extensive use of statistical analysis on the human skeletal material in the Pickwick report (Newman and Snow 1942) no other body of material received any such treatment. This was true not only for Pickwick but for most other WPA-TVA and other current reports.

Orr's study of the material culture found at the Kincaid site includes a commendable use of statistical tests to evaluate the uniformity of the trait frequencies in the various parts of that complex site (Orr 1951). In 1948 a study of canid skeletons that had been recovered from archaeological sites from Alaska to Alabama was published (Haag 1948). It was as sophisticated a statistical analysis as might be conceived at the time. It was patterned after biological studies that employed an analysis of variance and tests of the significance of differences in osteological characters. Such tests, at that time, were less than 10 years old. The dog study employed mensurational data of which there are only limited counterparts in archaeological research. Hence even this document was not followed by a heightened awareness of the need for statistical treatment. More obvious should have been the examples set by the physical anthropologists.

Sampling, particularly surface collecting rarely merited description in most site reports but the *Archaeological Survey in the Lower Mississippi Alluvial Valley* was one of the few documents with a thorough treatment of this aspect of field work (Phillips et al. 1951:42–43). In most survey accounts, the number of artifacts (usually potsherds) that constituted an "adequate sample" was wholly arbitrary. Probably to facilitate percentage comparisons an adequate sample was usually taken to be one hundred. Although objectivity may often be evoked, rarely could a sampler reject the tendency to pick up decorated or rim sherds more often than plain. In fact, some surveys simply discarded or ignored plain sherds and based comparisons on decorated sherd counts.

Few people have been more influential in advocating probability theory than has A. C. Spaulding (1960). Now, at the end of 50 years he is still chiding and admonishing (Spaulding 1985). Although the stern finger still points ahead, at least proper sampling strategy is regularly used now to assure that much of our data can remain meaningful for the future.

A criticism often voiced about WPA-TVA archaeology is that it was so poorly documented. It was not documentation but the concepts and strategies of the archaeology (read field work) that were flawed (Haag 1985). Despite the gloomy outlook described by Spaulding (1985), CRM contractors have been forced to employ an understandable sampling technique because few of these projects could encompass 100 percent excavation of a single site or of all the sites in a survey. Usually these projects are performed by a variety of persons in a given area and thus, perforce, the results must be couched in similar terms following similar methods. This may be a small beginning but it is begun. A good review of sampling theory has been presented by Ragir (1975).

The Shift to Ecological Concerns

Screening.—One of the now basic activities in acceptable field work is screening and its implications. Screening is by no means a new technique and is another item in our debt list to Old World archaeology. It is actually the turn to ecology that has demanded screening and other such recovery procedures. As our commitment to the ecological approach has increased we have not been content with simple statements about rainfall and temperature under which the peoples of a given culture existed, but all other aspects of man's relationships with his environment are pertinent. Thus we screen our diggings for minutia that includes bone fragments, teeth remains, and any other biotic residues that could give clues to the flora and fauna that may have been factors in the culture bearer's interface with the environment. Plant parts, seeds, and even pollen become highly important indicators. All of this concern has demanded an adjustment in our field collecting techniques and we have seen a truly remarkable change in this direction.

A fundamental concern in the Mississippi Valley is alluvial geology. The early work of H. N. Fisk on the geologic history of the Mississippi led each resident archaeologist to try to correlate his site's beginnings with the meander sequence of the river (Fisk 1944). At the 1932 Conference for Southern Prehistory held in Birmingham, Winslow Walker suggested use of successive changes in river channels as a guide to chronology. Kniffen (1936) was correlating stream channels with specific archaeological markers 50 years ago this spring. Ford was then brought into an awareness of the potential, but it was Phillips who meticulously assayed a sample of Lower Mississippi Valley sites relative to the Fiskian model (Phillips et al. 1951:295–306). In recent decades the work of Saucier (1974, 1977, 1981) has given us renewed faith in the method with his detailed modifications and corrections of Fisk's monograph. The future is bright for this paradigm in the Mississippi Valley.

New Trends.—Many other innovations of the past half century have affected field work. The specializations, such as historical archaeology, underwater archaeology, and CRM archaeology have developed narratives of their own. The archaeologist's image of himself has changed because of his increased reliance upon the physicist, the chemist, the geologist, and the biologist. More pronounced have been improvements on old field techniques in such areas as site surveying and site mapping (Plog et al. 1978). Magnetometry (Steponaitis and Brain 1976), resistivity, and remote sensing are routinely employed now (McManomon 1984). Our future is one in which computer literacy will be demanded of all, but computers will never teach us to think. We will make progress only through intellectual leaders continuing to point the way. Writing in 1975 Griffin (1976:38) said: "The great contrast between the archaeological picture of 1925 and today is a remarkable achievement. Hopefully, the interpretive structure and the results will continue to improve." Ten years later we can only echo that hope. Even the modality of Spaulding's universe of archaeological practitioners need not be ineluctable.

Literature Cited

Bell, R. E.
  1951 Dendrochronology at the Kincaid Site. In *Kincaid: A Prehistoric Illinois Metropolis,* by F.-C. Cole, pages 233–292. University of Chicago Press, Chicago.
  1952 Dendrochronology in the Mississippi Valley. In *Archaeology in the Eastern United States,* edited by J. B. Griffin, pages 345–351. University of Chicago Press, Chicago.

Bennett, J. W.
  1945 *Archaeological Exploration in Jo Daviess County, Illinois.* University of Chicago Press, Chicago.

Cole, F.-C.
  1951 *Kincaid: A Prehistoric Illinois Metropolis.* University of Chicago Press, Chicago.

Cole, F.-C., and T. Deuel
  1937 *Rediscovering Illinois.* University of Chicago Press, Chicago.

Daniel, G.
1967 *Origins and Growth of Archaeology.* T. Crowell, New York.

Fisk, H. N.
1944 Geological Investigations of the Alluvial Valley of the Lower Mississippi River. *Mississippi River Publication* 52. War Department, Corps of Engineers, U. S. Army, Vicksburg.

Ford, J. A.
1962 A Quantitative Method for Deriving Cultural Chronology. *Pan American Union Technical Manual* 1. Washington, D. C.

Griffin, J. B.
1976 A Commentary on Some Archaeological Activities in the Mid-Continent. *Mid-Continental Journal of Archaeology* 1:5–38.

Haag, W. G.
1948 An Osteometric Analysis of Some Aboriginal Dogs. *University of Kentucky Reports in Anthropology* 7(3). Frankfort.
1961 Twenty-Five Years of Eastern Archaeology. *American Antiquity* 27:16–23.
1974 The Adena Culture. In *Archaeological Researches in Retrospect,* edited by G. R. Willey, pages 119–145. Winthrop, Cambridge.
1985 Federal Aid to Archaeology in the Southeast, 1933–1942. *American Antiquity* 50:272–280.

Hawley, F.
1938 Tree Ring Dating for Southeastern Mounds. In An Archaeological Survey of the Norris Basin in Eastern Tennessee, by W. S. Webb. *Bureau of American Ethnology Bulletin* 118:359–362. Washington, D. C.

Kidder, A. V.
1924 *An Introduction to the Study of Southwestern Archaeology with a Preliminary Account of the Excavations at Pecos.* Phillips Academy, Andover.

Kniffen, F. B.
1936 A Preliminary Report on the Mounds and Middens of Plaquemines and St. Bernard Parishes, Lower Mississippi River Delta. In Lower Mississippi River Delta, by R. J. Russell et al. *Louisiana Department of Conservation, Geological Bulletin* 8:407–422. Baton Rouge.

McManomon, F. P.
1984 Discovering Sites Unseen. In *Advances in Archaeological Method and Theory,* edited by M. B. Schiffer, 7:233–292. Academic Press, New York.

Newman, M. T., and C. E. Snow
1942 Preliminary Report on the Skeletal Material from Pickwick Basin, Alabama. In An Archaeological Survey of Pickwick Basin in the Adjacent Portions of the States of Alabama, Mississippi, and Tennessee. *Bureau of American Ethnology Bulletin* 129:393–507. Washington, D. C.

Orr, K. G.
1951 Change at Kincaid: A Study of Cultural Dynamics. In *Kincaid: A Prehistoric Illinois Metropolis,* by F.-C. Cole, pages 293–359. University of Chicago Press, Chicago.

Phillips, P., J. A. Ford, and J. B. Griffin
  1951 Archaeological Survey in the Lower Mississippi Alluvial Valley, 1940–1947. *Papers of Peabody Museum of Archaeology and Ethnology Harvard University* 25.

Plog, S., F. Plog, and W. Wait
  1978 Decision Making in Modern Surveys. In *Advances in Archaeological Method and Theory*, edited by M. B. Schiffer, 1:383–421. Academic Press, New York.

Ragir, S.
  1975 A Review of Techniques for Archaeological Sampling. In *Field Methods in Archaeology*, by T. R. Hester, R. F. Heizer, and J. A. Graham, pages 181–200. Palo Alto.

Saucier, R. T.
  1974 Quarternary Geology of the Lower Mississippi Valley. *Arkansas Archaeological Survey, Publications in Archaeology, Research Series* 6. Little Rock.
  1977 Geological Analysis. In *Teoc Creek, a Poverty Point Site in Carroll County, Mississippi*, by J. Connoway, S. McGahey, and C. H. Webb. *Mississippi Department of Archives and History, Archaeological Report* 3:90–105.
  1981 Current Thinking on Riverine Processes and Geologic History as Related to Human Settlement in the Southeast. In *Traces of Prehistory, Papers in Honor of William G. Haag. Geoscience and Man* 22:7–18. Baton Rouge.

Spaulding, A. C.
  1960 Statistical Description and Comparison of Artifact Assemblages. In *The Application of Quantitative Methods in Archaeology*, by R. F. Heizer and S. F. Cook, *Viking Fund Publications in Anthropology* 28:60–90. University of Chicago Press, Chicago.
  1985 Fifty Years of Theory. *American Antiquity* 50:301–308.

Stahle, D. W., and D. Wolfman
  1985 The Potential for Archaeological Tree-Ring Dating in Eastern North America. In *Advances in Archaeological Method and Theory* edited by M. B. Schiffer, 8:279–302. Academic Press, New York.

Steponaitis, V. P., and J. P. Brain
  1976 A Portable Differential Proton Magnetometer. *Journal of Field Archaeology* 3:455–463.

Webb, W. S., and D. L. DeJarnette
  1942 An Archaeological Survey in Pickwick Basin in the Adjacent Portions of the States of Alabama, Mississippi, and Tennessee. *Bureau of American Ethnology Bulletin* 129.

Webb, W. S., and J. B. Elliott
  1942 The Robbins Mounds, Sites Be3 and Be14, Boone County, Kentucky. *University of Kentucky Reports in Anthropology* 5(5). Frankfort.

Webb, W. S., and C. E. Snow
  1945 The Adena People. *University of Kentucky Reports in Anthropology* 6. Frankfort.

Willey, G. R., and J. A. Sabloff
  1974   *A History of American Archaeology.* Freeman, San Francisco.

Woodbury, R. B.
  1960   Nelson's Stratigraphy. *American Antiquity* 26:98–99.
  1985   Regional Archaeological Conferences. *American Antiquity* 50:434–444.

Eoliths, Archaeological Ambiguity, and the Generation of "Middle-Range" Research

Introduction

During the past decade or so, archaeologists have become increasingly involved in the search for propositions that securely relate the archaeological record as it is discovered to the processes that formed that record. More and more archaeological work has focused on what Binford (1981, 1984) terms "middle-range" research: research that emphasizes the study of extant systems in which both processes and the results of those processes can be observed. The immediate goal of much of this work is the isolation of diagnostic "signatures" whose recognition in the archaeological record can inform us of the processes that led to the formation of that record. Secure recognition of such signatures, many believe, would allow archaeologists not only to distinguish patterns resulting from natural phenomena from those resulting from human behavior, but also to build more secure theoretical approaches to cultural dynamics (Binford 1983; Raab and Goodyear 1984).

Contemporary archaeologists see this approach as having grown from recently recognized difficulties in the interpretation of archaeological materials. Traditional archaeologists, Binford (1981) tells us, did not conduct middle-range work, a view with which Raab and Goodyear (1984) concur. What I will show here is that middle-range research, and in particular research directed toward the extraction of signatures diagnostic of formation processes, is very much a part of "traditional archaeology." I will argue that work of this sort is routinely spawned by situations in which archaeologists recognize perplexing ambiguity in the patterning presented to them by archaeological data. I will establish that middle-range research, including the actualistic studies that routinely form the heart of such research, has been part of the archaeologists' tool kit since the establishment of prehistoric archaeology as a discipline. Finally, I will suggest that what distinguishes contemporary archaeology is not the conduct of actualistic studies in the context of middle-range research, but is instead the extremely wide range of archaeological settings whose meaning is perceived as being ambiguous.

To establish these points, I will examine situations in which interpretive ambiguity was built in from the very beginning: the archaeological search for the earliest occupants of Europe after it had been established in 1859 that people had coexisted with now-extinct Pleistocene mammals. I will then turn to a similar search currently underway in North America. My goal is not to present a thorough history and analysis of the debate over eoliths and related phenomena, or even of the specific cases I examine, but is instead to show how perceived ambiguity led prehistorians to conduct actualistic research in a mid-range setting.

Some Historical Background

Elsewhere, I have discussed in detail how it came to be accepted, in 1859, that our ancestors had coexisted with a wide array of now-extinct Pleistocene mammals (Grayson 1983), and only a few aspects of that process need to be stressed here.

First, hand axes played a crucial role in the recognition of a deep human antiquity. That people had produced stone items of this sort had not been questioned since about the year 1700, as a result of the demise of the older concept of fossils as including a diverse array of materials of distinctive shape and composition from on and in the ground (Grayson 1983; Rudwick 1972). Thus, the debate over human antiquity that occurred between about 1810 and 1859 did not involve the processes that shaped the distinctive lithic objects found amongst the remains of extinct mammals, but instead how those undoubted artifacts came to be found amongst those bones and teeth. As I shall discuss, the nature of the objects that were to be involved in the search for even earlier, Tertiary hominids in England and Europe was of a very different nature, and here it was not stratigraphic context but the processes that formed the objects themselves that became the focus of discussion.

Second, although Darwin's *Origin of Species* was published in the same year that it became widely accepted that people had existed in the Pleistocene, the two events were not causally connected, and it was routinely recognized that a deep human antiquity was compatible with both evolutionist and creationist positions. As a result, the acceptance of a Pleistocene human existence opened the temporal gates, since in both evolutionist and creationist perspectives, there was no reason to suspect that even earlier hominids would not be found. It was suspected, however, that those earlier hominids would be western Asian in origin. By the late 1850s a series of Miocene-aged great apes, including *Dryopithecus,* was known from Europe (Lartet 1837a, 1837b, 1856). It was widely believed by evolutionary biologists that those great apes represented either a direct human ancestor or a divergent line (after the human divergence) from the ancestral primate stock. In the creationist view, people could have been called into being soon after the higher primates had first appeared. Either way, the known paleontological record suggested that hominid bones and artifacts of at least Miocene age were a very real possibility.

The key distinction between evolutionist and creationist perspectives as regards deeper hominid history resided in the predictions these positions made about ancient hominid morphology. Evolutionist views held that these hominids should look very much like nonhuman primates—Huxley's "lower pithecoid form" (Huxley 1863:159). Creationist views, on the other hand, predicted that the earliest hominid bones and teeth should look very much like their modern counterparts. These predicted differences in skeletal morphology, however, did not extend to artifacts. Although one might adhere to the biblical notion of fall from grace, such an argument had to be couched in terms that dealt with moral issues (e.g., J. W. Dawson 1894). The archaeological record allowed no choice as regarded the history of tools: as one went further back in time, tools became cruder and cruder in form, as shown conclusively by straightforward stratigraphic and faunal correlations of artifact-bearing deposits in western Europe and England.

Thus, by the early 1860s, western scientists expected not only that late Tertiary artifacts would be found, but that they would be of an exceptionally crude nature, perhaps so crude that they could be distinguished from the natural lithic background only with difficulty. This view was accepted by both evolutionists and by many creationists and was, in this sense, philosophically neutral.

The Search for Tertiary Hominids in Europe

It was, then, no tremendous surprise when the first report of a Tertiary human presence appeared. In 1863, Jules Desnoyers (1863a:1082) reported the discovery of "incisions, striations, and cuts" on a series of bones of extinct mammals from Pliocene deposits at Saint-Prest, near Chartres, some 80 km southwest of Paris. Only human hands, he felt, could have produced these marks.

Although Desnoyers soon found himself involved in a minor debate over the age of the cut marks (Robert 1863; Desnoyers 1863b), it was Charles Lyell who paid the most detailed attention to these specimens. Lyell visited Saint-Prest within a month of Desnoyer's presentation of his results, and published his detailed consideration of the cut specimens in an appendix to the third edition of his *Antiquity of Man* (Lyell 1863; see also Grayson in press).

Lyell found both the form and position of the cuts curious. Many of them, he observed, "exhibit several subordinate and parallel fine striae or lines such as the irregularities of a jagged flint knife or hatchet would produce" (1863:510). Lyell was aware, however, that remains of the extinct beaver *Trogontherium* had been found in the Saint-Prest deposits and suspected that beaver-gnawing could have been responsible for at least some of the marks. Using an approach that had been pioneered much earlier in the century by William Buckland (1823; see also Rupke 1983), Lyell had bone and antler specimens placed in a porcupine (*Hystrix* sp.) cage in the London zoo and carefully observed the nature of the resultant gnaw marks. Although Edouard Lartet saw similarities between those marks and cuts he had attributed to human activities on specimens from caves in the Dordogne region (Lyell 1863), Lyell noted that the individual tooth marks on the modern materials could not be observed on those from Saint-Prest.

Lyell (1863:515) concluded that because "the art of deciphering the cuts and other marks observable on fossil bones [was] so much in its infancy," it was premature to attribute the Saint-Prest cuts to human hands. To solve the problem, he suggested that a diligent search be made for stone tools wherever such cut bones were found, even though any associated stone artifacts might be difficult to detect because "tools of so remote a period may have been of so rude a description" (1863:515). Others echoed this conclusion (e.g., Gervais 1864–1866).

The Discovery of Eoliths in France, 1867–1885

It did not take long for the diligent search to be made. At the second session of the *Congrès international d'anthropologie et d'archéologie préhistoriques* (cited below as the "International Congress"), held in Paris in August 1867, the Abbé Louis Bourgeois (1868) claimed that he had discovered stone tools at the base of the Miocene-aged *Calcaire de Beauce* in deposits exposed in the small town of Thenay, some 45 km east of Tours. Although classic hand axes were absent and his specimens were crude, he argued that a human role in the creation of these objects could not be doubted. Not only were they fully similar to those observed in later contexts, belonging to the same functional categories, but they showed "all the signs by which human action is recognized" (Bourgeois 1868:71). Those "signs" included fine retouch, symmetrical notching, use wear, and, above all, the replication of basic morphological forms. In addition, he observed that many showed crackled surfaces suggestive of burning, and he inferred that only human-caused fires could account for this phenomenon.

Gabriel de Mortillet (1883, 1885) was later to express sardonic pleasure at the fact that a French priest was the first to argue for stone tools in an unquestionably Tertiary context, as if this discovery represented a major coup for evolutionary views. But as I have noted, Bourgeois' discovery was fully compatible with a creationist position, and Bourgeois (1868) declared himself unable to choose between the two views. Initial reaction to the facts of the case, however, were varied. De Mortillet (1868b) accepted at least some, noting that their crudeness was in line with their age, as did the Danish archaeologist Worsaae (in de Mortillet 1868b). However, neither the French geologist Hébert, who had worked with Rigollot at Saint-Acheul during the 1850s (Grayson 1983), nor the Swedish archaeologist Nilsson saw traces of human action in these specimens (de Mortillet 1868b).

Bourgeois was not deterred by this mixed reception. In 1869, he opened a new pit at Thenay, duplicating his previous results (Bourgeois 1869), and he repeated his arguments at the Sixth International Congress, held in Brussels in 1872 (Bourgeois 1873). To him, the presence of fine retouch, symmetrical notching, use wear, burning, occasional bulbs of percussion, and the presence of clear morphological groups, implying manufacture according to plan, all combined to demonstrate a human role in the production of the Thenay specimens. He not only provided illustrations of his specimens for the first time (Figures 1, 2), but also

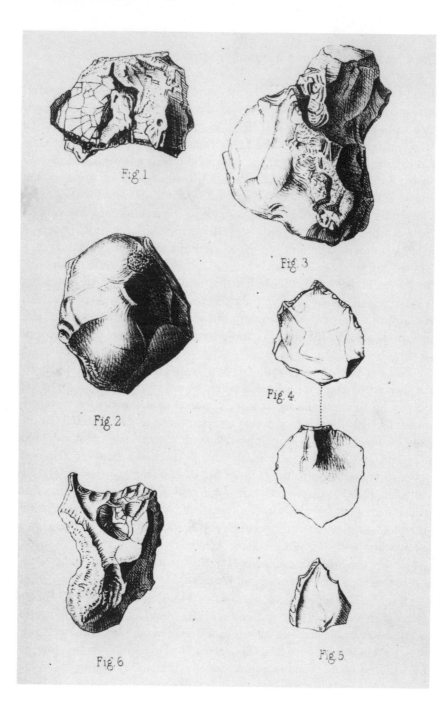

Figure 1 Crackled and fractured Tertiary flints from Thenay (from Bourgeois 1873).

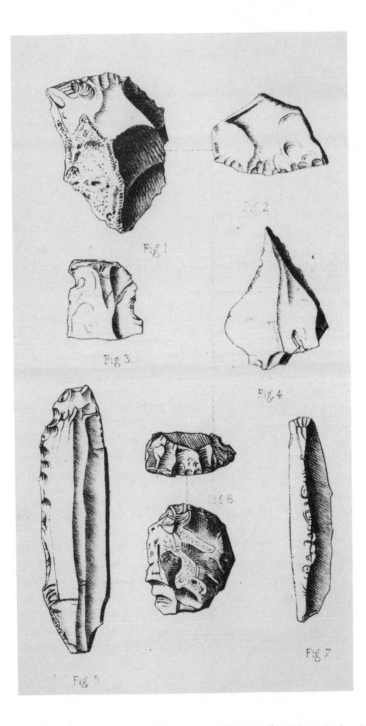

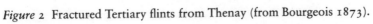

Figure 2 Fractured Tertiary flints from Thenay (from Bourgeois 1873).

requested that a commission be appointed to evaluate his collection (Bourgeois 1873).

After examining the specimens for less than 30 minutes, the 15-member commission rendered a split decision: nine agreed that one or more of the specimens was worked, five were extremely sceptical, while one simply could not decide (Bourgeois 1873, 1877). Even those who accepted some of the objects as artifacts could not agree on which specific ones were artifactual.

The problem was evident. There was no *a priori* reason to reject a human presence in the Tertiary, but presuppositions concerning what such ancient tools should look like implied that they should have been extremely crude, one step away from, as Cartailhac (1873:312) noted, "man armed with unworked stone." If they were that crude, the problem became one of distinguishing them from stone that had been fractured naturally. What was clearly needed, the young Marcellin Boule observed in 1880, was "an absolute criterion of intentional work" (in Chantre 1884:389); but such was not yet available. Lyell's hope that the lack of such a criterion for the recognition of worked bone could be remedied by the discovery of Tertiary stone tools was quickly proving overly optimistic.

While Bourgeois' reputation as a sound and cautious scholar, and de Mortillet's outspoken support of his position (de Mortillet 1868a, 1868b, 1873, 1879), made Thenay the most frequently discussed of the Tertiary sites during the 1870s, there was a wide variety of other claimants. Of these, two merited, and got, serious consideration during that decade.

Although the possible presence of Tertiary artifacts in the Aurillac (Cantal) region of south-central France was first signalled by Tardy (1869, 1870), it was the Aurillac pharmacist J.-B. Rames who put this area on the archaeological map. In 1877, de Mortillet (1883) later recalled, Rames sent him flint specimens from deposits exposed on the volcanic hill of Puy Courny, near Aurillac, that were analogous to those found at Thenay. Encouraged by de Mortillet, Rames continued his work and discovered a number of specimens from the upper Miocene strata of Puy Courny that de Mortillet felt were definitely worked; these de Mortillet exhibited at the 1878 Universal Exposition held in Paris (de Mortillet 1879, 1883; see also Rames 1884).

The other widely discussed claim for Tertiary artifacts during these years was based on a series of localities near Lisbon that had been brought to light during the early 1860s by the Portuguese geologist Carlos Ribeiro. Although Ribeiro initially used the presence of artifacts to assign these deposits to the Quaternary, objections by French geologists led him to reanalyze this assignment and to place the deposits in the Miocene and Pliocene (Ribeiro 1867). This reassignment, of course, meant that he had discovered Tertiary implements, and he published this conclusion in Lisbon in 1871 and presented it to the Sixth International Congress in Brussels in 1872 (Ribeiro 1873a, 1873b; see Figure 3). He provided a larger series of specimens for the 1878 Universal Exposition, where de Mortillet placed them alongside specimens from Thenay and Puy Courny as proof of Tertiary hominids (de Mortillet 1878; see also Cartailhac 1881). At the Ninth International Congress, held in Lisbon in 1880, Ribeiro presented his case again, only to see a nine-member commission appointed to judge his material reach a split decision: some members, including John Evans, rejected the evidence; others, including de Mortillet, accepted it fully (Ribeiro 1884).

By the early 1880s, then, lithic objects from three areas had been accepted by many as evidence for Tertiary hominids in Europe: Thenay, Puy Courny, and the Lisbon sites. In 1881, Gabriel de Mortillet and his son, Adrien, included Tertiary artifacts into their classification of the European past, introducing the term "Eolithique" to refer to the simple stone tools of the Tertiary (de Mortillet and de Mortillet 1881).

It was in 1883, however, that the notion of Tertiary hominids was introduced to a broader French-speaking public by de Mortillet, who devoted 102 pages of his *Le Préhistorique* to a detailed discussion of "Tertiary Man." This discussion analyzed 26 locales that had been suggested to provide possible evidence for Tertiary hominids. Of these, de Mortillet rejected all but the three I have discussed.

This is not the place to analyze de Mortillet's archaeology in detail (but see Hammond 1980 and Sackett 1981). It is important to realize, however, that *Le Préhistorique* was not just a book about prehistory: it was an evolutionary and antireligious book about prehistory (for insight into de Mortillet's background, see Cartailhac 1901 and Reinach 1899). In it, he continued to develop his classification of the European archaeological record in terms of a unilineal set of phases through which our ancestors had passed on their upwards biological and cultural evolutionary journey. This system required that the human voyage had begun with beings whose tools and morphology were extremely primitive, and the eolithic sites provided him with just such evidence. "It is thus extremely natural," he observed (1883:183), "that at an epoch so far removed from us, we find only an industry reduced to its simplest expression." It was

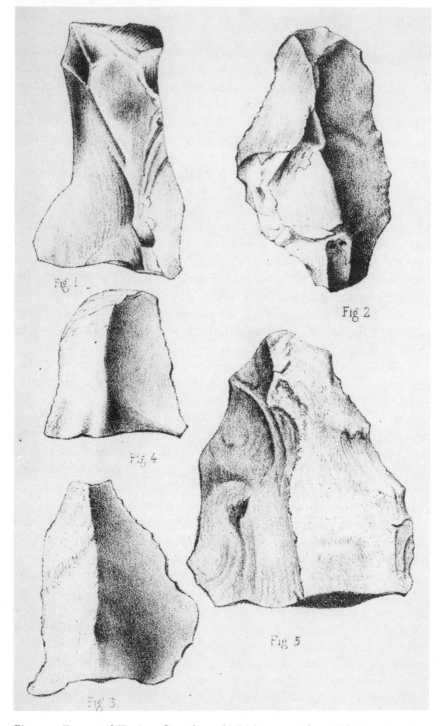

Figure 3 Fractured Tertiary flints from the Lisbon area (from Ribeiro 1873a).

one thing for de Mortillet's system to require an Eolithic; it was quite another to demonstrate its existence, and as I have noted, de Mortillet's enthusiasm for sites like Thenay was not shared by such experts as John Evans.

The initial arguments concerning the eoliths consisted almost entirely of assertions that the objects were, or were not, artifactual. Those arguing for the existence of Tertiary stone tools needed to convince the rest of the scientific community that their precise examples represented just such tools. The scientific community that needed to be convinced, however, did not have to convince anyone of anything: all they had to do was to disagree with the assertion that the items had been worked. Thus, while Bourgeois and Ribeiro spent pages discussing their sites, and de Mortillet many more pages supporting them, experts such as Evans (1872:574; 1878:637) could dismiss them in a sentence: "Though eventually works of man will, in all probability, be discovered in beds older than these Quaternary gravels . . . I cannot at present accept the views of Abbé Bourgeois and others as to their occurring in the Pliocene beds of St. Prest, near Chartres, and in the Miocene beds at Thenay, near Pontlevoy."

Those who accepted the Tertiary sites responded to the situation in the only ways available to them. They continued the search for ever-more convincing examples (e.g., de Mortillet 1873, 1879). In addition, they began to make arguments that depended not simply on intuitive assessments of the artifactual nature of those specimens, and on perceived similarities to Quaternary implements, but that rested instead on objective morphological evidence.

By the late 1870s, supporters of eoliths were couching that support in terms of a set of diagnostic attributes that infallibly allowed the recognition of a human role in the fracture of stone. For instance, both Cartailhac (1881) and de Mortillet (1883) noted that in evaluating Ribeiro's materials in 1878, they found human manufacture to be well-established "not only by their general form, which can be deceiving, but above all, more conclusively by their clear striking platforms and well-developed chonchoids of percussion, sometimes double, in relief on one surface, hollow on the other" (in Ribeiro 1884:94–95).

This set of diagnostic attributes took full form in de Mortillet's *Le Préhistorique* (1883), in which he devoted six pages to a discussion of the "characteristics of intentional work" (1883:79) in lithic materials. Here, he carefully defined three attributes that, especially when used jointly, allowed the secure identification of stone that had been percussion-flaked by human hands: striking platform (*plan de frappe*), bulb of percussion (*chonchoïde de percussion;* de Mortillet rejected the term "bulb"), and eraillure scars (*esquillement de percussion*). "The existence of these three characters on the same specimen . . . can leave no doubt as to the intentional manufacture of that specimen," he observed (1883:82), but even the presence of the bulb of percussion alone can allow secure diagnosis of a human role. Accordingly, in his discussion of Ribeiro's material, de Mortillet carefully illustrated a flint flake that showed a clear striking platform, positive and negative bulbs of percussion, and an eraillure scar (de Mortillet 1883:98).

If de Mortillet believed that the precise enunciation of a set of attributes that allowed the secure recognition of human lithic work would convince those that did not believe, he was incorrect. Instead, his specification of those attributes led immediately to the search for nonhuman phenomena that could produce the same results.

Adrien Arcelin, who had done important work at Solutré and whose accomplishments in helping demonstrate the reality of an Egyptian Paleolithic were warmly received by de Mortillet (de Mortillet 1879; Smith 1966), was one of those who accepted the challenge. Arcelin (1885a) did not disagree that human work could produce the attributes presented by de Mortillet, but he did disagree with the logical status de Mortillet had inferred for them. To demonstrate that they could not be used as true diagnostics, Arcelin turned to lower Eocene deposits in the Macon region of eastern France. Although the age of these deposits clearly precluded a human role in the production of anything found in them, Arcelin presented a series of objects from these beds that replicated the Tertiary items that had been accepted as artifacts. He even discovered a *grattoir* that was "as perfect as any Quaternary or Neolithic scraper" (Arcelin 1885a:202). His scraper was not, he emphasized, an Eocene tool: the unifacial retouch was mostly fresh and had been produced long after deposition. Arcelin suggested that he had "surprised nature in the process of manufacturing a perfect scraper" (1885a:202).

Nature, then, could make objects that looked just like tools. Since this was the case, it was far better to call on nature than on hominids to account for similar objects from such sites as Thenay and Puy Courny than to infer that an otherwise unknown intelligent being had produced them. It was context, he argued, that provided the real criterion of intelligent intervention: situations like those presented by the Eolithic sites, in which a few specimens showing striking platforms, eraillure scars, and bulbs of percussion could be selected from among thousands or millions of pieces of flint, simply did not provide that context.

That de Mortillet (1885) was frustrated by this attack is suggested by the fact that he began his response by accusing Arcelin of being motivated by theological concerns. De Mortillet's defense, however, was built on other issues. Where Arcelin had noted that the eoliths had been carefully culled from nonworked material, de Mortillet responded that the pseudoeoliths had been equally carefully culled. Where Arcelin argued that one convincing naturally formed artifact-mimic shed doubt on all eoliths, de Mortillet argued that one convincing eolith solved the problem and removed the value of the mimics. Where Arcelin asserted that the context in which eoliths were found was precisely the kind of context in which mimics were to be expected, de Mortillet responded that ethnographic data (see de Quatrefages 1885) showed this to be precisely the kind of situation in which real artifacts were to be expected.

In short, all de Mortillet could do in this situation was to argue that it was plausible that the eoliths were artifacts and to assert that this was, in fact, exactly what they were. His stipulation of diagnostic attributes in 1883 was meant to allow him to prove that eoliths were artifacts, yet these attributes were not even mentioned in his response to Arcelin. On the other hand, all Arcelin needed to do was to establish that eoliths could be produced naturally, not that they had been so produced; having shown that "all the characteristics of purposeful working of flint by an intelligent being can be accidently reproduced by unconscious causes . . . the accidental and natural origin of the claimed worked, fissured, or decorticated flakes from Tertiary sites can be logically maintained as well as the contrary opinion" (Arcelin 1885b:308; see also Arcelin 1886). It was not enough for de Mortillet to establish that the eoliths could be tools, but it was enough for Arcelin to establish, through middle-range research, that they could be mimics, and this move helped push the French and Portuguese Eolithic sites out of the realm where they could be judged scientifically with the knowledge at hand, a position that had clearly been reached in France by the late 1880s (e.g., Boule 1889).

The debate over these sites was far from over by the late 1880s, but the major battles were, and the information that would be needed to resolve the issue had become clear. Most important to me here are the stages through which this debate advanced. The simple assertion of human work led immediately to the simple assertion that the specimens were not worked, and then to an attempt by the supporters of eoliths to define diagnostic attributes—signatures—of a human role. Once stated, the diagnostics became the focus of contention, and a search was initiated to discover the range of phenomena that could produce those diagnostics, with observations of stone modification in geological deposits that were so old that hominids could not have played a role. It was quickly recognized that more than one process could produce the diagnostics, and the sites involved lost much of their force as a result. What remained was the knowledge generated by the debate in spite of the fact that the root issue was left unresolved.

The same process can be seen not only in the case of Saint-Prest, as I have discussed, but also in the discussion that surrounded many of the minor sites listed by de Mortillet in 1883 (see, for instance, the discussion of the cut bones of the Miocene sirenian *Halitherium* in Bourgeois 1868 and 1873, Delfortrie 1869, and de Mortillet 1883, in which the demonstration that carnivorous fishes could produce similar cut marks eliminated these specimens as evidence for Tertiary hominids). Later but extraordinarily similar episodes were to produce even greater amounts of knowledge in the attempt to probe possible diagnostic attributes of human manufacture.

The Discovery of Eoliths in England on the Kent Plateau, 1885–1900

The second round of enthusiasm for a set of possible Tertiary artifacts was British and began just as widespread support for the French and Portuguese sites was waning. The crucial British discoveries were made by Benjamin Harrison, a grocer from Ightham, Kent, some 40 km southeast of London. From the 1850s to his death in 1921, Harrison was, in his own words, a "flint hunter" (Harrison 1904:5), but it was in 1885 that he began to find what appeared to be very crude stone tools in gravel patches on the surface of the Chalk Plateau above the Darent River (Harrison, in Prestwich 1892; Harrison 1904). He soon interested the famed geologist Joseph Prestwich in his discoveries, and it was Prestwich who made known their potential significance.

In a series of papers published between 1889 and 1895, Prestwich (1889, 1891, 1892, 1895a, 1895b) described and illustrated Harrison's specimens (Figure 4). Even though he acknowledged that many of the Plateau specimens "exhibit the very rudiments of artificial work, and are often difficult to distinguish from natural forms" (1891:134), he was convinced that he was dealing with artifacts. With this conviction, Prestwich now focused on determining their possible antiquity. He concluded that while an early Quaternary date seemed most likely, a Tertiary age

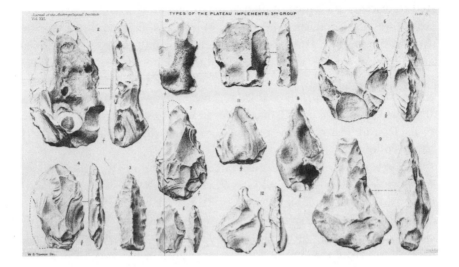

Figure 4 Plateau eoliths (from Prestwich 1892).

was possible. However, unlike the situation with the French and Portuguese sites, the Plateau specimens were initially all surface finds. Both Paleolithic and Neolithic implements were known from the same surface, raising the possibility that Prestwich's geology had merely established their maximum age. In 1892, for instance, Prestwich was able to report that a specimen had been found at a depth of 5 ft (1.5 m), and he stressed that the Plateau eoliths were stained much the same color, even on their chipped edges, as the unbroken flints of the drift. John Evans disagreed thoroughly with this assessment. There were, he felt, two different sorts of materials in Harrison's collection: those that were artifacts but that did not differ "from the ordinary forms" (in Prestwich 1892:271) of Paleolithic age found on the surface, and a large series that were not artifacts at all. Evans (in Prestwich 1892:271) avowed himself "to be among those who attributed the apparent chipping of their edges to an agency of Nature rather than to that of man." That is, those specimens that were acceptable were of Paleolithic age, but those that were not of this age were not acceptable. Pitt-Rivers and Boyd Dawkins agreed (in Prestwich 1892).

The mixed reception given the Plateau eoliths made it clear to Prestwich that acceptable specimens buried deep in the drift had to be found. Accordingly, in conjunction with the 1895 meetings of the British

Association for the Advancement of Science, a four-man committee (Evans, Harrison, Prestwich, and H. G. Seeley) was appointed to excavate the Plateau deposits. Harrison's (1895) report of the results was brief: he noted that one of the two pits provided a large number of worked specimens beneath a depth of 5½ ft (1.7 m), while the second produced a few worked objects at a depth of 8 ft (2.4 m). That the committee had actually failed to reach a consensus, however, is clear: Seeley (in Cunnington 1898) later indicated that neither he nor Evans believed that any artifacts had been found.

Harrison's work on the Kent Plateau earned him part of the Geological Society of London's Lyell Geological Fund award in 1895 (Woodward 1895), but arguments as to exactly what he had found were to continue for years. Prestwich's death in 1896 removed the most prestigious supporter the Plateau eoliths had found, but the debate went on. A move toward understanding the natural processes that could fracture stone soon developed. In 1898, for instance, William Cunnington demonstrated that eolithic chipping had been produced on undoubted Paleolithic implements, and thus must have postdated the manufacture of those implements. A. S. Kennard immediately objected to attributing the flaking to natural causes "when no attempt had been made to show what those causes were, and how and when they operated" (in Cunnington 1898:299). G. Coffey (1901) soon produced a series of specimens chipped by wave action on the beaches of northern Ireland and suggested that the Plateau eoliths had been produced by the same process. W. J. Knowles (1902:757) soon demanded to know, if the Plateau objects were not artifacts, "what force in nature can dress so many objects alike with chipping that has all the appearance of being artificial in character?"

To this point, parallels with the earlier French situation were strong: the initial assertion of the artifactual nature of materials of great, but not unexpected, antiquity, followed by assertion by archaeological experts that the materials could have been produced in other ways as well, followed by the call for more information on the ways in which flint could, and could not, fracture naturally. Whether a defender of the eoliths would have stipulated attributes diagnostic of human manufacture for them, and exactly what kinds of actualistic studies would have been generated by the Plateau eolith controversy by itself, however, will never be known. Developments in Belgium swept the British materials out of their local setting and engaged them in an international debate.

The Discovery of Eoliths in Belgium, 1887–1910

One of the members of the 1872 commission charged with evaluating the Thenay specimens was Gustave Neyrinckx. Neyrinckx voted against Bourgeois, but he nonetheless played a major role in the history of the eolith controversy. In 1868, he had discovered Paleolithic implements associated with a Pleistocene fauna in a railroad cut near Mesvin, approximately 50 km southwest of Brussels (Cornet and Briart 1873). In 1885, the geologist Emile Delvaux reported that the Mesvin deposits actually contained two stratigraphically distinct sets of deposits: Chellean tools, and, beneath them, a large set of implements similar to those from Thenay. Delvaux (1885) argued that although these tools were associated with lower Eocene deposits, they were early Quaternary in age and that they represented the earliest tools known from Belgium, suggesting the name Mesvinian for them.

Emile de Munck (1885) soon reminded Delvaux of Arcelin's discovery that many processes were now known to produce pseudoartifacts. De Munck's caution was not lost on Delvaux, but others were intrigued by the initial report. In 1887, Adolphe Cels reported that he had found not only Mesvinian artifacts in basal Quaternary sediments at Spiennes, near Mons, but that he had found an even cruder set in lower Eocene deposits here. Delvaux (in Cels 1887) immediately responded that any such tools must have been redeposited, and he cited de Munck (1885) in observing that before any fractured flint could be taken as artifactual, "it must be shown that a natural agency could not have caused that fracture" (in Delvaux and Houzeau de Lehaie 1887:195).

Caution in this matter was also advocated by Aimé Rutot. Rutot was an engineer, geologist, and conservator at the Musée d'Histoire naturelle de Belgique, and actively involved in the production of the geological map of Belgium. Remarkably productive, he published in excess of 650 items, many of which are lengthy monographs and books and many of which deal with the prehistory of Belgium. He did not live an uncomplicated life. Around the turn of the century, he was accused of having purchased large numbers of fraudulent specimens for his museum (he had, in fact, unknowingly done so: see de Heinzelin 1959) and resigned from the Société d'anthropologie de Bruxelles as a result. During his later years, he drifted toward mysticism, speaking with the dead and little celebrated by his fellow scientists (Stockmans 1966).

Rutot initially rejected Cels' lower Eocene artifacts and was skeptical of the Mesvinian specimens (Rutot 1887). Less than a decade later, however, he reversed his position on the Mesvinian (Rutot 1896, 1897), and soon reported new Mesvinian sites (Rutot 1898a), produced a functional classification of Mesvinian implements (Rutot 1898b), argued that de Munck's stream-bed artifacts were of such infrequent occurrence that they did not affect the Mesvinian, and called attention to similar materials reported by Prestwich in England (Rutot 1898c; see also Cels 1889).

Rutot quickly found an even earlier, basal Quaternary industry from the Lys valley of West Flanders. Named the Reutelian, after the small town of Reutel (Rutot 1899a), this industry was marked by simpler implements than the Mesvinian and by a higher frequency of striking tools, and a lower frequency of *grattoirs,* than was characteristic of the Mesvinian. Shortly after, he announced the discovery of a transitional Reutelo-Mesvinian industry (later called the Mafflian) at the small town of Maffles, some 50 km west of Brussels (Rutot 1899b). This discovery gave Rutot a complete developmental sequence from Reutelian through Mesvinian into the classic Paleolithic, and in 1900 he reported that Reutelo-Mesvinian industries were widespread in north-central Belgium (Rutot 1900a; see Figures 5 and 6).

Thus, by the turn of the century, Rutot had defined three basal Quaternary industries, each marked by a distinctive set of tool types and, generally, by a particular stratigraphic placement. The Mesvinian itself was seen as immediately ancestral to the Acheulean, through a transitional industry that he equated with the French Chellean (although his use of this term varied through time, as did his definition of the pre-Chellean industries; see Rutot 1897, 1899a, 1902c). His visits to England (where he equated the Plateau eoliths with the Mesvinian) and France convinced him that identical sequences existed in these countries as well. And, while the Reutelian was seen as basal Quaternary, he soon reported a series of crude, heavily patinated implements from West Flanders that he argued were Pliocene in age (Rutot 1900b, 1900c, 1901b, 1902d).

In this flurry of papers, Rutot's claim to have discovered basal Quaternary and upper Tertiary artifacts rested largely on assertions that the specimens were, in fact, artifacts, and on illustrations of those specimens. As he found more and more, and older and older, materials, doubts began to grow that all these specimens had been worked by human hands. At the International Congress of 1900, held in Paris, Rutot's presentation of his work was met with caution. Evans was skeptical because "there are many natural causes that can . . . produce the appearance of retouching" (in Rutot 1902c:116–117), while the French prehistorian Louis

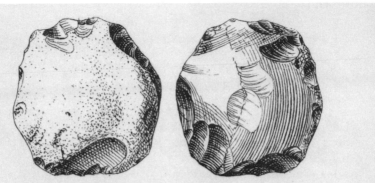

Fig. 20. — Disque. Silex brun foncé. Molenorelsthoek.

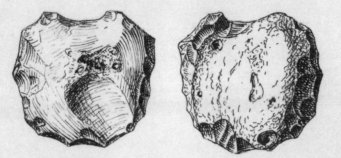

Fig. 21. — Disque. Silex gris brun. Reutel.

Fig. 22 — Grattoir à dos simple. Silex gris foncé. Hollebeek.

Figure 5 Reutelian eoliths (from Rutot 1899a).

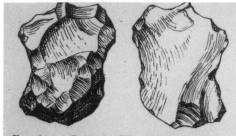
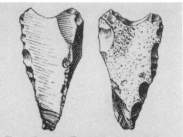

FIG. 61. — Grattoir. Silex gris jaune pâle. Kayaert-Molen (N. Westroosebeek). Mesvinien.

FIG. 62. — Grattoir à encoche. Silex gris foncé. Staden Berg (Tranchée du chemin de fer). Mesvinien.

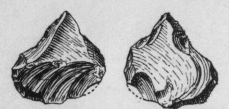

FIG. 63. — Poinçon (?). Silex jaune. Hollebeek. Mesvinien.

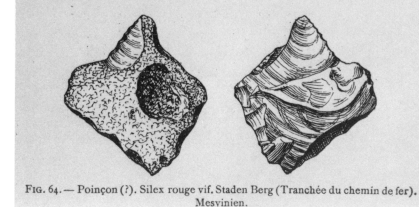

FIG. 64. — Poinçon (?). Silex rouge vif. Staden Berg (Tranchée du chemin de fer). Mesvinien.

Figure 6 Mesvinian eoliths (from Rutot 1899b).

Capitan noted that his experiments on the effects of shock and pressure on flint had produced results that closely replicated human work (in Rutot 1902c). Although Rutot had greater support in Belgium, even here he found a significant number of critics (see, for instance, the discussions in Rutot 1900a, 1901a).

In response to these criticisms, Rutot (1900a) began to specify in detail the attributes that allowed him to distinguish stone flaked by nature from that flaked by human hands. Natural flakes, he argued, have prominent, sharp edges that, if broken, show irregular breaks scattered randomly across both faces. Flakes utilized by people, on the other hand, show methodical retouch all along the usable edge, retouch that is easily seen under magnification, while many also have their sharp edges reduced so as to allow easy handling (alteration that he called "accommodation").

Although Rutot was being pushed toward clearer specification of those attributes he considered to be diagnostic of human work, just as de Mortillet had been so forced, it was his attempt to document the existence of the Reutelian-to-Mesvinian sequence in other areas, and particularly in France, that brought the issue to a head.

His detailed involvement on the French scene began in 1900, in conjunction with his trip to Paris for the Twelfth International Congress. Here, he was able to see materials from both Thenay and Puy Courny and, while he rejected the burned flints of Thenay, he was convinced that the retouched pieces from both sites were artifactual. The Thenay specimens he equated with the Reutelo-Mesvinian; those from Puy Courny (and the Portuguese site of Otta, which he had not seen) with the Mesvinian. These were far older, of course, than anything he had discovered in Belgium. However, the developmental sequence they displayed, from the lower Micene Reutelo-Mesvinian to the upper Miocene of Puy Courny, was identical to the much later Belgian sequence. Rutot (1900c) suggested that the Miocene had been the scene of a trial run, that a "mysterious precursor" (1900c:19) had existed at that time, only to become extinct. In the upper Pliocene, a "second humanity, better endowed" (1900c:19) had appeared and thrived. Evidence for this second humanity existed not only in Belgium, but also in France: Rutot (1900c) discovered Reutelian materials during his visit to Saint-Prest.

The French could not have disagreed more with Rutot's characterization of these sites. In 1900, Mahoudeau and Capitan (1901) had excavated at Thenay to obtain study specimens for the École d'anthropologie. The crackled flints they retrieved were submitted to Adolphe

Carnot, director of the École nationale des Mines, whose laboratory experiments on the burning of local flints convinced him that the Thenay materials had not been subjected to fire. More important to Rutot's position was Capitan's analysis of the possible stone tools. Of the 2500 pieces of flint they recovered, 30 "vaguely recalled" (Mahoudeau and Capitan 1901:149) known tool types, but Capitan arrayed several kinds of evidence against such an interpretation. In the Seine valley, he observed, the rapid movement of water produced retouched and fractured flints that often simulated human work, while his studies also showed that soil creep and temperature variation could duplicate the Thenay objects. In addition, he reported the results of a series of experiments he had performed in which blocks of flint were dropped or crushed against one another, producing "crushing, flaking, and retouching considered by some experts as characteristic of human work" (1901:152). The conclusion was clear: "in our present state of knowledge, seeing proof of intentional work in the Thenay flints represents a methodological error that results from inadequate observation" (1901:153).

Laville also disagreed with Rutot about Saint-Prest. Asked by Rutot to collect specimens for him, Laville (1901:288) could see nothing that was not "strongly problematic." "More than one time," he observed (1901:288), "I rejected, and then picked up again, the samples I had resolved to send" to Rutot. Laville could find no indication of artifacts in the deep deposits of Saint-Prest.

In response, Rutot removed his basal Quaternary sequence from the Paleolithic: these industries were Eolithic, and, unlike Paleolithic implements, eoliths were not made to preconceived forms. Only two attributes could be used to diagnose such artifacts: methodical retouch nonrandomly placed on an edge, and "accommodation" (Rutot 1902b). He also rejected each of the processes that Capitan had suggested could produce his eoliths naturally. There was, for instance, no evidence for anything but tranquil flooding at his sites, and the same appeared true in France. At Cergy, along the Oise River northwest of Paris, Rutot (1902a) had observed a mixed assemblage of eolithic industries, but he had also found fragile, reworked Eocene shells in the same deposits. Had torrential waters produced the eoliths, the shells would not have been so well-preserved. Besides, the reason that the best of Capitan's specimens from the Seine gravels looked like artifacts was that they *were* artifacts; the same was true for materials from coastal settings, where specimens thought to have been produced by waves were actually reworked tools (Rutot 1902b).

Capitan's discussion of the processes that could produce artifact-mimics, however, was just the beginning. In 1902, Stanislaus Meunier described the results of freeze and thaw in flint gravels observed in Normandy. This process, he argued, produced flakes that looked not only like eoliths, but also like some of the simpler Paleolithic implements. Boule (1903a) carefully brought Meunier's results to the readers of the journal *L'Anthropologie,* and this work elicited the most detailed statement Rutot had as yet made as to how eoliths were to be infallibly recognized. Edges had not only to be retouched, but the removed flakes had to be roughly parallel and unifacial; accommodation had to be opposite the cutting edge. These attributes, he observed, were absent from Meunier's specimens (Rutot 1904).

Rutot's report of pre-Chellean materials, and of well-preserved Eocene shells, at Cergy (Rutot 1902a, 1902b) ran directly counter to the results of the work that Laville had conducted here since 1895 (Laville 1898, 1899). His response to Rutot was blunt. Not only did he (Laville 1902b:748) reject "the Reutelian, Reutelo-Mesvinian, and Mesvinian . . . as pure fantasy" for the Paris area, but he also noted that all the shells in this deposit were heavily rolled. Rutot's statement otherwise was, if not false, then *"more than extraordinarily exaggerated"* (1902a:555; emphasis in original).

Rutot (1903) soon expressed regret that he had not saved the well-preserved Eocene shells from Cergy; but Laville was soon to give him much more to regret. This contribution was not brought to the scientific community directly by Laville, but by Boule, who was no fan of Rutot ("an apostle with faith only in his own renovating genius" Boule [1903c:704] said of Rutot). It is not surprising, therefore, that it was to Boule that Laville turned with a new discovery that seemed to provide the key for putting an end to all discussions about eoliths.

Boule reported this discovery in 1905. Boule noted that he had often thought about conducting experiments on the natural fracture of flint (in Chantre 1884), and was pleased when Laville told him that just such experiments were taking place near the town of Mantes, west of Paris. Here, the Mantes cement works produced its product by mixing clay, chalk, and water in a huge vat, the mixture stirred by a revolving metal rake, and the mass moving "at the speed of the Rhone in flood" (Boule 1905:261). Although an attempt was made to remove all flint nodules from the chalk prior to its addition to the mixture, many were missed, and these were subjected to "thousands of mutual shocks" (1905:262) during the 29-hour period of mixing. When the machine was stopped,

Figure 7 A Mantes eolith (from Boule 1905).

the flints were removed and placed in a pile to be used in concrete.

It was in this pile that the discovery was made. "In just a few minutes," Boule (1905:262) reported, "my companions and I were able to make a superb collection including the most characteristic forms of eoliths . . . we have pieces fully similar to those designated by Rutot as *percuteurs, rabots, grattoirs, retouchoirs, silex à encoches*. Certain examples, of extraordinary perfection, appear to have been the object of fine work, of 'methodical and repeated retouch'." This last phrase was Rutot's very own statement of one of his diagnostic attributes of eoliths (Rutot 1904:7; see Figures 7 and 8).

Boule realized that this discovery would not convince the true "eolithologists" (Boule 1903b), "conversions of this sort being very difficult" (Boule 1905:263), nor did he claim that none of the eoliths were artifacts. His point was a simpler one: to observe the "practical difficulty, often the impossibility [of] distinguishing the effects of rudimentary intentional work from the effects of natural agents" (Boule 1905:265–266).

Rutot responded heatedly to these criticisms. Since there is no natural analog to the cement machines, he argued, any similarities between flints from the machines and the eoliths are meaningless (Rutot 1905). Even so, the false eoliths did not reproduce his materials (Rutot 1906), and if further proof that the eoliths were artifacts were needed, it could be found in the Tasmanians, whose stone tools were perfectly eolithic in form (Rutot 1908b). He also became abusive. The opponents of eoliths—Laville's name figured quite prominently—were the victims of a "new form of mental illness," which he termed "antiéolithisme" (Rutot 1906/1907:22; see also Rutot 1908a and Laville 1908). Under attack himself for having accepted forged artifacts, Rutot (1906:19) accused Boule (1905) of providing fraudulent illustrations, in which "the pencil of the retoucher takes on more importance" than what was really there (several of Boule's photographs were, in fact, heavily retouched). Boule deeply resented these personal attacks (Boule 1907), but Rutot's caustic approach most certainly cost him support he might otherwise have had.

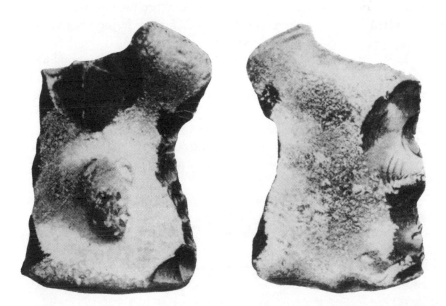

Figure 8 A Mantes eolith (from Boule 1905).

That support included Capitan who, in 1902, had visited Rutot and accepted his eolithic industries (Anon. 1903; Capitan 1904, 1905) but who, although remaining cautiously optimistic about some eolithic materials after 1905 (e.g., Capitan 1906; Capitan and Marty 1924), did not support Rutot again.

Rutot was not moved. In 1907, he announced the discovery of a new eolithic industry, the Fagnien, in Oligocene deposits at Boncelles, near Liège (Rutot 1907, 1909). This announcement, however, also proved harmful to his cause. In 1910, Henri Breuil published the discovery of what appeared to be perfectly good eoliths from the estate of Belle-Assise, near Clermont (Figure 9). These eoliths, however, were from the base of Eocene deposits, just as Arcelin's had been (as Breuil observed), and included examples in which the eoliths were still partially attached to the block from which they were being removed. Among those who observed these specimens in place was Capitan, who showed them to Rutot without telling him of their basal Eocene age. Rutot not only felt that they had been worked, but thought that some were so well made that they belonged to the Eolithic-Paleolithic transition. Rutot's Boncelles material, Breuil noted, was fully analogous to the Belle-Assise mimics, and Breuil (1910:406) concluded that his material, much of which bore striking platforms and bulbs of percussion, demonstrated clearly that "the criterion needed to distinguish these natural productions from flints truly utilized by man or even worked in rudimentary fashion has yet to be found and probably does not exist."

Breuil's attack cost Rutot much of the waning support that remained (compare, for instance, the statements in MacCurdy 1905, 1907, and 1910 with those in MacCurdy 1924). Even Rutot's own statements became much more subdued (e.g., Rutot 1918): the demonstration that natural causes could duplicate what he had found had placed his sites, like Thenay and Puy Courny before them, in a scientific holding area, even though no one had demonstrated, or even tried to demonstrate, that his eoliths were of natural origin.

The reaction in England, however, was different. Not only had Rutot attacked the French directly, through his misuse of de Mortillet's classification and his attempts to show that French archaeologists had missed a significant part of the record, but the English were far more concerned with their own eoliths than with the continental forms. As a result, the English response was milder, and focused on the Kent materials.

Although milder, that response was nonetheless immediate. The

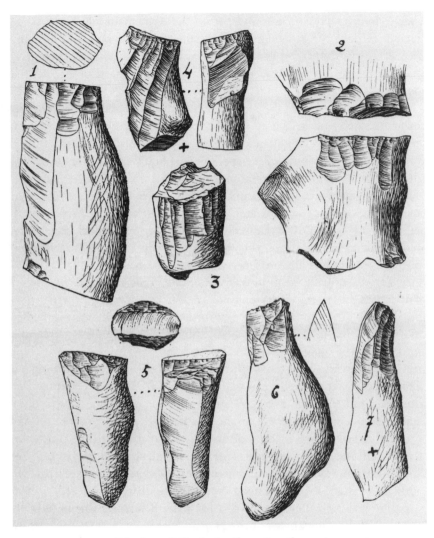

Figure 9 Eocene eoliths from Belle-Assise (from Breuil 1910).

journal *Man* for 1905 contained six articles dealing with the Mantes results (Abbott 1905; Dalton 1905; Kendall 1905; Larkby 1905; Obermaier 1905; Warren 1905b). Larkby, for instance, measured the edge angles on a series of pseudoeoliths from a cement factory in Kent, finding those angles to range primarily from 25° to 90°, and compared these figures to those from a sample of the Kent eoliths, which he found to lie primarily between 45° and 72°. An explanation for this difference in range, he felt, had to be found before the Kent materials could be rejected. Perhaps the most significant result of Boule's paper in England, however, was that it led the geologist S. Hazzledine Warren (1905a) to publish the results of experimental work on flint fracture that he had been conducting since the late 1890s.

Warren's work was the most detailed yet conducted in this area. His basic question was a simple one: "Can we . . . prove that the chipping must have been done by man, and could not have been done by nature?" (1905a:338). He stipulated six mechanisms that seemed capable of producing eoliths: people, wave abrasion, water abrasion by torrents, subsurface soil pressure, the pressure and drag of ice, and wear-and-tear on the surface of the ground. Water abrasion he felt accounted for virtually all of Rutot's material: examination of large series of river gravels provided insensible gradations from eoliths to forms clearly not artifactual, and Boule's results had confirmed this observation.

The Plateau eoliths, however, were a different matter. These he felt could have been caused by subsurface soil pressure. His own experiments, including the use of a screw press to simulate natural pressure, had shown that mechanical pressure could produce flakes with parallel retouch that simulated eoliths. In nature, the required pressure could readily be generated by the slow movement of deposits along an incline. This process, which had been discussed in less detail by Capitan (Mahoudeau and Capitan 1901), Warren (1905a:349) termed "soil abrasion." At a depth of 6 ft (1.8 m), he calculated, blocks of stone could be pressed together with a force of greater than a ton, in turn producing both striations on the surfaces of the raw material and pressure-flaked edges. Warren observed, as Cunnington (1898) had before him, that the surfaces of many of the Plateau eoliths were, in fact, striated, and he carefully provided illustrations of such striated forms. Warren also observed that the edge angles of the Plateau eoliths were identical to those he had flaked by mechanical pressure, while the trend of the ripple marks on flake surfaces were also identical. These detailed similarities, he felt, could not be fortuitous, and he concluded that the Plateau eoliths could be explained by the foundering of chalk deposits and by the subsurface pressures that accompanied that foundering (Warren 1905a; see Rutot 1908a for his sarcastic response to Warren).

Warren's work was just the beginning of "middle-range" studies conducted in England to more fully understand the nature of eoliths. In 1909, for instance, Alfred Schwartz and H. R. Beevor delivered the results of their experiments to the Manchester Literary and Philosophical

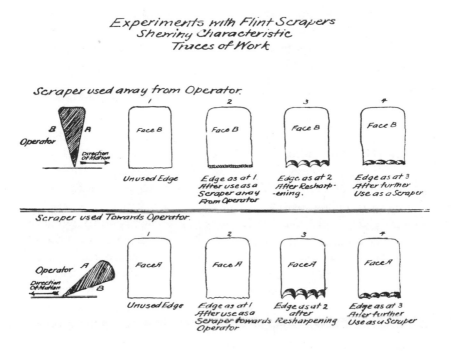

Figure 10 Use-wear analysis by Schwartz and Bccvor (1909).

Society. They provided their own list of diagnostic attributes for the secure recognition of human lithic work, a list that included the presence
of convincing use-wear and evidence for resharpening. In order to assess
these matters, they manufactured their own tools, using them, for instance, as scrapers and knives. Use for specific functions, they implied,
left specific traces, and they illustrated the use-wear patterns produced
by scrapers pulled toward and away from the body (Figure 10). Resharpening of scrapers could be detected by observing the angle of the scrap-
ing edge: each time resharpening occurred, a more acute angle was produced. Unlike Warren (1905a, 1905b), they concluded that the Plateau
eoliths were true artifacts.

The scope and depth of such work that would have been generated
in England by the Plateau eoliths after 1909 cannot be judged, because
in 1910 yet another case of potentially early material was brought to
light in England. This episode was to involve a wide range of geologists
and prehistorians, and to produce yet another round of research directed

toward learning the relationship between patterns of rock breakage and the processes that produced that breakage. This round, however, was to prove more far-reaching than earlier ones, in large part because it built more directly on work that had been recently conducted to probe previously discovered eoliths, and because to some extent it was conducted by the same people who had been involved in that earlier work.

The Crag Pre-Paleolithic, 1910–1940

This new episode was initiated by J. Reid Moir, whose work focused on the area surrounding Ipswich, in Suffolk, on the east coast of southern England. Here, in the Gipping River Valley, a lengthy stratigraphic sequence had been exposed. This sequence included the London Clay, a marine deposit assigned to the Eocene and lower Pliocene, and, above it, the Red Crag, a shelly marine sand now assigned to the basal Pleistocene (Funnell and West 1977), but then variously assigned to the latest Pliocene and early Quaternary, or to the basal Quaternary alone. It was in these deposits that Moir worked.

Moir's pivotal discovery was made on 3 October 1909, when he found what he thought to be a stone tool in backdirt left from excavations in the Red Crag and London Clay near Ipswich. Intrigued by this find, he soon located further examples beneath the Red Crag, on the surface of the London Clay (Moir 1911, 1919b).

Moir divided his objects into several classes (choppers, scrapers, and beak-shaped implements) and argued that, because flaking was not confined to their edges, they were transitional between the eoliths proper and true Paleolithic tools. As a result, he termed them "pre-palaeoliths," and the argument that they were morphologically transitional soon became an important part of his defense of their artifactual nature (Moir 1911, 1914).

Because his discovery came on the heels of Boule's Mantes discussion, Breuil's work at Belle-Assise, and Warren's experimental results, and because Warren immediately informed Moir that the sub-Red Crag specimens appeared to be of natural origin (Moir 1911), Moir knew from the outset that his materials would be carefully scrutinized, and that actualistic research would be likely to play a major role in the outcome. Moir himself conducted crude experiments to support the artifactual nature of his specimens, placing flint nodules in a sack and shaking "them violently about . . . for some considerable time" (1911:20), and to observe that the results bore no resemblance to his pre-paleoliths.

Soon, similar finds were reported from beneath the Norwich Crag to the north (Clarke 1912). More importantly, Moir gained an important ally in the renowned evolutionary biologist Sir E. Ray Lankester. Fully familiar with the geology of the Red Crag deposits, Lankester (1865, 1870) brought two additional attributes to Moir's side: extremely high scientific visibility and the powers of analytic description one would expect of an internationally famed embryologist. Lankester put these attributes to use in a series of well-placed papers (Lankester 1912b, 1912c, 1914, 1921).

Lankester's work focused on the one class of sub-Crag specimens whose complex form and high degree of redundancy seemed to require human manufacture. These were Moir's beak-shaped implements, or, as Lankester termed them, in the best of biological descriptive tradition, "rostro-carinates," because of the combination of central keel (carina) and beak-shaped end (rostrum) that they displayed. In 1912, Lankester, taking an approach also familiar in the biological world, derived an ideal form of this implement—"a shape at which the prehistoric workman was aiming" (1912c:294; Figure 11)—and used that ideal form as the basis of a descriptive terminology that could be used in the analysis of separate specimens. He then illustrated 10 rostro-carinates and described them in tremendous detail, down to the separate blows that had removed each flake.

Lankester soon had in his possession a rostro-carinate that approached the ideal form more closely than any other he had seen. Found at the base of the Norwich Crag in 1911, this object became Lankester's "test-specimen" because its complexity seemed explicable only through human manufacture (Figure 12). He devoted an entire monograph to its detailed description, including 14 illustrations, some with overlays displaying the roughly 40 separate blows that had produced the object (Lankester 1914).

While Lankester was throwing his full support behind Moir, others were taking a very different approach, and Moir soon found a dogged critic within the ranks of his own group, the Prehistoric Society of East Anglia. This critic was F. N. Haward, an engineer who had studied stone-tool manufacture with the Brandon flint knappers. In a visit to one of Clarke's Norwich sites, Haward extracted a series of battered, striated, and chipped flints that ranged from those that appeared completely unworked to those that appeared artifactual. Given the wide variety of forms here, Haward (1912) argued that natural processes could

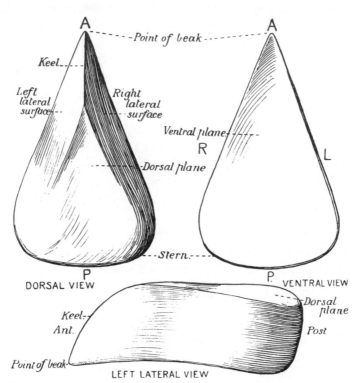

FIG. 1.—Diagrams showing the ideal form aimed at by the makers of the Rostro-carinate flint implements or " Eagle's Beaks " (Becs d'aigle). A, anterior ; P, posterior ; R, right ; L, left.

Figure 11 The rostro-carinate ideal form as reconstructed by Lankester (1912c).

account for them all. He then introduced the concept of "chip and slide," in which a stationary flint is flaked as a block of material slides over it, to account for the Norwich specimens. Freeze and thaw, wetting and drying, and foundering were among the processes that could cause the required movement, and the pressure generated at the base of the Norwich Crag—up to 4.27 tons per square foot, he calculated—would be more than sufficient to allow the chipping to occur. Both the Norwich and Ipswich specimens, he felt, "were made by Nature and not Man" (Haward 1912:192). These arguments he then expanded to cover the Plateau eoliths (Haward 1914) and the rostro-carinates themselves (Haward 1919; for responses, see Clarke 1916; Moir 1918b, 1919a; Barnes 1920; see also Haward 1921).

Haward's work quickly led Moir to use both his sack experiments and a set of experiments conducted with a screw press to derive a series of attributes felt diagnostic of human work (Moir 1912b). These attributes included the fact that flakes removed by human hands were at a constant angle to one another; that human flaking sharpened an edge, as opposed to blunting it; that people removed flakes at vertical, not oblique, angles; that fortuitous flake scars often cross-cut, or truncated, one another; that hinge fractures are more common on fortuitous flakes; and, that humanly struck flakes are longer and narrower than fortuitous ones (Moir 1912a, 1912b, 1919b; Figure 13).

At the same time, everyone agreed that there was "an extraordinary lack of precise information" (Lankester 1912a:249; see also Schwartz 1914) as regards the properties of flint and its natural fracture, and that this lack had to be removed were much progress to be made in resolving the issues raised by the Plateau eoliths and the sub-Crag specimens. S. H. Warren agreed, and was busily doing all he could to meet the challenge.

Warren (1913) not only applied Moir's diagnostic attributes to flaked objects of known origin, finding that they misidentified many of his specimens (see also Moir 1913a), but he also published a remarkably detailed discussion of natural flint fracture. Drawing both on his earlier work and on Haward's, Warren (1914) presented the results of seven separate sets of experiments that he had performed to fracture flint by percussion and by pressure. His work was done with sufficient precision that he was able to provide scattergrams showing the relationship be-

Figure 12 The Norwich Crag test-specimen (from Lankester 1914).

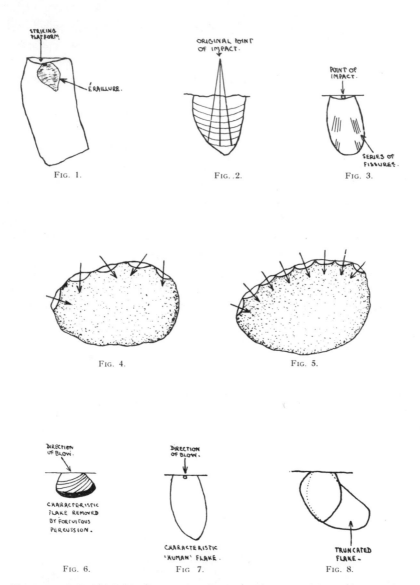

Figure 13 J. Reid Moir's diagnostic criteria for the recognition of human stone tool work (from Moir 1919b).

tween kinetic energy applied and the area of chip removed in percussion, and between vertical pressure applied and the depth of the resulting chip (Figure 14). He also examined such qualitative attributes as the presence or absence of bulbs of percussion and eraillure scars, producing fre-

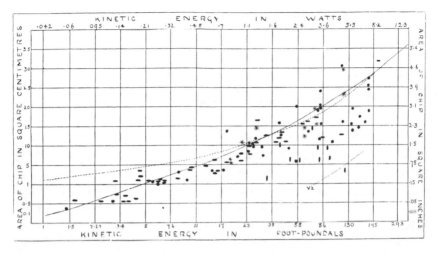

Figure 14 The relationship between energy applied in percussion and the size of the resultant flake, as calculated by Warren (1914).

quency distributions displaying the combinations of those attributes on eight separate samples, ranging from 83 to 369 specimens in size, of known human and natural origin. These distributions taught a clear lesson: not only did the absence of a bulb and eraillure scar not imply the absence of human manufacture, as was well known, but flakes with both attributes could be selected from naturally fractured stones if one looked long enough. Measuring edge angles, Warren found that these were concentrated at 60°–65° in both human and mechanical percussion flaking, but also showed that edge angles produced by mechanical pressure were identical to those on the Plateau eoliths. Both these and the sub-Crag materials, he suggested, could well have been produced by nature.

Moir was unmoved by this detailed contribution: his *Antiquity of Man in East Anglia* (1927) repeats many of the same criteria he used in 1912 and does not mention Warren's name. Indeed, Moir soon widened the scope of pre-Crag artifacts to include bone specimens. In 1915, he reported the discovery of a series of heavily mineralized bone objects, all but one of which had been broken across the grain. Moir quickly found that he could not work fossilized bone, and concluded that the breaks must have occurred while the bone was fresh. Fortuitous percussion, he discovered experimentally, produced irregular breaks that were totally unlike those displayed by his specimens. Subjecting fresh bone to the forces of his screw press, however, provided different results: two of his specimens fractured along the grain; then, for reasons he did not understand, "the lines of cleavage suddenly swept round in a curve and made their way out at the side of the bone" (Moir 1915:127). Although he found this peculiar, these fractures did not replicate his sub-Crag materials, which he concluded were artifactual.

At first, reaction to this middle-range research and to the sub-Crag specimens was generally negative. In 1913, for instance, W. J. Sollas reported that he had found rostro-carinates on a beach in southern England, where they had apparently been produced by wave action. While Moir (1913b; see also Anon. 1914) and Lankester (1921) objected that Sollas' specimens looked like artifacts because they were artifacts, Boule quickly took Sollas' side. In 1912, he and Breuil had visited the Ipswich sites, and Boule (1915) summarized both their reactions when he concluded that the sub-Crag materials were of natural origin.

Moir attempted to remove such objections by providing examples of rostro-carinates from other parts of the world, including areas in which wave action could not have produced them (Moir 1916, 1918a), and by stressing that those objects formed the technological ancestors of Paleolithic hand axes (Moir 1914, 1916, 1920). A remarkable shift in attitude toward the sub-Crag material did occur, however, with the discovery of the Foxhall artifacts and, to a lesser extent, the Piltdown discovery.

The Foxhall finds resulted from a piece of excellent detective work by Moir. Working from Collyer's 1867 publication in which he had described a human mandible found in 1855 at an estimated depth of 16 ft (4.9 m) within the Red Crag at Foxhall, near Ipswich, Moir relocated the quarry pit that had provided the jaw. As a result, in 1919 he located what he felt to be two separate living surfaces within the Red Crag. Although he treated the mandible itself with appropriate caution, the apparent stone tools on these two levels were surrounded by sand and were not in contact with one another, thus apparently eliminating the natural geological processes that could produce artifact-mimics. Moir (1921) concluded that these surfaces were occupied during episodes of retreat of the Red Crag sea.

The Foxhall and Piltdown discoveries softened attitudes toward the sub-Crag materials. Piltdown had been reported to the scientific community in a series of papers between 1913 and 1918 (Dawson and Woodward 1913, 1914, 1915; A. S. Woodward 1918). As they were then interpreted, the Piltdown finds included cranial remains from two individuals, a series of stone tools (including possible eoliths), a large bone implement fashioned from a proboscidean femur, and a series of non-human paleontological materials. The mammalian remains (some of which may well have been Red Crag specimens: see Weiner 1955) suggested a late Pliocene or early Pleistocene age, thus making the Piltdown complex roughly equivalent in age to the sub-Crag implements. The Piltdown remains were shown to be fraudulent in 1953 (Weiner et al. 1953), but were, of course, widely accepted at the time.

Moir announced his discovery of bone tools beneath the Red Crag on 3 March 1915, a scant three months after the Piltdown bone implement had been reported. He was quite explicit that the Piltdown discovery "in a measure prepared the way for the more easy acceptance of the claim" (Moir 1915:116–117) he was making for bone artifacts beneath the Red Crag. Indeed, it seems very likely that it was the Piltdown bone implement that led Moir to search for similar material beneath the Red Crag in the first place.

In addition, Piltdown created a context in which the criteria for recognition of the presence of hominids on artifactual grounds could be relaxed. As MacCurdy (1924:327) stated: "when a human skull is found associated with rudely worked flints, the nature of which might be questioned if occurring alone, the burden of proof is at once shifted from those who believe them to have been utilized by man to those who would call them the work of Nature." Whether or not the Piltdown discovery would have brought about a shift in attitude toward Moir's material by itself cannot be known, however, because Foxhall played such a major role.

The Foxhall finds excited the interest of a number of British archaeologists, including M. C. Burkitt, who informed Breuil of the discovery. Breuil visited Ipswich again, and the visit changed his opinion. He found Foxhall to contain "a true industrial level" (Breuil 1922:228), the living surfaces showing none of the attributes required for the natural production of flakes, and the flakes themselves showing all the characters of true artifacts. Having accepted material from within the Red Crag, Breuil also accepted that from beneath the Crag, noting that the Foxhall level "undoubtedly contributed to my acceptance of the earlier one" (1922:228).

Breuil was not alone. In 1920, Sollas accepted the Foxhall and sub-Crag specimens, excluding the rostro-carinates (which Breuil also excluded), noting that the Piltdown hominid might have been the maker of these artifacts (Sollas 1920). He later observed that "the discovery at Foxhall" relieved him "of all doubts" as regards the sub-Crag material

(Sollas 1924:104). A commission of the International Institute of Anthropology, including C. Fraipont, MacCurdy, and Capitan, agreed completely: the sub-Crag specimens "absolutely demonstrated" (Capitan 1923:67) a Tertiary hominid (see also Capitan 1922 and Anon. 1923). Burkitt (1921), Osborn (1921), and many others concurred.

The great weakness in Moir's position was that he had not found human bones with his material. As a result, his material was open to attack (indeed, even the possible eoliths from Piltdown were questioned: Weiner 1955). Boule (1923) continued to argue that they could have been produced naturally, while Warren (1921, 1923b) was busy reporting an Eocene rostro-carinate. In addition, Warren (1922) not only reported striations on the Foxhall flints, suggestive of subsurface pressure, but also that those objects appeared redeposited (Warren 1923a; see the response by Moir 1922, and Barnes and Moir 1923). In 1926, Etienne Patte, following a suggestion made by Boule, examined the flint nodules from a cement factory at Beaumont, northwest of Paris, and reported a full run of eoliths that duplicated those discussed by Moir, including rostro-carinates. Perhaps the heaviest blow, however, was delivered by Moir's one-time ally, A. S. Barnes. Barnes, who had repeatedly sided with Moir over the years (e.g., Barnes 1920; Barnes and Moir 1923), and who, as A. S. Schwartz, had defended the Plateau eoliths before the war (Schwartz and Beevor 1909), now took a very different approach.

Barnes (1938, 1939a, 1939b) began his attack simply enough. He reviewed the natural processes known to cause flint fracture, observed that these could produce results mirrored in eolithic sites, and outlined a series of experiments that he had performed to simulate the effects of pressure on flint, experiments that replicated "the so-called tools of Tertiary man" (1939b:109). As an objective criterion to allow the distinction between naturally and humanly flaked stone, he advanced the "angle platform-scar," or edge-angle, previously discussed by Larkby (1905), Warren (1914), and others. In stone tools, he argued, that angle should be acute, both for effective use and to allow control during flake removal; edge angles in naturally fractured flints, on the other hand, would often be obtuse.

Barnes measured this angle on seven groups of naturally broken flints (900 measurements), eight groups of eoliths (1700 measurements), and 19 groups of stone tools (2600 measurements). He found that 75% of his known artifacts had edge angles of less than 90°, while this angle exceeded 90° in 75% of his naturally broken specimens. And what of the eoliths? At Boncelles, 40% of the specimens had obtuse edge angles; the comparable figure for the Plateau eoliths was 40%; for Puy Courny, 62%, and, for the Red and Norwich Crag materials, 70%. The numbers spoke for themselves.

Moir kept up the battle (Moir 1932, 1939; Burchell and Moir 1935, 1944), but this spate of actualistic studies had turned the tide. Warren's observations of striations on the Foxhall flints, Patte's discovery of sub-Crag forms in the Beaumont cement mixer, Barnes' quantitative analysis of edge angles, and other, similar studies were once again showing that the patterns present on Moir's specimens could, indeed, have been produced by nature. As Breuil was later to note, some of the flakes from the Crag might be accepted, but "their cutting angle is generally against it" (Breuil and Lantier 1965:56).

A Brief Retrospective

How are these materials treated today? With the exception of some of the Mesvinian materials, which were artifactual, all of Rutot's eolithic industries are rejected; the broken flints are attributed to natural processes (Bourdier 1957; de Heinzelin 1957). Thenay and Puy Courny are likewise treated as having provided only naturally altered materials (Bourdier 1976; Breuil and Lantier 1965). However, some of the cut bone and antler from Saint-Prest, the very material that started it all over a century ago, is still seen as possibly archaeological (Bourdier 1976; Bourdier and Lacassagne 1963), although the Saint-Prest deposits are now placed squarely in the Pleistocene (Bourdier 1976).

The Kent Plateau eoliths are seen as natural (Breuil and Lantier 1965; Roe 1981); Roe (1981:116) notes that "'not proven' is the kindest possible verdict" for Moir's material. Coles (1968:30) finds Foxhall "the most perplexing of all the East Anglian sites," and suggests artifacts might, in fact, be present.

A Modern Ambiguity: The Calico Hills Site

The search for eoliths and similarly ambiguous traces of ancient peoples is restricted neither to the past nor to Europe. The history of the attempt to demonstrate a Pleistocene human occupation at the Calico Hills site helps to place the setting, or at least one of the settings, that generates "middle-range" research in broader perspective.

The Calico Hills site, in the Mohave Desert of southeastern California, was located in the early 1960s as a result of work conducted by R. D. Simpson and L.S.B. Leakey (Leakey et al. 1970; Simpson 1980, 1982). Soon, Leakey et al. (1968) reported the discovery of over 170 artifacts in the fan deposits that comprise the site, and suggested a likely age of 50,000 to 80,000 years B.P. By 1983, over 11,000 possible stone tools had been collected (Budinger 1983), while the age of the site had crept backwards to ca. 200,000 years B.P. (Bischoff et al. 1981). An international conference held to evaluate the Calico material in 1970, including a possible hearth that had been excavated in 1968 (Bischoff et al. 1984), produced opinions that were far more negative than positive about the artifactual nature of the lithics from the site (Schuiling 1972; see Budinger 1983 for an excellent review of the Calico materials).

The most widely cited evaluation of the Calico Hills site is that provided by Haynes (1973). Leakey et al. (1968) observed that the Calico specimens selected as artifacts have well-defined bulbs of percussion, while some have faceted striking platforms and approximately 30 (of the 170 then available) show eraillure scars. Haynes (1973; see also Haynes 1969 and Haynes in Leakey et al. 1970) observed that these possible artifacts had been culled from thousands of rejected pieces, and suggested that all of these items might have been naturally produced geofacts, formed at least in part as a result of their journey from the source of the raw material in the Calico Hills. He outlined five natural processes, from tectonic stress fracturing to erosion and redeposition, that could have played a role in their natural origin, and recommended detailed study of the fan to determine the potential of such a deposit to produce and contain geofacts.

Haynes' paper led most of the archaeological community to dismiss the Calico objects as being of natural origin. Although work continued (Simpson 1978; Schuiling 1979), Calico found few strong defenders during the 1970s. Research on the Calico materials began to become more broadly productive toward the end of this decade, however, largely as a result of detailed critiques of the artifacts that appeared at this time.

In 1979, Payen (in Taylor and Payen 1979; see also Payen 1982) returned to Barnes' criterion for distinguishing naturally from humanly fractured stone. Using a sample of over 14,000 measured angles on 54 groups of flaked objects of known origin, Payen replicated Barnes' initial results. Applying this test to the Calico materials, including a series of 83 objects selected by Leakey as "prime," Payen found the weighted average platform-scar angles of Leakey's prime tools to be 87°, compared to 88° for Calico materials rejected as natural, and 72° for known artifacts. Finding no significant differences between those Calico specimens selected as artifacts and those rejected as such, Payen held the entire complex to be naturally produced.

In response, Patterson (1983) published a detailed discussion of the criteria for determining the attributes of man-made lithics. Lamenting the fact that lithic technology remained an immature field and calling for more, and more detailed, studies of natural and cultural rock fracture, Patterson forwarded a series of key attributes that, used as a set, would allow the probability of human manufacture of a set of lithics to be objectively assessed. These attributes included high frequencies of bulbs of percussion, eraillure scars, and ripple marks, and the presence of prepared striking platforms and of unifacial, parallel flake scars. Single attributes, he suggested, could not accurately diagnose such objects (see also Duvall and Venner 1979, and Patterson 1980).

At the same time that Patterson (1983) was proposing this set of diagnostic attributes, Budinger (1983) was applying them in a general way to the Calico materials to support his argument that the site does, in fact, contain artifacts. In November 1984, Budinger announced that the geologist S. Schumm was about to begin a series of controlled experiments meant to duplicate stream and debris flow parameters in order to determine "if any type of artifact-like objects can be formed by rock-on-rock impacts in fluvial/alluvial environments" (Budinger 1984:6). The debate over the Calico Hills specimens, in short, has begun to produce "middle-range" research.

Ambiguity and the Generation of Middle-Range Research

This paper has been largely descriptive, but little more than description seems needed to make the point. In every case I have examined here, and in many others that I have not (debates over the meaning of faunal materials from Old Crow and Olduvai provide excellent examples), the sequence of events that occurred was virtually identical. An initial assertion of the artifactual nature of an ancient piece of stone or bone was quickly followed by an equally bold assertion that the specimen involved had been naturally produced. That denial was followed by the detailed provision of a set of attributes by which natural modification could be distinguished from that produced by people, and those attributes were then used to argue the artifactual nature of the contested specimens. Debate then focused on the supposedly diagnostic attributes. Those supporting a human role in the formation of the objects routinely used actualistic studies to make their interpretation appear plausible. Those opposing a human role, however, used such research in a very different way, to show that known noncultural processes could produce attributes extremely similar, if not identical, to those possessed by the items in question. Thus, they used actualistic studies to conduct "middle-range" research directed toward establishing the processes that had caused the patterns exhibited by a group of objects.

It is common to treat the debates over eoliths and their kin as "entertaining but in the event unproductive controversies" (Roe 1981:27), but it should be clear that these debates were not unproductive. Even though the Old World cases I have examined did not establish the presence of Tertiary hominids in England or Europe, the "middle-range" research they generated greatly enriched our knowledge of matters that are of crucial importance to archaeologists.

These cases also demonstrate that it is wrong to assert that "traditional archaeology did not recognize the need for, nor even the possibility of developing, middle-range research" (Binford 1981:86). Binford (1981) has suggested that middle-range research advances as knowledge is gained that allows the proper use of arguments by elimination; his critique of Morlan's analysis of the Old Crow bone assemblage provides a concise example of this approach in action. Rejecting earlier criteria for the identification of a human role in producing fractured bone at Old Crow, Morlan (1980) adopted as his prime diagnostic trait the presence of proboscidean limb bones broken while fresh: only the midshaft sections of such bones, he argued, exceeded the size range of bones on which carnivore damage could be expected, and only people could produce such breaks. Binford immediately objected. "To what extent," he asked (1981:180), "do you think we are capable of listing all the possible causes of broken and flaked elephant bones." He argued strongly that discovering such causes required middle-range research directed toward elephant bone taphonomy, including the study of modern elephant carcasses subjected to various processes of disturbance, and the analysis of "known paleontological assemblages where the presence of man can be ruled out on historical grounds" to see if broken and flaked elephant bones do, in fact, occur outside of archaeological settings.

In suggesting this approach, Binford recommended that we follow the same path taken by Arcelin in 1885 (a,b), Breuil in 1910, Warren in 1921, and by many others whose work I have discussed. Boule's cement-machine investigations, Warren's remarkable experimental studies of flint fracture, and Barnes' analysis of chipping angles are all middle-range analyses in which attempts were made to establish links between processes and results, and those links then used to probe the meaning of the archaeological record. "If actualistic research can be cited showing that what is observed in the archaeological record is not referable to a suggested cause," Binford (1981:85) tells us, "then one basis for myth-making will be eliminated," and it should be clear that this is exactly what many of the individuals I have discussed were doing. Research of this sort is, then, very much a traditional part of archaeology. Given that the discipline of prehistoric archaeology became established in the middle 1860s (Laming-Emperaire 1964; Grayson 1983; Gruber 1965), such research has been a standard tool of prehistorians since the beginning.

It is, of course, abundantly clear that archaeologists have not applied such an approach to all the settings in which they work. The settings I have examined here are those in which considerable ambiguity was not only recognized, but often even expected, in the materials under analysis. The recent history of actualistic research conducted for "middle-range" purposes suggests that such research is routinely produced in response to perceived interpretive ambiguities in the archaeological record. Indeed, just as Arcelin surprised nature in the process of making an eolith, my analysis suggests that we are now surprising archaeologists in the process of making "middle-range" research, as a response to the ambiguities perceived at such places as Calico, Old Crow, and Olduvai. What distinguishes contemporary archaeologists from those who went before is the scope of the archaeological situations that are now perceived of as being ambiguous. Unlike those we follow, we see ambiguity virtually everywhere, in part because of the kinds of questions we are now asking, and "middle-range" research is flourishing as a result. "Middle-range" research, however, is eternal in archaeology; what changes are our perceptions of the archaeological record and of the ambiguities it offers.

Acknowledgments

For crucial help rendered along the way, my very sincere thanks to Robson Bonnichsen, Fred E. Budinger, Jr., Sarah K. Campbell, Margot Dembo, Robert C. Dunnell, Stephanie D. Livingston, David J. Meltzer, L. A. Payen, Bruce E. Raemsch, Ann Felice Ramenofsky, David Rhode, Alden Sievers, David H. Thomas, and Robert S. Thompson.

Literature Cited

Abbott, W.J.L.
  1905 Machine-made Eoliths. *Man* 5:146–148.

Anonymous
  1903 Communications Diverses. *Bulletin de la Société d'anthropologie de Bruxelles* 21:lxxxiii.
  1914 [Palaeoliths, exhibited and discussed]. *Quarterly Journal of the Geological Society of London* 70:ii–xi.
  1923 Les Silex d'Ipswich: Conclusions de l'enquête de l'Institut internationale d'anthropologie. *Revue anthropologique* 33:53–67.

Arcelin, A.
  1885a Silex tertiaires. *Materiaux pour l'histoire primitive et naturelle de l'homme* 19:193–204.
  1885b Silex tertiaires. *Materiaux pour l'histoire primitive et naturelle de l'homme* 19:303–308.
  1886 Sur le craquelage de silex. *Materiaux pour l'histoire primitive et naturelle de l'homme* 20:567–569.

Barnes, A. S.
  1920 Note on the Paper by Mr. F. N. Haward on "The Origin of the Rostrocarinate Industry." *Proceedings of the Prehistoric Society of East Anglia* 3:259–260.
  1938 Les outils de l'homme tertiaire en Angleterre; Etude critique. *L'Anthropologie* 48:217–236.
  1939a De la manière dont la nature imite le travail humain dans l'éclatement de silex. *Bulletin de la Société préhistorique française* 36:74–89.
  1939b The Difference between Natural and Human Flaking in Prehistoric Flint Implements. *American Anthropologist* 41:99–112.

Barnes, A. S., and J. R. Moir
  1923 A Criticism of Mr. S. Hazzeldine Warren's Views on Eoliths. *Man* 23:51–55.

Binford, L. R.
  1981 *Bones: Ancient Men and Modern Myths.* Academic Press, New York.
  1983 *In Pursuit of the Past.* Thames and Hudson, New York.
  1984 *Faunal Remains from Klasies River Mouth.* Academic Press, New York.

Bischoff, J. L., M. Ikeya, and F. E. Budinger, Jr.
  1984 A TL/ESR Study of the Hearth Feature at the Calico Archaeological Site, California. *American Antiquity* 49:764–774.

Bischoff, J. L., R. J. Shlemon, T. L. Ku, R. D. Simpson, R. J. Rosenbaum, and
   F. E. Budinger, Jr.
   1981   Uranium-series and Soil-geomorphologic Dating of the Calico Archae-
          ological Site, California. *Geology* 9:576–582.

Boule, M.
   1889   [Review of] Arcelin, L'Homme tertiaire (Revue des questions scienti-
          fiques, 13ᵉ année, 1ʳᵉ livraison.). *Revue d'anthropologie* 18:216–217.
   1903a [Review of] Meunier (St.): Sur quelques formes remarquables prises par
          des silex sous l'effet de l'éclatement spontané par la gelée (Comptes
          rendus de Congrès des sociétés savantes de 1902. Sciences, p. 198).
          L'Anthropologie 14:527–529.
   1903b [Review of] Rutot (A.): Les "cailloux" de M. Thieullen (Extr. des Mém-
          oires de la Société d'anthropologie de Bruxelles, t. XXI, 1903). *L'An-
          thropologie* 14:706–707.
   1903c [Review of] Rutot (A.): Quelques découvertes paléontologiques nou-
          velles (Extr. de Bull. de la Société belge de géologie, t. XVII, pp. 188–
          197). *L'Anthropologie* 14:702–704.
   1905   L'Origine des éolithes. *L'Anthropologie* 16:257–267.
   1907   Les polémiques relatives aux éolithes. *L'Anthropologie* 18:486–487.
   1915   La paléontologie humaine en Angleterre. *L'Anthropologie* 26:1–67.
   1923   *Fossil Men*, translated by J. E. Ritchie and J. Ritchie. Oliver and Boyd,
          Edinburgh.

Bourdier, F.
   1957   Pre-Chelléen. *Lexique stratigraphique internationale*, fascicule 4b:96–
          97.
   1976   Les premières industries humaines dans le Nord-ouest. In *La préhistoire
          française, 1: Les civilisations paléolithiques et mésolithiques de la
          France*, edited by H. de Lumley, pages 804–809. Editions de Centre
          national de la recherche scientifique, Paris.

Bourdier, F., and H. Lacassagne
   1963   Précisions nouvelles sur la stratigraphie et la faune du gisement villa-
          franchien de Saint-Prest (Eure-et-Loir). *Bulletin de la Société géologique
          de France* series 7, 5:446–453.

Bourgeois, L.
   1868   Etude sur des silex trouvés dans les depôts tertiaires de la commune de
          Thenay, près Pontlevoy (Loir-et-Cher). *In* Congrès international d'an-
          thropologie et d'archéologie préhistoriques. In *Compte rendu de la* 2ᵐᵉ
          session, Paris, 1867 pages 67–75.
   1869   Sur des silex taillés trouvés dans les depôts miocènes a Thenay. *Bulletin
          de la Société géologique de France* series 7, 26:901–902.
   1873   Sur les silex considérés comme portant les marques d'un travail humain
          et découverts dans le terrain miocène de Thenay. *In* Congrès interna-
          tional d'anthropologie et d'archéologie préhistoriques. *Compte rendu
          de la 6ᵉ session, Bruxelles, 1872* pages 81–94.
   1877   La question de l'homme tertiaire. *Revue des questions scientifiques*
          2:561–575.

Breuil, H.
   1910   Sur la présence d'éoliths à la base de l'eocène parisien. *L'Anthropologie*
          21:385–408.

1922   Les industries pliocènes de la région d'Ipswich. *Revue anthropologique* 32:226–229.

Breuil, H., and R. Lantier
1965   *The Men of the Old Stone Age.* St. Martin's Press, New York.

Buckland, W.
1823   *Reliquiae Diluvianae; or, Observations on the Organic Remains Contained in Caves, Fissures, and Diluvial Gravel, and on other Geological Phenomena Attesting the Action of an Universal Deluge.* Murray, London.

Budinger, F. E., Jr.
1983   Evidence for Pleistocene Man in America: The Calico Early Man Site. *California Geology* 36:75–82.
1984   Calico Debitage. *Friends of Calico Newsletter* 6(4):5–7.

Burchell, J.P.T., and J. R. Moir
1935   The Evolution and Distribution of the Hand-axe in North-east Ireland. *Proceedings of the Prehistoric Society of East Anglia* 7(2):18–21.
1944   The Irish Stone Age. *Man* 44:55–56.

Burkitt, M. C.
1921   Congress at Liège. *Proceedings of the Prehistoric Society of East Anglia* 3(3):453–457.

Capitan, L.
1904   La question des éolithes. *Revue de l'Ecole d'anthropologie* 14:240–246.
1905   Les éolithes, d'après Rutot. *Revue de l'Ecole d'anthropologie* 15:274–279.
1906   Le Congrès international d'anthropologie préhistorique de Monaco (1906). *Revue de l'Ecole d'anthropologie* 16:261–282.
1922   Les silex tertiaires d'Ipswich. *Revue anthropologique* 32:126–136.
1923   Rapport de Dr. Capitan. *Revue anthropologique* 33:58–67.

Capitan, L., and Marty
1924   Nouvelles observations sur les silex pontiens du Puy Courny et du Puy de Boudieu (Cantal). *L'Anthropologie* 34:287–289.

Cartailhac, E.
1873   Association française pour l'avancement des sciences: session de Lyon. *Materiaux pour l'histoire primitive et naturelle de l'homme* 8:285–368.
1881   Notes sur l'archéologie préhistorique en Portugal. *Bulletins de la Société d'anthropologie* series 3, 4:281–291.
1901   Gabriel de Mortillet. *L'Anthropologie* 9:601–612.

Cels, A.
1887   Essai d'une classification des instruments quaternaires en silex et considérations préliminaires sur l'existence de l'homme à l'époque tertiaire dans les environs de Spiennes. *Bulletin de la Société d'anthropologie de Bruxelles* 6:156–182.
1889   Sur une note de M. Prestwich relative à des instruments de silex. *Bulletin de la Société d'anthropologie de Bruxelles* 8:189–192.

Chantre, E.
  1884 Discussion sur le gisement de Thenay. In *Association française pour l'avancement des sciences, Compte rendu de la 13ᵉ session, seconde partie: Notes et mémoires* pages 370–391.

Clarke, W. G.
  1912 Implements of Sub-Crag Man in Norfolk. *Proceedings of the Prehistoric Society of East Anglia* 1(2):160–168.
  1916 The Norfolk Sub-Crag Implements. *Proceedings of the Prehistoric Society of East Anglia* 2(2):213–222.

Coffey, G.
  1901 Naturally Chipped Flints for Comparison with Certain Forms of Alleged Artificial Chipping. *British Association for the Advancement of Science Report* 71:795.

Coles, J. M.
  1968 Ancient Man in Europe. In *Studies in Ancient Europe: Essays Presented to Stuart Piggott,* edited by J. M. Coles and D.D.A. Simpson, pages 17–43. Leicester University Press, Leicester.

Collyer, R. H.
  1867 The Fossil Human Jaw from Suffolk. *Anthropological Review* 5:221–229.

Cornet, F. L., and A. Briart
  1873 L'homme de l'age du Mammouth dans la province de Hainaut. In Congrès international d'anthropologie et d'archéologie préhistoriques. In *Compte rendu de la 6ᵉ session, Bruxelles, 1872* pages 250–269.

Cunnington, W.
  1898 On Some Palaeolithic Implements from the Plateau-Gravels and Their Evidence Concerning "Eolithic" Man. *Quarterly Journal of the Geological Society of London* 54:291–300.

Dalton, O. M.
  1905 Machine-made Eoliths. *Man* 5:123.

Dawson, C., and A. S. Woodward
  1913 On the Discovery of a Palaeolithic Human Skull and Mandible in a Flint-Bearing Gravel, Overlying the Wealden (Hastings Beds) at Piltdown, Fletching (Sussex). *Quarterly Journal of the Geological Society of London* 69:117–150.
  1914 Supplementary Note of a Palaeolithic Human Skull and Mandible at Piltdown (Sussex). *Quarterly Journal of the Geological Society of London* 70:82–99.
  1915 On a Bone Implement from Piltdown (Sussex). *Quarterly Journal of the Geological Society of London* 71:144–149.

Dawson, J. W.
  1894 *The Meeting-place of Geology and History.* Revell, New York.

de Heinzelin, J.
  1957 Boncelles, Mafflien, Mesvinien, Reutelien, and Reutelo-Mesvinien. In *Lexique stratigraphique international,* fascicule 4b:18, 50, 63–64, 152.
  1959 Déclassement de la collection Dethise. *Bulletin de l'Institut royal des sciences de Belgique* 35(11):1–27.

Delfortrie, E.
1869 Les ossements entaillés et striés du miocène aquitanien. *Actes de la Société linnéenne de Bordeaux* 27:261–262.

Delvaux, E.
1885 Excursion de la Société à Spiennes, et à Harmignies, le 5 septembre 1885. *Bulletin de la Société d'anthropologie de Bruxelles* 4:176–208.

Delvaux, E., and A. Houzeau de Lehaie
1887 Sur l'état des terrains dans lesquels M. Cels a découvert des silex taillés par l'homme tertiaire en Belgique. *Bulletin de la Société d'anthropologie de Bruxelles* 6:188–197.

de Mortillet, G.
1868a Homme tertiaire. *Matériaux pour l'histoire positive et philosophique de l'homme,* 4ᵉ année:179–182.
1868b L'Homme dans les temps géologiques. *Bulletin de la Société géologique de France* series 2, 25:180–185.
1873 Sur l'homme tertiaire. *Bulletins de la Société d'anthropologie* series 2, 8:671–684.
1878 Sur les pierres taillées de l'époque tertiaire trouvées par M. Ribeiro dans le Portugal. *Bulletins de la Société d'anthropologie* series 3, 1:428–429.
1879 L'Homme tertiaire à l'Exposition. *Revue d'anthropologie* 8:116–118.
1883 *Le Préhistorique.* Reinwald, Paris.
1885 Silex tertiaires intentionnellement taillés. *Materiaux pour l'histoire primitive et naturelle de l'homme* 19:252–263.

de Mortillet, G., and A. de Mortillet
1881 *Musee préhistorique.* Reinwald, Paris.

de Munck, E.
1885 Recherches sur les silex eclatés sous l'influence des agents atmospheriques et sur ceux retouchés et taillés accidentellement. *Bulletin de la Société d'anthropologie de Bruxelles* 4:259–265.

de Quatrefages, A.
1885 L'Homme tertiaire: Thenay et les îles Andamans. *Materiaux pour l'histoire primitive et naturelle de l'homme* 19:97–107.

Desnoyers, J.
1863a Note sur des indices materiels de la coexistence de l'homme avec l'*Elephas meridionalis* dans un terrain des environs de Chartres, plus anciens que les terrains de transport quaternaires des vallées de la Somme et de la Seine. *Comptes rendus hebdomadaires de l'Académie des sciences* 56:1073–1083.
1863b Réponse à des objections faites au suject de stries et l'incisions constatées sur des ossements de mammiféres fossiles des environs de Chartres. *Comptes rendus hebdomadaires de l'Académie des sciences* 56:1199–1204.

Duvall, J. G., and W. T. Venner
1979 A Statistical Analysis of Lithics from the Calico Site (SBCM 1500A), California. *Journal of Field Archaeology* 6:455–462.

Evans, J.
1872 *The Ancient Stone Implements, Weapons, and Ornaments, of Great Britain.* Appleton, New York.
1878 *Les ages de la pierre: Instruments, armes et ornements de la Grande-Bretagne.* Baillière, Paris.

Funnell, B. M., and R. G. West
1977 Preglacial Pleistocene Deposits of East Anglia. In *British Quaternary Studies,* edited by F. W. Shotton, pages 247–266. Clarendon Press, Oxford.

Gervais, P.
1864–1866 De l'ancienneté de l'homme. *Académie des sciences et lettres de Montpellier, Mémoires de la section des sciences* 6:177–208.

Grayson, D. K.
1983 *The Establishment of Human Antiquity.* Academic Press, New York.
In press The First Three Editions of Charles Lyell's *Geological Evidences of the Antiquity of Man. Archives of Natural History.*

Gruber, J.
1965 Brixham Cave and the Antiquity of Man. In *Context and Meaning in Cultural Anthropology,* edited by M. E. Spiro, pages 737–802. Free Press, New York.

Hammond, M.
1980 Anthropology as a Weapon of Social Combat in Late Nineteenth-Century France. *Journal of the History of the Behavioral Sciences* 16:118–132.

Harrison, B.
1895 High-level Flint-drift of the Chalk: Report of the Committee, Consisting of Sir John Evans (Chairman), Mr. B. Harrison (Secretary), Professor J. Prestwich, and Professor H. G. Seeley. *British Association for the Advancement of Science Report* 65:349–351.
1904 *An Outline of the History of the Eolithic Flint Implements.* Privately published, Kent.

Haward, F. N.
1912 The Chipping of Flints by Natural Agencies. *Proceedings of the Prehistoric Society of East Anglia* 1(2):185–193.
1914 The Problem of the Eoliths. *Proceedings of the Prehistoric Society of East Anglia* 1(4):347–359.
1919 The Origin of the "Rostro-carinate Implements" and Other Chipped Flints from the Basement Beds of East Anglia. *Proceedings of the Prehistoric Society of East Anglia* 3(1)118–146.
1921 The Fracture of Flint: A Reply to the Criticisms of Prof. A. S. Barnes. *Proceedings of the Prehistoric Society of East Anglia* 3(3):448–452.

Haynes, C. V.
1969 The Earliest Americans. *Science* 166:709–715.
1971 Time, Environment, and Early Man. *Arctic Anthropology* 8:3–14.
1973 The Calico Site: Artifacts or Geofacts? *Science* 181:305–311.

Huxley, T. H.
1863 *Evidence as to Man's Place in Nature.* Williams and Norgate, London.

Kendall, H.G.O.
1905 Eoliths and Pseudo-eoliths. *Man* 5:163–165.

Knowles, W. J.
1902 On Objects of the Plateau Kind from the Interglacial Gravels of Ireland. *British Association for the Advancement of Science Report* 72:756–757.

Laming-Emperaire, A.
1964 *Origines de l'archéologie préhistorique en France.* A. and J. Picard, Paris.

Lankester, E. R.
1865 On the Crags of Suffolk and Antwerp (Part I). *Geological Magazine* 2:103–106.
1870 Contributions to a Knowledge of the Newer Tertiaries of Suffolk and Their Fauna. *Quarterly Journal of the Geological Society of London* 26:493–514.
1912a The Investigation of Flint. *Nature* 90:331–333.
1912b The Sub-Crag Flint Implements. *Nature* 90:249–250.
1912c On the Discovery of a Novel Type of Flint Implements below the Base of the Red Crag of Suffolk, Proving the Existence of Skilled Workers of Flint in the Pliocene Age. *Philosophical Transactions of the Royal Society of London,* series B, 202:283–336.
1914 Description of the Test Specimen of the Rostro-carinate Industry Found beneath the Norwich Crag. *Royal Anthropological Institute Occasional Papers* 4.
1921 A Remarkable Flint Implement from Selsey Bill. *Proceedings of the Royal Society of London,* series B, 92:162–167.

Larkby, J. R.
1905 Machine-made Eoliths. *Man* 5:123.

Lartet, E.
1837a Note sur les ossements fossiles des terrains tertiaires de Simorre, de Sansan, etc., dans le département de Gers, et sur la découverte recente d'une machoire du singe fossile. *Comptes rendus hebdomadaires de l'Académie des sciences* 40:85–93.
1837b Nouvelles observations sur une machoire inférieure fossile, crue d'un singe voisin de gibbon, et sur quelques dents et ossements attribués à d'autres quadrumanes. *Comptes rendus hebdomadaires de l'Académie des sciences* 40:583–584.
1856 Note sur un grand singe fossile qui se rattache au groupe des singes supérieurs. *Comptes rendus hebdomadaires de l'Académie des sciences* 43:219–223.

Laville, A.
1898 Le gisement chelléo-moustierien à corbicules de Cergy. *Bulletins de la Société d'anthropologie* series 4, 9:56–69.
1899 "Coup de poings" avec talon et poignée réservés, disque, coin et dents d'Asiniens! des couches à corbicules de Cergy. *Bulletins de la Société d'anthropologie* series 4, 10:80–88.

1901 Coupe de la carriére de Saint-Prest, silex taillés. *Bulletins de la Société d'anthropologie* series 5, 2:285–291.

1902a Coquilles tertiaires éocènes roulées dans le gravier pléistocène de Cergy (Seine-et-Oise). *Bulletins de la Société d'anthropologie* series 5, 3:555–559.

1902b Réponse à M. Rutot sur son étude géologique et anthropologique du gisement du Cergy. *Bulletins de la Société d'anthropologie* series 5, 3:742–749.

1908 Réponse à la note de M. Rutot: "Un cas intéressant d'anti-éolithisme." *Bulletin de la Société belge de géologie, de paléontologie, et de hydrologie* 21:132–134.

Leakey, L.S.B., R. D. Simpson, and T. Clements
1968 Archaeological Excavations in the Calico Mountains, California: Preliminary Report. *Science* 160:1022–1023.

1970 Man in America: The Calico Mountains Excavations. In *Brittanica Yearbook of Science and the Future,* pages 64–79. Encyclopedia Brittanica, Chicago.

Lyell, C.
1863 *The Geological Evidences of the Antiquity of Man with Remarks on Theories of the Origin of Species by Vatiation.* Third edition. Murray, London.

MacCurdy, G. G.
1905 The Eolithic Problem: Evidences of a Rude Industry Antedating the Paleolithic. *American Anthropologist* 7:425–479.

1907 Some Phases of Prehistoric Archaeology. *Science* 25:125–139.

1910 Recent Discoveries Bearing on the Antiquity of Man in Europe. In *Smithsonian Institution Annual Report 1909* pages 531–583.

1924 *Human Origins: A Manual of Prehistory.* Volume 1. Appleton, New York.

Mahoudeau, P.-G., and L. Capitan
1901 La question de l'homme tertiaire à Thenay. *Revue de l'Ecole d'anthropologie* 11:129–153.

Moir, J. R.
1911 The Flint Implements of Sub-Crag Man. *Proceedings of the Prehistoric Society of East Anglia* 1(1):17–43.

1912a The Natural Fracture of Flint. *Nature* 90:461–463.

1912b The Natural Fracture of Flint and Its Bearing upon Rudimentary Flint Implements. *Proceedings of the Prehistoric Society of East Anglia* 1(2):171–185.

1913a Problems of Flint Fracture. *Man* 13:54–56.

1913b The Sub-Crag Flints. *Geological Magazine* new series, 10:553–555.

1914 A Defence of the "Humanity" of the Pre-river Valley Implements of the Ipswich District. *Proceedings of the Prehistoric Society of East Anglia* 1(4):368–374.

1915 A Series of Mineralized Bone Implements of a Primitive Type from below the Base of the Red and Coralline Crags of Suffolk. *Proceedings of the Prehistoric Society of East Anglia* 2(1):116–131.

1916 On the Evolution of the Earliest Palaeoliths from the Rostro-carinate Implements. *Journal of the Royal Anthropological Institute* 46:197–220.

1918a Some Flint Implements of the Rostro-carinate Form from Egypt. *Man* 18:3–6.

1918b The Fracturing of Flints by Natural Agencies in Geological Deposits. *Proceedings of the Prehistoric Society of East Anglia* 2(4):575–578.

1919a A Few Notes on the Sub-Crag Flint Implements. *Proceedings of the Prehistoric Society of East Anglia* 3(1):158–161.

1919b *Pre-Palaeolithic Man.* Harrison, Ipswich.

1920 The Transition from Rostro-carinate Flint Implements to the Tongue-shaped Implements of River-terrace Gravels. *Philosophical Transactions of the Royal Society of London,* section B, 209:329–350.

1921 Further Discoveries of Humanly-fashioned Flints in and beneath the Red Crag of Suffolk. *Proceedings of the Prehistoric Society of East Anglia* 3(3):389–430.

1922 The Ice-Age and Man: A Note on Man, 1922, 5. *Man* 22:52–54.

1927 *The Antiquity of Man in East Anglia.* Cambridge University Press, Cambridge.

1932 The Culture of Pliocene Man. *Proceedings of the Prehistoric Society of East Anglia* 7(1):1–17.

1939 Eolithic Man. *Man* 39:96.

Morlan, R. E.
1980 Taphonomy and Archaeology in the Upper Pleistocene of the Northern Yukon Territory: A Glimpse of the Peopling of the New World. *Archaeological Survey of Canada Paper* 94.

Obermaier, H.
1905 Is it Certain that Eoliths are Made by Man? *Man* 5:177–179.

Osborn, H. F.
1921 The Pliocene Man of Foxhall in East Anglia. *Natural History* 21:565–576.

Patte, E.
1926 Une nouvelle fabrique industrielle d'éolithes reproduisant des types de pliocène anglais. *L'Anthropologie* 36:1–13.

Patterson, L. W.
1980 Comments on a Statistical Analysis of Lithics from Calico. *Journal of Field Archaeology* 7:374–377.

1983 Criteria for Determining the Attributes of Man-made Lithics. *Journal of Field Archaeology* 10:297–307.

Payen, L. A.
1982 Artifacts or Geofacts at Calico: Application of the Barnes Test. *In* Peopling of the New World, edited by J. E. Ericson, R. E. Taylor, and R. Berger. *Ballena Press Anthropological Papers* 23:193–201.

Prestwich, J.
1889 On the Occurrence of Palaeolithic Flint Implements in the Neighbourhood of Ightham, Kent, Their Distribution and Probable Age. *Quarterly Journal of the Geological Society of London* 45:270–297.

1891 On the Age, Formation, and Successive Drift-Stages of the Valley of the Darent; with Remarks on the Palaeolithic Implements of the District, and on the Origin of Its Chalk Escarpment. *Quarterly Journal of the Geological Society of London* 47:126–163.
1892 On the Primitive Characters of the Flint Implements of the Chalk Plateau of Kent, with Reference to the Question of Their Glacial or Pre-Glacial Age. *Journal of the Anthropological Institute* 21:246–276.
1895a Nature and Art. *Geological Magazine* new series 2:375–376.
1895b The Greater Antiquity of Man. *Nineteenth Century* 37:617–628.

Raab, L. M., and A. C. Goodyear
1984 Middle-Range Theory in Archaeology: A Critical Review of Origins and Applications. *American Antiquity* 49:255–268.

Rames, J.-B.
1884 Géologie de Puy Courny: Eclats de silex tortonien du bassin d'Aurillac (Cantal). *Materiaux pour l'histoire primitive et naturelle de l'homme* 18:385–406.

Reinach, S.
1899 Gabriel de Mortillet. *Revue historique* 69:67–95.

Ribeiro, C.
1867 Note sur le terrain quaternaire du Portugal. *Bulletin de la Société géologique de France* series 2, 24:692–717.
1873a Sur des silex taillés découverts dans les terrains miocène et pliocène du Portugal. *In* Congrès international d'anthropologie et d'archéologie préhistoriques. In *Compte rendu de la 6ᵉ session, Bruxelles, 1872* pages 95–100.
1873b Sur la position géologique des couches miocènes et pliocènes du Portugal qui contiennent des silex taillés. *In* Congrès international d'anthropologie et d'archéologie préhistoriques. In *Compte rendu de la 6ᵉ session, Bruxelles, 1872* pages 100–104.
1884 L'Homme tertiaire en Portugal. *In* Congrès international d'anthropologie et d'archéologie préhistoriques. In *Compte rendu de la neuvième session à Lisbonne 1880* pages 81–118.

Robert, E.
1863 Sur l'origine récente des traces d'instruments tranchants observés à la surface de quelques ossements fossiles. *Comptes rendus hebdomadaires de l'Académie des sciences* 56:1157–1158.

Roe, D. A.
1981 *The Lower and Middle Palaeolithic Periods in Britain.* Routledge and Kegan Paul, London.

Rudwick, M.J.S.
1972 *The Meaning of Fossils.* American Elsevier, New York.

Rupke, N. A.
1983 *The Great Chain of History: William Buckland and the English School of Geology (1814–1849).* Clarendon Press, Oxford.

Rutot, A.

1887 Sur des silex taillés prétendument trouvés dans le landenien inférieur aux environs de Mons. *Bulletin de la Société d'anthropologie de Bruxelles* 6:414–421.

1896 Sur la découverte d'un nouveau gisement de silex taillés à l'est de Spiennes. *Bulletin de la Société d'anthropologie de Bruxelles* 15:56–64.

1897 Les conditions d'existence de l'homme et les traces de sa presence au travers des temps quaternaires et des temps moderns en Belgique. *Bulletin de la Société d'anthropologie de Bruxelles* 16:24–76.

1898a Sur la découverte d'immenses gisements de silex taillés dans la Flandre occidentale. *Bulletin de la Société d'anthropologie de Bruxelles* 17:354–355.

1898b Sur l'age des gisements de silex taillés découverts sur le territoire des communes de Haine-Saint-Pierre, Ressaix, Epinois, etc., Canton de Binche, Province de Hainaut (Belgique). *Bulletin de la Société d'anthropologie de Bruxelles* 17:231–354.

1898c Sur les silex mesviniens de la Flandre occidentale. *Bulletin de la Société d'anthropologie de Bruxelles* 17:382–383.

1899a Note sur la découverte d'importants gisements de silex taillés dans les collines de la Flandre occidentale: Comparaison de ces silex avec ceux du Chalk Plateau du Kent. *Mémoires de la Société d'anthropologie de Bruxelles* 1899–1900(1).

1899b Sur la découverte de nombreux instruments d'industrie reutelo-mesvinienne dans les carrières de Maffles (près d'Ath). *Bulletin de la Société d'anthropologie de Bruxelles* 18:cxxx–cxxxi.

1900a Sur l'aire de dispersion actuellement connue des peuplades paléolithiques en Belgique. *Bulletin de la Société d'anthropologie de Bruxelles* 19:xlvii–lvii.

1900b Sur l'existence de silex utilisés d'age tertiare dans le calloutis de base de moséen, renfermant l'industrie reutelienne. *Bulletin de la Société d'anthropologie de Bruxelles* 19:cxx–cxxi.

1900c Sur l'homme préquaternaire. *Mémoires de la Société d'anthropologie de Bruxelles* 1900–1901(3).

1901a Sur l'homme préquaternaire. *Bulletin de la Société d'anthropologie de Bruxelles* 19:cv–cvii.

1901b Sur une preuve de l'existence de l'homme sur la crête de l'Artois avant la fin du Pliocène. *Bulletin de la Société belge de géologie, de paléontologie, et de hydrologie (Procès-Verbaux)* 15:29–33.

1902a Etude géologique et anthropologique du gisement de Cergy (Seine-et-Oise). *Mémoires de la Société d'anthropologie de Bruxelles* 1901–1902(4).

1902b Les industries primitives. Défense des éolithes. Les actions naturelles possibles sont inaptes à produire des effets semblables à la retouch intentionelle. *Mémoires de la Société d'anthropologie de Bruxelles* 1901–1902(2).

1902c Sur la distribution des industries paléolithiques dans les couches quaternaires de la Belgique. *In* Congrès international d'anthropologie et d'archéologie préhistoriques. In *Compte rendu de la douzième session, Paris 1900* pages 79–117.

1902d Sur l'existence de l'homme préquaternaire sur la crête de l'Artois. *Bulletin de la Société d'anthropologie de Bruxelles* 20:lix.

1903 Les "cailloux" de M. Thieullen. *Mémoires de la Société d'anthropologie de Bruxelles* 1902–1903(3).
1904 Sur la cause de l'éclatement naturel de silex. *Mémoires de la Société d'anthropologie de Bruxelles* 1904(1).
1905 Toujours les éolithes. *Bulletin de la Société d'anthropologie de Bruxelles* 24:clxiii–clxxxiii.
1906 Eolithes et pseudo-éolithes. *Mémoires de la Société d'anthropologie de Bruxelles* 1906(1).
1906/1907 Un cas intéressant d'antiéolithisme. *Bulletin de la Société belge de géologie, de paléontologie, et de hydrologie (Procès-Verbaux)* 20:22–33.
1907 Un grave problème: Une industrie humaine datant de l'époque oligocène: Comparison des outils avec ceux des Tasmanians actuels. *Bulletin de la Société belge de géologie, de paléontologie, et de hydrologie, Mémoires* 21:439–482.
1908a A propos des éolithes du Cantal: Un deuxième cas intéressant d'antiéolithisme. *Bulletin de la Société belge de géologie, de paléontologie, et de hydrologie (Procès-Verbaux)* 21:104–109.
1908b La fin de la question des éolithes. *Bulletin de la Société belge de géologie, de paléontologie, et de hydrologie (Procès-Verbaux)* 21:211–217.
1909 Une industrie éolithique antérieure à l'Oligocène supérieur ou Aquitanien. *In* Congrès préhistorique de France. In *Compte rendu de la quatrième session - Chambery 1908* pages 90–104.
1918 *La Préhistoire, Première partie: Introduction à l'étude de la préhistoire de la Belgique.* Les naturalistes belges, Bruxelles.

Sackett, J.
1981 From de Mortillet to Bordes: A Century of French Paleolithic Research In *Toward a History of Archaeology,* edited by G. Daniel, pages 85–99. Thames and Hudson, London.

Schuiling, W. C. (editor)
1972 *Pleistocene Man at Calico.* San Bernardino County Museum Association, San Bernardino.
1979 *Pleistocene Man at Calico.* San Bernardino County Museum Association, San Bernardino.

Schwartz, A. S.
1914 Some Suggestions for Organised Research on Flint Implements. *Proceedings of the Prehistoric Society of East Anglia* 1(4):449–454.

Schwartz, A. S., and H. R. Beevor
1909 The Dawn of Human Invention: An Experimental and Comparative Study of Eoliths. *Memoirs and Proceedings of the Manchester Literary and Philosophical Society* 53(8):1–34.

Simpson, R. D.
1978 The Calico Mountains Archaeological Site. *In* Early Man in America from a Circum-Pacific Perspective, edited by A. L. Bryan. *Occasional Papers of the Department of Anthropology, University of Alberta* 1:218–220.
1980 The Calico Mountains Site: Pleistocene Archaeology in the Mojave Desert, California. In *Early Native Americans: Prehistoric Demography, Economy, and Technology,* edited by D. L. Browman, pages 7–20. Mouton, The Hague.

1982 The Calico Mountains Archaeological Project: A Progress Report. *In* Peopling the New World, edited by J. E. Ericson, R. E. Taylor, and R. Berger. *Ballena Press Anthropological Papers* 23:181–192.

Smith, P.E.I.
1966 Le Solutréen en France. *L'Institut de préhistoire de l'Université de Bordeaux Mémoire* 5.

Sollas, W. J.
1913 The Formation of 'Rostro-carinate' Flints. *British Association for the Advancement of Science Report* 83:788–790.
1920 A Flaked Flint from the Red Crag. *Proceedings of the Prehistoric Society of East Anglia* 3(2):261–267.
1924 *Ancient Hunters.* Third edition. Macmillan, London.

Stockmans, F.
1966 Notice sur Aimé Rutot. *Académie royale de Belgique, Annuaire* 132:3–123.

Tardy, M.
1869 [Sur un silex taillé du Cantal]. *Bulletins de la Société d'anthropologie* series 2, 4:703–705.
1870 Sur un silex taillé de Cantal. *Bulletin de la Société géologique de France* series 2, 27:358–360.

Taylor, R. E., and L. A. Payen
1979 The Role of Archaeometry in American Archaeology: Approaches to the Evaluation of the Antiquity of *Homo sapiens* in California. *Advances in Archaeological Method and Theory* 2:239–283.

Warren, S. H.
1905a On the Origin of "Eolithic" Flints by Natural Causes, Especially by the Foundering of Drifts. *Journal of the Royal Anthropological Institute of Great Britain and Ireland* 35:337–364.
1905b On the Origin of Eoliths. *Man* 5:179–183.
1913 Problems of Flint Fracture. *Man* 13:37–38.
1914 The Experimental Investigation of Flint Fracture and Its Application to Problems of Human Implements. *Journal of the Royal Anthropological Institute of Great Britain and Ireland* 44:412–450.
1921 A Natural 'Eolith' Factory beneath the Thanet Sand. *Quarterly Journal of the Geological Society of London* 76:238–253.
1922 The Red Crag Flints of Foxhall. *Man* 22:87–89.
1923a Sub-soil Pressure Flaking. *Proceedings of the Geologists' Association* 34:153–175.
1923b The Sub-soil Flint Flaking Sites at Grays. *Proceedings of the Geologists' Association* 34:38–42.

Weiner, J. S.
1955 *The Piltdown Forgery.* Oxford University Press, Oxford.

Weiner, J. S., K. P. Oakley, and W. E. Le Gros Clark
1953 The Solution of the Piltdown Problem. *British Museum (Natural History) Bulletin: Geology* 2(3):141–146.

Woodward, A. S.
   1918   Fourth Note on the Piltdown Gravel, with Evidence of a Second Skull
          of *Eoanthropus dawsoni. Quarterly Journal of the Geological Society
          of London* 73:1–10.

Woodward, H.
   1895   Award of the Lyell Geological Fund. *Quarterly Journal of the Geolog-
          ical Society of London* 51:xliv–xlvi.

Don D. Fowler University of Nevada

Conserving American Archaeological Resources

In 1974 William D. Lipe (1974) presented a "Conservation Model for American Archaeology." Influenced by the natural sciences and environmental concerns of the day, he reminded archaeologists that archaeological sites comprise a finite, nonrenewable resource rapidly being obliterated throughout the land. The core of Lipe's model, styled a "conservation ethic" by many, lies in the statement that we should "treat [archaeological] salvage, especially of the emergency kind, as the last resort—to be undertaken only after all other avenues of protecting the resource have failed" (Lipe 1974:243).

This paper reviews attempts to develop a workable conservation ethic in American archaeology. Lipe's statement is not an ethic *per se* but an ideal procedure that should follow from an ethic. I take such an ethic to be a set (or sets) of ideals and values that fosters and encourages actions by the citizenry, government officials *and* archaeologists and in turn stimulate *effective* preservation, conservation, and protection of extant cultural resources for the future. It is easy to say what such an ethic should be. It has, in various ways, been stated as an intended public policy in both state and national legislation. Unfortunately, policies flowing from such an ethic have been equivocal at best. Ethical principles and policies, like morals, exist only when expressed through positive and consistent actions. The major concern of this paper is to explore why an archaeological conservation ethic is *not* imbued in the minds of the American public to any extent, and hence, not fully expressed in positive actions. The approach to this question is through an historical overview of some developments in American archaeology over the past two centuries.

In 1929 Fay-Cooper Cole (1929) and Neil Judd (1929) published papers on the problems as they then perceived them of establishing and implementing an adequate program of archaeological site conservation in the United States. Cole's paper, "The Conservation of Public Sites," was focused on the Midwest. Therein he used the engaging and oft-repeated metaphor that sites destroyed by vandalism or land-development are, "pages torn from the book . . . of prehistory—pages that can never be rewritten." Cole noted that in one Illinois county, 655 "pages," primarily burial mounds were known; all save 50 had, by 1929, been despoiled, "torn from the book" (Cole 1929:11–12).

Judd's paper, "The Present Status of Archaeology in the United States," painted a similarly melancholy picture for the Southwest and the United States generally. In both writers' eyes, the problems of site destruction and the lack of effective public conservation measures had assumed near-critical proportions. Both considered legislative solutions. Cole (1929:13) considered legislation, "to prevent the opening or destruction of any . . . site except by qualified archaeologists. But [he then continued], experience has taught us that legislation is of little avail unless those affected by it are convinced of its desirability." Judd (1929:406) was even less sanguine: "Legislation affecting private property is not readily passed, especially if it appears inconsequential to the legislative mind."

Cole thought a massive public education program might help create a conservation ethic. Judd doubted it. An education program, he said, "to create a public sentiment so intense and sincere as to guard from further spoliation ancient Indian remains either on private lands or other lands [is] a task not readily achievable, if achievable at all" (Judd 1929:405).

Cole offered two arguments for site conservation. One was economic and directed toward local business leaders in the Midwest. He pointed to money he thought would be spent by tourists to see properly excavated and displayed private or public outdoor museums or archaeological parks, such as the Serpent Mound in Ohio. His second argument is the key premise of research and education, our debt to the future: "We owe it to our children and to future generations to preserve the mounds and other prehistoric sites, and to hand on to them the most nearly complete record possible" (Cole 1929:14).

Judd was so despondent that he offered no solutions, but he did make an important and seemingly quixotic point: public indifference to archaeological conservation does not mean indifference to archaeological results; a significant segment of the public is fascinated by what archaeology tells it of exotic times, places, and cultures. Thus we see in these two papers the elements of the archaeological conservationist's dilemma: many people are deeply interested in what archaeology tells them, but they are not imbued with either urges or ideals that lead them to actively support actions to conserve the sources of interest: the sites. It is the thesis of this paper that the dilemma still exists. The reasons for it exist, I think, in how archaeology has developed in the United States within the larger context of the dynamics of American sociocultural development.

Since about 1780 in North America, those scholars called antiquarians, and later, archaeologists, have taken as their concern the physical remains of autochthonous cultures and what they can be made to tell about past lifeways. The "telling" requires that the remains and their interrelationships continue intact until disassembled and interpreted by properly knowledgeable persons, to wit, archaeologists. Others have been concerned only with "relics"—objects fascinating to many, hence valuable things to be acquired by whatever means. Such objects have been, and are, fondled, gloated over, and placed in geometric designs in picture frames. Being prestational objects, like Kwakiutl coppers and Trobriands kula necklaces and armbands, they increase in value every time they change hands, especially if the middlemen are Christie's or Sotheby Parke Bernet. Still others, concerned to develop the landscape in the name of God, Progress, Manifest Destiny, Mommon, or all of the above, have viewed the physical remains as simply impediments to be levelled as expeditiously as possible. It is against these competing and conflicting desires, and against deeply held ideas about the "sanctity" of private property, that we must judge the archaeologists' dilemma.

The recognition that (1) archaeological sites are "containers of information" (Fowler 1982:19); (2) relevant to an understanding of the American aboriginal past; and (3) that such understanding is a worthwhile scholarly endeavor, began probably with Thomas Jefferson, often called the parent of American archaeology (Willey 1968:32) for his excavation of a burial mound, as reported in his *Notes on the State of Virginia* (Jefferson [original 1784] 1944:222–225). Jefferson's stratigraphic approach was quite modern, although seldom emulated in America until about 1910 (Spier 1931), as was his purpose in excavating the site: to test an explicit hypothesis about burial practices. Having set another precedent, not always followed, of conducting an excavation and promptly publishing the results, Jefferson did not take the next step. He did not issue a call to *conserve* archaeological sites for future study or appreciation, although he did develop field guides for recording archaeological sites, as well as ethnographic and linguistic data (Fowler 1975:21; Ronda 1984:113–132). The first step in that direction seems to have been taken by the directors of the Ohio Land Company, who, when platting the future town of Marietta in 1788, "reserved . . . the two truncated pyramids and the great mound, with a few acres attached to each, as a public square" (Squier and Davis 1848:75, n. 2, map 26; Atwater 1820:134–135). As site destruction accelerated in the 19th century, there were laments. In 1820 Caleb Atwater (1820:121, 123) noted that "the destroying hand of man has despoiled [many Ohio mounds] of their contents and entirely removed them." In 1845, Caleb Goldsmith Forshey (1845:39) described "artificial mounds" on Prairie Jefferson, Louisiana, and wrote: "The levelling hand of American industry is fast obliterating these dumb, yet eloquent records of the past . . .[and hence] the necessity of early attention and accurate description is needed." In 1848 Squier and Davis (1848:xxxix) issued a similar lament and call for action:

> The importance of a complete and speedy examination of the whole field cannot be overestimated. The operation of the elements, the shifting channels of the streams, the levelling hand of public improvement, and most efficient of all, the slow but steady encroachments of agriculture, are fast destroying these monuments of ancient labor, breaking in upon their symmetry and obliterating their outlines. Thousands have already disappeared, or retain slight and doubtful traces of their former proportions.

In fact, in the 1840s, an effort to study the sites before they disappeared was the only realistic alternative. The institutional and intellectual frameworks for systematic and concerted action did not exist. They soon, however, began to be developed.

From its founding in 1846 the Smithsonian Institution has been deeply involved in the study of Indian antiquities. The most notable early efforts included Squier and Davis' (1848) great "Mounds" report, the still-useful overview of North American prehistory by Haven (1856), and various field manuals to guide archaeological and ethnographic research issued by or through the Institution after 1847 (Fowler 1975:22; Hinsley 1981:34–36). The ways in which Indians and Indian artifacts and sites were interpreted by the Smithsonian and the other great natural history museums founded in the 19th century (Barber 1980; P. J. Lyon 1969) were also to have deep, if implicit, effects on the development of a true conservation ethic, as discussed below. Discovery and description by Army topographical engineers (Goetzmann 1959: 109–260) of the spectacular "ruins" in the newly acquired American Southwest after 1846 (e.g., the 1849 report by Simpson, 1964), stimulated much interest and speculation, but no calls for conservation of the sites.

After the Civil War, there was a renewed interest in the ruins of the Southwest, stimulated by the first detailed studies of them, especially the reports of Putnam (1879), Jackson (1875), and Holmes (1876). There was the beginning of a perception that as more and more Anglos moved into the Southwest, looting and vandalism of sites increased, but calls for conservation did not begin until the following decade.

The post-Civil War period also saw the advent of a new phenomenon, professional collectors in the service of the still-nascent natural history museums. Museums in both the United States and Europe were hastening to fill up their collections and exhibit cases. An example was Edward Palmer (McVaugh 1956), employed by both the Peabody Museum at Harvard and the Smithsonian to make extensive archaeological and ethnographic collections in the American West. His excavation methods were little different than those of "amateur" collectors elsewhere (Fowler and Matley 1978:22). Palmer's and others' collecting was regarded as quite acceptable at Harvard and the Smithsonian, as long as they worked for American museums. But collectors in the employ of foreign museums (and they were numerous in the 1870s) raised American chauvinistic hackles.

In 1879 John Wesley Powell, by an adroit bit of legislative legerdemain, founded the Bureau of Ethnology under the auspices of the Smithsonian. His principal purpose was to "organize anthropological research in America" (Powell 1881:xi), especially extensive programs of salvage ethnography and linguistics. For Powell and his staunch backer Lewis Henry Morgan, archaeology was a low priority, except in the Southwest. Smithsonian Secretary Spencer F. Baird, however, thought otherwise. Alarmed by the incursions of foreign collectors and domestic looting of eastern "mounds," in 1881 Baird forced a "Mounds Program" on Powell (Meltzer 1985:350). Morgan sarcastically wrote to Powell, congratulating him on his elevation to the "Chair of Archaeology," saying that the need to study rapidly disappearing cultures and languages "is more important just now" (L. H. Morgan to J. W. Powell, April 15, 1881, BAE Collection, National Anthropological Archives, Washington, D.C.). Nonetheless, Powell was forced to acquiesce. The Mounds Program (Thomas 1894) did ultimately answer the long-nagging question of "who were the Mound Builders," but its principal purpose in Baird's eyes was essentially a salvage effort: to get the "goodies" into the Smithsonian before they ended up in the museums of London, Paris, or Berlin. There was no real concern to develop a program of archaeological site conservation; that would fill up museum cases.

Although there was not a movement toward systematic conservation in the actions of museum collectors or most museum administrators, changes were underway soon after 1880. Conservation of both natural resources (McConnell 1954; Graham 1971; Van Hise 1921) and historic buildings and places (Hosmer 1965) began to be of increasing concern. So, too, did archaeological conservation, although it was often to remain separate from natural resource conservation and preservation of the "built environment" for many years (King et al. 1977:20). In 1872 the U.S. Congress (U.S. Code 1984a) acted to set aside the Yellowstone region as the world's first national park. Such an action, setting aside a portion of the public domain for the benefit of the people, was to have important implications for archaeology in the years ahead. The action of the Congress in 1888 (U.S. Code 1984b), empowering the government to use the eminent domain power (Bosselman et al. 1973) to acquire private property (i.e., the Civil War battlefields of Gettysburg, Shiloh, Antietam), did not have a similar impact on archaeology. In 1896 the Supreme Court (U.S. Supreme Court 1896) upheld the "taking" (with just compensation, as required by the Constitution) of the battlefields because they are places of "overweening national significance." To date, the power has never been exercised, on the federal level, to acquire or protect archaeological sites (Fowler 1982:30). As indicated, however, the public domain, which was quite another matter, was put under Congressional control regarding its disposition.

The roots of modern archaeological conservation efforts lie in Boston. In 1879 the Archaeological Institute of America was founded there, and the Institute sent the ethnohistorian Adolph Bandelier (1883) to the Southwest. His work (Lange and Riley 1966; Lange et al. 1970–1975) and that of the Bureau of Ethnology under Powell's direction (Fowler and Fowler 1969), stimulated interest and concern among Bostonians. In 1882 a group of prominent Bostonians presented a petition to the U.S. Congress, laying out the historical importance of Southwestern archaeological sites and imminent threats thereto. They "prayed that at least some of these extinct cities or pueblos, carefully selected, with . . . land reservations attached . . . may be withheld from public sale and their antiquities and ruins be preserved, as they furnished invaluable data for the ethnological studies now engaging the attention of our most learned scientific, antiquarian, and historical students" (Wilder and Slafter 1882:3777). The petition died in committee, but the cause of archaeological conservation had become a matter of public concern, at least in Boston. Areas other than the Southwest also demanded attention. Between 1883 and 1885 Frederic Ward Putnam, of Harvard University, working with Alice Fletcher, Francis Parkman, and others, raised $6000 to purchase, in the name of the Harvard Peabody Museum, the Great Serpent Mound site in southern Ohio. The site was preserved, and in 1900, turned over to the Ohio Archaeological and Historical Society to be maintained, as it still is, as an archaeological park (Putnam 1890; Dexter 1965). In 1886 the Boston philanthropist Mary Hemenway provided funds for the celebrated Hemenway Southwestern Expedition, led by the brilliant, but erratic, Frank Hamilton Cushing (Brandes 1965:134–158; Mark 1980:96–130). Cushing's report of his work and increasing awareness of the ongoing work in the Southwest by the Smithsonian excited much attention and stimulated further thoughts of archaeological conservation in Boston and other parts of the East.

Some years earlier, in 1873, F. W. Putnam had become the permanent Secretary of the American Association for the Advancement of Science. He held the post for 25 years. As Secretary he came to wield considerable influence on American science in general and anthropology in particular (Mark 1980:21–27). In 1888 in further pursuit of federal protection of archaeological sites, Putnam appointed Alice Fletcher and Tille E. (later Matilda Coxe) Stevenson as the Committee on the Preservation of Archaeological Remains on the Public Lands. After consulting with J. W. Powell and others, they recommended preservation of the great ruins in Chaco Canyon in New Mexico; the sites in Canyon DeChelly, Walnut Canyon, some sites in the Verde Valley and the "Cavate Lodges in the cinder cone 8 miles east of Flagstaff," in Arizona; sites in the Mancos drainage in southwestern Colorado; also the "Pueblos, which are not on treaty reservations" in Arizona and New Mexico, "the old Mandan and Arickaree villages . . . in Dakota Territory, when they shall cease to be inhabited by the Indians"; and several other isolated sites in the Southwest and Alaska (Fletcher and Stevenson 1888:1). Recognizing that all they had recommended would be difficult to convince Congress and the public, they proposed "to inaugurate the precedent of preserving archaeologic [sic] remains upon the Public Domain" by submitting a bill to preserve only one tract. The tract they suggested was an area of "cavate dwellings" and "stone pueblos . . . on the Rio Grande west of Santa

Fe" (Fletcher and Stevenson 1888:2), basically the area of Canyon de los Frijoles. However, by January 1889, Bostonians had made a decision to "inaugurate the precedent" by petitioning Congress to set aside the Casa Grande ruins in Arizona. The petition, signed by Mary Hemenway, Francis Parkman, Edward Everett Hale, Oliver Wendell Holmes, and 10 other Boston luminaries, asked Congress to set aside and protect, "from destruction or injury . . . the ancient and celebrated ruin of Casa Grande, an ancient temple of the prehistoric age of the greatest ethnological and scientific interest . . ." (Ames et al. 1889). Congress agreed (U.S. Code 1984c) and appropriated $2000 for repairs and protection. A Presidential Executive Order in 1892 established a 480-acre reserve around Casa Grande (Sullivan 1947:140; Van Valkenburgh 1962). Repair and stabilization work was delegated to the Bureau of Ethnology (Mindeleff 1897; Fewkes 1912), thus initiating federal involvement in archaeological conservation, later to be highly developed by the National Park Service. Thus the first national archaeological reservation was achieved (Lee 1970:16–20). Canyon de los Frijoles would have to wait for federal protection until the creation of Bandelier National Monument in 1916.

Two weeks before the Bostonians submitted their petition to Congress, on December 18, 1888, rancher Richard Wetherill and his brother-in-law Charles Mason of Mancos, Colorado, were hunting stray cattle on the Mesa Verde, and found instead Cliff Palace and Spruce Tree House (McNitt 1966:23–28; Fletcher 1977:91–171). Soon known to the world through the Wetherill's "excavations," tourist visits, and Nordenskiöld's (1893) investigations, the spectacular ruins of the Mesa Verde excited much interest. Their continued exploitation became the catalyst for the establishment of a Colorado women's group, the Cliff Dwellers Association. The Association led the long and ultimately successful campaign to have Mesa Verde made a national park. In the 1890s the boundlessly energetic Edgar Lee Hewett began his long archaeological career (Chauvent 1983:35) of adroit administration, effective lobbying, and mediocre field work. He was soon in the thick of the fight (Hewett 1906) to protect archaeological sites in the Southwest.

A new nationwide chapter organization of the Archaeological Institute of America helped promote public awareness and lobbying pressure. In 1902, the newly created American Anthropological Association set as a major priority passage of federal legislation to accord general protection for archaeological sites on public lands. The complex story behind the passage of the 1906 Antiquities Act (U. S. Code 1984d) has been ably chronicled by Ronald Lee (1970) and need not be repeated here. What is important for our purpose is that the campaigns for the legislation and for Mesa Verde, which became a National Park 22 days after the 1906 Act became law (Lee 1970:80), created for the first time considerable public awareness of and sympathy for archaeological conservation, at least in the West. Second, the Act put the federal government in the archaeological conservation business permanently—at least in theory. Actual conservation came primarily through the power granted to the President to establish, by Executive Order, national monuments of historic and scientific importance. By 1920 a dozen major archaeological sites, all in the Southwest, had been so designated (Lee 1970, table 1). The provision in the Act requiring permits and appropriate expertise to excavate sites on public lands was another matter. It basically was not enforced, as Judd (1924:429) and others bitterly noted in 1924. Archaeologists soon learned that a legislative Act does not a Conservation Ethic create.

In reviewing the actions that led to the passage of the 1906 Antiquities Act and the creation of Mesa Verde National Park, two things are apparent. One, the public's attention was focused on spectacular sites, not on smaller, run-of-the-mill sites. In theory, protection for both the spectacular and the small sites was accorded through the permitting process of the Antiquities Act; but, in fact, there was little if any effective protection either accorded or possible. Second, the Act dealt, necessarily, only with the public lands. The federal eminent domain power was exercised to acquire battlefields and ultimately places of great historic interest, but not prehistoric places. Prehistoric sites on private land could be purchased, as was the Great Serpent Mound. But such actions were not forthcoming until the 1920s.

One of the key developments in the organization of American archaeology in the first part of this century was the establishment in 1919 of the Committee on Statewide Archaeological Surveys of the Division of Anthropology and Psychology, National Research Council (Guthe 1930). Between 1920 and 1937 the Committee played a major role in stimulating research and professionalism. Committee members played crucial roles in the founding of the Society for American Archaeology in 1934, and laid the foundation for what emerged in 1945 as the Committee for the Recovery of Archaeological Remains (Marlowe 1983).

When the Anthropology and Psychology Division was created as part of the National Research Council in 1919 (Wissler 1920:1), various projects were proposed. One was a plan to stimulate statewide archaeological surveys in the Midwest, initially in Illinois, Indiana, Iowa, and

Missouri, comparable to ongoing surveys in Alabama, New York, and Wisconsin (Wissler 1922:233). The idea was to encourage existing state historical societies, academies of science, universities, etc., to undertake county by county surveys. The Committee provided guidance in data recording techniques and standards (Wissler 1923), as well as encouraged the formation of new statewide archaeological societies, e.g., in Michigan in 1922 and Tennessee in 1924 (Kidder 1926:313). Soon the Committee became a national clearing house for archaeological information and began publishing in the *American Anthropologist* reports on archaeological work throughout the country (Wissler 1922; Kidder 1925a, 1925b, 1926; Guthe 1928–1934, 1935). The task of reporting fieldwork was soon taken up by the newly founded journal *American Antiquity*.

A central concern of the Committee was archaeological conservation and how it might be achieved. Committee members and correspondents began documenting site destruction. Mills (1922:401) reported that at Mound City, Ohio, less than half of the extensive mound complex reported by Squier and Davis (1848:54–55) remained. Judd (1924:428) reported rampant vandalism throughout the Southwest: "most residents of the Southwest regard it as their inalienable right to dig for 'relics' in any ruin that tempts their enthusiasm. The spirit has rarely been contested." One Indian trader in western New Mexico was reportedly filling an order for 1000 pieces of pottery (presumably Mimbres wares) from sites on public lands. As previously noted, there was apparently no attempt to enforce the Antiquities Act (Judd 1924:429). Similar horror stories abounded throughout the country (Cole 1929; Judd 1929).

The Committees further encouraged the formation of state archaeological societies, particularly in the midwest, hoping to productively channel the activities of "relic hunters." There were successes but results overall were mixed. Positive actions included the establishment in 1922–1923 of the Missaukee Archaeological Reserve in Michigan and the appropriation in 1922 of $50,000 by the Illinois legislature to begin the long effort to conserve the Cahokia mound group. Between 1929 and 1932, Moundville, the great Mississippian complex in western Alabama, was purchased with funds raised by public subscription and private mortgages (Peebles et al. 1981:437–438). Still, no overarching conservation ethic was established, though definite gains were made.

The 1920s also saw the beginning of new trends that would deeply influence the conduct of American archaeology for several decades. In this period the federal government accelerated planning for flood control and hydroelectric development on the nation's rivers. Archaeologists began to recognize that such activities would drown enormous numbers of archaeological sites situated in and adjacent to river valleys. The first step in "river basin salvage archaeology" seems to have been taken in 1924 when Gerard Fowke, using Smithsonian funds, salvaged sites threatened by construction of Wilson Dam at Muscle Shoals, Alabama (Lyon 1982:12). By the end of the decade Mark R. Harrington was beginning salvage archaeology of sites to be inundated by Lake Mead, soon to rise behind Boulder (now Hoover) Dam on the lower Colorado River (Shutler 1961). These activities set the stage for the much larger scale developments in river basin salvage archaeology of the 1930s and later decades.

The 1930s was a truly remarkable time in American archaeology. The onset of the Depression was a boon for archaeology in many respects. The New Deal make-work agencies needed to put lots of laborers to work in a hurry. Archaeology was made to order for the task, as its equipment costs were minimal, and money could be spent largely on labor. Bright young archaeologists suddenly found themselves in charge of crews of 100 or more (Setzler and Strong 1936:301). The history of 1930s "WPA and TVA Archaeology" is amply chronicled elsewhere (Fagette 1983; Haag 1985; Lyon 1982; Marlowe 1983); it is useful here to examine other developments during the 1930s relating to efforts at archaeological conservation.

Under a 1933 reorganization of the federal government, the National Park Service assumed control of all national monuments, most national battlefields, and other historic places owned by the government. It also assumed new responsibilities for archaeological conservation (Kelly 1940). In 1935 Congress passed the Historic Sites Act (U.S. Code 1984e), the cornerstone of the federal preservation "system." The Act made historic preservation and archaeological conservation a matter of federal policy and designated the National Park Service as the primary agency for implementation of that policy (Fowler 1982:5–6). Over the next decade, the Park Service, federal development agencies, and professional archaeologists worked out the basic tripartite partnership that was to guide the post-World War II River Basin Survey program (Jennings 1985:282–283) and that continues to structure "contract archaeology" nearly a half-century later.

The 1930s was a time of great increased efforts to conserve archaeological resources, though focused on specific sites and localities. The successful effort to purchase and conserve the Moundville complex in

Alabama was mentioned previously. Other such examples in the 1930s included two developments in Indiana. In 1930 the Adena-Hopewell earthworks at Anderson, Indiana, were acquired by the Madison County Commissioners and turned over to the state, becoming Mounds State Park (Beuhrig and Hicks 1983:37; Lilly 1937:37). Also in Indiana, the pharmaceuticals manufacturer Eli Lilly became increasingly interested in antiquities after 1930. He provided funding and long-time support for the Indiana Historical Society, purchased the Angel Mounds, and supported the work of Glenn Black there for many years (Black 1967; Griffin 1971; Lilly 1937; Ruegamer 1981:262–297). Lilly's interest in and support for archaeology continued over the next five decades. In other states archaeological conservation took other paths. For example, in North Carolina a state archaeological society was established in 1933 and worked with the University of North Carolina on a statewide survey. The Society helped secure passage of an "Indian Antiquities Act" in the 1935 legislature. Clearly mindful of the "taking issue" relating to private property, discussed above, the original statute (State of North Carolina 1981) forbade improper excavation on public lands, but only "urged" private landowners to engage in archaeological conservation in concert with the state. The state bought the Frutchey Mound site in 1937 to insure its conservation (Wauchope 1941:1, 4); the site is now Town Creek Indian Mound State Historic Site (Burke 1983:1).

One further example of what can be accomplished by concerted cooperation between amateur and professional archaeologists is that which is established in Missouri. The Missouri Archaeological Society was founded in 1934 and remains one of the most active in the country, stimulated especially through the work of the late Henry W. Hamilton and Carl H. Chapman. The Society's first major conservation effort was the "Old Fort," a rare Hopewellian ceremonial complex in central Missouri (Chapman 1948:4) acquired for protection by the state in 1937–1938 (Berry 1939:3–5). Subsequently the Society, in cooperation with the University of Missouri developed a long-range statewide program of survey and excavation (Chapman 1955, 1985). There are a few states where the cause of archaeological conservation and study and citizen involvement therein is taken quite seriously. Missouri is in the vanguard of such states.

The final development of note during the 1930s was, of course, the founding of the Society for American Archaeology. Thirty-one persons signed the charter of the Society late in the evening of December 28, 1934 (McKern 1935:146). Among the Society's original objectives were "the conservation of archaeological data and the elimination of the commercialization of archaeological objects" (Griffin 1985:263). Stating objectives, however, does not in itself make them realities. There remained the problem of establishing a conservation ethic in the mind of the public and trying to bring about effective means of achieving conservation. The salvage programs in the river basin offered one means of conservation, as understood in 1935, that is, the conservation of knowledge through the proper excavation of sites and publishing the results. It was to remain the principal means of conservation, outside specifically protected areas, for years to come. The federal-professional partnership solidified and did provide the beginnings of an organizational framework to work more effectively toward conservation, but a number of steps remain to be taken. Professional thinking about archaeological conservation at the end of the 1930s is perhaps best summarized by a subcommittee report of the National Research Council Statewide Survey Committee, chaired by W. Duncan Strong (Marlowe 1983:1). The report (Guthe 1939) is a comprehensive yet pragmatic guide for the conduct of archaeological projects. It can still be read with profit in courses on archaeological method. The report concludes with an eloquent plea for archaeological conservation (Guthe 1939:529).

> Not only should each site opened be excavated with the greatest care, the material completely studied, and the results fully published, but also certain sites in every area should be fully preserved for research in the future as new techniques are developed. . . . [Conservation] activities should extend from the National Park Service . . . to the State Historical Societies and municipalities. They will advance the growth of national consciousness as well as scientific progress, and should receive every encouragement.

By late 1944, as the efforts of World War II began to wind down, government planners began dusting off war-shelved plans and formulating new ones. Between 1945 and 1950 as these plans began to be implemented, it was clear that the American landscape and city- and town-scapes were undergoing radical transformations. Urban renewal, the interstate highway system, long-distance gas and oil pipelines, and water control projects of all sizes were underway or about to be implemented. Concern over urban renewal and its devastating impacts on the built environment led to the chartering of the National Trust for Historic Preservation in 1949 (Mulloy 1976:3–88). The major problem facing archaeologists was the water control projects planned for the Missouri, Colorado, Columbia, and Tennessee basins. Some 108 projects were planned for the Missouri basin alone. The Basic Needs Committee and the Planning Committee of the SAA began working on the problem in late 1944 (Roberts 1955:7; Johnson 1951; Brew 1947, 1961; Jennings 1985:281–282). It was agreed that the most effective way for the archaeological profession to influence the course of government planning for, and funding of, "emergency" archaeology was through an independent committee. The Committee for the Recovery of Archaeological Remains (CRAR), sponsored by the SAA, the American Anthropological Association, and the American Council of Learned Societies, began work in 1945 (Marlowe 1983; Brew et al. 1958; Brew 1961:3). What emerged was the River Basin Survey program in which the key players were CRAR, professionals in universities and museums, the Smithsonian Institution, the National Park Service (principally through the Interagency Archaeological Salvage Program), and the federal construction agencies, the Bureau of Reclamation, the Corps of Engineers, and others (Brew 1947, 1961; Roberts 1955; Jennings 1985).

Soon, archaeologists were also forced to grapple with problems of archaeological salvage along highways and pipeline rights-of-way (Wendorf 1954–1957, 1956) as well. Throughout this period, we see the continued expansion of the "conservation through salvage" ethic implemented in advance of land-altering projects that had its roots in the 1920s (Jennings 1985). This ethic is best reflected in the title of a paper by J. O. Brew (1961), "Emergency Archaeology: Salvage in Advance of Technological Progress." To proponents of a different conservation ethic 15 years later, "salvage" was a pejorative term (Fowler 1982:3). But such an attitude reflects the philosophy of "presentism": projecting current attitudes and values into the past (Stocking 1965). Those of us who worked in the Glen Canyon (Jennings 1966) between 1957 and 1963, including William Lipe and Alexander Lindsay, Jr. (who would later play key roles in the development of the present day conservation ethic [Lipe 1974; Lipe and Lindsay 1974]), were saddened that the archaeological sites in the canyons would be (and were) drowned beneath the waters of Lake Powell. Although we had no thoughts of flinging ourselves in front of cement buckets at the Glen Canyon Dam to stop construction, neither did anyone else at the Navajo Project in New Mexico or in the Missouri River Basin. Why? *Zeitgeist:* the spirit of the times was still "Technological Progress." Archaeological conservation then meant, as it had in the 1930s and '40s, conservation of knowledge through salvage rather than by conserving the sites intact for the future (Reaves 1974:5).

By 1970–1971, archaeologists began to be caught up in the emerging "environmental movement." Although the roots of the movement were at least a century old, as we have seen (Glacken 1956), now the movement became increasingly urgent; the times began to be perceived as perilous. Urban renewal was creating more blight than it cured in many cities; lakes and rivers caught on fire; interstate highways generated congestion and smog; air was still free, but often not breatheable; pesticides threatened fragile ecosystems; the Bureau of Reclamation, yet again, proposed to drown the Grand Canyon; and "Spaceship Earth," seen from the moon, suddenly was both a grand, yet very small and finite speck of matter in space. The term "cultural resources" began to be used to describe archaeological sites, recognizing that sites, like other nonrenewable earth resources, were in danger of being forever destroyed, hence, worthy of protection and conservation (Davis 1972). The age-old idea of stewardship of the earth and its resources, always part of the Western tradition but often ignored (Glacken 1967), came again to the forefront. There was a concerted effort to shift the direction of public thinking about the environment back into stewardship channels, symbolized best in the language and procedures of the 1969 National Environmental Policy Act (NEPA) (U.S. Code 1984g), and, for cultural resources, in the 1966 Historic Preservation Act (U.S. Code 1984f). In 1972 Hester Davis (1972) declared that accelerating destruction of archaeological sites had produced a state of "crisis." In 1973 in Fayetteville, Arkansas, and in 1974 in Denver, Colorado (Lipe and Lindsay 1974), federal, contract, and academic archaeologists met to grapple with the complexities of the emerging federal "preservation system" (McGimsey 1972; King et al. 1977:65–83; Fowler 1982:4–29). A few months after the Denver conclave the Airlie House seminars (McGimsey and Davis 1977) were held, setting forth a framework for the conduct of "Cultural Resources Management" (Fowler 1982).

The National Environmental Policy Act (U.S. Code 1984g) presented planners and developers with a startling set of directives: do more than simply calculate cost/benefit ratios for your "undertakings"; consider all alternatives, including project redesign, to *avoid* important natural and cultural resources; think seriously about whether or not the project is really needed at all; if it is, plan ways to "mitigate" "adverse impacts" that will affect resource integrity. How to implement these directives vis-à-vis cultural resources was the concern of many papers published after 1974 in the American Society for Conservation Archaeology *Newsletter* and *Reports,* and latterly in *Contract Abstracts and CRM Archeology* and its successor *American Archeology.* Lipe's (1974) "conservation model" reflects the stewardship concept behind the NEPA directives: "treat salvage, especially of the emergency kind, as the last resort—to be undertaken only after all other avenues of protecting the resource have failed." As indicated at the outset of this paper, I don't think Lipe's "model" is a conservation ethic; it is, rather, a policy or a procedure that should flow from an ethic. It is a matter of equivocation whether attempts to implement this policy have worked. Well-intentioned conservation-oriented "noncollection" procedures leave artifacts in place to be picked up by looters; Flags marking sites are smashed beneath heavy equipment treads, together with the sites they are set out to protect. And, more often than not, salvage is a cheaper form of mitigation than avoidance and long-range protection (Fitting 1982:184–188). Deliberate looting of artifacts for money has also accelerated, despite passage of the 1979 Archaeological Resources Protection Act (U.S. Code 1984h), encouraged by the illicit activities of prominent soap opera stars, professional football players, and country-western singers, as reported in national magazines. One is almost forced to conclude that site destruction, like the poor, will always be with us.

We return then to our starting point. In the best of all possible archaeological worlds, all sites would be kept intact by an enlightened public and its representatives until carefully and properly disassembled by trained archaeologists, and the knowledge gained thereby passed on to scholars and the eager, curious, appreciative enlightened public. But such a Panglossian vision has only been rarely achieved. Since 1820 American archaeologists have watched, in increasing despair, as looting, the elements, and the "levelling hand of Progress" have despoiled thousands of archaeological sites. Conservation has worked through the creation on public lands of archaeological reservations, monuments, and parks. On private lands conservation has been primarily through purchase, beginning in 1883 and continuing down to the present efforts of the Archaeological Conservancy. There are, and have been, practitioners of an archaeological conservation ethic. The complex ramifications of implementing such an ethic in present-day United States have recently been explored by professionals (Green 1984; Schiffer and Gumerman 1977); but we have yet to achieve a real and lasting national conscience about the need for conservation. Why is there such public indifference, despite legislation and public education programs? The deeply held American opposition to anything standing in the way of "Progress," i.e., making money, is one part of the answer. But I think there are other deep reasons as well. I think the crux of the matter is implicit in a statement in Neil Judd's (1929:404) paper:

> The United States is the only major power in the world, perhaps the only American republic, that does not reserve in behalf of its nationals a prior right to all material records of its prehistoric past, wherever and however found. It will surprise many to learn that Mexico, in proportion to national wealth, leads the world in Federal effort toward the conservation, and investigation, of her archaeological heritage. In marked contrast, we of the United States ... make a very feeble gesture indeed toward preservation of such aboriginal works as have survived from pre-Colonial days.

Judd went on to wonder why, but gave no answer. I think the answer is because the prehistory of Mexico has been made the prehistory of all the Mexican people. Jacques Lafaye (1976) has brilliantly shown how both pre-Hispanic and Hispanic cultures, Mexico's two pasts, symbolized by the Plumed Serpent and the Sainted Virgin, *Quetzalcoatl* and *Guadelupe,* have been syncretized and integrated within Mexican nationalistic ideology over the past 300 years. The great National Anthropology Museum in Mexico City is a triumphal monument to the Mexican people, their cultures, and their syncretized past. Prehistory and history do not mean, symbolically, what they mean in the United States. Here, prehistory is the past of Native Americans, not Euroamericans. There has been no syncretism; no amalgamation of these pasts. Rather there has been, and remains, separation and ambivalence. The ambivalence is reflected in art and literature (Billington 1981; Dahl 1961; Dickason 1984; Honour 1975; Mitchell 1981) and in other intellectual constructs, including reconstructions of Indians' pasts (Fowler 1983; Gero 1985). The ambivalence is symbolized also by the fact that, since the 19th century, things Indian have been placed in museums of natural history. Artifacts are considered to be scientific specimens, not humanistic documents. Only latterly have they become works of art. This separation is further symbolized by the fact that even today contemporary Indian art works are shown in the Smithsonian Natural History Museum; contemporary Euroamerican art is shown in the Hirshhorn. No matter how scientifically and educationally useful are the "Indian halls" of the great natural history museums of Washington, New York, Chicago, Denver, Los Angeles, and elsewhere (and they *are* very useful to Indians and non-Indians alike), they are not comparable in their purposes nor symbolism to the Mexico City Museum, or the museums of other countries that celebrate nationalistic ideas and aspirations. The true museological equivalents of Mexico City's masterpiece are the museums of American History and Air and Space at the Smithsonian, and Colonial Williamsburg and Henry Ford's museum at Dearborn, Michigan. *They* celebrate American national ideology and aspiration.

Elsewhere, I and others (Fowler 1983; Trigger 1984; see also the papers in Cleere 1984) have discussed uses of the past by nation states for ideological and chauvinistic purposes. Where such uses are positive, as in Mexico, they result in such things as Mexico's great museum. Where they are negative, other results accrue. In 19th century United States, mythical pasts about Toltecs, Aztecs, and Mound Builders covertly at least supported denigration of American Indians and the imperialistic ideology of Euroamerican expansion at Indian expense. It took archaeologists a long time to disprove these myths. However, Indian pasts and Euroamerican pasts remain separate. There are, I think, two major reasons for this continued separation. One is that professional archaeologists communicate in print primarily with each other (Sabloff 1985:231–232) and much less often with the general public. The second is that in the United States the prehistoric past is not integrated with the Euroamerican past, in part because Native Americans are not in the mainstream of the American sociopolitical system, as they are in Mexico. Hence, making a case for conservation of the prehistoric past, when that past is publically perceived as "quaint" and "curious" rather than a matter of roots, is difficult.

Archaeologists, and many others, take a broader view, centering on the concept that *all* cultural traditions, all pasts, have equal validity. On some levels, the United States does celebrate and honor its many rich and diverse ethnic heritages. But most people and most politicians regard themselves as members of a specific ethnic group, or social class. *Their* past is *their* roots. Other's pasts are interesting, curious, possibly fascinating, but not something to abrogate the sacredness of private property for, nor even necessarily a reason to obey laws protecting cultural resources, for and of all the people, on public lands. It has not yet been made a matter of conscience.

Even preservation of historic sites and buildings, places that *are* part of the Euroamerican past, has become a matter of conscience only for a minority, albeit a larger minority than those committed to preserving the Native American past. Historic preservationists have been most successful only when they can demonstrate, or develop legal tools to allow, preservation to become a matter of economic gain.

Can we, in fact, achieve a true archaeological conservation ethic and make it truly effective in the country? We've tried, hard, for over a century. We have won some and we have lost some. Given the present high visibility of archaeology, a set of federal laws (U.S. Code, 1984d-i) undreampt of by Cole and Judd, and an established concern for preservation of all our cultural resources, we have an unparalleled opportunity. We also have a professional and human obligation to continue to use all the means at our disposal to achieve such an ethic by continuing and expanding the work begun by our predecessors a century ago.

Acknowledgments

Several colleagues kindly provided information for this paper, including Thomas D. Burke, Carl H. Chapman, Hester Davis, Calvin Cummings, Dena Dincauze, Kathleen Gilmore, Jacob W. Gruber, Alfred E. Johnson, William Johnson, Roger E. Kelly, Kristian Kristiansen, Cheryl Ann Munson, Robert W. Neuman, Nan Rothschild, Vincas Steponaitus, David Watters, Fred Wendorf, and J. Ned Woodall. Carl Chapman, Carol Condie, Hester Davis, Jesse D. Jennings and Cheryl Munson offered valuable critiques of an earlier version of the paper. My thanks to all; errors of omission and commission remain my responsibility.

Literature Cited

Ames, O., J. G. Whittier, M. Hemenway, *et al.*
   1889   Memorial of Oliver Ames, John G. Whittier, Mary Hemenway, and Others, Praying Legislation for the Protection from Destruction of the Ancient Ruin of the Temple Casa Grande, Situated in Pinal County, near Florence, Arizona. *Congressional Record, 50th Congress, 2nd Session*, page 1454. [Also *Senate Miscellaneous Document 60.*]

Atwater, C.
   1820   Description of the Antiquities Discovered in the State of Ohio and Other Western States. *Transactions and Collections of the American Antiquarian Society* 1:105–267.

Bandelier, A. F.
   1883   Report on the Ruins of the Pueblo of Pecos. *Papers of the Archaeological Institute of America: American Series* I. Boston.

Barber, L.
   1980   *The Heyday of Natural History, 1820–1870.* Doubleday & Company, Inc., Garden City.

Berry, B.
   1939   The "Old Fort" in Saline County. *The Missouri Archaeologist* 5(1):3–5.

Beuhrig, J. E., and R. Hicks
   1983   A Comprehensive Survey of the Archaeological Resources of Mounds State Park, Anderson Indiana, with a Proposed Resources Management Plan. *Ball State University Archaeological Resources Management Services, Reports of Investigations 6.*

Billington, R. A.
   1981   *Land of Savagery, Land of Promise: The European Image of the American Frontier in the 19th Century.* W.W. Norton & Co., New York.

Black, G. A.
   1967   *Angel Site: An Archaeological, Historical, and Ethnological Study.* 2 volumes. Indiana Historical Society, Indianapolis.

Bosselman, F., D. Cullies, and J. Branta
   1973   *The Taking Issue: An Analysis of the Constitutional Limits of Land Use Control.* Council on Environmental Quality, Washington, D. C.

Brandes, R.
   1965   Frank Hamilton Cushing: Pioneer Americanist. Doctoral dissertation, University of Arizona, Tucson.

Brew, J. O.
   1947   Symposium on River Valley Archaeology. *American Antiquity* 12:209–225.
   1961   Emergency Archaeology: Salvage in Advance of Technological Progress. *American Philosophical Society Proceedings* 105(1):1–10.

Burke, T. D.
   1983   Reflections on a Decade of North Carolina's State Archaeology Program. Paper on file, North Carolina Division of Archives and History, Raleigh, N.C.

Chapman, C. H.
   1948   Archaeological Survey of Missouri. *The Missouri Archaeological Society News Letter* 19:2–4.
   1955   Retrospect and Prospect. *Missouri Archaeological Society News Letter* 88:1–2.
   1985   The Amateur Archaeological Society: A Missouri Example. *American Antiquity* 50:241–248.

Chauvent, B.
   1983   *Hewett and Friends: A Biography of Santa Fe's Vibrant Era.* Museum of New Mexico Press, Santa Fe.

Cleere, H. (editor)
   1984   *Approaches to the Archaeological Heritage: A Comparative Study of World Cultural Resource Management Systems.* Cambridge University Press, Cambridge.

Cole, Fay-Cooper
1929   The Conservation of Public Sites. *In* National Research Council, Report of the Conference on Midwestern Archaeology, Held in St. Louis, Missouri, May 18, 1929. *National Research Council Bulletin* 74:11–15.

Dahl, C.
1961   Mound-Builders, Mormons, and William Cullen Bryant. *The New England Quarterly* 34(2):178–190.

Davis, H.
1972   The Crisis in American Archaeology. *Science* 176:267–272.

Dexter, R. W.
1965   Contributions of Frederic Ward Putnam to Ohio Archaeology. *Ohio Journal of Science* 65(3):110–117.

Dickason, O. P.
1984   *The Myth of the Savage and the Beginnings of French Colonialism in the Americas.* University of Alberta Press, Edmonton.

Fagette, Paul H., Jr.
1983   New Deal Archaeology: The Impact of the New Deal Relief Programs on Archaeology, 1933–1942. Paper presented at the Pacific Coast Branch, American Historical Association, San Diego, California, August 1983.

Fewkes, J. W.
1912   Casa Grande, Arizona. *Twenty-eighth Annual Report of the Bureau of American Ethnology,* pages 25–179.

Fitting, J. E.
1982   The Status of Rescue Archeology in North America. In *Rescue Archaeology: Papers from the First New World Conference on Rescue Archaeology,* edited by R.L. Wilson and G. Loyola, pages 173–190. The Preservation Press, Washington, D. C.

Fletcher, A., and T. E. Stevenson
1888   *Report of the Committee on the Preservation of Archaeologic Remains on the Public Lands Presented to the Council of the American Association for the Advancement of Science August, 1888.* Separate on file Tozzer Library, Harvard University.

Fletcher, M. S. (editor)
1977   *The Wetherills of the Mesa Verde: Autobiography of Benjamin Alfred Wetherill.* Fairleigh Dickinson University Press, Rutherford.

Forshey, C. G.
1845   Description of Some Artificial Mounds on Prairie Jefferson, Louisiana. *American Journal of Science and Arts* 49:38–42.

Fowler, D. D.
1975   Notes on Inquiries in Anthropology: A Bibliographic Essay. In *Toward a Science of Man: Essays in the History of Anthropology,* edited by T.H.H. Thoresen, pages 15–32. Mouton Publishers, The Hague.
1982   Cultural Resources Management. In *Advances in Archaeological Method and Theory,* edited by M.B. Schiffer, 5:1–50. Academic Press, New York.

1983 Uses of the Past: Archaeology in the Service of the State. Paper presented at the XIth International Congress of Anthropological and Ethnological Sciences, Vancouver, B. C.

Fowler, D. D., and C. S. Fowler
1969 John Wesley Powell, Anthropologist. *Utah Historical Quarterly* 37(2):152–172.

Fowler, D. D., and J. F. Matley
1978 The Palmer Collection from Southwestern Utah, 1875. *University of Utah Anthropological Papers* 99:17–42.

Glacken, C. J.
1956 The Origins of the Conservation Philosophy. *Journal of Soil and Water Conservation* 11(2):63–66.
1967 *Traces on the Rhodian Shore: Nature and Culture in Western Thought from Ancient Times to the Eighteenth Century.* University of California Press, Berkeley.

Goetzman, W. H.
1959 *Army Exploration in the American West, 1803–1863.* Yale University Press, New Haven.

Graham, F., Jr.
1971 *Man's Dominion: The Story of Conservation in America.* McGraw-Hill, New York.

Green, E. L. (editor)
1984 *Ethics and Values in Archaeology.* The Free Press, New York.

Griffin, J. B.
1971 A Commentary on an Unusual Research Program in American Anthropology. In *Glenn A. Black Laboratory of Archaeology Dedication Volume,* pages 1–6. Indiana University, Bloomington.
1985 The Formation of the Society for American Archaeology. *American Antiquity* 50:261–271.

Guthe, C.
1928–1934 Archaeological Field Work in North America, 1927–33. *American Anthropologist* 30:501–534; 31:332–360; 32:342–374; 33:283; 34:476–509; 35:483–511; 36:595–598.
1930 The Committee on State Archaeological Surveys of the Division of Anthropology and Psychology, National Research Council. In *Proceedings of the 23rd International Congress of Americanists (1928),* pages 52–59.
1935 Archaeological Field Work in North America during 1934. *American Antiquity* 1(1):47–66; 1(2):113–140.
1939 The Basic Needs of American Archeology. *Science* 90 (2345):528–530.

Haag, W. G.
1985 Federal Aid to Archaeology in the Southeast, 1933–1942. *American Antiquity* 50(2):272–280.

Haven, S. F.
1856 Archaeology of the United States, or, Sketches Historical and Bibliographical, of the Progress of Information and Opinion Respecting Ves-

tiges of Antiquity in the United States. *Smithsonian Contributions to Knowledge* 8:1–159.

Hewett, E. L.
1906 Preservation of American Antiquities: Progress during the Past Year; Needed Legislation. *American Anthropologist* 8:109–114.

Hinsley, C. M., Jr.
1981 *Savages and Scientists: The Smithsonian Institution and the Development of American Anthropology, 1846–1910.* Smithsonian Institution Press, Washington, D. C.

Holmes, W. H.
1876 A Notice of the Ancient Ruins of Southwestern Colorado, examined during the Summer of 1875. *Bulletin of the United States Geological and Geographical Survey of the Territories,* volume 2 (Bulletin 1):3–24.

Honour, H.
1975 *The New Golden Land: European Images of America from the Discoveries to the Present Time.* Pantheon Books, New York.

Hosmer, C. R., Jr.
1965 *Presence of the Past.* Putnam, New York.

Jackson, W. H.
1875 Ancient Ruins in Southwestern Colorado. *Bulletin of the United States Geological and Geographical Survey of the Territories* volume 1 (Bulletin 1, 2nd series):17–38.

Jefferson, T.
1944 [1784] Notes on the State of Virginia. In *The Life and Selected Writings of Thomas Jefferson,* edited by Adrienne Koch and William Peden, pages 187–288. The Modern Library, New York.

Jennings, J. D.
1966 Glen Canyon: A Summary. *University of Utah Anthropological Papers* 81 (Glen Canyon Series 31).
1985 River Basin Surveys: Origins, Operations, and Results, 1945–1969. *American Antiquity* 50(2):281–296.

Johnson, Frederick
1951 *The Inter-Agency Archaeological Salvage Program in the United States.* Committee for the Recovery of Archaeological Remains, Washington, D. C.

Judd, N. M.
1924 Report on Illegal Excavations in Southwestern Ruins. *American Anthropologist* 226(4):428–432.
1929 The Present Status of Archaeology in the United States. *American Anthropologist* 31(4):401–418.

Kelly, A. R.
1940 Archaeology in the National Park Service. *American Antiquity* 5(4):274–282.

Kidder, A. V.
1925a Notes on State Archaeological Surveys during 1924. *American Anthropologist* 27:581–587.

1925b Anthropological Work of Museums and Other Institutions during 1924. *American Anthropologist* 27:587–597.
1926 Archaeological Work by State Agencies in 1925. *American Anthropologist* 28:679–694.

King, T. F., P. P. Hickman, and G. Berg
1977 *Anthropology in Historic Preservation: Caring for Culture's Clutter.* Academic Press, New York.

Lafaye, J.
1976 *Quetzacoatl and Guadalupe: The Formation of Mexican National Consciousness, 1531–1813.* University of Chicago Press, Chicago.

Lange, C. H., and C. L. Riley (editors)
1966 *The Southwestern Journals of Adolph E. Bandelier.* Volume 1 (1880–1882). University of New Mexico Press, Albuquerque, School of American Research and Museum of New Mexico Press, Santa Fe.

Lange, C. H., C. L. Riley, and E. M. Lange (editors)
1970–1975 *The Southwestern Journals of Adolph F. Bandelier.* Volume 2 (1883–1884); volume 3 (1885–1888). University of New Mexico Press, Albuquerque; School of American Research and Museum of New Mexico Press, Santa Fe.

Lee, R. F.
1970 *The Antiquities Act of 1906.* U.S. Department of the Interior, National Park Service, Washington, D. C.

Lilly, E.
1937 *Prehistoric Antiquities of Indiana.* Indiana Historical Society, Indianapolis.

Lipe, W. D.
1974 A Conservation Model for American Archaeology. *The Kiva* 39:213–245.

Lipe, W. D., and A. J. Lindsay, Jr. (editors)
1974 Proceedings of the 1974 Cultural Resource Management Conference, Federal Center, Denver, Colorado. *Museum of Northern Arizona, Technical Series* 14.

Lyon II, E. A.
1982 New Deal Archaeology in the Southeast: WPA, TVA, NPS, 1934–1942. Doctoral dissertation, Louisiana State University.

Lyon, P. J.
1969 Anthropological Activity in the United States, 1865–1879. *Kroeber Anthropological Society Papers* 40:8–37.

Mark, J.
1980 *Four Anthropologists: An American Science in Its Early Years.* Science History Publications, New York.

Marlowe, Greg
1983 Preservation and Profession in American Archaeology: From "Basic Needs" to the Committee for the Recovery of Archaeological Remains. Paper presented at the Pacific Coast Branch, American Historical Association San Diego, California, August, 1983.

McConnell, G.
1954 The Conservation Movement—Past and Present. *Western Political Quarterly* 7:463–478.

McGimsey III, C. R.
1972 *Public Archeology.* Seminar Press, New York and London.

McGimsey III, C. R., and J. H. Davis (editors)
1977 *The Management of Archeological Resources: The Airlie House Report.* Society for American Archaeology Special Publication, Washington, D. C.

McKern, W. C. (editor)
1935 The Society for American Archaeology Organization Meeting [and] the Constitution and By-Laws and Rules of Procedure of the Society. *American Antiquity* 1(2):141–151.

McNitt, F.
1966 *Richard Wetherill, Anasazi: Pioneer Explorer of Southwestern Ruins.* Revised edition. University of New Mexico Press, Albuquerque.

McVaugh, R.
1956 *Edward Palmer: Plant Explorer of the American West.* University of Oklahoma Press, Norman.

Meltzer, D. J.
1985 North American Archaeology and Archaeologists, 1879–1934. *American Antiquity* 50:349–360.

Mills, W. C.
1922 Exploration of the Mound City Group, Ross County, Ohio. *American Anthropologist* 24:397–431.

Mindeleff, C.
1897 The Repair of Casa Grande Ruin, Arizona, in 1891. *Fifteenth Annual Report of the Bureau of Ethnology,* 1893–94, pages 315–349.

Mitchell, L. C.
1981 *Witnesses to a Vanishing America: The Nineteenth Century Response.* Princeton University Press, Princeton.

Mulloy, E. D.
1976 *The History of the National Trust for Historic Preservation, 1963–1973.* The Preservation Press, Washington, D.C.

Nordenskiöld, G.
1893 *The Cliff Dwellers of the Mesa Verde.* P.A. Thorstedt & Sonen, Stockholm.

Peebles, C. S., M. J. Schoeninger, V. P. Steponaitus, and C. M. Scarry
1981 A Precious Bequest: Contemporary Research with the WPA-CCC Collections from Moundsville, Alabama. *In* The Research Potential of Anthropological Museum Collections, edited by A-M. Cantwell, J. B. Griffin, and N. A. Rothschild. *Annals of the New York Academy of Sciences* 376:433–447.

Powell, J. W.
1881 Report of the Director. *First Annual Report of the Bureau of Ethnology,* pages xi-xxxiii.

Putnam, F. W.
   1879 Archaeology. *U.S. Geographical Survey West of the 100th Meridian, Report.* Volume 7. Washington.
   1890 The Serpent Mound of Ohio. *Century Magazine* (April):871–888.

Reaves, R. W., II
   1974 Conservation: The New Imperative for American Archeology. Manuscript on file, National Park Service, Federal Center, Denver, CO.

Roberts, F.H.H., Jr.
   1955 The Inter-Agency Archaeological and Paleontological Salvage Program. *Missouri Archaeological Society News Letter* 96:7–10.

Ronda, J. P.
   1984 *Lewis & Clark among the Indians.* University of Nebraska Press, Lincoln.

Ruegamer, L.
   1981 *A History of the Indiana Historical Society, 1830–1980.* Indiana Historical Society, Indianapolis.

Sabloff, J. A.
   1985 American Antiquity's First Fifty Years: An Introductory Comment. *American Antiquity* 50:228–236.

Schiffer, M. B., and G. Gumerman (editors)
   1977 *Conservation Archaeology.* Academic Press, New York.

Setzler, F. M., and W. D. Strong
   1936 Archaeology and Relief. *American Antiquity* 1(4):301–309.

Shutler, R., Jr.
   1961 Lost City: Pueblo Grande de Nevada. *Nevada State Museum Anthropological Papers* 5.

Simpson, J. H.
   1964 *Navaho Expedition: Journal of a Military Reconnaissance from Santa Fe, New Mexico to the Navaho Country Made in 1849.* University of Oklahoma Press, Norman.

Spier, L.
   1931 N.C. Nelson's Stratigraphic Technique in the Reconstruction of Prehistoric Sequences in Southwestern America. In *Methods in Social Science,* edited by S. A. Rice, pages 275–283. University of Chicago Press, Chicago.

Squier, E. G., and E. H. Davis
   1848 Ancient Monuments of the Mississippi Valley Comprising the Results of Extensive Original Surveys and Explorations. *Smithsonian Contributions to Knowledge* 1.

State of North Carolina
   1981 Indian Antiquities, Archaeological Resources and Unmarked Human Skeletal Remains Protection. *General Statutes of North Carolina* 70:5–40.

Stocking, G. W., Jr.
   1965 On the Limits of "Presentism" and "Historicism" in the Historiography of the Behavioral Sciences. *Journal of the History of the Behavioral Sciences* 1:211–218.

Sullivan, T. A. (compiler)
  1947 *Proclamations and Orders Relating to the National Park Service Up to January 1, 1945.* U.S. Department of the Interior, Washington, D. C.

Thomas, C.
  1894 Report on the Mound Explorations of the Bureau of Ethnology. *Twelfth Annual Report of the Bureau of Ethnology, 1890–91,* pages 3–730.

Trigger, B. G.
  1984 Alternative Archaeologies: Nationalist, Colonialist, Imperialist. *Man,* new series, 19(3):355–370.

United States Code
  1984a *An Act to Set Apart a Certain Tract of Land near the Headwaters of the Yellowstone River as a Public Park, 1887*2. Title 16, Section 21 (17 Statute 32–33).
  1984b *An Act to Authorize Condemnation of Lands for Sites of Public Buildings and for Other Purposes, 1888.* Title 40, Section 258 (25 Statute 357).
  1984c *Repair of the Ruin of Casa Grande, Arizona, 1889.* Title 16, Section 431n (25 Statute 961).
  1984d *An Act for the Preservation of American Antiquities, 1906.* Title 16, Sections 461–467 (Public Law 59–209, 34 Statute 666).
  1984e *Historic Sites, Buildings, and Antiquities Act, 1935.* Title 16, Section 461–67 (Public Law 74–292; 49 Statute 666).
  1984f *National Historic Preservation Act, 1966.* Title 16, Section 470 (Public Law 89–665; 80 Statute 915).
  1984g *National Environmental Policy Act, 1969.* Title 42, Section 4321 et seq. (Public Law 91–190; 83 Statute 852).
  1984h *Archaeological Resources Protection Act, 1979.* Title 16, Section 470aa–el. (Public Law 96–95; 93 Statute 728).
  1984i *National Historic Preservation Act Amendments of 1980.* Title 16, Section 470 (Public Law 96–515; 94 Statute 2987).

United States Supreme Court
  1896 *United States vs. Gettysburg Electric Railway Company.* 16 U.S. 668 ff. (1896).

Van Hise, C. R.
  1921 History of the Conservation Movement. In *The Conservation of Natural Resources in the United States,* pages 2–14. Macmillan Co., New York.

Van Valkenburgh, S.
  1962 The Casa Grande of Arizona as a Landmark on the Desert, a Governmental Reservation and a National Monument. *The Kiva* 27(3):1–31.

Walker, E. S.
  1955 *The Great Reconnaissance: Soldiers, Artists and Scientists on the Frontier, 1848–1861.* Little Brown & Co., Boston.

Wauchope, R. (editor)
  1941 Frutchey Mound Excavations. *Archaeological Society of North Carolina Newsletter* 6(January):1, 4.

Wendorf, F. (editor)
  1954–1957 *Highway Salvage Archaeology.* 3 volumes. New Mexico State Highway Department and Museum of New Mexico, Santa Fe.

1956 *Pipeline Archaeology; Reports of Salvage Operations in the Southwest on El Paso National Gas Company Project, 1950–53.* Laboratory of Anthropology, Santa Fe; Museum of Northern Arizona, Flagstaff.

Wilder, M. P., and E. F. Slafter
1882 Petition to the U.S. Congress. *Congressional Record, 47th Congress, 1st Session (1882)*, page 3777.

Willey, G. R.
1968 One Hundred Years of American Archaeology. In *One Hundred Years of Anthropology*, edited by J. O. Brew, pages 29–53. Harvard University Press, Cambridge.

Wissler, C.
1920 Opportunities for Coordination in Anthropological and Psychological Research. *American Anthropologist* 22:1–12.
1922 Notes on State Archaeological Surveys. *American Anthropologist* 24:233–242.
1923 State and Local Archaeological Surveys: Suggestions in Method and Technique, Prepared by the Chairman of the Committee on State Archaeological Surveys, Division of Anthropology & Psychology, National Research Council. *State Historical Society of Iowa, Bulletin of Information* 11. Iowa City, IO.

Archaeology, History, and Culture

Early in the winter of 1839, John Stephens, special envoy for President Van Buren, visited the extensive ruins of Copan. Seeing for the first time the monkeys high in the trees above and listening to their incessant chatter, he noted how "these mockeries of humanity . . . with the strange monuments around us . . . seemed like wandering spirits of the departed race guarding the ruins of their former habitations" (Stephens 1841:103). Later, as he sat on the edge of the monumental wall that supported the large plaza, he

> strove in vain to penetrate the mystery by which we were sur-
> rounded. Who were the people who built this city? In the ruined
> cities of Egypt, even in the long-lost Petra [which he had earlier vis-
> ited and described], the stranger knows the story of the people
> whose vestiges are around him. America, say historians, was
> peopled by savages; but savages never reared these structures, sav-
> ages never carved these stones. We asked the Indians who made
> them, and their sole answer was 'Quien sabe?' 'who knows?' There
> were no associations connected with the place; none of those stirring
> recollections which hallow Rome [and] Athens; but architecture,
> sculpture, and painting, all the arts which embellish life, had flour-
> ished in this overgrown forest; orators, warriors, and statesmen,
> beauty, ambition and glory, had lived and passed away, and none
> knew that such things had been, or could tell of their past existence.
> Books, the records of knowledge, are silent on this theme. The city
> was desolate. No remnant of the race hangs round the ruins, with
> traditions handed down from father to son, and from generation to
> generation. It lay before us like a shattered bark in the midst of the
> ocean, her masts gone, her name effaced, her crew perished, and
> none to tell whence she came, to whom she belonged, how long on

her voyage, or what caused her destruction; her lost people to be traced only by some fancied resemblance in the construction of the vessel, and, perhaps, never to be known at all. . . . All was mystery, dark, impenetrable, mystery, and every circumstance increased it [Stephens 1841:104–105].

Although Daniel Wilson was to coin the term itself a decade later and its final demonstration to wait another decade, it was of "prehistory" and the problems of its reconstruction that Stephens was thinking as he viewed, romantically, the ruins almost obliterated by the jungle. Beyond history, behind history, before history, in the absence of some contemporary record that was the base line of archaeology and the stimulus and guide for its pursuit, he was asking how to form the syntax of human behavior from the physical rubble of the lived moment? With the explosion of data that followed the discovery of prehistory early in the 1860s, with the expansion of human time which that discovery created, that problem of translation, of making the mute stones speak, became more pressing. Although there were (as in the lavishly published *Reliquiae Aquitanicae* of Lartet and Christy in 1875) attempts to contemporize the bone and stone artifacts from the Perigord caves, in general the language was limited to the prose of chronology.

In his popular and titillating history of archaeology Michaelis (1908) would write that while it was "the archaeology of the spade and its results" which were his subject, his archaeology was "the archaeology of art; . . . the products of civilization in so far as they express no artistic character . . . will only be mentioned incidentally" (Michaelis 1908:xiii). In the Americas, however, both by definition derived from a historic bias and by experience, the past was artless. Concealed by its lack of a historical base and represented for the most part only by an artifact inventory whose simplicity merely corroborated the uncivilized state of the American aborigine, the prehistoric past seemed a vast plain of savagery, whose monotony was only occasionally—and literally—relieved by monuments of art; the mounds of the Ohio Valley, for example, whose character defied explanation and whose creators seemed (and for some still seem) to have come from another world.

By the time that Samuel Haven, the librarian of the American Antiquarian Society, brought together the disparate information on America's aboriginal past in his review of the history of American archaeology a brief fifteen years after Stephens (Haven 1856), the romantic enthusiasm had been forced from a local antiquarian interest into the more precise definition of a scientific problem. It is not too much to say that Haven created a "general anthropology" out of the mass of information and misinformation, which had accumulated from the earliest European contacts, about the aboriginal inhabitants of the New World, the Indian. His "archaeology" or "ethnology"—the words themselves deceive us in the semantic mutations even into the present—sought to explore "the ethnological position and social advancement of the people by whom our soil was occupied in ages beyond the reach of history" as a necessary prerequisite to an understanding of the "customs, arts, and civil condition of those mysterious races" (Haven 1856:2). Thus the data piling up from archaeology, linguistics, craniology, and ethnography were to be synthesized in order to elucidate not only the fast-disappearing Indian but also to recreate the condition of those who had preceded him as the indigenous inhabitants of the continent. That aim—magisterial as much for its comprehensiveness as for its speculative caution—could only have been so confidently defined in that exuberant generation preceding the calamity of the Civil War, when in the first maturing of the new nation, in the fruits of its declaration of intellectual independence from the Old World, in a fervent nationalism which was pushing its interests and its peoples into the lands of the West whose promise had been trumpeted by Josiah Gregg's *Commerce of the Prairies* (Gregg 1844; Horgan 1979), all problems seemed surmountable and everything was possible.

And the Indian was central. For the new American, searching for a past upon which to build a unique present rooted in a native soil, the Indian became a significant albeit a contradictory figure. A continuing threat to territorial expansionism, he was still, as Jefferson had made him, a symbol of the particular spiritual strength which the New World had produced and which was to characterize the New Society. Savage though he was, his original nature despoiled by the worst of civilization, the idealization of his essential nobility, his strength and independence provided a tradition as well as a past for the created American as he sought an ethnic identity alongside those which Romanticism was exalting in Europe.

As Stephens pondered the meaning of his monuments submerged in the human void of the enclosing jungle, archaeology itself was experiencing a quickened excitement and heightened interest as it moved from the fantasies of the collector to the more sober and more conservative goals of the naturalist and historian. The 1840s—the "mad forties" as one historian labels the decade—saw the beginnings of a professional interest in archaeology born of a promise that a real history of humanity could be written beyond speculation. The decipherment of Egyptian hieroglyphics and the Assyrian cuneiform scripts extended literate history back into the period of Creation; and the liberation of Greece from the Turks inaugurated an investigative program that fitted well the Romantic yearnings to probe the sources of western traditions of individualism and freedom. Even more, a generation of explorers were finding in the caves and gravels of Europe the evidences for a human past far older even than the Egyptians and Assyrians who according to the Bible were as old as time itself. Closer to home, there were the accumulating evidences of the pre-European inhabitants of America.

Early on, the existence of the material remains of the aboriginal inhabitants of the continent were seen as evidences for the reconstruction of history. It was a history for which the material remains seemed the only record. That such fragments of an unknown past could form the foundation upon which a history might be built was already recognized, as the colonies and then the states and then the nation sought some form of historical validation for a newly emerging sense of identity apart from a European past. Jefferson's reading of the history of an Indian mound from its carefully scrutinized contents is well known, a part of the folk-lore of the history of American archaeology. Following the lead of an interest in local antiquities that had already led to the organization of societies for their collection and conservation in Europe, similar organizations were formed locally during the early years of the nation when the search for an intellectual independence followed rapidly the attainment of political independence. And while such organizations in both their libraries and their cabinets were catholic in their historical interests, all saw in the past of the Indian an important element for an understanding of an American history. They saw too in the Indian presence something of importance in the formation of the national character. "Our principal objects are to COLLECT and PRESERVE," noted Isaiah Thomas in the 1814 report of the recently founded American Antiquarian Society (Thomas 1820:39). While members were urged to collect "antiquities of our country, whether of nature or art," there was a particular interest in "articles of Indian fabrication . . . with some account of the place of their deposit, probable age, supposed use, and any other matter which may elucidate their history" (Fiske 1820:43). While the founders of the Society saw the preservation of materials of their own time useful for some future historian, it was the relicts of their aboriginal predecessors that were vital for a knowledge of the past. Nor were they unaware of the difficulties of the task, of achieving understanding in the face of so fragmentary a record. Commenting on the difficulty of discovering the "true character" of "uncivilized nations" in the present; that is, of realizing an cthnography, the Society's editor perceived the continuing archaeological problem: "if it be thus difficult to take the picture of the living man, what must be the labour of drawing a portrait of him from the works of his hand, which for ages have been mouldering away" (Anonymous 1820:5–6).

By the 1840s, the importance for an understanding of the history and through it of the character of the American, was receiving institutional support. As its first major publication, the newly established Smithsonian Institution published in 1848 the results of the mound researches of Squier and Davis (1848). Undoubtedly the result of the expressed concern of the Smithsonian's energetic director Joseph Henry for the preservation of the rapidly disappearing evidences of the American Indian was only the most expressive evidence of the increased awareness of a scientific responsibility. Urging the New York State regents to establish a museum for the collection and preservation of artifacts, Lewis H. Morgan wrote, also in 1848, that though "the vestiges of our Indian predecessors are very limited" a museum for their preservation was necessary. For even though it "would seem to enlarge but slightly the bounds of human knowledge, yet it would be . . . a memento of the Red Race who preceded us. If the scholar of after years should ask of our age an account of our predecessors, such a collection would be the most acceptable answer it could render. It would enable the Red Race to speak for itself through these silent memorials" (Morgan 1848a:6). And a few weeks later, in presenting his own collection to the newly established Historical and Antiquarian Collection, he (1848b:84–86) was both more perceptive and more precise in stating the importance of such "vestiges."

> Governments owe it to themselves, and to succeeding generations, to make these collections. . . . The low state of the most useful arts among them detracts greatly from the interest with which the scanty vestiges of their civilization would otherwise be invested. Such specimens as we discover are rude to the last degree in their construction, and bespeak a social condition of extreme simplicity. Still there is no condition of man, however rude, in which he is not surrounded by mementoes of his handywork. . . . Artificial contrivances are inseparable from the social state; and when these specimens of human ingenuity are brought together, they unlock the social history of the people from whom they come. In this view especially, the artificial remains of our Indian predecessors, . . . possess an intrinsic value, and should be sought out and preserved as the unwritten history of their social existence.

That is quite a statement! Morgan's enthusiasm was but a single and local expression of the romantic frenzy of the 1840s in which the Indian played a major role. For the nascent *science* of ethnology, itself a product of the bursting ethnic chauvinism, which had supplanted the universalism of the Enlightenment, America was central. As Squier noted in 1849 in his summary of the results of the new science: here alone "can we find brought in so close proximity, the representatives of races and families of men, of origins and mental constitutions so diverse; . . . upon this continent is found a grand division of the human race whose history is involved in night, and the secret of whose origin and connections affords a constant stimulus to investigations of a strictly ethnological character" (Squier 1849:386). American science, he went on to say, had a particular responsibility in making ethnology its own, since the presence of the Indian in almost an unadulterated state provides the best opportunity for the study of ethnological problems such as racial origins, the meaning of diversity, the process of racial change, and the relationship between racial type and environment. Henry Schoolcraft, already the foremost authority on the Indian, stressed the uniqueness of the Indian for an understanding of a national, a distinctly *American* character. To the New Confederacy of the Iroquois at its third annual "Council" where he spoke at Morgan's invitation on August 14, 1845, he provided the *raison d'etre* for the interests of these truly *new* Americans:

> [Your] field of inquiry is broad, [he proclaimed,] and it is to be trodden in various ways. . . . You aim at general objects and results, but pursue them, through the theme and story of that proud and noble race of the sons of the Forest, whose name, whose costume and whose principles of association you assume. . . . There is in the idea of your association, one of the elements of a peculiar and national literature. And whatever may be the degree of success, which characterizes your labors, it is hoped they will bear the impress of American heads and American hearts. We have drawn our intellectual sustenance, it is true, from noble fountains and crystal streams [of Europe]. . . . [However] it is time, in the course of our national developments, that we begin to produce something characteristic of the land that gave us birth. No people can bear a true nationality, which does not exfoliate, as it were from its bosom, something that expresses the peculiarities of its own soil and climate. In building its intellectual edifice, . . . there must come from the broad and deep quarries of its own mountains, foundation stones, and columns and capitals, which bear the impress of an indigenous mental geognosy. And where! when we survey the length and breadth of the land, can

a more suitable element for the work to be found, than is furnished by the history and antiquities and institutions and love, of the free, bold, wild, independent, native hunter race? . . . We descry, as we plough the plain, the well chipped darts which pointed their arrows, and the elongated pestles, that crushed their maze [sic]. We exhume from their obliterated and simple graves, the pipe of steatite, in which they smoked, and offered incense to those deities, and the fragments of the culinary vases, around which the lodge circle gathered to their forest meal. Mounds and trenches and ditches, speak of the movement of tribe against tribe, and dimly shadow forth the overthrow of nations. There are no plated columns of marble; no tablets of inscribed stone—no gates of rusted brass. But the MAN himself survives, in his generation. He is a WALKING STATUE before us. His looks and his gesture and his language remain. And he is himself an attractive *monument* to be studied. Shall we neglect him, and his antiquarian vestiges, to run after foreign sources of intellectual study? Shall we toil amid the ruins of Thebes and Palmyra, while we have before us the monumental enigma of an unknown race? Shall philosophical ardor expend itself, in searching after the buried sites of Nineveh, and Babylon, and Troy, while we have not attempted, with decent research, to collect, arrange and determine, the leading data of aboriginal history and antiquities? [Schoolcraft 1846:5–7]

Since the first coming of the Pilgrims early in the 17th century, the remains of these indigenes had long been recognized and sought (Wecter 1941). The search for artifacts, with their particular fascination as touchstones with the past, provided the American tradition a part of the "romance" which colored in popular imagination the activity of both the professional archaeologist as "scientist" and the amateur with his collections. Jefferson's ideal (strengthened by the romantic enthusiasms which accompanied the realization of nationhood) did not so much vanish as it was vanquished by the politics of empire and the sense of a manifest destiny which supported it. The image of the Indian so popularly expressed by Longfellow's Hiawatha and Cooper's noble savages of the forests remained impressed in memory. Savages they may have been, cruel they often were, but they were human and their virtues of nobility and independence were important components of an emerging American character. They occupied a legitimate place in the progress of humanity and a special one for the realization of the American soul. In the assumption of progress, however, it was their past that was important, for it was a discernible way-station on the inevitable road to the present. Thus, it was history that was the investigative goal; and it was to know the past, both particular and general, to feel this particular past, that the Indian was to contribute his mite.

Throughout the 19th century the Indian, living or dead, was an historical symbol. The unconcealed ideological conflicts which by mid-century underlay the arguments over the builders of the mounds or the origins of the Indians or the nature of Nature itself etch more deeply the importance of the Indian as spiritual ancestor. The historical disjunction, however, the real discontinuity between the aboriginal past and the immigrant present, between the nobility of the ideal and the corruption of the living present raised real problems in the reconstruction of the past, problems themselves that the varied speculations of aboriginal history illustrate. The lack of historical documentation at the same time, however, emphasized the importance of the artifact. It alone was unquestioned testimony to the past. Through it alone was the past something other than a mental construction. The artifact was the anchor to floating speculation and fantasy.

Whatever the disagreements over the process of history, it was clear that the material relics of the prehistoric past, which Euro-American occupation was revealing with increasing frequency, provided important (perhaps the only) clues to a past whose extent in time had hardly been realized. Everywhere, as with Stephens, their existence prompted the historical question. In his popular synthesis later in the century, Foster modestly compared himself, as he gazed "upon the works of that mysterious people known as the Mound-builders," with Gibbon who "among the ruins of the Roman capital first conceived the idea of writing the history of the decline and fall of that empire" (Foster 1873:iii).

The problem was one of method rather than goal: how to convert the artifact into historical documentation. In an expanded chronological frame for which ethnohistorical account and speculative history were the poorest of guides, how to give tongue to artifactual fragment.

The living Indian, in the guise of an idealized "savage" occupied a special niche in the course of history. Linked to the exotic savages beyond the world of the European tradition, their ways of life—and they themselves as "living fossils" like the elephant and rhinoceros—were seen as a part of nature, and as such, to be studied as natural history rather than as art. As products of nature, they served, like their analogs in geology and palaeontology, as the keys to unlock the gates to the long unrecorded history of humanity, a universal history of continuing progress.

Both an institutionalized and professionalized natural history and geology thus seemed quite naturally to provide the methodological guides, as they set the limits of the investigative problem for the interpretation of the artifactual evidence. Unlike the development of a traditional archaeology in Europe whose methodology and goal were drawn from what we may loosely term the "humanities," those of the newly emerging prehistoric archaeology were an exfoliation of the natural sciences and, in particular, of geology (Grayson 1983; Gruber 1965). In America particularly, the assumption of the Indian as a "man of nature" categorized studies of him as a part of natural history. In the instructions to the naturalists accompanying the succession of government-sponsored explorations to the West beginning with that of Lewis and Clark in 1803, those for the collection of information on the Indian were always included with the schedules for the gathering of data on zoology, botany, and geology. It was naturalists, like Jeffries Wyman, for example, who initiated the reasonably controlled excavations for the contextual recovery of artifacts.

What such a methodological bias meant, of course, was that the problems that had been defined within natural history and geology were those which were unquestionably carried over to the extant fragments of aboriginal behavior (past and present), which could be collected and physically preserved.

"Natural history" had as its initial goal a holistic description of particular (and presumably historically unrelated) organic forms in what today we might refer to as their ecological and behavioral context. In the post-Linnean zeal for a classificatory system, which might somehow reproduce the order of Creation, the emphasis had been shifted toward increasingly precise descriptions of the organic and classificatory typologies as abstractions from living complexity. The investigative locus had shifted from field observations and collections by the naturalist to the description and classification in the "laboratory" by the professional botanist or zoologist. The result if not indeed the goal was to recreate the hierarchical "scale of nature" which, naively ethnocentric, imposed a particular logic upon what was assumed to be the divine design of Creation. For example, as popular and perceptive as was Darwin's *Journal* as "natural history," it was his painstaking study of the barnacles that was considered by his colleagues to be his most important scientific work and for which he received the Copley Medal from the Royal Society. It was such a classificatory emphasis, Linnean in its origins leading to a universe of reified abstractions, which, following the lead of the English and, in particular, the French, clearly separated prehistoric researches from classical archaeology in seeming to provide a scientific cachet to the activities of the prehistorian. As in palaeontology, the classificatory hierarchy of formal complexity was easily converted to a chronological progression which the discoveries in the caves and gravel terraces of Europe seemed so clearly to confirm. Classification, its value to science notwithstanding, is analytical and aholistic in its essence although not necessarily in its result; however heuristic or instrumental its intent, its effect was to shift an interpretive emphasis from system to part.

For the historical problem, that is for the construction of a diachronic record of aboriginal occupation and the associated problems relating to the Indian, it was geology and its then more spectacular off-spring palaeontology that provided the more relevant model. In these days scientific break-throughs approaching the nature of revolution seem to occur with a frequency made more bewildering by the esoteric nature of the information they require. Therefore, it may be difficult to feel the excitement with which an expanding literate middle class met the discoveries in palaeontology during the first half of the last century. The occasion required more than the reconstruction of organic worlds long gone, occupied by such mind-boggling creatures as the dinosaurs or the gigantic Moa or the Megatherium from the fragmentary evidences of fossil teeth or fragments of limb bones or whatever. It was the explosion of time that was so wondrous—and, of course, so worrying and, to many, so threatening. It was the use of the fossil to lay out a progression of life forms through the pages of history written by the succession of geological strata which everywhere the canals and the housing tracts and railways of an industrializing and urbanizing Europe were revealing. So challenging, so promising was the increase of the data from the earth for the answering of the questions of earth history, that there was a revival of the Baconian injunction to describe what is as the necessary prerequisite to the construction of systems. To recall the particular semantics, natural history must precede natural philosophy. Thus for what was essentially a new science, whose injunctions were adopted by the prehistorian, the initial demand was for the accumulation of precise data from observation uncluttered by speculation or ideological bias. As Lyell had done a generation earlier in revitalizing geology, Squier defined the empiricism from which the recreation of the Indian's prehistory must proceed. At the outset of the survey of Indian mounds which he and Davis pursued, he (1847:135) wrote:

> All preconceived notions were abandoned, and the work of research commenced, as if no speculations had been indulged in, nor any

thing before been known, respecting the singular remains of antiquity scattered so profusely around us. It was concluded that, either the field should be entirely abandoned to the poet and the romancer, or, if these monuments were capable of reflecting any light upon the grand archaeological [problem] connected with the primitive history of the American continent, the origin, migration, and early state of the American race, that then they should be carefully and minutely, and above all, systematically investigated.

And so were the idols of the cave to be banished.

The key concepts in this new method for the translation of the artifact into meaningful historical statement were those of stratigraphic sequence and the index fossil. Both were transferred directly from geology to the building of a prehistory in which the artifact, so much a part of nature and so removed from its modern counterpart was treated as fossil. The construction of the artifact type provided the index "fossil" which served to identify the stratum. As in palaeontology the positional identity of the type—the conjunction of type and stratum—provided the real evidence to support theories of historical progress, which had become important components of the ascendant 19th century ideology generally accepted, in its various guises, by professional and laymen alike. Where excavation procedures were insufficient to demonstrate stratigraphic sequence or where the conditions of deposition did not lead to stratigraphic segregation, the artifact type itself, fitted into a scheme of technological progress, became the indicator of its place in the temporal sequence. The logic of the method was not peculiar to archaeology. Tested effectively and with spectacular success in geology, it had been taken over, concept and method together, by the nascent professionalizing prehistory, earning thereby alliance with "real" science. Pitt-Rivers, vastly underrated in the history of archaeology both as methodologist and field archaeologist, was an effective spokesman for the method. Interested in weaponry, of which he had a large collection, he had already in the 1850s used the principle of technological improvement or progress as the essential principle on which to base the arrangement of his collection (Pitt-Rivers 1906). It was a principle documented seemingly with such apparent force in comparative ethnography and in the historical record as virtually to force its application to the data of prehistory. Furthermore, his careful excavations were designed to collect artifacts from carefully controlled stratified contexts. Always, however, the context was stratigraphic. The close analogy between prehistoric archaeology and an older palaeontology extends to the level of synthesis as well.

Whereas it was the laboratory and the professional comparative anatomist who supplanted the naturalist in the construction of the more abstract plan of Nature, it was the museum and the curator that supplanted
the localized collector in the search for a more precise definition of the
human past and, through it, the path to the present.

It was these uses of artifact type and stratigraphic position that defined the main lines of archaeological research for the next century. The
research results served to provide the documentation to support the generally accepted assumption of a universally applicable progress, which
somehow generated a continuing improvement in the human condition
and which could be best demonstrated in technology. The rapid shift to
a machine economy during the century provided some logic to an often
unrealized technological bias. For the archaeologist, however, it was the
artifacts that were so large a part of his database and whose "reality"
his method emphasized, and that strengthened such a bias in the search
for a scientific or positivistic concept of both history and culture. The
effect was that in Europe and subsequently in America, the archaeologist
reified—and to a large extent personified—the artifact as a piece of behavior in much the same way that the palaeontologist used his organic
fragments as if they were the whole organism. Though presumably representing the whole, each part was both aholistic and atextual in any but
a relatively limited temporal sense. Too often a chronology based upon
an artifact type with an assumed universal applicability led to controversy, which only emphasized the limitations of the type concept and the
extent of ideological bias. It was the misplaced trust in the universal validity of the type as a time-marker that, as Meltzer (1983) has so interestingly described, was so central an issue in the great debate surrounding Abbott's "palaeoliths" from the Trenton gravels. So much heat was
expended in that great debate that, as with Squier earlier, a deep freeze
descended upon archaeological speculation of any sort. Subsequently, the
discipline became increasingly concerned with an observational and descriptive precision in which an emphasis upon the object and its physical
context robbed it of any but the faintest of a human flavor.

By the end of the century, the archaeology of the Indian had become
fully professionalized. In the work of the Smithsonian-centered Bureau
of American Ethnology, with its congressional mandate to preserve the
remnants of the race against foreign acquisition in the forefront, there
was a no nonsense approach to both the recovery and preservation of
the archaeological materials. Although throughout the country, local collectors still accumulated artifacts and displayed them to the curious, ac-

tive programs of survey and excavation were instituted and field methods refined to document developmental sequences whose local historicity was demonstrable in stratified deposits. That very professionalism—the emergence of a science of archaeology rooted in positivism—precluded speculation in its emphasis upon the data themselves. I emphasize again, however, that what was observed were the artifacts, only bits and pieces of a culture, upon which was placed too heavy a burden of meaning. As Trigger (1980) has suggested, the development of American archaeology had transformed the Indian from person to object. Morgan's Indian, real or ideal, and Schoolcraft's spiritual ancestor had disappeared. Their cry for heritage had been smothered by the silence of the stone—mute once again.

Despite the occasional and often highly speculative attempts to relate artifact to function through the use of an ethnographic analogy based upon stages of human progress assumed to have a universal validity, the central aim of both archaeology and ethnology—of anthropology itself—was the history of the species beyond history. More particularly a new nationalism, inspired by both political and economic success, revived interest in the colonial period; and in that interest archaeology was recruited as a supplement to ethnohistory to document the ethnic conditions within which the earliest scenes of Euro-American settlement were enacted.

It was as an adjunct of political history that anthropological (i.e., prehistoric) archaeology was, and by many is still, regarded. It had as little to do with the "high culture" of the classical archaeologist as it had to do with what in this century distinguished anthropology as a discipline in its own and particular right—an understanding of that which was universally regarded as peculiar to the species: culture, however difficult it became to reduce that concept to a precise definition. The history in whose service archaeology was pressed was, however, in the main ethnic history. It was the same history of "peoples," of their migrations and shifting geography that underlay contemporary territorial realities as well as aspirations to which both linguistics and "racial" anthropology were also making their contributions. Like the particulars of vocabulary or physical form, the material fragments in the archaeologist's kit, preserved through time, were the name tags of a timeless human convention adding the detail of time to that of space. "Culture" in the Tylorean sense, these fragments might be, but culture they were not.

While it is surely a dangerous time-bound exercise to create heroes in intellectual history, it is, as Stocking (1963) so usefully demonstrated,

Franz Boas who deserves the credit for the invention of the concept of culture as something particular and systemic. The emphasis given to Tylor's definition notwithstanding, it was Boas who gave to the concept a particularity and a vitality that made it possible to approach culture as an organic whole, the expression of the total way of life of a socially prescribed human group rather than as an assemblage of isolated bits and pieces of human behavior. In him, the concept was a product of an earlier, persistent, and essentially German theme born of German Romanticism in which a human group, the *Volk,* possessed a historical unity and particularity expressed in the total range of everyday behavior. So successful—may one say so satisfying?—was the shift to such a concept of culture as an investigative focus justified by its humanness that within half a century, Tylor's assemblage of bits and pieces had been replaced in the Anglo-American tradition by a Boasian holism. Arguing for a more highly structured approach to the concept of culture, Hocart, in a somewhat defiant tone, drew upon a newer version of the organic model.

In introducing his analysis of the structure of human society, he (1970:3) wrote:

> The present work definitely abjures the method of Tylor and his successors, the composite picture made up of scattered fragments. It takes peoples as a whole, even as the zoologist studies his animals as a whole. Like the zoologist it dissects the specimens and lays bare the structure of the different societies. This intensive anatomy means a limitation in extent. It is better to do a few societies thoroughly than a vast number superficially.

Even as example, Hocart is an appropriate testimony to the change in attitude just because he was neither Boasian nor American.

Although the impact on Boas' thinking of his year-long stay with the Eskimo has been subjected to various interpretations (e.g., Stocking 1965), there can be little doubt that it strengthened his deeply felt sense of the organic unity of *a* behavioral system: *a culture.* He was unlike his English contemporaries whose sense of a universal history was driven by the concept of progress or his newly acquired American colleagues with their tradition based upon the collection of fragments of culture. He had experienced as a young man a culture system in being and in practice. His were the ideas mined from Herderian Romanticism and forged in the crucible of intensive field work. They demanded his suspicion of cultural evaluations based upon any arbitrary and ethnocentric criteria, and, even more, the idea of a universal progressive series which was the result. He attacked the implicit assumption that underlay the goals and methods of classical archaeology: that it is "culture" in the vulgar sense of the fine arts and literature and music that distinguishes civilized man from his savage ancestor. He provided the evidences for the sensitivity of the Eskimo to music and poetry; and concluded (Boas 1887a:385) that "these few examples will show that the mind of the 'savage' is sensible to the beauties of poetry and music, and that it is only the superficial observer to whom he appears stupid and unfeeling." Later he was to make the same point with reference to art (Boas (1897; 1916; 1927).

Boas attacked more directly the view of the Indian traditionally derived from a nostalgia for a past that never was or the realities of experience with peoples whose way of life had been destroyed by a century of forced acculturation. To find the Indian, to study his customs, "we must visit him in his village, where he lives undisturbed by the contact with Europeans, according to his ancient customs" (Boas 1888:628). It is in this shift of perspective away from behavioral chaos (which was the product of Euro-American expansion along a constantly shifting frontier) to a system of internally consistent behavior that the beginnings of a Boasian anthropology are discerned. For the Indian this shift in perspective would require a remembered past transformed into an ethnographic present.

Furthermore every behavioral expression, every part of a system, can be understood only through an analysis of its role in that system. This view provides a new means of interpreting the artifact, which even more than the datum of the ethnographer is an atextual fragment. Against the notion that, somehow, the Indian or the "savage" anywhere was characterized by a mental state qualitatively different from that of "modern" man and, therefore, to be studied and understood in a manner also different, Boas continually proclaimed and taught that whatever the particular condition of physical life, however great the varieties of human experience, mankind, past and present, was a unity. This unity derived not because of a common historical ascent through universal stages of qualitative development but rather from a basic commonality of thought, imagination, and concern. Recalling that great experience of his youth with the Eskimo forty years earlier (and it is always important to remember that Boas was only a 24-year-old middle-class assimilating urban German Jew when he went out to the Eskimo), he (Boas 1927:2) wrote:

Anyone who has lived with primitive tribes, who has shared their joys and sorrows, their privations and their luxuries, who sees in them not solely subjects of study to be examined like a cell under the microscope, but feeling and thinking human beings, will agree that there is no such thing as a 'primitive mind,' a 'magical' or 'pre-logical' way of thinking, but that each individual in 'primitive' society is a man, woman, a child of the same kind, of the same way of thinking, feeling and acting as man, woman or child in our own society.

It was in his controversy with Otis Mason that early on Boas pressed the methodological point. Against Mason's museum-oriented typological and geographical arrangement of specimens, Boas argued that it was in the "history" of the object alone that one could discern its meaning (see Hinsley 1981:98–100; Boas 1887b). History again! But for Boas—both museum collector and field ethnographer—history was context. It was the history of the older natural history in which each living organism was described in its living context. Alone the object was dead, as dead as the bird skin or fossil on the systematist's table, as dead as the cadaver on the anatomist's dissecting bench. To be understood the object must be seen alive, in the context of the behavioral system of which it was a single expression. Implement or song, monument or tale, material or idea— each element in the behavioral system took its meaning from its sociology, from the role it played in a uniquely human system of behavior; and it was to that system that the renovated term "culture" was applied.

Beyond the expressed differences with respect to the manner in which objects should be displayed in a museum or, even more, the understanding to which such bits of information so arranged should contribute, the Mason/Boas controversy illustrates the just emerging conflict between the museologist and the academic "ethnologist," between the demands of the conservator and the interpreter, between the positivist and the theorist. It is but a single aspect of the more general and never successfully resolved conflict between the empiricist and the theorist in the fields of science. Within anthropology, it reflects a conflict between an object emphasis and one of system or structure. Although often stated as a conflict between the material and nonmaterial expressions of human behavior, the discussion goes beyond that. The early students of anthropology could and would regard kinship terminology or language characteristics as isolated bits and pieces to be arranged along some developmental line in much the same way as that which seemed natural for the physical artifact. Few students of archaeology, faced with the more immediate problem in the acquisition of their data, saw the need to engage in the cerebral acrobatics of the theorists of culture. For their part, cultural anthropologists found the shuffling of ceramic sherds or the creation of artifact typologies dull and boring. When archaeologists approached culture, they tended to see it as an assemblage of discrete traits reified by the discreteness of the objects with which they dealt; and, in the field, the cultural anthropologist, tended to focus upon concepts reified in the language of his informant rather than the particulars of everyday life. That there may be—that there are—good reasons for such a difference in approach to a common investigative problem should not conceal the fact that such a difference did exist to the limitation of understanding in both archaeology and cultural anthropology. Other than a recognition by each that the object was a part of culture, there was no sense of what I would call a "sociology of material culture." Despite differences attached to the value of the artifact as a cultural document, there was no recognition that the object itself played a role in the structure of behavior, in the culture.

Early on Boas adumbrated a "cultural archaeology" founded upon the utility for the understanding of a particular culture's historical continuity, that is, a concept of the cultural whole which brought into clearer focus its temporal, its historical, dimension. To a reading audience who were in a state of continuous excitement over the finds at Knossos and Nineveh which were extending through archaeology the temporal limits of the western literate tradition, Boas (1902:1) pointed out the promise of an archaeology in the New World and the method for realizing it.

> While the archaeology of the Mediterranean country and a large portion of Asia deals with the early remains of peoples that possessed a literature, and whose history is partly known from literary sources, we find in America, almost exclusively, remains of a people unfamiliar with the art of writing, and whose history is entirely unknown. The problem, therefore, with which we are dealing is allied to the problem of the prehistoric archaeology of the Old World. The method that is pursued in dealing with the ancient remains of the lake-dwellers, of the kitchen-middens, and of other prehistoric sites, of which we have no literary knowledge, must be pursued in investigations in American archaeology. But even in this case the conditions are not quite comparable. The ancient culture of the people who left their remains in Europe has completely disappeared, and has given way to civilization of modern type. It seems probable that the remains found in most of the archaeological sites of America were left by a people similar in culture to the present Indians. For this reason, the ethnological study of the Indians must be considered

as a powerful means of elucidating the significance of the archaeological remains. It is hardly possible to understand the significance
of American archaeological remains without having recourse to ethnological observations, which frequently explain the significance of
prehistoric finds.

Having said this, Boas then went on to ignore it, using the rest of
his short article to describe the manner in which archaeological materials
from various sites could be used, much in the manner of historical and/
or comparative linguistics, to reconstruct the historical movements of
distinct ethnic units. I do not wish to claim too much for Boas. In these
early years his objective was history; but it was a history more vital than
the schemes hatched by his contemporaries in their book-filled studies
and nurtured by a rational faith in a universal and unilineal progression-
ism. A recognition of his sense of the organic holism of past and present
in the culture of a given society should not conceal the importance which
he attached to the reconstruction of human history as an anthropological
(i.e., ethnological) goal nor the method of cultural analysis as the means
to track the process of cultural change. History for him was not the
metaphysical director of human events but rather itself an expression of
cultural process. The problems of his ethnology were essentially historical ones, a temporal extension of a cultural geography that had worked
well in the time-restricted area of historical linguistics. What Boas added
is a wider range of behavioral attributes or expressions, which together
in a systematic fashion constitute his culture. Thus he concludes the same
brief programmatic essay with the expectation that "if archaeology in
America is applied hand in hand with ethnological [i.e. cultural geo-
graphical] and linguistic methods, it will be a most powerful help in un-
ravelling the history of the continent" (Boas 1902:6). A culture was now
an internally consistent assemblage whose additions and subtractions *in
situ* can be traced through time. It is thus the comparison of the past, via
archaeology, with the present, via ethnography, which could provide the
measure of change; but it is always change within a particular culture
rather than change vis a vis a universal human state. The reconstruction
of these cultures of the past was still a long way off, shunted aside in part
by Boas' distrust of the manner through which the whole had so easily
been inferred by the cultural evolutionists and the grand theorists of cultural change who followed in the wake of the revolutionary discoveries
of Brixham Cave, the Somme Valley, and the caves of the Perigord.

Nor did his students pick up the suggestion of a "cultural archaeology," seeking rather, in both ethnography and archaeology, to refine

more precisely and interpret more cautiously the disappearing evidences of both past and present. Instead of serving as an aid to reconstruction of cultural sequences, archaeology, embroidered with a greater precision, continued as a hand-maiden to history—whether particular or universal. An archaeology of the now-particularized culture was but a blip on the historical screen. Given the fragmentary nature of the archaeological data, it was more reasonable, more scientific, to retain a concept of culture that stressed its parts and ignored the coherence which enlivened the whole and part in the continuing behavior of the human group. As a Boasian "culture" itself moved center stage and became academicized, the archaeological specimen, so disjointed, so asystemic in *its* reality, came to be used as isolated text to supply the temporal dimension which acculturative disorganization had destroyed. In the search for a cultural whole (the ethnographic present), which could serve as a base-line for the understanding of the dynamic systems which were the localized cultures, it was not so much existing practice which read meaning into the object from present to past but rather the reverse. As Boas used his collected texts as an oral literature from which untainted practice might be recovered, so too did Kroeber use Peruvian ceramics (those special ones of museum quality) as another kind of document for the reconstruction of a culture long gone. Just as language, however, lacked an ethnography of speech, so did the artifacts of the archaeologist lack their ethnography of use. Deprived of a social context, of a life within a vital system of behavior, they were lifeless indeed.

For the development of a fruitful relationship between archaeology and ethnography during this period of fumbling for a workable concept of culture, these years at the turn of the century were in fact a crossroads. In the succeeding decades, archaeology moved toward increasing the precision of its data. Except for limited excursions in the establishment of temporal sequences through carefully controlled stratified associations and limited spatial relationships, it extended its concern with the artifact as object. It was the artifact type that changed through time or space rather than the behavioral system of which it was the material manifestation. At the same time, the "culturalist" was moving more and more toward the idea of a culture as an abstraction whose essential structure could best be seen in comprehensive ideational systems, such as religion, cosmology, and social organization. For such an approach, the artifact was too much a fragment, too immediate and ephemeral in its meaning, to be a useful clue to the understanding of the whole; indeed, it seemed to stress too much the act of doing rather than the art of thinking. Within, then, what was still conceived of as a unified field—the hallmark of the new American anthropology—archaeology and cultural anthropology moved further and further from one another, neither in fact understanding the particular bias which its data and its methodology produced.

The interesting question is, why did neither Boas nor his students pick up on what was a significant methodological observation, namely the importance of context for the understanding of the object on the one hand and the important "sociological" or systemic role that the material object played in a behavioral whole? There is, of course, no single answer to such a question. In part, the Boasian concept of culture itself was too much an abstraction, still too far removed from ethnographic reality, too "romantic," too theoretical, too difficult to handle analytically. Boas' own ethnography in the Pacific Northwest was a disappointing aftermath to his experience with the Central Eskimo. Although there was still cultural practice, both social and cultural systems were too fragmented, too broken for the essential structure to be part of the ethnographer's experience. One wonders to what extent a cultural archaeology would have more readily emerged if Boas' field experiences had occurred within the more "wholesome" communities of the Southwest, where the ruins of the past and the life of the present formed much more clearly a single reality.

More significant and more subtle were the effects of the different loci of anthropological attention, particularly the museum and the university. By the first decade of the 20th century, they had become the major centers of anthropological activity. The materials of prehistoric archaeology, as I have noted before, were parts of natural history collections rather than in collections of classical antiquities, which were the direct outcome of an interest in the classical past within the humanities tradition. While the former, because of their Indian associations, usually were considered national and public property, the latter were in private and academic hands. There was a humanistic bias against the crude materials that American archaeology contributed. The stones were mute, but only because they seemed to have little worth saying. In an orientation which saw culture still as civilization, which saw language as the most important characteristic of man and, incidentally, for whom the lack of literacy, i.e., the lack of a written language, was an embarrassment, where there were still available for collection kinship systems and mythologies and laws and beliefs, the apparently crude implements in the archaeology of North America must have seemed hardly worth while in the search for culture. Is this suspicion of the technological process itself not a reflection of a social bias common to the 19th century during which, in England for example, even participation in trade barred one from being a gentleman? It seemed hardly possible that these crude instruments of a simple technological level could say anything significant about the overall cultural system in which the work of the mind was considered so much more important than that of the hand.

Such a bias was a reflection of a concept of cultuure (even of the living), which was insufficiently concerned with the more mundane matters of survival: the means manufactured and employed to squeeze sustenance from an unyielding environment. It was only later, much later, that cultural analysis permitted an appreciation of the interrelationships that exist between the material and the nonmaterial: the distribution of artifact types or raw materials of one sort or another tell us not only something about the historical relationships between ethnic units (whatever they may be) but, much more significantly, about the patterns of trade and the economic relationships which they foster; or that the sizes, shapes, and distributions of house plans (stark as they may be in the scant evidence of their existence) demonstrate something of the social organization of the group; or that the detailed analysis of artifact collections (as collections rather than types) can say something significant about the microchanges in life styles through time. To make such extrapolations of the sort which have renovated prehistoric archaeology in the decades following the formation of this Society, it was necessary to conceive of culture as a unity in which each of its expressions, material or ideational, participated in a set of continuous relationships of man to man, man to nature, and man to his imagined universe. It was this that I believe was central to Boas' vision and through which he saw the promise of an American anthropology.

To sum up this synoptic review, we may say that until there was a concept of culture as itself a comprehensive and consistent system of behavior (at whatever level or at how many levels that system operates) archaeological activity (and in fact ethnography itself) could be little more than a way of "collecting." There may have been particular goals of the collection, i.e., the establishment of chronologies for particular kinds of objects, but the acquisition of knowledge was essentially "positivistic" in that it was accumulative without any "informing principle." With the emergence of a concept of culture as system and with that sense of system as a cognitive background or kind of mental template, the collection of information in the field as well as the definition of problem occurred within that frame so that the "center of gravity" of the data shifted from the object itself to its meaning within the system. Until that shift in the investigative orientation occurred, where there was a problem orientation in archaeology it could only be a very limited one that emerged from and was limited by the field data themselves. One of the virtues of the "marxist" introduction into anthropology and archaeology is that it does provide an *a priori* view to which the investigation and the acquisition of field data can be directed. The danger of course is that the "system" comes to exist as an overriding truth to which the data are sought only as illustration rather than as test. In this sense, there is a parallel with the way in which the Aristotelian method was converted in the late Medieval period wherein the tentative became permanent, the ephemeral became real.

In his novel, *World of Wonders,* Robertson Davies has one of his characters give a definition of historical truth which is an apt take-off point for a not uncommon attitude for the use of archaeological data by archaeologists (1977:59):

> The truth of the past is to be seen in museums, and what is it? Dead things, sometimes noble and beautiful, but dead. And cases and cases of coins, and snuff boxes, and combs, and mirrors that won't reflect any more, and clothes that look as if the wearers had all been midgets, and masses of frowsy tat that tells us nothing at all.

Dead as they may be, however stilled their voices, these artifacts contain in themselves the multiple realities of human existence through time. As always it is the archaeologist's task to make them speak, to reveal to the present the life of the past. As archaeologists absorb a sense of culture and as ethnographers extend their concept of system to erase the traditional line between "material" and "nonmaterial" we bring light to Stephens' "dark, impenetrable mystery." That past becomes ours.

Literature Cited

Anonymous
    1820 Archaeologia Americana. *Transactions and Collections of the American Antiquarian Society* 1:5–6.

Boas, Franz
    1887a Poetry and Music of Some North American Tribes. *Science* 9:383–385.
    1887b The Occurrence of Similar Inventions in Areas Widely Separated. *Science* 9:485–486.

1888 The Indians of British Columbia. *Popular Science Monthly* 32:628–635.

1897 Decorative Art of the Indians of the North Pacific Coast. *Bulletin of the American Museum of Natural History* 9:123–176.

1902 Some Problems in North American Archaeology. *American Journal of Archaeology* new series, 6:1–6. [Reprinted in Boas 1940:525–529.]

1916 Representative Art of Primitive People. In *Holmes Anniversary Volume*, pages 18–23. Washington, D. C. [Reprinted in Boas 1940:535–540.]

1927 *Primitive Art.* Oslo.

1940 *Race, Language and Culture.* New York.

Davies, Robertson
1977 *World of Wonders.* New York and London.

Fiske, Oliver
1820 Abstract of an Address to the Members of the American Antiquarian Society, 1819. *Transactions and Collections of the American Antiquarian Society* 1:41–46.

Foster, J. W.
1873 *Prehistoric Races of the United States of America.* Chicago.

Grayson, Donald K.
1983 *The Establishment of Human Antiquity.* New York.

Gregg, Josiah
1844 *Commerce of the Prairies, or the Journal of a Santa Fe Trader.* New York.

Gruber, Jacob W.
1965 Brixham Cave and the Antiquity of Man. In *Context and Meaning in Cultural Anthropology,* edited by M. E. Spiro, pages 373–402. New York.

Haven, Samuel F.
1856 Archaeology of the United States. *Smithsonian Contributions to Knowledge* 8:1–168.

Hinsley, Curtis M., Jr.
1981 *Savages and Scientists: The Smithsonian Institution and the Development of American Anthropology, 1846–1910.* Washington, D. C.

Hocart, A. M.
1970 *Kings and Councillors,* edited by Rodney Needham. Chicago. [Originally printed in Cairo, 1937.]

Horgan, Paul
1979 *Josiah Gregg and His Vision of the Early West.* New York.

Lartet, Edouard, and Henry Christy
1875 *Reliquiae Aquitanicae: Being Contributions to the Archaeology and Paleontology of Perigord and the Adjoining Provinces of Southern France,* edited by Thomas Rupert Jones. London.

Meltzer, David J.
    1983   The Antiquity of Man and the Development of American Archaeology. In *Advances in Archaeological Theory and Method,* edited by Michael B. Schiffer, 6:1–51. New York.

Michaelis, A.
    1908   *A Century of Archaeological Discoveries,* translated by Bettina Kahnwahler. London.

Morgan, Lewis H.
    1848a Communication of October 31, 1848. In *2nd Annual Report of the Regents of the State University of New York,* page 6.
    1848b Communication of November 13, 1848. In *2nd Annual Report of the Regents of the State University of New York,* pages 84–91.

Pitt-Rivers, A. Lane-Fox
    1906   *The Evolution of Culture and Other Essays,* edited by J. L. Myres. Oxford.

Schoolcraft, Henry
    1846   *An Address Delivered before the* WAS-AH HO-DE-NO-SON-NE *or New Confederacy of the Iroquois.* Rochester. [Pamphlet.]

Squier, E. G.
    1847   Observations on the Aboriginal Monuments of the Mississippi Valley. *Transactions of the American Ethnological Society* 2:134–207.
    1849   American Ethnology. *The American Review, A Why Journal* 9:385–398.

Squier, E. G., and E. H. Davis
    1848   Ancient Monuments of the Mississippi Valley. *Smithsonian Institution Contributions to Knowledge* 1.

Stephens, John L.
    1841   *Incidents of Travel in Central America, Chiapas, and Yucatan.* 2 volumes. New York.

Stocking, George W., Jr.
    1963   Franz Boas and the Culture Concept in Historical Perspective. *American Anthropologist* 68:867–882.
    1965   From Physics to Ethnology: Franz Boas' Arctic Expedition as a Problem in the Historiography of the Behavioral Sciences. *Journal of the History of the Behavioral Sciences* 1:53–66.

Thomas, Isaiah
    1820   Abstract of a Communication Made to the Society by the President at the Annual Meeting in Boston, 1814. *Transactions and Collections of the American Antiquarian Society* 1:32–40.

Trigger, Bruce G.
    1980   Archaeology and the Image of the American Indian. *American Antiquity* 45:662–676.

Wecter, Dixon
    1941   *The Hero in America.* New York.

Prehistoric Archaeology and American Society

Introduction

Understanding the history of American archaeology requires coming to terms with some harsh truths about Euro-American society past and present. American prehistoric archaeology, like American anthropology as a whole, originated in a colonial milieu. The 19th century saw the expansion of white settlement from the Appalachian Mountains to the Pacific Ocean. Yet, despite the massive pandemics of European diseases that had devastated the native population of the New World since the 16th century, white settlement was not the peaceful occupation of a "virgin" or "empty" land. It involved the constant use of military force to conquer and control peoples who, while being too fragmented politically to prevent themselves from being overwhelmed by military force, tenaciously resisted Euro-American efforts to dominate their lives (Prucha 1977; Washburn 1973, 1975; Patterson 1972).

Prehistoric archaeology has traditionally been interpreted as a discipline uninfluenced by contemporary social values. It has generally been believed that archaeological findings lack social or political significance and are irrelevant to everyday life. Such a view does not, however, explain why in many totalitarian societies the interpretation of archaeological data has been subjected to strict political control; nor does it account for the obvious role that archaeology has played in promoting many nationalistic ideologies (Miller 1956; Sklenář 1983; Trigger 1984a). Recent studies indicate that even seemingly whimsical interpretations of archaeological data reflect the values and social commitments of individual archaeologists (Bintliff 1984). This accords with the more general observation that what people believe about the present conditions their understanding of the past, just as what they hold to be true about the past influences their views of the present (Collingwood 1946). It is therefore unlikely that American archaeology has been uninfluenced by the ideology of American society and more particularly by the values of the more conservative elements of the middle class to whom such studies have particularly appealed.

Yet the development of archaeology, like that of the other social sciences, has been shaped by the acquisition of new analytical skills and an increasing amount of factual knowledge, as well as by social factors. Although I do not deny the significance of relativist arguments (Leone 1982; Hodder 1982), the social sciences are never simply passive reflections of contemporary society or mere embodiments of the personal prejudices of their practitioners. On the contrary, in situations where political and religious controls do not intervene, their findings have helped to alter public opinion in significant ways. For example, in the mid-20th century ethnology played a notable role in promoting more liberal and individualistic views of social conduct as well as in combatting racism in America (Stocking 1974). Hence this paper will seek to document the dialectical relationship between American society and prehistoric archaeology within a historical framework that combines elements of both positivist and relativist approaches.

Early American Archaeology

For almost 500 years the encounter between European colonists and Native North Americans has been influenced by a pervasive and enduring European ethnocentrism. From the beginning, Europeans were convinced of their religious, technological, and cultural superiority. Authors who unstintingly lauded the "noble savage" were few and far between (Lescarbot 1907–1914). At first Europeans assumed that the superiority of their customs would be equally evident to Native Americans. They also thought that native people would quickly learn to live and think like Europeans and eventually would be able to take their place in the lower echelons of colonial society (Vaughan 1982:927–929). When it became obvious that Indians were unwilling to surrender their land and submit to European domination, they were perceived as a threat to colonization and denounced as savages fit only to be killed or enslaved. In the 17th century religious reasons were advanced to justify such aggression (Porter 1979:91–115).

Beginning in the 18th century, the low cultural status of native peoples and their refusal to be assimilated were explained more "scientifically" in terms of alleged biological inferiority (Vaughan 1982). At first, under the rationalist influences of the American enlightenment (Gorenstein 1976:87), this inferiority was attributed to environmental factors and thought to be reversible in the long run. Later it was claimed to be biologically innate and irreversible; first by the polygenists, who viewed Native Americans as a separately created species that was inferior to Europeans, and later by Darwinian evolutionists who argued that, because natural selection acting slowly over the centuries had not equipped native people for life in more complex societies, it was now impossible for them ever to adapt successfully to civilized ways (Stanton 1960). This latter view absolved white Americans of any moral responsibility for what was perceived as the rapidly approaching extinction of the American Indian (Hinsley 1981:10).

By the 1840s, the embryonic study of American archaeology was drawn into an association with ethnology, linguistics, and physical anthropology as components of a new discipline of anthropology that had as its goal to study Native Americans (Gruber 1967:5–9). These four fields were united by a cultural evolutionary perspective that interpreted Native Americans as living examples of what Europeans had been like in prehistoric times (Resek 1960:133). Anthropology thus became the study of peoples who were believed to be unchanging; while history investigated groups that had evolved into civilizations (Wolf 1982). The dichotomy between history and the specialized social sciences that were concerned with Western societies on the one hand and anthropology on the other therefore expressed in disciplinary terms the popular view that Native Americans were incapable of becoming civilized and hence were doomed to extinction. It also created a significant barrier between prehistoric archaeology, which studied the cultural remains of Native Americans and was regarded as a branch of anthropology, and Classical, Egyptian, and Mesopotamian archaeology, which were allied to historical (or at least art historical and epigraphic) disciplines. The archaeological study of the ancient civilizations of the New World remained the domain of anthropology for the technical reason that these groups appeared to be nonliterate, even though a large number of 19th-century scholars acknowledged that these societies had otherwise attained a level of development comparable to that of the ancient kingdoms of Egypt and Mesopotamia (Wilson 1862). These academic arrangements reflected the popular conviction that no Amerindian people had ever been truly civilized.

Diverse factors contributed to the development of an interest in the prehistoric archaeology of North America. Little notice appears to have been taken of prehistoric remains prior to the late 18th century (for an exception, see Ribes 1966). Between the 16th and 18th centuries the concern with pre-European times was largely restricted to archaeologically unsubstantiated speculations about where Native Americans had originated and along what routes they had reached North America (Pagden 1982). As in Europe, the first remains to attract substantial scholarly attention were monuments, such as mounds, earthworks, and rock carvings, although collections of artifacts found by farmers and builders also began to be amassed. Yet large scientific collections were not established anywhere in North America prior to the 19th century. For a long time little distinction was made between archaeological and ethnographic specimens.

The first substantial stimuli to an interest in North American archaeology were the many large mounds and earthworks that were encountered as European settlement pushed west of the Appalachians in the late 18th century. These mounds challenged the popular view that all of the native inhabitants of North America had been primitive and uncreative. Yet few Euro-Americans were prepared to interpret these finds as evidence of the creative abilities of North American Indians. The mounds and earthworks were accommodated with a primitive view of these Indians by claiming that they had been built by some vanished people, variously identified as Scandinavians, Hindus, Toltecs, or Israelites. Such speculations easily became part of white American folklore in the 19th century, since they accorded with the popular image of native people as bloodthirsty savages. Mound builder myths were propagated in popular studies and novels and through the teachings of Joseph Smith became a significant component in a major religious movement. Yet they also stimulated much empirical archaeological research and helped to encourage the scientific development of American archaeology throughout the 19th century (Silverberg 1968).

Increasing private and public support for the systematic collection of artifacts also reflected the scientific interests of Americans during the 19th century. Archaeological studies developed alongside investigations of geology and natural history. The latter researches among other things served to identify the exploitable resources of recently acquired territories, while ethnological investigations of traditional Indian life were seen as a basis for devising policies to deal with Indians who were coming under white control in increasing numbers. As early as 1799 the American Philosophical Society, as one of its many scientific projects, had solicited information about prehistoric fortifications, tumuli, and Indian artifacts (Willey and Sabloff 1980:28). In the years that followed, private institutes, whose membership consisted largely of professional men, and public research centers, such as the Smithsonian Institution and natural history museums, were founded in major cities across the United States to encourage a wide range of scientific studies, including archaeology (McKusick 1970:2; Connolly 1977; Killan 1980). The American Antiquarian Society, which was established in 1812, encouraged a more specialized interest in archaeology (Gorenstein 1976:89–90). Many of these institutions established journals and monograph series in which accounts of serious archaeological research began to be published. The results were highly variable. Members of the Davenport Academy of Science in Iowa were duped by finds of inscribed roofing slates and stone elephant pipes into supporting the idea that the mound builders had been contemporary with extinct megafauna (McKusick 1970). On the other hand, Joseph Henry, the physicist who became director of the Smithsonian Institution, used the prestige of that establishment to curb speculation and encourage description and classification by American archaeologists (Haven 1856). He also sought to disseminate information about recent advances in European archaeology to as wide an American audience as possible (Morlot 1861). The quality of American archaeology increased as growing numbers of archaeologists, many of whom had been trained in the natural sciences, found full-time employment, first in museums and then in university anthropology departments during the last decades of the 19th century.

Although archaeology developed within the general context of anthropology, archaeologists could not claim, as ethnologists did, that their work was of potential benefit to anyone. Instead they had to justify their research in terms of its humanistic interest. Thus an enduring image was created of archaeology as a subject that had little social significance and of archaeologists as enthusiasts who were pursuing studies that were of little practical value. On the whole American archaeologists were a conservative lot. They remained predominantly male and of Anglo-Saxon origin; which was very different from ethnology, where women and ethnic minorities played a much more significant role. Prehistoric archaeologists also had less contact with native people than did ethnologists. Yet because of their considerable interest in how artifacts were made and used and because some anthropologists engaged in both ethnographic and archaeological research, they had more contact with native people at this time than they were to have later during the culture-historical period (Willey and Sabloff 1980:50–51).

The attention that was paid to the systematic study of Indian artifacts in the course of the 19th century partly reflected a growing interest in prehistoric archaeology in Europe. Yet it was also motivated by a romantic conviction that white Americans had a duty to preserve a record of the race that they were supplanting on the North American continent. Henry Schoolcraft and others saw this as involving the collection not only of archaeological material but also of ethnographic specimens, oral traditions, and linguistic data (Hinsley 1981:20). A softer and more romantic image of Indians gradually replaced that of the bloodthirsty savage in areas where white hegemony was firmly established (Keiser 1933:101–143; Monkman 1981). Yet these views continued to reflect the conviction that the Indians were an inferior race whose passing was foreordained by manifest destiny. Their cultural inferiority was also taken for granted by leading evolutionary anthropologists. These included John Wesley Powell, the first director of the Bureau of American Ethnology, even though he was personally well-disposed towards native people and sought to promote government policies that he believed would protect them (Hinsley 1981:287).

The 19th century witnessed a burgeoning amateur interest in North American archaeology (Killan 1980, 1983). Many individuals began to collect artifacts and to ponder what they had been used for and how they had been made. Although large numbers of artifacts were encountered in the course of agricultural activities and construction work, this interest was not an inevitable response to such finds. It did not, for example, occur in French Canada, where beginning in the 1840s there was considerable religious opposition to the study of natural history and where nationalistic and religious sentiments impeded the emergence of a more romantic view of native people (Smith 1974). Significantly, however, in the 1850s there was much interest in Quebec, especially among Jesuit scholars, in the archaeological study of sites associated with French missionary activity in the 17th century (Martijn 1978; Trigger 1981a:70).

An increasing amateur interest helped professional archaeology to expand by encouraging the creation of more full-time positions in museums and universities. Informed amateur archaeologists also assisted professional ones and provided an audience for their publications. Growing interest in prehistoric archaeology also led to the preservation of major monuments, such as the Great Serpent Mound in Ohio, which was saved from total destruction and restored by means of a public subscription organized by Frederic W. Putnam (1890) in 1886, and Casa Grande, which the United States federal government reserved as a public site in 1889 (Fowler 1982:5).

Yet just as ethnographic material was displayed to the Euro-American public in museums as trophies appropriated from conquered peoples, the exhibition of prehistoric artifacts symbolized white control of the soil from which these objects were recovered. Both types of evidence served not only to satisfy white curiosity about native people, who were now assumed to be part of America's past or to be rapidly becoming so, but also to illustrate their primitiveness and hence to make clear the historical circumstances that had led to their subjugation. Within the context of a unilinear evolutionary perspective, this material was assumed to show what European society had been like millennia ago. Thus at the same time that Indian relics were displayed as evidence of the inherent inability of native people to progress and become civilized, they also demonstrated the progress that Europeans had made in their climb from savagery to civilization.

The low esteem in which Native Americans were held was further dramatized by displaying ethnographic and archaeological collections in museums of natural history, alongside minerals, fossils, stuffed animals, and dried plants, rather than together with European and Near Eastern antiquities in museums of fine arts. This arrangement not only physically expressed the distinction between anthropology and history but also implied that "primitive" humans remained more akin to the natural world than to civilized people. Hence on many levels these displays symbolized to white Americans their assumed superiority and justified their treatment of native people as the working out of a providential, if ruthless, historical order (Trigger 1985).

Few, if any, 19th century archaeologists consciously perceived their work in precisely these terms. Yet the subliminal importance of these concepts for structuring reality is evident from the powerful influence that they exerted on the interpretation of archaeological data. Because evolutionary anthropologists believed that native peoples represented the most primitive and therefore the earliest levels of cultural development, they assumed that the archaeological record in North America would reveal little evidence of internal cultural transformations. It was frequently asserted that artifacts of exceptional quality had been manufactured after European contact when iron tools became available (McGuire 1899). Thus native cultures were pictured as having been exceedingly primitive in prehistoric times.

Because of this there was little interest in working out cultural chronologies as a basis for objectively demonstrating either cultural change or the lack of it. While some American archaeologists sought to discover an American equivalent to the European Paleolithic, finds of an American Paleolithic, like the mound builder remains, were normally assigned to a vanished non-Indian people by those who accepted their validity. Most archaeologists, however, assumed a shallow time depth for the human occupancy of the New World and explained alleged American Paleolithic sites as the stone-processing workshops of later cultures (Meltzer 1983).

Although a considerable number of archaeologists were familiar with the principles of stratigraphy and typology (or seriation), as these had been developed for chronological purposes in Europe, the application of these techniques remained extremely limited and played no significant role in regional syntheses of archaeological data (Trigger 1980:664). Instead, professional as well as amateur archaeologists mainly sought to determine how artifacts had been made and for what purposes they had been used. It was widely assumed that there had been considerable ethnic and cultural continuity during the prehistory of the various parts of North America and hence that local ethnographic data provided the best source of information for interpreting finds from each region. When major alterations were obvious in the archaeological record, these were attributed to ethnic changes brought about by tribal migrations from one region to another, rather than to internal transformations of cultures (Parker 1916). This version of the direct historical approach was championed as a research strategy by the Bureau of American Ethnology, under Powell's directorship, as part of the expression of an evolutionist commitment to the unity of all forms of anthropological study (Meltzer 1983). Towards the end of the 19th century, influenced by a growing interest in a culture area approach among ethnologists, archaeologists began to study the geographical distribution of different types of pottery, stone tools, and other types of artifacts and to define culture areas on the basis of archaeological data (Willey and Sabloff 1980:77; Trigger 1978:88). While these studies promoted an understanding of geographical variations in artifact distributions as well as a rudimentary awareness of prehistoric adaptations to different kinds of natural environments, American archaeologists did not systematically control for temporal variation. Hence they conflated material from many different periods and cultural groupings. This approach both reflected and reinforced the assumption that native cultures had generally been static in prehistoric times.

What happened in American archaeology at this time foreshadowed what was to happen later in other colonial settings, such as southern Africa, Australia, and New Zealand (Fagan 1981; Posnansky 1982; Mulvaney 1981; Gathercole 1981). In each of these places it was assumed that native cultures had changed little, if at all, in prehistoric times. The view that nonliterate societies were fossilized entities, incapable of progress and therefore doomed to extinction, was rationalized in terms of Darwinian evolution and presented as a world view of human development by the English prehistorian John Lubbock (Lord Avebury), whose book *Pre-historic Times* was widely read in America and went through seven editions between 1865 and 1913. The findings of American archaeology thus reflected and reinforced a racist view of Native Americans that was shared not only by vast numbers of white Americans at all social levels but also by an international scientific community that was increasingly influenced by racist explanations of human behavior (Trigger 1984a).

Culture-Historical Archaeology

Yet American archaeology did not remain a passive victim of these social stereotypes. By the early 20th century it was becoming obvious that the archaeological record in certain parts of North America varied radically from one period to another. In the eastern United States, where archaeological research had gone on for almost 100 years, it appeared as a confused palimpsest in which one prehistoric culture had been superimposed on another, even though these cultures were only vaguely defined and their relative sequence frequently remained uncertain. As a result of the first confirmed Paleo-Indian finds in the 1920s, it also became evident that the Indian occupation of North America had lasted far longer than most archaeologists had hitherto imagined (Willey and Sabloff 1980: 121–123).

In 1913, the ethnologist Berthold Laufer (1913) identified a lack of chronological control as the most serious weakness of American archaeology. During the same decade researchers began to employ stratigraphy and seriation to work out the prehistoric chronology of the southwestern United States (Nelson 1916; Kidder 1924; Kroeber 1916; Spier 1917). At the same time they also defined cultural variation more systematically and in far greater detail than archaeologists had done before. As a result, prehistoric times came to be viewed as a mosaic of archaeological cultures, each of which was established on the basis of inventories of carefully defined artifact types and had its geographical and temporal boundaries empirically delimited. This culture-historical approach to synthesizing archaeological data gradually became standard practice across the United States (Ritchie 1944; Ford and Willey 1941). The results were in many respects similar to those achieved in European archaeology by Gordon Childe in *The Dawn of European Civilization* (1925).

Yet the culture-historical approach evolved very differently in Europe and America. In America, archaeological cultures were delineated after an awareness of temporal variation in the archaeological record had supplemented a longstanding preoccupation with geographical variations. In Europe, they were identified after a growing recognition of geographical variation in the archaeological record supplemented a unilinear evolutionary approach that hitherto had been concerned almost exclusively with studying temporal change. In spite of historical interconnections, the concept of the archaeological culture appears to have developed convergently as a response to the very different problems that archaeology was facing on either side of the Atlantic Ocean (Trigger 1978:75–95).

During the 1920s and 1930s amateur archaeologists became more numerous and well-organized and trafficking in artifacts increased. This produced at least two important countermeasures. In 1934 government, academic, and museum archaeologists formed the Society for American Archaeology, whose aims were to promote closer relations among professional archaeologists and between them and amateurs, as well as to combat "the commercialization of archaeological objects." The two-tiered membership that was maintained until a single category of membership was established in 1942 was intended to assert the leadership of professional archaeologists over amateurs in the society. The Historic Sites Act of 1935 also authorized the Secretary of the Interior to protect archaeological sites.

Public funds had been made available for archaeological research by the Bureau of American Ethnology already in the 19th century, largely as a result of public interest in the mound builders, but most of the funding for archaeological research came from private sources. In 1921 the National Research Council formed a committee on State Archaeological Surveys to encourage the organization of such units (Gorenstein 1976:94). Already in the late 1920s some publicly funded salvage archaeology was undertaken in connection with the construction of Boulder (Hoover) Dam (Fowler 1982:9). During the economic depression of the 1930s, relatively large sums of money were made available for archaeological research by various United States federal government relief agencies through cooperating institutions, such as federal and state park services, museums, and universities. The labor-intensive nature of archaeological fieldwork made it a desirable form of employment for unskilled laborers. Large numbers of sites were excavated in salvage operations carried out in areas that were to be inundated as a result of dam construction. Other excavations were initiated simply to provide jobs, particularly in the southeastern United States (Willey and Sabloff 1980:115, 127).

The vast expansion of archaeological activity that came about as a result of these projects provided a training ground for a future generation of professional archaeologists, who worked as crew supervisors. It also produced enough new information to make possible the first large-scale culture-historical synthesis for the eastern United States (Ford and Willey 1941). Vastly increased manpower allowed large areas of sites to be excavated for the first time, and this in turn resulted in a new emphasis on noting the archaeological context in which artifacts were found and recording settlement pattern data. The recovery of artifacts for study ceased to be the only significant objective of excavations.

The social context of these developments remains obscure. How even a small share of public funds came to be appropriated for prehistoric archaeological research rather than being used for utilitarian projects such as road building is a problem of American social history that is worthy of detailed study. Were certain archaeologists well-placed to influence government allocations? Did amateur support for archaeologists help to promote government action? To some degree the decision must have been influenced by prehistoric archaeology's increasing stature as an academic discipline, especially since the execution of many of these projects was entrusted to archaeologists employed in universities. It is also likely that it was motivated by a growing sense of responsibility to conserve the past that had developed within the context of historical archaeology, especially as manifested in the privately funded restoration work being carried out at Colonial Williamsburg and Greenfield Village.

While these projects were particularly valued because they reinforced establishment views about Euro-American history, they provided a model for studying other remains from the past as part of America's national heritage. The attention paid to prehistoric archaeology was also a continuation of an earlier interest in conserving spectacular native sites, in perhaps the same spirit that spectacular landscapes were considered to be worthy of preservation as national parks. Prehistoric archaeology was also favored as a means of government-sponsored employment because it was labor intensive, digging techniques could be learned quickly, and it produced nothing to compete with private industry. Although there was growing concern in the 1930s with improving the administration of Indian policy in the United States (Redfield et al. 1936), there is no evidence that government-sponsored archaeology programs reflected a significantly improved view of the historical role of native people or of their position in American society.

What happened in the United States at this time was not inevitable. Despite shared economic depression, government support for archaeological projects was not forthcoming in Canada, where there was no publicly supported salvage archaeology until the International St. Lawrence Seaway Project was undertaken in the 1950s. In part, this difference reflects the dearth of professional archaeologists in Canada during the 1930s.

Yet the development of a culture-historical approach to American archaeology, with its emphasis first on chronology and later on cultural context, eventually altered and enhanced the view that archaeologists had of Native Americans. Hitherto native cultures had been generally assumed to have been static, and striking transformations in the archaeological record were interpreted as replacements of one ethnic group by another. As detailed chronologies were constructed, it was frequently observed that such an interpretation was untenable, since evidence of substantial continuity was evident alongside that of change. While migrations were still invoked to account for what appeared to be abrupt changes, diffusion was now relied on to explain more gradual ones (Adams et al. 1978).

These more gradual changes implied that Native North Americans had been capable of altering their way of life as new ideas and items of material culture became available. Yet archaeologists were unwilling to go further and concede that they had been able to innovate on their own. Most significant new traits, such as corn, pottery, burial mounds, and metal-working, were thought to have reached North America by way of eastern Siberia or from Mesoamerica rather than been invented by North American Indians (Trigger 1980). Few archaeologists would have agreed with Kidder (1962:344) when he described the Pueblo cultures as a largely indigenous development within the southwestern United States that only in its early stages had depended on a few ideas of external origin. Hence Native North Americans were regarded as creative only to the minimum extent that was necessary to adjust ideas about their behavior to a current understanding of the archaeological record.

Except in the southwestern United States, where dendrochronology supplied accurate dates for sites back to the beginning of the Christian era, archaeologists also applied what now appear to be very short chronologies to their archaeological sequences. For example, in New York State, the late Archaic Period, which is radiocarbon dated as early as the third millennium B.C., was estimated to have begun around A.D. 300 (cf. Ritchie 1944:10; Ritchie 1965). Because of this, radical transformations of the archaeological record appeared to follow each other in such rapid succession that there was little likelihood that these changes had come about as the result of internal social processes. Such chronologies both reflected and reinforced the traditional assumption that Native Americans were uncreative.

Yet cultural transformations were now clearly documented in the archaeological record, which refuted the 19th-century view that Native North Americans were totally uncreative. Was this change in archaeological interpretation a necessary adjustment of ingrained beliefs to accommodate the discordant findings of archaeological research? Was it partly the result of Boasian anthropology's laudable efforts to refute racist interpretations of human behavior? Or did it reflect a lessening antipathy among Euro-Americans towards native people, whose numbers were assumed to be inevitably declining and who at the beginning of the 20th century posed less of a threat to white American society than they had done at any time in the past?

While most American prehistoric archaeologists were trained and worked in anthropology departments, they were more absorbed by the technical details of their own research and had less significant contact with ethnology at this time than at any other period in the history of American archaeology. Interaction between professional archaeologists and native people was also more limited than at any time in the past. Gorenstein (1976:95) has suggested that the chasm between archaeology and ethnology was widened by the need for professional archaeologists to establish stronger working relationships with amateur archaeologists, which resulted in greater emphasis on material remains. For all of these reasons archaeologists were mainly interested in recovering and classifying their data, reconstructing patterns of material culture, establishing cultural chronologies, and explaining cultural changes in terms of exogenous factors that operated through diffusion and migration (Willey and Sabloff 1980:126–127). It therefore seems likely that the minimal acceptance of changes in prehistoric American cultures was mainly an adjustment of cherished beliefs to fit new archaeological facts. It cannot be denied, however, that this alteration in viewpoint occurred in an intellectual environment that was no longer strongly opposed to such changes.

Processual Archaeology

By making the study of internal change central to its interpretation of archaeological data, processual archaeology, as formulated by Lewis Binford (1962) and his followers, implicitly eliminated the remaining stigmatization of native people as uncreative. Thus, for the first time native and nonnative Americans were placed on an equal level as far as archaeological interpretation was concerned. Only amateur archaeologists, such as Barry Fell, have continued to denigrate native people by attributing major elements of their cultural heritage to prehistoric visitors from the Old World (cf. Fell 1982; Vastokas and Vastokas 1973). In thus breaking with the past, processual archaeology realized the creative potential of the ecological and settlement approaches that had preceded and helped to create it. Both of these approaches stressed the importance of studying cultures as functionally integrated and adaptive systems (Willey and Sabloff 1980:146–155). Yet from the beginning, processual archaeology ignored the potential benefits of this achievement because of its emphasis on generalization as being the principal goal of archaeology (Binford 1967; Watson et al. 1971:3–19). This was illustrated in Paul Martin and Fred Plog's *The Archaeology of Arizona* (1973), where the authors suggested that generalizations about human reactions to stress that were derived from the ecological study of prehistoric archaeological data might be used to understand the behavior of underprivileged black and Mexican groups living in the ghettos of modern Arizona cities (Martin and Plog 1973:364–368). Many processual archaeologists also laid great stress on the relevance of prehistoric archaeology for solving current problems (Ford 1973; Fritz 1973; see also Jennings 1973). In doing so, they proposed to use data concerning the heritage of Native Americans as a basis for formulating generalizations that were relevant for the management of Euro-American society.

The emphasis on nomothetic, or generalizing, goals in prehistoric archaeology reflected the low status of history and the humanities in utilitarian-oriented, mid-20th-century American society and the desire of American archaeologists to conform to a more prestigious model of scholarly behavior, especially as the National Science Foundation became a major source of funding. Similar concerns shaped the development of all the social sciences in the 1960s and early 1970s (Bronowski 1971:195; Kolakowski 1976:229). More specifically, by adopting this new orientation with its nomological and utilitarian pretensions, archaeologists sought to make their own field, which had tended to be atheoretical and descriptive, more closely resemble ethnology. In this manner, a branch of anthropology that generally was regarded as lacking rigor (Kluckhohn 1940; Binford 1962) attempted with considerable success to upgrade its academic credentials within both anthropology and the social sciences generally. On the other hand, archaeology left itself open to the charge that its nomological orientation was a new and intellectually more subtle technique for exploiting the material remains of Native North American prehistory to serve the interests of Euro-American society (Trigger 1980). In this, as well as in its neoevolutionary orientation, processual archaeology bears a close resemblance to the unilinear evolutionism of the 19th century. Its tendency to regard the study of North American prehistory primarily as a means of generalizing about human behavior suggests that the significance of native people to archaeologists had not changed. While no longer denying that a common humanity unites prehistoric archaeologists and the people whose cultural remains they study, most processual archaeologists remained as spiritually alienated from Native Americans as their predecessors had been in the 19th century.

This alienation was not, however, only between archaeologists and Native Americans. In their pursuit of nomothetic goals, many archaeologists espoused an unacceptably narrow view of science, inherited from Julian Steward (1955:179). Science was defined in terms of formulating rules that explain similarities and regularities in data. In this manner, Steward distinguished science from history, which he viewed as being concerned with trying to account for the unique and idiosyncratic aspects of human behavior. Steward was perhaps unduly influenced by claims advanced by late 19th-century historians, such as Leopold von Ranke, that the first duty of their discipline was to ascertain what had actually happened in the past rather than to explain it (Carr 1962:2–3). Yet, in this manner, a false dichotomy was created between history and science. Most scientific disciplines are concerned with explaining the differences as well as the similarities in the phenomena they study (Salmon 1982:125–126). Idiographic and nomothetic explanations are viewed as being two different aspects of science and any attempt to explain, as opposed merely to chronicle, the past counts as a scientific enterprise. Marxist archaeologists, in particular, insist on viewing history as a scientific discipline in which generalizing and particularizing are indissoluably linked (Childe 1947, 1979). Whether or not one accepts Marxism's basic assumptions about human behavior, this approach demonstrates that it is possible to eliminate the gap between science and history by insisting that science must be concerned with the specific as well as the general and that historical interpretation involves explaining particulars as well as generalization. The dichotomy between history and science reflected a parochial view that happily now appears to be on the decline among American prehistoric archaeologists.

The emphasis on nomothetic goals also widened the gap between the study of Old World and New World archaeology in North America. In the past, the two fields were separated by their subject matter, which studied developmental traditions that most professional archaeologists believed had little if any historical relationship to one another and therefore were of no mutual interest within the framework of a culture-historical approach. One would have expected the comparative scientific orientation of processual archaeology to have unified these two branches of archaeology, especially as a growing number of American students trained in processual archaeology began to do research in the eastern hemisphere. Yet, while some excellent comparative work has been done (Adams 1966) and ideas have been exchanged (Weeks 1979), this has not occurred to any substantial degree. The problem now appears to be an antipathy that results from processual archaeologists believing that traditional Old World archaeology is handicapped by its old-fashioned humanistic orientation. Mutual exchanges of information in the respective journals of these two branches of American archaeology (*American Antiquity* and the *Journal of American Archaeology*) will not overcome this alienation. That would require archaeologists on both sides to abandon their exaggerated distinctions between social science, history, and humanism and to recognize that all three approaches can contribute significantly to a scientific understanding of prehistoric and ancient times throughout the world.

There has been an enormous escalation in archaeological activities and in the number of professional archaeologists in North America since the 1960s. The initial growth occurred in universities, where many archaeologists found employment in the general educational expansion that occurred after World War II. After university expansion slowed in the early 1970s, archaeologists continued to find employment in government posts and private consulting firms, as ideas of cultural resource management gained wider public support and government concern with protecting cultural heritage expanded from sites and buildings that were relevant to Euro-American history to include more Native American remains (Fowler 1982:2–12). At the same time, there was a massive (if now threatened) increase in overall government funding of archaeological research. This permitted a diversification of archaeological activities, including systematic regional surveys that provided new kinds of information about the past and allowed a more scientific selection of sites for excavation. The employment of many specialists from the physical and biological sciences to recover and analyze data also contributed to a more detailed understanding of the environmental settings, economies, and ecology of prehistoric cultures (Schiffer 1978–1985).

Recent decades have witnessed the expansion of archaeological activities related to cultural resource management, which seeks to apply managerial skills to achieve goals set through the political process for regulating important aspects of the "national heritage" (Wildesen 1980:10). By its very nature the political process is partisan rather than scientific; however much scientific findings may be taken into consideration. The problems encountered in trying to establish criteria for judging the significance of archaeological sites reflect all of the ambiguities about native people in American society as well as within archaeology as a profession. They also reflect public disagreements about the extent to which current resources should be used to study and conserve the remains of the past. Should native people alone have the right to decide what should be done with prehistoric sites? Since even those native people who claim this exclusive right disagree among themselves, should secular or religious considerations predominate? Or ought the remains of the past to be regarded as the common heritage of all Americans? Should their scientific, recreational, or educational value be of primary concern? These issues have made prehistoric remains the object of growing political controversies involving native peoples, developers, and archaeologists. Various alliances form with respect to specific issues. It is by no means certain that these disputes will ever result in a broadly based consensus concerning the management of cultural resources. Moreover, programs begun in an era of affluence may be regarded with increasing disfavor by the tax payer if they are perceived as consuming public resources at the expense of more valued activities or as impeding economic development. A stable policy with respect to Native American cultural remains is also unlikely to develop in the absence of a public consensus that would grant native people an acceptable place in American society.

Major difficulties have also arisen coordinating the increasingly problem-oriented research of academic archaeologists with cultural resource management. The responsibility of cultural resource management archaeologists to preserve cultural remains for future generations of Americans often does not accord with the wishes of academic archaeologists to excavate and study specific sites. Nor has it been possible to establish norms by which the performance of either academic or contract archaeologists can be evaluated or to arrest the destruction of the vast majority of archaeological sites, which calls the whole conservation ethic into question. Associations have been founded to represent the specific interests of new categories of archaeologists: The Society of Professional Archaeologists in 1975, followed by the American Society for Conservation Archaeology.

Perhaps the most important long-term result of cultural resource management will be to break down the barrier between prehistoric and Euro-American-oriented historical archaeology. This has already happened to a considerable degree as large numbers of anthropologically trained archaeologists have found employment excavating historical sites. In so doing they have injected a strong social science component (South 1977) into what had hitherto been a humanistically oriented pursuit (Noël Hume 1969). On the other hand, historical archaeology has as yet only marginally been incorporated into anthropological training programs; a clear indication that the 19th-century dichotomy between history and anthropology still powerfully influences the academic community. In the long run, however, prehistoric archaeology may be challenged to maintain its position in view of much greater public interest in historical archaeology.

D. D. Fowler (1982) has noted that in preservation archaeology dealing with historic sites a substantial portion of the allocated funds is used for the dissemination of public information about the projects; whereas in prehistoric research such funds are almost nonexistent. He interprets this as evidence of a failure by prehistoric archaeologists to see the need to communicate with the public or, except at the most technical level, among themselves. There has been little discussion of the responsibility of prehistoric archaeologists to transmit information about their findings to native people or to Euro-Americans, although the latter through taxes support most of these activities (Ford 1976).

In the United States the isolation of prehistoric archaeology mirrors the continuing absence of widespread interest in the history of native peoples. Much of what interest there is in prehistoric times centers on sensational claims by nonprofessionals about Atlantis, Noah's Ark, and Tutankhamen's curse, or the ancient cosmonauts that are part of the extraterrestrial salvationism that has become a prominent feature of American fantasy life as the threat of nuclear destruction has increased (Feder 1984). Even serious archaeological coverage seems largely directed to the exotic civilizations of Mesoamerica and the Old World. Relatively few articles about North American archaeology appear in mass circulation journals such as the *National Geographic Magazine* and *Archaeology*, while the now defunct *Early Man*, which sought to popularize North American archaeology, attracted only a few thousand subscribers. The popularization of archaeology in North America has not yet achieved the level of sophistication reached in Great Britain where, as a result of prolonged close relations between professional archaeologists and producers, excellent radio and television programs are regular, not isolated, events (Jordan 1981). This kind of broadcasting may not be possible in a society where the mass media are as commercially oriented as they are in the United States. Brian Fagan (1977:349) noted a lack of coverage of Native American archaeology and of native people generally during the bicentennial celebrations of American Independence in 1976. While the historical event being commemorated is one with which Native Americans have traditionally been associated only to a limited degree, their exclusion from a celebration intended to reaffirm national unity is not without social and political significance.

Nor is the continuing alienation of prehistoric archaeology from native people without its influence on the discipline. This is particularly evident in the deleterious effects of a nomothetic orientation. Processual archaeology, despite the claim that it seeks to understand all aspects of prehistoric behavior, has largely limited the range of questions that it asks to those features of prehistoric economies and social hierarchies that can be explained in terms of general postulates about human activities. It has generally ignored iconography, religious beliefs, and other culturally specific aspects of human behavior that can probably be accounted for in detail only by employing the direct historical approach. Yet these are the kinds of human behavior that are of greatest interest to the general public and to native people. Far from encouraging a comprehensive interest in the past, processual archaeology has so far cultivated a narrow and restricted view of human behavior (Trigger 1984b).

Finally, archaeological explanations offered since the early 1970s evidence a strong concern with population growth and limited resource availability as major factors shaping cultural change. It has been observed that this in turn reflects current anxieties in middle-class American society about unchecked population growth, environmental destruction, and the depletion of nonrenewable resources (Trigger 1981b). It would appear to be symptomatic of the continued indifference of processual archaeology towards Native Americans that the discipline now uses data concerning Native Americans to address general problems about human behavior and processes of social change that are of current interest to Euro-American society rather than making the study of Native American prehistory its primary goal. This situation is the more striking because the two concerns need not be antithetical. Because of this, it appears that archaeologists have turned from using their discipline to rationalize Euro-American prejudices against native people, as they did in the 19th century, to simply ignoring native people as an end of study in themselves. Their rejection of the value of a historical view of the past may help to explain why so few native people want to become archaeologists or are interested in the results of archaeological research.

Processual archaeology developed at a time when the native population of North America was growing rapidly and native people were becoming militant in their efforts to regain control of their own social, economic, and political destiny. It was also a period when Indians were being identified as "natural ecologists" by middle-class Euro-Americans who were increasingly preoccupied with conservation. This view has produced a more favorable popular image of Native Americans that native leaders have been able to manipulate in their struggles with the dominant society (Martin 1978:157–188). Finally, there is emerging a pan-Indian identity that makes the archaeological remains of any one native group or from any period a matter of concern to all living Native Americans. While many archaeologists question the historical validity of such claims (Rosen 1980), they reflect a powerful new ethnic consciousness that is uniting or reuniting disparate and sometimes formerly hostile groups and like other such movements is attributing new meanings to the past (Hertzberg 1971).

In recent years, some native people have sought to control or prevent the archaeological study of prehistoric burials or even prehistoric sites in general, often on religious grounds. Yielding to such pressures is a far less expensive way for governments, businessmen, and the general public to display concern for native people than granting their demands for more far-reaching economic and political changes. Hence archaeologists, as a small and relatively powerless group, that is highly dependent on government and government-legislated financing, find it difficult to check a growing threat to archaeology as they know it. One example of legislation establishing the rights of native people to control their cultural heritage are the provisions guaranteeing them access to and use of sacred sites contained in the American Indian Religious Freedom Act passed in 1978 (Fowler 1982:33). Some archaeologists are now forming groups to oppose in the courts laws that grant Native Americans the power to determine the fate of any excavated skeletal remains and the artifacts associated with them (Bard 1984). Such legislation challenges traditional Euro-American views that archaeological sites belong solely to private owners or to the government. It also challenges the belief hitherto shared by most archaeologists that, because their research aims to produce knowledge for public benefit, they have a moral right of access to the archaeological documentation of the past (Johnson et al. 1977:91–92). Many archaeologists view the idea that living native peoples should control the use of sites as threatening the future of their discipline or major aspects of it. The threat is perceived as being especially serious in view of the escalating rate at which the archaeological record is being destroyed by commercial and recreational activities in North America.

Some native people are religious fundamentalists in the sense that they affirm traditional accounts of Amerindian origins to the exclusion of all other accounts. In general, these people are not interested in archaeological findings and they may be among those most opposed to the collection of archaeological data. Archaeologists can probably no more convince such people of the value of archaeological research than they have been able to win the approval of Christian fundamentalists, who have long rejected and opposed the findings of Paleolithic archaeology. Other native people, who are inclined to adopt a more scientific view, however, may see in archaeology a way to achieve a more detailed, accurate, and favorable view of their past. Among these is the Pueblo of Zuni, which has sponsored its own program of archaeological research (Ferguson 1984). This positive view of archaeology has been encouraged to some degree by the minor but valuable role that archaeologists have played in giving expert testimony on behalf of Native Americans in land

claims litigation (Ford 1973). Yet native people in general have been re-
pelled by the negative attitudes toward them that have been reflected in
interpretations of archaeological data, and in particular by the continuing lack of concern among archaeologists to study the past as a record
of Native American history and culture.

The cultural needs of Native Americans for a better understanding
of their history and the reciprocal need of archaeologists for their support create a powerful incentive for archaeologists to overcome their prolonged estrangement from the people whose past they study. Gaining the
support of native people does not simply involve the popularization of
archaeological findings or the writing up of archaeological conclusions
in a different format, as some archaeologists have implied (Binford
1967:235). Nor is it enough to employ native people on excavations;
although their participation in all aspects of archaeological research is
highly desirable. It also requires that archaeologists pay attention to topics other than those involving explanation in terms of general assumptions about human behavior. The investigation of more culturally specific
aspects of human behavior using the direct historical approach would
emphasize developmental continuities between prehistoric and historic
times and thus draw archaeologists, ethnologists, and linguists closer together in a new cooperative association. While there is some evidence of
movement in this direction (Gibbon 1984:169–176), for the most part it
remains hesitant and highly defensive towards processual archaeology.
More studies of this sort would enrich rather than diminish the explanatory power of archaeology at the same time that it would expand the
scope of Native American history. Historically oriented archaeological
research can also contribute to reshaping social attitudes and help to
bring to an end the marginalization of native people with respect to
North American society that began with the attitudes adopted by European settlers 400 years ago.

Conclusions

Anthropologists have traditionally viewed themselves as objective scholars or as favorably inclined toward Native Americans. Yet, in the 19th
century, anthropology was deeply colored by colonization and uncon-
sciously helped to rationalize it by reaffirming white stereotypes of Indians as primitive, unevolved people. Only recently have significant numbers of anthropologists become critically aware of the social significance

of their studies. Because of their relative lack of contact with native people, archaeologists were influenced by popular stereotypes to an even greater degree than were ethnologists. Yet while archaeology has been shaped to a considerable degree by middle-class Euro-American values, it has not been completely determined by them. Archaeologists, despite their generally conservative orientation, have displayed some ability to transcend their social circumstances and even to alter social perceptions. Archaeology can no more be practiced independently of society than can other disciplines. Yet the evidence suggests that relativism complicates rather than excludes a positivist approach. If archaeology is to play a role that is more significant in terms of both the social sciences and American society as a whole, it is essential that archaeologists understand and take account of the social significance of their discipline.

Literature Cited

Adams, Robert McC.
 1966 *The Evolution of Urban Society.* Aldine, Chicago.

Adams, W. Y., D. P. van Gerven, and R. S. Levy
 1978 The Retreat from Migrationism. *Annual Review of Anthropology* 7:483–532.

Bard, Kathryn
 1984 Reburial an Issue in California Again: New Law Poses a Threat to Effective Archaeological Research. *Early Man* 4(4):1–2.

Binford, Lewis R.
 1962 Archaeology as Anthropology. *American Antiquity* 28:217–225.
 1967 Comment. *Current Anthropology* 8:234–235.

Bintliff, J. L.
 1984 Structuralism and Myth in Minoan Studies. *Antiquity* 58:33–38.

Bronowski, Jacob
 1971 Technology and Culture in Evolution: Introduction to Symposium on Technology and Social Criticism. *Philosophy of the Social Sciences* 1:195–206.

Carr, E. H.
 1962 *What is History?* Vintage, London.

Childe, V. Gordon
 1925 *The Dawn of European Civilization.* Kegan Paul, London.
 1947 *History.* Cobbett, London.
 1979 Prehistory and Marxism. *Antiquity* 53:93–95.

Collingwood, R. G.
 1946 *The Idea of History.* Oxford University Press, Oxford.

Connolly, John
   1977   Archeology in Nova Scotia and New Brunswick between 1863 and
          1914 and Its Relationship to the Development of North American Ar-
          cheology. *Man in the Northeast* 13:3–34.

Fagan, Brian M.
   1977   *Elusive Treasure: The Story of Early Archaeologists in the Americas.*
          Scribner's, New York.
   1981   Two Hundred and Four Years of African Archaeology. In *Antiquity and
          Man: Essays in Honour of Glyn Daniel,* edited by J. D. Evans, B. Cun-
          liffe, and Colin Renfrew, pages 42–51. Thames and Hudson, London.

Feder, Kenneth L.
   1984   Irrationality and Popular Archaeology. *American Antiquity* 49:525–
          541.

Fell, Barry
   1982   *Bronze Age America.* Little, Brown, Boston.

Ferguson, T. J.
   1984   Archaeological Ethics and Values in a Tribal Cultural Resource Man-
          agement Program at the Pueblo of Zuni. In *Ethics and Values in Ar-
          chaeology,* edited by E. L. Green, pages 224–235. Free Press, New
          York.

Ford, John A., and Gordon R. Willey
   1941   An Interpretation of the Prehistory of the Eastern United States. *Amer-
          ican Anthropologist* 43:325–363.

Ford, R. I.
   1973   Archeology Serving Humanity. In *Research and Theory in Current Ar-
          cheology,* edited by Charles Redman, pages 83–93. John Wiley, New
          York.
   1976   The State of the Art in Archeology. *In* Perspectives on Anthropology
          1976, edited by A.F.C. Wallace et al. *American Anthropological Asso-
          ciation, Special Publication* 10:101–115. Washington, D.C.

Fowler, D. D.
   1982   Culture Resources Management. In *Advances in Archaeological
          Method and Theory,* edited by M. B. Schiffer, 5:1–50. Academic Press,
          New York.

Fritz, J. M.
   1973   Relevance, Archeology, and Subsistence Theory. In *Research and
          Theory in Current Archeology,* edited by C. L. Redman, pages 59–82.
          John Wiley, New York.

Gathercole, Peter
   1981   New Zealand Prehistory before 1950. In *Towards a History of Archae-
          ology,* edited by Glyn Daniel, pages 159–168. Thames and Hudson,
          London.

Gibbon, Guy
   1984   *Anthropological Archaeology.* Columbia University Press, New York.

Gorenstein, Shirley
   1976   History of American Archaeology. *In* Perspectives on Anthropology
          1976, edited by A.F.C. Wallace et al. *American Anthropological Asso-
          ciation, Special Publication* 10:86–100. Washington, D.C.

Gruber, J. W.
1967   Horatio Hale and the Development of American Anthropology. *Proceedings of the American Philosophical Society* 111:5–37.

Haven, Samuel F.
1856   Archaeology of the United States. *Smithsonian Contributions to Knowledge* 8(2). Washington, D.C.

Hertzberg, H. W.
1971   *The Search for an American Indian Identity: Modern Pan-Indian Movements.* Syracuse University Press, Syracuse.

Hinsley, C. M., Jr.
1981   *Scientists and Savages: The Smithsonian Institution and the Development of American Anthropology, 1846–1910.* Smithsonian Institution Press, Washington.

Hodder, Ian
1982   *The Present Past: An Introduction to Anthropology for Archaeologists.* Batsford, London.

Jennings, J. D.
1973   The Social Uses of Archaeology. *Addison-Wesley Module in Anthropology* 41. Reading, Massachusetts.

Johnson, E. (compiler)
1977   Archeology and Native Americans. In *The Management of Archaeological Resources: The Arlie House Report,* edited by C. R. McGimsey III and H. A. Davis, pages 90–96. Special Publication of the Society for American Archaeology, Washington, D.C.

Jordan, Paul
1981   Archaeology and Television. In *Antiquity and Man: Essays in Honour of Glyn Daniel,* edited by J. D. Evans, B. Cunliffe, and Colin Renfrew, pages 207–213. Thames and Hudson, London.

Keiser, Albert
1933   *The Indian in American Literature.* Oxford University Press, New York.

Kidder, A. V.
1924   An Introduction to the Study of Southwestern Archaeology, with a Preliminary Account of the Excavations at Pecos. *Papers of the Southwestern Expedition, Phillips Academy* 1. New Haven.
1962   *An Introduction to the Study of Southwestern Archaeology, with an Introduction on "Southwestern Archaeology Today" by Irving Rouse.* Yale University Press, New Haven.

Killan, Gerald
1980   The Canadian Institute and the Origins of the Ontario Archaeological Tradition, 1851–1884. *Ontario Archaeology* 34:3–16.
1983   *David Boyle: From Artisan to Archaeologist.* University of Toronto Press, Toronto.

Kluckhohn, Clyde
1940   The Conceptual Structure in Middle American Studies. In *The Maya and Their Neighbors,* edited by C. L. Hay, pages 41–51. Appleton-Century, New York.

Kolakowski, Leszek
  1976 *La philosophie positiviste.* Denoël, Paris.

Kroeber, A. L.
  1916 Zuni Potsherds. *Anthropological Papers of the American Museum of Natural History* 18(1):7–37.

Laufer, Berthold
  1913 Remarks. *American Anthropologist* 15:573–577.

Leone, M. P.
  1982 Some Opinions about Recovering Mind. *American Antiquity* 47:742–760.

Lescarbot, Marc
  1907–1914 *The History of New France,* translated by W. L. Grant. 3 volumes. The Champlain Society, Toronto.

Lubbock, John (Lord Avebury)
  1913 *Prehistoric Times as Illustrated by Ancient Remains and the Manners and Customs of Modern Savages.* 7th edition. Williams and Norgate, London.

Martijn, Charles
  1978 Historique de la recherche archéologique au Québec. *Recherches Amérindiennes au Québec* 7(1–2):11–18.

Martin, Calvin
  1978 *Keepers of the Game: Indian-Animal Relationships and the Fur Trade.* University of California Press, Berkeley and Los Angeles.

Martin, Paul, and Fred Plog
  1973 *The Archaeology of Arizona: A Study of the Southwest Region.* The Natural History Press, Garden City, New York.

McGuire, J.
  1899 Pipes and Smoking Customs of the American Aborigines, Based on Material in the U.S. National Museum. *Annual Report of the Board of Regents of the Smithsonian Institution, Report of the U.S. National Museum* 1:351–645, Washington, D.C.

McKusick, Marshall
  1970 *The Davenport Conspiracy.* The University of Iowa, Iowa City.

Meltzer, D. J.
  1983 The Antiquity of Man and the Development of American Archaeology. In *Advances in Archaeological Method and Theory,* edited by M. B. Schiffer, 6:1–51. Academic Press, New York.

Miller, Mikhail
  1956 *Archaeology in the U.S.S.R.* Atlantic Press, London.

Monkman, Leslie
  1981 *A Native Heritage: Images of the Indian in English-Canadian Literature.* University of Toronto Press, Toronto.

Morlot, Adolphe von
  1861 General Views on Archaeology. *Annual Report of the Smithsonian Institution for 1860,* pages 284–343, Washington, D.C.

Mulvaney, D. J.
  1981 Gum Leaves on the Golden Bough: Australia's Palaeolithic Survivals Discovered. In *Antiquity and Man: Essays in Honour of Glyn Daniel,* edited by J. D. Evans, B. Cunliffe, and Colin Renfrew, pages 52–64. Thames and Hudson, London.

Nelson, N. C.
  1916 Chronology of the Tano Ruins, New Mexico. *American Anthropologist* 18:159–180.

Noël Hume, Ivor
  1969 *Historical Archaeology.* Alfred A. Knopf, New York.

Pagden, Anthony
  1982 *The Fall of Natural Man: The American Indian and the Origins of Comparative Ethnology.* Cambridge University Press, New York.

Parker, Arthur C.
  1916 The Origin of the Iroquois as Suggested by Their Archaeology. *American Anthropologist* 18:479–507.

Patterson II, E. P.
  1972 *The Canadian Indian: A History Since 1500.* Collier-Macmillan, Don Mills.

Porter, H. C.
  1979 *The Inconstant Savage: England and the North American Indian, 1500–1660.* Duckworth, London.

Posnansky, Merrick
  1982 African Archaeology Comes of Age. *World Archaeology* 13:345–358.

Prucha, F. P.
  1977 *A Bibliographical Guide to the History of Indian-White Relations in the United States.* University of Chicago Press, Chicago.

Putnam, F. W.
  1890 The Serpent Mound of Ohio. *Century Magazine* 39:698–703.

Redfield, Robert, Ralph Linton, and M. J. Herskovits
  1936 Outline for the Study of Acculturation. *American Anthropologist* 38:149–152.

Resek, Carl
  1960 *Lewis Henry Morgan: American Scholar.* University of Chicago Press, Chicago.

Ribes, René
  1966 Pièces de la période archaïque trouvées vers 1700 dans la région de Bécancour. *Cahiers d'archéologie Québecoise* 2(1):22–34.

Ritchie, William A.
  1944 The Pre-Iroquoian Occupations of New York State. *Rochester Museum of Arts and Sciences, Memoir* 1. Rochester.
  1965 *The Archaeology of New York State.* The Natural History Press, Garden City, New York.

Rosen, Lawrence
  1980 The Excavation of American Indian Burial Sites: A Problem of Law and Professional Responsibility. *American Anthropologist* 82:5–27.

Salmon, M. H.
    1982   *Philosophy and Archaeology.* Academic Press, New York.

Schiffer, Michael B. (editor)
    1978–1985   *Advances in Archaeological Method and Theory.* Volumes 1–8.
        Academic Press, New York.

Silverberg, Robert
    1968   *Mound Builders of Ancient America: The Archeology of a Myth.* New
        York Graphic Society, New York.

Sklenář, Karel
    1983   *Archaeology in Central Europe: The First 500 Years.* Leicester Univer-
        sity Press, Leicester.

Smith, Donald B.
    1974   *Le Sauvage: The Native People in Quebec Historical Writing on the
        Heroic Period (1534–1663) of New France.* (Mercury Series, 6) Na-
        tional Museum of Man, History Division, Ottawa.

South, Stanley
    1977   *Method and Theory in Historical Archaeology.* Academic Press, New
        York.

Spier, Leslie
    1917   An Outline for a Chronology of Zuñi Ruins. *Anthropological Papers of
        the American Museum of Natural History* 18(3):207–331, New York.

Stanton, William
    1960   *The Leopard's Spots: Scientific Attitudes Toward Race in America,
        1815–59.* University of Chicago Press, Chicago.

Steward, Julian H.
    1955   *Theory of Culture Change: The Methodology of Multilinear Evolution.*
        University of Illinois Press, Urbana.

Stocking, George W., Jr.
    1974   *A Franz Boas Reader: The Shaping of American Anthropology, 1883–
        1911.* University of Chicago Press, Chicago.

Trigger, Bruce G.
    1978   *Time and Traditions: Essays in Archaeological Interpretation.* Colum-
        bia University Press, New York.
    1980   Archaeology and the Image of the American Indian. *American An-
        tiquity* 45:662–676.
    1981a Giants and Pygmies: The Professionalization of Canadian Archaeology.
        In *Towards a History of Archaeology,* edited by Glyn Daniel, pages 69–
        84. Thames and Hudson, London.
    1981b Anglo-American Archaeology. *World Archaeology* 13:138–155.
    1984a Alternative Archaeologies: Nationalist, Colonialist, Imperialist. *Man*
        19:355–370.
    1984b Archaeology at the Crossroads: What's New? *Annual Review of An-
        thropology* 13:275–300.
    1985   The Past as Power: Anthropology and the North American Indian. In
        Who Owns the Past?, edited by Isabel McBryde, pages 11–40. Oxford
        University Press, Melbourne.

Vastokas, J. M., and R. K. Vastokas
  1973 *Sacred Art of the Algonkians: A Study of the Peterborough Petroglyphs.*
  Mansard Press, Peterborough.

Vaughan, A. T.
  1982 From White Man to Red Skin: Changing Anglo-American Perceptions
  of the American Indian. *American Historical Review* 87:917–935.

Washburn, Wilcomb E. (compiler)
  1973 *The American Indian and the United States: A Documentary History.*
  4 volumes. Random House, New York.

Washburn, Wilcomb E.
  1975 *The Indian in America.* Harper and Row, New York.

Watson, P. J., S. A. LeBlanc, and C. L. Redman
  1971 *Explanation in Archeology: An Explicitly Scientific Approach.* Columbia University Press, New York.

Weeks, Kent (editor)
  1979 *Egyptology and the Social Sciences.* Cairo: American University in
  Cairo Press.

Wildesen, L. E.
  1980 Cultural Resource Management: A Personal View. *Practicing Anthropology* 2(2):10, 22–23.

Willey, Gordon R., and J. A. Sabloff
  1980 *A History of American Archaeology.* 2nd edition. Freeman, San Francisco.

Wilson, Daniel
  1862 *Prehistoric Man: Researches into the Origin of Civilization in the Old
  and the New World.* 2 volumes. Macmillan, London.

Wolf, Eric
  1982 *Europe and the People without History.* University of California Press,
  Berkeley and Los Angeles.

Edgar Lee Hewett and the School of American Research in Santa Fe 1906–1912

As is the case in most sciences, the history of American archaeology has been largely written by the participants themselves. Generally speaking, these histories fall into several categories. There are, first, the general survey histories, such as Gordon Willey and Jeremy Sabloff's *A History of American Archaeology* (1974) or Ignacio Bernal's *A History of Mexican Archaeology* (1980). These usually adopt a scheme of periodization defined chiefly by changing methodology, theory, and purpose. Willey and Sabloff, for instance, following suggestions of Douglas Schwartz (1967, 1968), present four periods: the speculative (1492–1840); the classificatory-descriptive (1840–1914); the classificatory-historical (1914–1940); and the explanatory (1940–present). Alternatively, Gene Rogge, in a recent (1983) unpublished dissertation, has followed the lead of George C. Moore (1973) in suggesting a four-period scheme based on both intellectual concerns and definable scholarly communities within archaeology. In their conception, one can identify an early community, focused institutionally on the American Ethnological Society between 1830 and 1860, and centered intellectually on the problem of the origin and identity of the Native Americans. This institutional-intellectual paradigm, according to Rogge and Moore, subsequently underwent three identifiable transformations, ending with a primary emphasis, since about 1965, on processual archaeology, among certain influential circles of the Society for American Archaeology.

Such surveys are useful and necessary. They are supplemented by regional histories, such as James E. Fitting's regionally organized volume, *The Development of North American Archaeology* (1973), or Douglas Schwartz's *Conceptions of Kentucky Prehistory* (1967); and by works which center on a single locus or group of sites, such as Robert and Florence Lister's recent retrospective and analytical study, *Chaco Canyon* (1981). In addition, some students have focused on specific issues, such as David Meltzer's study of "The Antiquity of Man and the Development of American Archaeology," which appeared at the same time (1983) as Donald Grayson's longer study of the same set of issues in the European context (*The Establishment of Human Antiquity*). Finally, biographies, memoirs, and autobiographical accounts—written and, increasingly, oral histories—constitute a growing corpus of valuable materials. Archaeologists, like anthropologists in general, have turned out to be among the most historically self-conscious of scientists; so much so, in fact, that the challenge to the historian is to avoid getting lost in the masses of information, data, and memories, in order to sketch as clearly as possible the larger outlines. We can begin to do so with the following questions: (1) What, if any, patterns in its history distinguish archaeology from the histories of other sciences? (2) What characteristics have marked archaeology as practiced in the United States from archaeology practiced elsewhere?

In this paper I am arguing, through a brief case study, that archaeology as it has developed in this country has been sociologically distinct in at least one significant way. In a recent history of British archaeology, entitled *A Social History of Archaeology* (1981), Kenneth Hudson demonstrated the persistent difficulties in drawing clear lines between the amateur and the professional and the ways in which this problem of boundary demarcation has influenced funding and method. In the American historical context porousness is also evident, greatly exacerbated by a strong democratic ideology of openness in science (Hinsley 1981:34–63) and, even more importantly, by the shifts of demographic and economic power accompanying the nation's growth and expansion over time. These factors have impeded all efforts at centralized professional control. American archaeology, in consequence, has historically been a decentralized and somewhat unruly undertaking, subject to regional, local, even individual outbreaks of innovation, enthusiasm, and defiance of established authority.

There is no clearer case of this than Edgar Lee Hewett's determined effort to establish the School of American Archaeology (now the School of American Research) in Santa Fe, New Mexico, in the early years of the 20th century. At the time of Hewett's appearance American anthropology was dominated by a handful of individuals and institutions: the

Bureau of American Ethnology and Smithsonian Institution; Frederick Putnam at the Peabody Museum at Harvard; Franz Boas at the American Museum and Columbia; and to a lesser degree, Frederick Starr at the University of Chicago and George Dorsey at the Field Museum. The balance of entrenched professional power lay in the Northeast, while the rest of the country, notably the Southwest, had for some decades provided good hunting grounds for northeastern archaeologists and ethnologists. Within this context Hewett's story unfolded.

In 1901 Charles P. Bowditch, a Boston investor and patron of Central American studies at Harvard's Peabody Museum, convinced the Boston-based Archaeological Institute of America to establish a Central American fellowship in order to train an individual in linguistics, ethnography, and epigraphy of the Mayan region. Alfred Tozzer held the fellowship for four years; then, in 1905, he joined the Harvard faculty, leaving a vacancy in the fellowship.

Bowditch was willing to continue supporting the fellowship and wanted the Institute to deepen its involvement in New World studies, particularly in the Mayan region. As he had done four years previously, Bowditch looked in 1905 to Boas and Putnam for advice. The choice was small, but Boas suggested Robert H. Lowie, a student at Columbia who had not yet decided on his major fields. Boas had set Lowie to work with the aging Adolph Bandelier (for whom Boas had arranged an adjunct position in the anthropology department at Columbia, familiarizing students with Spanish literature on the New World). Bowditch agreed with Boas' suggestion that the new Fellow should concentrate on the linguistics and archaeology of the province of Oaxaca: "a most promising enterprise," thought Boas. He recommended Lowie as "a most conscientious and intelligent all round man" for the ethnology of Central or South America (Boas to Bowditch, 1 July 1905, CPB). According to their plan Lowie would spend the summer of 1906 reading and formulating problems; the fall would be passed with Boas in New York, followed by six months with Eduard Seler in Berlin. Thus by the summer of 1907 Lowie would be ready for the field: "A young man could find no better chance of getting a start in scientific investigation," wrote Boas (to Bowditch, 21 July and 30 September 1905, CPB). In November, though, Lowie suddenly overturned the careful plans by withdrawing, citing financial and personal considerations. Boas and Bowditch were left with a single alternative candidate, about whom neither was enthusiastic: Edgar Lee Hewett. Boas was particularly glum: "The prospect in regard to

Mr. Hewitt [sic] does not appeal to me at all," he confided to Bowditch, "particularly after listening to a lecture which he gave here a week or so ago before our Ethnological Society" (Boas to Bowditch, 13 November 1905, CPB).

While Boas and Bowditch pondered the unexpected and uncomfortable prospect of having a fellowship without acceptable candidates, Hewett organized a campaign. His key supporter was Jesse Walter Fewkes, already a central part of what would become Hewett's Southwest-Washington axis. Fewkes wrote to Bowditch in high praise of his friend in December. After Christmas, Francis Kelsey of the University of Michigan, a rising star in the Institute, talked with Hewett about the fellowship and came away favorably impressed (Fewkes to Bowditch, 15 December 1905; Kelsey, to Bowditch, 28 December 1905, CPB). The support from Fewkes was probably discounted in Cambridge, since Fewkes had been banished from Harvard's Museum of Comparative Zoology in 1889 by Alexander Agassiz for publishing some materials without permission. But Fewkes had since built a second career as an archaeologist with strong loyalties institutionally to the Smithsonian and regionally to the Southwest. At this juncture, in late 1905, he made an important move: he submitted an alternative plan for the prospective Fellow, and it was on the basis of this plan that Hewett took the position. The Fewkes plan was indeed designed for Hewett. Rather than begin field work in Mexico after the kind of training Boas had intended for Lowie, Hewett was to embark immediately on a single year's work: three or four months of "original researches" in the ruins of the Southwest and northern Mexico, and the remainder of the time in "preliminary reconnaissance" of fields of future work in Mexico, with an eye to establishing an Institute school in Mexico City. Time permitting, Fewkes advised visiting San Juan Teotihuacan, Tezcoco, Mitla, Palenque, and other sites (Fewkes to Bowditch, 10 January 1906, CPB). It would be a year of survey, constant movement, and "politicking"—Hewett's strengths. As to the Boas-Bowditch plan for a man of university training, Fewkes could barely hide his disdain: "It has been evident to me for some years," he wrote, "that our universities have failed to build up a school of American Archaeology, and have not turned out first class scholars in this department" (Fewkes to Bowditch, 4 January 1906, CPB).

At the Institute's meetings in December 1905, Hewett was appointed Fellow in American Archaeology for one year, with the expectation that he would lay the foundation for an American school, probably in Mexico, on the model of the Institute's schools in Athens and Rome. He was clearly on trial. Some, such as Alice Fletcher, seemed cautiously pleased with the outlook (Fletcher to Bowditch, 6 January 1906, CPB), but Boas was already washing his hands of a man he did not trust. Asked his opinion of the plans, Boas responded curtly: "It seems to my mind that a man of the type of Hewett will probably have his own definite plan for field-work, and that it would be wiser to ask him to state what he wants to do and, if his plan seems good, to approve it" (Boas to Bowditch, 10 January 1906, CPB). To Putnam he was more explicit: The proposed reconnaissance by Hewett would be useless to the Institute, though it might help Hewett's career; in any case, he advised, Hewett should stick strictly to archaeology (Boas to Putnam, 7 February, 1906, CPB). Hewett accepted both the plan and the position.

The new Committee on American Archaeology for the Institute consisted of three members (Bowditch, Putnam, and Boas) whose chief functions were to oversee Hewett and work toward founding an American school. Of the three, Putnam was the most malleable and sympathetic toward the Fewkes plan, partly because it coincided with his long-standing interest in historical migrations between the Southwest and Mexico, and partly because Putnam was an individual of great tolerance and patience. He was also ill at the time (e.g., Putnam to Hewett, 8 February 1906; Putnam to Bowditch, 7 and 22 February 1906, CPB). Whenever possible Hewett preferred to circumvent Bowditch and Boas, whose dislike was apparent. Thus when Bowditch left in January 1906 for his winter home in Santa Barbara, California, appointing the ailing Putnam as temporary chairman, Hewett felt the reins slacken. With the help of Francis Kelsey, he took his own lead.

Hewett firmly believed that if American archaeology were ever to receive the attention and financial backing it deserved within the Institute or in American society generally, the Institute would have to appeal to and take advantage of local enthusiasms, regional pride, important individual egos, and the untrained but ardent talents springing up in the urban centers of the Midwest and Southwest, and on the West Coast. Charles Lummis had shown the way in Los Angeles, building his South West Society in three short years into the bumptious strapling of the Institute federation; Lummis referred to the Society as the "new and remote western brat" of the Institute (Lummis to Norton, 9 December 1906, AIA). As feared by the Institute's president, Yale professor Thomas Day Seymour, the Institute's center of gravity was steadily migrating from the respectable confines of the East Coast and pushing westward past Detroit. Charles Eliot Norton, the Harvard professor and Boston gentleman who had founded the Institute in 1879, wrote that he saw a "great calamity" and "grave danger" in domination by midwesterners and hoped that such a "revolution" could be avoided (Norton to Bowditch, 29 December 1906, AIA). Kelsey, the vigorous new corresponding secretary of the Institute, personified and promoted this "nationalizing," which was quickly leaving the eastern men outnumbered and outmaneuvered. Seymour told Bowditch that he was convinced that Kelsey "does not value a high standard for the work of the Institute so much as he does 'influence' with the masses . . .[but] no man from the faculties of Harvard, Yale, or Columbia could draw such an audience as he in Kansas, Missouri, or Utah" (Seymour to Bowditch, 26 May 1906, CPB).

Due to his institutional placement Kelsey became the central figure in the maneuverings in the Institute after 1906; he was principally responsible for Hewett's rise to prominence. As secretary of the Institute Kelsey engaged in an enormous flow of correspondence. He devised plans of reorganization, established a wide acquaintanceship, and encouraged the formation of new Institute affiliates across the country. All of this drew much power to him. When President Seymour died a few days before the Christmas meetings in 1907, Kelsey emerged as the logical successor. The Kelsey presidency, which lasted through 1912, provided optimal conditions for Hewett's expansive plans, for those intentions conformed well to Kelsey's own ideas and methods. Until late 1910, when serious accusations of unprofessional conduct were leveled against Hewett, Kelsey supported him faithfully; only in 1912, when he saw that Hewett's ever-growing ambitions were to extend beyond Central America and the Southwest, did Kelsey noticeably cool toward him. What had held him to Hewett?

Kelsey's view of the future of classical studies and archaeology in the United States centered regionally on the western half of the country and socially on new urban business wealth between St. Louis and Los Angeles. A professor of classical studies at the University of Michigan, Kelsey enjoyed independent wealth and dabbled in business investments at various times. He was proud of these ventures, for Kelsey had great respect for men of business acumen and action. In this regard, of course, he merely shared a favorite bias of his generation, but it was a preference with some import. As an officer of the Archaeological Institute Kelsey came to view himself as a broker between business and science, a man who spoke fluently both the language of efficiency and practical investment and the dialect of university archaeology. While he liked to present his services to the Institute as labors of love performed at sacrifice to his family and career, it is clear that Kelsey greatly enjoyed the travel, hotels, official stationery, secretarial services, committee meetings, and judgments over others—in sum, the exercise of worldly power by a man of affairs. His admiration for the aggressive business world and his desire to associate with the movers and shakers of American enterprise (without, however, sacrificing his persona as reflective scholar) are transparent in his words and actions. Throughout them run the complementary themes of time pressure and physical movement: Kelsey's constant hurry was his assertion of vigor and importance.

Kelsey actually had little interest in American archaeology. With few exceptions among the founders and leaders of the Institute, New World studies had always been something of an afterthought. Henry W. Haynes, an influential Boston enthusiast of archaeology, had expressed the prevailing sentiment in 1889 when he wrote to Norton: "I should not like to maintain that there is practically nothing more to be learned in respect of the past of the native races of America. If people are willing to spend their money in an attempt after this, even if it is a futile one, it seems to me more respectable than to waste it in ignobler ways—, surely we can never hope to get such people to give it for classical archaeology" (Haynes to Norton 22 April 1889, AIA). Over the next quarter of a century, as the need for a broader financial base for archaeology led to national expansion of the Institute, it also became apparent that local interests west of the Mississippi, or even west of the Alleghenies, could be kindled by appeal to local, regional, national, even hemispheric heritage. This support, once established, could then be channeled or partly siphoned off to sustain classical archaeology. In other words, men like Kelsey who had no personal commitment to American studies could nonetheless promote them as a catalyst in the West in order to aid what they considered ultimately more worthwhile investigations. This was less a matter of deceit than a question of pragmatic manipulation. Kelsey was clear on this point as early as 1906, when he wrote to Seymour (15 May 1906, AIA):

> In Colorado, Utah, New Mexico and other states of the West, there is a large body of college men from the East who cherish the classical traditions. Naturally enough the first impulse of the people in this region is along the lines of immediate interest; but I am convinced that the interest in American Archaeology, which is a field almost barren of the ideal, will lead to the development of an interest along the lines of the Institute's present work in classical and Oriental lands.

Kelsey's general strategy for arousing interest and permanent support in the western cities was to grant greater financial autonomy to these affiliates and encourage them to undertake regional projects, build museum collections, and preserve local sites on their own with oversight from the national organization. Annual spring lecture tours by recognized Institute scholars in archaeology and linguistics would stimulate the locals by giving a sense of access to cosmopolitan discourse. In this context of western boosterism Hewett became a prized spokesman for the Institute.

Needless to say, the vision shared by Kelsey and Hewett directly contradicted the professionalism in science that Boas had been struggling to define since the 1890s. His institutional paradigm for anthropology called for transcending local and "amateur" practitioners, who could only, he felt, obstruct proper scientific discourse among accredited professionals. In 1902 Boas wrote to Charles D. Walcott of his concern that "the emotional interest in the welfare of the local bodies may outweigh among many individuals the more general interest in the advancement of science" (21 January 1902, FB). It was a conviction that grew with time for Boas; understandably he saw Hewett's activities as regressive.

Given such deep differences in perspective and purpose, it did not take long for misunderstanding to arise around Hewett. Bowditch, Putnam, and Boas had assumed that following a few weeks of library preparation the new Fellow would take immediately to the field in the Southwest and Mexico. But Kelsey and Hewett had their own ideas. In the absence of clear instructions from Putnam, in February Kelsey encouraged Hewett to remain in Washington until early March, lobbying for final passage of the Antiquities Act of 1906 and for the national charter of the Institute. Hewett then spent three months organizing support for an Institute affiliate in Colorado, helping the Land Office survey Mesa Verde, lecturing in Salt Lake City, and overseeing some archaeological field work of the South West Society. By mid-May, when Bowditch returned to Boston from California, Hewett had yet to begin his work for the fellowship. Bowditch exploded. He accused Kelsey of overextending his purview as secretary of the Institute, lectured Hewett on his failure to report his activities properly, and ordered him to Mexico immediately (Bowditch to Kelsey, 25 May 1906; Bowditch to Hewett, 25 May, 1906, AIA). Kelsey responded vigorously, defending Hewett's work as a "reasonable effort to conserve remains for future generations and to submit them to scientific scrutiny rather than the depredations of commercial excavation." As for the Colorado Society work, Kelsey explained: "I per- ceived that in the Middle West the interests of cultural as distinguished from professional education were losing ground, and it seemed that the establishment of affiliated societies of the Institute might be made an effective means of combating certain prevailing tendencies. . . . [I]n the future the development of the work of the Institute in the Middle West will be reckoned a not insignificant factor in favor of higher culture stan- dards." He accused Bowditch, furthermore, of trying to impose a regi- men on Hewett: "In the aggregate the best results for any good cause are secured by giving the right sort of man a full opportunity." Finally, he suggested that Bowditch's bias toward Central America led him to slight the Southwest, especially Colorado (Kelsey to Bowditch, 1 June 1906, AIA). Hewett reacted in the same spirit, arguing that his work con- formed to Putnam's instructions, if not to Bowditch's expectations.

The first six months of 1906 thus established the central opposition: Kelsey and Hewett, the western boosters, against Boas, Bowditch, and Putnam, the eastern establishment. Over the next three years an increas- ingly bitter hostility rigidified the two camps and their allies. Charles Lummis and Alice Fletcher soon joined with Hewett in important alli- ances, as did Sylvanus Morley somewhat later; while Roland B. Dixon and, more cautiously, Alfred Kroeber sided with the Boas group. Between July 1906 and the end of 1907 jockeying for strength and position in the Institute and in the young western societies occurred. Kelsey pushed through a reorganization scheme that increased the power of the central and western affiliates; in the same period, working with Fletcher, he ex- panded the American Committee from three to nine members, thereby diluting the power of the Boas-Bowditch faction. Ultimately, by support- ing Hewett's interests and tolerating increasingly outrageous machina- tions in Committee affairs, he forced their resignations not only from the Committee but from the Institute altogether. Bowditch resigned first, fol- lowed by Boas, Tozzer, and Dixon, and finally Putnam. All were gone by the end of 1910, leaving Hewett, Fletcher, and Kelsey in full charge of the Institute's American work through the new school in Santa Fe.

Alice Fletcher's role in these months was critical and revealing, as Joan Mark has partly indicated (1980:82–86). Deeply impressed by Hewett's survey work in Mexico in the summer of 1906, she wrote to Bowditch of his "sterling qualities" (29 August 1906, CPB). In December Fletcher presented to the American Committee a plan (it was actually Hewett's) that included a culture-area map, a director of American Ar- chaeology, and a school in the Southwest. Predictably, Hewett was named director. The following summer (1907) he took A. V. Kidder and Morley to Colorado for the famous first field school, and in October Bowditch resigned as chair of the Committee. Fletcher took his place. In December 1907 the Institute's annual meeting gave approval for the School, and Hewett spent much of 1908 gathering support in the West for the School and lobbying among groups in Colorado, New Mexico, and Utah. At a meeting of the American Committee in November 1908, with only five of the nine members present, Boas, Putnam, and Bowditch (still members of the Institute) voted to block the proposed School; Fletcher then outflanked them and reversed the decision by mailing out ballots to the absent members (including Kelsey and Lummis) who voted with Hewett and her (Mark 1980:83).

Although frustrated with the direction of affairs and furious at Hewett, Bowditch still tried other tacks to get Mayan studies into competent hands. Hewett's appointment as director left the possibility that the now-vacant fellowship position could be directed once again to Central America. In October 1908 Bowditch and W. K. Bixby of St. Louis agreed to contribute $3000 annually for five years for Mayan archaeology, hopefully at Palenque; Morley was appointed the Institute's Fellow with great expectations. In a complex series of events, however, over the first half of 1909 Bowditch was replaced as a contributor, the Bowditch-Bixby contract was annulled, and Morley, who Bowditch had hoped would work with some independence, came under Hewett's influence as well. Although Putnam and Bowditch constituted the subcommittee to supervise Central American work, Kelsey, Fletcher, and Hewett had once again succeeded in excluding them from critical decisions.

As relationships worsened between 1909 and 1912, the eastern men wrote privately and publicly of their deep concern for the future of American archaeology under Hewett. Bowditch was so distressed that he began writing memoranda to himself entitled "My Reasons for Distrusting Dr. Edgar L. Hewett" and "My Reasons for No Longer Trusting Miss Alice C. Fletcher" (CPB). As he had done on a previous occasion, Boas went public by printing at his own expense *Correspondence between Edgar Lee Hewett and Franz Boas* (1910), an appeal to the scientific community that revealed Boas's faith in its democratic judgment where questions of honor and integrity arose. "There are certain things which I at least cannot put up with, and that is a general deterioration of the character of scientific work," he told Tozzer. "I have never compromised with slipshod and untruthful methods in science, and that is what we are up against in this case . . ." (Boas to Tozzer, 18 November 1910, AMT).

After visiting Hewett's summer camp in 1908 for six weeks, Tozzer issued a troubling criticism of Hewett's lack of plan and superficial methods. In reviewing the case against Hewett in 1910, Tozzer pointed to Hewett's self-aggrandizing political and publicity campaigns, his lack of knowledge even of southwestern archaeology, his baleful influence on young men such as Morley and J. P. Harrington and, most recently, his presentation as his own the discoveries of Herbert Spinden regarding the chronological development of Mayan art. Tozzer (to Gardiner M. Lane, 28 October 1910, [draft], AMT) continued:

> The main criticism in all the excavations made by Hewett is the lack of any well-defined and comprehensive plan of work which would settle once and for all certain broad questions still remaining unanswered concerning the archaeology of the Pueblo region. His work is seemingly done where it will yield the best results from the point of view of collections and spectacular plans and restorations. There has been, as far as I know, little correlation in the many small bits of digging here and there undertaken by Hewett but in almost every case there has resulted a good pottery collection while the work has thrown very little light upon the more important questions of migrations etc. etc. In other words, the various pieces of excavation, although in most cases fairly well done, have been made with a view to tangible results for his Museum rather than for scientific data of a more valuable sort. . . .
>
> As for Hewett's standing among the American archaeologists I can say, I think, with truth that with the exception of certain people connected with the Bureau of Ethnology and the Smithsonian at Washington together with personal friends in the west there is not a person connected with a scientific institution in the country which is doing work in American anthropology who approves of Hewett's work.
>
> . . . I feel very strongly the evil effect of Hewett's work not only upon the good name of the Institute and of Archaeology in general but more especially on that of American Archaeology which has been endeavoring slowly to emerge from the rather forlorn state resulting from unscientific methods and untrained investigators.

Tozzer inherited the interests, biases, and professional definitions of his mentors, Boas, Putnam, and Bowditch (Hinsley, 1984). Concerned with national professionalization—the "broader," theoretical questions of the sciences of anthropology—they had no sympathy with local needs or sensitivities. The young Alfred Kidder, by contrast, struck a more balanced judgment, writing to his friend Tozzer (undated [ca. November 1910], AMT):

It strikes me that he is just about what we had already thought him to be: a man nervously active, too much in a hurry to do any one thing with any thoroughness, a rather consistent limelight hunter, an inveterate politician and lobbyist, a man who would rather wreck a thing than not run it himself. On the other hand he *does* get things accomplished, he is a great arouser of interest and collector of money (he has formed branches all through the West) and I can't see that he does the science any great harm except to cheapen it, perhaps, by rather jingoish methods and advertising. The great question seems to be whether it is better to have work (of a sort) done with a good deal of hurrah and perhaps in a slipshod manner, or to have it left undone for the time being. I don't see who else could do exactly what he is doing at the rate he is doing it.

Kidder's words move us beyond vituperation to glimpse the distinctly American set of conditions that created the Hewett controversy. As Boas and the others reiterated with disgust, Hewett was indeed a politician in the sense that he appealed to local pride and personal vanities in an effort, as he saw it, to preserve the archaeological heritage from the forces of modern American commerce and greed. In order to do so he had to appeal to those forces; he did pander to the press, and he did make his science accessible to the public. Hewett confronted an old problem, particularly apposite to archaeology in an industrial, expansive, capitalist democracy. In 1848 Joseph Henry of the Smithsonian had warned Squier and Davis against appealing to public recognition rather than seeking, through scientific journals, "that commendation which it is the privilege of only the learned few to grant . . ." (Henry to Ephraim Squier, 23 June 1847, EGS). The voices of academic professionalism now railed against Hewett's work as "superficial" and "unprofessional," to which Hewett could and did respond with equal vigor: the eastern men were willing to colonize the archaeology of the West, willing to let it lie unexplored or even suffer destruction at the hands of tourists, marauders, robbers, or developers, until they had trained men to do the job "thoroughly." In the meantime the strong civic pride of the leaders of New Mexico, Utah, and Colarado would remain untapped by archaeologists or preservationists. Hewett could only view such an attitude as self-serving and short-sighted.

In the end there was more slander than communication. Returning from the annual meetings in Toronto in December 1908, Tozzer was exasperated and drained by his conversations with Fletcher and Hewett. The latter was "simply impossible and cannot understand our side of the question. I told him at the end of our interview that it was simply the difference between New Mexico and Boston" (Tozzer to Bowditch, 5 January 1909, CPB).

We need not accept Tozzer's verdict, however. Rather, consider for a moment Sylvanus Morley, who straddled the debate, with a foot in each camp. Trained by Tozzer at Harvard, he worked closely with Hewett in the Southwest and at Quirigua before establishing his own remarkable career in Central American epigraphy and archaeology. In some ways it was Morley who realized Bowditch's hopes. Tozzer and Bowditch worried excessively over Hewett's influence on the young Morley. They might have recognized from their own close personal relationship that anthropological training involves emotional support and camaraderie as much as intellectual disciplining. In this respect it is enlightening to read Morley's diary for these years, for it provides yet another picture of Hewett.

By the beginning of 1908 Morley had decided on a career in archaeology, but he had also fallen deeply in love with Alice Williams, granddaughter of New Hampshire Senator Ralph Gallinger. He feared that he could never make enough money in archaeology to gain the Senator's approval for the marriage. Here the diary (SGM) for February 24, 1908, in Washington picks up the story.

So I told Mr. H. I felt as though I really must talk of the personal side of it with him. We sat down on one of the benches between the old and new National Museums and there I asked him. He said that far from being a hindrance he would use all his influence to have her come with me [to the field in Mexico]. He said a lot more about how happy his own married life had been with Mrs. Hewett in the field, and I can't put it down here—there's not room, but, I shall remember it all vividly until my dying day for it was the first time I had ever been assured I could support my wife and myself with my work. He said though he thought she had better not go down to Mexico with us the first year but wait until we had made a sanitary camp. That would make Alice and I get married about the 1st of June a year from the coming one. . . . After that I said Mr. Hewett will you tell Sen. G. this, and after making arrangements for him to call at the Normandie Annex about 7:30 we parted and I returned to the hotel where I found little woman [Alice] by herself and I broke the good news to her. By and by Ralph G. and his wife came over. . . . [Mr. Hewett] came about 8. and after a short call with Alice I called the Senator down. Mr. Hewett didn't stay long but he told things straight to Alice's grandfather and succeeded in convincing him of how two could live by it. He went after a 15 or 20 minute call, perhaps it was a half an hour, and then Little Woman and I went down to the New Willard where we had a bangup supper, one of the very happiest meals I have ever eaten. . . . It has been perhaps the happiest day of my life This 24 of Feb.

The history of American archaeology has included many a February 24th, many moments like Morley's. While it is impossible to measure the strength of the bond created between two individuals, a rich and full history of American archaeology must not ignore such factors. It must move constantly between personal intimacy, small group encounters, bureaucratic battles, exciting field discoveries, and methodological and theoretical breakthroughs. Such history covers the spectrum from intensely private to brilliantly public science.

Part of the process of professionalization in any discipline involves the creation of an accepted view of the past for group cohesion and identity. Such history has several uses: it helps to define the terms of entry into (or exclusion from) the profession, to validate the boundaries of acceptable method and behavior, and to frame current debate and future direction. Nor does such history remain stagnant; as the profession grows and changes, its history is rewritten, commonly by elders, to take the new growth into the consensual account. Not surprisingly, history rooted in intramural soil usually displays signs of its origins in its language, structure, and perspective. Characteristically one sees, for example, a tendency toward historical explanation that omits extramural influences in favor of an internal, linear causality. In part this may be merely a consequence of close focus; in some instances, though, causality can be altogether lost in the desire to produce a coherent sequence of progressive knowledge in the profession.

The historian standing outside the profession asks somewhat different questions. It is not, however, precisely the matter of "presentism vs. historicism" that distinguishes the archaeologist *cum* historian from the historian of archaeology. Both have in fact their "presentist" agendas, and these color their histories; but those agendas may differ markedly. To my mind, the imbroglio over Hewett and the founding of the School of American Archaeology in Santa Fe suggests various groups of questions, all of them interrelated. In the first place, it reminds us that the debate between preservationists and conservationists that awakened Hewett's generation to the need for state policy regulating use of natural resources had an analog in archaeology: the antiquities preservation movement, in other words, was part of a larger cultural change in American society. Furthermore, it is a still unresolved issue. Who in the end served the interests of the public insofar as southwestern archaeology was concerned—Boas or Hewett? "The great question," Kidder wrote, "seems to be whether it is better to have work (of a sort) done," or to leave it undone—and risk continued looting and commercial development.

Secondly, the evolution of institutional structures out of individual energy and personality, which is so characteristic of this transformative period of U.S. history in general and anthropology in particular (e.g., J. W. Powell's Bureau of Ethnology, Boas' Columbia University department, Hewett's School) raises another set of questions. The institution (whether department, museum, school, or bureau) unquestionably augmented the individual voice and magnified personal power. Institutional support on a continuing basis, however, might also entail risking vulnerability to patron whim and influence, and thus involve compromise with external forces. On the other hand, failure to create or join some such structure virtually doomed an individual to intellectual oblivion in the post-Civil War generations. As in other fields of endeavor, the day of the autonomous intellectual was rapidly drawing to a close. Hewett's struggle was, in this light, more than merely a bid for employment, for the imperative to institutionalize had become irresistible; such were the new terms of struggle and survival.

Finally, we confront the puzzles of people like William K. Bixby, Bowditch, and the urban rich of Colorado Springs, Santa Fe, and Los Angeles whom Hewett and Charles Lummis tapped for support. Curiously, we know very little of those who paid for so much of American archaeology: their motivations, expectations, or influences on its development. The subject has a special claim to attention, for it connects the "internal" history of this scientific and humanistic enterprise—one that has traditionally enjoyed a broad base of public sympathy and interest—with the larger sociological conditions of its growth.

In addressing these rich and complex issues, the historian and the archaeologist need each other's mutually corrective influence and nagging reminders of partiality. So much of the text, after all, is unwritten; and so much of the context lies beyond the immediate archaeological horizon.

Literature Cited

Archival collections cited in the text are identified by the following acronyms.

AIA   Papers of the Archaeological Institute of America, Colgate University, Hamilton, New York (on temporary loan)

AMT   Alfred M. Tozzer Papers, Peabody Museum Archives, Harvard University, Cambridge, Massachusetts

CPB   Charles P. Bowditch Papers, Peabody Museum Archives, Harvard University, Cambridge, Massachusetts

EGS   Ephraim G. Squier Papers, Library of Congress, Washington, D.C.

FB   Franz Boas Papers, American Philosophical Society, Philadelphia, Pennsylvania

SGM   Sylvanus G. Morley Diary, Carnegie Institute of Washington Collection, Peabody Museum Archives, Harvard University, Cambridge, Massachusetts

Bernal, I.
1980   *A History of Mexican Archaeology.* Thames and Hudson, London.

Boas, F.
1910   *Correspondence between Edgar Lee Hewett and Franz Boas.* Privately printed.

Fitting, J. (editor)
1973   *The Development of North American Archaeology.* Pennsylvania State University Press, University Park.

Grayson, D. K.
1983   *The Establishment of Human Antiquity.* Academic Press, New York.

Hinsley, C. M.
1981   *Savages and Scientists: The Smithsonian Institution and the Development of American Anthropology, 1846–1910.* Smithsonian Institution Press, Washington, D.C.
1984   Wanted: One Good Man to Discover Central American History. *Harvard Magazine* 87(2):64A–64H.

Hudson, K.
1981   *A Social History of Archaeology: The British Experience.* MacMillan, London.

Lister, R., and F. Lister
1981   *Chaco Canyon.* University of New Mexico Press, Albuquerque.

Mark, J.
1980   *Four Anthropologists: An American Science in Its Early Years.* Science History Publications, New York.

Meltzer, D. J.
1983   The Antiquity of Man and the Development of American Archaeology. In *Advances in Archaeological Method and Theory,* edited by M. B. Schiffer, 6:1–51. Academic Press, New York.

Moore, G. C.
1973   A Comparison of the Effectiveness of Social and Topical Criteria in Identifying Scholarly Communities. Master's thesis, Department of Anthropology, Cornell University, Ithaca, N.Y.

Rogge, A. E.
   1983   Little Archaeology, Big Archaeology: The Changing Context of Archae-
          ological Research. Doctoral dissertation, Department of Anthropology,
          University of Arizona.

Schwartz, D. W.
   1967   *Conceptions of Kentucky Prehistory.* University of Kentucky Press, Lex-
          ington.
   1968   North American Archaeology in Historical Perspective. *Actes du XIe
          Congrès Internationale d'Histoire de Sciences,* 2:311–315. Warsaw and
          Cracow.

Willey, G., and J. Sabloff
   1974   *A History of American Archaeology.* Thames and Hudson, London.
          [Reprinted 1980.]

New Looks at Past Problems

Contemporary Hunter-Gatherer Archaeology in America

Introduction

When invited to prepare a paper on "state-of-the-art" hunter-gatherer studies in American archaeology, I jumped at the chance, and began my attempt to pull together an impartial, overarching synthesis. This approach seemed vastly preferable to merely grinding a few personal axes. After probing the literature and polling several colleagues, however, it became crystal clear that any consensus on this volatile topic remains a long way away.

So I am back to grinding my own axes. No attempt has been made to synthesize the voluminous literature, and no claim is made for completeness. What follows is a decidedly idiosyncratic view of Americanist approaches to the archaeological record of extinct hunter-gatherers. This paper highlights some things done well, a couple of things done poorly, and things still in need of doing.

Some Cheers

After reviewing a spate of recent grant proposals and listening to several papers delivered at the 50th meeting of the Society for American Archaeology, I am convinced that "mid-range" and "optimal foraging" have become the twin archaeological buzzwords of the eighties.

Setting the optimal foragers momentarily aside, I begin by toasting the builders of archaeological mid-range theory. In elemental form, mid-range theory attempts to link our ideas about the world to the world itself, assigning meaning to our empirical observations (Clarke 1973:8;

Schiffer 1976; Binford 1977:2–10, 1981:21–30; Sullivan 1978; Thomas, et al. 1979; Smith and Winterhalder 1981:7; Hayden and Cannon 1984a). Mid-range theory is a way to build our perception of the past, an intellectually independent exercise from building a general theory designed to explain that past (Binford 1981:29; Thomas 1983a:17).

Much theory at the mid-range consists of operational definition, specifying precise relationships between a concept and a class of empirically observable phenomena (Thomas 1970, 1972; Campbell 1973; Binford 1977). Today, even the most basic concepts in hunter-gatherer studies are being rethought and (when necessary) redefined.

Take the deceptively simple notion of the base camp (or residential base). Assigning behavioral meaning to this concept is not difficult: base camps form "the hub of all subsistence activities" for modern hunter-gatherers (Binford 1980:9), the locus of most processing, manufacturing, and maintenance. One can readily enumerate key characteristics shared by most base camps: domestic dwellings, site furniture, specialized utilitarian structures and outdoor work spaces, service centers, diversified tool fabrication and repair, child rearing, diversified food consumption, and so forth.

Although a suitable starting point, these behavioral definitions are not archaeologically operational because the concept "base camp" has yet to be successfully articulated with archaeologically grounded observations (Thomas 1983a:73–79). Doing so requires unambiguous signatures linking "domestic dwellings," "site furniture," and "tool fabrication and repair," to archaeologically observable criteria. These criteria must then themselves be articulated to define an archaeologically recognizable "base camp."

The attempt to "operationalize" archaeology's basic concepts is not, as Salmon (1982:150) suggests, some sort of misguided manifesto "to demand complete operational definition of all terms as a first step in the construction of an archaeological theory" nor "to perform reductions of the expressions in which these terms occur to expressions that contain only terms capable of operational definition." To my knowledge, nobody has advocated this procedure for archaeology.

Rather, such definitions—what Grayson (1982) calls the "if and only if" statements of mid-range theory—provide the building blocks by which behavioral correlates are translated into archaeologically observable consequences; this search seems to be the most profitable line of inquiry within hunter-gatherer studies over the past decade. Nevertheless, many such signatures remain vaguely defined, and relatively few substantive applications have appeared in print (e.g., Speth 1983; Thomas 1983a, 1983b; see also Hayden and Cannon 1984a). James O'Connell (personal communication) correctly suggests that the most exciting and potentially innovative applications of mid-range theory exist in doctoral dissertation form, and I fully expect the present generation of graduate students to reap the full harvest of such advances.

As Grayson points out earlier in this volume, mid-range linkage has been an important aspect of archaeological inquiry for more than a century; quite obviously mid-range theory building hardly began with Lewis Binford. But Binford's research did, for the first time, articulate a tactical argument about how mid-range theory fits into an overall research strategy of learning about the past. Even some severe critics of the New Archaeology acknowledge the importance of mid-range theory building (e.g., Trigger 1984:294).

Regardless, massive confusion remains about the role of mid-range theory in contemporary archaeology. Perhaps because of this uncertainty, Binford has frequently resorted to explanatory analogy, describing research at the mid-range as seeking "a kind of Rosetta Stone: a way of 'translating' the static, material . . . found on an archaeological site into the vibrant life of a group of people who in fact left them there" (Binford 1983a:24; see also Binford 1979a:19, 1981:25, 1982:49; 1983b:67, 389).

The Rosetta Stone, of course, led directly to the decipherment of ancient Egyptian hieroglyphs, and this analogy illustrates how such research is actually being conducted in today's archaeology. In the case of hieroglyphics, scholars first needed to break the demotic code using the Rosetta Stone; then, once the symbols could be translated, anyone could draw upon the now-readable texts to piece together a picture of what happened in ancient Egypt. (For details regarding the discovery and ultimate deciphering of the Rosetta Stone, see Andrews 1981.) So too in contemporary archaeology. Mid-range theory building attempts to "break the codes" of meaning in material cultural residues. General theory, which addresses explanation of the past as it is understood through mid-range linkages, attempts to explain why the past is the way it appears to have been. Although the specifics of mid-range research remain logically independent of general theory, the overall direction of mid-range theory building is clearly a function of one's general theoretical bent. In this sense, development of both theoretical bases proceeds hand-in-hand.

The following section provides a perspective on the growing pains and epistemological shifts within today's archaeology, as told in four little proverbs.

Proverb One   *'Tain't what a man don't know that hurts him, it's what he knows that just ain't so.*—Frank McKinney Hubbard

Mere discovery of the Rosetta Stone was the least instructive step toward ultimately understanding ancient Egyptian. This three-quarter ton basalt "fact," now enshrined in the British Museum, decidedly did not speak for itself. Full decipherment of ancient Egyptian hieroglyphs required nearly a quarter century of concerted effort by dozens of scholars working on the clues carved thereon.

The role of discovery is likewise vastly overrated in archaeology; these facts remain as mute as the Rosetta Stone. Faunal analysts, for instance, suffer no shortage of archaeological facts. The problem is to read what such facts tell us about the past. In one classic case (see Binford 1978:9–10), Theodore White (1952) empirically observed that upper limb bones of food animals were often missing from American Plains Indian sites, a pattern he attributed to differential destruction in the manufacture of bone grease. Some years later, confronted by a similar pattern of differential destruction at Suberde, a seventh millennium B.C. Neolithic village in Turkey, the investigators dreamed up the "schlepp" effect: discarding upper limb bones at the butchering site and using lower limb bones to drag the meat-bearing hides back home (Daly 1969:151). In a third instance, a similar relative shortage of limb bones at a late ninth-century A.D. Saxon farm was attributed to dressing and export for market (Chaplin 1971:135–138).

Such initial efforts at behavioral interpretation commonly approached their "facts" through simple pattern recognition and *ad hoc* reasoning. Although some research produced useful data, most achievements remain merely symbolic *tours de force*, crippled by archaeological codes that have yet to be cracked.

This research is typical of the 1960s and 1970s in American archaeology, an enthusiastic era during which archaeologists boldly penetrated most areas of ecological interest. We now know that many tacit assumptions of this period were simplistic or downright wrong (see also Binford 1981:13–20; Dunnell 1982:510–511, 525–528; Grayson 1984:xix,

171, 179). During the past 15 years, American archaeology has outgrown its Age of Aquarius.

Or consider the study of seasonality, another empirical domain rich
in archaeological facts: lots of seeds, plant parts, pollen, phytoliths, and
animal bones. Archaeologists and biologists have spent decades wringing
the last shred of seasonal minutae from such facts (e.g., Howard 1929;
Thomson 1939; Clark 1952:25–289, 1954). The apogee of such studies
was reached by the massively ambitious Tehuacan Valley project (see esp.
Byers 1967). Richard MacNeish's Tehuacan Valley research—regional in
scope and ecological in orientation—became the flagship of interdisciplinary archaeology (Thomas 1974:60–62, 1979:69–73, 245–246,
256–257, 330–333), defining a niche unique in the history of our field.

History aside, however, we must now question many conclusions
derived from the Tehuacan project: (1) "Here [at Coxcatlan Cave] . . .
was a hardened deer antler fragment, indicating a winter dry-season occupation (MacNeish et al. 1972:363). (2) "The lower levels of Zone XIV
in Activity Areas A through D, with evidence of nopal and tetecho fruit,
pochote pods and seeds, definitely seem to be winter season" (MacNeish
et al. 1972:368). Such conclusions invariably ignored the formation processes involved: how did these season-specific ecofacts end up into the
archaeological record? Almost never is relevance of an organism's demise
related to a tangible aspect of human behavior.

Most archaeologists now realize that simple enumeration of "seasonal indicators" (or abence thereof) on a site or surface no longer provides sufficient grounds for assigning season of occupation (Monks
1981; Andresen et al. 1981; Grayson and Thomas 1983; Grayson
1984:174–177). Many seasonal assignments at Tehuacan are undoubtedly correct; but without understanding a great deal more about the precise formation events involved, we may never know which estimates are
right.

Contemporary archaeology is also taking a hard look at the meaning of lithic and ceramic assemblages. Most regional studies of prehistoric hunter-gatherers require that residential areas be operationally distinguished from areas used logistically. While base camps can sometimes
be separated from procurement areas on the basis of site structure, assemblage level signatures remain ill-defined and the available base camp
diagnostics are notoriously difficult to apply (Binford 1979a, 1979b; R.
Gould 1980:126; Thomas 1983a:78–79).

Nevertheless, archaeologists over the past two decades have not hes-
itated from routinely making such behavioral assignments. Smaller, less

diverse assemblages have commonly been interpreted as areas of diurnal extraction ("locations"). Larger, more diverse assemblages are often equated with residential utilization ("base camps"). Assemblages of intermediate size and diversity are conventionally viewed as logistic settlements ("field camps"). Although rarely spelled out, the tacit equation of absolute assemblage diversity with discrete settlement types underlies many so-called behavioral interpretations in contemporary hunter-gatherer studies (Aikens 1970:191; Longacre and Reid 1971; MacNeish et al. 1972; Judge 1973:199; Thomas 1973:173; O'Connell 1975:24–26; Reher 1977:29–33; Bettinger 1977:13; Elston 1982:194, 196, 199, to list but a few).

This line of reasoning is incorrect. In many (if not most) archaeological assemblages, sample diversity is a direct, linear function of sample size. Jones, Grayson, and Beck (1983) have convincingly demonstrated the "treacherous" relationship between class richness and sample size in archaeological assemblages (see also Beck 1984; G. Jones 1984; Thomas, 1983a, 1983b).

Assemblage diversity is hardly unrelated to site function, but the exact nature of that relationship can be appreciated only by focusing on relative (not absolute) diversity. When data from Gatecliff Shelter were scrutinized in this fashion (Thomas 1983b:419–431), we found that, irrespective of how assemblage size or diversity were measured, these two variables persistently maintained a strong, linear relationship. Based strictly on a knowledge of sample size at Gatecliff Shelter, one can predict the degree of the artifact diversity contained in these assemblages with an accuracy ranging between 75 and 95 percent. Raw assemblage diversity is useless in interpreting archaeological patterning at Gatecliff Shelter.

This is not a remote "methodological" concern; sample size bias impacts the everyday business of archaeology. So long as archaeologists continue to assess site function this way, our knowledge of prehistoric hunter-gatherer cultural geography will depend heavily on archaeological field strategy. Dig all of a large site, and we perceive it as a base camp; dig half of the same site, and you have a field camp; take a surface collection, and most archaeologists will tell you it is a location.

The size/diversity issue dramatically underscores the need to explore the way in which we perceive patterning within the archaeological record. Such knowledge may, at times, temporarily tie our interpretive hands. As one colleague grumbles, "fine, but all this mid-range stuff gets in the way of telling a good story." Maybe our "good stories" will be somewhat shorter, but it seems preferable to exercise a degree of interpretive restraint than to blither on about what simply is not so. This is what mid-range inquiry is all about.

Proverb Two *Aristotle could have avoided the mistake of thinking that women have fewer teeth than men by the simple device of asking Mrs. Aristotle to open her mouth.*
                                               —Bertrand Russell

Effective theory building involves an interplay between empirical and intellectual domains (Salmon 1982:155–156; Thomas 1983a:8–23). The relationship between mid-range theory building and progress on substantive archaeological issues is evident in recent work on the economic anatomy of prey species. As part of his on-going Nunamiut studies, Binford (1978) developed a series of anatomical utility indices (MGUI), which provide a way of approaching butchering, processing, transport, and consumption in the archaeological record.

Binford applied these indices to prehistoric faunal assemblages at Olduvai Gorge (Binford 1981) and from the Klasies River mouth (Binford 1984). Speth (1983) found that Nunamiut-derived utility indices assisted in interpreting bison remains at the Garnsey site in New Mexico. Using a somewhat different approach, Thomas and Mayer (1983) employed the same utility indices to analyze a bighorn kill/butchering feature at Gatecliff Shelter. Todd, Rapson, and Ingbar (1985) are currently exploring Binford's indices in an extremely fine-grained application on faunal materials from the Bugas-Holding site in Wyoming. Lyman (1985) also has recently reexamined Binford's MGUI utility indices and (as will be the case with so much of today's mid-range theory) his results suggest that the indices are decidedly first generation approximations. If upheld by future research, Lyman's results suggest that differential destruction may be a greater problem than initially anticipated. While these early applications will doubtless be superceded by later developments, mid-range investigations are beginning to pay off in our understanding of what went on at specific sites.

Another focus of mid-range theory building looks at the mechanics of bone fracture. Earlier investigators had argued that a spiral pattern of long bone fracture provided an unambiguous way to detect human involvement (Dart 1957; Sadek-Kooros 1972): if true, these spiral bone signatures could be taken as diagnostic of an early human presence in cases where lithic artifacts are ambiguous (or absent). These early pattern recognition studies have fostered a number of well-controlled mid-range experiments, and we now know that spiral fracturing can readily be produced by nonhuman agents as well (Myers et al. 1980; Brain 1981; Binford 1981; Hanes 1983; Lyman 1984). Spiral fracture is a poor diagnostic trait of human butchery.

We pointed earlier to the Tehuacan Valley project as the epitomy of enthusiastic 1960s reconstructionist archaeology. Central to this research was the valiant and pioneering attempt to monitor intrasite covariability of features, artifacts, and ecofacts. Tehuacan Valley researchers expended prodigious efforts piece-plotting artifacts that allegedly defined clear-cut activity areas within caves and shelters. More than six dozen such "living floor maps" were ultimately published, all of them guided by three fundamental and explicit assumptions: (1) ecofacts found on a given surface are sufficient to define season of occupation; (2) artifacts and ecofacts found on the same surface define synchronous events; (3) intrasite spatial patterning is sufficient to define specific activity sets (MacNeish et al. 1972:7). None of these assumptions can be accepted in light of contemporary mid-range theory.

Proverb Three   *The medium is the message.*—Marshall McLuhan

Mid-range theory is an observational language, in a way to convert statics to dynamics, lacking specific empirical content and intellectually independent of general theory (Binford 1981:29; 1982:48; 1983a). Similarly, the message on the Rosetta Stone is an unglamorous decree passed by a general council of priests assembled at Memphis to celebrate the first anniversary of the coronation of King Ptolemy V. As a text, the Rosetta Stone contributed little to actual understanding of ancient life. In both cases, it is the redundant patterning and underlying systematic articulation of parts that infuse them with significance. This lack of empirical content has created great confusion among contemporary archaeologists; as Raab and Goodyear (1984) emphasize, "middle range theory" means (at least) two very different things in today's archaeology.

Middle range theory *sensu* Binford.—"The function of mid-range theory . . . is to bridge the gap between [the known,] observable archaeological contexts and [the unknown,] nonobservable systemic contexts.

This is why mid-range theory is necessary to provide relevance and meaning to the archaeological objects" (Thomas 1979:402).

Middle range theory *sensu* Merton.—"It is intermediate to general theories of social systems which are too remote from particular classes of social behavior, organization and change to account for what is observed. . . . Middle-theory involves abstractions, of course, but they are close enough to observed data to be incorporated in propositions that permit empirical testing" (Merton 1968:39).

In simplest terms, Merton advocated a limited form of general theory, directly applicable to an empirically observable, intermediate level. Binfordian mid-range theory, by contrast, seeks invariant linkages between the archaeological record and the behavior that produced it.

Debate as to proper use of the term *middle range* (or mid-range),[1] while of historical interest, remains tangential to theory building in archaeology. I cannot agree with Raab and Goodyear (1984), who argue that only Merton's sociological definition is germane to archaeology. Both brands of theory building are relevant to current inquiry, and archaeologists are already making progress in both directions (Salmon 1982:176–177), although the results are often confused with each other.

Proverb Four   *What we need is a flexible plan for an everchanging world.*—Jerry Brown

Thomas Young made the first significant contribution toward deciphering ancient Egyptian. But Young was not a linguist; he was a physicist and physician who became interested in hieroglyphs only after having read about the discovery of the Rosetta Stone and its unknown language. At the age of 41, he began to work on decipherment during a summer vacation. The rest of his life was spent re-tooling, working out innovative methods of code-breaking and broadening his scope by studying copies of other hieroglyphic inscriptions.

Archaeologists are likewise showing a healthy willingness to redefine and re-tool. Binford (1983a) has spoken of his "disconsolate self-reflection" after a year of pattern recognition work on Mousterian materials. Stumped, his solution was to try another tack, traveling to the Arctic to live with Eskimo hunters: "My reasons for going there were little more specific at that stage than that it could hardly fail to be a good educational experience" (Binford 1983a:100–101). As it turned out, this shot-in-the-dark elevated mid-range theory to the forefront of contemporary archaeological thinking.

Other archaeologists find it necessary to switch directions for more specific reasons. In 1977, Mark Cohen published *The Food Crisis in Prehistory,* which argued that changes in hunter-gatherer food procurement strategies through the Pleistocene could be viewed in Boserupian terms, representing a compensation for growing population rather than mere "technological" progress (see also Cohen 1981).

Critics blasted Cohen's appeal to population pressure as the primary mechanism for explaining culture change (e.g., Cowgill 1975; Hassan 1981; Price and Brown 1985:14); this was an objection to the general theory being proposed. Skeptics also emphasized the lack of direct archaeological evidence for population growth and crowding. How would we know if Cohen was right or wrong? How can population size or density be observed in archaeological contexts (Dunnell 1979:443; 1982:524)? These are mid-range level problems.

Rather than simply reiterate the same tired position, Cohen pursued an innovative, constructive course by seeking direct indices to measure the consequences of population pressure in the archaeological record. As it turned out, contemporary paleopathological research had derived several such measures, including both generalized stress indicators (Harris lines, enamel hypoplasias, etc.) and specific trace-element/carbon-isotope analysis of dietary composition (Buikstra and Cook 1980). Thus, physical anthropologists had been unwittingly engaged in nascent mid-range theory building, beginning to translate such formerly elusive concepts as stress and social status into archaeologically observable terms. Cohen grasped the significance of such studies to his own population pressure argument, and, although an archaeologist, he was instrumental in organizing a symposium to pool available data and stimulate additional relevant research (Cohen and Armelagos 1984; Cohen 1985). Moreover, Cohen is presently excavating a cemetery in Belize, generating his own paleopathological data and helping to shape future innovations most directly relevant to population growth and pressure.

I find this direction both refreshing and stimulating. It illustrates a practical way for archaeologists to establish the necessary operational linkages between behavioral and empirical worlds. It likewise highlights the often-overlooked point that mid-range theory building need not be restricted to ethnoarchaeology; there are compelling reasons to look further afield. Valid mid-range theory can (and must) be derived from experimentally controlled contexts, from ethnohistorical documentation, from extant museum collections—even from select segments of the archaeological record itself (Jochim 1976, 1981; Schalk 1981; Kelly 1983, 1985; Keene 1981; Smith and Winterhalder 1981; Thomas 1981, 1983a; Trigger 1984). Mid-range theory is, after all, where you find it (Thomas, 1983a:18).

Self-conscious development of mid-range theory is less than ten years old, but we are well on the way toward cracking the codes linking static material culture to the behavior that produced it. For that, we offer cheers.

A Few Boos

But all is not well with Americanist hunter-gatherer studies. Mid-range theory building is today hampered by its uneveness, and some of the more critical needs are not being seriously addressed by those best equipped to do so.

The archaeological record of hunter-gatherers is dominated by stone and bone. Whereas considerable progress has been made in the analysis of faunal remains, the same cannot be said for the study of lithic assemblages. Hunter-gatherer archaeology today requires a comprehensive body of mid-range theory addressed specifically at material consequences of lithic procurement, production, utilization, and discard. We now have *Bones* (Binford 1981), but its comprehensive companion volume *Stones* seems a very long way off.

Those skilled in production and analysis of stone can make a vital contribution toward understanding extinct hunter-gatherer societies. Although advances are being made in this direction, contemporary lithic studies seem in danger of chasing rainbows rather than providing archaeology with the theory so obviously lacking.

That lithic studies fail to live up to advanced billing is not news; several observers have lamented the strongly empiricist, atheoretical character of recent lithic studies (Dunnell 1980a:466–467, 1982:515, 1984:496; Schiffer 1979:15–16; Binford 1979a:23–24). The subject could be skipped entirely were it not for recent publications touting the supremacy of "anthropological" or "cognitive" approaches to stone tool technology (esp. Flenniken 1984; Young and Bonnichsen 1984). My boo of the year goes to the latter day school of "anthropological" flintknappers, some of whom seem consumed in a game of macho rocksmanship.

After reading that "flintknapping is currently on an exciting threshold in anthropology" (Flenniken 1984:192), one feels compelled to ask why is it now necessary to define a school of "anthropological flintknapping" at all? As influential as he was, Don Crabtree never made any lofty and public pretenses at being an anthropologist: he was first an archaeologist and then a lithics man (see Binford 1979b).

A primary focus of "anthropological" flintknapping appeals to an outdated analogic reasoning that claims to project replicative studies into the prehistoric past. A widely circulated review article outlines the "formal procedures" by which replicative experiments are to be conducted: the first step is to correctly identify the technique(s) involved; then this technique is controlled for several variables, ultimately reproducing "a statistically valid sample"; finally, experimental results are compared technologically with prehistoric controls to assess validity. "If valid, the replicator has reproduced a tangible aspect of prehistoric human behavior and demonstrated the reality of that behavior" (Flenniken 1984:197).

Some framework. Viewed this way, Thor Heyerdahl "reproduced a tangible aspect of prehistoric human behavior" by floating around the Pacific on the Kon Tiki. Heyerdahl did not "demonstrate the reality" of the past; he simply showed one possible way of accomplishing a task. The same is true of the replicative scenario. There is absolutely no assurance that mere familiarity with specific techniques of lithic reduction will automatically lead to accurate interpretation of the past. In fact, Young and Bonnichsen (1984:135)—themselves vocal proponents of "cognitive" flintknapping—warn of the dangers involved: "the modern day flintknapper is unduly influenced by his personal knowledge of how artifacts are made. . . . He interprets prehistoric artifacts in terms of his own production code, which does not encompass the total range of possible cross-cultural tool manufacturing procedures."

Instead of addressing the nature of lithic variability, contemporary "anthropological" flintknappers flash back to the V. Gordon Childe school of ethnic history (1928; see also Binford 1983a:84–85). Modern flintknappers can (and should) contribute handily toward archaeological studies of hunter-gatherers by defining sets of unambiguous signatures that translate the statics of prehistoric stone tools to the dynamics that produced them. But rather than doing this, current directions suggest a return to the strictly normative objectives of fifty years ago. Young and Bonnichsen (1984:135) argue that "of the many important problems that the archaeologist may wish to address, there is one that is more basic than the others—how to isolate prehistoric cultural groups." Flenniken

(1984:199) agrees: "The problem now and for the future lies in the identification, description, demonstration, and use of flaked stone tool reduction techniques (debitage and end products) as cultural markers" (see also K. L. Jones 1984). Not only would this approach artificially limit the scope of inquiry, but a mono-minded focus on "cultural markers" would also single out one of contemporary archaeology's least interesting topics. It is true that decades ago, archaeologists assumed that a test pit or surface sherd sample could be taken as "typical" of a site; sites, in turn, were seen as "typical" of a culture. But today, most American archaeologists are wary of equating kinds of artifacts with ethnic groups; most also recognize that the complexity of site structure and regional patterning render the concept of "typical" useless (except in an extremely limited cultural chronological context). "Possessing a small, side-notched, and basally concave arrowhead does not make you a Ute any more than owning a Volvo makes you a Swede" (Sheets 1975:369).

"Anthropological" flintknappers are out of synch with contemporary archaeology. Consider the ultimate reasoning behind so-called "replicative system analysis" (from Flenniken 1984:199): (1) It is easier to teach children aged three to six years to make stone tools than adults. "Language was of little value, only confusing the incipient knapper." (2) These children were not taught a specific reduction technique, but rather techniques to produce a variety of lithic materials into intended end products. "These techniques were . . . a patterned response and *indicative of that specific group of knappers potentially representing a distinct cultural group*" [emphasis added]. (3) Therefore, "if these cultural patterns of flaked stone tool reduction were identified, then the behavior that created them would be identified, lending credence to the identification of a potentially distinct cultural group." This programmatic statement ignores the significant body of ethnographic and ethnoarchaeological literature documenting the complex enculturative frameworks in which young human beings learn what they know (e.g., Hayden and Cannon 1984b:326–327).

This ultranormative thinking, if contagious, would undermine the solid achievements already made by flintknappers over the past two decades. A case in point is Flenniken's (1981) analysis of the worked vein quartz industry at the Hoko River site in northwestern Washington. When published, this investigation stood on its own, an innovative and worthwhile study of a little understood industry. But instead of building solid methodology in this direction, the new logic of "anthropological" flintknapping extended his analysis like this: 2500 years ago young Indians at Hoko River learned to manufacture hafted microlithic knives at the knee of the master. Because the "reduction sequence or technique, i.e., debitage" is "culturally determined," lithic "cultural markers" can be recognized that are both necessary and sufficient to define the cultural group at Hoko River. If reduction sequences are diagnostic of specific cultural groups, it must follow that those manufacturing this kind of debris belong to that same "potential cultural group." Does this mean that Flenniken (who can produce identical vein quartz debris) is, by definition, a "potential" Hoko River Indian who lived 2500 years ago? If so, then we certainly have entrée into cognitive archaeology. But if not, how can this be a distinctive, unambiguous signature to "identify" prehistoric cultures? This is, after all, the same flintknapper who also replicated the Lindenmeier Folsom points (Flenniken 1978). Would analysis of this experimental debris prove that he is also an 11,000-year-old Folsom Indian?

Underlying the issue of "cultural markers" is a more distressing fundamental conceit: the so-called "anthropological" flintknappers possess the inside track to truth. Not only would they myopically focus their own research on ethnic group identification, they go so far as to assert that "archaeologists have no business classifying prehistoric artifacts unless they take manufacturing technology into account" (Young and Bonnichsen 1984:153; see also Epstein 1975:234; Green 1975:159; Flenniken and Raymond in press). By maintaining that a strictly technological approach is *a priori* superior to any other way of monitoring prehistoric behavior, they would tie the hands of archaeology by restricting the questions to be asked and the methods used to answer them.

Let me emphasize in the strongest possible terms that this is not a blanket indictment of lithic studies. It could not be more obvious that an understanding of what stone tools mean is essential to virtually every inquiry involving prehistoric hunter-gatherers. Many promising new directions are evident: defining the spatial correlates of flintknapping and quarrying (Gallagher 1980; Newcomer and Sieveking 1980; Binford and O'Connell 1984); developing regional approaches to lithic variability (Magne 1983; Camilli 1983; Kelly 1983, 1985; Cross 1983); establishing explicit "if and only if" linkages between observed behaviors and the traces they produce on stone tools (Hayden 1979; Greiser and Sheets 1979; Keeley 1980; Holly and Del Bene 1981; Vaughan 1985); isolating the role of raw materials in determining lithic variability (Straus 1980; Flenniken 1981; Sussman 1985); developing staging models for understanding lithic products and by-products (Magne and Pokotylo 1981;

Magne 1983), distinguishing natural damage from cultural modification (Patterson 1983; see also Grayson, this volume); defining biases in differential recovery of lithic assemblages (Kalin 1981; Nicholson 1983); determining the role of post-depositional factors that influence stone tools (Flenniken and Haggerty 1979); identifying organic residues on stone tools (Anderson 1980; Loy 1983); developing techniques such as retrofitting to distinguish *in situ* work areas from secondary, redeposited midden (Cahen et al. 1979; Cahen and Keeley 1980; Newcomer and Sieveking 1980; Hofman 1981; Fladmark 1982; Behm 1983; Bowers et al. 1983; Stevenson 1985). It is a sad and curious comment on the state of "anthropological" flintknapping that many of today's most innovative approaches are being developed by people not necessarily well known for their ability to break rocks.

The point is this: research pursued in contemporary hunter-gatherer studies is not specific to (or removed from) flintknappers. These are problems of anthropological archaeology in general (Binford 1979b:24; Knudson 1978). Lithic specialists are quite capable of exploring the organization of lithic technology as a coping strategy. Lithic specialists do themselves and their field a disservice when they try to focus on isolated and largely irrelevant objectives. But they must participate in (and learn from) the mid-range dialog or they will continue to seek "fine-grained solutions to coarse-grained questions" (Cross 1983:101–102).

For that, we can only offer boos.

And Some Mixed Reviews

Recent history amply documents how easily archaeologists can be seduced and sidetracked by slick techniques; to some, *any* theory may be considered to be better than no theory at all. Although bandwagonism has generally met with little long-term success in the past (Thomas 1978; Dunnell 1979:444), the contemporary literature of optimal foraging theory warns that archaeologists may once again be in danger of buying their theory straight off-the-rack.

Although the potential of foraging theory for archaeology was occasionally overstated by early proponents, many recent discussions present more balanced views of both costs and benefits involved (Bettinger 1980; Smith and Winterhalder 1981, 1985; Winterhalder 1981, 1983; Durham 1981; Smith 1983; O'Connell and Hawkes 1984). Today, applications of optimal foraging theory to human populations command the serious attention of the anthropological community. But as knowledgeable advocates readily admit, premature and half-baked applications to the data of archaeology can only hamper and demean the potential of evolutionary ecology in general.

Numerous applications of optimal foraging models to strictly archaeological data have appeared (Bayham 1979; Perlman 1980; Yesner 1981; Winterhalder 1981; Bettinger and Baumhoff 1982; O'Connell and Hawkes 1981; O'Connell et al. 1982; Smith 1983:633; Simms 1984; K. T. Jones 1984). A detailed examination of the empirical support for such "tests" is now overdue. Rather than attempting that evaluation here, however, I concentrate on four logical and procedural issues raised by appeals to evolutionary ecology in the strictly archaeological context: (1) Can evolutionary ecology supply a general theoretical framework adequate for interpreting the archaeological record? (2) Can optimal foraging models be adequately "tested" against strictly archaeological data? (3) Can archaeology afford the price of empirical reductionism? (4) Is there merit in a hierarchial approach to archaeological explanation? I urge archaeologists to consider each question before hitching too many horses to an optimal foraging bandwagon.

Is Evolutionary Ecology the Answer to Archaeology's General Theoretical Drought?

Nearly a decade ago, Binford (1977:1–10) deplored the lack of theory building in American archaeology at both mid-range and general theoretical levels. Although significant progress has been made at the mid-range, the problem remains acute with regard to general theory (Dunnell 1980a:477; 1983:535; Salmon 1982:140; Meltzer 1979; Trigger 1984).

Some archaeologists are now turning to evolutionary ecology to provide this theory. The underlying logic of applying optimal foraging theory to archaeology seems to go like this. Because archaeologists embrace such a huge empirical domain, a variety of intellectual strategies may be required. Much of the relatively recent archaeological record was created under conditions rather similar to those observed ethnographically. Provided that one is aware of the behavioral dynamics and understands how those dynamics are reflected in the statics of the archaeological record, there is every likelihood of success in accounting for the general structure of the archaeological record in behavioral terms. Mid-range theory is critical to this endeavor; mature general theory may not be.

More remote segments of the archaeological record lack adequate behavioral linkages; the conditions were too dissimilar to assume the uniformitarianism necessary to render behaviorally observed theory relevant. In such cases, available mid-range theory must be simultaneously intertwined with a general theory of human behavior in order to distinguish, or even conceive, likely alternatives. To some, optimal foraging theory offers a way to solve just this problem (Winterhalder 1981; Smith 1983:626–627, 1984). Evolutionary ecology embodies theory at the general level, anchored in assumptions derived from basic postulates of natural selection theory. This explicit optimization approach uses mathematical and graphic representations for the rigorous deduction of testable hypotheses. Evolutionary ecology is a thriving field—just look at recent issues of *Nature* and *Science*—with generality and testability capable of drawing adherents who seek a way to explain human variability.

Albert Goodyear (personal communication) points out that current debate about relevance of optimal foraging models to archaeology provides "a pretty fair description of what Merton called middle range theory." Consistent with Merton's (1968:39–45) views, optimal foraging theory is neither whole nor unified, but it is general and provides some measure of explanatory power. Whereas specific applications remain provisional and partitive (i.e., directed at limited aspects of the cultural system), the endeavor has the promise of moving toward a general, unified theory of human behavior, provided the assumptions hold and the applications survive empirical scrutiny.

Is It Realistic to "Test" Optimal Foraging Models against Archaeological Data?

Viewed this way, evolutionary ecology may indeed offer a degree of general theoretical guidance, but enthusiasm must be tempered against the realities of the archaeological record. A number of ethnographic applications of optimal foraging models have appeared in recent years, ranging from qualitative, "heuristic" modeling to quantitative empirical testing: the work of Winterhalder (1977, 1980, 1981) on the Boreal Forest Cree; research on the Aché of Paraguay (Hawkes et al. 1982; Hill and Hawkes 1983); Hames and Vickers (1982) on Amazonian groups, O'Connell and colleagues on the Alyawara (O'Connell and Hawkes

1981; Hawkes and O'Connell 1981) and Smith (1980, 1981) on the Inuit.

Perhaps the greatest appeal of such models is their potential to bring testability and falsifiability to bear on real data (Krebs et al. 1983; Roth 1983; Winterhalder 1981:32–33). Although many such "tests" have been conducted by biologists, application to human populations has only just begun. As Smith (1983:648) readily acknowledges, "rigorous tests assume that most variables are under experimental control—a condition that few ethnographers, and no paleoanthropologists, are capable of meeting."

Optimal foraging theory provides a set of predictions (X) about how actors should behave under circumstances Y. The ecologist can determine the explanatory power of such projections by observing and recording behavior in a quantitative manner; he can simultaneously measure the state of the environment, to see if X and Y covary as predicted.

O'Connell and Hawkes (1981) did this by applying optimal foraging models to plant use by the modern Alyawara. An optimal diet model provided predictions X: If Alyawara collectors forage optimally, then resources taken in each patch will depend on the relative energy return per unit of handling time and the average return from collecting in that patch. Resources yielding a return higher than the average for a patch should be included in the diet; resources with lower returns should not. Stated in formal algebraic terms, these propositions generated specific expectations expressed in kcal/forager hour (O'Connell and Hawkes 1981:108).

"Situation Y" in this case reflects environmental state: degree of rainfall, relative temperature, and, most importantly, geographic distribution and condition of available plant communities, all in one place at a single point in time (i.e., near Bendaijerum between 1974 and 1975; see O'Connell and Hawkes 1981, fig. 5.3).

Covariation of X and Y was monitored across a series of Alyawara foraging events observed by O'Connell. On 11 visits to sandhill patches, energy returns were indeed well above average for the patch: "foraging behavior in this habitat is clearly consistent with the predictions of the optimal diet model" (O'Connell and Hawkes 1981:109). But foraging in mulga woodland produced different results: "Alyawara foraging behavior in these . . . events fails to fit the optimal diet prediction about the threshold at which lower-ranked resources will be added" (O'Connell and Hawkes 1981:109). The investigators suggest that future modeling include cost-benefit analyses of manufacturing and maintaining processing gear.

There is no question that optimal foraging models do indeed open up potentially fruitful lines of inquiry, although specific aspects of this application have been criticized (Durham 1981:225; Balme 1983; Martin 1983:615–616). Either the foraging models stand up to observable behavior or they do not. When models fail to fit reality, they can be refined or discarded; this is the strength of the optimal foraging effort in anthropology.

Observing behavior through an archaeological filter, however, is quite another matter. Encouraged by their ethnographic successes, O'Connell and Hawkes (1981:114–116) proffered some optimal foraging-based projections about long-term change in diet and land use in Australia:

> We propose that the onset of arid conditions 17,000–18,000 BP led to critical reductions in the abundance of high-ranked foods and favored the adoption of more expensive items, including seeds. Once the technogy for processing seeds was available, it was possible for Aborigines to move to previously uninhabited . . . parts of the continent [O'Connell and Hawkes 1981:115].

They argue that these projections command special attention from archaeologists because:

> Hunter-gatherer subsistence can be viewed profitably in terms of the same general theory now being applied by evolutionary ecologists to the study of feeding strategies. . . . The value of such theory lies in its role as a reference dimension, as a source of testable hypotheses about the organization of subsistence-related behavior in a wide range of environmental, technological, and social circumstances [O'Connell and Hawkes 1981:116].

As expressed earlier relative to Cohen's (1977) research on population pressure, one must ask how these propositions and their alternatives are to be tested against the archaeological record. Assuming that archaeologists are not simply to swallow theory on faith, how, specifically, would one know if optimal foraging propositions about the past are right or wrong?

Shifting empirical referent from ethnographic to archaeological data means that neither behavior nor environment is observed directly: two additional steps are always required to test the same proposition. Before optimal foraging theory, or any other general theory, can be brought to bear on archaeological data, it is necessary to infer past behavior from the archaeological record, and also to infer past environmental states from the paleoenvironmental record. Only then can archaeologists examine whether the inferred behaviors and conditions covary according to theory.

The Australian example requires comprehensive cultural and paleoenvironmental chronologies, an accurate picture of (1) who lived where (and when), and (2) what plants and animals were (and were not) available for inclusion in the diet. This is a tall order, and currently available data simply do not measure up. The authors of a recent synthesis clearly recognize the problem: climatic changes in Australia over the past 16,000 years "must have affected human life, but the data are inadequate to document what happened. . . . Almost no data are available on the prehistoric plants used at various times, and fauna has not been shown to be a sensitive enough marker to be related directly to these climatic variations" (White with O'Connell 1982:99). No testability here.

Verifying or rejecting the O'Connell and Hawkes propositions also requires solid evidence about which plants and animals were and were not actually consumed by prehistoric people. Those "testing" optimal foraging projections archaeologically must be careful to avoid the now-outmoded wishing-will-make-it-so euphoria of the 1960s and 1970s: grinding stones and seed processing were once considered to be isomorphic; projectile points once equaled hunting; pine nut hulls in a hearth were, at one time, sufficient to define a fall occupation. While recent mid-range research on sample size/sample diversity, seasonality, size sorting and intrasite patterning, regional assemblage variability, taphonomy, and post-depositional modifications proceed apace, such progress itself carries with it the sober realization that archaeological data are more intractable than was appreciated in the first two decades of the new archaeology.

Relative to the O'Connell and Hawkes propositions, one must keep in mind that mere presence of bones and seeds in an archaeological site is no longer considered to be valid evidence of consumption. Further, one must document the procurement and processing strategies applied to these resources; how are seeds processed and how does such processing show up in the archaeological record? It is especially critical to show that particular technologies were not in use at certain points in time. Likewise, one must distinguish areas being exploited residentially from those used only on a logistical basis.

Empirical and theoretical problems are rife in the Australian data (as elsewhere): "even in the areas of most intensive research, the number of analysed sites is very small [and] . . . the sampling of subsistence data within sites has also been very limited. . . . These analyses may not give us the full picture" (White with O'Connell 1982:133–134). No testability here either.

One might object that this is simply one more empirical cautionary tale. We just have not dug enough yet! While this is absolutely true—and one hopes that the O'Connell and Hawkes discussion will foster additional relevant field work—the important point is this: even if such data were forthcoming tomorrow, monumental interpretive problems effectively prohibit "testing" and "verification" of these actor-specific suggestions.

Progress is being made in both data acquisition and mid-range theory building. But let us not fool ourselves into thinking that the O'Connell and Hawkes propositions have been "verified" or even "tested." This simply has not happened (and almost certainly will not happen within the foreseeable future). And yet, one archaeologist is already arguing (prematurely) that the O'Connell and Hawkes hypotheses about late and post-Pleistocene behavior lend "support" to theoretical arguments about the way the world worked (Cohen 1985:102). Contemporary grant proposals and doctoral dissertations are already being propped up with such alleged "support" from optimal foraging theory. This is appeal-to-authority reasoning. To some, the fact that hypotheses happen to derive from optimal foraging models somehow lends them a degree of *a priori* support. This is not so; until rigorously subjected to empirical data of the past, the models of evolutionary biology have no greater degree of explanatory power in archaeology than any other notion someone might dream up.

Some candid proponents of optimal foraging theory recognize the problems: "Applying such theory presumes that the archaeological record is reasonably clear concerning what prehistoric folks did, and the task is then to *explain* it. But in fact, such an assumption is almost completely wrong in many important instances" (Eric Smith, personal communication; see also Smith 1983:640; Winterhalder 1983). Only by building the necessary mid-range linkages can we hope to obtain sufficiently accurate ways of perceiving the past. This is an entirely different objective from general theories like evolutionary ecology, which attempt to explain that past. In fact, investigators serious about ultimately applying optimal foraging models to archaeology can most profitably spend their time building necessary mid-range theory—and some are doing just that (Simms 1983, 1984; K. T. Jones 1983, 1984).

This is not to discourage proposals such as those put forward by O'Connell and Hawkes (1981), but rather to emphasize the poverty of "testability" and "falsifiability" as arguments warranting application of optimal foraging models to archaeology. Such propositions may well serve as "rough analogies" for the archaeologist, "more as a way of looking at things than as a source of rigorous quantitative models" (Bettinger 1983:640; see also Stini 1983). Optimal foraging models can, and have, provided us with another source of good ideas, some "interesting and non-obvious insights" (Cashdan 1982:1308–1309), a series of "counterintuitive" proposals (O'Connell et al. 1982:234.)

One must seriously question whether archaeological data can ever achieve the resolution required for any degree of "empirical support or refutation" of short-term decision-making theory at the level of the organism (Smith 1983:640). This is certainly not possible now, and those familiar with contemporary archaeological and paleoenvironmental records will have difficulty seeing how to distinguish between foraging optimally or foraging any other way. It is likewise difficult to be optimistic that archaeologists can immediately address the sufficiently broad range of issues that must be addressed when employing optimal foraging theory.

This shortcoming is hardly the fault of optimal foraging theorists. This is uniquely an archaeological problem originating from the specifics of the archaeological record and the immaturity of theory at the mid-range—not from the contents of evolutionary ecology. But if we as archaeologists cannot adequately satisfy a criterion of falsifiability on data from the past, then the greatest appeal of optimal foraging theory falls by the wayside.

Costs and Benefits of Reductionism

The tenets of evolutionary ecology are explicitly reductionistic, and reductionism can be a good thing. In fact, methodological reductionism ("the ability to account for the widest possible range of phenomena with the smallest possible set of laws and units"; Dunnell 1980b:49) constitutes the very goal of scientific inquiry.

Smith (1983) argues that methodological reductionism in evolutionary ecology provides a useful starting approach (a "shortcut" to understanding) without pretending to provide what S. Gould and Lewontin (1979) term "Panglossian" conclusions about the operation of the real world (see also Hawkes and O'Connell 1985; Smith and Winterhalder 1985). The analytical frame is deliberately simplified to specify a currency, a goal, a set of constraints, and a set of options. Decision-making categories are further simplified, ignoring such factors as perception and predation, to provide "simpler and more tractable" ways of asking questions and recognizing responses.

The focus is on strategic rules rather than on particular tactics (Krebs et al. 1983:165). Foraging models are not intended or suited to describe the interaction of all, or even a large number of variables that might affect subsistence related behavior. "They help one make an informed guess, or more precisely, a set of likely hypotheses . . . these hypotheses lead to predictions which can be tested against real data" (Hawkes and O'Connell in press; see also O'Connell and Hawkes 1984:530).

Selective methodological reductionism can indeed define a workable research strategy, but Dunnell (1980b:49) cautions about the dangers of encroaching "empirical reductionism, in which the phenomena of one field are 'reduced' to functions of those in another." It is this empirical brand of reductionism that further clouds the archaeological potential of optimal foraging models. The agenda of evolutionary ecology requires an explicit "optimization" approach to make the models operational. Such optimization, by definition, telescopes large-scale evolutionary trends down to the level of individual actors, thereby empirically reducing macroevolutionary phenomena to a microevolutionary level.

Theory constructed at one level of resolution cannot necessarily be smoothly transferred to other levels. Empirical testing of optimal foraging models is aimed only at the microevolutionary locus of decision-making: the individual actor. Explanation at a macroevolutionary scale requires the added assumption that the outcome of individual decision-making is strictly additive. Price (1982:716) succinctly summarizes this view:

"The long run" is nothing more than a continuous series of short runs, of nows, placed end to end and—if a "long run" is to be discerned at all—linked by an uninterrupted positive feedback loop; whatever the "payoffs" of a given trait, these are and must be in the now only.

Empirical reductionism remains highly controversial in today's evolutionary biology (Maynard Smith 1978; Lewontin 1979; S. Gould and Lewontin 1979; Krebs et al. 1983; Myers 1983; Smith 1983:626–627), and additional doubts are raised when such prime-mover arguments are applied to human beings (Lee 1979:434; Durham 1981; Binford 1983a:221–222; Jochim 1983:164; Keene 1983; Martin 1983; Moore 1983:183; Smith 1983:627; Brown 1985:205–206; Schrire 1984:11–12; Sih and Milton in press). The assumptions underlying optimal foraging models remain "rich in the need of empirical verification" (Winterhalder 1981: 34).

Evolutionary biology likewise employs natural selection as its primary explanatory mechanism, and the relevance of natural selection to human populations is another hotly debated topic (Goldschmidt 1959; Rappaport 1971; Sahlins 1976; Dunnell 1980b; Adams 1981; Price 1982; Binford 1983a:221–222; Eldredge 1985; Carneiro, in press). The outcome of this dialog will largely condition the relevance of optimal foraging models in anthropology.

These difficulties arise relative to contemporary human populations, and the problem is vastly compounded in the archaeological record, where "individuals" are analytically invisible. Given a strikingly similar prospect, paleontologists have recently engaged in a painful self-reassessment, attempting to define the foundations of their own nomothetic evolutionary science (S. Gould 1980a, 1980b). How relevant this exegesis will be for theory construction in archaeology remains to be seen. At a minimum, there are important parallels and lessons involved (Dunnell 1981:445, 1982; Binford 1983a:23).

S. Gould (1980a:96–97) argues that theoretical excitement in paleontology has been cyclical, the major peaks correlated with infusion of fresh biological concepts. "We take the evolutionary concepts formulated for us by students of modern populations and we try to show that ancient ones lived by the same rules. But where does this lead beyond exemplification based on imperfect data?" (S. Gould 1980a:98). Traditional paleontology, Gould argues, assumed an "unadventurous" posture relative to biology, too often passively transferring the orthodoxies of microevolutionary theory across vast stretches of time and multiple levels into the domain of macroevolution.

Tired of their second-rate, subservient status, some ask: "Why be a paleontologist if we are condemned only to verify imperfectly what students of living organisms can propose directly?" (S. Gould and Eldredge 1977:149). Many paleontologists reject this empirically reductionistic view, and maybe archaeologists should do the same.

There is a direct and obvious parallel to the relationship between archaeology and anthropology. Some perceive a "peak of excitement" coming to archaeology from an infusion of principles from evolutionary ecology. Perhaps so, but properly viewed, the excitement should be largely restricted to the domain of students of modern populations. When these notions are grafted onto the archaeological record, one must ask (to paraphrase Gould), where does this lead beyond exemplification based on imperfect data?

Hierarchical Explanation in Archaeology?

The paleontological alternative to reductionism is hierarchy, a world not perceived as a smooth and seamless continuum, but as a series of ascending levels. Hierarchies organize individuals within levels of authority, usually with each level subordinate to the next higher level, and ruling over the next lower level (S. Gould 1980b:121; Vrba and Eldredge 1984:146). A hierarchical approach requires the identification of analytical individuals, each having spatiotemporal boundedness, and characterized by births, histories, and deaths. Although the organism is the "paradigmatic" individual, genomes, populations, and species can also be treated as individuals of focus, nested within each other at ascending levels of the genealogical hierarchy.

The so-called "new evolutionary synthesis" maintains that the principles of evolution (mutation, adaptation, natural selection) may be valid and sufficient, but they work in different ways, on different materials, at different levels, and cannot be smoothly extrapolated from one to another (S. Gould 1980a:106). Many scientists working on both ends of the genealogical hierarchy—paleontologists and molecular biologists alike—now question the effectiveness and propriety of viewing population-level processes of natural selection and genetic drift as sole determinants in evolution (Eldredge and Salthe 1984:184). Many seek a "bounded independence" for macroevolution: unity in a body of principles common to all levels, diversity in the different working of these principles upon the material at different levels (S. Gould 1980a:107).

Explanatory success for paleontology resides at the level of species, relatively high in the hierarchy. Within this framework, paleontologists are free to explore rates or tempos of evolution, differential success of species, and explanations of trends. Basic processes (e.g., mutation and selection) enter into explanations at all scales; in this sense there may remain a "general theory of evolution"; but the processes are viewed as working in different ways on diverse levels. This is hardly to suggest that all evolutionists accept the Gould-Eldredge-Stanley views on macroevolution and the fossil record (see Charlesworth et al. 1982 for one such contrary view).

What does all of this mean for archaeology? Perhaps nothing should we pursue a path of strictly reductionistic, extra-archaeological explanation. But should archaeologists define their own version of macroevolutionary theory, then the distinctive parallel between behavioral optimization theories and the archaeological record is clear.

While surely lacking a coherent body of *in situ* general theory, archaeologists might galvanize behind the belief, as Dunnell (1982:528) has so succinctly expressed it, that archaeology is not ecology, evolution, central place theory, optimization theory, information theory, or any other kind of theory: "Archaeology is first and foremost archaeology if only by virtue of the archaeological record."

A hierarchial perspective may define where archaeologists and optimal foraging theorists must part company. At one level, optimal foraging models explicitly define the organism as the "paradigmatic" individual; optimization explanations are deliberately (and correctly) reduced to an organism-specific level. Optimal foraging theory could have real potential at the level of microevolution; but can models of optimal organismic foraging necessarily be extrapolated to higher levels in the hierarchy? It remains to be seen how factors such as nutrition, food storage, imperfect knowledge, backup and famine strategies, intragroup competition, risk, seasonal variability, and higher level cooperation influence such organism-specific decision making (Keene 1983:146–147; Jochim 1983).

It may be necessary to look elsewhere for ways to explain long-term macroevolution, which necessarily involves adaptive processes only manifest archaeologically. To the extent that they may prove successful in explaining human behavior, principles of optimal foraging may well work in different ways at various levels in the hierarchy of cultural evolution. The explanatory potential of archaeology resides at a relatively high level in the hierarchy, and explanations at one hierarchical level cannot necessarily be smoothly extrapolated to another level.

An unresolved question remains: What are the demes, species, and monophyletic taxa of archaeology (see Dunnell 1980b:86) and how are they hierarchically interrelated? Phases, traditions, co-traditions, and "cultures" have in the past functioned as archaeology's higher level "individuals" (*sensu* Vrba and Eldredge 1984). Phases, for instance, exhibit spatiotemporal boundedness, and they can be characterized by births, histories, and deaths. This traditional archaeological hierarchy, however, is defined on the normative basis of shared culture, and we learned long ago that projectile point and pottery types have little to do with people or their adaptive processes. Except in the relatively low level case of cultural chronology, Americanist archaeology has largely shifted from a normative to an adaptive perception of "culture" (Binford 1962; Thomas 1979); but on-the-ground definition of higher level adaptive "individuals" has not begun. To proceed meaningfully with a hierarchical view of cultural evolution, it is necessary to define new phenomenological entities that are adaptively significant, uniquely archaeological "individuals," nested within each other at ascending levels of a genealogical hierarchy.

Once the archaeological equivalent of genomes, populations, and species can be treated as individuals of focus, archaeologists will be free to explore rates or tempos of evolution, differential success of local groups, and explanations of trends. Basic Darwinian processes may enter into explanations at all scales (in this sense, anthropology may yet achieve a "general theory of cultural evolution"); but the processes must be viewed as working in different ways on the characteristic materials of each of the diverse levels.

General theory building in archaeology receives mixed reviews. Should archaeologists choose to follow the lead of their paleontological cousins, defining a distinctly archaeological hierarchy of the evolutionary process, we may find rave reviews awaiting at the sixtieth birthday of the Society for American Archaeology.

Acknowledgments

In approaching this paper, I asked for assistance from a number of friends and colleagues, and thank each for providing advice, reprints, and unpublished manuscripts. I am particularly grateful to Robert L. Bettinger, Lewis Binford, Albert Goodyear, Donald K. Grayson, Brian Hayden, James F. O'Connell, Eric A. Smith, and Bruce Winterhalder for detailed, sometimes lengthy comments and criticisms. I also appreciate assistance and comments from Mark Cohen, Robert Dunnell, Niles Eldredge, Thomas Hester, Cynthia Irwin-Williams, J. Alan May, David Meltzer, Jerry Sabloff, Michael Schiffer, and John Speth. Given the diversity of perspectives, insights, and backgrounds involved here, it is hardly surprising that no consensus emerged regarding American hunter-gatherer studies. Still, their opinions are probably an accurate reflection of reality: there really is no consensus! Unlike paleontology, we lack "synthesis," much less "antithesis."

I also thank Margot Dembo and Fred Wayne for help in pulling the manuscript together. Special thanks also to Lorann S. A. Pendleton, for providing ideas, references, and helping out in all possible ways.

Note

[1]In this paper, as elsewhere, I use the terms "middle range" and "mid-range" interchangeably to designate the theory building effort programmatically mapped out by Lewis Binford in 1977, and elaborated several times since then. Two terms are involved because somewhere in the editorial process of my 1979 textbook, I managed to add a hyphen and drop a syllable, creating "mid-range" from Binford's original "middle range" (Thomas 1979). This transliteration was wholly unintentional, and I retain my original usage primarily for reasons of personal preference and consistency (see also Thomas 1983a, 1983b). While not necessarily advocating its widespread adaptation—I really do not care what people *call* it—the new phrase itself does serve to emphasize that Binfordian "mid-range theory" is very different from Merton's (1968) "middle range theory."

Literature Cited

Adams, Richard N.
   1981 Natural Selection, Energetics, and "Cultural Materialism." *Current Anthropology* 22(6):603–624.

Aikens, C. Melvin
   1970 Hogup Cave. *University of Utah Anthropological Papers* 93.

Anderson, Patricia C.
   1980 A Testimony of Prehistoric Tasks: Diagnostic Residues on Stone Tool Working Edges. *World Archaeology* 12(2):181–194.

Andresen, John M., Brian F. Byrd, Mark D. Elson, Randall H. McGuire, Ruben G. Mendoza, Edward Staski, and J. Peter White
   1981 The Deer Hunters: Star Carr Reconsidered. *World Archaeology* 13(1):31–46.

Andrews, Carol
  1981   *The Rosetta Stone.* British Museum Publications, Ltd., London.

Balme, J.
  1983   Review of *Hunter-Gatherer Foraging Strategies,* edited by Bruce Winterhalder and E. A. Smith. *Mankind* 13:438–440.

Bayham, Frank E.
  1979   Factors Influencing the Archaic Pattern of Animal Exploitation. *Kiva* 44:219–235.

Beck, Charlotte
  1984   Steens Mountain Surface Archaeology: The Sites. Doctoral dissertation, University of Washington, Seattle.

Behm, Jeffery A.
  1983   Flake Concentrations: Distinguishing between Flintworking Activity Areas and Secondary Deposits. *Lithic Technology* 12(1):9–16.

Bettinger, Robert L.
  1977   Aboriginal Human Ecology in Owens Valley: Prehistoric Change in the Great Basin. *American Antiquity* 42(1):3–17.
  1980   Explanatory/Predictive Models of Hunter-Gatherer Adaptation. In *Advances in Archaeological Method and Theory,* edited by M. B. Schiffer, pages 257–310. Academic Press, New York.
  1983   Comment on "Anthropological Applications of Optimal Foraging Theory: A Critical Review" by Eric Alden Smith. *Current Anthropology* 24(5):640–641.

Bettinger, Robert L., and M. A. Baumhoff
  1982   The Numic Spread: Great Basin Cultures in Competition. *American Antiquity* 47:485–503.

Binford, Lewis R.
  1962   Archaeology as Anthropology. *American Antiquity* 28:217–225.
  1977   General Introduction. In *For Theory Building in Archaeology,* edited by Lewis R. Binford, pages 1–10. Academic Press, New York.
  1978   *Nunamiut Ethnoarchaeology: A Case Study in Archaeological Formation Processes.* Academic Press, New York.
  1979a Interview. *Flintknappers' Exchange* 2(1):19–25.
  1979b Organization and Formation Processes: Looking at Curated Technologies. *Journal of Anthropological Research* 35(3):255–273.
  1980   Willow Smoke and Dogs' Tails: Hunter-Gatherer Settlement Systems and Archaeological Site Formation. *American Antiquity* 45(1):4–20.
  1981   *Bones: Ancient Men and Modern Myths.* Academic Press, New York.
  1982   Objective-Explanation-Archaeology 1980. In *Theory and Explanation in Archaeology: The Southampton Conference,* edited by C. Renfrew, M. Rowlands, and B. A. Seagraves. Academic Press, London.
  1983a *In Pursuit of the Past: Decoding the Archaeological Record.* Thames and Hudson, London.
  1983b *Working at Archaeology.* Academic Press, New York.
  1984   *Faunal Remains from Klasies River Mouth.* Academic Press, New York.

Binford, Lewis R., and James F. O'Connell
  1984   An Alyawara Day: The Stone Quarry. *Journal of Anthropological Research* 40:406–432.

Bowers, Peter M., Robson Bonnichsen, and David Hotch
   1983   Flake Dispersal Experiments: Noncultural Transformation of the Archaeological Record. *American Antiquity* 48:553–572.

Brain, C. K.
   1981   *The Hunters or the Hunted? An Introduction to African Cave Taphonomy.* University of Chicago Press, Chicago.

Brown, James A.
   1985   Long-term Trends to Sedentism and the Emergence of Complexity in the American Midwest. In *Prehistoric Hunter-Gatherers: The Emergence of Cultural Complexity,* edited by T. Douglas Price and James A. Brown, pages 201–231. Academic Press, New York.

Buikstra, Jane and Della C. Cook
   1980   Paleopathology: An American Account. *Annual Review of Anthropology* 9:433–470.

Byers, Douglas S.
   1967   *The Prehistory of the Tehuacan Valley, Volume One: Environment and Subsistence.* University of Texas Press, Austin.

Cahen, Daniel, and Lawrence H. Keeley
   1980   Not Less than Two, Not More than Three. *World Archaeology* 12(2):166–180.

Cahen, D., L. H. Keeley, and F. L. Van Noten
   1979   Stone Tools, Toolkits, and Human Behavior in Prehistory. *Current Anthropology* 20(4):661–684.

Camilli, Eileen
   1983   Site Occupational History and Lithic Assemblage Structure: An Example from Southeastern Utah. Doctoral dissertation, University of New Mexico, Albuquerque.

Campbell, Donald T.
   1973   Natural Selection as an Epistemological Model. In *A Handbook of Method in Cultural Anthropology,* edited by Raoul Naroll and Ronald Cohen, pages 51–85. Columbia University Press, New York.

Carneiro, Robert L.
   In press   The Role of Natural Selection in the Evolution of Culture.

Cashdan, Elizabeth
   1982   Review of *Hunter-Gatherer Foraging Strategies,* edited by B. Winterhalder and E. A. Smith. *Science* 216:1308–1309.

Chaplin, R. S.
   1971   *The Study of Animal Bones from Archaeological Sites.* John Willey and Sons, New York.

Charlesworth, Brian, Russell Lande, and Montgomery Slatkin
   1982   A Neo-Darwinian Commentary on Macroevolution. *Evolution* 36(3):474–498.

Childe, V. Gordon
   1928   *The Most Ancient East: The Oriental Prelude to European Prehistory.* Kegan Paul, London.

Clark, J. G. D.
  1952 *Prehistoric Europe: The Economic Basis.* Methuen, London.
  1954 *Excavations at Star Carr: An Early Mesolithic Site at Seamer near Scarborough, Yorkshire.* Cambridge University Press, Cambridge, U. K.

Clarke, David L.
  1973 Archaeology: The Loss of Innocence. *Antiquity* 47:6–18.

Cohen, Mark N.
  1977 *The Food Crisis in Prehistory.* Yale University Press, New Haven.
  1981 Pacific Coast Foragers: Affluent or Overcrowded? *In* Affluent Foragers: Pacific Coasts East and West, edited by Shuzo Koyama and David Hurst Thomas. *Senri Ethnological Studies* 9:275–295.
  1985 Prehistoric Hunter-Gatherers: The Meaning of Social Complexity. In *Prehistoric Hunter-Gatherers: The Emergence of Cultural Complexity,* edited by T. Douglas Price and James A. Brown, pages 99–119. Academic Press, New York.

Cohen, Mark N., and George J. Armelagos (editors)
  1984 *Paleopathology at the Origins of Agriculture.* Academic Press, New York.

Cowgill, George
  1975 On Causes and Consequences of Ancient and Modern Population Changes. *American Anthropologist* 77:505–525.

Cross, John R.
  1983 Twigs, Branches, Trees, and Forests: Problems of Scale in Lithic Analysis. In *Archaeological Hammers and Theories,* edited by James A. Moore and Arthur S. Keene, pages 87–106. Academic Press, New York.

Daly, Patricia
  1969 Approaches to Faunal Analysis in Archaeology. *American Antiquity* 34(2):146–153.

Dart, Raymond A.
  1957 The Osteodontokeratic Culture of *Australopithecus Prometheus. Transvaal Museum Memoir* 10. Pretoria.

Dunnell, Robert C.
  1979 Trends in Current Americanist Archaeology. *American Journal of Archaeology* 83:438–449.
  1980a Americanist Archaeology: The 1979 Contribution. *American Journal of Archaeology* 84:463–478.
  1980b Evolutionary Theory and Archaeology. In *Advances in Archaeological Method and Theory,* edited by Michael B. Schiffer, 3:35–99. Academic Press, New York.
  1981 Americanist Archaeology: The 1980 Literature. *American Journal of Archaeology* 85:430–445.
  1982 Americanist Archaeological Literature: 1981. *American Journal of Archaeology* 86:509–529.
  1983 A Review of the Americanist Literature for 1982. *American Journal of Archaeology* 87:521–544.
  1984 The Americanist Literature for 1983: A Year of Contrasts and Challenges. *American Journal of Archaeology* 88:489–513.

Durham, William
    1981 Overview: Optimal Foraging Analysis in Human Ecology. In *Hunter-Gatherer Foraging Strategies,* edited by Bruce Winterhalder and Eric Alden Smith, pages 218–232. University of Chicago Press, Chicago.

Eldredge, Niles
    1985 Comments on "Evolutionary Approaches to the Study of Human Diversity." Paper presented at the 50th anniversary symposium of the Society for American Archaeology, Denver.

Eldredge, Niles, and Stanley N. Salthe
    1984 Hierarchy and Evolution. *Oxford Surveys in Evolutionary Biology* 1:184–208.

Elston, Robert G.
    1982 Good Times, Hard Times: Prehistoric Culture Change in the Western Great Basin. *In* Man and Environment in the Great Basin, edited by David B. Madsen and James F. O'Connell, pages 186–206. *Society for American Archaeology Papers* 2.

Epstein, Jeremiah
    1975 Comments. In *Lithic Technology: Making and Using Stone Tools,* edited by Earl Swanson, pages 233–236. Mouton Publishers, The Hague.

Fladmark, K. R.
    1982 Microdebitage Analysis: Initial Considerations. *Journal of Archaeological Science* 9:205–220.

Flenniken, J. Jeffrey
    1978 Reevaluation of the Lindenmeier Folsom: A Replication Experimentation in Lithic Technology. *American Antiquity* 43(3):473–480.
    1981 Replicative Systems Analysis: A Model Applied to the Vein Quartz Artifacts from the Hoko River Site. *Laboratory of Anthropology Reports of Investigations* 59. Washington State University, Pullman.
    1984 The Past, Present, and Future of Flintknapping: An Anthropological Perspective. *Annual Review of Anthropology* 13:187–274.

Flenniken, J. Jeffrey, and Anan W. Raymond
    In press Morphological Projectile Point Typology: Replication Experimentation and Technological Analysis. *American Antiquity.*

Flenniken, J. Jeffrey, and J. Haggerty
    1979 Trampling as an Age in the Formation of Edge Damage: An Experiment in Lithic Technology. *Northwest Anthropological Research Notes* 13:208–214.

Gallagher, J. P.
    1980 Experimental Flake Scatter-Patterns: A New Interpretive Technique. *Journal of Field Archaeology* 7:345–352.

Goldschmidt, Walter
    1959 *Man's Way.* The World Publishing Company, Cleveland.

Gould, Richard A.
    1980 *Living Archaeology.* University of Cambridge Press, Cambridge.

Gould, Stephen J.
    1980a The Promise of Paleobiology as a Nomothetic Evolutionary Discipline. *Paleobiology* 6(1):96–118.

1980b Is a New and General Theory of Evolution Emerging? *Paleobiology* 6(1):119–130.

Gould, Stephen J., and Niles Eldredge
1977 Punctuated Equilibria: The Tempo and Mode of Evolution Reconsidered. *Paleobiology* 3:115–151.

Gould, Stephen J., and Richard C. Lewontin
1979 The Spandrils of San Marco and the Panglossian Paradigm: A Critique of the Adaptationist Programme. *Proceedings of the Royal Society, London,* series B, 205:581–598.

Grayson, Donald K.
1982 Review of *Bones: Ancient Men and Modern Myths,* by Lewis R. Binford. *American Anthropologist* 84:439–440.
1984 *Quantitative Zoology: Topics in the Analysis of Archaeological Faunas.* Academic Press, New York.

Grayson, Donald K., and David Hurst Thomas
1983 Seasonality at Gatecliff Shelter. *In* The Archaeology of Monitor Valley, 2: Gatecliff Shelter, by David Hurst Thomas. *Anthropological Papers of the American Museum of Natural History* 59(1):434–438.

Green, James P.
1975 McKean and Little Lake Technology: A Problem in Projectile Point Typology in the Great Basin of North America. In *Lithic Technology: Making and Using Stone Tools,* edited by Earl Swanson, pages 159–172. Mouton Publishers, The Hague.

Greiser, Sally T., and Payson D. Sheets
1979 Raw Materials as a Functional Variable in Use-wear Studies. In *Lithic Use-wear Studies,* edited by Brian Hayden, pages 289–296. Academic Press, New York.

Hames, Raymond B., and William Vickers
1982 Optimal Diet Breadth Theory as a Model to Explaining Variability in Amazonian Hunting. *American Ethnologist* 9:357–378.

Hanes, Gary
1983 Frequencies of Spiral and Green-bone Fracture on Ungulate Limb Bones in Modern Surface Assemblages. *American Antiquity* 48:102–114.

Hassan, Fekri
1981 *Demographic Archaeology.* Academic Press, New York.

Hawkes, Kristen, Kim Hill, and James O'Connell
1982 Why Hunters Gather: Optimal Foraging and the Aché of Eastern Paraguay. *American Ethnologist* 9:379–398.

Hawkes, Kristen, and James F. O'Connell
1981 Affluent Hunters? Some Comments in Light of the Alyawara Case. *American Anthropologist* 83(3):622–626.
In press Optimal Foraging Models and the Case of the !Kung. *American Anthropologist.*

Hayden, Brian (editor)
1979 *Lithic Use-wear Studies.* Academic Press, New York.

Hayden, Brian, and Aubrey Cannon
1984a The Structure of Material Systems: Ethnoarchaeology in the Maya Highlands. *Society for American Archaeology Papers* 3.
1984b Interaction Inferences in Archaeology and Learning Frameworks of the Maya. *Journal of Anthropological Archaeology* 3(4):325–367.

Hill, Kim, and Kristen Hawkes
1983 Neotropical Hunting among the Aché of Eastern Paraguay. In *Adaptive Responses of Native Amazonians,* edited by R. Hames and W. Vickers, pages 139–188. Academic Press, New York.

Hofman, Jack L.
1981 The Refitting of Chipped-stone Artifacts as an Analytical and Interpretive Tool. *Current Anthropology* 22:691–693.

Holly, G., and T. Del Bene
1981 An Evaluation of Keeley's Microwear Approach. *Journal of Archaeological Science* 8:337–352.

Howard, Hildegarde
1929 The Avifauna of Emeryville Shellmound. *University of California Publications in Zoology* 32:378–383.

Jochim, Michael
1976 *Hunter-Gatherer Subsistence and Settlement: A Predictive Model.* Academic Press, New York.
1981 *Strategies for Survival: Cultural Behavior in an Ecological Context.* Academic Press, New York.
1983 Optimization Models in Context. In *Archaeological Theory and Hammers,* edited by James A. Moore and Arthur S. Keene, pages 157–172. Academic Press, New York.

Jones, George T.
1984 Prehistoric Land Use in the Steens Mountain Area, Southeastern Oregon. Doctoral dissertation, Department of Anthropology, University of Washington, Seattle.

Jones, George T., Donald K. Grayson, and Charlotte Beck
1983 Artifact Class Richness and Sample Size in Archaeological Surface Assemblages. *In* Lulu Linear Punctated: Essays in Honor of George Irving Quimby, edited by R. C. Dunnell and D. K. Grayson. *Anthropological Papers of the Museum of Anthropology, University of Michigan* 72:55–73.

Jones, Kevin L.
1984 Lithic Waste Flakes as a Measure of Cultural Affinity: A New Zealand Case Study. *Lithic Technology* 13(3):71–83.

Jones, Kevin T.
1983 Forager Archaeology: The Aché of Eastern Paraguay. In *Carnivores, Human Scavengers, and Predators: A Question of Bone Technology,* edited by G. M. LeMoine and A. E. MacEachern, pages 171–191. Archaeological Association, University of Calgary, Calgary, Alberta, Canada.
1984 Hunting and Scavenging by Early Hominids: A Study in Archaeological Method and Theory. Doctoral dissertation, Department of Anthropology, University of Utah, Salt Lake City.

Judge, W. J.
1973 *Paleoindian Occupation of the Central Rio Grande Valley in New Mexico.* University of New Mexico Press, Albuquerque.

Kalin, Jeffrey
1981 Stem Point Manufacture and Debitage Recovery. *Archaeology of Eastern North America* 9:134–172.

Keeley, Lawrence H.
1980 *Experimental Determination of Stone Tool Uses: A Microwear Analysis.* University of Chicago Press, Chicago.

Keene, Arthur S.
1981 *Prehistoric Foraging in a Temperate Forest: A Linear Programming Model.* Academic Press, New York.
1983 Biology, Behavior, and Borrowing: A Critical Examination of Optimal Foraging Theory in Archaeology. In *Archaeological Theory and Hammers,* edited by James A. Moore and Arthur S. Keene, pages 137–155. Academic Press, New York.

Kelly, Robert L.
1983 Hunter-Gatherer Mobility Strategies. *Journal of Anthropological Research* 39(3):277–306.
1985 Hunter-Gatherer Mobility and Sedentism: A Great Basin Pilot Study. Doctoral dissertation, Department of Anthropology, University of Michigan, Ann Arbor.

Knudson, Ruthann
1978 Experimental Lithicology: Method and Theory. *Lithic Technology* 7(3):44–46.

Krebs, J. R., D. W. Stephens, and W. J. Sutherland
1983 Perspectives in Optimal Foraging. In *Perspectives in Ornithology,* edited by G. A. Clarke and A. H. Brush, pages 165–216. Cambridge University Press, Cambridge.

Lee, Richard B.
1979 *The !Kung San.* Cambridge University Press, Cambridge.

Lewontin, Richard C.
1979 Fitness, Survival, and Optimality. In *Analysis of Ecological Systems,* edited by D. H. Horn, R. Mitchell, and G. R. Stairs, pages 3–21. Ohio State University Press, Columbus.

Longacre, William A., and J. Jefferson Reid
1971 Research Strategy for Locational Analysis: An Outline. *In* The Distribution of Prehistoric Population Aggregates, edited by George J. Gumerman. *Prescott College Anthropological Reports* 1:103–110.

Loy, Thomas
1983 Prehistoric Blood Residues: Detection on Tool Surfaces and Identification of Species or Origin. *Science* 220(4603):1269–1271.

Lyman, R. Lee
1984 Broken Bones, Bone Expediency Tool, and Bone Pseudotools: Lessons from the Blast Zone around Mount St. Helens, Washington. *American Antiquity* 49:315–333.

1985 Bone Frequencies: Differential Transport, *in situ* Destruction, and the MGUI. *Journal of Archaeological Science* 12:221–236.

MacNeish, Richard S., Melvin L. Fowler, Angel Garcia Cook, Frederick A. Peterson, Antoinette Nelken-Terner, and James A. Neely
1972 *The Prehistory of the Tehuacan Valley, Volume Five: Excavations and Reconnaissance.* University of Texas Press, Austin.

Magne, Martin P. R.
1983 Lithics and Livelihood: Stone Tool Technologies of Central and Southern Interior British Columbia. Doctoral dissertation, University of British Columbia, Vancouver.

Magne, Martin P., and David Pokotylo
1981 A Pilot Study in Bifacial Lithic Reduction Sequences. *Lithic Technology* 10:34–47.

Martin, John
1983 On the Estimation of Sizes of Local Groups in a Hunting-Gathering Environment. *American Anthropologist* 85:612–629.

Maynard Smith, John
1978 Optimization Theory in Evolution. *Annual Review of Ecology and Systematics* 9:31–56.

Meltzer, David J.
1979 Paradigms and the Nature of Change in American Archaeology. *American Antiquity* 44(4):644–657.

Merton, Robert K.
1968 *Social Theory and Social Structure.* The Free Press, New York.

Monks, G. G.
1981 Seasonality Studies. In *Advances in Archaeological Method and Theory,* edited by Michael B. Schiffer, 4:177–240. Academic Press, New York.

Moore, James A.
1983 The Trouble with Know-it-alls: Information as a Social and Ecological Resource. In *Archaeological Hammers and Theories,* edited by J. A. Moore and A. Keene, pages 173–191. Academic Press, New York.

Myers, J. P.
1983 Commentary on Perspectives in Optimal Foraging. In *Perspectives in Ornithology,* edited by G. A. Clarke and A. H. Brush, pages 216–221. Cambridge University Press, Cambridge.

Myers, Thomas P., Michael R. Voorhies, and R. George Corner
1980 Spiral Fractures and Bone Pseudotools at Paleontological Sites. *American Antiquity* 45:483–489.

Newcomer, M. H., and G. de G. Sieveking
1980 Experimental Flake Scatter-Patterns: A New Interpretative Technique. *Journal of Field Archaeology* 7:345–352.

Nicholson, B. A.
1983 A Comparative Evaluation of Four Sampling Techniques and of the Reliability of Microdebitage as a Cultural Indicator in Regional Surveys. *Plains Anthropologist* 28:273–281.

O'Connell, James F.
  1975 The Prehistory of Surprise Valley. *Ballena Press Anthropological Papers 4.*

O'Connell, James F., and Kristen Hawkes
  1981 Alyawara Plant Use and Optimal Foraging Theory. In *Hunter-Gatherer Foraging Strategies,* edited by Bruce Winterhalder and Eric Alden Smith, pages 99–125. University of Chicago Press, Chicago.
  1984 Food Choice and Foraging Sites among the Alyawara. *Journal of Anthropological Research* 40(4):504–535.

O'Connell, James F., Kevin T. Jones, and Steven R. Simms
  1982 Some Thoughts on Prehistoric Archaeology. *In* Man and Environment in the Great Basin, edited by David B. Madsen and James F. O'Connell. *Society for American Archaeology Papers* 2:227–240.

Patterson, Leland W.
  1983 Criteria for Determining the Attributes of Man-made Lithics. *Journal of Field Archaeology* 10:297–307.

Perlman, Stephen M.
  1980 An Optimum Diet Model, Coastal Variability, and Hunter-Gatherer Behavior. In *Advances in Archaeological Method and Theory,* edited by M. B. Schiffer, 3:257–310. Academic Press, New York.

Price, Barbara J.
  1982 Cultural Materialism: A Theoretical Review. *American Antiquity* 47(4):709–741.

Price, T. Douglas, and James A. Brown
  1985 Aspects of Hunter-Gatherer Complexity. In *Prehistoric Hunter-Gatherers: The Emergence of Cultural Complexity,* edited by T. Douglas Price and James A. Brown, pages 3–20. Academic Press, New York.

Raab, L. Mark, and Albert C. Goodyear
  1984 Middle-Range Theory in Archaeology: A Critical Review of Origins and Applications. *American Antiquity* 49(2):255–269.

Rappaport, Roy
  1971 Nature, Culture, and Ecological Anthropology. In *Man, Culture and Society,* edited by Harry L. Shapiro, pages 237–267. Oxford University Press, New York.

Reher, C. A.
  1977 Settlement and Subsistence along the Lower Chaco River. In *Settlement and Subsistence along the Lower Chaco River: The CGP Survey,* edited by Charles A. Reher, pages 7–113. University of New Mexico, Albuquerque.

Roth, Eric Abella
  1983 Comment on "Anthropological Applications of Optimal Foraging Theory: A Critical Review" by Eric Alden Smith. *Current Anthropology* 24(5):646.

Sadek-Kooros, Hind
  1972 Primitive Bone Fracturing: A Method of Research. *American Antiquity* 37(3):369–382.

Sahlins, Marshall
1976 *Culture and Practical Reason: The Use and Abuse of Biology.* University of Chicago Press, Chicago.

Salmon, Merrilee H.
1982 *Philosophy and Archaeology.* Academic Press, New York.

Schalk, Randall F.
1981 Land Use and Organizational Complexity among Foragers of Northwestern North America. *In* Affluent Foragers: Pacific Coasts East and West, edited by Shuzo Koyama and David Hurst Thomas. *Senri Ethnological Studies* 9:53–76.

Schiffer, Michael B.
1976 *Behavioral Archaeology.* Academic Press, New York.
1979 The Place of Lithic Use-wear Studies in Behavioral Archaeology. In *Lithic Use-wear Analysis,* edited by Brian Hayden, pages 15–25. Academic Press, New York.

Schrire, Carmel (editor)
1984 *Past and Present in Hunter Gatherer Studies.* Academic Press, New York.

Sheets, Payson D.
1975 Behavioral Analysis and the Structure of a Prehistoric Industry. *Current Anthropology* 16(3):369–391.

Sih, Andrew, and Katharine A. Milton
In press Optimal Diet and Theory: Should the !Kung Eat Mongongos? *American Anthropologist.*

Simms, Steven R.
1983 Comment on "Anthropological Applications of Optimal Foraging Theory: A Critical Review," by Eric Alden Smith. *Current Anthropology* 24(5):646.
1984 Aboriginal Great Basin Foraging Strategies: An Evolutionary Analysis. Doctoral dissertation, Department of Anthropology, University of Utah, Salt Lake City.

Smith, Eric Alden
1980 Evolutionary Ecology and the Analysis of Human Foraging Behavior: An Inuit Example from the East Coast of Hudson Bay. Doctoral dissertation, Department of Anthropology, Cornell University, Ithaca.
1981 The Application of Optimal Foraging Theory to the Analysis of Hunter-Gatherer Group Size. In *Hunter-Gatherer Foraging Strategies,* edited by B. Winterhalder and E. A. Smith, pages 35–65. University of Chicago Press, Chicago.
1983 Anthropological Applications of Optimal Foraging Theory: A Critical Review. *Current Anthropology* 24(5):625–651.
1984 Anthropology, Evolutionary Ecology, and the Explanatory Limitations of the Ecosystem Concept. In *The Ecosystem Concept in Anthropology,* edited by Emilio F. Moran, pages 51–85. Westview Press, Boulder.

Smith, Eric Alden, and Bruce Winterhalder
1981 New Perspectives on Hunter-Gatherer Socioecology. In *Hunter-Gatherer Foraging Strategies,* edited by Bruce Winterhalder and Eric Alden Smith, pages 1–12. University of Chicago Press, Chicago.

1985 On the Logic and Application of Optimal Foraging Theory: The Brief Reply to Martin. *American Anthropologist* 87(3):645–648.

Speth, John
1983 *Bone Kills and Bone Counts: Decision Making by Ancient Hunters.* University of Chicago Press, Chicago.

Stevenson, M. G.
1985 The Formation of Artifact Assemblages at Workshop/Habitation Sites: Models from Peace Point. *American Antiquity* 50:63–81.

Stini, W. A.
1983 Comment on "Anthropological Applications of Optimal Foraging Theory: A Critical Review," by Eric Alden Smith. *Current Anthropology* 24(5):646–647.

Straus, Lawrence G.
1980 The Role of Raw Materials in Lithic Assemblage Variability. *Lithic Technology* 9(3):68–72.

Sullivan, A. P.
1978 Inference and Evidence in Archaeology: A Discussion of Conceptual Problems. In *Advances in Archaeological Method and Theory,* edited by Michael B. Schiffer, 1:183–222. Academic Press, New York.

Sussman, Carole
1985 Microwear on Quartz: Fact or Fiction? *World Archaeology* 17(1):101–111.

Thomas, David Hurst
1970 Archaeology's Operational Imperative: Great Basin Projectile Points as a Test Case. *University of California (Los Angeles) Archaeological Survey Report* 12:27–60.
1972 The Use and Abuse of Numerical Taxonomy in Archaeology. *Archaeology and Physical Anthropology of Oceania* 7(1):31–49.
1973 An Empirical Test for Steward's Model of Great Basin Settlement Patterns. *American Antiquity* 38(2):155–176.
1974 *Predicting the Past: An Introduction to Anthropological Archaeology.* Holt, Rinehart and Winston, Inc., New York.
1978 The Awful Truth about Statistics in Archaeology. *American Antiquity* 43(2):344–345.
1979 *Archaeology.* Holt, Rinehart and Winston, Inc., New York.
1981 Ethics and the Contemporary Museum of Anthropology. *In* The Research Potential of Anthropological Museum Collections, edited by Anne-Marie Cantwell, James B. Griffin, and Nan A. Rothschild. *Annals of the New York Academy of Sciences* 376:575–578.
1983a The Archaeology of Monitor Valley, 1: Epistemology. *Anthropological Papers of the American Museum of Natural History* 58(1):1–194.
1983b The Archaeology of Monitor Valley, 2: Gatecliff Shelter. *Anthropological Papers of the American Museum of Natural History* 59(1):1–552.

Thomas, David Hurst, and Deborah Mayer
1983 Behavioral Faunal Analysis of Selected Horizons. *In* The Archaeology of Monitor Valley, 2: Gatecliff Shelter, by David Hurst Thomas. *Anthropological Papers of the American Museum of Natural History* 59(1):353–391.

Thomas, R. B., Bruce Winterhalder, and S. McRae
   1979   An Anthropological Approach to Human Ecology and Adaptive Dynamics. *Yearbook of Physical Anthropology* 22:1–46.

Thomson, D. F.
   1939   The Seasonal Factor in Human Culture. In *Proceedings of the Prehistoric Society for 1939* 5(2):209–221.

Todd, Lawrence C., David J. Rapson, and Eric E. Ingbar
   1985   Glimpses of Organization: Integrating Site Structure with Analysis of Assemblage Content. Paper presented at the 50th meeting of the Society for American Archaeology, Denver.

Trigger, Bruce
   1984   Archaeology at the Crossroads: What's New? *Annual Review of Anthropology* 13:275–300.

Vaughan, Patrick C.
   1985   *Use-Wear Analysis of Flaked Stone Tools.* University of Arizona Press, Tucson.

Vrba, Elisabeth S., and Niles Eldredge
   1984   Individuals, Hierarchies and Processes: Towards a More Complete Evolutionary Theory. *Paleobiology* 10(2):146–171.

White, J. Peter with James F. O'Connell
   1982   *A Prehistory of Australia, New Guinea and Sahul.* Academic Press, New York.

White, T. E.
   1952   Observations on the Butchering Techniques of Some Aboriginal Peoples, I. *American Antiquity* 17(4)337–338.

Winterhalder, Bruce
   1977   Foraging Strategy Adaptations of the Boreal Forest Cree: An Evaluation of Theory and Models from Evolutionary Ecology. Doctoral dissertation, Department of Anthropology, Cornell University, Ithaca.
   1980   Trapping Practices. *American Naturalist* 115:870–879.
   1981   Optimal Foraging Strategies and Hunter-Gatherer Research in Anthropology: Theory and Models. In *Hunter-Gatherer Foraging Strategies,* edited by B. Winterhalder and E. A. Smith, pages 13–35. University of Chicago Press, Chicago.
   1983   The Analysis of Hunter-Gatherer Diet: Stalking an Optimal Foraging Diet. Paper prepared for Wenner-Gren Symposium No. 94: "Food Preferences and Aversions," held at Cedar Cove, Cedar Key, Florida.

Yesner, David
   1981   Archaeological Applications of Optimal Foraging Theory: Harvest Strategies of Aleut Hunter-Gatherers. In *Hunter-Gatherer Foraging Strategies,* edited by Bruce Winterhalder and Eric Alden Smith, pages 148–170. University of Chicago Press, Chicago.

Young, David E., and Robson Bonnichsen
   1984   Understanding Stone Tools: A Cognitive Approach. *University of Maine (Orono), Peopling of the Americas Process Series* 1.

Origins of Food Production
in the New World

> *We now know that man was sufficiently civilized to cultivate the ground at an immensely remote period.*
> --Charles Darwin (1897:336)

Introduction

Scholarly interest in the origins of food production began with stage concepts in the early history of the social sciences (G. Wright 1971). However, Darwin's (1896, 1897) interest in the process of domestication and De Candolle's (1959 [orig. 1886]) emphasis on antecedent conditions and forms of evidence signaled an early shift from speculation to a more balanced presentation of natural and cultural issues. By the end of the 19th century a biological and anthropological effort was established to understand "living artifacts" (Anderson 1960:74): species so symbiotic with humans that, in many cases, we now cannot survive without each other. Despite an early start, notable progress falls into a more compact time span, approximately the past fifty years.

I focus on plants because herding economies developed in the New World only in a relatively localized context: camelids from high elevations in the Andes. Otherwise, domesticated food animals, such as guinea pigs in ancient Peru and dogs and turkeys in Mesoamerica, were important only as an adjunct to agricultural economies.

Sometimes specialized definitions distinguish degrees of involvement in food production. "Agriculture" is usually applied to situations involving artificial fields of cultivars or domesticates that yield the majority of foods or calories that sustain people, although crops on a lesser scale may be as crucial in subsistence if seasonal or episodic resource shortage is a problem (Minnis 1985:316). "Gardening" or "horticulture" are terms sometimes applied to smaller scale production that may be combined with considerable use of wild foods. Here I am interested not only in agriculture but also in lesser investments in food production in order to consider the earliest actions, such as cultivation and domestication, that necessarily preceded any major involvement in this new economy. By "domestication" I mean alteration of genotypes through human selection. By "cultivation" I mean selectively aiding plant growth or reproduction without necessarily any genetic effects.

Because I do not command the "infrastructure" of information in all the areas of potential interest, I have chosen to curtail discussion to primarily the midwestern United States, Mesoamerica, and South America, especially ancient Peru, all three of which are thought to have been locales where domestication occurred on a substantial scale. Because of text limitations, I am concerned not so much with particular details as with general issues. Other recent summaries cover current information for these New World regions (Pickersgill and Heiser 1978; Pearsall 1978; Ford 1981, 1985b; MacNeish 1977; 1984; MacNeish and Nelken-Terner 1983b; Stark 1981; Flannery 1968, 1973; Flannery et al. 1981; Wing 1978; Stone 1984). Inevitably in a paper of this sort many valuable pieces of research are not cited. Other synthetic papers should be consulted for more complete information.

First I establish a historical background, noting different characteristics of North, Middle, and South American studies. However, an adequate appreciation of the history of work on early food production cannot be subdivided to any great extent, not even by separation of the Old and New World literatures. Following examination of some aspects of the history of archaeological field research and of issues derived from botanical research, I consider recent methods that have had or may have a substantial impact—both archaeological and biological ones. Next I discuss problems surrounding interpretations of evidence. Explanations are discussed in the last section.

A Harvest from History

> *The traditions of ancient peoples, embellished by poets, have commonly attributed the first steps in agriculture and the introduction*

of useful plants to some divinity, or at least to some great emperor or Inca.—Alphonse de Candolle (1959:1)

The Fruits of Labor

In the 1930s archaeological field work began to contribute directly to research on the beginnings of agriculture. In comparison, key botanical field work should be traced to the twenties in view of the impact of Vavilov's (1949–1950) identification in 1926 of species distributions and geographic centers of variety, which he thought were centers of origin. Archaeological field projects specifically designed to collect data on the origins of agriculture only began in the late 1940s (G. Wright 1971:449). In different regions a combination of key early finds or problem-oriented field projects began creating the foundations of current knowledge both in the Old and New Worlds.

In 1947 Robert Braidwood (Braidwood et al. 1983) began Near Eastern research to assess Childe's (1951) ideas about the origins of food production. Braidwood's Near Eastern work provided a leading example in the discipline, but key research in the three regions considered here was underway at about the same time or earlier. In the New World in 1931 Gilmore discussed possible prehistoric domestication of certain eastern North American small seeded species at the Ozark Bluff sites, and in 1936 Jones analyzed Newt Kash Hollow collections from Kentucky and suggested a domestication process independent of other regions.

Three years later Manglesdorf and Reeves (1939) published their "tripartite" theory of the botanical origin of domesticated maize. In 1948 the discovery of Bat Cave maize (Manglesdorf and Smith 1949; Dick 1965) catalyzed a productive cooperation between Manglesdorf, engaged in breeding experiments to reconstruct ancestral maize, and archaeologists. The most notable collaboration was with Richard S. MacNeish, whose Mexican projects began in 1949 (MacNeish 1974; Manglesdorf 1974:147). In South America excellent preservation of plant remains at Peruvian preceramic coastal sites such as Aspero, excavated by Willey and Corbett (1954) in 1941, and Huaca Prieta, excavated by Bird in 1948, established a Late Archaic occurrence of some domesticates.

A quest for information was underway and became eminently successful. Dry caves and rockshelters with good preservation were particularly sought out for excavation by MacNeish and others. With the exception of the dry Peruvian coast, it was not until the inception of large-scale flotation at open-air sites in the Midwest (Streuver 1968; Asch and Asch 1985) that other archaeological contexts began to play a substantial role, one which has yet to be fully realized for the Latin American preceramic. As archaeological research targeted the origins of food production, the organization of research on major projects was multidisciplinary, following the lead of Braidwood's projects. A major surge in New World research closely paced a period of growing ecological interest in the discipline, a mutually reinforcing circumstance (Willey and Sabloff 1974:151–156, 178–192; Brose 1973:106–110), and the continued growth of ethnobotany has been important as well (Ford 1978).

South America.—This continent was interpreted by Vavilov (1949:1950:42–43) as containing a highland center of origin of domesticates. Sauer (1952:40–61) argued there was more than one "hearth" of domestication and added part of the tropical lowlands in northwestern South America for certain root crops. Unfortunately, South America has not played the same role in research as Mesoamerica (and, recently, the Midwest) because the dry Peruvian coast, which has produced the greatest amount of preceramic information (Lanning 1967; Patterson 1971a,b; Moseley 1975; Pozorski 1983), is not a location where the earliest evidence of domestication was anticipated or discovered. The coast mainly sheds light on the introduction and adoption of domesticates and their roles vis à vis marine foods (Moseley 1975; Quilter and Stocker 1983). It is commonly accepted that most domesticates appearing in coastal sites (e.g., gourds and two types of squashes by about 3000–2000 B.C. and cotton and *Canavalia* beans by about 2500 B.C. [MacNeish, Patterson, and Bowman 1975:29; Moseley 1975:21, 23; Whitaker 1983]) did not originate there (Pickersgill and Heiser 1978). Of particular interest in the coastal record is the indication of settled communities, some with substantial public architecture, prior to any thorough reliance on food production, e.g., maize (Moseley 1975).

In the Andean highlands information on domesticates is rapidly accumulating (Pires-Ferreira et al. 1976; MacNeish 1977, 1978:171–231; Pearsall 1978; Lynch 1980a; Rick 1980; MacNeish et al. 1983). In most cases, sequences from rockshelters and caves suggest seasonal Archaic occupation (but see Rick, 1980 and 1984, for an argument for sedentary puna hunters). Domesticates are reported from Guitarrero Cave by about 6000 B.C. (Lynch 1980a) and in the Ayacucho sequence by about

5000 B.C. and perhaps earlier (MacNeish and Nelken-Terner 1983a:9–10). The concept of vertical environmental and economic zonation, so important in ethnohistoric communities (Murra 1972), has figured in discussions of transhumant Archaic subsistence patterns (Lynch 1971, 1973). There are many gaps facing any attempt at synthesis of the highland substantive record and possible causes of change (MacNeish 1977, 1978). I doubt that in the near future any comprehensive scheme will gain the wide acceptance of the Mesoamerican synthesis because of the large highland area involved and the expected role of changes elsewhere, such as in the montaña zone.

In the humid lowlands of South America problems of poor preservation have impeded investigations until recently. New techniques are now being applied, such as phytolith analysis (Pearsall 1982), flotation (Lippi et al. 1984), and isotopic bone analysis (Roosevelt 1980; van der Merwe et al. 1981). However, we still lack a record of primary domestication.

Mesoamerica.—The Mesoamerican record, principally a tribute to the efforts of MacNeish, derives mainly from his projects in dry caves or rockshelters in Tamaulipas (MacNeish, 1958), Chiapas (MacNeish and Peterson 1962), and the Tehuacan Valley (Byers 1967; MacNeish et al. 1975). Research elsewhere has added important data (e.g., Flannery et al. 1981; Flannery 1983; Niederberger 1976; see summary in Stark 1981). Most recently MacNeish and several colleagues (MacNeish and Nelken-Terner 1983b; Zeitlin 1984) have investigated open-air preceramic sites along the Belizean coast, which he interprets as indicating Archaic seasonal settlement-subsistence shifts with a riverine or coastal component.

The long Tamaulipas and Tehuacan sequences remain the backbone in our picture of change. They have been interpreted as showing a slow shift from hunting and gathering by small bands to increasing food production, with sedentary communities appearing only after several millennia had elapsed. Domesticates appear at Tehuacan by 5000 B.C., but villages are not clearly indicated until about 1500 B.C. Hunting and gathering patterns are reconstructed as involving seasonal rotation, but movement across marked altitudinal gradients has not figured in interpretations to the same extent as in the Andes. However, we have so little information except from highland interior valleys that it is unclear if more vertical movement may have characterized Archaic adaptations along the watersheds leading down to the tropical lowlands. The Mesoamerican synthesis has incorporated settlement pattern change, dietary estimates, and population estimates, with particular valleys treated as relevant regions or "universes" of analysis.

Always noteworthy in the Mesoamerican highlands has been its contrast with the Near East in regard to the sequence of sedentary patterns and domestication. Mesoamerica supplies a contrast in which seasonal mobility continued much longer and food production grew in importance more slowly, requiring several millennia until fully sedentary, agricultural communities were evident. Note that sedentism is a complex concept: settlement re-use (i.e., settlement permanence) and length of occupation episodes at settlements are two facets of the concept which can vary from each other (Eder 1984). In this paper I use "fully sedentary" in the sense of year-round occupation by at least some members of a group.

Midwestern North America.—Mesoamerica can be said to have been the flagship of research on the origins of agriculture until recently, when investigations of the U.S. Eastern Woodlands Archaic Period have become prominent (Phillips and Brown 1983; Ford 1985b). The latter research has benefitted from increased field investigations spurred by contract archaeology, coupled with use of new techniques. Archaic settlement pattern reconstructions for some well-studied areas, such as the Lower Illinois Valley, have identified localized hunting-gathering subsistence focused along major drainages, with re-use of many camp sites and at least semi-sedentary occupation by Middle Archaic times, ca. 6000–3000 B.C. (Brown and Vierra 1983).

In Eastern North America domesticates were acquired, but only in part, from elsewhere (Ford 1981, 1985a). By about 5000 B.C., a Mesoamerican container and seed cultivar (*Cucurbita pepo*) is present, and domestication of at least one local species (*Iva annua*) is indicated by about 2000 B.C. (Conard et al. 1984; Asch and Asch 1985; Ford 1985a). Other eastern agricultural complex species were cultivated or domesticated by Hopewell times (Middle Woodland) and formed a rather consistent element of the diet, along with wild resources, such as nuts and fauna (Ford 1979; Asch and Asch 1985; Watson 1985). Maize agriculture does not become widespread until the Late Woodland Period and subsequently dominates subsistence in the Mississippian Period. As will be discussed below, the time of maize's first appearance in the Midwest is controversial. Particularly interesting in the Archaic and Woodland sequences are indications of variation among localities in the dietary roles of cultivars (Asch and Asch 1985; Watson 1985).

Discussion of the Three Areas

According to what we now know, both the Midwest and the Pacific coast of Peru contrast with Mesoamerica in that they have some localities where sedentary or nearly sedentary communities precede any substantial food production, as does a degree of corporate organization in community relations (Mosely 1975; Brose 1979; Charles and Buikstra 1983; Brown and Vierra 1983; Emerson and McElrath 1983; Asch and Asch 1985). For some years it has been theorized that in Mesoamerica sedentary communities might have appeared earlier in the tropical lowlands than in the highlands, but this possibility has not yet been demonstrated conclusively (Stark 1981; but cf. MacNeish and Nelken-Terner 1983b).

Despite my avoidance of any detailed survey of the early occurrences of particular cultivars, it is striking that either *Cucurbita pepo* and/or *Lagenaria siceraria* appear quite early in the Archaic in all three areas. Both species may have been important as containers, although the seeds also were eaten (Ford 1981; Heiser 1985:63–67). The earliest bottle gourd known is from Mesoamerica (e.g., ca. 7000 B.C. in Tamaulipas), but it is not clear if this implies a single center of origin (Ford 1985a; Pickersgill and Heiser 1978:146). The plant occurs on the coast in northwest Peru between 6000–4000 B.C. (Richardson 1972:267) and in the highland Ayacucho sequence between 6700–5000 B.C. (MacNeish and Nelken-Terner 1983a:9).

It is notable that cultivars with a non-food use more speedily gained acceptance in multiple areas than maize, the use of which spread widely in Latin America within a few millennia of its earliest record as a Mesoamerican domesticate. Galinat (1985:276) treats the slower northward spread of maize as an effect of the environmental requirements of the early domesticated forms. Dates of maize occurrence in the U.S. Southwest are subject to some dispute (Berry 1985; Ford 1985a), but many early occurrences may not antedate the first millennium B.C. when *Cucurbita pepo* also appears (Ford 1985a; but see Betancourt and Davis 1984 concerning a possibly slightly earlier appearance of *Zea* pollen). The earliest maize occurrences in the Eastern Woodlands also are disputed (Schoenwetter 1979, 1985) but postdate the earliest squash (Ford 1985a). The wide importance of container plants indirectly supports Anderson's (1952:136–150) "dump heap" idea of early domestication since both are weedy "camp followers."

Another general observation is that there is no indication that vertically transhumant subsistence patterns (Lynch 1973) were critical for domestication in all the areas considered. It has been suggested that cultivation and domestication of species like *Iva annua* would require planting outside riverine floodplain locales in the interfluve "uplands" (Asch and Asch 1978). Perhaps some river valley versus uplands situations in the Eastern Woodlands involved sufficient zonation that selection and genetic control mechanisms across those boundaries were important; but no case can be made that transhumance *per se* was critical. Unfortunately, it is still unclear which regions of the Eastern Woodlands played a critical role in local domestication (Ford 1985a). Within highland Mesoamerican valleys seasonal movement to different resource zones has not been reconstructed as involving more than valley bottom to valley flank relocations. Thus, harvesting mechanisms and seasonality appear to have been more prevalent factors in the domestication process than vertical transhumance, although the latter is tied to seasonality.

Grist for the Mill

In the history of botanical research, one of the recurring problems for archaeologists is the complexity of botanical identifications and interpretations. Although major hurdles remain in the study of domestication, botanists have contributed comparative studies of wild and domesticated forms to identify traits that might have been selected first during domestication. One outcome is the observation that harvesting characteristics may determine an early step in domestication of some plants, such as selection for indehiscent seeds (e.g., maize, beans) or loss of germination delay mechanisms (e.g., *Chenopodium berlandieri*).

Embedded in the proliferation of botanical studies have been debates that cause problems for archaeologists as "consumers" of botanical expertise. Clearly the outstanding example involves maize. "The maize wars" have taken place for over a decade (Beadle 1980; Galinat 1978, 1983; Iltis 1983; Manglesdorf 1974, 1983; Flannery 1973; Ford 1983). They involve competing interpretations of the earliest maize in the Tehuacan Coxcatlan Phase (5000–3400 B.C.). Manglesdorf (1974, 1983) views it as wild corn, now extinct. The opposite position, within which there are also competing genetic scenarios (Ford 1983), treats a teosinte as the ancestral form, with the implication that the earliest macrofossil maize now known is already a primitive domesticate. Teosinte as the ancestor is now the majority view.

Thus, for corn, as well as common beans, we now have very early finds that appear already domesticated (although there were many subsequent improvements). For beans, early seed samples, even those dating to 6800–6200 B.C. in Guitarrero Cave, Peru (Kaplan 1980, 1981), are said to be morphologically like modern ones. This has led to a second generation of discovery problems. Despite the great success of expeditions to find evidence of the steps leading to domestication and food production, for many species we cannot yet trace early domestication archaeobotanically nor can we chart changing antecedent use of wild forms very well. Studies of Midwestern species, such as *Iva annua* (Asch and Asch 1978) and *Helianthus annuus* (Yarnell 1978), now are arguably more successful in tracing the shift from wild use to cultivation and domesticated forms than studies of some key tropical species. This likely results from different methods of data collection (e.g., large scale flotation in the Midwest). In the Andean and Mesoamerican highlands the period 6000–10,000 B.C. is more crucial for the study of domestication than was previously appreciated, although this has been implied by the circumstantial evidence for plant cultivation in the El Riego Phase in the Tehuacan Valley, ca. 5000–7000 B.C. (MacNeish 1967; Smith 1967).

Complex botanical judgments are illustrated by studies of *Chenopodium berlandieri*, which has had a checkered history as a putative domesticate in the Eastern Woodlands (Asch and Asch 1977; Fritz 1984; B. D. Smith 1984; Wilson 1981). Current data suggest that this plant was domesticated by about 2000 years ago in Early Woodland times (B. D. Smith 1984), either introduced from Mexico or developed locally (Asch and Asch 1985). For other eastern agricultural complex species (Ford 1981; Asch and Asch 1985), better information has supported the idea of autochthonous domestication or cultivation in that region (not all the economic species show morphological evidence of domestication; Ford 1985a). Some of the evidence for domestication of *Chenopodium* concerns distributions of wild ancestral forms; but it is clear from Asch's and Asch's (1985) thoughtful review that there are many uncertainties since modern distributions may reflect other factors, which are hard to control: environmental change, modern disturbance, and evolutionary change in the species itself, both that we might label "endogenous" and that derived from backcrossing with domesticated forms.

Some botanical studies raise the issue of temporal resolution. Beadle's (1980:114) breeding experiments suggest to him approximately five major independent gene differences between maize and teosinte, which might not require lengthy domestication prior to significant improvement in the plant's economic value. Galinat (1983:133) speculates that the selection process he reconstructs leading from teosinte to early maize could have occurred in 100 plant generations: thus, "the rate of evolution under domestication in geologic time would appear as instantaneous" (1983:122). Similarly rapid human selection favoring larger seed size in common beans through preservation technology is proposed by Kaplan (1981).

The prospect of discerning a "rapid" process of change is never a pleasing one for archaeologists. The archaeobotanical visibility of the domestication process will vary among species, depending on their maturation rates, reproductive habits, and the complexity of the genetic changes in question, in addition to other factors linked to human behaviors. However, alterations in settlement pattern, diet, and demography will prove as crucial in understanding subsistence transitions as details in the selection process (cf. Flannery 1973).

"The Problem" and Problems

V. G. Childe's (1951:59–86) notion of the "Neolithic Revolution" helped motivate research on the origins of agriculture. In his view domesticated species were critical enabling resources for settled village life, which in turn was a prerequisite for early civilizations: the "Urban Revolution." Thus, the problem of domestication was of paramount concern. Due to subsequent research, domestication has become an element in a linked series of processes. Braidwood's (1952) "incipient" food producers were presumed to have begun cultivating plants or managing animals, resulting in domestication. Preceding cultivators was a "broad spectrum revolution" in which hunter-gatherers added more species to their diets (Flannery 1969:77). The processes of intensified predation, cultivation, and domestication were recognized as partly intertwined with an independent process: sedentarization. Sedentism became more prevalent following food production, but also antedated it, at least in the Near East (Flannery 1972). Sedentism was linked, minimally, to abundant localized resources (whether agricultural or not) because otherwise groups would have had to move to new resource areas.

Preconditions for development of agriculture have been recognized, both environmental and technological. Beyond the necessity of access to ancestral species pointed out by de Candolle (1959), Flannery (1973) emphasized the critical role of appropriate variability in wild populations (see also Rindos 1984). Also, prior predation by hunter-gatherers established key aspects of the exploitative technology (such as tools, storage facilities, or processing techniques; Flannery 1969).

A complicating substantive point is that there likely were not "centers" of origin of domesticates in many cases (Harlan 1971), but, rather, more complex distributions of ancestral forms. Multiple domestications of some closely related species may have occurred (Pickersgill and Heiser 1978; Eshbaugh et al. 1983; Pickersgill 1984). Consequently, an emerging food production economy that developed in a particular region must also be seen as a mosaic over time, growing with the adoption of domesticates from other human groups to assemble a diversified food production package. Granted, carbohydrate staples are a critical feature of predominantly agricultural lifeways. Nevertheless, many factors encourage diversified food production: (1) nutritional balances, (2) food variety, (3), in some regions, ecological factors such as the "imitative" structure of tropical swiddens in which intercropping provides some of the soil and nutrient protection of the tropical forest (Harris 1972:188), and (4) the resiliency that is offered by a variety of species with differing seasonality and environmental requirements.

In sum, a historical perspective of research on the transition to food production must incorporate (1) a surprising quantity of successful field work, (2) growing botanical information and a better appreciation of botanical issues, and (3) reworking and expansion of the topics considered directly relevant to the transition. Future work promises more of the same but with even greater success due to new methods, as discussed in the next section, in which I note several particularly important advances (see Wing and Brown 1979; Gilbert and Mielke 1985 for paleodietary compendia).

New Methods Reap New Data

> *For each species we need . . . a varied research, in which sometimes one process is employed, sometimes another; and these afterwards combined and estimated according to their relative value.*
> —Alphonse de Candolle (1959:8)

Flotation.—One "revolutionary" (Watson 1976:79) methodological innovation to recover small vegetal items already has been noted. Large-scale flotation or water separation is the oldest of what might be termed the "new" methods and already is well known and widely used (for history of technique, see Watson 1976). Applied on a sufficient scale, it provided a major breakthrough, especially in the Midwest where the greatest amount of new data has been acquired (Asch and Asch 1985). While archaeological occurrences of some species (e.g., small seeded ones) can scarcely be assessed without flotation, it has proven equally valuable in increasing recovery of identifiable broken plant parts (e.g., squash). Aside from adaptations of the method, the major technical problem encountered has been one of standardization of procedures (Watson 1976; Munson 1981; Wagner 1982; Pendleton 1983).

Phytolith Analysis.—Phytolith analysis can provide information on economic plants, environment, and agricultural practices (Pearsall 1982; Rovner 1983). New World archaeological applications date to about 1970, and much basic taxonomic and taphonomic research remains to be done (Pearsall 1982; Rovner 1983). As a consequence, it is premature to judge the contribution of phytolith studies to the origins of agriculture (*contra* Roosevelt 1984b). However, it is reasonably clear that there will be a substantial benefit in certain contexts (Piperno and Clary 1984). In particular, Ecuadorian (Pearsall 1978) and Panamanian (Piperno 1984) research have developed criteria (phytolith shapes, shape frequencies, and surface morphologies) to distinguish maize in those tropical environments. Concern over disturbance, preservation, and contamination (Dunn 1983; Roosevelt 1984b:10) is legitimate and is being addressed in basic research (Piperno 1984). Except for the problem of modern airborne additions to samples, contamination issues seem to have been exaggerated for microscopic data (including pollen) compared to macrofossils (Flannery 1973:272).

Accelerator Radiocarbon Dating.—Radiocarbon dating of small plant samples directly with tandem accelerator mass spectrometry (TAMS) is quite new, but overviews have been published (Bennett et al. 1978; Bennett 1979; Pavlish and Banning 1980; Browman 1981; Long et al. in press). TAMS measures the abundance of ^{14}C isotopes rather than isotope decay activity; hence, smaller samples can be dated. A much more recent (or ancient) intrusive sample can be identified directly. Accelerator dates already have played a critical role in establishing the chronology of rare early plant finds (Conard et al. 1984; Wendorf et al. 1984; Long et al. 1985; Lynch et al. 1985). However, the method is so recent that we do not have a large body of applications to provide guidance concerning any unanticipated problems (cf. Wendorf et al. 1984).

Stable Isotopic and Elemental Assays.—Another extremely valuable methodological advance derives from the nutritional dictum "you are what you eat." Chemical bone assays provide dietary information be-cause diets differ as nutrient bases for bone or tooth formation (other tissues may be analyzed as well if they are preserved). These chemical studies constitute a very rapidly developing subject, and recent reviews by specialists should be consulted for particulars and the full range of methods (Browman 1981:268–280; Bumsted 1981; Huss-Ashmore et al. 1982; Sillen and Kavanagh 1982; van der Merwe 1982; Klepinger 1984; Gilbert 1985). Here, three techniques will be identified briefly because of their current and potential impact on studies of early agriculture through assessment of animal versus plant foods or of the dietary role of maize. However, there are a number of general points about chemical assays which warrant mention first.

Although there may be exceptions, appropriate human skeletal se-ries are required to determine the diets of populations. Also needed in some cases are samples of associated fauna to provide independent con-trols on diagenesis and regional variation. The methods transcend some of the temporal and locational limits of conventional botanical and faunal data. Archaeological bone composition reflects an average of ap-proximately the last 6–10 years of food consumption (Bumsted, personal communication). Thus, among the various kinds of dietary evidence now available there is a progression in "dietary time" represented: from fecal analysis (Callen 1967; Heizer and Napton 1969; Bryant and Williams-Dean 1975), to botanical and faunal samples in floors or some strata of brief accumulation, to isotopic and elemental bone assays (and dental attrition and pathology, considered in the next subsection). Certain as-pects of chemical bone analyses, which rely on faithful effects of food consumption, also avoid the taphonomic dilemmas that afflict evalua-tions of other dietary samples, e.g., differentials between faunal and flo-ral remains.

However, bone chemical analyses are "species-blind." Only in fa-vorable circumstances, requiring associated data, is it possible to infer the contribution of particular species to the diet. Instead, analyses usu-ally identify the relative contributions of major food groups (Bumsted in press). Clearly, then, these very powerful approaches to dietary research are most effective in combination with traditional sources of data.

Plant-animal dietary or animal measures have primarily involved (1) strontium, (2) nitrogen isotope, or (3) carbon isotope measurement. Al-though others of potential value exist, such as magnesium or barium assays, they lack as much controlled research to demonstrate their strengths and weaknesses (Sillen and Kavanagh 1982:69, 82; Klepinger

1984:80–81). Strontium (Sr) is a regionally variable trace element affected by "biopurification" in connection with calcium (Ca) intake in the food chain. Plants generally do not discriminate metabolically between Ca and Sr, but mammals do. Consequently, in a food chain terminating in carnivores, they will contrast with herbivores in Sr/Ca levels in bone mineral. The balance of plants and terrestrial animals in human diets may be inferred by comparison of human bone Sr/Ca levels to those of carnivores and herbivores in a region. Diagenesis, sex-linked differences due to preganancy, the skeletal parts of choice for analysis, and the effects of some marine foods that accumulate Sr are major problems for applications of the method.

Terrestrial versus marine dietary components have been analyzed using the proportion of stable nitrogen isotopes, $^{15}N/^{14}N$ (Schoeninger et al. 1983), and of stable carbon isotopes, $^{12}C/^{13}C$ (Chisholm et al. 1982), in bone collagen. Marine organisms generally have much higher ^{15}N levels, and yield ^{13}C levels in consumers similar to those of C4 plants (see below). Schoeninger et al. (1983:1383) note that (1) nitrogen isotope studies can complement the more ambiguous carbon isotope information in certain mixed diets, and (2) although use of marine foods may make strontium levels difficult to interpret, nitrogen or carbon isotopes can identify the marine component.

Stable carbon isotope studies also have proven extremely useful in certain New World analyses involving maize. Because plants differ in their photosynthetic pathways, they differ in carbon isotopic fractionation. Consequently, as proportionate dietary components, different plants create different "isotopic signatures" in consumers (van der Merwe 1982:599) once account is taken of metabolic fractionation by the consumer (or, rather, by the body part of the consumer, since tissues can differ in isotopic ratios). The C3 pathway in plants (C3 for 3-carbon molecules formed in photosynthesis) discriminates more strongly against ^{13}C than does the C4 pathway (forming a 4-carbon molecule during photosynthesis) or the CAM pathway (acronym for Crassulacean acid metabolism). The latter two may yield similar values for ^{13}C. In an environment in which the C3 pathway predominates in plant life, such as much of North America, the adoption of maize agriculture as a substantial element in subsistence is detectable because maize is a C4 plant with much higher concentrations of ^{13}C. These effects are observable provided marine fauna are not part of the diet since they, too, have higher ^{13}C values.

Dental Dietary Inferences.—Analogous to use-wear studies of artifacts, dental anthropologists have long used dental wear to infer dietary patterns (Molnar 1972; Powell 1985). Milled grains are expected to constitute a "gritty" diet contributing to wear, but unfortunately other factors may create similar effects (Anderson 1965; Molnar 1972). Recently measures have been developed and tested using angles of dental wear created in consumption of processed agricultural foods compared with animal or animal and wild plant foods (B. H. Smith 1984). Potentially such controlled wear analysis could be applied to populations with unknown diets, provided a sufficient sample of reasonably complete non-pathological dentitions were available.

That dental pathology can play a direct role in revealing diet has been recognized for some time. Frequent consumption of sticky carbohydrate agricultural foods can increase the incidence of caries compared to other diets. Turner's (1979) comprehensive comparative study of hunter-gatherers, mixed economies, and agriculturalists reveals a strong relationship between caries rates and general type of diet; it is also clear that cariogenic variation among foods requires attention, among other factors (Powell 1985), to account for variability in caries rates *within* a general category of diet. Among Turner's data, extremes in caries rates within a diet category can even approach caries means for other diet categories.

Discussion

Methodological breakthroughs and refinements mean renewed hope for research on transitions to food production, with the prospects even more favorable because of synergism. Added sources of information can complement traditional data, as has been routinely pointed out in reviews of methods (Rovner 1983:258; Goodman et al. 1984; Schoeninger et al. 1983). However, controlled comparisons among methods and "basic" research on methods are needed to integrate results because discrepancies among suites of evidence are a growing problem. Rovner's (1983:258) plea for matched archaeobotanical samples of different kinds will have to be generalized to achieve controlled documentation of the limits and contributions of different methods. Not one of our current methods of reconstructing diets is broadly feasible because of the inherent spottiness of appropriate data or limitations in inferences from the methods themselves.

Taken together, recent methodological advances yield an impressive arsenal compared to the situation of even fifteen years ago. Flotation, isotopic and elemental assays, and accelerator dating in particular have already proven of great value in subsistence studies. Practically, the addition of new methods poses clear dilemmas: the cost of first-rate research is increasing, and institutional structures and budgets supporting archaeology currently cannot meet the need for more specialists and laboratories.

Winnowing the Evidence

Childe, with a sparkle in his eye, remarked that it would be exactly with the interpretation of the evidence for the transition that we would have our greatest difficulty.
—Braidwood, Braidwood, and Howe (1983:7)

Over a decade ago Flannery (1973:271) urged reasonable scepticism for "claims for domestication based on a single burned seed, a single trampled rind, or a single crumpled pod." The quality of physical evidence has two facets, its amount (especially in relation to subsistence species as population), and the validity of associations of domesticates with other data (Flannery 1973:272). The two points are not independent because invalid associations will not be abundant or consistent in a variety of circumstances (e.g., Wendorf et al. 1984). However, minor use of a domesticate or cultivar, which is possible very early in food production, may not produce consistent associations either.

In 1973 Flannery (1973:272) criticized the competition to find "the oldest domesticated plant," although that was a natural outcome of the quest for evidence in the early history of research. In 1985 we still face some of the same problems in evaluating evidence (compare Pickersgill, 1984:115 with Smith, 1980:110; Lynch, 1980b:303; and Kaplan, 1980:145). Given the need for good contexts, the vagaries of preservation and discovery, and interest in the broader cultural context of the earliest cultivation and selection, the importance of early rare finds will not disappear. As I noted above, for many key species we now need yet older sequences, particularly of procurement of wild ancestral forms.

The need to acquire early dietary evidence is further saddled with the problems of determining domestication from phenotypic characteristics. Plant remains will be dried, charred, or otherwise altered and preserved (corrections may be required, e.g., Asch and Asch 1985); even so, they may not be the appropriate parts for identifying some key morphological character(s), and not all genetic changes will be reflected in morphology. In several respects the same problems affect analyses of fauna. Identification of domesticates among Andean camelids is especially difficult (Pires-Ferriera et al. 1976; Wing 1978).

Deliberate actions to aid plant growth and reproduction may have been undertaken with wild forms, and it has long been recognized that such cultivation would be important in the development of domesticates and agriculture. Cultivation, especially if it involves the saving and planting of seeds (or other parts), can rapidly bring to bear strong selection for characters favorable to humans as well as establishment of what Rindos (1984) has called the "agroecology." However, domestication also may be an inadvertent by-product of human action (Anderson 1952:136–150; Lynch 1973; Rindos 1984). The reconstruction of behaviors along the sequence leading to food production is tricky, since a satisfying descriptive record (which we know to be skimpy anyway) must confront a process that "begins small," and for which the earliest evidence is likely to be highly inferential. The problems surrounding identification of the earliest domesticates are not acute for overall goals since we have other behavioral data, but they are chronic because such identification provides a crucial link to the genetic effects of past behaviors.

In the past 10 to 15 years issues of evidence have transcended "the oldest domesticated plant" problem. Difficulties have arisen in reconciliation of multiple kinds of evidence. For example, in the Midwest the long-standing idea of independent plant domestication has been juxtaposed against the occurrence of introduced domesticates, ultimately derived from Mesoamerica. At present the great antiquity of squash (*Cucurbita pepo*), thought to have been cultivated first mainly for containers and seeds (originally the flesh was thin and bitter; Whitaker and Cutler 1965), has led to recognition that an introduced squash-gourd complex antedated domestication of indigenous species (Ford 1981, 1985a).

However, this fact does not necessarily account for local domestication of other plants as food sources. The container plants are weedy "camp followers," which may have been important as tools more than as foods; they imply no major investment in gardens or fields. The subsequent eastern agricultural complex, which was oriented toward oily or starchy seeds, represents a more sizable effort in food production. It is generally accepted now that simple procedures in cultivation could originate independently (Bronson 1977:28), given appropriate circumstances. Consequently, I do not consider it highly significant that some "container" cultivars reached the Midwest and were grown prior to domestication of native plants. More important than which domesticates came first is the question of selective pressures that favored investment in food cultivars.

An ongoing question has involved the possible early appearance of maize in the Midwest along with the squash-gourd complex. This plant was potentially a carbohydrate staple; certainly it served this role much later in the Eastern Woodlands. With pollen evidence, the earliest and strongest case for maize occurs in Horizon 6 at Koster, ca. 3000 B.C. (Schoenwetter 1974, 1979, 1985). In addition, Schoenwetter (1985) notes two other instances of *Zea* pollen at Midwestern sites later in the Archaic. The Koster early maize pollen is now considered by many to be a possible case of contamination, especially following accelerator radiocarbon dating of yet earlier maize macroremains floated from Koster deposits (Conard et al. 1984; Asch and Asch 1985). Phytoliths from related Middle Archaic deposits at Koster (Horizon 6) did not provide strong evidence to support the pollen, as only one of seven samples produced grass phytoliths that might indicate maize (Rovner 1983:253). Phytolith analysis at Koster was done prior to recent advances in the analysis of maize phytoliths and was not accompanied by extensive study of local grasses.

Even later occurrences of Midwestern maize have been called into question. Maize was once viewed as an economic prerequisite to Hopewell social developments (Spaulding 1955:20; Griffin 1960, 1967:183; Brown 1977:171). Following widespread flotation beginning in the late 1960s, plant macroremains showed maize was only a minor element in Middle Woodland diet (Ford 1979). Stable carbon isotope analysis of human bone has corroborated that it was not a major dietary element until Late Woodland and Mississippian times (van der Merwe and Vogel 1978; Bender et al. 1981). More recently doubts have been expressed about the validity of the association of maize with Hopewell (Middle Woodland) after accelerator dating of some samples with "good" context indicated they were intrusive (Conard et al. 1984).

At issue is how long particular resources were available to people, to what extent they used them, and whether these facts bear any correlation to social, demographic, trade, settlement pattern, or other changes. For example, if Midwestern intensification of food production was important because of increased effective population densities by Hopewell times, as is sometimes suspected (Ford 1979), then why was maize so unimportant if present? Later, similar factors are thought to have been significant in a subsistence shift to Mississippian maize agriculture. Maize is superior in caloric yield per hectare to eastern agricultural complex plants (Asch and Asch 1978). Certainly some allowance must be made to achieve locally well-adapted varieties, but it is unclear how much time might be required. Although at Koster there has been concern with archaeological contamination of flotation and pollen field samples (Conard et al. 1984), in many respects the wider problem may prove to be one of contamination that occurs independent of excavation (Keepax 1977). Clearly there is a growing interest in cultural and natural processes that establish associations (Wood and Johnson 1978; Schiffer 1983).

As in the Midwest, suites of evidence do not agree concerning maize in the Valdivia Phase (3000–1500 B.C.) in the coastal Ecuadorian sequence. There, phytoliths (Pearsall 1978, 1982), caries rates (Turner 1978), carbon isotopes (Burleigh and Brothwell 1978:359; cf. Bumsted 1981), macrofossils (beans [Damp et al. 1981] and maize in the subsequent phase [Lippi et al. 1984]), settlement pattern (Damp 1984:109–110), and a pottery seed impression (Zavallos et al. 1977; cf. Lippi et al. 1984:119; Roosevelt 1980:63) fuel a debate, which ranges from establishing the presence of the cultivar to its dietary role. Distinction of these points is critical, because the presence of a cultivar need not imply agricultural subsistence.

It seems clear from the Midwestern and Ecuadorian cases that there are significant new problems in adjudicating different kinds of evidence (concerning evaluations of evidence, see Harlan and De Wet 1973; Ford 1984; Roosevelt 1984b). In situations in which contradictory conclusions are reasonable depending on the reliance placed on particular methods or "facts," underlying assumptions or "paradigms" about early agriculture can come into play. How variable should we expect subsistence to be among different sites in an area or among subregions? Can we expect a staple cultigen used in one region to play a similar major role if it is available elsewhere?

In cases where basic assumptions about economic practices are brought to bear to evaluate complex or contradictory evidence, they should be made clear. For example, although it cannot be denied there is a strong argument for an Archaic *Zea* pollen association at Koster (Schoenwetter 1979, 1985), diachronic subsistence data currently argue against such an early appearance since no occurrence of maize is well documented for over a millenium subsequently. The unstated assumption is that food production involving a storable caloric staple would have favored use of a more productive cultivar (maize) over less productive eastern agricultural complex plants (i.e., in caloric yield per hectare) that were used. Thus, I would not expect maize to have been so long neglected in favor of local seed cultivars. Expectations such as this "efficiency" assumption also structure explanations of the origins of agriculture.

Food for Thought

> *... after all these years of work on the problem of how and why agriculture began, I see no final answers.*
> —R.S. MacNeish (1974:233 but cf. 1984)

Explanations of the changes leading to food production have been varied, and they both depend on and affect our notion of what it is we need to explain. Adequate explanations must address not simply domestication, which may begin for a variety of reasons and in diverse circumstances, but a subsistence transformation toward food production. Because of the increasingly detailed understanding of what the "Neolithic Revolution" involved, explanations have become more diverse to accomodate different ideas about the roles of various processes in the development of food production. Binford's (1968) paper was a turning point due to its focus on clear identification of stimuli to alter complex hunter-gatherer systemic relationships. Modern "theories" are usually rather complex in their entirety, but without too much violence many can be distilled to an initiating or driving causal factor. Redman (1978:89–140), Myers (1971), G. A. Wright (1971), Rindos (1984), Roosevelt (1984a), and MacNeish (1984) provide typologies of explanations. Here I group theories into three sets ("Push," "Pull," and Social models), noting some of the problems facing each.

Explanatory Models

"Push" Models.—"Push" models are founded on population-resource relationships. In an extension of Boserup's (1965) argument that food production systems are elastic, hunter-gatherer labor intensification leading to food production is seen as a response to less favorable population/resource ratios (Christenson 1980; Clark and Yi 1983). This kind of approach is the most promising in my judgment (Stark 1981), but it requires attention to the specific configuration of local conditions, a step which often is problematic. Among the possible factors producing population/resource imbalances, population growth is often singled out. It has been argued that sedentarization could contribute to population growth through decreased birth spacing (Binford 1968; Lee 1972; Sussman 1972; Binford and Chasko 1976). Bronson (1977), and others (e.g., Johnson 1977) have noted that sedentarization, which may be affected by a localized attractive resource, also saves travel costs. However, sedentarization has been viewed as an *effect* of population growth as well, since denser packing of foraging groups in a region or key resource zone may increasingly restrict the territory available to each, leading to lessened mobility and more intensive exploitation (Charles and Buikstra 1983; Brown and Vierra 1983; Braun and Plog 1982:508).

Others maintain that over long periods human population was not as successfully regulated as the short time-depth of modern hunter-gatherer studies suggests (Ammerman 1975; Cohen 1977). This assertion requires a broad geographic perspective since population levels may vary greatly among particular localities. Declining returns to labor with higher populations is the expected result, rather than "pressure" in the sense of carrying capacity (Stark 1981). All groups need not experience population growth, which need not be viewed as a constant. Furthermore, not all groups need necessarily adopt intensification practices in response to population growth; however, those groups that do will maintain higher population numbers, thus locking in the change.

Population growth has been discussed as an important variable in all three regions considered here. The Near Eastern broad spectrum revolution and New World Archaic Period resource diversification are then way-stations in a larger process that under certain conditions leads to food production (cf. Hayden 1981a). Consequently, the study of the origins of agriculture has become five parts understanding hunter-gatherers and five parts understanding the first cultivators, domesticators, and farmers.

Processes of environmental change, seen by Childe (1951) as a key factor in the Neolithic Revolution, are still discussed in some "push" models, although usually they play a less direct role than in his "oasis" theory (Moore 1982; Binford 1968; Butzer 1978; H. E. Wright 1977; Hesse 1982). Environmental changes are potentially important because they may affect population-resource balances and/or the costs and benefits of different resource strategies for predation versus production. At present, environmental change plays a greater role in some explanations of Midwestern Archaic subsistence shifts than in the two other regions considered here. Hypsithermal climate and vegetation, plus changes in floodplain geomorphology, are the factors which have received the most attention (see summaries in Brown and Vierra 1983; Styles et al. 1983).

Another dimension of environmental change is risk or unpredictability in procurement strategies, which may lead to subsistence stress (Flannery 1973; Ford 1977; Harris 1977; Hayden 1981a, 1981b; Braun and Plog 1982; Hesse 1982). In a sense, exposure to some risks is dependent on overall population levels; otherwise fewer people would occupy only a few resource-rich, stable locales and would thus avoid many risks. Nevertheless, risk issues recast population-resource balances in a very different framework than a straight population growth argument, since diminished returns to labor (or food shortages) are only episodic. Oscillating or fluctuating perturbations are particularly characteristic of some climatic and regional conditions, although all environments entail some risk. Periodic stresses due to fluctuating conditions are another expression of a population-resource imbalance concept since low points in cycles of food availability can regulate population size, whether we identify annual low points or ones dependent on multi-year spans.

Often risk is discussed in unsatisfactorily broad terms: risk duration and frequency are critical. Protracted stress invites emigration, while risk from very infrequent stresses makes hedging strategies extremely costly since a given individual (or group) may never experience the stress. Frequent stresses are more likely to be offset by technological changes, such as elaboration of food storage (to which many key domesticates are well suited). Thus, cultural solutions to frequent food supply stresses may favor cultivation and domestication linked to food storage. Among the three regions considered, the Midwest is the most problematic in regard to such risk, although winter food storage clearly would have been important because of climatic conditions. Unfortunately it remains to be demonstrated that comparable risk or stress conditions had not existed previously in human prehistory. Hence, population levels are likely to have been an important additional factor.

Non-intensification options for population/resource problems exist, too, such as emigration or more food storage to even out periods of abundance and scarcity (Binford 1968). However, Hayden (1981b) points out that preservation and storage often do entail added labor. At present, the full labor costs of subsistence options are extremely poorly specified, in part because of inattention to processing, preservation, and storage efforts.

Sedentarization, population-resource imbalances, and environmental risk can be investigated empirically, but it cannot yet be claimed that any one of them has been either satisfactorily verified or discredited as a primary causal factor for food production. (Subsequent effects on agricultural intensification are less controversial for the first two factors.) It will be difficult to disentangle the three, as they are thought to have some interdependent effects. Because returns to labor for different subsistence strategies are so poorly defined empirically, "push" arguments have tended to rely on identification of population growth antecedent to (and accompanying) the growth of food production or to appeal to climatic conditions as evidence of "risk." In neither case is the specificity of the argument very convincing. Demographic explanations, which have been the most popular, have also met with substantive opposition. Here it is interesting to focus on the early Mesoamerican record as an illustration of empirical problems.

Recently, Flannery (1973, 1983) questioned the role of population growth. However, the issue is far from clear, as a brief review of Mesoamerican Tehuacan Valley data indicates. Flannery (1983) adopts one measure of population size: the number of sites, in order to compare the El Riego (7000–5000 B.C.) and Abejas phases (3400–2300 B.C.). Rather than consider the total number of sites, he uses only one of the site types since mobile groups may leave several seasonal sites. He notes that the number of macroband camps scarcely differs between the two phases. In fact, site numbers, which can be graphed on several different ways for the Ajuereado, El Riego, Coxcatlan, and Abejas phases (Figure 1) do not behave very consistently, and neither numbers of surface sites (or components) nor macroband sites (or components) change much in the Archaic after the Ajuereado Phase.

Most important, Flannery points out that so few sites were recovered from each phase that we have no convincing index of population numbers in any case. One might use this reasoning to argue that site numbers are too low for *any* conclusion. However, there is another, more troublesome feature of the measure he adopts.

Population growth in the Tehuacan Valley cannot be so easily dismissed, because a process of sedentarization characterizes the sequence, one aspect of which is growth of macroband seasonal camps. Consequently, it is at least as relevant to consider site area as site numbers in assessment of demographic change. In contrast to site numbers, mean site area is strongly patterned (Figure 2). All measures increase, some dramatically, except for mean microband site (or component) area and mean cave or rockshelter site (or component) area. (The latter two exceptions are expected. Microbands are thought to represent small, minimal social units, and cave or rockshelter sites are physically constrained.) The pattern of increase in site area contrasts with the steadily decreasing length of the phases, 3000, 2000, 1600, and 1200 years, respectively.

Those familiar with the Tehuacan data will realize that identification of separate components is not always straightforward (Stark 1981). Until we know more about the largely unexcavated open-air sites, we cannot gauge reoccupation and length of occupation. These sites, so crucial to population estimates, also will be important to examine more closely for comparison to dietary data in cave sites. The reliability of caves and rockshelters for subsistence reconstruction has been called into question (Farnsworth et al. 1985) because there are discrepancies between isotopically reconstructed diets and (1) MacNeish's dietary estimates extrapolated from cave macrofossil food remains and (2) Anderson's (1965) dental wear analyses. Unfortunately, skeletal samples yielding appropriate chemical data were so few that the isotope information is tantalizing rather than conclusive. Even if the isotopic plant food measure is representative, it does not clarify what plant foods might have created the results nor how the plants were obtained. Maize is one among a variety of possible C_4 or CAM foods in the Tehuacan Valley.

In any case, it is by no means clear that Tehuacan data contravene population growth as a contributing factor in the origin and growth of food production there. But even if we accept the idea of population growth in the Tehuacan Valley, it is difficult to specify its implications. A significant problem confronts demographic arguments. True, there is always difficulty in archaeological population estimates (Cook 1972; Hassan 1981:63–93), and these problems are exacerbated for mobile hunter-gatherers. More problematic, however, is that regional information alone is not adequate. We cannot yet establish that demographic dynamics are confined to the units such as valleys within which current estimates are constructed. Indeed, there are strong reasons to think they were not and should not be expected to have been, given the low population densities (Wobst 1974). This issue is well illustrated by Flannery's (1983) discussion of the Mesoamerican Archaic, where he notes evidence for exchange among regions (see also Stark 1981).

Given that wider contacts were maintained, if population-resource imbalances affected populations in the Tehuacan Valley, why did groups remain there and intensify their efforts, e.g., in cultivation? Hunter-gatherers in other somewhat comparable situations are known to have relocated seasonally over distances that, if applied to the Tehuacan Val-

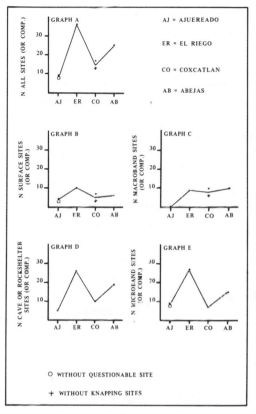

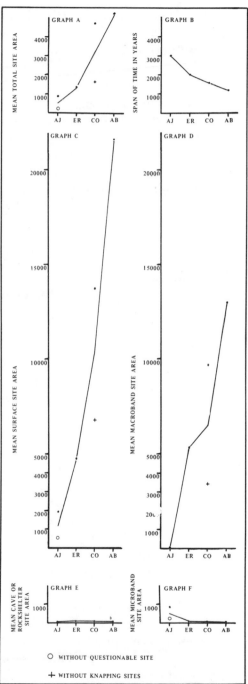

Figure 1 (above) Graphs show numbers per phase of those Archaic Tehuacan sites that had areal measurements. Most surface sites are macroband sites. Most cave or rockshelter sites are microband sites. Several Coxcatlan sites are knapping stations for which temporal placement is less clear. The graph arbitrarily passes midway between points that include and exclude these more problematic sites.

Figure 2 (right) Graphs show total site or component area (in square meters) per Archaic Phase in the Tehuacan Valley.

ley, might take them outside the valley entirely (e.g., over 50 miles annually [Philip Weiss, personal communication, with reference to southern Paiute data in Kelly 1964]).

Arguments about population growth in Tehuacan or the role of winter season storage (Stark 1981:361) are potentially misplaced if Tehuacan was not a demographic "universe" and until we have more information about population density and resources in surrounding regions, plus travel costs. "Open" hunter-gatherer social systems offer safety valves for population-resource imbalances; therefore we need demographic estimates and resource information over large areas if we are to firmly establish population growth arguments.

"Pull" Models.—Some ecological, systemic approaches focus on natural variability in food resources and the interactive effects of human exploitation. The "pull" models are similar to what Minnis (1985:334) has termed an "opportunity" model for the introduction of agriculture to the U.S. Southwest. Another example is Reidhead's (1980:175–177) model in which maize is incorporated into agriculture (in Ohio) because it was a superior resource in return for labor compared to local options. With "pull" models attractive benefits of proto-domesticates or early domesticates increased use of those resources, resulting eventually in food production (cf. Bronson 1977:36; Rindos 1984).

Flannery (1968) pointed to plant mutations as an initial "kick" that altered ecological relations and thus homeostatic hunter-gatherer settlement-subsistence systems. Some question whether a few specific mutations could fuel long-term patterns of change (Myers 1971; Harris 1977:195; Stark 1981). Nevertheless, Flannery et al. (1981:55) have reported that it is possible to simulate the transition to food production in the Oaxaca Valley without recourse to population "pressure" or environmental change. In their view annual rainfall variation affecting wild resource yield, combined with natural variability in plant populations, prompted a series of gradual subsistence shifts leading to an agricultural lifeway. This sort of fluctuation in environmental parameters *is* a form of environmental change, and consequently, this particular argument is a "hybrid" model.

More research in plant genetics eventually may offer some help in how we conceptualize the selective pressures affecting domestication and the sequencing of plant changes. Much discussion to this point has focused on particular mutations seen in single morphological traits. Genetic studies may reveal a more complex picture (Galinat 1983). At least we can agree that the genetic process is not confined to the morphological traits identifiable with archaeobotanical samples.

Although these mutualistic, genetically oriented scenarios are presently sketchy, they must confront two issues. What prods the process along? Can it be reduced to a series of shifts in cost/benefit equations of different subsistence options, such as those employed in optimal foraging (Winterhalder and Smith 1981) or niche breadth models (Christenson 1980)? These models hold that species are added to the diet in order of energy costs (measured by the energy required to discover, capture, and process an item compared with nutritive gain). Complicating these models are differences in kinds of nutritive contributions (Reidhead 1980), seasonality, nonfood uses, and storage issues, to name a few (Martin 1983; Keene 1983). The point is that both genetic changes and availability changes encouraged by people alter the economic values of species.

In genetic-ecological models the minimal role for population growth is that of a "gatekeeper" preventing reversal to greater use of wild resources. Population growth prior to subsistence shifts could increase the rate at which groups capitalized on any changed food production potentials, with the change process seen as fundamentally interactive with plant (or animal) populations. On one level one cannot quarrel with the genetic scenarios. Obviously domestication is dependent on genetic change in plants (or animals). The critical issue is whether a species' increasing economic attractiveness alone offsets the labor of cultivation, processing, and storage, or whether we need to address other incentives.

Another problem for genetic-ecological scenarios is why the origin of food production is delayed until relatively recently in human prehistory. There is no a priori reason to assume that species variability and desirable mutations could not have been evident much earlier in some locales. The timing of food production is, of course, important for any explanations since antecedent conditions are at stake. Models founded on population growth currently are the most promising in regard to the timing issue because of (1) overall evidence for human population growth, albeit slow during the Paleolithic, (2) the rather pervasive occurrence of occasional environmental stresses (Hayden 1981b), and (3) the evidence for pre-agricultural hunter-gatherer intensification (Moore 1982; Clark and Yi 1983).

Social Models.—A third major school of thought among explanations looks to social factors to create the demands leading to intensification of food procurement and ultimately food production (Flannery

1973:284; Bender 1978, 1985). In a sense this is both a pull and push model, as both social opportunities and demands act to encourage food production. Group rituals, leadership, or other social obligations, that is, internal social demands and opportunities, are viewed as linked to social reproduction. In view of the emphasis on socially mediated reproduction this "social" explanation is no less ecological than others. However, the social model reshapes "the problem" to be one of identifying reasons for social changes. Again, sedentarization is one factor of potential importance because it may contribute to stabilization of group membership and restrictions on social interaction.

Key evidence for social models would consist of (1) early indications (prior to food production) of group rituals or group projects embodied in fixed facilities and/or (2) social differentiation of more specialized leadership or status. Bender (1985) argues that in the Midwest, on the coast of Peru, and in the Near East evidence of at least the first sort exists. For Mesoamerica there is no early evidence supporting the social incentive theory although a possible Late Archaic open plaza in Oaxaca suggests we should pay more attention to open-air sites. Also, Mesoamerican Archaic evidence has not been found at a wide variety of locations because lowland evidence is quite limited. It is unreasonable to discount social organizational explanations simply because the Mesoamerican case currently offers no obvious support.

However, evidence for this model is weak, and it will be exceedingly difficult to demonstrate direct support for it. Evidence of social change in itself could reflect territorial and group symbolic identification (cf. Charles and Buikstra 1983) ensuing from other demographic causes. Obviously more "social archaeology" is needed, but so, too, are attempts to rule out other causes.

Discussion

In many respects the conceptual achievements of the past half century of research are symbolized by the "box and arrow" literature that displays complex feedbacks among the different processes thought to be important in the origins of food production (Harris 1977; Redman 1977, 1978; Hassan 1981:209–229). There is hope we can move beyond multifactoral flow charts which, while they are more than a primordial explanatory "soup," are far from readily testable models. In the cumbersome accomodation of multiple factors attractive to so many of us, we lose the ability to partition variability and effects. In short, we are not in a position to effectively link complex models with data because the models are neither quantified nor explicit in their material expectations.

I hope to be shown short-sighted, but I do not expect that the future holds great diversification in the *kinds* of causal factors that are thought to have prompted the appearance and growth of food production. What I expect is that more subtle modeling will succeed in pinning down causal variables within regional contexts where environmental conditions can be more explicitly identified. However, it remains to be seen if environmental reconstructions can achieve the detail needed for rigorous analysis of subsistence strategies. Quantified comparisons of subsistence options (both empirical and simulated) are vital for clarification of the selective pressures that favored cultivation, domestication, and agriculture. Such quantification presents a difficult research endeavor, as hunter-gatherer subsistence studies already reveal (Hayden 1981b; Reidhead 1980). There will be an important role for more studies like the economic analysis of sumpweed (*Iva annua*) by Asch and Asch (1978) or Flannery's (1973) comparison of maize and mesquite.

I contend that we cannot convincingly explain the origins of agriculture without accepting or discrediting environmental and demographic "push" variables. Obviously they must operate in conjunction with ecological factors: the changing relative costs and benefits of different food resources. The possible role of social factors has been underrated, but because of problems in testing for these effects, this alternative should also spur more careful research to eliminate competing explanations. Although I doubt that social factors will prove to explain the early origins of food production, there are indications that it could constitute a strong contributing factor to the intensification of food production.

In an essay of this sort, inevitably many important topics have been neglected. The timing of agricultural origins, the rate and degree of incorporation of cultivars in diets (as opposed to simply their appearance), and reasons for nonadoption of cultivars (or agriculture) are prominent examples. Also, I have devoted little attention to the intensification of food production. I would argue that these topics are likely to be clarified by better testing of explanatory models for the origins of food production. Some of the same economic and ecological variables applicable to origins are pertinent to the questions I have neglected. By the same token, however, there is no reason that research on these topics should not be highly informative for "pristine" agricultural origins. I am forced to conclude that current evidence does not rule out the operation of a few underlying demographic, economic, and environmental variables that favored the growth of food production in all three regions examined. Cultivation and domestication per se, however, may be undertaken for diverse reasons, as the widespread use of container plants indicates.

In closing, I would like to express my congratulations to the protagonists in a half century of research on the origins of agriculture. Their work gives ample grounds for satisfaction because we now have a rich fund of knowledge; but in their work I count most valuable the signs of how much more awaits.

Acknowledgments

I thank the SAA 50th Anniversary Committee for their invitation to prepare an assessment of research on this gargantuan subject. Several people were generous in suggesting information, loaning materials, and/or providing vital criticism from which I have benefitted and without which I could not have coped. I thank Neal Ackerly, George Armelagos, Nancy Asch, Pamela Bumsted, Geoffrey Clark, Richard Ford, Robert Gasser, Paul Fish, Austin Long, David Meltzer, Paul Minnis, Michael Moseley, James Schoenwetter, Holly Smith, Christy Turner, Patty Jo Watson, and Philip Weiss. Unfortunately, none of them bears the blame for errors or deficiencies in the paper, which only I can claim.

Literature Cited

Ammerman, Albert J.
  1975 Late Pleistocene Population Dynamics: An Alternative View. *Human Ecology* 3(4):219–234.

Anderson, Edgar
  1952 *Plants, Man and Life*. Little, Brown and Company, Boston.
  1960 The Evolution of Domestication. In *Evolution after Darwin*, edited by Sol Tax, 2:67–84. University of Chicago Press, Chicago.

Anderson, James E.
  1965 Human Skeletons of Tehuacan. *Science* 148:496–497.

Asch, David L., and Nancy B. Asch
  1977 Chenopod as Cultigen: A Re-evaluation of Some Prehistoric Collections from Eastern North America. *Mid-Continental Journal of Archaeology* 2(1):3–45.
  1978 The Economic Potential of *Iva annua* and Its Prehistoric Importance in the Lower Illinois Valley. *In* The Nature and Status of Ethnobotany, edited by Richard I. Ford. *University of Michigan, Museum of Anthropology, Anthropological Papers* 67:300–341.

1985 Prehistoric Plant Cultivation in West-Central Illinois. *In* Prehistoric Food Production in North America, edited by Richard I. Ford. *University of Michigan, Museum of Anthropology, Anthropological Papers* 75:149–203.

Beadle, George W.
1980 The Ancestry of Corn. *Scientific American* 242(1):112–119.

Bender, Barbara
1978 Gatherer-Hunter to Farmer: A Social Perspective. *World Archaeology* 10:204–222.
1985 Emergent Tribal Formations in the American Midcontinent. *American Antiquity* 50(1):52–62.

Bender, Margaret M., David A. Baerreis, and Raymond L. Steventon
1981 Further Light on Carbon Isotopes and Hopewell Agriculture. *American Antiquity* 46(2):346–353.

Bennett, C. L.
1979 Radiocarbon Dating with Accelerators. *American Scientist* 67:450–457.

Bennett, C. L., R. P. Beukens, M. R. Clover, D. Elmore, H. E. Gove, L. Kilius, A. E. Litherland, K. H. Purser
1978 Radiocarbon Dating with Electrostatis Accelerators: Dating of Milligram Samples. *Science* 201:345–347.

Berry, Michael S.
1985 The Age of Maize in the Greater Southwest: A Critical Review. *In* Prehistoric Food Production in North America, edited by Richard I. Ford. *University of Michigan, Museum of Anthropology, Anthropological Papers* 75:279–307.

Betancourt, Julio L., and Owen K. Davis
1984 Packrat Middens from Canyon de Chelly, Northeastern Arizona: Paleoecological and Archaeological Implications. *Quaternary Research* 21:56–64.

Binford, Lewis R.
1968 Post-Pleistocene Adaptations. In *New Perspectives in Archeology*, edited by S. R. Binford and L. R. Binford, pages 313–341. Aldine Publishing Co., Chicago.

Binford, Lewis R., and W. J. Chasko, Jr.
1976 Nunamiut Demographic History: A Provocative Case. In *Demographic Anthropology: Quantitative Approaches*, edited by Ezra B. W. Zubrow, pages 63–143. University of New Mexico Press, Albuquerque.

Bird, Junius B.
1948 Preceramic Cultures in Chicama and Viru. *In* A Reappraisal of Peruvian Archaeology, edited by Wendell C. Bennett. *Memoirs of the Society for American Archaeology* 14:21–28.

Boserup, Ester
1965 *The Conditions of Agricultural Growth: The Economics of Agrarian Change under Population Pressure*. Aldine Publishing Company, Chicago.

Braidwood, Robert J.
  1952 From Cave to Village. *Scientific American* 187:62–66.

Braidwood, Linda S., Robert J. Braidwood, and Bruce Howe
  1983 Introduction. In *Prehistoric Archeology along the Zagros Flanks*, edited by L. S. Braidwood, R. J. Braidwood, B. Howe, C. A. Reed, and P. J. Watson, pages 1–22. The Oriental Institute of the University of Chicago. Chicago.

Braun, David P., and Stephen Plog
  1982 Evolution of "Tribal" Social Networks: Theory and Prehistoric North American Evidence. *American Antiquity* 47(3):504–525.

Bronson, Bennet
  1977 The Earliest Farming: Demography as Cause and Consequence. In *Origins of Agriculture*, edited by Charles A. Reed, pages 23–48. Mouton Publishers, The Hague.

Brose, David S.
  1973 The Northeastern United States. In *The Development of North American Archaeology: Essays in the History of Regional Traditions*, edited by James E. Fitting, pages 84–115. Anchor Press, Garden City, New York.
  1979 A Speculative Model of the Role of Exchange with the Prehistory of the Eastern Woodlands. In *Hopewell Archaeology: The Chillicothe Conference*, edited by David S. Brose and N'omi Greber, pages 3–8. The Kent State University Press, Kent, Ohio.

Browman, David L.
  1981 Isotopic Discrimination and Correction Factors in Radiocarbon Dating. In *Advances in Archaeological Method and Theory*, edited by Michael B. Schiffer, 4:241–295. Academic Press, New York.

Brown, James A.
  1977 Current Directions in Midwestern Archaeology. *Annual Review of Anthropology* 6:161–179.

Brown, James A., and Robert K. Vierra
  1983 What Happened in the Middle Archaic? Introduction to an Ecological Approach to Koster Site Archaeology. In *Archaic Hunters and Gatherers in the American Midwest*, edited by James L. Phillips and James A. Brown, pages 165–195. Academic Press, New York.

Bryant, Vaughn M., Jr., and Glenna Williams-Dean
  1975 The Coprolites of Man. *Scientific American* 232(1):100–109.

Bumsted, M. Pamela
  1981 The Potential of Stable Carbon Isotopes in Bioarchaeological Anthropology. *In* Biocultural Adaptation—Comprehensive Approaches to Skeletal Analyses, edited by Debra L. Martin and M. Pamela Bumsted. *Department of Anthropology Research Reports* 20:108–127. University of Massachusetts, Amherst.
  In press Past Human Behavior from Bone Chemical Analsyis—Respects and Prospects. *Journal of Human Evolution*.

Burleigh, Richard, and Don Brothwell
  1978 Studies on Amerindian Dogs I: Carbon Isotopes in Relation to Maize in the Diet of Domestic Dogs from Early Peru and Ecuador. *Journal of Archaeological Science* 5:355–362.

Butzer, Karl W.
  1978   Changing Holocene Environments at the Koster Site: A Geoarchaeolog-
         ical Perspective. *American Antiquity* 43:408–413.

Byers, Douglas S. (editor)
  1967   *The Prehsitory of the Tehuacan Valley, Volume 1: Environment and
         Subsistence*. University of Texas Press, Austin.

Callen, Eric O.
  1967   Analysis of the Tehuacan Coprolites. In *The Prehistory of the Tehuacan
         Valley, Volume 1: Environment and Subsistence*, edited by Douglas S.
         Byers, pages 261–289. University of Texas Press, Austin.

Charles, Douglas K., and Jane E. Buikstra
  1983   Archaic Mortuary Sites in the Central Mississippi Drainage: Distribu-
         tion, Structure, and Behavioral Implications. In *Archaic Hunters and
         Gatherers in the American Midwest*, edited by James L. Phillips and
         James A. Brown, pages 117–145. Academic Press, New York.

Childe, V. Gordon
  1951   *Man Makes Himself*. The New American Library, New York. [Origi-
         nally published in 1936.]

Chisholm, Brian S., D. Erle Nelson, and Henry P. Schwarcz
  1982   Stable Carbon Isotope Ratios as a Measure of Marine versus Terrestrial
         Protein in Ancient Diets. *Science* 216:1131–1132.

Christenson, Andrew L.
  1980   Change in the Human Food Niche in Response to Population Growth.
         In *Modeling Change in Prehistoric Subsistence Economies*, edited by
         Timothy K. Earle and Andrew L. Christenson, pages 31–72. Academic
         Press, New York.

Clark, Geoffrey, and Seonbok Yi
  1983   Niche-Width Variation in Cantabrian Archaeofaunas: A Diachronic
         Study. In Animals and Archaeology, 1: Hunters and Their Prey, edited
         by Juliet Clutton-Brock and Caroline Grigson. *British Archaeological
         Reports, International Series* 163:183–208. Oxford, England.

Cohen, Mark Nathan
  1977   *The Food Crisis in Prehistory*. Yale University Press, New Haven.

Conard, Nicholas, David L. Asch, Nancy B. Asch, David Elmore, Garry Gove,
    Meyer Rubin, James A. Brown, Michael D. Wiant, Kenneth B. Farns-
    worth, and Thomas G. Cook
  1984   Accelerator Radiocarbon Dating of Evidence for Prehistoric Horticul-
         ture in Illinois. *Nature* 308:443–446.

Cook, Sherburne F.
  1972   Prehistoric Demography. *Addison-Wesley Modular Publication* 16.

Damp, Jonathan E.
  1984   Environmental Variation, Agriculture, and Settlement Processes in
         Coastal Ecuador (3300–1500 B.C.) *Current Anthropology* 25(1):106–
         111.

Damp, Jonathan E., Deborah M. Pearsall, and Lawrence T. Kaplan
  1981   Beans for Valdivia. *Science* 212:811–812.

Darwin, Charles
1896, 1897   *The Variation of Animals and Plants under Domestication.* 2 volumes. D Appleton and Company, New York.

de Candolle, Alphonse
1959   Origin of Cultivated Plants. 2nd edition. Hafner Publishing Co. New York [Second edition originally printed 1886.]

Dick, Herbert W.
1965   Bat Cave. *The School of American Research, Monograph* 27. Santa Fe.

Dunn, Mary Eubanks
1983   Phytolith Analysis in Archaeology. *Mid-Continental Journal of Archaeology* 8(2)287–301.

Eder, James F.
1984   The Impact of Subsistence Change on Mobility and Settlement Pattern in a Tropical Forest Foraging Economy: Some Implications for Archaeology. *American Anthropologist* 86(4):837–853.

Emerson, Thomas E., and Dale L. McElrath
1983   A Settlement-Subsistence Model of the Terminal Late Archaic Adaptation in the American Bottom, Illinois. In *Archaic Hunters and Gatherers in the American Midwest,* edited by James L. Phillips and James A. Brown, pages 219–242. Academic Press, New York.

Eshbaugh, W. Hardy, Sheldon I. Guttman, and Michael J. McLeod
1983   The Origin and Evolution of Domesticated *Capsicum* species. *Journal of Ethnobiology* 3(1):49–54.

Farnsworth, Paul, James E. Brady, Michael J. DeNiro, and Richard S. MacNeish
1985   A Re-evaluation of the Isotopic and Archaeological Reconstructions of Diet in the Tehuacan Valley. *American Antiquity* 50(1):102–116.

Flannery, Kent V.
1968   Archaeological Systems Theory and Early Mesoamerica. In *Anthropological Archeology in the Americas,* edited by Betty J. Meggers, pages 67–87. Anthropological Society of Washington, Washington, D. C.
1969   Origins and Ecological Effects of Early Domestication in Iran and the Near East. In *The Domestication and Exploitation of Plants and Animals,* edited by Peter J. Ucko and G. W. Dimbleby, pages 73–100. Gerald Duckworth & Co., Ltd., London.
1972   The Origins of the Village as a Settlement Type in Mesoamerica and the Near East: A Comparative Study. In *Man, Settlement, and Urbanism,* by Peter J. Ucko, Ruth Tringham, and G. W. Dimbleby, pages 23–53. George Duckworth and Co., Ltd., London.
1973   The Origins of Agriculture. *Annual Review of Anthropology* 2:271–310.
1983   Settlement, Subsistence, and Social Organization of the Proto-Otomangueans. In *The Cloud People: Divergent Evolution of the Zapotec and Mixtec Civilizations,* edited by Kent V. Flannery and Joyce Marcus, pages 32–36. Academic Press, New York.

Flannery, Kent V., Joyce Marcus, and Stephen A. Kowalewski
1981   The Preceramic and Formative of the Valley of Oaxaca. In *Supplement to the Handbook of Middle American Indians, Volume 1: Archaeology,*

edited by Jeremy A. Sabloff assisted by Patricia A. Andrews, pages 48–93. University of Texas Press, Austin.

Ford, Richard I.
1977 Evolutionary Ecology and the Evolution of Human Ecosystems: A Case Study from the Midwestern U.S.A. In *Explanation of Prehistoric Change,* edited by James N. Hill, pages 153–184. University of New Mexico Press, Albuquerque.
1978 Ethnobotany: Historical Diversity and Synthesis. *In* The Nature and Status of Ethnobotany, edited by Richard I. Ford. *Museum of Anthropology, University of Michigan, Anthropological Papers* 67:33–49.
1979 Gardening and Gathering: Trends and Consequences of Hopewell Subsistence Strategies. In *Hopewell Archaeology: The Chillicothe Conference,* by David S. Brose and N'omi Greber, pages 234–238. The Kent State University Press, Kent, Ohio.
1981 Gardening and Farming before A.D. 1000: Patterns of Prehistoric Cultivation North of Mexico. *Journal of Ethnobiology* 1(1):6–27.
1983 The Evolution of Corn Revisited. *The Quarterly Review of Archaeology* 4(4):12–13, 16.
1984 Prehistoric Phytogeography of Economic Plants in Latin America. *In* Pre-Columbian Plant Migration, edited by Doris Stone. *Papers of the Peabody Museum of Archaeology and Ethnology, Harvard University* 76:175–183.
1985a Patterns of Prehistoric Food Production in North America. *In* Prehistoric Food Production in North America, edited by Richard I. Ford. *University of Michigan, Museum of Anthropology, Anthropological Papers* 75:341–364.
1985b [Editor.] Prehistoric Food Production in North America. *University of Michigan, Museum of Anthropology, Anthropological Papers* 75.

Fritz, Gayle J.
1984 Identification of Cultigen Amaranth and Chenopod from Rockshelter Sites in Northwest Arkansas. *American Antiquity* 49(3):558–572.

Galinat, Walton C.
1978 The Inheritance of Some Traits Essential to Maize and Teosinte. In *Maize Breeding and Genetics,* edited by D. B. Walden, pages 93–111. John Wiley and Sons, Inc., New York.
1983 The Origin of Maize as Shown by Key Morphological Traits of Its Ancestor, Teosinte. *Maydica* 28:121–138.
1985 Domestication and Diffusion of Maize. *In* Prehistoric Food Production in North America, edited by Richard I. Ford. *University of Michigan, Museum of Anthropology, Anthropological Papers* 75:245–278.

Gilbert, Robert I., Jr.
1985 Stress, Paleonutrition, and Trace Elements. In *The Analysis of Prehistoric Diets,* edited by R. I. Gilbert, Jr., and J. H. Mielke, pages 339–358. Academic Press, New York.

Gilbert, Robert I., Jr., and James H. Mielke (editors)
1985 *The Analysis of Prehistoric Diets.* Academic Press, New York.

Gilmore, Melvin R.
1931 Vegetal Remains of the Ozark Bluff-Dweller Culture. *Papers of the Michigan Academy of Science, Arts, and Letters* 14:83–102.

Goodman, Alan H., Debra L. Martin, George J. Armelagos, and George Clark
   1984 Indications of Stress from Bone and Teeth. In *Paleopathology at the Origins of Agriculture,* edited by Mark Nathan Cohen and George J. Armelagos, pages 13–49. Academic Press, New York.

Griffin, James B.
   1960 Climatic Change: A Contributory Cause of the Growth and Decline of Northern Hopewell Culture. *Wisconsin Archaeologist* 41:21–33.
   1967 Eastern North American Archaeology: A Summary. *Science* 156(3772):175–191.

Harlan, Jack R.
   1971 Agricultural Origins: Centers and Noncenters. *Science* 174:468–474.

Harlan, Jack R., and J.M.J. de Wet
   1973 On the Quality of Evidence for Origin and Dispersal of Cultivated Plants. *Current Anthropology* 14(1–2):51–62.

Harris, David R.
   1972 The Origins of Agriculture in the Tropics. *American Scientist* 60(2):180–193.
   1977 Alternative Pathways toward Agriculture. In *Origins of Agriculture,* edited by Charles A. Reed, pages 179–243. Mouton Publishers, The Hague.

Hassan, Fekri A.
   1981 *Demographic Archaeology.* Academic Press, New York.

Hayden, Brian
   1981a Research and Development in the Stone Age: Technological Transitions among Hunter-Gatherers. *Current Anthropology* 22(5):519–548.
   1981b Subsistence and Ecological Adaptations of Modern Hunter/Gatherers. In *Omnivorous Primates,* edited by R.S.O. Harding and G. Teleki, pages 344–422. Columbia University Press, New York.

Heiser, Charles B., Jr.
   1985 Some Botanical Considerations of the Early Domesticated Plants North of Mexico. *In* Prehistoric Food Production in North America, edited by Richard I. Ford. *University of Michigan, Museum of Anthropology, Anthropological Papers* 75:57–97.

Heizer, Robert F., and Lewis K. Napton
   1969 Biological and Cultural Evidence from Prehistoric Human Coprolites. *Science* 165:563–568.

Hesse, Brian
   1982 Animal Domestication and Oscillating Climates. *Journal of Ethnobiology* 2(1):1–15.

Huss-Ashmore, Rebecca, Ian H. Goodman, and George J. Armelagos
   1982 Nutritional Inference from Paleopathology. In *Advances in Archaeological Method and Theory,* edited by Michael B. Schiffer, 5:395–474.

Iltis, Hugh H.
   1983 From Teosinte to Maize: The Catastrophic Sexual Transmutation. *Science* 222:886–894.

Johnson, Gregory A.
1977 Aspects of Regional Analysis in Archaeology. *Annual Review of Anthropology* 6:479–508.

Jones, Volney H.
1936 The Vegetal Remains of the Newt Kash Hollow Shelter. *In* Rockshelters in Menifee County, Kentucky, edited by W. S. Webb and W. D. Funkhouser. *University of Kentucky, Reports in Archaeology and Anthropology* 3(4)147–165.

Kaplan, Lawrence
1980 Variation in the Cultivated Beans. In *Guitarrero Cave: Early Man in the Andes,* by Thomas F. Lynch, pages 145–148. Academic Press, New York.
1981 What Is the Origin of the Common Bean? *Economic Botany* 35(2):240–254.

Keene, Arthur S.
1983 Biology, Behavior, and Borrowing: A Critical Examination of Optimal Foraging Theory in Archeology. In *Archaeological Hammers and Theories,* edited by James A. Moore and Arthur S. Keene, pages 137–155. Academic Press, New York.

Keepax, Carole
1977 Contamination of Archaeological Deposits by Seeds of Modern Origin with Particular Reference to the Use of Flotation Machines. *Journal of Archaeological Science* 4:221–229.

Kelly, Isabel
1964 Southern Paiute Ethnography. *Department of Anthropology, University of Utah, Anthropological Papers 69.*

Klepinger, Linda L.
1984 Nutritional Assessment from Bone. *Annual Review of Anthropology* 13:75–96.

Lanning, Edward P.
1967 *Peru before the Incas.* Prentice-Hall, Inc., Englewood Cliffs, New Jersey.

Lee, Richard B.
1972 Population Growth and the Beginnings of Sedentary Life among the !Kung Bushmen. In *Population Growth: Anthropological Implications,* edited by Brian Spooner, pages 329–343. MIT Press, Cambridge.

Lippi, Ronald D., Robert McK. Bird, and David M. Stemper
1984 Maize Recovered at La Ponga, an Early Ecuadorian Site. *American Antiquity* 49(1):118–124.

Long, A., D. J. Donahue, A.J.T. Jull, and T. Zabel
In press Tandem Accelerator Mass Spectrometry Applied to Archaeology and Art History. In *Application of Science in Examination of Works of Art, Fifth International Seminar, September 1983.* Boston Museum of Fine Art.

Lynch, Thomas F.
1971 Preceramic Transhumance in the Callejon de Huaylas, Peru. *American Antiquity* 36:139–148.

1973   Harvest Timing, Transhumance, and the Process of Domestication. *American Anthropologist* 75(5):1254–1259.

1980a *Guitarrero Cave: Early Man in the Andes.* Academic Press, New York.

1980b Guitarrero Cave in its Andean Context. In *Guitarrero Cave: Early Man in the Andes,* by Thomas F. Lynch, pages 293–320. Academic Press, New York.

Lynch, Thomas F., R. Gillespie, John A. J. Gowlett, and R.E.M. Hedges
1985   Chronology of Guitarrero Cave, Peru. *Science* 229:864–867.

MacNeish, Richard S.
1958   Preliminary Archaeological Investigations in the Sierra de Tamaulipas, Mexico. *Transactions of the American Philosophical Society* 48:6. Philadelphia.

1967   A Summary of the Subsistence. In *The Prehistory of the Tehuacan Valley, Volume 1: Environment and Subsistence,* edited by Douglas S. Byers, pages 290–309. University of Texas Press, Austin.

1974   Reflections on My Search for the Beginnings of Agriculture in Mexico. In *Archaeological Researches in Retrospect,* edited by Gordon R. Willey, pages 207–234. University Press of America, Washington, D. C.

1977   The Beginnings of Agriculture in Central Peru. In *Origins of Agriculture,* edited by Charles A. Reed, pages 753–801. Mouton Publishers, The Hague.

1978   *The Science of Archaeology?* Duxbury Press, North Scituate, Massachusetts.

1984   The Origins of Agriculture and Settled Life. Manuscript in files of R. S. MacNeish, Boston, Massachusetts.

MacNeish, Richard S., and Antoinette Nelken-Terner
1983a Introduction to Preceramic Contextual Studies. In *Prehistory of the Ayacucho Basin, Peru, Volume 4: The Preceramic Way of Life,* by R. S. MacNeish, R. K. Vierra, A. Nelken-Terner, R. Curie, and A. Garcia C., pages 1–15. University of Michigan Press, Ann Arbor.

1983b The Preceramic of Mesoamerica. *Journal of Field Archaeology* 10(1):71–84.

MacNeish, Richard S., and Frederick A. Peterson
1962   The Santa Marta Rock Shelter, Ocozocoautla, Chiapas, Mexico. *Papers of the New World Archaeological Foundation* 14. Provo, Utah.

MacNeish, Richard S., Melvin L. Fowler, Angel Garcia Cook, Frederick A. Peterson, Antoinette Nelken-Terner, and James A. Neely
1975   *The Prehistory of the Tehuacan Valley, Volume 5: Excavations and Reconnaissance.* University of Texas Press, Austin.

MacNeish, Richard S., Robert K. Vierra, Antoinette Nelken-Terner, Rochelle Lurie, and Angel Garcia Cook
1983   *Prehistory of the Ayacucho Basin, Peru, Volume 4: The Preceramic Way of Life.* The University of Michigan Press, Ann Arbor.

MacNeish, Richard S., Thomas C. Patterson, and David L. Browman
1975   The Central Peruvian Prehistoric Interaction Sphere. *Papers of the Robert S. Peabody Foundation for Archaeology* 7. Phillips Academy, Andover, Massachusetts.

Manglesdorf, Paul C.
1974 *Corn: Its Origin, Evolution and Improvement.* The Belknap Press of Harvard University Press, Cambridge, Massachusetts.
1983 The Mystery of Corn: New Perspectives. *Proceedings of the American Philosophical Society* 127(4):215–247.

Manglesdorf, Paul C., and R. G. Reeves
1939 The Origin of Indian Corn and Its Relatives. *Texas Agricultural Experiment Station Bulletin* 574:1–315.

Manglesdorf, P. C., and C. E. Smith, Jr.
1949 New Archaeological Evidence on Evolution in Maize. *Botanical Museum Leaflets, Harvard University* 13:213–247.

Martin, John F.
1983 Optimal Foraging Theory: A Review of Some Models and Their Applications. *American Anthropologist* 85(3):612–629.

Minnis, Paul
1985 Domesticating People and Plants in the Greater Southwest. *In* Patterns of Prehistoric Food Production in North America, edited by Richard I. Ford. *University of Michigan, Museum of Anthropology, Anthropological Papers* 75:309–339.

Molnar, S.
1972 Tooth Wear and Culture: A Survey of Tooth Function among Some Prehistoric Populations. *Current Anthropology* 34:175–190.

Moore, A.M.T.
1982 Agricultural Origins in the Near East: A Model for the 1980's. *World Archaeology* 14(2):224–236.

Moseley, Michael Edward
1975 *The Maritime Foundations of Andean Civilization.* Cummings Publishing Company, Menlo Park, California.

Munson, Patrick J.
1981 Note on the Use and Misuse of Water-separation ("Flotation") for the Recovery of Small-scale Botanical Remains. *Mid-Continental Journal of Archaeology* 6(1):123–126.

Murra, John V.
1972 El "control vertical" de un maximo de pisos ecologicos en la economia de las sociedades andinas. In *Visita de la provincia de Leon de Huanaco (1562),* 2:429–476. Universidad Hermilio Valdizan, Huanaco, Peru.

Myers, J. Thomas
1971 The Origins of Agriculture: An Evaluation of Three Hypotheses. In *Prehistoric Agriculture,* edited by Stuart Struever, pages 101–121. The Natural History Press, Garden City, New York.

Niederberger, Christine
1976 Zohapilco: Cinco milenios de ocupación humana en un sitio lacustre de la Cuenca de Mexico. *Colección Científica, Arqueología* 30. Instituto Nacional de Antropología e Historia, Mexico.

Patterson, Thomas C.
1971a Population and Economy in Central Peru. *Archaeology* 24:316–321.

1971b The Emergence of Food Production in Central Peru. In *Prehistoric Agriculture,* edited by Stuart Struever, pages 181–207. The Natural History Press, Garden City, New York.

Pavlish, L. A., and E. B. Banning
1980 Revolutionary Developments in Carbon-14 Dating. *American Antiquity* 45(2):290–297.

Pearsall, Deborah H.
1978 Phytolith Analysis of Archaeological Soils: Evidence for Maize Cultivation in Formative Ecuador. *Science* 199:177–178.
1982 Phytolith Analysis: Applications of a New Paleoethnobotanical Technique in Archaeology. *American Anthropologist* 84(4):862–871.

Pendleton, Michael W.
1983 A Comment Concerning "Testing Flotation Recovery Rates." *American Antiquity* 48(3):615–616.

Phillips, James L., and James A. Brown
1983 *Archaic Hunters and Gatherers in the American Midwest.* Academic Press, New York.

Pickersgill, Barbara
1984 Migrations of Chili Peppers, *Capsicum* spp., in the Americas. *In* Pre-Columbian Plant Migrations, edited by Doris Stone. *Papers of the Peabody Museum of Archaeology and Ethnology* 76:105–123.

Pickersgill, Barbara, and Charles B. Heiser, Jr.
1978 Origins and Distribution of Plants Domesticated in the New World Tropics. In *Advances in Andean Archaeology,* edited by David L. Browman, pages 132–165. Mouton Publishers, The Hague.

Piperno, Dolores R.
1984 A Comparison and Differentiation of Phytoliths from Maize and Wild Grasses: Use of Morphological Criteria. *American Antiquity* 49(2):361–383.

Piperno, Dolores R., and Karen Musum Clary
1984 Early Plant Use and Cultivation in the Santa Maria Basin, Panama: Data from Phytoliths and Pollen. *In* Recent Developments in Isthmian Archaeology: Advances in the Prehistory of Lower Central America, edited by Frederick W. Lange, *in* Proceedings 44 International Congress of Americanists, Manchester, 1982, general editing by Norman Hammond. *BAR International Series* 212:85–120.

Pires-Ferreira, Jan, Edgardo Pires-Ferreira, and Peter Kaulicke
1976 Preceramic Animal Utilization in the Central Andes. *Science* 194:483–490.

Powell, Mary Lucas
1985 The Analysis of Dental Wear and Caries for Dietary Reconstructions. In *The Analysis of Prehistoric Diets,* edited by R. I. Gilbert, Jr., and J. H. Mielke, pages 307–338. Academic Press, New York.

Pozorski, Sheila
1983 Changing Subsistence Priorities and Early Settlement Patterns on the North Coast of Peru. *Journal of Ethnobiology* 3(1):15–38.

Quilter, Jeffrey, and Terry Stocker
  1983 Subsistence Economies and the Origins of Andean Complex Societies. *American Anthropologist* 85(3):545–562.

Redman, Charles L.
  1977 Man, Domestication, and Culture in Southwestern Asia. In *Origins of Agriculture,* edited by Charles A. Reed, pages 523–541. Mouton Publishers, The Hague.
  1978 *The Rise of Civilization: From Early Farmers to Urban Society in the Ancient Near East.* W.H. Freeman and Company, San Francisco.

Reidhead, Van A.
  1980 The Economics of Subsistence Change: Test of an Optimization Model. In *Modeling Change in Prehistoric Subsistence Economies,* edited by Timothy K. Earle and Andrew L. Christenson, pages 141–186. Academic Press, New York.

Richardson, III, James B.
  1972 The Pre-Columbian Distribution of the Bottle Gourd (*Lagenaria siceraria*): A Re-evaluation. *Economic Botany* 26:265–273.

Rick, John W.
  1980 *Prehistoric Hunters of the High Andes.* Academic Press. New York.
  1984 Punas, Pundits, and Prehistory: Comment on Wheeler's Review of "Prehistoric Hunters of the High Andes." *American Antiquity* 49(1):177–180.

Rindos, David
  1984 *The Origins of Agriculture: An Evolutionary Perspective.* Academic Press, Inc., New York.

Roosevelt, Anna Curtenius
  1980 *Parmana: Prehistoric Maize and Manioc Subsistence along the Amazon and Orinoco.* Academic Press. New York.
  1984a Population, Health, and the Evolution of Subsistence: Conclusions from the Conference. In *Paleopathology at the Origins of Agriculture,* edited by Mark Nathan Cohen and George J. Armelagos, pages 559–583. Academic Press, New York.
  1984b Problems Interpreting the Diffusion of Cultivated Plants. *In* Pre-Columbian Plant Migrations, edited by Doris Stone. *Papers of the Peabody Museum of Archaeology and Ethnology, Harvard University* 76:1–18.

Rovner, Irwin
  1983 Plant Opal Phytolith Analysis: Major Advances in Archaeobotanical Research. In *Advances in Archaeological Method and Theory,* edited by Michael P. Schiffer, 6:225–266. Academic Press, New York.

Sauer, Carl O.
  1952 *Agricultural Origins and Dispersals.* American Geographical Society, New York.

Schiffer, Michael B.
  1983 Toward the Identification of Formation Processes. *American Antiquity* 48(4):675–706.

Schoeninger, Margaret J., Michael J. DeNiro, and Henrik Tauber
   1983 Stable Nitrogen Isotope Ratios of Bone Collagen Reflect Marine and Terrestrial Components of Prehistoric Diet. *Science* 220:1381–1383.

Schoenwetter, James
   1974 Principal Results of Palynological Studies at Koster: Summary Statement. Manuscript, Arizona State University Palynology Laboratory, Tempe, Arizona.
   1979 Comment on "Plant Husbandry in Prehistoric Eastern North America." *American Antiquity* 44(3):600–601.
   1985 Methodology and Maize Pollen. Paper presented at the 50th Annual Meeting of the Society for American Archaeology, Denver, Colorado.

Sillen, Andrew, and Maureen Kavanagh
   1982 Strontium and Paleodietary Research: A Review. *Yearbook of Physical Anthropology* 25:67–90.

Smith, B. Holly
   1984 Patterns of Molar Wear in Hunter-Gatherers and Agriculturalists. *American Journal of Physical Anthropology* 63:39–56.

Smith, Bruce D.
   1984 *Chenopodium* as a Prehistoric Domesticate in Eastern North America: Evidence from Russell Cave, Alabama. *Science* 226:165–167.

Smith, C. Earle, Jr.
   1967 Plant Remains. In *The Prehistory of the Tehuacan Valley, Volume 1: Environment and Subsistence,* edited by Douglas S. Byers, pages 220–260. University of Texas Press, Austin.
   1980 Plant Remains from Guitarrero Cave. In *Guitarrero Cave: Early Man in the Andes,* by Thomas F. Lynch, pages 87–119. Academic Press, New York.

Smith, Patricia, Ofer Bar-Yosef, and Andrew Sillen
   1984 Archaeological and Skeletal Evidence for Dietary Change during the Late Pleistocene/Early Holocene in the Levant. In *Paleopathology at the Origins of Agriculture,* edited by Mark Nathan Cohen and George J. Armelagos, pages 101–136. Academic Press, New York.

Spaulding, Albert C.
   1955 Prehistoric Cultural Development in the Eastern United States. In *New Interpretations of Aboriginal American Culture History,* pages 12–27. Anthropological Society of Washington, Washington, D.C.

Stark, Barbara L.
   1981 The Rise of Sedentary Life. In *Supplement to the Handbook of Middle American Indians, Volume 1: Archaeology,* edited by Jeremy A. Sabloff assisted by Patricia A. Andrews, pages 345–372. University of Texas Press, Austin.

Stone, Doris (editor)
   1984 Pre-Columbian Plant Migration. *Papers of the Peabody Museum of Archaeology and Ethnology, Harvard University* 76.

Struever, Stuart
   1968 Flotation Techniques for the Recovery of Small-scale Archaeological Remains. *American Antiquity* 33(3):353–362.

Styles, Bonnie W., Steven R. Ahler, and Melvin L. Fowler
    1983   Modoc Rock Shelter Revisited. In *Archaic Hunters and Gatherers in the American Midwest,* edited by James L. Phillips and James A. Brown, pages 261–297. Academic Press, New York.

Sussman, Robert W.
    1972   Child Transport, Family Size, and Increase in Human Population during the Neolithic. *Current Anthropology* 13:258–259.

Turner II, Christy G.
    1978   Dental Caries and Early Ecuadorian Agriculture. *American Antiquity* 43(4):694–697.
    1979   Dental Anthropological Indications of Agriculture among the Jomon People of Central Japan, X: Peopling of the Pacific. *American Journal of Physical Anthropology* 51(4):619–635.

van der Merwe, Nikolaas J.
    1982   Carbon Isotopes, Photosynthesis, and Archaeology. *American Scientist* 70:596–606.

van der Merwe, Nikolaas J., Anna Curtenius Roosevelt, and J. C. Vogel
    1981   Isotopic Evidence for Prehistoric Subsistence Change at Parmana, Venezuela. *Nature* 292:536–538.

van der Merwe, Nikolaas J., and J. C. Vogel
    1978 ^{13}C Content of Human Collagen as a Measure of Prehistoric Diet in Woodland North America. *Nature* 276:815–816.

Vavilov, N. I.
    1949–1950   Phytogeographic Basis of Plant Breeding. *Chronica Botanica* 13:13–54.

Wagner, Gail E.
    1982   Testing Flotation Recovery Rates. *American Antiquity* 47(1):127–132.

Watson, Patty Jo
    1976   In Pursuit of Prehistoric Subsistence: A Comparative Account of Some Contemporary Flotation Techniques. *Mid-Continental Journal of Archaeology* 1(1):77–100.
    1985   The Impact of Early Horticulture in the Upland Drainages of the Midwest and Midsouth. *In* Prehistoric Food Production in North America, edited by Richard I. Ford. *University of Michigan, Museum of Anthropology, Anthropological Papers* 75:99–147.

Wendorf, Fred, Romuald Schild, Angela E. Close, D. J. Donahue, A.J.T. Jull, T. H. Zabel, Hanna Wieckowska, Michal Kobusiewicz, Bahay Issawi, Navil el Hadidi
    1984   New Radiocarbon Dates on the Cereals from Wadi Kubbaniyah. *Science* 225:645–646.

Whitaker, Thomas W.
    1983   Cucurbits in Andean Prehistory. *American Antiquity* 48(3):576–585.

Whitaker, Thomas W., and Hugh C. Cutler
    1965   Cucurbits and Cultures in the Americas. *Economic Botany* 19:344–349.

Whiting, Alfred F.
  1944   The Origin of Corn: An Evaluation of Fact and Theory. *American Anthropologist* 46(4):500–515.

Willey, Gordon R., and Jeremy A. Sabloff
  1974   *A History of American Archaeology.* W. H. Freeman and Company, San Francisco.

Willey, Gordon R., and John M. Corbett
  1954   Early Ancon and Early Supe Culture. *Columbia Studies in Archaeology and Ethnology* 3.

Wilson, Hugh D.
  1981   Domesticated *Chenopodium* of the Ozark Bluff Dwellers. *Economic Botany* 35:233–239.

Wing, Elizabeth S.
  1978   Animal Domestication in the Andes. In *Advances in Andean Archaeology,* edited by David L. Browman, pages 167–196. Mouton Publishers, The Hague.

Wing, Elizabeth S., and Antoinette B. Brown
  1979   *Paleonutrition: Method and Theory in Prehistoric Foodways.* Academic Press, New York.

Winterhalder, Bruce, and Eric Alden Smith (editors)
  1981   *Hunter-Gatherer Foraging Strategies: Ethnographic and Archeological Analyses.* The University of Chicago Press, Chicago.

Wobst, H. Martin
  1974   Boundary Conditions for Paleolithic Social Systems: A Simulation Approach. *American Antiquity* 39:147–178.

Wood, W. Raymond, and Donald Lee Johnson
  1978   A Survey of Disturbance Processes in Archaeological Site Formation. In *Advances in Archaeological Method and Theory,* edited by Michael B. Schiffer, 1:315–381. Academic Press, New York.

Wright, Gary A.
  1971   Origins of Food Production in Southwestern Asia: A Survey of Ideas. *Current Anthropology* 12(4–5):447–477.

Wright, Herbert E., Jr.
  1977   Environmental Change and the Origin of Agriculture in the Old and New Worlds. In *Origins of Agriculture,* edited by Charles A. Reed, pages 281–318. Mouton Publishers, The Hague.

Yarnell, Richard A.
  1978   Domestication of Sunflower and Sumpweed in Eastern North America. *In* The Nature and Status of Ethnobotany, edited by Richard I. Ford. *University of Michigan, Museum of Anthropology, Anthropological Papers* 67:289–299.

Zavallos M., Carlos, Walton C. Galinat, Donald W. Lathrap, Earl R. Leng, Jorge G. Marcos, and Kathleen Klump
  1977   The San Pablo Corn Kernel and Its Friends. *Science* 196:385–389.

Zeitlin, Robert N.
  1984 A Summary Report on Three Seasons of Field Investigations into the Archaic Period Prehistory of Lowland Belize. *American Anthropologist* 86(2):358–369.

Henry T. Wright University of Michigan

The Evolution of Civilizations

Introduction

The year 1985 marks not only the 50th anniversary of the founding of
the Society for American Archaeology, but also the 30th anniversary of
the publication of Julian Steward's *Theory of Culture Change* (1955)
which included his "Culture Causality and Law: A Trial Formulation of
the Development of Early Civilizations" (1949). Few American anthropologists are unfamiliar with either the volume or the paper, and both
have exerted a decisive influence on research directions for three decades.
It is appropriate at this time to assess what has been accomplished during
these years and to ask where the study of the early civilizations may be
going. Such a task, however, is immense, and in this brief paper I will
not attempt to cover the range of problems or areas discussed by Steward. Instead, I will limit myself to regional studies of the first steps toward complexity—the development of chiefdoms and primary states—
in four major regions: Mesopotamia, the Indus Valley, Mesoamerica, and
the central Andes. Two developments covered by Steward will be excluded. Egypt will not be discussed, since regional research is only just
beginning there. China may have had such research, but regrettably the
author has no access to the primary data, so this area cannot receive the
coverage it certainly deserves.

Steward sought to compare the early civilization of the arid zones in
order to discover "cross-cultural regularities" which could be formulated
as "trial laws" for future testing. He was quite familiar with the work of
Karl Wittfogel and V. Gordon Childe, and it is not surprising that he
emphasized (and the field researchers who followed him sought data on)
irrigation, craft specialization, and exchange. At the present time, there

seems to be wide consensus regarding the role of irrigation in the rise of the early civilizations. As Steward himself noted (1977), it contributed to productive stability and increasing differentials of family wealth, but irrigation systems were small until the rise of the early empires; such systems probably did not require the kind of management that Wittfogel (1957) discussed. Regarding the crafts, processual perspectives on industrial analysis, and use-wear analyses are revolutionizing our understanding at the present moment, and it is not possible to provide a uniform evaluation of the role of craft specialization in the early civilizations. Broad patterns of exchange are now well known, but the study of the dynamics of exchange is almost dormant at the moment, probably because we lack both useful economic models and comparable sampling of exchange by-products from multiple sites in one area needed to test such models. I will leave these three areas of enquiry for another paper.

Instead, I will focus on three issues that were important in Steward's formulation, but which have only become major objects of research in recent years. These are sociopolitical control hierarchies, population changes, and conflict, particularly conflict between polities. These variables are fundamental to Robert Carneiro's consideration of the origins of states (1970), a construct which has guided recent research in many areas. This paper too will consider the development of states, defined here as cultural entities with both internal and external specialization of the central control apparatus (Wright 1977), a definition which subsumes classical definitions based on legitimate force. However, other topics and other explanatory constructs will also be discussed. The following presentation will also attempt to consider some of the variability, as well as the regularities, in this rather limited sample of civilizations. In considering each case, I will touch briefly on the broad structure of the environment and on the present extent of regional work. Then, I will discuss changing patterns of regional integration up to the level of the early empires, illustrating key changes with settlement maps and rank-size graphs (Johnson 1981). Finally, I will turn to the evidences of control hierarchy, population change, and conflict, presented in generalized time charts. After the four cases have been presented, it will be possible to assess progress and say a few words about the future.

Mesopotamia

It is easy to think of the heartland of southwest Asian state development as a relatively homogenous "land between two rivers," but this ignores not only the contrast between the grassy steppes of northern Mesopotamia and the alluvial desert and marshes of the south (which lack sufficient rainfall for grain cultivation), but also that between the river valleys and the wooded Zagros and Taurus mountains and the plateau beyond to the northeast. These different regions have been complementary at least since the beginnings of agriculture (Flannery 1965), and both exchange and conflict between mountains and lowlands continue up to the present day. It would be difficult to evaluate ideas about the development of early Mesopotamian civilization without data from all these regions. In all, the mainstays of agriculture throughout early Mesopotamia were wheats, barleys, sheep, goats, and cattle, with additional complementarities being the investment of cereal in animals and the use of cattle as draft animals. In general, there were more payoffs in extensive production coupled with exchange than in intensification, even under irrigation conditions.

The first modern regional archaeological survey to be completed and published on Mesopotamia was the Diyala Basin project undertaken in 1957 by Robert McC. Adams (with assistance from Thorkild Jacobsen and Fuad Safar) under the joint sponsorship of the University of Chicago and the Iraq Directorate-General of Antiquities (Adams 1965). During the next decade this was followed by other surveys of earlier sites by Adams and Nissen (1972), Gibson (1972), Johnson (1973) and Sumner (1972). More recent surveys have been undertaken by teams from Britain, Canada, Denmark, France, Iran, Iraq, Italy, the Netherlands, Saudi Arabia, Turkey, and the United States, some involving detailed coverage on foot rather than by vehicle. New publications with detailed maps, site catalogs, artifact studies, and even ethnoarchaeological and geomorphological studies, appear every year. Nevertheless, examination of Figure 1 shows that survey coverage is biased toward the south. This is in part a result of the greater difficulty of survey in the less arid, grass-covered north, and in part a result of the more complicated modern political situation in the north. Furthermore, many areas known to have had major early settlements from more extensive surveys and casual visits by archaeologists have not yet been carefully surveyed. Nevertheless, using both the available survey and excavation data, it is possible to evaluate social and political changes during the late 5th to early 3rd mil-

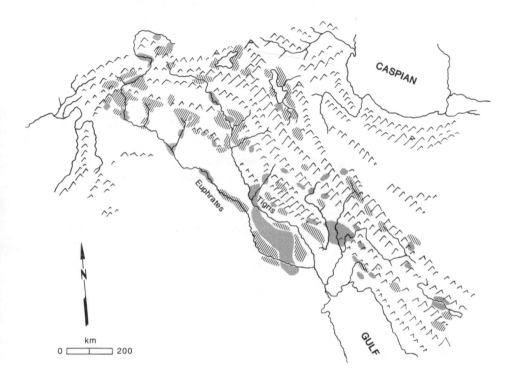

Figure 1 Archaeological survey in Greater Mesopotamia to 1985. Stippled areas mark complete surveys for which published period maps and site tabulations are available. Hatched areas are some of the important tracts for which only partial survey data or none at all are available.

lennia B.C. in portions of Mesopotamia.

By 4500 B.C., along the lower Euphrates valley in Iraq, in the foot-hill valleys of southwestern Iran, and in larger valleys on the southern Zagros in Iran, there were larger centers with populations of 1000 to 3000, which dominated networks of smaller settlements. Excavation on some of these larger centers revealed central platforms supporting ritual buildings, segregated elite residences with large storage structures, and indications of socially segregated cemeteries (Wright and Pollock 1985). This pattern was a resilient one for there had been at least one previous cycle of the development of such centers in the lowlands. In contrast, on the steppes of Assyria and Syria and in the adjacent highlands to the north and east, there were clusters of smaller settlements, but no evidence as yet of larger dominating centers. Either these were simpler societies or the larger centers remain undetected, buried beneath the remains of im-

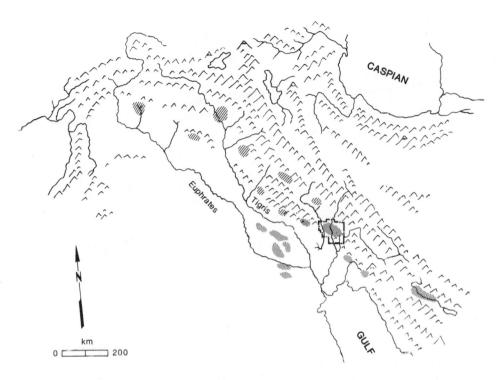

Figure 2 Major settled zones of the mid to late 5th millennium B.C. (the Late 'Ubaid Period) in Greater Mesopotamia. Stippled areas are those dominated by larger centers; hatched areas are those lacking present evidence of such centers, and which therefore may have sustained simpler societies. The Susiana plain, detailed in Figures 3, 5, and 6, is marked by a dash-dot line.

mense later cities. Figure 2 shows the distribution of both the larger pre-state stratified societies, what may be termed complex chiefdoms, nucleated in what is to be the southern part of the zone of early state development, as well as some of the lesser known contemporary societies elsewhere.

Southwestern Iran provides us with an example of a region whose radical transformations in integrative patterns can be outlined. The Suse Phase was a late example of the pre-state stratified societies just discussed (Dollfus 1978; Pollock 1984; Wright 1984). As Figure 3 shows, the major center of Susa dominated a series of local settlement clusters to the north, south, and east, each of which had a small center spatially interposed between Susa and most of the component villages and hamlets of the cluster. Susa itself was a new foundation on the west edge of the Susiana plain far from the older centers it replaced, with public buildings

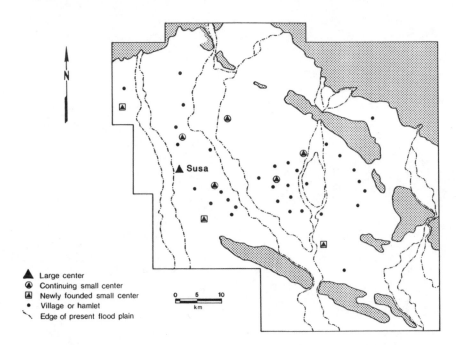

Figure 3 The Susiana plain during the Suse Phase (adapted from Wright 1985, fig. 6). The stippled areas are rugged terrain generally above 200 meters.

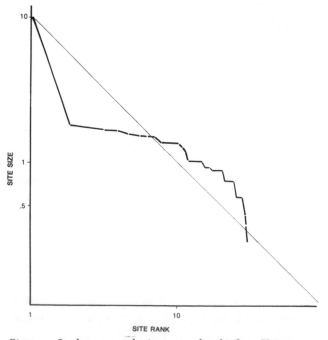

Figure 4 Settlement rank-size curve for the Suse Phase.

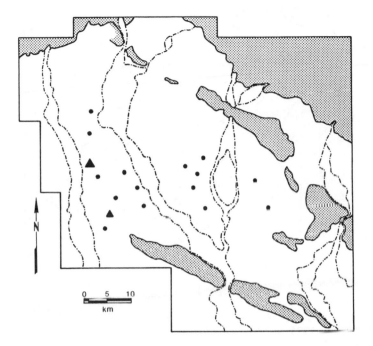

Figure 5 The Susiana plain during the terminal Suse Phase (adapted from Johnson 1973, fig. 15).

and storage facilities on a huge central platform. Also newly founded were three additional small centers to the south and west, perhaps border centers. A population of 8000 to 12000 is reasonable for the Suse Phase. The rank-size curve for this settlement pattern (Figure 4) with its large major center and several more or less equal-sized minor centers, is termed "primo-convex" and, as we shall see, is characteristic of both pre-state and early state settlement configurations (Johnson 1981, in press). During Terminal Suse Phase times, this settlement network disintegrates (Figure 5). Susa remains a major center, but many smaller settlements, as well as those on the edge of the plain, were abandoned leaving a few disconnected clusters of settlement (Johnson 1973:87–90).

By the beginning of the succeeding Early Uruk Period, Susa had been at least partially abandoned and other settlements had grown considerably, resulting in a compact pattern of more or less equally spaced centers, not greatly varying in size (Figure 6). The rank-size graph for this kind of settlement configuration is convex (Figure 7). This suggests a

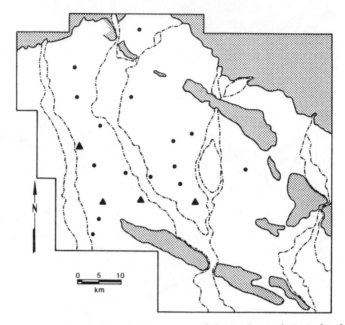

Figure 6 The Susiana plain at the beginning of the Early Uruk Period (adapted from Johnson 1973, fig. 16, table 35).

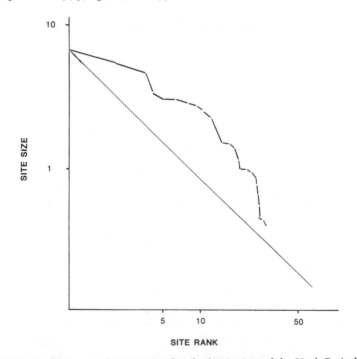

Figure 7 Settlement rank-size curve for the beginning of the Uruk Period.

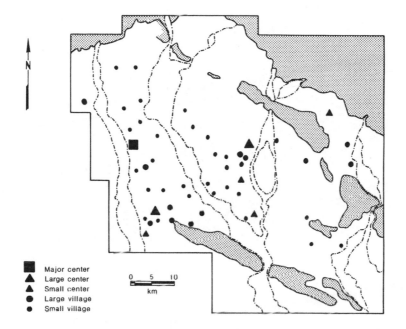

N

Major center
Large center
Small center
Large village
Small village

0   5   10
km

Figure 8 The Susiana plain during the Middle Uruk Period (adapted from Johnson 1973, fig. 19).

balance between poorly integrated, perhaps even competitive, centers. Unfortunately there are almost no data from excavations relevant to this period, and such a proposition remains untested.

By the end of the Early Uruk Period, Susa had grown and re-established its dominant position on the Susiana Plain. There is evidence of administrative agencies directly involved with control of the food supply and of centralization of the crafts (Johnson in press; Wright 1985). By Middle and Late Uruk times there was an elaborate control hierarchy involving villages, agricultural estates, subsidiary towns and the main center of Susa, with both centrally controlled and locally negotiated craft production and distribution networks (Wright et al. 1980) (Figure 8). Technologies for record-keeping were developed and steps toward true writing are made before the end of the Uruk Period (Le Brun and Vallat 1978).

Stepping back and considering all of Greater Mesopotamia in the Middle Uruk Period, we see that southwestern Iran is only one small element in a nexus of emergent states (Figure 9). The lower Euphrates

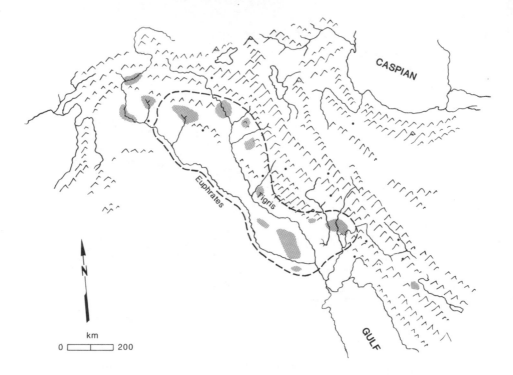

Figure 9 Major settled zones of the mid-4th millennium B.C. (the Middle and Late Uruk Periods) in Greater Mesopotamia. The dots are known Late Uruk outposts on communication routes. The dashed line indicates the approximate limits of imperial installations emplaced by the Dynasty of Agade, ca. 2300 B.C.

alluvium has gone through a similar history of growth, though complicated by major shifts in river channels at various times. In Terminal 'Ubaid times, several large, dense clusters of similar-sized centers, comparable in pattern to the small Early Uruk cluster on the Susiana, developed on a joint Tigris-Euphrates channel well to the north of Uruk (Adams 1981:61). Later a large, hierarchically organized settlement network developed around Uruk itself (Adams and Nissen 1972; Johnson 1975, 1980). Similar Terminal 'Ubaid and Uruk developments may be taking place around Nineveh on the upper Tigris, Tell Brak on the Khabur, and elsewhere in the north. There is no reason why these networks, based on highly productive dry farming rather than irrigation, could not have been as complex as those in the south (Weiss 1983). This nexus of ten or more interacting polities, extending 1200 kilometers from northwest to southeast, with populations ranging from 25,000 to perhaps 100,000 may have been dominated by Uruk itself for a period of time at the end of the Uruk Period. Also at this time, there was a great elaboration in record-keeping technologies throughout Mesopotamia (Schmandt-Besserat 1979). After this period of domination, however, these societies underwent centuries of fission and reintegration before the emergence of effective imperial administration late in the 3rd millennium B.C.

Changes through time in control hierarchies, population, and conflict are shown in Figure 10. In this and subsequent similar illustrations (Figures 17, 24, 32) absolute dates, rather than C-14 age-determinations are noted. Phase or period names are in a terminology familiar to most anthropologists, even if no longer current among specialists. My best assessments of the number of levels of the central political control hierarchies are based on evidence of settlement hierarchy, different types of administrative technology, public architecture, and iconography on var-

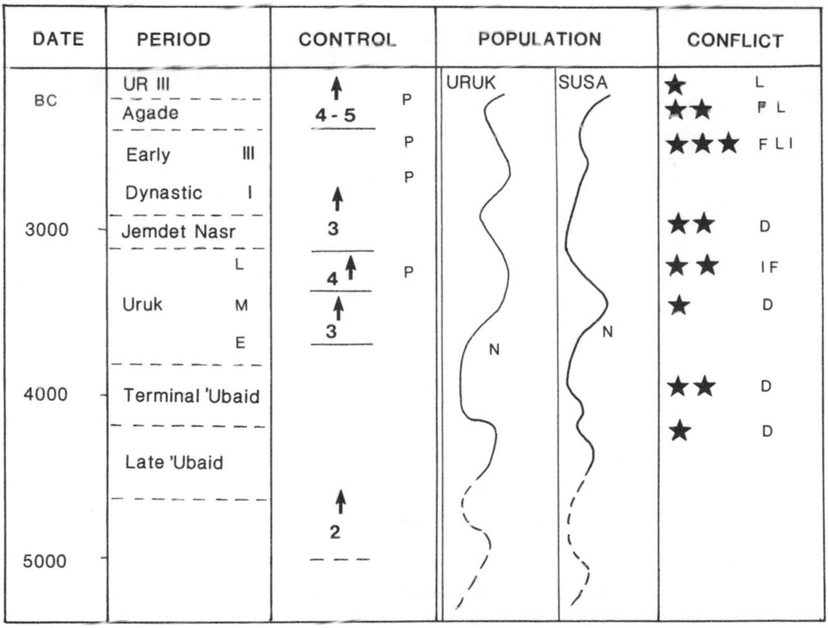

Figure 10 Changes through time in control hierarchies, population, and conflict in Mesopotamia. Control column: 2–5 = number of levels of the central political control hierarchies; P = palatial residences. Population column: curve = relative population changes based upon settlement areas; N = period of rapid nucleation. Conflict column: stars = intensity of conflict; sources of assessment: D = destruction and major settlement abandonment; F = major fortifications; I = iconic representations; L = written sources.

ious sites. Relative population changes are based upon site area estimates for one component region in the particular case. The intensity of conflict is indicated by one to three stars.

In Mesopotamia, the later 5th millennium was one in which two level control hierarchies were widespread, though locally (perhaps after periods of collapse when competing centers were being reintegrated under the control of a major center) three-level hierarchies may have operated. At the end of the millennium, during the time when settlement units were fragmented, it seems likely that every center competed with all others, and there was little or no control of one settlement by another. In the second quarter of the 4th millennium, during the Early Uruk Period, centers of unprecedented size grew to dominate the larger settlement clusters. There is evidence of centralized control of the economy—focused in elaborate buildings—indicating specialized administration. State emergence with at least three levels of control hierarchy is suggested (Johnson in press). During the middle of the 4th millennium, the settlement networks and the administrative technology indicate at least four to five levels of control hierarchy in several of the areas of Middle Uruk florescence.

During this period of increasingly centralized control, population fluctuates greatly. Curves are presented for both the Uruk area on the Euphrates and the somewhat marginal Susa area. Both have relatively high population levels during the later 5th millennium. With major river channel shifts the Euphrates drops off first; the Susa area drops somewhat later. Subsequent nucleation along the Tigris-Euphrates channel is so rapid and the resulting site density is so high, it is difficult to believe this is a result of local migration and biological reproduction, but precise population estimates will not be possible without samples of site histories and domestic architecture. Growth also occurs, perhaps somewhat later, on the Susiana Plain, but estimated relative populations do not surpass those of the late 5th millennium until after the state is established at the end of the Early Uruk Period. Finally, it is interesting to note that the Uruk area continues to grow during Late Uruk times, while the Susa area and other marginal centers collapse after brief periods of prosperity.

Is there any indication that conflict between polities correlates with periods of increasing population? The evidence indicates a complex relationship. During the late 5th millennium, the abandonment of marginal land and the occasional destruction of centers—even Susa is destroyed at least once at the height of its prosperity—indicate episodes of raiding among the complex chiefdoms. The close packing of centers at the beginning of the Early Uruk Period argues for competition, but there is little direct evidence of actual conflict, even with the rapid nucleation of population with state emergence. It is only during the Late Uruk Period that we again see settlement abandonment, destruction, the emplacement of what appear to be southern Uruk outposts in Syria (Strommenger 1979) and in the Zagros (Weiss and Young 1975), and representations of fighting and captives (Amiet 1961:251). The Mesopotamian evidence does not seem to support the proposition that population growth produces conflict and that in turn this conflict leads to the conquest and agglomeration of smaller societies into states.

The Indus Valley

This area is broadly similar to Mesopotamia, with a single great arid valley lying below rugged mountains and distant, mineral-rich plateaus. However, there are important differences in detail. The rivers' channels are entrenched in some places (Fairservis 1961) and affected by faulting in others (Raikes 1964; Lambrick 1967), and irrigation of much of the interfluvial terrain was impossible before recent times. The nearby mountains are more arid than the Zagros, and societies of the higher valleys would have depended on irrigation as did their lowland neighbors. Differences aside, the early production systems in this area used domestic plants and animals, which were similar to those of Mesopotamia.

Efforts at systematic coverage of the archaeological landscape were begun long ago (Fairservis 1956) and work by French, Indian, Italian, Pakistani, and United States teams continues, but there is little publication of detailed site maps and catalogs (Figure 11). A commendable exception to this lack of published regional studies is the work of M. Rafique Mughal (1980) on an eastern tributary of the Indus largely abandoned for more than three millennia. Since it is not possible to construct a broad overview of pre-state societies throughout the Indus area, I will go directly to a consideration of the Cholistan evidence, analyzed by Michael J. Adler (n.d.), in a manner comparable to that used above for Mesopotamia, referring where necessary to evidence from excavated sites in nearby areas.

The earliest recognized occupation along the abandoned channel surveyed by Mughal is that of the Hakra Period of the late 5th and early 4th millennia B.C. Hierarchically organized societies certainly existed

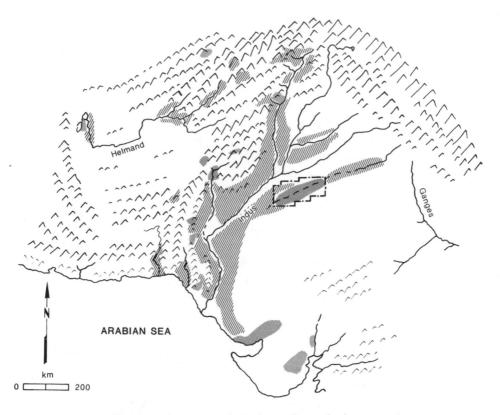

Figure 11 Archaeological survey in the Indus Valley and adjacent regions to 1985. The stippled areas are those for which fairly complete survey information exists. Hatching marks possibly important tracts for which little survey data are available; however, in contrast to Figure 1, the author's lack of personal familiarity has prevented the exclusion of much interfluvial desert and permanent marsh. The Cholistan area, detailed in Figures 12 and 14, is marked by a dash-dot line.

much earlier in the foothills west of the Indus (Jarrige 1981), and it is not surprising that Hakra settlements exhibit marked size differences between larger centers covering 15 to 27 hectares—indicating populations of 1500 to 5000 in each center if Mesopotamian housing densities prevailed—and smaller settlements. Unfortunately, studies of actual ancient channels with remote sensing are not yet available for Cholistan. It is possible, however, to impose hypopthetical channels with the amplitude of modern channels in the nearby Punjab onto the archaeological settlement distributions. The reconstruction shown in Figure 12 has two main channels, with some sites being watered by canals of 5 to 10 kilometers

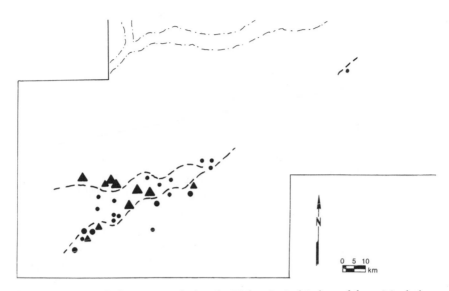

Figure 12 The Cholistan area during the Hakra Period (adapted from Mughal 1980, fig. 2, table 2.)

in length. Several centers are on each suggested channel, and the packing of centers is close but irregular. Keeping in mind that Hakra covers a rather long period and that some of these settlements are probably not contemporary, the pattern is similar to that of the very beginning of the Early Uruk Period, just before the period of state emergence. The rank-size graph (Figure 13) is markedly convex, as we expect with poorly integrated competing centers.

The focus of the Early Harappan settlement of the late 4th millennium B.C. is upstream from that of the Hakra settlements. There is a large center on the upstream end of the settlement cluster dominating the location where the river bifurcation or canal offtake would have been. There are several smaller centers just downstream, and a concentration of village-sized settlements yet further downstream (Figure 14). Once again, the period is relatively long and some of these sites may not be contemporary, but the pattern is similar to those of Early Uruk settlement clusters in Mesopotamia. The rank-size curve (Figure 15) for the entire set of Early Harappan sites is only slightly convex, and that for the area within 20 kilometers of the main center is close to the normal rank-size relation, indicating a well-integrated settlement system. Evidence from elsewhere on the Indus alluvium indicates that this is the period when items of administrative technology such as seals become widespread, and

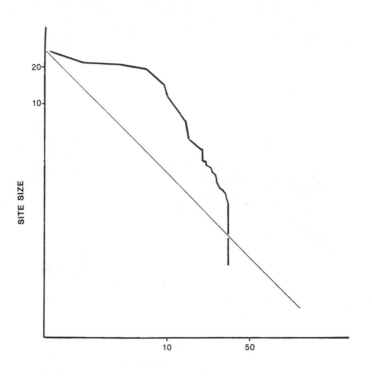

Figure 13 Settlement rank-size curve for the Hakra Period.

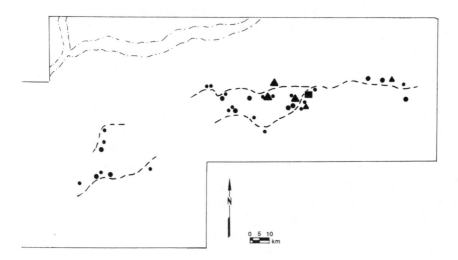

Figure 14 The Cholistan area during the Early Harappan Period (adapted from Mughal 1980, fig. 2, table 4).

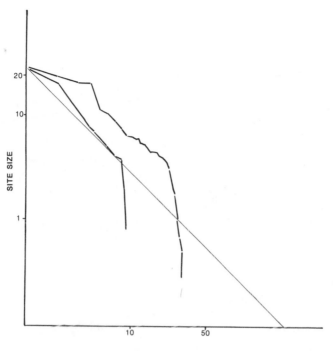

Figure 15 Settlement rank-size curve for the Early Harappan Period. The upper line includes all sites; the lower line includes only sites within 20 km of the major center.

when centers have planned layouts and substantial public works, even though there is much diversity in crafts and access to exotic materials (Mughal 1972; Durrani 1981). It is reasonable to suggest that primary states developed during this period. Cholistan was perhaps marginal to more important centers of state development, whose distribution is at present difficult to map. In Figure 16, an effort is made to indicate some possible centers, though no doubt there were others yet unknown. The scale of the network, perhaps ten discrete polities scattered over 900 kilometers from northeast to southeast, is comparable to that of the somewhat earlier Middle Uruk nexus in Mesopotamia.

A very tentative time chart is present in Figure 17. Two levels of central control hierarchy are suggested for the Hakra period, with three levels emerging sometime during the Early Harappan. Both assessments are based on settlement evidence alone. Based upon architectural and

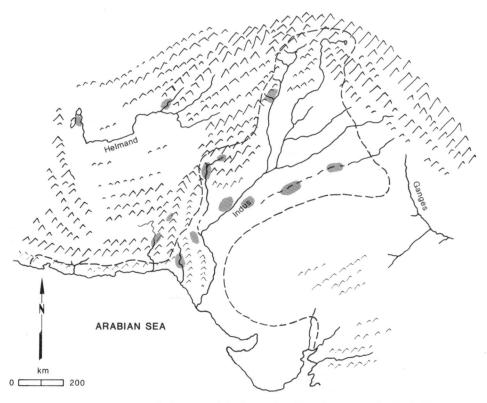

Figure 16 Known settled zones of the late 4th millennium B.C. (the Early Harappan Period) in the Indus valley and adjacent areas. The dashed line indicates the approximate limit of the Mature and Late Harappan community network of the middle and late 3rd millennium B.C.

artifactual evidence as well, the Mature Harappan would have had four, five or even six levels depending on the extent to which the whole Indus system, including far-flung dependencies over the Hindu Kush (Frankfort and Pottier 1978), was actually a single integrated polity. The relative population curve suggests that there was less population during Early Harappan times than during Hakra times. However, the time periods are long, and people may have moved about. It is possible that relative assessments of regional population may not be directly comparable to those for Mesopotamia. The evidence for conflict is sporadic. The Hakra settlements have little indication of destruction, but subsequent Early Harappan sites are often fortified and some were burned or abandoned, suggesting widespread conflict. Thus, on the face of things, more com-

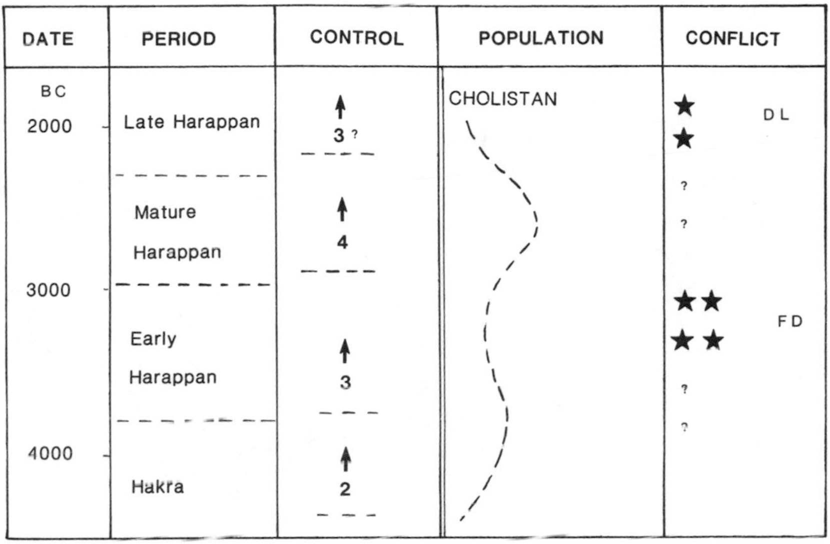

DATE	PERIOD	CONTROL	POPULATION	CONFLICT
BC 2000	Late Harappan	↑ 3 ?	CHOLISTAN	★ ★ D L
				?
	Mature Harappan	↑ 4		?
3000				★★ ★★ F D
	Early Harappan	↑ 3		?
4000				?
	Hakra	↑ 2		

Figure 17 Changes through time in control hierarchies, population, and conflict in the Indus. Control column: 2–4 = number of levels of central political control hierarchies; Population column: curve = relative population changes based on settlement areas. Conflict column: stars = intensity of conflict; sources of assessment: D = destruction and major settlement abandonment; F = major fortifications; L = written sources.

plex regional control hierarchies seem to have emerged in a time of reduced population and increased conflict. Certainly, however, more regional surveys using more refined chronologies are necessary.

Mesoamerica

The central portion of Mesoamerica is a world totally different from those discussed previously. It is a broken mosaic of basins, ranges, and strips of coastal plain, with environments varying from arid desert to tropical lowlands. The few large rivers do not have extensive aggraded valleys; transportation is difficult everywhere. Furthermore, the productive systems developed in Mesoamerica used few domestic animals, but a wealth of domestic plants whose productivity can be greatly increased through such practices as multiple cropping, fertilization, and intensive cultivation techniques.

Regional archaeological survey is much more difficult in Mesoamerica than in the lands previously discussed. Many sites are marked only

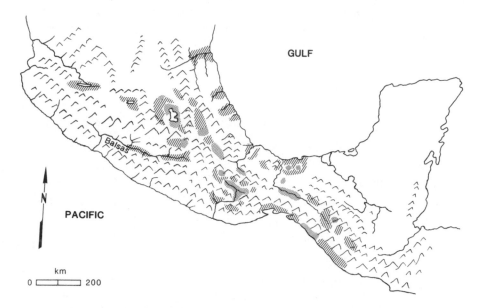

Figure 18 Archaeological survey in central Mesoamerica to 1985. Stippled areas mark intensive surveys for which published period maps and, in most cases, site tabulations are available. Hatched areas are some of the important tracts for which only incomplete survey data or none at all are available.

by potsherds and rubble, and it is advisable to walk every tract on foot. In spite of the difficulties much survey has been undertaken and much is available in fully published form. The techniques of field-walking and air photography in widespread use today were developed in the Teuacan Valley beginning in 1961 (Sanders 1965) by the teams of William Sanders of Pennsylvania State University and Rene Millon of the University of Rochester. During the next decade, further surveys were undertaken in the Basin of Mexico by Parsons (1971) and others; in Puebla by the teams of MacNeish et al. (1972) and Garcia Cook (1972, 1977); in Oaxaca by Spores (1972) and Blanton (1978) and Blanton et al. (1982); in Veracruz by Sisson (1970); and in Chiapas by Lowe (1959) and others. Mexican and U.S. teams are at work today on additional and much improved surveys. The completed surveys are biased toward the major highland valleys (Figure 18). This is understandable, for these are the tracts most likely to be damaged by modern urbanization and agriculture. A fuller understanding of the development of civilization in Mesoamerica, however, will require more regional surveys in the smaller

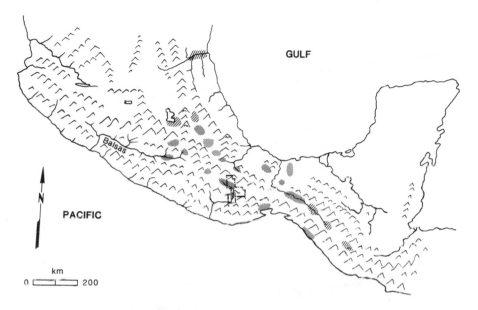

Figure 19 Known settled zones of the early 1st millennium B.C. (the earlier Middle Formative Period) in central Mesoamerica. Stippled areas are those dominated by larger centers. Hatched areas are those lacking present evidence for such centers, and which therefore may have supported simpler societies. The Valley of Oaxaca, detailed on Figures 20 and 21, is marked by dash-dot lines.

valleys and the difficult forested coastal areas. The available survey evidence and that from various excavations can be assembled into an overview of pre-state societies during the Middle Formative Period.

By about 800 B.C., from Chiapas to Puebla, in highland valleys and on both coasts, the larger tracts of fertile land had settlement networks with one or more larger centers, each with public buildings on platforms organized around a central plaza (Figure 19). Those of the Middle Formative centers known from excavation have evidence of a range of elaboration in both domestic housing and in mortuary treatment. Elite individuals were certainly buried in or near the ceremonial structures, and in some cases they appear to have lived in segregated residential areas. In many of these networks, nearby hamlets must have been directly tributary to these centers (Brumfiel 1976; Steponaitis 1981), and there is evidence that exotic materials were obtained by major centers and redistributed to smaller settlements (Wheeler 1975), often for the manufacture of artifacts in the widespread Olmec style (Flannery 1968). This pattern

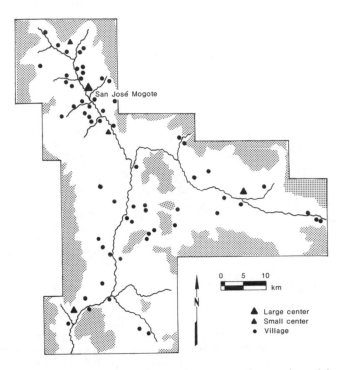

Figure 20 The Valley of Oaxaca during the Rosario Phase (adapted from Feinman et al. 1985, fig. 7).

had developed during the preceding Early Formative Period. Though there is evidence of the overthrow of centers and rise of new elites, the social pattern, and the elaborate iconography that must have communicated elite privilege (Drennan 1976b), proved durable. It seems likely that these were complex chiefdoms with two and sometimes three levels of control hierarchy and with populations ranging from a thousand to more than 9000 individuals (Heizer 1960).

Oaxaca is here taken as an example of the development from societies of the sort just outlined toward more complex forms because we have both high quality survey data, much of it fully published, as well as precisely recovered excavation data from a range of both larger and smaller surveyed sites. During the Rosario Phase of the earlier Middle Formative Period, the major center of the Valley of Oaxaca at San Jose Mogote in the northern arm of the valley was refurbished (Figure 20). The public buildings were reconstructed on a massive scale (Flannery and

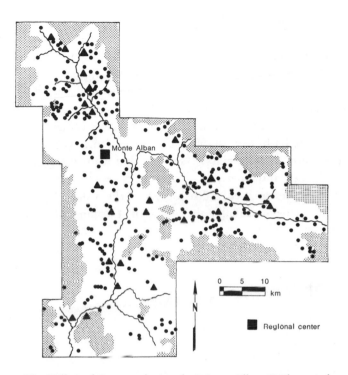

Figure 21 The Valley of Oaxaca during the Monte Alban II Phase (adapted from Feinman et al. 1985, fig. 11). Dots represent village occupation sometimes recording several adjacent hamlets or villages.

Marcus 1983:59). Immediately around San Jose Mogote was a dense cluster of hamlets. Small subsidiary centers with only a few mounds and limited evidence of elite residence in this period existed beyond this cluster (Drennan 1976a). A similar settlement network existed in the south arm of the valley, though a detailed survey of its center is not yet available. These two units, each with about 2000 inhabitants, were separated by a sparsely inhabited area in the center of the valley, suggesting that they were independent and perhaps antagonistic. A rank-size curve for any one cluster would have a concave or "primo-convex" form; one for the several clusters in and around the Valley of Oaxaca combined might have a convex distribution.

In the succeeding early Monte Alban I Phase, major changes take place, though unfortunately neither maps nor graphs are yet available. San Jose Mogote and other Rosario Phase centers are abandoned. Population is nucleated both on top of the high peak of Monte Alban overlooking the juncture of the three arms of the valley and in a dense cluster of hamlets around the foot of Monte Alban. Monte Alban appears at this time to be three spatially discrete settlements. Blanton (1978:37–40) has suggested that it was founded as a result of a confederation between three centers of formerly independent chiefdoms. However there is little excavation evidence with which such a proposition might be evaluated. By Late Monte Alban I times, the plaza of the great center and its major public buildings had been established (Flannery and Marcus 1983:87–91), several kilometers of massive surrounding walls were begun (Blanton 1978:52–54), and a network of secondary centers developed as population became more evenly distributed in the valley (Blanton et al. 1982:37–69). This is probably the period of state emergence in the area of Oaxaca.

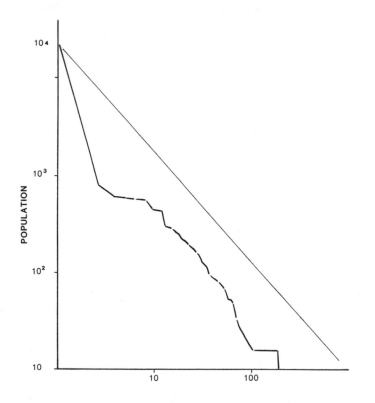

Figure 22 Settlement rank-size curve for the Monte Alban II Phase.

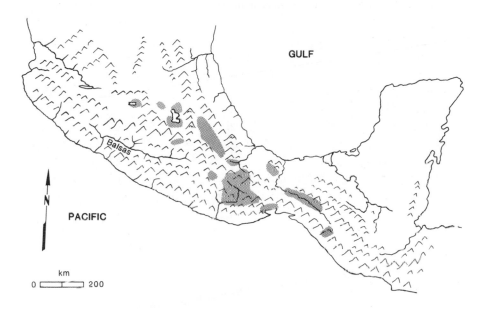

Figure 23 Known settled zones of the later 1st millennium B.C. (the Late Formative Period) in central Mesoamerica.

By Monte Alban II times (Figure 21) the hierarchical pattern of society is fully formed, with successively smaller elite residences and temples at subsidiary and local centers (Flannery and Marcus 1983). By this time there is evidence of Monte Alban control well beyond the confines of the Valley of Oaxaca, and it is possible that established population is being moved out of the valley into newly conquered regions, as is discussed below. The rank size graph shows a "primo-convex" curve with Monte Alban much larger than any other center, as one expects of a transregional center controlling many diverse regions (Figure 22).

Stepping back at this point and looking at central Mesoamerica during the Terminal Formative Period about 100 B.C., just before the rise of Teotihuacan to transregional status (Figure 23), it seems clear that there were a number of large polities in existence, though the political complexity of most remains poorly defined, and some may yet be unrecognized. On present evidence, the network of perhaps six large primary states spanned a distance of about 1100 kilometers, from the Basin of Mexico to the Peten. However, there is not much evidence of a continuation of the direct interaction of Early and Middle Formative times over

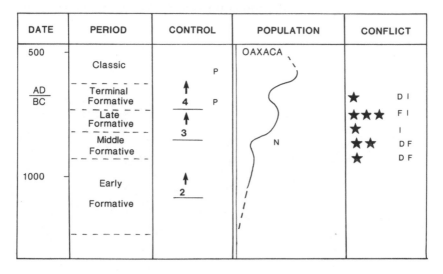

Figure 24 Changes through time in control hierarchies, population, and conflict in central Mesoamerica. Control column: 2–4 = number of levels of central political control hierarchies; P = palatial residences. Population column: curve = relative population changes based on site area; N = period of rapid nucleation. Conflict column: stars = intensity of conflict; sources of assessment: D = destruction and major settlement abandonment; F = major fortifications; I = iconic representations.

this broad geographical span until the ascendency of Tikal and Teotihuacan during the Classic Period.

The pattern of the development of control hierarchies is presented in simplified form in the third column of Figure 24. Two levels of control are demonstrable for the later Early Formative and earlier Middle Formative. A brief phase at the end of the Middle Formative may have had three levels, but four-level hierarchies were probably established by Late Formative times. The population curve indicates that the shift to three and thence four levels occurs during a period of rapid population growth, so rapid that it must be due to nucleation rather than to local biological reproduction alone. With full consolidation of the state and expansion beyond the confines of the valley in Terminal Formative times, there was apparently a drop in population in the valley, perhaps because of colonization. Conflict occurs throughout this sequence. Even during the time of the earlier Middle Formative chiefdoms there were shifts in the locations of centers, destruction layers, and mutilated pieces of bodies, all indicating raiding. The move to Monte Alban itself, with attendant nucleation on some of the poorer tracts in the Valley of Oaxaca, may well represent a confederation in response to pressure by hostile forces. Certainly the new lords of Monte Alban constructed fortifications, and embellished their center with representations of slain and mutilated elite individuals (Marcus 1983a:90–96), suggesting that a major concern was the destruction of opposing elites. Finally, there is concrete archaeological evidence that Monte Alban II forces conquered and controlled centers outside the Valley and imposed strongpoints on these areas (Spencer 1982; Redmond 1983). Conquest glyphs at Monte Alban apparently record such campaigns (Marcus 1983b:106–108). It is notable that the state building process in central Mesoamerica was very rapid in comparison with other areas. It is possible that rapid nucleation is related to the benefits that rulers could gain from forced intensification of food production in maize centered production systems. Complex control hierarchies develop in a time of increasing warfare and nucleating population.

The Central Andes

The regional structure of the Andes, with its juxtaposition of mountains and lowlands, shows a superficial resemblance to that of the Old World cases cited above. However, the Pacific coast is a series of small river valleys separated by very arid desert, and the mountains have very strong vertical zonation, passing rapidly from subtropical river valleys—tributaries of the Amazon—to Alpine punas. To the east are vast rain forests. Early Peruvians had adopted or developed very different suites of crops to accommodate this extreme diversity, but several, maize in the lower areas and various tubers at high altitudes, had potential for increased productivity with intensification. The domestication of camelids facilitated transport and thus exchange between regions. Under any circumstances, however, travel was not easy in the central Andes, particularly across the trend of the mountains.

The north coast of Peru is the birthplace of modern archaeological survey. The Virú Valley project of W. Duncan Strong, Clifford Evans, James A. Ford, Donald Collier, and Gordon Willey, with strong encouragement from Julian Steward himself, produced the first comprehensive regional study with a detailed—albeit not total—surface survey, aided by the magnificent architectural preservation in the dry coastal areas (Willey 1953). Unfortunately, this outstanding beginning was not immediately pursued. Work by D. Browman, L. Lumbreras, C. Morris, M.

Figure 25 Archaeological survey in the central Andes to 1985. Stippled areas mark intensive surveys for which published period maps and site tabulations are available. Hatched areas are some of the larger important tracts for which only partial survey data or none at all are available.

Moseley, J. Parsons, D. Proulx, and others, much of which remains unpublished, was underway by 1970. Survey coverage (Figure 25) has been spotty and many important valleys on both the coast and the highlands await systematic survey and publication. Nonetheless, a broad picture of Andean development during the Early Horizon and First Intermediate Period can be assembled from existing excavation and survey evidence.

By 800 B.C. the valleys of the north coast had long traditions of sedentary life and social differentiation (Figure 26). Many had a major center with characteristic platforms, courtyards, and other structures; some of these had associated elaborate residences. Both the buildings and

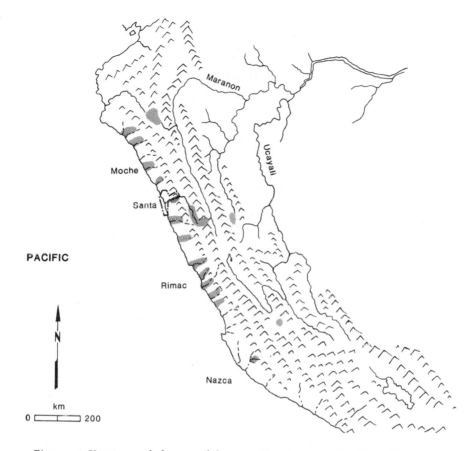

Figure 26 Known settled areas of the 1st millennium B.C. (the Early Horizon) in the central Andes. The Santa Valley, detailed in Figures 27 and 29, is marked by a dash-dot line.

items of daily use, such as ceramics and fabrics, had the characteristic Chavin iconography widespread throughout the central Andes (Benson 1971). Smaller settlements with a few platforms, or with only modest huts are widespread, and some valleys have small fortifications. A few such centers are known from the inner valleys of the Andes, and it seems likely that future survey in these more difficult areas will reveal similar settlement systems throughout these valleys and perhaps even in the rainforests. While these societies were probably a mixture of various types of chiefdoms, those to the south (which participated to some extent in the same exchange and iconographic systems) seem to have lacked large centers and probably had little or no permanent control hierarchy.

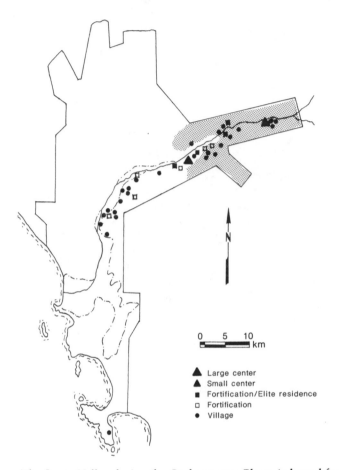

Figure 27 The Santa Valley during the Cayhuamarca Phase (adapted from Wilson 1985, figs. 23–25).

A well-documented case of development from such a basis is provided by David Wilson's (1985) recently completed survey of the Santa Valley. Here, data are available for a total coverage on foot of the valley and adjacent desert from the coast well into the mountains. Though Santa is well watered and is geologically well preserved, it is small, and Wilson argues that it was not itself a center of primary state formation. It is nonetheless interesting as an illustration of developmental processes in an area affected by nearby primary states. By the Cayhuamarca Phase of the later Early Horizon (Figure 27), a society of the sort outlined above was well established. There are two ceremonial centers, the upstream one perhaps founded earlier. Neither was a major population center, but both had nearby elite residential areas. There are a number of fortified centers, some with elite residences, and many small villages and hamlets. The rank-size curve is primo-convex like that of the Suse Phase in Iran (Figure 28). Study of subsistence and population shows that the upper valley had to bring food from elsewhere, probably the lower valley, precluding persistent intravalley conflict, and placement of fortifications indicates that the threat was from other valleys.

This pattern continued, with local movement of centers and other settlements, for many centuries. Indeed, by the 1st century A.D. when states were probably emerging in the Moche and Chicama valleys to the north, Late Suchimancillo Phase settlement was qualitatively similar to Cayhuamarca, though there are more settlements, and the subsidiary centers were more regularly spaced (Figure 29). The rank-size curve (Figure 30) is convex showing that these centers were little different in size and were perhaps competitive with one another, even though actual conflict in such a small valley would be unlikely. In the succeeding Guadalupito Phase, the settlement pattern was centered in the lower valley and reorganized with Moche-style center and village architecture and craft goods. Conquest and absorption in the Moche state of later First Intermediate times seems likely.

The Moche state was one of several multivalley polities along the

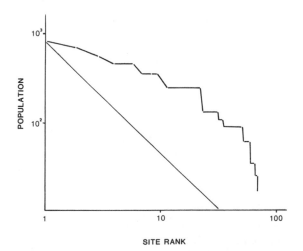

Figure 28 Settlement rank-size curve for the Cayhuamarca Phase.

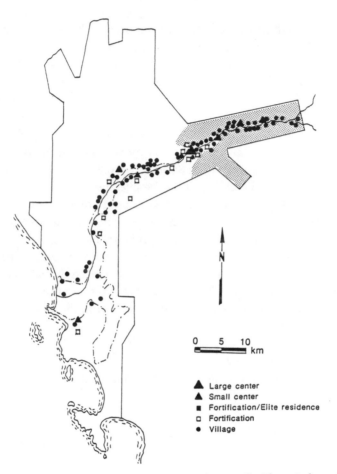

Figure 29 The Santa Valley during the Late Suchimancillo Phase (adapted from Wilson 1985, figs. 87–89). Dots mark village occupation sometimes recording several adjacent villages or hamlets.

coast (Figure 31). Several of the richer mountain valleys and basins, certainly Titicaca (Kolata 1982) and perhaps Cajamarca and other even less well-known valleys, had complex hierarchical organization, but many subsequently important highland regions were inhabited only by village societies (Isbell 1983). The network of ten or more primary states spanned at least 1200 kilometers.

The time chart (Figure 32) shows the suggested development of central control hierarchies for the Virú Valley, which should be closely linked to developments in Moche-Chicama. There is a long period of two level hierarchies, though perhaps, as elsewhere, with the occasional emergence of three levels, beginning in the Initial Period. Three level central control hierarchies are indicated by settlement hierarchy, by the architecture of the castillos, by mortuary evidence, and by exchange evidence, for at least the late Gallinazo Phase of the middle First Intermediate Period. The multivalley Moche polity must have had at least four levels, probably five, judging from public architecture. Relative population curves are presented for both Virú (though it is based only on a sample of sites) and Santa. Gallinazo state emergence appears to occur in a period of local population decline, but at that time population was climbing in the marginal Santa Valley. With Moche expansion, population dropped in Santa, though it was nucleated and reorganized, and rises in Virú (and no doubt Moche itself). Throughout this time there is evidence of periodic conflict. During the long pre-state period, there were fortifications and even some iconographic evidence of conflict, probably raiding between valleys. The abandonment and destruction of settlements are widely attested on the north coast early in the First Intermediate Period at the time of primary state emergence. For the Moche polity itself, there

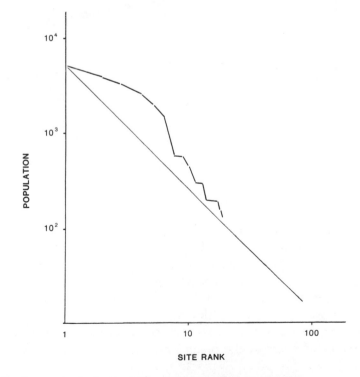

Figure 30 Settlement rank-size curve for the Late Suchimancillo Phase.

Figure 31 Known settled zones of the early 1st millennium A.D. (the First Intermediate Period) in the central Andes. The dashed line marks approximate limits of Middle Horizon Wari-related administrative installations of the late 1st millennium A.D.

is similar evidence, plus graphic representation of battles and captives in art. Thus, this limited north coast evidence indicates that, after a long period of conflict among complex chiefdoms, states emerge in areas of intense conflict and reduced population, but that with state consolidation, population was brought in from marginal areas, probably to staff the tributary apparatus. Clearly, full publication of already completed surveys in various north coast valleys and adjacent highland areas would do much to improve this preliminary assessment of the case.

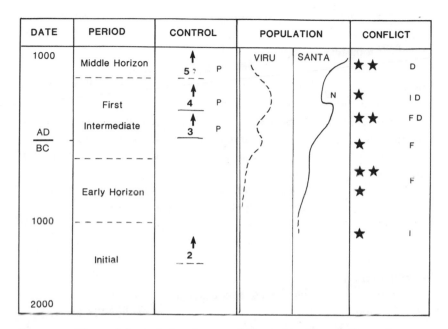

DATE	PERIOD	CONTROL	POPULATION		CONFLICT
1000	Middle Horizon	↑ 5 ? P	VIRU	SANTA	★★ D
		↑		N	★ I D
	First	4 P			★★ F D
AD	Intermediate	↑ 3 P			★ F
BC					★★ ★ F
	Early Horizon				★
1000					★ I
	Initial	↑ 2			
2000					

Figure 32 Changes through time in control hierarchies, population, and conflict in the Central Andes. Control column: 2–5 = number of levels of the central political control hierarchies; P = palatial residences. Population column: curve = relative population changes based on architecture and site areas; N = period of rapid population nucleation. Conflict column: stars = intensity of conflict; sources of assessment: D = destruction and major settlement abandonment; F = major fortifications; I = iconic representations.

Concluding Remarks

Clearly a tremendous amount of regional study has been accomplished during the past three decades, although even more remains to be done. Steward would probably be happy with what has been accomplished, even though it forces modification of some of his ideas. For example, there are indeed "regularities" in Steward's sense, but those which can be documented with our more precise archaeological record are not always in accord with those he perceived:

1. Pre-state societies with two to three levels of control hierarchy persisted for centuries, with intense competition and much replacement of centers and no doubt of paramounts, but with little or no increase in sociopolitical complexity.

2. State emergence occurs in limited areas with dense concentrations of similar-sized centers, often with populations dispersed and reduced as a result of long term competition and increasing overt conflict.

3. Correlated with the emergence of three to four level central control hierarchies, rapid population nucleation occurs, probably at the expense of defeated or threatened neighbors.

4. Coincident with these changes, the intensity of conflict increases, and in some cases one can document that raiding is replaced by organized warfare with the conquest and reorganization of surrounding areas.

We need not pursue subsequent developments. These points are enough to indicate that the gradual development that Steward perceived in the coarse-grained data available to him, and that Carneiro predicted on the basis of theoretical considerations, did not occur. State emergence is a relatively rapid, though of course not instantaneous, transformation following on a period of cyclical conflict and limited growth. The parallels between independent cases encourage further efforts to construct general explanations for these phenomena, however they are defined.

This raises a challenge for those who study the development of early civilization. The regularities set forth by Steward, and the models constructed by Wittfogel, Carneiro, and others, have guided a great deal of fruitful research leading to knowledge about the material forces important in the rise of complex chiefdoms and states. What constructs, however, will guide us in the future? These several decades of research have given us a good start in understanding material changes precedent to state formation. We have some provocative theoretical constructions regarding hierarchy formation (Johnson 1982; Reynolds 1984) and the ideological changes which facilitate such transformation (Kus 1981). However, we lack constructs which specify the relations between particular material changes and particular changes in the ideology and organization of control. This writer has argued that the central problem is why the conditions of competition within and between elites lead in some cases to a reformulation of the strategies for control (Wright 1977). However, until a more rigorous object-language can be developed to replace ordinary language statements about "power," "authority" and so on, we will have no way of expressing the principles we dimly perceive, nor of deducing testable consequences from such expressions.

Whatever our guiding constructs will be, both regional survey and large site excavation will continue within the constraints of funding, and both classical and newly devised propositions will be evaluated against this evidence. If regional surveys and small site studies are not pursued vigorously during the next two decades we may lose any possibility of retrieving the data on demography, production, and conflict needed to test both the constructs of Steward and those emerging in our day. If large site excavations are not undertaken with greater attention to representative sampling, comprehensive recovery of daily debris, and the development of very fine scale—seasonal to decadal—chronologies, we cannot hope to understand the emergence of social stratification, competition among elites, and other such processes (Fried 1967; Adams 1981; Haas 1982). One trend that transcends all these diverse approaches is an increasing interest in truly integrated archaeological and ethnohistoric studies. Such studies allow the assessment of the roles of ethnicity, ideology, and the fine details of sociopolitical processes, which are difficult to evaluate unambiguously for the earlier civilizations known solely from archaeological research. Both the later imperial phases of the early civilizations and the more recent examples of primary and secondary state formation are increasingly the object of research by anthropological archaeologists and ethnohistorians together.

Such interests raise several issues. First, few of us are trained ethnohistorians. We do not know much about the special techniques used to interpret oral and written sources; it is easy to impose ethnocentric biases in such circumstances. Second, and even more grave, integrated archaeological and ethnohistoric research involves the definition, even the control, of historical knowledge of great importance to living people. Neither such conjoint research nor ordinary archaeology can be done in today's world solely by outsiders. Fortunately, the modern tradition of regional archaeological research has never been the monopoly of one group of archaeologists. Though North American archaeologists have been involved in the initation of regional survey in many areas, both locally based archaeologists and visitors from many countries have been increasingly involved in regionally oriented studies. There has also been increasing cooperation in the fight against the illegal trade in antiquities, which leads to so much destruction of data crucial to knowledge of the past. If the challenges of landscape destruction are to be met, and knowledge of the past evolution of the cultural ecosystem on this planet is to be developed, such trends in international cooperation, as well as international funding of such endeavors, must continue.

Acknowledgments

The author is deeply indebted to David J. Meltzer, who has given me the opportunity to compose this piece and has been exceptionally patient with my frailties. The present draft has profited from comments by Robert McC. Adams, Richard E. Blanton, Joyce Marcus, and Arthur Saxe but the weaknesses are the author's alone. Unfortunately the paper was revised while many of the area specialists were in the field and unable to respond to pleas for help. Therefore, coverage of the cases depends greatly on my spotty personal knowledge. Any comments or suggestions for additions will be gratefully incorporated in future efforts to deal with this topic.

Literature Cited

Adams, Robert McC.
   1965   *Land Behind Baghdad.* University of Chicago Press, Chicago.
   1981   *The Heartland of Cities.* University of Chicago Press, Chicago.

Adams, Robert McC., and Hans J. Nissen
   1972   *The Uruk Countryside.* University of Chicago Press, Chicago.

Adler, Michael J.
   n.d.   An Investigation of Pre-Harappan State Formation. Paper on file at the Museum of Anthropology, University of Michigan, Ann Arbor.

Amiet, Pierre
   1961   *La Glyptique Mesopotamienne Archaique.* Editions du Centre National de la Recherche Scientifique, Guethner, Paris.

Benson, Elizabeth P., editor
   1971   *The Dumbarton Oaks Conference on Chavín.* Dumbarton Oaks Research Library and Collection, Washington, D. C.

Blanton, Richard
   1978   *Monte Alban: Settlement Patterns of the Ancient Zapotec Capital.* Academic Press, New York.

Blanton, Richard E., Stephen Kowalewski, Gary Feinman, and Jill Appel
   1982   Monte Alban's Hinterland: The Prehistoric Settlement Patterns of the Central and Southern Part of the Valley of Oaxaca, Mexico. *Memoirs of the Museum of Anthropology, University of Michigan* 15. Ann Arbor.

Brumfiel, Elizabeth
   1976   Regional Growth in the Eastern Valley of Mexico: A Test of the "Population Pressure" Hypothesis. In *The Early Mesoamerican Village,* edited K. V. Flannery, pages 234–249. Academic Press, New York.

Carneiro, Robert L.
   1970   A Theory of the Origin of the State. *Science* 169:733–738.

Dollfus, Geneviéve
　1978　Djaffarabad, Djowi, Bendebal: Contribution de l'étude de la Susiane au Veme millénaire et au début du IVeme millénaire. *Paléorient* 4:141–167.

Drennan, Robert D.
　1976a　Fabrica San Jose and Middle Formative Society in the Valley of Oaxaca. *Memoirs of the Museum of Anthropology, University of Michigan* 8. Ann Arbor.
　1976b　Religion and Social Evolution in Formative Mesoamerica. In *The Early Mesoamerican Village*, edited by K. V. Flannery, pages 345–368. Academic Press, New York.

Durrani, Farzand Ali
　1981　Rehman Dheri and the Birth of Civilization in Pakistan. *Bulletin of the Institute of Archaeology, University of London* 18:194–207.

Fairservis, Walter
　1956　Excavations in the Quetta Valley, Pakistan. *Anthropological Papers of the American Museum of Natural History* 45(2). New York.
　1961　The Harappan Civilization: New Evidence and More Theory. *Novitates of the American Museum of Natural History* 2055. New York.

Feinman, Gary M., Stephen A. Kowalewski, Laura Finsten, Richard E. Blanton, and Linda Nicholas
　1985　Long-term Demographic Change: A Perspective from the Valley of Oaxaca, Mexico. *Journal of Field Archaeology* 12:333–362.

Flannery, Kent V.
　1965　The Ecology of Early Food Production in Mesopotamia. *Science* 147:1247–1256.
　1968　The Olmec in the Valley of Oaxaca: A Model for Inter-regional Interaction in Formative Times. In *The Dumbarton Oaks Conference on the Olmecs*, edited by Elizabeth P. Benson, pages 79–110. Dumbarton Oaks Research Library and Collection, Washington, D. C.

Flannery, Kent V., and Joyce Marcus
　1983　*The Cloud People*. Academic Press, New York.

Frankfort, Henri-Paul, and M.-H. Pottier
　1978　Sondage préliminaire sur l'etablissement protohistorique harrapéen et post-harrapéen de Shortugai. *Ars Asiatique* 34:29–86.

Fried, Morton
　1967　*The Evolution of Political Society*. Random House, New York.

Garcia Cook, Angel
　1972　Investigaciones Arqueológias en el Estado de Tlaxcala. *Communicaciones, Proyecto Puebla-Tlaxcala* 6.
　1977　Lo Teotihuacano en Puebla. *Communicaciones, Proyecto Puebla-Tlaxcala* 14.

Gibson, McGuire
　1972　*The City and Area of Kish*. Field Research Publications, Coral Gables.

Haas, Jonathan
　1982　*The Evolution of the Prehistoric State*. Columbia University Press, New York.

Heizer, Robert F.
  1960   Agriculture and the Theocratic State in Lowland Southeastern Mexico. *American Antiquity* 26:215–225.

Isbell, William H.
  1983   State Origins in the Ayacucho Valley, Central Highlands, Peru. Paper presented at the American Anthropological Association Annual Meeting, Washington, D. C.

Jarrige, Jean-Francois
  1981   Economy and Society in the Early Chalcolithic/Bronze Age of Baluchistan: New Perspectives from Recent Excavations in Baluchistan. In *South Asian Archaeology 1979* pages 93–114. Dietrich Reiner, Berlin.

Johnson, Gregory A.
  1973   Local Exchange and Early State Development in Southwestern Iran. *Anthropological Papers of the Museum of Anthropology, University of Michigan* 51. Ann Arbor.
  1975   Locational Analysis and the Investigation of Uruk Local Exchange Systems. In *Ancient Civilizations and Trade,* edited by Jeremy Sabloff and C. C. Lamberg-Karlovsky, pages 285–331. University of New Mexico Press, Albuquerque.
  1980   Spatial Organization of Early Uruk Settlement Systems. In *L'Archéologie de l'Iraq: Perspectives et limites de l'interpretation anthropologique des documents,* edited by M.-T. Barrelet. *Colloque internationale du C.N.R.S.* 580:233–264. Centre National de la Recherche Scientifique, Paris.
  1981   Monitoring Complex System Integration and Boundary Phenomena with Settlement Size Data. In *Archaeological Approaches to the Study of Complexity,* edited by Sander E. van der Leeuw, pages 143–188. A. E. van Giffen Instituut voor Prae- en Protohistorie, Amsterdam.
  1982   Organizational Structure and Scalar Stress. In *Theory and Explanation in Archaeology,* edited by Colin Renfrew, Michael J. Rowlands, and B. A. Segraves, pages 389–421. Academic Press, New York.
  In press   The Changing Organization of Uruk Administration on the Susiana Plain. In *Archaeological Perspectives on Iran: From Prehistory to the Islamic Conquest,* edited by Frank Hole. Smithsonian Institution Press, Washington, D. C.

Kolata, Alan
  1982   Tiwanaku: Portrait of an Andean Civilization. *Field Museum of Natural History Bulletin* 53(8):13–18.

Kus, Susan M.
  1981   The Context of Complexity. In *Archaeological Approaches to the Study of Complexity,* edited by Sander E. van der Leeuw, pages 197–227. A. E. van Giffen Institut voor Prae-en Protohistorie, Amsterdam.

Lambrick, H. T.
  1967   The Indus Flood Plain and the "Indus" Civilization. *Geographical Journal* 133(4):483–495.

Le Brun, Alain, and Francois Vallat
  1978   L'origine de l'écriture à Suse. In *Cahiers de la Délégation Archéologique Francaise en Iran* 8:11–59.

Lowe, Gareth W.
 1959 Archeological Exploration of the Upper Grijalva River, Chiapas, Mexico. *Papers of the New World Archeological Foundation 3.* Provo, Utah.

MacNeish, Richard S., Frederick A. Peterson, and James A. Neely
 1972 The Archaeological Reconnaissance. In Excavations and Reconnaissance. In *The Prehistory of the Tehuacan Valley,* edited by Richard S. MacNeish, 5:341–495. University of Texas Press, Austin.

Marcus, Joyce
 1983a The First Appearance of Zapotec Writing and Calendrics. In *The Cloud People,* edited by K. V. Flannery and J. Marcus pages 91–96. Academic Press, New York.
 1983b The Conquest Slabs of Building J, Monte Alban. In *The Cloud People,* edited by K. V. Flannery and J. Marcus pages 106–108. Academic Press, New York.

Mughal, M. Rafique
 1972 Present State of Research on the Indus Valley Civilization. In *Proceedings of the International Symposium on Moenjo Daro,* pages 1–28. National Book Foundation, Karachi.
 1980 *Archaeological Surveys in Bahawalpur.* Department of Archaeology and Museums, Karachi.

Parsons, Jeffrey
 1971 Prehistoric Settlement Patterns in the Texcoco Region, Mexico. *Memoirs of the Museum of Anthropology, University of Michigan 3.* Ann Arbor.

Pollock, Susan
 1984 Style and Information: An Analysis of Susiana Ceramics. *Journal of Anthropological Archaeology* 2:354–390.

Raikes, Robert L.
 1964 The End of the Ancient Cities of the Indus. *American Anthropologist* 66(2):284–299.

Redmond, Elsa M.
 1983 A Fuego y Sangre: Early Zapotec Imperialism in the Cuicatlan Canada, Oaxaca. *Memoirs of the Museum of Anthropology, University of Michigan* 16. Ann Arbor.

Reynolds, Robert G.
 1984 A Computational Model of Hierarchical Decision Making Systems. *Journal of Anthropological Archaeology* 3(3):159–189.

Sanders, William T.
 1965 *The Cultural Ecology of the Teotihuacan Valley.* Department of Sociology and Anthropology, University Park, Pennsylvania.

Schmandt-Besserat, Denise
 1979 An Archaic Recording System in the Uruk-Jemdet Nasr Period. *American Journal of Archaeology* 83:19–48.

Sisson, Edward B.
  1970 Settlement Patterns and Land Use in Northeastern Chontolpa, Tabasco, Mexico: A Progress Report. *Ceramicas de Cultura Maya* 6:41–54.

Spencer, Charles S.
  1982 *The Cuicatlan Canada and Monte Alban.* Academic Press, New York.

Spores, Ronald
  1972 An Archaeological Settlement Survey of the Nochixtlan Valley, Oaxaca. *Vanderbilt University Publications in Anthropology* 1. Nashville.

Steponaitas, Vincas
  1981 Settlement Hierarchies and Political Complexity in Non-Market Societies: The Formative Period in the Valley of Mexico. *American Anthropologist* 83:320–362.

Steward, Julian
  1955 Culture Causality and Law: A Trial Formulation of the Development of Early Civilizations. In *A Theory of Culture Change,* pages 178–209. Free Press, Glencoe.
  1977 Wittfogel's Irrigation Hypothesis. In *Evolution and Ecology,* edited by J. C. Steward and Robert F. Murphy, pages 85–99. University of Illinois Press, Urbana.

Strommenger, Eva
  1979 Ausgrabungen der Deutschen Orient Gesellschaft in Habuba Kabira. In *Archaeological Reports from the Tabqa Dam Project—Euphrates Valley, Syria,* edited by David N. Freedman, pages 63–78. American Schools of Oriental Research, Philadelphia.

Sumner, William
  1972 *Cultural Development in the Kur River Basin, Iran.* University Microfilms, Ann Arbor.

Weiss, Harvey
  1983 Excavations at Tell Leilan and the Origins of North Mesopotamian Cities in the Third Millennium B.C. *Paléorient* 9(2):39–52.

Weiss, Harvey, and T. Cuyler Young, Jr.
  1975 The Merchants of Susa. *Iran* 13:1–17.

Wheeler, Jane C.
  1975 Formative Mesoamerican Exchange Networks with Special Reference to the Valley of Oaxaca. *Memoir of the Museum of Anthropology, University of Michigan* 7. Ann Arbor.

Willey, Gordon R.
  1953 Prehistoric Settlement Patterns in the Virú Valley, Perú. *Bureau of American Ethnology Bulletin* 155.

Wilson, David J.
  1985 Prehispanic Settlement Patterns in the Lower Santa Valley, North Coast of Peru: A Regional Perspective on the Origins and Development of Complex Society. Doctoral dissertation, Department of Anthropology, University of Michigan, Ann Arbor.

Wittfogel, Karl
 1957   *Oriental Despotism.* Yale University Press, New Haven.

Wright, Henry T.
 1977   Recent Research on the Origin of the State. *Annual Review of Anthropology* 6:379–397.
 1984   Prestate Political Formations. In *On the Evolution of Complex Societies: Essays in Honor of Harry Hoijer 1982,* edited by Timothy K. Earle, pages 41–77. Undena Press, Los Angeles.
 1985   Preliminary Excavations of IVth Millennium Levels on the Northern Acropolis of Susa: 1978. *National Geographic Research Reports* 19:725–734.

Wright, Henry T., and Susan Pollock
 1985   Regional Socio-economic Organization in Southern Mesopotamia: The Middle and Late Fifth Millennium B.C. In *La Mesopotamie: pré- et protohistoire,* edited by J.-L. Huot. Editions du Centre Nationale de Recherche Scientifique, Paris.

Wright, Henry T., Richard W. Redding, and Naomi Miller
 1980   Time and Process in an Uruk Rural Center. In L'Archéologie de l'Iraq: Perspectives et limites de l'interpretation anthropologique des documents, edited by M.-T. Barrelet. *Collogue internationale du C.N.R.S. 580.* Centre National de la Recherche Scientifique, Paris.

Current Trends and Future Prospects

Archaeological Applications of Mathematical and Formal Methods

Introduction

This paper is about archaeological uses of mathematical or formal logical techniques and concepts that go beyond the simple tabulation and inspection of measurements, counts, and proportions. Actually, the point at which even these simple operations become more than routine is a bit vague, and I will not hesitate to discuss some aspects of their use and misuse. I include statistics as a subset of mathematics. The connection with computer applications is more tenuous. Computers present us with a body of extremely useful technology, partly for implementing mathematical and logical techniques, and partly for quite different purposes.

It is useful to think rather distinctly of three broad categories: archaeological observations, analytical methods, and sociocultural theory. Analytical methods provide the connections between observations and theory. Some theory is expressed directly in mathematical terms, but, as I will argue below, at present the vast majority of archaeological uses of mathematical and formal techniques pertain to the domain of analytical methods or to the design of data collection.

There is room for improvement in many of the mathematical techniques themselves, both in general terms and in developing techniques based on models that more closely approximate realistic archaeological situations. I will not, however, say much about the mathematics. One reason is that only a few of us will participate directly in this. Most of the developments will continue to be made by statisticians and applied mathematicians who have little or no contact with archaeological problems. Even the exceptions, although they will be very important, will be produced by the few persons who combine a practical sense of archaeological conditions with the capacity for creative mathematics, or who are at least able to communicate well with mathematicians. A second reason is that the realms of data and theory are far more in need of improvement. At present it is all too easy to find examples where the power and sophistication of the mathematics far outstrip both the relevance and reliability of the data and the depth or interestingness of the theory. It can be something like using a Rolls Royce to pull a wooden plow to cultivate nettles and thistles.

Improvement of mathematical techniques will remain a specialized task, but most of us can contribute to better theory, and all of us can, and indeed *must*, take pains to improve our data. It is a serious mistake to think that mathematical analysis, by and large, is theory-building. It is a disastrous mistake to think that sophisticated analysis obviates the need for data of very much higher quality than archaeologists have customarily obtained.

I will begin with a very brief discussion of the bearing of computers on formal techniques. After that, I will elaborate on the relations between mathematical analysis and sociocultural theory. Then I will discuss some of the most serious problems about data quality. Finally, I will offer an assessment of the current situation for some major topics in mathematical and formal approaches.

Computers

The impact of the affordable personal computer has been genuinely revolutionary. For decades computers were really used by only a minority of archaeologists. Quite suddenly this has changed. Most archaeologists are now accustomed to using computers for word processing, many are using database management systems, and interest in computer graphics is growing very rapidly. The continuously plummeting cost of computing has reached the point where, for a one-time investment of a few thousand dollars, one can acquire the hardware and software to do quite interesting things, with no further major expense except one's own time. Also, except perhaps in the climatic extremes of arctic cold or tropical heat and humidity, it is feasible to do very substantial computing in the field, without having to worry much about links to a mainframe at some home base.

We hear a lot about "user-friendly" software. It is at least equally important to note the great increase in "computer-friendly" archaeologists. The relevance of this for mathematical and formal methods is that many (though by no means all) of the useful techniques are not feasible without the aid of computer technology, and that awe of computers should no longer either impede their use nor distract us from down-to-earth pragmatic evaluation of results.

Relations Between Analysis of Data and Sociocultural Theory

Most applications of statistics and other mathematical concepts and techniques in archaeology fall into one of two quite distinct categories. One is designing research, summarizing important aspects of data, and generally manipulating data in ways that will bring out the aspects most relevant for specific purposes, especially for making well-warranted culture-historical inferences and for evaluating and improving sociocultural theory. The other is the direct use of mathematics for expressing sociocultural theory.

A surprisingly high proportion of the archaeological literature about mathematical and formal methods concentrates on the methods themselves and has very little or nothing to say about explicit sociocultural theory (except insofar as some general theoretical propositions may be included in the assumptions that justify certain models or procedures). Other publications use *results* of mathematical and/or formal methods to test, support, challenge, or suggest theoretical propositions, but the theory itself is rarely couched in mathematical terms. Finally, only a few publications use mathematics directly for expressing sociocultural theory. In fact, outside of simulation and modeling and applications of ideas from mathematical geography, I cannot think of good examples.

The split is not simply due to different workers with different interests. I find the distinction very evident in my own work. There have been a number of papers (e.g., Cowgill 1968, 1970, 1972, 1974, 1977, 1982) that examined aspects of various formal procedures in some detail. There was explicit concern that the results of these procedures should be useful for some important archaeological purposes, but almost nothing about specific topics in theory. In other papers (e.g., Cowgill 1975, 1979, 1983) I have addressed various issues in sociocultural theory, but have made almost no use of explicit mathematics. In my 1975 paper on population, the equation $p_t = p_0 (1 + r)^t$ was central to some of the points that I made, but it was relegated to a footnote. In the other papers a few inequalities and ordinal relationships were important, but I did not see any need to go beyond the words of ordinary English to express them. The only paper that combines substantial use of formal techniques and substantial discussion of theory is Cowgill et al. (1984) and in that paper we emphasized difficulties in connecting theory with results of formal analyses.

If I tried, perhaps I could come up with theory that was more mathematical, but the fact is that I have not been motivated to do so. The concepts and issues in theory that interest me do not come from reading or reflecting on mathematical concepts. Many of them come, of course, from the writing and talk of other archaeologists. Most of the rest of them come from the work of other social scientists, to some extent social anthropologists, but especially social and economic historians.

There will always be some people who will fix on any newly fashionable mathematical idea that comes along, treating it as a hammer for which there must be some archaeological nails somewhere. These efforts should not be altogether discouraged; some of them may prove useful. Most of them, however, result only in gimmicks and the occasional bandwagon, and we do well to regard the enthusiasts with skepticism.

The most promising efforts to express aspects of theory in mathematical or quasi-mathematical terms have been in the fields of mathematical and economic geography, and the simulation of sociocultural systems (e.g., Clarke 1977; Hodder 1978a, 1978b; Hodder and Orton 1976; Renfrew and Cooke 1979; Sabloff 1981; Smith 1976). However, many of the former have been highly controversial (such as attempts to apply central place models), and the more thoughtful simulation efforts have ended by stressing how very much more we need to know to make the models good enough to be very enlightening (e.g., Aldenderfer 1981).

Paleodemography makes highly effective use of a substantial body of applied mathematics. However, the mathematics are concerned with describing and estimating vital rates and population structures, and the central problem of all demography, contemporary as well as paleo, is devising sociocultural theory that can explain, rather than merely describe, population changes. So, in this case as well, the mathematics pertain to data analysis rather than to sociocultural theory.

Thus, formal methods are extremely useful for the ordering and analysis of archaeologically recovered traces of ancient activities, but the problems of connecting the results with sociocultural theory remain formidable. I see two reasons for this, one of which is peculiar to archaeology. Sociocultural theory is about people, societies, and cultural traditions, but the objects and deposits we can actually observe have very complex relations to the things theory is about. Archaeologists have always more or less known this, and some have felt that the difficulties were overwhelming and retreated from trying to do serious sociocultural interpretation. Others have dealt with the problem by greatly underestimating it. Some of the "new archaeology" efforts of the 1960s seem to have been covertly guided by a "Hansel and Gretel" model: like the trail of breadcrumbs in the woods, people of the past thoughtfully left trails of objects to mark out just what they did where. One of the great merits of the work of Michael Schiffer (1972, 1976, 1983) is that he has made us far more aware than we were that observable structure in the archaeological record is not just an incomplete, biased, and partially disordered reflection of structure in ancient sociocultural phenomena. There are many things, natural processes as well as ancient ways of dealing with discards, that can introduce new and different patterning. This means that there is usually a long and complex road between the identification and description of structure in the archaeological record and its accepted interpretation in terms of ancient sociocultural phenomena. Formal techniques can help us to move along this road, but the central insights must come from ethnoarchaeology, experimental archaeology, and taphonomy.

The second problem in connecting results of formal analyses with theory is one that we probably share with all the sciences; certainly with all the social sciences. It is, I hope, widely understood that valid objections to an "inductive" or "empiricist" approach do not hinge on the possibility of making archaeology purely deductive—of somehow sidestepping or transcending the need for inductive steps. They are ineluctible parts of the theory-building process in any science that claims to be truly about anything outside our minds. The controversy, instead, is between those who assume that the kinds of inductive steps that are most useful for theory are easy and obvious and those who argue instead that the steps are hard and not obvious. The former believe that usually "the facts speak for themselves." The difficulties with this idea have been discussed at length by other archaeologists, notably by Lewis Binford (1985 and earlier), and I will not further belabor the point. Of course, we should not be too dogmatic; many highly relevant and useful inductions, especially in everyday life, really are simple and obvious. But many others are not. This is especially the case as one approaches theoretical frontiers.

I will make one further observation on this. I do not think that the tendency for empiricists to hesitate to generalize "before all the facts are in" is necessarily due to intellectual timidity; of being, as Kent Flannery (1967) once put it, "deathly afraid of being wrong." If the implications of data are simple and obvious, then faulty conclusions will be due mainly to faulty data, rather than to faulty reasoning. Furthermore, there is no great problem about what kinds of data are needed. The only large task is to go out and get them. If, however, the relevant inductions are not obvious and not simple, then heuristics become a major problem. It is important to begin reasoning while the data are imperfect and highly incomplete, partly because the reasoning itself is problematic and should be a subject of discussion within the archaeological community, and partly because not all the kinds of relevant data are obvious. Our early inductive efforts are immensely valuable in leading us to recognize new aspects of data that are highly relevant for theory.

Granted, then, that some kind of hard reasoning has to mediate between "raw" data (more properly, observations interpreted in terms of very widely shared and accepted concepts) and the construction and testing of explicit theory, we can ask where mathematics fits in. A view that was implicit in much of the "new archaeology" literature of the 1960s, and that probably still persists, is that statistical and/or other mathematical methods can provide most of the hard reasoning. In other words, although "the facts" do not speak for themselves, there are statistical and mathematical techniques which, when applied to the data, will generate results whose relevance for theory *is* obvious and unproblematic.

I do not think this is so. I am especially skeptical of the variant that suggests that the harder and more abstruse the math, the easier all the rest of the reasoning will be. Often, the formal part of developing implications that are highly relevant for theory can be very simple, perhaps no more than computing and displaying some well-chosen percentages.

Have I said anything very surprising? Doubtless many who never cared for math anyhow will feel that they already understood the limits of formal approaches. But I am not suggesting that mathematical and statistical methods are of limited value; I am saying that they only complement other kinds of hard work; they do not substitute for other things. In particular, richness of mathematical concepts cannot remedy poverty of sociocultural concepts. The remedy for the latter has to come from a much greater acquaintance with the other social disciplines, most obviously sociocultural anthropology, but also and especially the work of historians.

To help us think better about the links between data and theory and the problems of induction, I propose that we distinguish the terms "uniformity" and "regularity." By a "uniformity" I mean a statistically warranted statement about a relationship or pattern between or among the values of two or more variables. The statement refers to the values of these variables that are exhibited by the elements of some population. However, usually we have only observed the values of the variables for the elements of a subset or sample of the population. By "statistically warranted" I mean that there is strong or at least satisfactory reason to think that the relationship observed in the sample is neither accidental nor an artifact of measurement errors or bias in sample selection; in other words, the observed relationship in the sample is difficult to explain unless a rather similar relationship occurs in the population.

In contrast, I suggest that we limit the term "regularity" to a logically deduced consequence of a coherent body of theory. Examples of uniformities include the observation that bodies that are free to move without constraint or friction, regardless of composition, move toward the center of the earth at a constant rate of acceleration; that tides rise and fall in very predictable patterns that are related to the positions of the Moon and Sun; and formulas that enable one to predict quite accurately the future positions of the planets. All of these become regularities only when they are deduced from a theory, such as the Newtonian laws of motion and gravitation.

Many writers (e.g., Tilly 1984:33) use the terms "regularity" and "uniformity" as synonyms. The idea of systematically contrasting them was suggested to me by Julian Steward's usage (Steward 1955:88). However, I should say at once that the contrast I am proposing is not the same as Steward's. For him, uniformities referred to resemblances between different societies that were explainable by the fact that the societies were linked by processes of cultural transmission, while regularities were resemblances that reflect the independent operation of causal processes in unrelated societies. Steward's contrast is important, and I have appropriated the term "uniformity" in a different sense only because I do not think that Steward's usage has been very widely adopted.

What I mean by a uniformity, then, is any empirically discovered pattern that does not seem to be accidental. Merely stating a uniformity does not get us very far toward understanding or explanation. "All ravens are black" is an example of a proposed uniformity. In contrast, a regularity is a pattern that is implied by some body of theory about the causal connections between various phenomena. If, for example, a body of biological and evolutionary theory implies that black ravens will be better adapted than ravens of other colors, and moreover implies that a trait can be explained by showing that it has adaptive value, then the statement "according to this theory, all ravens will be black" is a proposed regularity. It may be helpful to remember that the word "regularity" is derived from a Latin word meaning "rule," and thus it at least connotes, if it does not denote, the idea of something lawful. "Uniformity" seems to me a much more passive term, with no such connotation. (Note that "statistical laws" are not necessarily synonymous with uniformities. It is perfectly possible for a regularity to be a probabilistic statement.)

Now the point of all this is that the vast majority of statistical methods are concerned with (1) identifying uniformities in samples, (2) describing uniformities in samples, and (3) making the fullest and most effective use of sample evidence as it bears on what is reasonable to think about the extent to which similar uniformities may be present in populations represented by the samples. The issue is seriously confused because we are used to talking about statistical "hypothesis testing." In most cases, *statistical* hypotheses are about uniformities, and these should be thought of as quite distinct from *scientific* hypotheses, which are about regularities. Statistical hypothesis tests are usually concerned with how good the evidence is that some proposed uniformity actually exists in some sampled population. It may be fairly easy to see that simple statistics mostly involve the search for evidence of uniformities, but this is also true of most applications of more advanced techniques, such as principal components analysis, the general linear model, and discrete multivariate analysis. Nearly all social scientists, not just archaeologists, are too prone to treat the results of multivariate analysis as statements about *regularities,* when in fact in most cases they should be regarded as indications of *uniformities.* The results do not have any simple or direct bearing on regularities unless the investigator steps in strongly and knowingly to direct and constrain the analysis in the light of explicit theory.

To come at the same thing from a slightly different angle, everyone knows that "correlation is not causality." Introductory statistics texts commonly give examples of bivariate correlations that are not accidental but are nevertheless only explainable as the outcome of more complex multivariate causal links, such as the positive correlation between numbers of sandflies and sales of ice cream at the beach. Unfortunately, we too easily forget this when the statistics become more multivariate and complex. To be sure, many of the techniques can be used to get at regularities, *provided* all the variables likely to be relevant have been included, all have been well measured and appropriately expressed, and all plausible linear and nonlinear forms of functional relations between variables have been adequately imagined by the researcher and tested for by the mathematical model or models. But what if not all of the above has been well done? The result is likely to be something that sort of fits, that accounts for ("explains" in the quite peculiar sense of that term used by statisticians) perhaps 40% to 70% of the data variance—far more than could often be achieved by accident, but far less than we would like. It is a *dead wrong* strategy to take the outcome of such procedures as an imperfect *theory;* that is, as the best foundation upon which to build better theory. Unless theory was strongly used to guide the analyses from the beginning, statistical results should be taken as evidence for uniformities, and uniformities should be taken as symptoms of possible regularities. The statistical analysis is only one part of the inductive process.

My discussion bears on the Salmons' "statistical relevance" approach to scientific explanation (Salmon and Salmon 1979). I am enthusiastic about this approach, but, as the Salmons point out, *just* statistical relevance is not enough. It has to be coupled with postulates about causality. To use statistical relevance as the only criterion would lead to endlessly piling up well warranted uniformities, without ever getting to any regularities.

Please make no mistake about this. I am not denouncing statistical methods. Most emphatically, I am not, repeat not, suggesting that we should bypass or ignore them in trying to connect data and theory. There are plenty of examples, to be sure, where intelligent use of very simple statistics would have been far better than some ill-conceived attempt to use abstruse techniques. In general, however, statistics can be extremely useful to us. I am particularly attracted, as are many other archaeologists, to the "robust" techniques of "exploratory data analysis" (Tukey 1977; Mosteller and Tukey 1977; Mosteller et al. 1983), techniques that are often quite simple and well adapted to the nonnormality and general untidiness of much archaeological data. I simply urge that we not mistake the results of most statistical analyses for theory. We must understand that even when the results are expressed in law-like form, they are usually really uniformities that are useful clues about regularities, rather than themselves regularities. It is no mean task to identify and characterize uniformities; the fallacy lies in thinking that that is the only hard job that needs to be done to connect data and theory.

The distinction between uniformities and regularities also offers clarification of Flannery's (1973) well-known contrast between the "law and order" and the "serutan" (or systems) approaches. Spaulding (1973) was absolutely correct in insisting that exactly the same logic of verification applies to systems approaches as to any other body of theory. The difference is that the "law and order" approach, as described by Flannery, seems too narrowly inductive and is likely to mistake the accumulation of well-warranted uniformities for the building of theory.

What are the implications of my arguments? On the inductive side, we simply have to recognize that there is a gap between uniformities and theory that has to be bridged (or sometimes leapt) by creative imagination, by processes that are not likely to be reduced to algorithmic forms. On the deductive side, we should spend less time testing null hypotheses (whose rejection usually implies that an observed sample property is probably also a property of the relevant population) and more time assessing the fit between data and implications logically deduced from explicit theory. In doing so, it is not very useful to merely establish that the data fit the implications of theory better than would be expected by chance. It is far more useful to look at the discrepancies between data and theory. These discrepancies do not simply suggest that a theory urgently needs to be superseded by a better theory; they are apt to be among the best heuristic devices, as we re-enter the inductive phase of the scientific cycle, for suggesting how theory might be improved. Richard Gould (1980) calls this (rather unhappily I think) "argument by anomaly." It is probably better expressed as simply paying close attention to the residuals or discrepancies. One nice example is Robert Zeitlin's (1982) interpretation in sociopolitical terms of the ways in which proportions of obsidian from various sources fail to fit the implications of a simple gravity distance decay model.

Data and Data Analysis

So far I have talked about the relation between data analysis and theory. It is time to turn to the relation between observations and data analysis. Stephen Dyson has recently referred to "the criticism made by some Northern European archaeologists that archaeologists working in the Americas have overrefined their post-excavation analytical skills while not making comparable advances in field methods" (Dyson 1985:456). I disagree because I do not think our analytical skills are the least bit overrefined in relation to the demands made by the topics in culture history and theory with which we would like to deal. However, I strongly agree that there is far too often a disparity between the sophistication of the analyses and the quality of the data on which they are based. Sophisticated formal and mathematical techniques simply cannot remedy the problems caused by poor data. Mathematical concepts can, however, aid in a discussion of some of the problems.

First, there is the myth of "total survey coverage." Plog et al. (1978) show that although all the large and conspicuous sites may be reliably found in open landscapes, no surveys have yet reached the level of intensity at which a still more intensive survey fails to reveal additional inconspicuous but significant occurrences of archaeological data. In order to be able to even begin to compare the results of one survey with another, we must *routinely* describe the exact procedures used, and recognize that more intensive survey would always modify the picture.

Of course, a great deal of survey work does not even aspire toward total coverage; frequently some kind of sampling is used. If one must sample, I have only a few general guidelines to suggest. It would be good to do at least a quick preliminary coverage of the entire region, in order to locate all the large conspicuous occurrences; this will ensure that we do not miss Teotihuacan in a survey of the Teotihuacan Valley. Next, both statistical theory and practical expediency suggest that one should make the fullest possible use of sociocultural theory and prior knowledge of the region in order to stratify the survey area according to theoretically relevant criteria. Probability methods can then be used to select quadrats or transects that provide good representation of all strata, and more intensive survey done within these tracts. Such a scheme should provide fairly good estimates of the numbers of inconspicuous but common types of occurrences to be found in the different survey strata (Flannery 1976:159–160). There are at least two things this procedure cannot do well. First, it is a poor way to find out about occurrences that are inconspicuous and scarce (either throughout the region or within a specific stratum) but highly significant, such as Paleoindian remains. Second, it is a very poor way to find out about the spatial organization of sites relative to one another, unless the individual survey tracts are substantially larger than the largest meaningful spatial patterns. In fact, it is worse than poor, because attempts to treat fragments of patterns as whole patterns are very apt to result in outright misinformation.

There is no statistical scheme that can make regional survey by means of spatial sampling very good. It is always a very inferior alternative, to be resorted to only if imminent destruction of sites and limited resources leaves no possibility of complete or nearly complete coverage.

If spatial sampling must be done at all, then of course it should be done as effectively as possible. One should be clear about what kinds of information are to be maximized (or better, which losses are to be minimized). One family of strategies, often involving predictive modeling, is adapted to identifying the settings where sites are most likely to occur, in order to maximize the number of sites identified per person-day or per dollar of survey. Predictive modeling is thoroughly legitimate when it is used to identify high-risk localities that should be avoided by construction projects or to test and improve theory about reasons for site location choices. However, it cannot be legitimately used to "write off" unsurveyed areas as archaeologically insignificant. Furthermore, when it is used simply to maximize the number of sites located, it implies that we should look hardest where we already expect the most sites to occur, and this will lead to self-fulfilling prophecies and a very distorted picture of overall regional patterns. Predictive modeling is usually not good for designing regional surveys because, for most purposes, the sheer number of sites discovered is not the thing we want to maximize or optimize. Often, we want instead to optimize our knowledge of what is typical of each of the strata in the survey area, and to do this we must devote a substantial part of the survey effort to settings that we think are not very likely to contain many sites. Another purpose of survey is to find occurrences that are neither very typical nor very conspicuous, but are exceptionally valuable for culture history or exceptionally relevant for theory. Luck and intuition can help in this quest, but I think "luck" is mostly hard work, and "intuition" means being alert to the right hints. To find what is not common and not obvious, but very important, it helps to have good hunches, but there is just no substitute for lots of intensive survey.

One reason that I put so much emphasis on spatial sampling as an inferior option is the feeling that sampling has been much misused in cultural resource management work (Berry 1984). I suspect that there are powerful, even if sometimes subtle, pressures in favor of doing a survey quickly and not finding very much. Obviously it would never do, however, to produce a report that said "Well, we went out and poked around for a while in the survey area, never set foot on quite a bit of it, and didn't find much of anything." Therefore, some stuff about "stratified two-stage systematic unaligned 10% cluster sampling" should be thrown in, to bemuse bureaucrats and make the fact that it was a real quick and dirty job sound scientifically respectable. I know that a great deal of work has been done more responsibly than this, and that often the people involved have sincerely believed that explicit sampling designs would effectively provide all the relevant data for research questions and that fuller regional coverage would quickly reach a point of diminishing returns. Nevertheless, I do not think my caricature is too far from some of the work that has been done. The final word about spatial sampling is simply this: at least until we know very much more about regions and have very much stronger accepted theory than we now have, there is no possible sampling scheme for regional survey that could make the point of diminishing returns fall at much less than 100% coverage.

I have been referring to surveys intended to *discover* occurrences of archaeological data. How should one deal with an occurrence once it has been found? This brings me to a second pernicious myth: the "total collection." Excavation reports frequently state that deposits were screened, and specify the mesh size. Even statements of this kind leave many unanswered questions, such as how much time was allowed to screen a liter of material, how skilled were the screeners, and exactly what criteria were used to decide which of the material that did not pass through the screen was discardable junk. But at least such statements are better than nothing. Amazingly often, descriptions of intensive surface survey begin and end with the flat assertion that "everything" was collected. Such a statement could only be sensible for sites that bear little resemblance to any site I have ever worked on. Unless the surface is actually devoid of small objects altogether, there is simply no lower limit to the size of fragments to be found. A literal interpretation of the directive to collect *everything* would lead to days or weeks of crawling around on one square meter with magnifying glass and tweezers. I do not, of course, advocate such a procedure. The point is simply that there has to be some cutoff; some level below which fragments are too small and too insignificant to be collected. This is not a matter of choice. The only choice is whether to make the cutoff criteria explicit or to leave them inexplicit and unreported. The latter choice greatly increases the difficulty of trying to compare one survey report with another. Furthermore, absence of any discussion of this point creates the suspicion that the matter was never even considered by the field workers, and that cutoff choices may have been made very differently by different workers, or even by the same worker at different times. In other words, this is a major source of unreliability, in the technical sense, that is usually simply ignored.

One's reaction may be that any responsible worker, told to collect "everything" from a specified tract, will spot and collect virtually all the important stuff, and that I am only talking about variations in how many additional unimportant little bits get collected. Suppose, however, that one worker consistently collects everything with a maximum linear dimension of 3 cm or more, but only sporadically anything smaller, while another worker consistently collects everything larger than 2 cm. Since small fragments tend also to be numerous, those between 2 and 3 cm will be a substantial proportion of all fragments. The fraction of objects in this size range will, however, differ in many ways from the fraction of all larger objects. For example, there will be a higher proportion of featureless body sherds, a higher proportion of lithic waste chips relative to fragments of finished artifacts, a lower proportion of sherds from thick-walled vessels, and so on. If everything that gets collected gets counted, then the extent to which the 2 to 3 cm fraction is collected will have a substantial impact on the proportions, as well as the absolute numbers, of important categories of objects. Use of weights rather than counts would reduce the impact of inconsistencies in size/significance cutoffs, but it would not make the problem go away.

The solution is simple, at least in principle. First, do not just tell workers to "collect everything." Establish explicit guidelines about how far to go in collecting the tiny and insignificant. Second, spend enough time on replications so that the workers learn how to get relatively similar results from the same surfaces, and so that one has a good statistical basis for determining the actual reliability of the work.

I am in the process of complicating my life by using recent intensive collections to get a better idea of the reliability of Teotihuacan Mapping Project surface collections. When that work is completed I will be able to document the arguments I have made above with actual examples, as well as having a far better basis for substantiating the degree of reliability of our quantitative data, rather than merely asking others to have faith in it. Meanwhile, I hope that the argument I have made will be clear and convincing in its own terms. I am amazed by the number of projects that "deal" with this problem by simply ignoring it and hurrying on to analyses and interpretations of data whose reliability remains undemonstrated and largely unconsidered.

Another problem is the "controlled" collection. The words sound good, but what do they mean? They can, of course, mean something, and it is a legitimate expression when one explains clearly and thoughtfully exactly which aspects of collection procedures were controlled, and how they were controlled. But writers often simply assert that collections were "controlled," as if we all understand and agree on the meaning of that term. This is, at best, obfuscation. Some of the energy spent on refining terms such as "chiefdom" would be better spent in thinking harder about what is meant by "controlled collection."

A fourth error is the belief that 100 or so objects will probably be enough for most statistical purposes. To illustrate the trouble with this, suppose we have collections of size 100 from each of a number of sites or loci. To give them the benefit of the doubt, suppose that each collection was obtained by processes that reasonably approximate simple random sampling, so that each can be regarded as a sample of a population consisting of all sherds in or on a site or specified part of a site; each sample representing a different population. Suppose we are interested in differences in the proportion of redware sherds. Common sense tells us that random samples of size 100 from a population with 10% redware sherds do not always contain exactly 10 examples; they often have 8 or 9 or 11 or 12, and sometimes they have 7 or fewer or 13 or more. Elementary statistical knowledge (e.g., Blalock 1979:197–198) enables us to be more exact and to calculate that about a fifth of such samples will have 7 or fewer objects of a category whose true proportion is 10%. Now consider an assemblage where the true proportion is 5%. A calculation shows that nearly one-fourth of the simple random samples of size 100 from such an assemblage will have 7 or more redware sherds. Thus, even when the true assemblage proportions differ by 5%, it is easy to get samples of size 100 in which the sample proportions do not reflect this difference or even reverse the order of the assemblage proportions.

If one only wants to reliably distinguish assemblages with, say, 20% of a given category from assemblages with 10% or 30%, then samples of size 100 may be adequate. But, unless we have defined extremely few categories, there are bound to be important categories that are never more than a few percent of any assemblage. For these categories, it will be critical to reliably distinguish assemblages with 10% from those with 5% or 15%. Samples of size 100 are at best marginal for this purpose. If we hope to reliably distinguish between true proportions that differ by only 3% or 4% in different assemblages, samples of size 100 are wholly inadequate.

A further serious consequence of small samples is that correlations between categories are not simply made less reliable. They are also systematically biased toward low absolute values. This effect, called "attenuation," is bound to be serious for collections of the sizes used for most correlation matrices by archaeologists. Spearman (1904) showed this many years ago. I discussed it in a not very accessible publication

(Cowgill 1970) but have never dwelt on it since. So far as I know, Nance (1985) is the only archaeologist who has ever picked up on it. Yet the implication of attenuation is that a large proportion of archaeological multivariate analyses that depend on correlations are seriously distorted by unrecognized effects of small collection sizes.

Still another effect of small collection size is that assemblage diversity is underestimated. Many categories that constitute a moderate proportion of an assemblage can easily fail to occur at all in a small collection. Kintigh (1984) and Jones et al. (1983) give vivid demonstrations of this. For example, if one category constitutes 3% of a population, the probability that it will be totally absent from a sample of size 100 is about 1 in 21. If several categories are this scarce in the population, the probability is very high that one or more of them will be absent in a sample of size 100.

There will remain many cases where we have to try to make the best of collections of 100 or fewer objects, simply because they're all we've got. We have to recognize, however, how desperately inadequate such collections are for most purposes, and we have to understand that the problem is not just unreliability. Small samples also cause serious distortions. We must be very much more conscious of the complications involved in comparing collections of diverse sizes, and we should try much harder to get larger collections. I realize that one's perceptions of the tradeoffs involved are significantly affected in the field by heat, cold, rain, difficulty of terrain, distance to vehicles, number of bags already filled, and the like. Nevertheless, from the viewpoint of subsequent analyses, the point of diminishing returns in collection size is nowhere near 100, unless there is exceedingly little intrinsic diversity in the assemblages themselves, so that very few categories have been defined and each category constitutes a fairly high proportion in at least some assemblages. I will not attempt to suggest a collection size at which diminishing returns set in, but I feel sure it would not be less than 300 objects for assemblages of even moderate diversity.

The final data problem I want to mention is insufficient attention to distinct depositional layers in excavation. This may seem an unexpectedly down to earth topic for a paper on mathematical and formal techniques, but one comes back over and over again to the fact that mathematics do not enable one to somehow rise above bad field techniques. If anything, the more sophisticated the analyses, the more exacting are the demands placed on the data. American archaeologists nearly all repeat the formula that "arbitrary levels were used only when no natural stratigraphy could be detected." This stock phrase conceals enormous differences in the care and skill with which the search for natural stratigraphy is conducted. Far too many of us are far too ready to resort to arbitrary levels. Field records, including the timely drawing of profiles, also often leave a great deal to be desired.

The State of Some Major Topics

My discussion of specific technical topics is necessarily brief and selective. I will try to say something useful in a few words about matters that deservedly receive whole chapters in review volumes.

Spatial Analysis

Spatial analysis is a domain strongly affected by scale. I suggest that the intra/intersite dichotomy is too crude and that at least three overlapping levels can usefully be distinguished. The largest, generally involving whole regions, is concerned with distances on the order of 1 to upwards of 1000 kilometers, and is dominated by concepts from economic and mathematical geography; especially by "central place" and other models of hierarchical patterns of site size, importance, and location.

I have two comments. One is that doubts about the importance of retail marketing in ancient societies do not challenge the potential value of some sort of central place model, since there are many other kinds of services and activities that may be associated hierarchically with specific places. Second, I am struck by the frequency with which arguments about whether a particular effort to apply a geographical model has in fact been "successful" are carried out without even a hint of the possibility that formal goodness of fit statistics might be appropriate. I suppose the reason is that it is exceedingly difficult to quantify the vague notion that some hierarchical spatial models fit the data better than others do. One has to assess the joint significance of deviations in both the hierarchy and the spatial locations, as well as often serious measurement ambiguities. Nevertheless, formal measures of the goodness of fit of spatial models should be given more attention.

At the other end of the spatial scale are studies involving distances on the order of 0.1 to perhaps as much as 100 meters. These usually involve small sites or individual structures or living surfaces within sites.

Investigations at this scale are dominated by the Schifferian transforms. If spatial patterning in the archaeological residues has been identified and described, what does it really tell us about who did what, where? It is crucial to dig and record in ways that will give the best possible chances for distinguishing between de facto, primary, and secondary refuse; and to do our utmost to discriminate layers reflecting a sequence of occupations, activities, processes, and events. Problem-directed ethnoarchaeology and experimental archaeology are essential.

The intermediate spatial level, concerned mostly with distances on the order of 10 to 10,000 meters, is the least well defined. It involves the study of large sites, especially cities, and also clusters of small sites and site catchment areas. Problems of redeposition are less serious than for smaller scale studies, but not negligible. Relevant theory depends strongly on the type of site, and for urban sites theory comes largely from the history and sociology of more recent nonindustrialized cities.

A serious technical problem in spatial studies, regardless of scale, is that most statistical techniques deal only with the values of two or more variables that jointly occur on each of a number of independent cases, without considering the spatial proximity of the cases. If, for example, a surface is divided into a number of cells and we know the number of endscrapers and the number of backed blades found in each cell, then it is easy to do a bivariate plot of their joint occurrence, which we can inspect to decide whether it would be appropriate to compute a correlation coefficient, a regression equation, and so on. But this approach ignores two questions: what are the consequences of making the spatial cells larger or smaller, and what is going on in the cells close to a given cell? Statisticians have done a good deal of work on these questions, but the results are harder to use and less well developed than the techniques that ignore spatial relations.

One question, of course, is whether an apparent spatial pattern could easily be just accidental. Berry et al. (1983) sketch what looks like an impressive technique to answer this question. However, many spatial patterns are clearly not altogether accidental, and we are more in need of ways to describe patterns. Whallon (1984) explains a key difficulty in many approaches: they derive from models that postulate processes operating *globally* over the study area, whereas realistic archaeological models must postulate multiple processes that are diverse in the shape and size of the affected areas, as well as diverse in their impacts on these areas. A great deal remains to be done to develop methods that are based on realistic models and that enable us to go with confidence much beyond our considerable inbuilt pattern-recognition abilities.

Problems of Multiple Processes

Problems of multiple processes are not limited to spatial analyses. Read (1985) argues in detail that statistical models generally presuppose populations generated by single processes; a presupposition that is rarely likely to be true of archaeological databases. Perhaps it would be better to take an "information" approach for a vague guiding model: the task can be seen as that of discriminating the archaeological "signal" of a target process amidst the confusion of noise, distortion, and crosstalk from the signals of other processes. I do not think, however, that this vague guiding model can easily be implemented by adopting well-developed communications engineering methods for filtering signals, such as Fourier techniques. One problem is that although such techniques postulate multiple concurrent processes, the processes are nevertheless, in a strong sense, global. That is, each process is seen as operating over the whole study area. The approach does not really take account of the possibility that totally different things may be happening in different places. It may be more profitable to think and experiment more about the archaeological consequences of single processes, in order to deduce the probable consequences of a mix or sequence of processes. Also, the common-sense recognition that some deposits are more informative than others can be made more exact by suggesting that we try hard to identify deposits that reflect the operation of relatively few processes, possibly only one process.

The problem of multiple processes recalls my earlier discussion of uniformities and regularities. Mechanically subjecting the kinds of data generated by customary archaeological procedures to standard multivariate statistical techniques is likely to yield ill-formed and nearly meaningless uniformities reflecting the confounded operation of diverse processes, rather than approximations to regularities in sociocultural phenomena.

Classification

A volume edited by Whallon and Brown (1982) provides a range of views about typology. One purpose of classification is data management.

Computer technology is increasingly relevant for this. Other purposes come under the general heads of organizing and expressing similarities and differences between objects in a single assemblage (that is, a data set that as near as possible pertains to people in close interaction doing much the same things over a relatively short time), similarities and differences between objects in different assemblages, and similarities and differences between assemblages. The similarities and differences that can be detected will depend on how objects are observed; how they are observed will depend on what we think it important to notice; and what we think it important to notice is fundamental and will depend on our research problems. We also have a choice of different ways to express similarity/difference patterns, and each choice is better for some problems than for others. Of course, ideal techniques have not yet been developed for most problems, and there are some techniques that are inferior for any reasonable problem. But techniques and observations are not fundamental; problems are fundamental, and they should guide our selection of techniques and observations. We have been saying this for 40 years now (Brew 1946). Most work on classification is still centered on a specific technique or dominated by a few of the reasonable purposes. It would be useful to look more systematically at the various implications for techniques of all the currently known reasonable purposes of classification.

Simulation

I have already said the main thing about simulation. It is one of the few mathematical or formal approaches that can be used not just to analyze data in ways relevant for theory but to actually express theory. Nevertheless I have been disappointed by most simulation efforts. Publications that never get beyond the verbal stage and that never quantify the proposed relationships or actually lead to a simulation also rarely get much beyond expressing some fairly simple ideas in nonsimple language (Lowe 1985 is an important exception). Many of the simulation efforts have taken ready-made computer systems whose built-in limitations and presuppositions were grossly (and sometimes grotesquely) mismatched with the phenomena the simulation was supposed to elucidate (I will not name awful examples, since I have avoided that elsewhere in this paper). I think the simulation bubble has broken now, and a more sober attitude prevails (e.g., Aldenderfer 1981; Cordell 1981).

An essential point about simulation is that it is not a body of socio-cultural concepts; it is a way to embody concepts. In most simulations, the concepts have come from some variant of systems theory. Contrary to the views in many quarters, I do not think that systems theory, at least the versions used by archaeologists, has furnished us with a very rich body of highly relevant concepts. It is useful up to a point, but it offers our imaginations very thin sustenance about sociocultural phenomena. We can only be nourished by reflection on ethnographic and historical data. If we have the knowledge and imagination to formulate better models and good enough data so that none of the key input values have to be wildly guessed, it should be technically feasible to create very useful simulations.

Conclusion

Both the number and sophistication of archaeological publications that are concerned with mathematical or formal methods are greater than they were a few years ago. However there are still very few, if any, mathematical or formal techniques that are applied by archaeologists both frequently and also in ways that are simultaneously technically correct, appropriate to data and problems, and highly useful. In that sense, the art is still in a weakly developed state. Most publications fit into one of three broad categories. First are those that make substantial use or mis-use of mathematical or formal techniques in the service (or alleged service) of significant theory. A second, and I think much larger category, consists of those publications that describe and advocate a technique, method, or approach; illustrating it with "data" that are either made up or of little intrinsic interest. The third and also large category consists of publications that criticize or defend other publications belonging to one of the first two categories. Some of the debate is needlessly argumentative or petty, but much of it raises important points. There is probably also somewhat better pre-publication review and screening than there was 20 years ago. I think it is harder for incorrect or inappropriate work to gain acceptance now than it was in the 1960s. This seems to me the major advance; not a long list of widely accepted accomplishments, but advances in the conceptualization of problems, the sophistication of experimentation, and the level of self-criticism.

However, in spite of the growing number of archaeologists who have some acquaintance with mathematical and formal methods, there remains a high proportion who either avoid these methods or who make serious errors in their attempts to apply them. It is unrealistic to expect most archaeologists to become mathematical experts, but we still sorely need better and more general teaching of some simple techniques and, above all, the basic logic of statistical inference. These are not topics that can be treated casually, nor can students be expected any longer to learn them on their own.

Finally, I will repeat what I have suggested throughout. Improvements in mathematical/formal techniques and their applications are much to be encouraged. But what we need above all are data, sociocultural theory, and understandings of the connections between archaeological evidence and past behavior that are all worthy of the techniques.

Acknowledgments

I thank David J. Meltzer and anonymous readers for a number of comments on the draft of this paper prepared for presentation in Denver. They have aided materially in the preparation of the final version.

Literature Cited

Aldenderfer, Mark S.
  1981 Computer Simulation for Archaeology: An Introductory Essay. In *Simulations in Archaeology*, edited by J. A. Sabloff, pages 11–49. University of New Mexico Press, Albuquerque.

Berry, Kenneth J., Kenneth L. Kvamme, and Paul W. Mielke, Jr.
  1983 Improvements in the Permutation Test for the Spatial Analysis of the Distribution of Artifacts into Classes. *American Antiquity* 48:547–553.

Berry, Michael S.
  1984 Sampling and Predictive Modelling on Federal Lands in the West. *American Antiquity* 49:842–853.

Binford, Lewis R.
  1985 "Brand X" Versus the Recommended Product. *American Antiquity* 50:580–590.

Blalock, Hubert M., Jr.
  1979 *Social Statistics*. McGraw-Hill, New York.

Brew, John O.
  1946 The Archaeology of Alkali Ridge. *Peabody Museum of Archaeology and Ethnology Papers,* 21. Cambridge, Massachusetts.

Clarke, David L. (editor)
  1977 *Spatial Archaeology*. Academic Press, New York.

Cordell, Linda S.
1981 The Wetherill Mesa Simulation: A Retrospective. In *Simulations in Archaeology,* edited by J. A. Sabloff, pages 119–141. University of New Mexico Press, Albuquerque.

Cowgill, George L.
1968 Archaeological Applications of Factor, Cluster, and Proximity Analysis. *American Antiquity* 33:367–375.
1970 Some Sampling and Reliability Problems in Archaeology. In *Archeologie et Calculateurs,* edited by J.-C. Gardin, pages 161–175. Centre National de la Recherche Scientifique, Paris.
1972 Models, Methods and Techniques for Seriation. In *Models in Archaeology,* edited by D. L. Clarke, pages 381–424. Methuen, London.
1974 Quantitative Studies of Urbanization at Teotihuacan. In *Mesoamerican Archaeology: New Approaches,* edited by N. Hammond, pages 363–396. Duckworth, London.
1975 On Causes and Consequences of Ancient and Modern Population Changes. *American Anthropologist* 77:505–525.
1977 The Trouble with Significance Tests and What We Can Do About It. *American Antiquity* 42:350–368.
1979 Teotihuacan, Internal Militaristic Competition, and the Fall of the Classic Maya. In *Maya Archaeology and Ethnohistory,* edited by N. Hammond and G. R. Willey, pages 51–62. University of Texas Press, Austin.
1982 Clusters of Objects and Associations between Variables: Two Approaches to Archaeological Classification. In *Essays in Archaeological Typology,* edited by R. Whallon and J. Brown, pages 30–55. Center for American Archaeology Press, Evanston, Illinois.
1983 Rulership and the Ciudadela: Political Inferences from Teotihuacan Architecture. In *Civilization in the Ancient Americas,* edited by R. Leventhal and A. Kolata, pages 313–343. University of New Mexico Press, Albuquerque.

Cowgill, George L., Jeffrey H. Altschul, and Rebecca S. Sload
1984 Spatial Analysis of Teotihuacan: A Mesoamerican Metropolis. In *Intrasite Spatial Analysis in Archaeology,* edited by H. Hietala, pages 154–195. Cambridge University Press, Cambridge.

Dyson, Stephen L.
1985 Two Paths to the Past: A Comparative Study of the Last Fifty Years of *American Antiquity* and the *American Journal of Archaeology. American Antiquity* 50:452–463.

Flannery, Kent V.
1967 Culture History vs. Culture Process: A Debate in American Archaeology. *Scientific American* 217:119–122.
1973 Archeology with a Capital "S." In *Research and Theory in Current Archeology,* edited by C. Redman, pages 47–58. Wiley, New York.

Flannery, Kent V. (editor)
1976 *The Early Mesoamerican Village.* Academic Press, New York.

Gould, Richard A.
1980 *Living Archaeology.* Cambridge University Press, Cambridge.

Hodder, Ian (editor)
1978a *The Spatial Organisation of Culture.* The University of Pittsburgh Press, Pittsburgh.

1978b *Simulation Studies in Archaeology.* Cambridge University Press, Cambridge.

Hodder, Ian, and Clive Orton
1976 *Spatial Analysis in Archaeology.* Cambridge University Press, Cambridge.

Jones, George T., Donald K. Grayson, and Charlotte Beck
1983 Sample Size and Functional Diversity in Archaeological Assemblages. *In* Lulu Linear Punctated: Essays in Honor of George Irving Quimby, edited by R. C. Dunnell and D. K. Grayson. *University of Michigan, Museum of Anthropology, Anthropological Papers* 72:55–73. Ann Arbor.

Kintigh, Keith W.
1984 Measuring Archaeological Diversity by Comparison with Simulated Assemblages. *American Antiquity* 49:44–54.

Lowe, John W. G.
1985 Qualitative Systems Theory: Its Utility and Limitations. *Journal of Anthropological Research* 41:42–61.

Mosteller, Frederick, Stephen E. Fienberg, and Robert E. K. Rourke
1983 *Beginning Statistics with Data Analysis.* Addison-Wesley, Reading, Massachusetts.

Mosteller, Frederick, and John W. Tukey
1977 *Data Analysis and Regression.* Addison-Wesley, Reading, Massachusetts.

Nance, Jack D.
1985 Reliability and Validity of Archaeological Measurement. Paper for the 50th Annual Meeting of the Society for American Archaeology, Denver, Colorado, 3 May.

Plog, Stephen, Fred Plog, and Walter Wait
1978 Decision Making in Modern Surveys. In *Advances in Archaeological Method and Theory,* edited by Michael B. Schiffer, 1:383–421. Academic Press, New York.

Read, Dwight W.
1985 The Substance of Archaeological Analysis and the Mold of Statistical Method: Enlightenment out of Discordance? In *Analysis of Archaeological Data Structures,* edited by C. Carr, pages 45–86. Westport Publishing Company, Kansas City.

Renfrew, Colin, and Kenneth L. Cooke (editors)
1979 *Transformations: Mathematical Approaches to Culture Change.* Academic Press, New York.

Sabloff, Jeremy A. (editors)
1981 *Simulations in Archaeology.* University of New Mexico Press, Albuquerque.

Salmon, Merrilee, and Wesley Salmon
1979 Alternative Models of Scientific Explanation. *American Anthropologist* 81:61–74.

Schiffer, Michael B.
  1972 Archaeological Context and Systemic Context. *American Antiquity*
    37:156–165.
  1976 *Behavioral Archeology.* Academic Press, New York.
  1983 Toward the Identification of Formation Processes. *American Antiquity*
    48:675–706.

Smith, Carol A. (editor)
  1976 *Regional Analysis, Volume I: Economic Systems.* Academic Press, New
    York.

Spaulding, Albert C.
  1973 Archeology in the Active Voice: The New Anthropology. In *Research
    and Theory in Current Archeology,* edited by C. Redman, pages 337–
    354. Wiley, New York.

Spearman, Charles
  1904 The Proof and Measurement of Association between Two Things.
    American Journal of Psychology 15:72–101.

Steward, Julian H.
  1955 *Theory of Culture Change.* University of Illinois Press, Urbana.

Tilly, Charles
  1984 *Big Structures, Large Processes, Huge Comparisons.* Russell Sage Foun-
    dation, New York.

Tukey, John W.
  1977 *Exploratory Data Analysis.* Addison-Wesley, Reading, Massachusetts.

Whallon, Robert
  1984 Unconstrained Clustering for the Analysis of Spatial Distributions in
    Archaeology. In *Intrasite Spatial Analysis in Archaeology,* edited by H.
    Hietala, pages 242–277. Cambridge University Press, Cambridge.

Whallon, Robert, and James A. Brown (editors)
  1982 *Essays on Archaeological Typology.* Center for American Archaeology
    Press, Evanston, Illinois.

Zeitlin, Robert N.
  1982 Toward a More Comprehensive Model of Interregional Commodity
    Distribution: Political Variables and Prehistoric Obsidian Procurement
    in Mesoamerica. *American Antiquity* 47:260–275.

Ruthann Knudson Woodward-Clyde Consultants, Walnut Creek, California

Contemporary Cultural Resource Management

Archaeological Resources as a Public Interest

Cultural resource management (CRM) is much more than archaeology, more than "public archaeology" or "contract archaeology" (Cleere 1984a, 1984b; Gruber this volume; Lipe 1984; Trigger this volume; cf. Workman 1985:1). In fact, there is a growing professionalization of cultural resource management that requires an eclectic suite of disciplinary interests and education and work experience. The archaeologists effectively began that move toward professionalization in the early 1970s, but it is now a much more complex, more broadly anthropological interdisciplinary practice. Perhaps most importantly, cultural resource management is the primary context within which most professional or avocational archaeologists address the public nature of the resources and their treatment (cf. Fowler 1981). This paper will focus first on that public aspect, then on the elements in present and future cultural resource management, and finally on some specific responsibilities and opportunities of archaeological practice within CRM.

Who owns an archaeological site? Or the materials from it, once they have been removed from that site? Or the records that retain information about site context? Who or what entity has primary rights in saying how archaeological sites, their included remains, and information about those remains are to be treated? These may sound like simplistic questions, but they are elementary to what we do as archaeologists and are not addressed even in introductory undergraduate archaeology textbooks (e.g., Sharer and Ashmore 1985; Thomas 1979).

The answer lies in part in the historical definition of land ownership and is a significant element in the sociopolitics of archaeology (Gero et al. 1983; Hanen and Kelley 1983; Leone 1981) and in the relationship of archaeology and patrimony (Cleere 1984 a, 1984 b, 1984 c; Fowler this volume; Wilson and Loyola 1982). In countries where there is a direct tie between the dominant current inhabitants of a landscape and the original inhabitants whose archaeological residues are available for study, the ownership of heritage resources is more frequently reserved to the state. In other countries, especially the United States, where the right of private land ownership is highly valued, conflicts over public versus private control over archaeological resources have arisen.

The United States lacks a clear legal definition of archaeological resource ownership. This is partly the result of the lack of genetic continuity between the dominant political community in the United States and prehistoric Americans, as Fowler and Trigger have discussed in this volume. However the problem is more directly a function of the history of the United States' separation from England 200 years ago.

During the late 1700s, when the Colonies were developing a constitution and a bill of rights in a frontier nation previously uninhabited by Euro-Americans, the issue of the ownership of the archaeological heritage was not addressed. Archaeological materials, largely unknown at that point, came with the land and were not identified as being of particular public value. In reaction to English royal rights developed from the feudal system, the right of private ownership of land was clearly established in the new American Bill of Rights as the "taking clause" of the Fifth Amendment: ". . . nor shall private property be taken for public use without just compensation." The land was private, the question of archaeological heritage resources within it was not addressed, therefore archaeological materials were privately owned.

A similar legal situation prevails in Canada, for many of the same historical reasons (Cinq-Mars 1984; Falkner 1977; Janes and Arnold 1983; Sutherland 1983). In contrast, in Australia the tradition of English common law prevails and the Crown reserves the ownership of all heritage resources including those within private property (McKinley and Jones 1979; Pearson and Temple 1984), just as they reserve all mineral rights to the Crown. A somewhat problematic situation is developing in Australia with the passage of legislation, such as the Aboriginal Land Rights (Northern Territories) Act and the Pitjantjatjara Act, which give Aboriginals both surface and mineral rights (and hence archaeological rights) to vast tracts of land (Berndt 1982; Knudson 1985).

Given the Fifth Amendment, the present federal, state, and local legal position about archaeological site ownership in the United States is that it is entailed by surface ownership. This is the basic position of the Antiquities Act of 1906 (P.L. 59–209, 34 Stat. 437, 16 USC 431–433). This Act expanded the public authority by asserting in Section 1 that the protection applied to any antiquity "on lands owned *or controlled* by the Government of the United States" (emphasis added) and thus provides a basis for extending coverage to any properties subject to federal authority (e.g., by lease, license, or right-of-way). However, the implementation of the present legal position is variable, and that is a key element to understanding our roles as archaeologists in this country. The most critical legal threshhold in contemporary and future archaeological resource management in the U. S. is not the Antiquities Act of 1906, "Moss-Bennett" (P.L. 93–291, 88 Stat. 174, 16 USC 469), or the Archeological Resources Protection Act (P.L. 96–95, 93 Stat. 721, 16 USC 470a), though each of these is an important contributor to the prevailing public value about archaeology. Rather, it is the National Environmental Policy Act (NEPA) (P.L. 90–190, 83 Stat. 852, 42 USC 4321) that has provided a land use and resource management legal mechanism that overrides the concept of private ownership (Blodgett 1978; Bosselman et al. 1973; Chambers 1985b). It is NEPA and other resource planning and management laws, regulations, and programs that are the major impetus behind "CRM archaeology," (Lipe 1978:143) and the concept of the public nature of all resources that underlies them. Everyone involved in using or conserving archaeological resources needs to understand this significant change in the United States' philosophy about its resources. Today and into the future, America's natural, social, and cultural resources are explicitly recognized as part of the public wealth and their treatment is a matter of public issue. This is true even from an international perspective, where "the international environmental movement is the expression of a fundamental change in human perceptions of life on earth," including "the cultural environment." (Caldwell 1984:3–4).

For a century archaeologists have lobbied Congress to pass legislation stating that archaeological resources are part of the public wealth. Many of the introductory general anthropology or archaeology textbooks comment on the importance of archaeological resources in providing information of public social value (e.g., Beals et al. 1975:16–19, 687–699). Lyon (1982) has provided the major Depression-era public archaeological practice. The concept is implicit in the Antiquities Act of 1906, and in the Reservoir Salvage Act of 1960 (P.L. 86–523, 74 Stat. 220, 16 USC 469–469c) and its amended 1974 form, but it is not clearly stated. Again, that is probably in large part a function of the lack of genetic continuity between the original inhabitants of the archaeological sites and the modern community (including the archaeologists) supporting excavation of the sites. In contrast, the Historic Sites Act of 1935 (P.L. 74–292, 49 Stat. 666, 16 USC 461–467) and the National Historic Preservation Act of 1966 (P.L. 89–665, 80 Stat, 915, 16 USC 470) included explicit statements of the public value of historic buildings (National Trust for Historic Preservation 1980, 1983); here there is cultural and kindred continuity between original and modern inhabitants. The Archeological Resources Protection Act of 1979 (P.L. 96–95, 93 Stat. 721, 16 USC 470a) states that "archaeological resources on *public lands and Indian lands* are . . . an irreplaceable part of the Nation's heritage" (Sec. 2(a); emphasis added), but does not address the broader issue. In contrast, NEPA (Section 101, emphasis added) states that

> (a) . . . it is the continuing policy of the Federal Government . . . to use all practicable means and measure . . . to foster and promote the general welfare, to create and maintain conditions under which [people] and nature can exist in productive harmony, and fulfill the social, economic, and other requirements of present and future generations of Americans.
> (b) . . . it is the continuing responsibility of the Federal Government to use all practicable means . . . to improve and coordinate Federal plans, functions, programs, and resources to the end that the nation may—
> (1) Fulfill the responsibilities for each generation as trustee of the environment of succeeding generations;
> (2) assure for all Americans safe, healthful, productive, and esthetically and *culturally* pleasing surroundings;
> (3) attain the widest range of beneficial uses of the environment without degradation, risk to health or safety, or undesirable and unintended consequences;
> (4) *preserve important historic, cultural, and natural aspects of our national heritage, and maintain, wherever possible, an environment which supports diversity and variety of individual choice;*
> (5) achieve a balance between population and resource use which will permit high standards of living and a wide sharing of life's amenities; and
> (6) enhance the quality of renewable resources and approach the maximum attainable recycling of depletable resources.
> (c) The Congress recognizes that each person should enjoy a healthful environment and that each person has a responsibility to contribute to the preservation and enhancement of the environment.

It is the fuller address of archaeological site management under the rubrics of NEPA, the 1980-amended National Historic Preservation Act (P.L. 96–515, 94 Stat. 2987, 16 USC 470), and planning laws such as the Federal Land Management and Policy Act of 1976 (FLPMA) (P.L. 94–579, 90 Stat. 2743, 43 USC 1701), the National Forest Management Act of 1976 (P.L. 94–588, 90 Stat. 2949, 16 USC 1600), and the Surface Mining Control and Reclamation Act of 1977 (P.L. 95–87, 91 Stat. 445, 30 USC 1201 et seq.), whose programs must in turn comply with NEPA, that is resulting in the implementation of a policy of public values for all archaeological sites. In addition, the increasing growth of historic archaeology, where there is more direct cultural and kindred continuity between the past and the present, supports this public perception of value. This is supplemented by passage of the American Indian Religious Freedom Joint Resolution of 1978 (AIRFA) (P.L. 95–341, 92 Stat. 469, 42 USC 1966) (Federal Agencies Task Force 1979) and the increasing political sophistication of the Native American community, and sharp Native American awareness of the continuity between their present community and many of the archaeological resources studied in this country (Holmes 1982).

As archaeologists, we have persuaded the major policymakers (and by implication the constituencies that vote them into office) of the public significance of archaeological resources (Knudson 1982). Once persuaded, the implementation of such policies will not leave anyone (including the archaeologists) out of the process of public accountability for the treatment of those resources.

Thus, "there is a worldwide moral consensus that the long-term conservation of a significant portion of our cultural past is good for the human community" (Knudson 1984:245–247). Management of our cultural resources will be conducted in a context of multiple public objectives, and archaeologists have an ethical responsibility to operate appropriately within that public context.

During the next fifty years most of the money that supports archaeology anywhere in the world will come either from public coffers, or from developers who are required by public law to conduct archaeology. Most of the projects that so involve and support archaeological inquiry will probably relate to broader public issues, and will deal with "archaeology" within the broader context of "cultural resource management," and even broader, within the context of environmental multiple-resource planning and management. The public will require that this money be spent effectively, and a normal complement to that is that the archaeological work be done efficiently and be ethical and productive in a publicly perceivable manner (see Keel 1979 for a similar statement).

The Scope of Contemporary Cultural Resource Management

The Concept of "Cultural" Resources

The term "cultural resource management" (CRM) was invented by anthropological archaeologists working in the National Park Service and other federal agencies in the early 1970s (Lindsay and Lipe 1974). It was a rebellion against the connotations of the term "salvage archaeology" (Lipe 1978:121–122; but see Dunnell 1985; Haag 1985; Haury 1985; Jennings 1985), a response to the requirements of the National Environmental Policy Act and other new planning and management directives, a reflection of 1960s archaeologists' traditional academic training, and a reaction to their task of managing prehistoric sites in the midst of living Native American communities. During the following decade (Dickens and Hill 1978; McGimsey and Davis 1977; Matheny and Berge 1976) the term was more consistently used as a synonym for "public archaeology," "contract archaeology," or "government archaeology."

However, within the last few years the term has been or is being adopted by a wide range of disciplinary interests, all of which focus on considerations about the protection of the cultural aspects of our lives. Today, in most contexts (generally federal, state, or local environmental or planning studies) CRM involves the things and behavior patterns that are important reflections of our traditional culture, the "complex whole which includes knowledge, belief, act, law, custom, and any other capabilities and habits acquired (by a human) as a member of society" (Tylor, quoted in Beals et al. 1975:704). The anthropological breadth of training and interest that underlie the original selection of the term "cultural" resource management is becoming reality.

Of the range of interests presently included under the CRM rubric, the structure of the environmental impact assessment is a useful illustration. The Council on Environmental Quality's regulations outlining the requirements of the Environmental Impact Statement (EIS) specify that there be a major section titled "Affected Environment," but they do not list the topics to be addressed in that section. Over the past fifteen years of EIS preparation there has come to be a standard outline of topics: air quality, geology, soils, surface and groundwater, aquatic and terrestrial biology, socioeconomics, land use and recreation, cultural resources, paleontological resources, visual resources, and noise. "Socioeconomics" is an umbrella term that includes social services, economics, demographics, public facilities, and fiscal impacts. It sometimes includes an assessment of social impacts that focuses on more traditional cultural values (e.g., U. S. Department of the Interior's [1983] assessment of the impacts of a proposed New Mexico generating station on traditional Navajo values). "Cultural resources," which in the early to mid-1970s were usually restricted to historic buildings and archaeological sites, now usually address these topics:

1. Terrestrial and marine prehistoric, historic, industrial, and commercial archaeological resources, focusing on those that are eligible for the National Register of Historic Places (36 CFR 800).

2. Formal (e.g., Fitch 1982) and vernacular (e.g., Brunskill 1982; Glassie 1975; Marshall 1981; Pillsbury and Kardos 1969; Wilson 1984) historic buildings or architecture, engineered construction (e.g., Fitz-Simons 1968–1973; Johnson 1985; U. S. Department of the Interior 1981), and cultural landscapes (e.g., Jakle 1980; Jellicoe and Jellicoe 1982; Melnicj 1980; Stilgoe 1982; Stipe 1980), again focusing on those that are eligible for the National Register of Historic Places (and appropriate for registration with the Historic American Buildings Survey [HABS], or the Historic American Engineering Record [HAER])

3. Traditional or cultural "intangible" values (Loomis 1983), including traditional Native American religious considerations in compliance with the American Indian Religious Freedom Act (e.g., Oregon Commission on Indian Services 1980), and other rural and/or urban folklife traditions and oral history (e.g., Chambers 1985a; Howell 1981; Huth 1941; McDaniel 1982; Sitton et al. 1983)

A similar list of environmental topics, and subtopics within "cultural resources," is used for most land use planning efforts around the country today. The management of the cultural resources that might be affected by a large project or require management planning is a complicated activity, no matter the project's size. It involves expertise in prehistoric, historic, and marine archaeology; archival research (U. S. National Archives and Records Service 1974:1), documentary, oral, architectural and engineering history (e.g., Karamanski 1985); anthropology; and folklife studies; as well as regionally or culturally specific expertise. The cultural resource impact assessments or management plans, including recommendations for mitigating any adverse impact, must be appropriate to the full range of other topical or disciplinary assessments and mitigation recommendations. A recommendation that a pipeline be moved to avoid a significant archaeological site may conflict strongly with a recommendation to avoid the visual impacts of cutting a new pipeline corridor through a forest rather than out in a grass meadow. Cultural resource management practitioners must therefore also have some familiarity with, and sensitivity to, all other environmental issues that are addressed in management and planning. In addition, to develop plans that result in affirmative and effective management of our prehistoric and historic archaeological resources, the practitioners must know about budgets, schedules, staffing, and effective communication with nonarchaeological decision-makers.

In 1980, as part of the National Historic Preservation Act Amendments, Congress instructed the U. S. Department of the Interior and the Library of Congress' American Folklife Center to

> submit a report to the President and the Congress on preserving and conserving the intangible elements of our cultural heritage. . . . This report shall include recommendations for legislative and administrative actions by the Federal Government in order to preserve, conserve, and encourage the continuation of diverse traditional prehistoric, historic, ethnic, and folk cultural traditions that underlie and are a living expression of our American heritage [P.L. 96–515, Section 502].

The *Cultural Conservation* study (Loomis 1983) is probably the prevailing definition of "cultural resources" in the federal government now and for the forseeable future. Its conceptual base is broadly anthropological, "cultural heritage" being defined as a range of tangible and intangible resources and values, explicitly including prehistoric and archaeological resources. A similar definition was used in a National Resource Council, Environmental Studies Board (1982) evaluation of cultural resource management needs of federal water projects. More recently, the California Heritage Task Force (1984) adopted this same broad definition of "cultural heritage resources" in making long-term recommendations about the direction of a statewide historic preservation or cultural resource management program.

The Concept of "Management"

Federal archaeological legislation (which has been developed in response to program design requests and lobbying efforts of archaeologists) has generally been reactive, a response to the threat of loss of a nonrenewable resource. The legislation and implement regulations provide rules about who and how one can consume one of those resources. They have never outlined a national program to inventory the universe of sites that exist, so that relative judgments can be made about which to save, which to use, and which to allow destroyed without conservation. This position probably reflects an internally focused preoccupation over the past century with the development of archaeology as a recognized profession with a unique set of methods, techniques, and ethics (Wildesen 1984). This position also recognized, until recently, a lack of approaches and tools to handle a nationwide database (cf. Spaulding 1985:307) and the still-prevailing professional and avocational emphasis on archaeological exploration and excavation (Gero 1985).

In contrast, the National Historic Preservation Act, NEPA, and the land use management legislation are proactive, and are directed to the identification and evaluation of a set of resources so that they can be affirmatively managed. Management is the prevailing national policy regarding how cultural resources should be treated, and that policy is being implemented through the federal agencies in response to the public's identification of these resources as having significant, long-term value. A key factor in this management effort is planning, and the National Historic Preservation Act (Section 102(a)(2) in the original 1966 Act, Section 101(b)(3) in the 1980-amended Act) requires that each state develop a "comprehensive statewide historic preservation plan." Over the past fifteen years a large database has been developed that tells us where sites are and are not located, and which of the known sites is more likely to have scientific, historic, or sociocultural significance (cf. King 1981). The database allows us to predict the distribution of important archaeological values, hence to make more managerial decisions about how we handle sites. All these are the basis for true planning.

The National Park Service has provided guidance for the development of statewide historic preservation plans (U. S. Department of the Interior 1980); the Advisory Council on Historic Preservation (1982) has drafted a statement of the kind of planning they believe is needed to provide a context for treatment decision-making; and the U. S. Army and National Park Service have recently contracted the development of a nationally applicable work outline for Army facility archaeological management planning (Knudson et al. 1983). Many state historic preservation plans have been drafted around the country (e.g., Brown et al. 1982; Lyneis 1982; Massachusetts Historical Commission 1980). All these are providing a context for making decisions about the treatment of individual resources on a basis other than site-by-site decisions.

Archaeological Responsibilities and Opportunities

All professional or avocational archaeologists have a responsibility to provide the general public with the most affirmative treatment of the archaeological resource base (sites, artifacts, samples, data, documentary records, reports) possible within the context of other cultural values and other resource management programs and policies today. There have been numerous discussions of the responsibilities of research-oriented archaeologists within a public contractual and managerial context (Brose 1985; Keel 1979; Lipe 1978; Knudson 1979; Portnoy 1978; Mayer-Oakes and Portnoy 1979; McGimsey and Davis 1977; U. S. Department of the Interior 1985;24–29), which includes both public tax dollars paid out by the National Science Foundation and private industry dollars paid out to acquire development authorization.

Affirmative treatment includes the responsibility of the archaeological practitioner to understand the needs of the agency or firm (client) financially supporting the investigation, and, with that understanding, to help develop and comply with a contract that meets those needs. Affirmative treatment also includes the responsibility of the archaeological practitioner to protect, and if possible to enhance, the research values of the archaeological resources insofar as is possible and appropriate given the client's needs and contract stipulations. It also includes the responsibility, insofar as possible, to return the essence of the generated research values to the public in a consumable form. Further, the form should be crafted in such a fashion that nonarchaeologists might gain insight into the public value of bringing an historical perspective to contemporary social issues.

At present, and for the forseeable future, archaeological resource management will be conducted in a context of "cultural resource management." It is thus a responsibility of the archaeological practitioner to be familiar with the range of professional, avocational, and client values under the umbrella that is CRM and with all the values associated with all other kinds of resource management that provide the context within which CRM operates! In addition to gaining knowledge and insight, given the sociopolitical context of archaeology, it is also a responsibility of archaeological practitioners to build coalitions with others working in CRM.

The good news is that the fulfillment of all these responsibilities is accompanied by an even broader range of opportunities. One of the most important is the tremendous enrichment of the research database that has come about over the past decade and the high likelihood that it will continue to grow significantly. As just one example, planning-oriented archaeological inventories have given us a large data set about site locations (and absences), a fundamental factor in formulating settlement or subsistence studies.

Given that database, there are opportunities for many future grant-supported projects that can make cost-effective use of the scarce research funds available from the National Geographic Society of the National Science Foundation (cf. Casteel 1980; Yellen et al. 1980; Yellen and Greene 1985). Further, the collection and evaluation of archaeological data in conjunction with the collection of other kinds of data (biological, geological) provides an opportunity for bringing enhanced multidisciplinary insights to our archaeological investigations. One example of such an opportunity was the EIS evaluation of the impact on cultural resources of a proposed electrical generating station (U. S. Department of Interior 1982, 1983) Another was the completion of a cultural resource and rescue program within the context of an ongoing construction project (Knudson 1983).

Archaeologists are generally trained as social scientists, if not specifically as anthropologists, or as historians, or in American Studies. As an anthropologically trained archaeologist, this author finds that archaeology in a CRM context provides a substantial enhancement of standard anthropological training and practice in that it forces the researchers to understand and operate effectively within the social, economic, and political subcultures of the companies and agencies with which they must work: federal offices, oil and gas developers, and engineering and architectural consultants, among others. Other anthropolological subdisciplinary practitioners are apparently also finding this to be true (Nelson and Paredes 1985; Opie 1983).

Lipe (1978:133) has commented that in the current context of archaeological practice one of the greatest needs may be the introduction of "more innovation." Drucker (1985:67) defines innovation as "the effort to create purposeful, focused change in an enterprise's economic or social potential," and comments that "innovation can be systematically managed—if one knows where and how to look." Drucker is discussing innovation in the business context of striving for competitive success, but given the public context of archaeology it seems that archaeological practitioners are striving for the same goal. That context provides the responsibility and also the opportunity for purposeful innovation. For instance, the balancing of the U. S. Army's limitation on funds with which to complete archaeological overviews and management plans on many of its installations against the innovative borrowing of concepts from decision analysis (e.g., Goddard 1984, Keeney and Raiffa 1976) to complete pre-field-inventory archaeological management planning is now leading to affirmative management of the significant prehistoric and historic archaeological resources on those installations (Constance Ramirez, 1985, Department of the Army, personal communication).

As Wildesen commented at the 50th annual meeting of the SAA while reading this paper for the author:

> Most important in the long run, we have an opportunity to make a difference. In our relatively young, entrepreneurial nation, we can help our fellow citizens understand the depth and value of the distant past, not as a narrow special-interest group, but as an integral part of our own contemporary ethno-socio-political-economic (e.g., cultural) milieu. By meeting our basic responsibilities, and taking advantage of our obvious opportunities, we can help to ensure, as the National Historic Preservation Act [as amended, Sec. 1(b)(2)] enjoins, "that the historical and cultural foundations of the Nation should be preserved as a living part of our community life and development in order to give a sense of orientation to the American people."

Acknowledgments

Many individuals (too numerous to identify) have been impetus and idea-developers for this paper. I particularly wish to acknowledge and thank Leslie Wildesen, who when I was unable to attend the 1985 meetings or even discuss the paper, took the responsibility for presenting the original draft of this paper and providing the presentation with a logical completion of my unfinished ideas.

Literature Cited

Advisory Council on Historic Preservation
 1982 Planning in Context (draft). Manuscript on file, Advisory Council on Historic Preservation, Washington, D.C.

Beals, Ralph L., Harry Hoijer, and Alan R. Beals
 1975 *An Introduction to Anthropology.* 5th edition. MacMillan Publishing Company, Inc., New York.

Berndt, R. M. (editor)
 1982 *Aboriginal Sites, Rights and Resources Development.* University of Western Australia Press, for the Academy of the Social Sciences in Australia, Perth.

Blodgett, John E. (editor)
 1978 *Environmental Protection: Legislation and Programs of the Environmental Protection Agency.* Library of Congress, Washington, D.C.

Bosselman, Fred, David Callies, and John Banta
 1973 *The Taking Issue: A Study of the Constitutional Limits of Governmental Authority to Regulate the Use of Privately-owned Land Without Paying Compensation to the Owners.* Council on Environmental Quality, Washington, D.C.

Brose, David S.
 1985 Good Enough for Government Work? A Study in "Grey Archeology." *American Anthropologist* 87(2):370–377.

Brown, Theodore M., Kay L. Killen, Helen Simons, and Virginia Wulfkuhle
 1982 *Resource Protection Planning Process for Texas.* Texas Historical Commission, Austin.

Brunskill, R. W.
 1982 *Illustrated Handbook of Vernacular Architecture.* Faber and Faber, London.

Caldwell, Lynton Keith
 1984 *International Environmental Policy: Emergence and Dimensions.* Duke University Press, Durham.

California Heritage Task Force
 1984 *California Heritage Task Force, a Report to the Legislature and People of California, Sacramento, August 1984.* Joint Legislative Publications Commission, Sacramento.

Casteel, Richard W.
 1980 National Science Foundation Funding of Domestic Archeology in the United States: Where the Money Ain't. *American Antiquity* 45(1):170–180.

Chambers, Erve (editor)
 1985a Practicing Folklore. *Practicing Anthropology* 1985(1, 2):4–24.
 1985b Social Factors in Federal Environmental Planning. *Practicing Anthropology* 1985(1,2):2.

Cinq-Mars, Jacques
 1984 A Critique of Rescue Archeology in the New World: Canada. Presentation at Second New World Conference on Rescue Archeology, Dallas.

Tape recorded, on file with Organization of American States, New York.

Cleere, Henry
  1984a [Editor.] *Approaches to the Archaeological Heritage; A Comparative Study of World Cultural Resource Management Systems.* Cambridge University Press, Cambridge.
  1984b World Cultural Resource Management: Problems and Perspectives. In *Approaches to the Archaeological Heritage; A Comparative Study of World Cultural Resource Management Systems,* edited by Henry Cleere, pages 1–11. Cambridge University Press, Cambridge.
  1984c [Moderator.] The Social and Political Realities of Rescue Archeology. Presentation at Second New World Conference on Rescue Archeology, Dallas. Tape recorded, on file with Organization of American States, New York.

Dickens, Roy S., Jr., and Carole E. Hill
  1978 *Cultural Resource Planning and Management.* Westfield Press: Boulder.

Drucker, Peter F.
  1985 The Discipline of Innovation. *Harvard Business Review* 85(3):67–72.

Dunnell, Robert C.
  1985 Archaeological Survey in the Lower Mississippi Alluvial Valley, 1940–1947: A Landmark Study in American Archaeology. *American Antiquity* 50(2):297–300.

Falkner, Ann
  1977 *Without Our Past? A Handbook for the Preservation of Canada's Architectural Heritage.* University of Toronto Press, in association with the Ministry of State for Urban Affairs and Publishing Centre, Supply and Services, Toronto.

Federal Agencies Task Force
  1979 *American Indian Religious Freedom Act Report, P. L. 95–341.* U. S. Department of the Interior, Washington, D.C.

Fitch, James Marston
  1982 *Historic Preservation: Curatorial Management of the Built World.* McGraw-Hill Book Company, New York.

FitzSimons, Neal
  1968–1973 *Engineer as Historian.* Committee on History and Heritage of American Civil Engineering, American Society of Civil Engineers, Kensington, Maryland.

Fowler, Peter J.
  1981 Archaeology, the Public and the Sense of the Past. In *Our Past Before Us, Why Do We Save It?* edited by David Lowenthal and Marcus Binney, pages 56–69. Temple Smith, London.

Gero, Joan M.
  1985 Socio-Politics and the Woman-at-Home Ideology. *American Antiquity* 50(2):342–350.

Gero, Joan M., David M. Lacy, and Michael L. Blakey (editors)
  1983 The Socio-Politics of Archaeology. *University of Massachusetts, Department of Anthropology, Research Report 23.*

Glassie, Henry
1975   *Folk Housing in Middle Virginia*. University of Tennessee Press, Knoxville.

Goddard, Haynes C.
1984   An Introduction to Uncertainty Analysis in Environmental Decision Making. *The Environmental Professional* 6(2):172–184.

Haag, William G.
1985   Federal Aid to Archaeology in the Southeast, 1933–1942. *American Antiquity* 50(2):272–280.

Hanen, Marsha P., and Jane H. Kelley
1983   Social and Philosophical Frameworks for Archaeology. *In* The Socio-Politics of Archaeology, edited by Joan Gero, David Lacy, and Michael L. Blakey. *University of Massachusetts, Department of Anthropology, Research Report* 23:107–117. Amherst.

Haury, Emil W.
1985   Reflections: Fifty Years of Southwestern Archaeology. *American Antiquity* 50(2):383–394.

Holmes, Barbara, editor.
1982   *American Indian Concerns with Historic Preservation in New Mexico*. New Mexico Archeological Council, Albuquerque.

Howell, Benita J.
1981   *A Survey of Folklife along the Big South Fork of the Cumberland River*. Department of Anthropology, University of Tennessee, Knoxville.

Huth, Hans
1941   *Report on the Preservation of Mountain Culture in Great Smoky Mountains National Park*. National Park Service, Washington, D.C.

Janes, Robert R., and Charles D. Arnold
1983   Public Archaeology in the Northwest Territories. *The Musk-ox* 33:42–48.

Jellicoe, Geoffrey, and Susan Jellicoe
1982   *The Landscape of Map, Shaping the Environment from Prehistory to the Present Day*. Van Nostrand Reinhold Company, New York.

Jennings, Jesse D.
1985   River Basin Surveys: Origins, Operations, and Results, 1945–1969. *American Antiquity* 50(2):281–296.

Johnson, Leland R.
1985   *The Davis Island Lock and Dam, 1870–1922*. U. S. Army Corps of Engineers, Pittsburgh.

Karamanski, Theodore J.
1985   Logging, History, and the National Forests: A Case Study of Cultural Resource Management. *The Public Historian* 7(2):27–40.

Keel, Bennie C.
1979   A View from Inside. *American Antiquity* 44(1):164–170.

Keeney, Ralph L., and Howard Raiffa
1976   *Decisions with Multiple Objectives: Perferences and Value Tradeoffs*. John Wiley and Sons, New York.

King, Thomas F.
  1981 Historic Preservation and Sociocultural Impacts: A Developing Relationship. *Practicing Anthropology* 4(1).

Knudson, Ruthann
  1979 Commentary: Management in Historic Preservation. *COPA Communication 1979* (March):2. [Committee on Public Archaeology, Society for American Archaeology.]
  1982 Basic Principles of Archaeological Resource Management. *American Antiquity* 47(1):164–166
  1983 *An Archaeological Test of the Lower Fort MacArthur Area (CA-LAN-1129H), West Channel/Cabrillo Beach Recreational Complex, Port of Los Angeles, San Pedro, California.* Woodward-Clyde Consultants, Santa Ana, California.
  1984 Ethical Decision Making and Participation in the Politics of Archaeology. In *Ethics and Values in Archaeology,* edited by Ernestene L. Green, pages 243–263. The Free Press, New York.
  1985 Book Review, "Aboriginal Sites, Rights and Resource Development," edited by R. M. Berndt. *American Anthropologist* 87(2):457–459.

Knudson, Ruthann, David J. Fee, and Steven E. James
  1983 *A Work Plan for the Development of Archeological Overviews and Management Plans for Selected U. S. Department of the Army DARCOM Facilities.* Woodward-Clyde Consultants, Walnut Creek, California.

Leone, Mark P.
  1981 Archaeology's Relationship to the Present and the Past. In *Modern Material Culture: The Archaeology of Us,* edited by Richard Gould and Michael Schiffer, pages 5–14. Academic Press, New York.

Lindsay, Alexander J., Jr., and William D. Lipe
  1974 Introduction. *In* Proceedings of the 1974 Cultural Resource Management Conference, Federal Center, Denver, Colorado, edited by William D. Lipe and Alexander J. Lindsay, Jr.. *Museum of Northern Arizona, Technical Series* 14:vii-xii.

Lipe, William D.
  1978 Contracts, Bureaucrats and Research: Some Emerging Problems of Conservation Archaeology in the United States. In *Archaeological Essays in Honor of Irving B. Rouse,* edited by Robert C. Dunnell and Edwin S. Hall, Jr., pages 121–147. Mouton Publishers, New York.
  1984 Value and Meaning in Cultural Resources. In *Approaches to the Archaeological Heritage: A Comparative Study of World Cultural Resource Management Systems,* edited by Henry Cleere, pages 1–11. Cambridge University Press, Cambridge.

Loomis, Ormond H. (coordinator)
  1983 *Cultural Conservation: The Protection of Cultural Heritage in the United States.* Library of Congress, Washington, D.C.

Lyneis, Margaret M. (coordinator)
  1982 *An Archaeological Element for the Nevada Historic Preservation Plan.* University of Nevada, for the Nevada Division of Historic Preservation and Archaeology, Las Vegas.

Lyon II, Edwin A.
1982 *New Deal Archaeology in the Southeast: WPA, TVA, NPS, 1934–1942.* Doctoral dissertation, Louisiana State University, Baton Rouge. [University Microfilms, Ann Arbor.]

Marshall, Howard Wight
1981 American Folk Architecture: A Selected Bibliography. *Publications of the American Folklife Center,* 9 Library of Congress, Washington, D. C.

Massachusetts Historical Commission
1980 *Cultural Resources In Massachusetts: A Model for Management.* Revised edition. Division of State Plans for Grants, Heritage Conservation and Recreation Service, U.S. Department of the Interior, Washington, D. C.

Matheny, Ray T., and Dale L. Berge
1976 Symposium on Dynamics of Cultural Resource Management. *U. S. Forest Service, Southwestern Region, Archeological Report* 10.

Mayer-Oakes, William J., and Alice W. Portnoy, editors.
1979 *Scholars as Contractors.* Interagency Archeological Services Division, Heritage Conservation and Recreation Service, U. S. Department of the Interior, Washington, D. C.

McGimsey III, Charles R., and Hester A. Davis
1977 *The Management of Archeological Resources: The Airlie House Report.* Society for American Archaeology, Washington, D.C.

McKinley, J. R., and K. L. Jones (editors)
1979 *Archeological Resource Management in Australia and Oceania.* New Zealand Historic Places Trust, Wellington.

Melnicj, Robert Z.
1980 Preserving Cultural and Historic Landscapes. *U. S. Department of the Interior, National Park Service, Cultural Resources Management Bulletin* 3(1):1–2, 6.

National Research Council, Environmental Studies Board
1982 *Assessing Cultural Attributes in Planning Water Resources Projects: Report of the Panel on Cultural Attributes in Water Resources Projects.* National Research Council, Washington, D.C.

National Trust for Historic Preservation
1980 *Preservation: Toward an Ethic in the 1980s.* The Preservation Press, Washington, D.C.
1983 *With Heritage So Rich.* The Preservation Press, Washington, D.C.

Nelson, Hal, and J. Anthony Paredes (editors)
1985 Government and Industry, "Any Comments on the Sociology Section, Tony?": Committee Work as Applied Anthropology in Fishery Management. *Human Organization* 44(2):177–186.

Opie, John
1983 The Uses of History in the Search for a Common Ground in the Environmental Debate: SOL/QOL Values. *The Environmental Professional* 5(3/4):260–272.

Oregon Commission on Indian Services
  1980 *American Indian Cultural Resources: A Preservation Handbook.* Oregon Commission on Indian Services, Salem.

Pearson, Michael, and Helen Temple (editors)
  1984 *Historical Archaeology and Conservation Philosophy.* Heritage Council of New South Wales, Sydney.

Pillsbury, Richard, and Andrew Kardos
  1969 A Field Guide to the Folk Architecture of the Northwestern United States. *Geography Publications at Dartmouth* 8. [Special Edition on Geographical Lore.]

Portnoy, Alice W. (editor)
  1978 *Scholars as Managers, or How Can the Managers Do It Better.* Interagency Archeological Services, Office of Archeology and Historic Preservation Division, Heritage Conservation and Recreation Service, U. S. Department of the Interior, Washington, D.C.

Sharer, Robert J., and Wendy Ashmore
  1985 *Fundamentals of Archaeology.* The Benjamin/Cummings Publishing Company, Inc., Menlo Park, California.

Sitton, Thad, George L. Mehaffy, and O. L. Davis, Jr.
  1983 *Oral History: A Guide for Teachers (and Others).* University of Texas Press, Austin.

Spaulding, Albert C.
  1985 Fifty Years of Theory. *American Antiquity* 50(2):301–308.

Stilgoe, John R.
  1982 *Common Landscape of America, 1580 to 1845.* Yale University Press, New Haven.

Stipe, Robert E. (editor)
  1980 *New Directions in Rural Preservation.* U. S. Department of the Interior, Washington, D.C.

Sutherland, Patricia D.
  1983 Discussant's Comments: Northern Archaeology Symposium, Pt. Two: Current Trends. *The Musk-ox* 33:92–93.

Thomas, David Hurst
  1979 *Archaeology.* Holt, Rinehart and Winston, New York.

U. S. Department of the Interior
  1980 *Resource Protection Planning Process.* Division of State Plans and Grants, Heritage Conservation and Recreation Service, U. S. Department of the Interior, Washington, D.C.
  1981 *Historic American Engineering Record Field Instructions.* National Park Service, U. S. Department of the Interior, Washington, D.C.
  1982 *Cultural Resources Technical Report for the Environmental Impact Statement on Public Service Company of New Mexico's Proposed New Mexico Generating Station and Possible New Town.* U. S. Department of the Interior, Bureau of Land Management, New Mexico State Office, Santa Fe.
  1983 *Final Environmental Impact Statement on Public Service Company of New Mexico's Proposed New Mexico Generating Station and Other*

Possible End Uses of the Ute Mountain Land Exchange. New Mexico State Office, Bureau of Land Management, U. S. Department of the Interior, Santa Fe.

1985 *A Review of the Unsuitability Criteria in Federal Coal Leasing.* Bureau of Land Management, Office of Surface Mining Reclamation and Enforcement, and Fish and Wildlife Service, U. S. Department of the Interior; Forest Service, U. S. Department of Agriculture, Washington, D.C.

U. S. National Archives and Records Service
1974 *Guide to the National Archives of the United States.* U. S. National Archives and Records Service, General Services Administration, Washington, D. C.

Wildesen, Leslie E.
1984 The Search for an Ethic in Archaeology: An Historical Perspective. In *Ethics and Values in Archaeology,* edited by Ernestene L. Green, page 3012. The Free Press, New York.

Wilson, Mary
1984 Log Cabin Studies. *U. S. Forest Service, Intermountain Region, Cultural Resource Report* 9.

Wilson, Rex L., and Gloria Loyola (editors)
1982 *Rescue Archeology: Papers from the First New World Conference on Rescue Archeology.* The Preservation Press, Washington, D.C.

Workman, William B., compiler
1985 Cultural Resource Management Archeology in Alaska: Current Status and Future Prospects. *Alaska Historical Commission Studies in History* 148.

Yellen, John E., and Mary W. Greene
1985 Archaeology and the National Science Foundation. *American Antiquity* 50(2):332–341.

Yellen, John E., Mary W. Greene, and Richard T. Louttit
1980 A Response to "National Science Foundation Funding of Domestic Archeology in the United States: Where the Money Ain't." *American Antiquity* 45(1):180–181.

Symbolic, Structural, and Critical Archaeology

Introduction

What is symbolic archaeology, structural archaeology, and critical archaeology? Given that they are different approaches to archaeology, what do they share? And given that these two approaches do not compose a uniform movement, what are the currents and cross-currents between them and mainstream archaeology?

Symbolic archaeology, structural archaeology, and critical archaeology are three quite different approaches to archaeological data. None of them is completely defined as yet. None grows directly out of either traditional (Leach 1973) or the new archaeology (Clarke 1973) and yet all three have drawn significant attention. The archaeologists involved in them appear to be involved in the same issues and operate with the same assumptions (Hodder 1982a, Spriggs 1984; Miller 1982b; Moore and Keene 1983). As these approaches are being defined it is becoming clear that they are not necessarily headed for similar analyses (Bender 1985, Patterson 1984). It is, however, clear to anyone who reads the archaeological literature today, that many archaeologists are concerned with meaning (Hodder 1982a, 1983), ideology (Kristainsen 1984; Paynter 1985; Handsman 1980, 1981, 1982), structure (Friedman and Rowlands 1977; Glassic 1975; Freidel 1981), and cognition (Deetz 1967) in past societies. In order to approach such areas through the archaeological record, ideas, models, and theories have been borrowed and explored from structuralism, cognitive anthropology, symbolic analysis, and Marxism (Baudrillard 1975, Gledhill 1981; Godelier 1977, 1978; Meillassoux 1972; Wallerstein 1976).

Symbolic, structural, and critical archaeology are chosen in this essay because their spokespersons are increasingly vocal and widely read, and because their differences are not as clear within the field as they should be. The point of this essay is not to address the origins of these approaches, whether they are mainly American or British, nor to identify schools of thought associated with universities or with particular scholars. The point is to identify the basic assumptions and to see how they are expressed in the five illustrations discussed and quoted below.

Four Issues

These three initiatives in archaeology can be understood by reference to four issues. The first one is the interactive or recursive quality of culture. Rather than supposing that culture, including the rules, behavior, and things produced, is borne by people in a fairly passive and unaware fashion, the assumption is that people create, use, modify, and manipulate their symbolic capabilities, making and remaking the world they live in. This does not necessarily mean the capacity to dominate, control, or even to change culture in directive or politically forceful ways. It is, however, an effort to see that, like language, its use shapes our lives, and our lives would be shapeless without it. The major impact in archaeology of this viewpoint comes in regarding material culture as an instrument in creating meaning and order in the world (Conkey 1982; Donley 1982; Kus 1982; Moore 1982; Parker Pearson 1982), and not solely as the reflection of economics, social organization, or ideology.

The importance of this point is well developed by John Barrett who attempts to adapt Giddens (1979, 1981, 1982a, 1982b) to archaeology.

> One attempt to break with functionalism involves shifting the focus of analysis from the consequences of human action to the intentions and motivations of that action. . . . In the theory of structuration, Giddens employs an analytical frame of the "time-space continuum" within which the actions of knowledgeable human subjects reproduce the institutional conditions of their own existence. Giddens means . . . discursive knowledge (which) encompass[es] the practical knowledge of "how to go on" . . ., it is knowledge which is drawn upon for, and reproduced in, human action. Here the subjects draw upon their reflexive experience of an objective world, which appears constituted as a meaningful cultural resource, and act upon those same external conditions to reproduce and transform them, bequeathing the results of that action as the conditions for future action [Barrett n.d.:5–9].

This is the recursive quality of culture, which sees people as actors, symbols as central to human existence, and material culture in context as analogous to language in its capacity to order human life.

The second crucial issue behind symbolic, structural, and critical archaeology is an emphasis on meaning. All approaches deny the kind of materialism which has over the years come to be associated with the new archaeology. As materialism was inherited from Leslie White, Julian Steward, reinterpreted through Marvin Harris and A. P. Vayda, and a host of other, largely American, scholars, it became a form of determinism that has been avoided by most British social anthropologists and all American symbolic anthropologists. The materialism which has been rejected by symbolic (Hodder 1985) and critical archaeology is that which is seen as a hierarchy of factors going from ecological, technological, and demographic considerations to social organization, and to a vaguely defined ideological or religious organization.

In a concrete historical sense in archaeology, the last twenty years' progress has revolved around the remarkably productive studies of the natural environment, domesticated plant and animal foods, and the tools, shelters, and techniques used to supply, support, reproduce, and control a population, society, and a whole culture. While sometimes taking potshots at these achievements, symbolic archaeology rejects the materialism that ignores meaning, the context of daily life, deliberate attempts to manipulate social relations, and the whole world of thought. On the other hand, the sources (Habermas 1971, 1981) of critical archaeology, which are here separate from the others, do not renounce a materialist tradition. Such archaeology argues that in any society where there are contradictions, conflict, or exploitation, to expect smooth functioning or adaptation as the new archaeology did, is to miss a major part of the culture. Ideology is the mechanism, the part of a cultural system that hides or masks the contradictions, and thus prevents active conflict from occurring (Althusser 1971; Barnett and Silverman 1979). Ideology has, until recently, never been defined in archaeology in any coherent or operational way.

How is culture conceived by these approaches to archaeology? Is it levels, a system, or like language? What interacts and where is cause? Barrett (n.d.) and the symbolic archaeologists (Miller 1982a; Tilley 1982, 1984) avoid the notion of levels in preference for a picture of people using symbols to negotiate reality on a moment by moment basis. Structuralists see a coherent set of symbols (oppositions) shaping daily life, but in the examples used below from Freidel and Schele (in press) and Deetz (1977; 1983) we can see they are not so concerned with how the oppositions are affected by use. For their part, critical archaeologists do conceive of levels in the Marxist sense, but see ideology as powerful in maintaining society, its coherence, and its continuity: ideology is what reproduces society intact.

The third issue that helps to define both symbolic and critical archaeology is a critique of the function of the past and scientific knowledge of it in society. Symbolic (Shanks and Tilley in press) and critical archaeology (Gero et al. 1983; Leone 1981a, 1981b; Meltzer 1981) assert the active role of the past in the society that is interested in it. Both approaches assert that the past, whether it be known through the sciences of the past, the vernacular media, myth, or through museums, is an active vehicle for communicating and composing meanings. Neither position will allow archaeology to assert scientific neutrality, or its role as the objective producer of accurate knowledge about the past (Wylie 1981, 1985), or even as a socially irrelevant pursuit. Symbolic archaeology asserts that since the past is a social creation, and that because it exists in most societies in endless variations, and further, that because archaeology produces one of these variations, the priviliged status of archaelogy must be examined for its own good. Where does its right to dominate come from? Why is the archaeological interpretation considered the only correct one?

Critical archaeology forcefully asserts with Marx that history is always produced in the service of class interests (Bloch 1977; Gero 1983; Wobst 1983). Furthermore, it asserts that appeals to scientific objectivity are likely to obfuscate discussion of the assumption of objectivity. Thus, an exploration of the political function of archaeology may produce both a consciousness of the social function of archaeology as well as a set of questions for archaeology to address that may be of greater social benefit. Thus, while symbolic archaeology on the one hand is aware that the past is a social construct and is just as dynamic a part of culture as language, critical archaeology, on the other hand, sees history as ideology, and likely to be pernicious if ignored. Therefore, attention to archaeology's ideological status may produce important, archaeologically answerable questions.

Fourth, from within symbolic archaeology has come a serious denial of the place of positivism in archaeological science (Hodder 1982a; Miller and Tilley 1984). Within critical archaeology the critique is less severe in its implications and more hopeful of sustaining the tradition of the later sixties and seventies. Symbolic archaeology is not willing to grant a culture-free status to the self-proclaimed self-watching abilities of Western scientific logic. There are two points: an unaware science is ignorant of its own culture. Further, since method is itself of cultural origin, it may ultimately not be possible to create or depend on a science of the past to produce any more than a strong interpretation. This does not imply that all pasts are equal, but it does imply that any science that believes itself to be active in the cross-cultural traditions or in the law-searching tradition, or in the tradition that regards an examination of its connection with modern society as mere social philosophy is blinding itself to the fundamental proposition of anthropology: we and our institutions are cultural creations, and we do not exist outside of culture.

Critical archaeology has not divorced itself so completely from the emphasis on scientific method developed over the last twenty years in archaeology. The word "critical" in any scholarly context means that the relations between the assumptions and discoveries of the discipline and their ties to modern life are a central concern and are subject to examination (Habermas 1971). Such examination automatically subjects the questions, methods, and discoveries of a science or discipline to questions which ask how the scientist's surroundings dictate the questions, influence the method, and predetermine either the results or, more usually, their meaning and interpretation. Nonetheless, critical studies do not hope for or cause the impoverishment of a science or discipline. The point is to produce neither a debilitating skepticism nor a pointless relativism.

The most prominent work done by British symbolic archaeologists is with different aspects of the Bronze Age of Northwest Europe. Hodder (1982b), Shanks and Tilley (1982) Tilley (1984), Shennan (1982), Kristiansen (1984), and Parker Pearson (1984) have taken a stratified society in which there were marked differences in access to wealth, and asked how was power justified, used, and perpetuated. Their analyses of the standard remains of the Bronze Age suggest that the rituals associated with burials, barrows, and utensils were used by the powerful to convince the less powerful of the existence of equality when that relationship was actually diminishing. The basic assumptions in these analyses are that stratification was based on unequal access to power, or goods, but is always tentative and must be justified or masked. Stratification is a dynamic, not a stable, relationship. The second assumption is that some material items, like those associated with burial, can be used, probably in ritual contexts, to convince all involved of the justice of the situation and thus to neutralize potential conflict, and so to continue society intact. This precis of the argument distills too much, however, to see the difference between a symbolic and a critical interpretation.

Hodder's (1982b) argument shows cogently what he is after. In the Dutch Neolithic there are a series of well-known phases marked by different settlement, subsistence, and ceramic patterns. Early on, settlements were nucleated, agriculture was intensive, and pottery was decorated in clearly bounded areas. Later, pottery decorations are related to each other (Hodder 1982b:165).

> The pottery designs of [phases] A to E has been described as incorporating increasing numbers of contrasts and oppositions. Complex communal burial and associated ritual are known throughout the early . . . phases. But in phases F and G . . . megaliths cease to be constructed. . . . The construction of tombs in the early [phases] argues for the presence of corporate groups and . . . the use of communal burial mounds and monuments . . . symbolize local competing groups and lineages in north and west Europe. . . . The tombs, and an ideology related to ancestors, may have functioned not only to legitimate dominant groups, but also to legitimate their traditional rights tied to one place [Hodder 1982b:170].

> [Given change to dispersed settlement, contradictions emerge between] dominant and subordinate groups to emphasize traditional, stable ties to ancestors, in the context of shorter term, expanding settlement. . . . [Consequently] the decrease in identifiable contrasts and categorical oppositions in the pottery forms and decoration of the late [phases] could have acted to deny the earlier social distinctions, and to emphasize connections and interrelationships. By expressing a decreased concern with categorization and by drawing less attention to the boundaries between these categories, a new pattern of social and economic relationships could be set up [Hodder 1982b:171].

> The material culture [burial, pots, axes] is organized into a complex series of categories and oppositions so that the associated activities can play a part in drawing attention to and legitimating individual rights in a context in which there is increasing potential for the disruption of those rights". . . . On the North European plain . . . groups manipulated burial, pottery and the symbols . . . in order to maintain traditional rights. . . . The new process of legitimization resolved the earlier contradictions . . .[as did the] symbolic distinctions in pottery and . . . the daily activities associated with . . . its use" [Hodder 1982b:175, 176].

Material culture was used by people in institutional settings to negotiate the change from stable, closely settled hierarchical groups to unstable, widely scattered, also hierarchical groups. The groups changed and so did people's places in and among them. Thus there had to be negotiation over place, which means that meaning changed and this was facilitated through the use of many items of material culture. This particular illustration of Hodder's work is important because of its emphasis on meaning and context, its emphasis, on the recursive quality of material culture, which in turn allows us to see that people as individuals, not as population aggregates, die, are buried, take part in rituals which are genuinely significant in their lives, make, use, and rely on pottery vessels to help define their lives, resolve conflicts within them, and furthermore, that this is an interpretation of elements of the archaeological record. The validity of this interpretation outside of a small part of Europe is irrelevant; its strength lies in its ability to take normally separated aspects of archaeological data, and to articulate the relationships that produced them. Consideration of burial, subsistence, ritual, settlement, and their changes over time in terms of the stresses, conflicts, and contradictions is not at all normal behavior among conventional archaeologists. Also, there is obviously a hypothesis behind the article. Hodder is opposed to variable testing of the kind that shreds the fabric of the past for an accuracy that has limited value in the present. Hodder's piece does not offer a conclusion with a stated degree of veracity; it offers an ending which is plausible, which can be expanded or changed by other archaeologists just as easily as could be done by using strict positivist procedures.

A Case of Structural Archaeology

In isolating symbolic archaeology as a topic, we have the benefit of discussing a form of archaeology that is being elaborated continually. Its major contributions involve an integration of the massive data on the Northwest European Neolithic. Its ethnoarchaeology (Donley 1982; Kus 1982; Moore 1982; Parker Pearson 1982) and its critique of the new archaeology are also, obviously, important. Upon examination, it is clear that symbolic archaeology's achievements cannot be isolated from the progress made by cognitive or structural archaeology.

Since symbolic archaeology exists as a movement contemporaneously with structural analyses, it is reasonable to ask what is its relationship to reconstructions of the New England mind set (Deetz 1977), the cognitive rules of folk housing in Virginia (Glassie 1975), Olmec cosmology (Furst 1968), or Maya cosmology (Freidel 1981)? A number of American archaeologists have been concerned with symbolic, or in a Parsonian framework, cultural issues for some time. For many, indeed most, culture is a level of meaning or thought that includes values, cosmology, patterns held unawares, or structures composed of oppositions. Such a reality exists alongside and is independent of social organization. Culture facilitates social reality. Further, these archaeologists do not find cause for change or stability in any one level of reality, but rather reinforcement between them. Most would agree with the recursive quality of material culture, but as an afterthought not as a basic operation to start with. For these archaeologists, it is culture or symbols that are recursive with changes in politics, settlement expansion, dynastic or governmental shift, or subsistence. Structural and cognitive scholars also would find a recursive relationship between archaeological constructions and the society of the archaeologists inevitable. Except for Kehoe (1984a, 1984b) none seems to have pursued it yet as a research strategy. All these archaeologists favor interpretation over the testing of precisely arranged variables, hypothesis fashion, as suggested by an approach from positivism.

When one reads Deetz, Glassie, Freidel, Furst, Hall, or some of the others, there is a horde of data, and tremendous emphasis on an idea of complex dimensions to fit all the archaeological pieces together. Such authors attempt to produce a whole that either corrects a previous error of archaeological fragmentation or because it replaces overly simple explanations of social change.

David Freidel's work on Maya cosmology is a useful example. He has been working for years on Maya iconographic images and, along with Linda Schele (Freidel and Schele in press), has tried to understand their meaning and textual place in terms of the changes in Maya society from the Preclassic to Classic to Postclassic, or for about a thousand years (roughly 200 B.C.–A.D. 800). Freidel and Schele begin by using changes in iconography to trace changes in the meaning of the symbols that are associated with political power.

> The Late Pre-classic symbolic model was based on the passage of Venus as Morning and Evening Star with the rising and setting of the sun. . . . They developed an amazingly effective cosmogram . . . which the community could verify by simply observing the sky. As the model was expanded and adapted . . . two processes of change stand out. The historical identities of Late Pre-classic rulers have not been found recorded in public space, suggesting that personal and historical identity of rulers did not require permanent verification in

the form of public monuments. Exactly the opposite is true of the Classic period. The legitimation of individual rulers through genealogy and supernatural charter and in public space with public participation seems to have been the prime motivation for the erection of public art in the Classic period. Those [later] rulers legitimized their positions by claiming identity as the gods of the cosmogram [Freidel and Schele in press:27–29].

This innovation in the Late Pre-classic period occurs in the context of a rapid and profound reorganization of Maya society in which a heretofore *de facto* elite becomes legitimate and acceptable to the general populace. The result is a greatly expanded access to labor and goods celebrated in the construction of massive centers [Freidel and Schele in press:31].

. . . the Lowland Maya were not in a position . . . to reverse strategies of production and trade, population growth and other indigenous factors reinforcing the trend towards increased social complexity. In the face of these dynamic social conditions, an ideal of social equality became increasingly untenable and finally underwent transformation to a model of reality which made elitism both rational and necessary. The social result was the explosive release of energy invested in central places celebrating the new order [Freidel and Schele in press:36].

[Freidel and Schele finish off with establishing the power of the symbols whose political use they have so effectively described.] As metaphor, the twin ancestors [Sun and Venus] provide a potent image for lateral blood ties between lineages, communities, and peoples adhering to the same myth cycle. As twins are of the same womb and blood, so all Maya are of the same ancestry and blood. Brotherhood lends itself to egalitarian values and their kinship sanctions. [In the Classic period they became ranked, and] this positioning provides a celestially correct cosmic model, with Morning and Evening Star above the rising and setting sun. . . . By asserting that time had passed between the birth of the twins, as given in the hieroglyphic texts at Palenque, the Maya displayed the principle of ranking, of inequality, in their icon and concept. . . . [Freidel and Schele in press:37].

The mass of data on the elements showing the iconography is not included in the excerpts. Were they presented, the clear use of structuralism to highlight oppositions would be unmistakable. Freidel proposes a social as well as a cultural revolution among the Lowland Maya; these are independent but simultaneous, mutually supporting, with neither causing the other. He insists that there is no need to depend on invasion or environmental disturbance on which to base the changes. Thus, along with the symbolic archaeologists, Freidel sees people thinking order into their world through the use of central, powerful, and pliable symbols. These symbols initiate behavior and rationalize it as well.

In Freidel and Schele's treatment of material culture is the understanding that material objects are recursive or forming. Friedel can be and is more clear than Hodder, Shanks, Tilley or Sheenan about how ritual life and shrines and temple structures shaped people's lives. He can be, since ethnohistoric texts exist to give a good idea of what Mayan cosmology was and what its manifestations were. No such help is available from the Neolithic of Northwest Europe. We have long had the evidence from linguistics, semiotics, and from structural and symbolic anthropology that cultural materials form; they are active ingredients in thought and behavior. Nonetheless, when the material record was defined as reflective of all aspects of behavior, the recursive quality of culture, including material culture, tended to be ignored or considered second, when at all.

Cognitive Archaeology

"Ignored" may be a better way to characterize how theory within the new archaeology handled material culture, and, indeed, culture as a whole. Even so, Binford's early and central move of defining material culture as being shaped by all levels of culture, and thus of reflecting all its components is an essential step in allowing Freidel to take Preclassic cylinders and Classic pyramids and postulate a cosmogram. True, the method Freidel employs is structuralist and its assumptions about what material culture encodes may simply coincide with the new archaeology's. They may be independent, but they are not contradictory. Yet, the recursive quality of the items is clearly seen by the symbolic and structural archaeologists, and it is not employed by materialist archaeologists.

The contrast in Freidel's position with Deetz (1977) and Glassie (1975), who are quite concerned with thought, is important because the latter do not explore the impact of symbolically constituted behavior back on the symbolic structure. Both Deetz and Glassie, one an archaeologist and the other a folklorist, are concerned with reconstructing the rules or cognitive patterns behind expressions of folk material culture. Their method is structuralist and they take the recursive quality of material culture more as a given, than as a topic for detailed description. Since Deetz employs Glassie, and uses archaeological data from New England in the 17th, 18th, and 19th centuries, he is a useful illustration of the two points they share with the symbolic archaeologists. Deetz is occupied with the consistency of thought (its power) that finds expression in a vast array of material items. He is committed to building a case strong enough to link large and diverse ranges of functionally unrelated items. He is willing to attempt this approach, using logic that takes a culturally specific opposition and finds replication in other cultural domains as evidence of accuracy. Deetz is no less scientific than Hodder, Freidel, or Levi-Strauss. He is less concerned with defining tests, but quite concerned with generality, which is just as much a part of science as measurement.

Deetz, Glassie, and Freidel, unlike the symbolic archaeologists, are unconcerned with the origins of their questions. Insofar as Deetz and Glassie are concerned with early American culture they are concerned with American society today. But they are not concerned with systematic examination of research categories, the locus of the oppositions found in the data, or the social function of the interpretation which they create. Indeed, there is no particular concern with why the American patterns they so cogently describe ceased, or why today is, or is not, their product.

Deetz begins his analysis by using Glassie (1975:189–190) to say that in Anglo-America when "the social, economic, political and religious conditions . . . changed . . . people adapted . . . , developing new modes of thought, and [then] the things they did, the artifacts they made, manifested the changes that had taken place in their minds" (Deetz 1981:14).

In Virginia, in New England, and throughout Anglo-America in the late 18th and 19th centuries, "individualism signals 'the point at which the face-to-face community dies' [Glassie 1975:190]. This important statement is based on observed changes in vernacular housing. This shift from corporate communal organization to lonely individualism is reflected in many aspects of the material world" (Deetz 1981:13).

> The shift from extensive to intensive structures [appearing to be random vs. symmetrically ordered] that accounts for shrinking chimneys, lowering ceilings and roofs, and tucking behind of ells and sheds in Virginia appears in New England not only in similar architectural changes but also in the disappearance of shared seating at meals, shared utensils, and the appearance of the very impersonal, private urn and willow design, which is profoundly different from both the earlier death's heads and cherubs, both of which extensively related the individual to the community by portraying a part of him or her as it passed by. Simple forms replace complex forms in the rapid change from multicolored ceramics to those predominantly

white and blue. In foodways, complex pottages and stews give way to discrete foodstuffs, served separate one from another. Like ceramics, gravestones, earlier made from slates, schists, and sandstones in a range of colors—blue, red, green, black and buff—also become uniformly white, carved from low grade local marbles. The disappearance of borders on louvres, doors and windows in houses is paralleled by the reduction in size and complexity of borders on gravestones, and at least a change in the average width and decorative elaboration of the marleys (edges) of plates and saucers toward less framed, more open forms. And the shift to symmetry reflected in central hall houses—tripartite and severely symmetrical—in all of the Anglo-American world is paralleled by the emergence of a symmetrical relationship between the individual and his or her material culture, utensils, foodstuffs, and burial pits [Deetz 1983:33].

To arrive at the synthesis of the profound conceptual changes that occurred in America during the 18th century and that peaked before 1800, Deetz used oppositions employed by Glassie to describe Middle Virginia folk housing, and applied them to ceramics, foodways, mortuary remains, and music. The oppositions are intellect/emotion, private/public, artificial/natural substance, scattered/clustered, extensive/intensive, complex/simple, framed/open, and nonsymmetry/symmetry. All these fall under Levi-Strauss' larger opposition order/chaos or culture/nature.

Deetz has taken an interpretation, which one could call legitimately a hypothesis, and tried it on data from New England, where he showed it has a strong ability to fit wide ranges of vernacular material culture. As the idea assumes generality, both in domains covered and in space, it becomes less particularistic but does not lose its ability to include local context. Deetz's current work in the historical archaeology of South Africa will provide a place to extend the idea. Once done outside of the American context, Deetz will, or may, face the worldwide impact of an organizational form for everyday life that stems from England and Holland, or from the colonial process. Dealing with our direct ancestors leads, naturally enough, to the tie to ourselves, which is one of the central issues in archaeology.

Critical Archaeology

As soon as any archaeologist assumes the recursive quality of culture and the active quality of material culture, it follows logically that archaeology may have some active impact on our own society. Just as myths about ancestors are verified through astronomical prognostication in the Bronze Age (Thorpe 1981) and in the Classic Maya, and were used to support local power structures, it may follow that our reconstructions of the past, which are verified through archaeological data, have a social function analogous to the ones we are postulating for ancient societies. Archaeology thus, may be more than a neutral and objective science.

How does an archaeologist explore the relationship just mentioned? And what will we know as a result? Such an exploration is known either as phenomenological self-reflection, or critical analysis, depending on the assumptions used. The assumption behind the first is that knowledge of another culture is always constituted through categories and methods that can never be freed from the scholar's culture. Thus, ethnographic, and, logically, archaeological, knowledge is always contingent. This produces the skeptical position which implies that if the distant other cannot be known independently, the effort at knowing is always going to be questionable. A critical analysis stems from a Marxist position and does not deny the possibility of knowing the other, ethnographic or archaeological. Rather, the position argues that all knowledge is class-based and histories are composed for class purposes. Science is a politically contingent enterprise. It is not just that science is part of its own culture, which is obvious with anthropology, but that it is subject to political and economic aims. An examination of those aims leads to knowledge of the political uses of science, and of the sources of the questions, methods, and results which the science produces. Stemming from this argument is the unwillingness of both symbolic and critical archaeologists to allow an unreflective positivism to assert the degrees of certainty with which its methods relate the past.

Critical archaeology, based on the work of Habermas (1971) and Lukacs (1971), does not join symbolic archaeology in such severe doubts about understanding the past. Its concern is with understanding pasts that are more relevant to its theoretical concerns. What are the pasts of those who have been denied a history: women, blacks, the Third World, workers? What is the past of ideology?

Two initial efforts that stem more from hermeneutical reading than from critical analysis have been made to disentangle deep prehistory from myth. They (Perper and Schrire 1977 and Landau 1984) illustrate why we should be concerned with the cultural basis of our work and what the results of disentanglement can be.

These [myths] allow us to see the hunting model for what it is: a mixture of biological facts and evolutionary concepts entangled in the constricting threads of western myth [the Genesis stories of eating of the tree of knowledge, and eating meat after the flood]. It is these mythic notions that distinguish the visions of human evolution . . . from those of modern ecologists and evolutionists for whom human behavior is not dominated by irrevocable actions, but is above all, a matter of constant adaptation, flexibility, and plasticity. . . . The most plausible ecological strategy would have been to avoid depending on only one foodstuff and to adapt a flexible, mixed diet. In truth, there need have been no single act, no primal trigger, no expulsion from Eden to set off an irreversible series of evolutionary changes. We need not have been shot into existence by one major dietary change [Perper and Schrire 1977:458].

[The myth entangled point of view,] that hunting transformed the ancestral primate into man is found in the seminal essay by Washburn and Avis. . . . [They argue that] a combination of tool-using and meat-eating were therefore key factors in producing man. . . . Ardrey finally says explicitly what Washburn, Campbell, and others only imply. He lays bare the essence of hunting for the anthropologist, by stating unequivocally that it lies at the center of human behavior today and that its effects were not only powerful but irreversible. In his terms, we hunted because we were human, but more important, we are human because we hunted. The hunting model is the counterpart of [the Genesis] myth. . . . [Perper and Schrire 1977:454].

In a more technically exhaustive analysis, Landau (1983; 1984:262–268) shows that

accounts of human evolution usually feature four important episodes: terrestriality, bipedalism, encephalization, or the development of the brain, intelligence, and language: and civilization, the emergence of technology, morals, and society. . . . [The order of these episodes] may vary between paleoanthropological accounts [but] they tend to fall into a common narrative structure [which] can also describe traditional literary forms such as the folktale or hero myth (Landau 1984:266–267].

[One part of the structure which produces the uniform narrative] is that history can be seen as a meaningful totality. Behind this lies the idea that scattered events of the past can be linked with the present in an overall continuous series . . .; a sequence of events . . . organized into an intelligible story with a beginning, a middle, and an end [Landau 1984:267].

[A second part of narrative structure] is that history can be seen as a series of critical moments and transitions. . . . This is especially true of Darwinian narratives, which, owing to their emphasis on natural selection, are often cast in terms of transformation through struggle. Events are not inherently crises, however, nor are they transitions, they acquire such value only in relation to other events in a series [Landau 1984:267].

[A third part of the narrative structure] is that history can be explained by arranging events into a sequence. Selecting events and arranging them sequentially involves considerations of causality . . .; what happens next often cannot be answered separately from the questions of how and why it happened and how it all turns out. Thus, although scientific explanations may invoke specific laws to account for events . . . , such explanations must be distinguished from explanatory effects produced simply by the sequential ordering of events. In other words, the task is to determine whether scientific explanations apparently based on natural laws are actually a function of narrative procedures [Landau 1984:267].

In turning to critical archaeology now, two changes are apparent in the analyses produced within a reflexive context (Wylie in press). The first is that the relationship between the present and interpretations of the past is assumed to be a political and economic one. And, second, it is also assumed that a past can be discovered or interpreted archaeologically that can comment on the origins and impact of that tie so that the ideological and class-centered nature of history is illuminated.

The two steps are well illustrated in the research of Handsman (1980, 1981, 1982) working on the historical archaeology of western Connecticut. He begins with a series of modern towns like Canaan and Litchfield, which from their outward appearance look like perfect 18th century New England villages, right out of stereotypes from Norman Rockwell, Grandma Moses, and traditional calendar scenes.

The New England urban village as a complex social place appeared around 1800 and "is marked by an increase in the disparity of the distribution of wealth within many villages, as well as the appearance of commercial and professional specialization" (Handsman 1981:5). The classic New England village replaced an earlier landscape made up of scattered farms with a few wide places in the road where there were nucleated settlements. Why then was the New England village defined as agrarian and used to hide the industrial process which accompanied it and why has that use continued? Why is "the modern system . . . constituted so as to segregate itself from what appeared before" (Handsman 1981:16)?

Handsman proceeds to argue that "modern America's past is not a more simplified version of itself but an entirely different [noncapitalist] world. . . . Thus the history of the village of Canaan is capable of being written . . . to reveal the structural discontinuities and then to explore the missing pieces" (Handsman 1981:18). To do so Handsman has isolated the classes of artifacts that show the processes of industrially based urbanization. These processes are explored because they are the origins of daily life today and because they sustain exploitation and are hidden behind an ideology that says the processes have existed since colonial times.

These industrial processes are recoverable archaeologically in a tavern midden (1750-1850) by reasoning that

> during the first century of its use, when the center village of Canaan did not exist between 1750 and 1850, the everyday lives of the inhabitants of the Lawrence Farmstead [the earlier use of the tavern] did not differ from one year to the next. The range of activities which took place, the equipment and facilities which were used during these activities, and the deposited activities from them will tend to be homogeneous from one analytical unit to the next.
>
> Once the process of settlement growth, socio-economic differentiation, and commercial and professional specialization begin, this principle of redundancy will disappear, to be replaced by everyday lives which are variable and non-redundant from one moment to the next. The associated archaeological record of everyday life at the tavern [a later use of the farmstead] should become more individuated . . . whether specific [archaeological] units are compared to one another or to units . . . of the earlier period [Handsman 1981:13–14].

Handsman (1981:14) reasons that undifferentiated deposits of ceramics, bottle glass, window glass, nails and construction hardware represent a homogeneous way of life, and that a greater degree of dispersion represents greater differentiation. And indeed "the earlier midden displays a coarse-grained structure while the later midden, reflective of a period of urbanization, is characterized by a fine-grained . . . individuated . . . highly differentiated . . . deposit" (Handsman 1981:13–14).

A critical archaeologist has taken a living environment, in this case the well-known New England village, and has shown that it was constructed to be and remains a mask. That makes it ideology in the Marxist sense. The center villages so commonly assumed to be unaltered since the 18th century are indeed 19th century representations created by an industrializing elite to ground itself and its large variation in wealth in an earlier agrarian era which valued independence, equality, and family. By extension, it may also be the case that many of the museum villages, historic houses, living farms, media presentations of the past, and virtually all popular uses of archaeology and history in this country are ideological. A critical archaeologist's task is to examine such environments that have an archaeological component and show which political and economic factors in the present have created them. Furthermore such a study should show how those factors are disguised within the setting from the past. Such economic or political factors are usually not well understood in the present and to illuminate them, is to give them a history through archaeology as Handsman has tried to do. He has established the switch to an industrial existence through archaeology, which was an existence the society had to deny by the use of settlement pattern and architecture. The denial was necessary because of the contradiction between the ideal of equality and the reality of substantial disparity in wealth and power. That denial prevents knowledge of shifting family relations, gender definition, wage relations, and property holdings. These factors, when given a history by a critical archaeologist, in turn contribute to an awareness of the role of capitalism in producing histories that disguise but do not educate (Lukacs 1971). The point in a critical archaeology is to understand the past in order to create a consciousness of modern society.

The question of consciousness is a central one in symbolic archaeology and in critical archaeology. The question stems from the problematic relationship between present and past. Awareness of the range of possibilities for influence of the present on interpreting the past, and of the recursiveness of history, makes apparent the problem of the appropriation of the past. Sensitivity to this problem has led Hodder (1984:25–32, 1985:1–26) to the position that all pasts are culturally constituted. If one of them is more accurately interpreted because it was derived from more rigorous methodology, then the practice that produces rigor must also be seen as culturally constituted and that such a basis for accuracy may be a bogus basis for authority. This is a paradoxical situation, which leads logically to suggesting that other peoples and classes develop their own pasts. Critical archaeology, on the other hand, presents an equally difficult course: to write the history of domination and resistance, which must by definition include the use of archaeology itself.

There is no question that symbolic, structural, and critical archaeologists feel that there are two developments in the new archaeology that are unfortunate. One is that it has become so rational it is dehumanized, and, as a result, it has diminished its ability to situate itself in its own society and has thus left archaeology vulnerable to a political critique. By "rational" is meant concern with the degree of certainty over conclusions, a concern which has tended in the 1970s and 1980s to restrict conclusions to subsistence, numbers of people, and numbers of things, and away from social relations, symbolic relations, and the role of humans and of tradition. Much of the best of archaeology has become not only mechanical but almost devoid of cultural context.

The unintended consequence of such heavy emphasis on a strict epistemology has been a deepening of the chasm between archaeology and its own society. There has been no concern within the materialist tradition in archaeology with how society shapes its own past. This is true too for more traditional Marxist archaeologists in Europe and America. When Trigger (1984a; 1984b) pointed out obvious misuses of the past, he also implied that there is no dominant conceptual apparatus within any kind of archaeology on which archaeologists can formulate a response to his descriptions. There is nothing in materialist theory that would tell us what to do in the face of the scandalous passivity toward our own society which characterizes archaeology today.

Thus, we can understand Hodder's assertion (1984) that hands are to be kept off other people's pasts, for our own epistemologies are so deadening. An analysis of the role of epistemology is the basis for the claim by critical archaeologists that teaching is political action. These two assumptions are behind an attempt to reach the public with an understanding of how a past is constructed, and of the history of the central economic relations of modern society. The utter irrelevance of most of historical archaeology today is taken to stand as witness to the power of capitalism to disguise its own history. Consequently, excavations have been opened to the public in several places in the United States on the East Coast (Leone 1983; Potter and Leone in press) and in Arizona, not just to satisfy public curiosity, or to justify spending public money on archaeology, but explicitly to show that the past is not dug up; we think up and with the past. Such an ideological quality is the basis for understanding that the past can be interpreted in a multitude of ways, including some that are quite manipulative.

The idea of awareness invites professionals or practicioners to ask themselves to see that in celebrating fifty years of the SAA, the celebration has to consist of decisions derived from current social practices. These are then used, largely unintentionally, to shape the celebration of the past. This celebration gives present reality a depth it may not have, and acts to perpetuate current relations into the future and inevitably must preclude challenges from those so excluded. We all know culture works this way, but we also know that it is our business to know this actively. And in the active consciousness is presumably greater choice as to whether simple duplication is our fate.

Acknowledgments

An essay with the same title as this one was read by the author at the 1985 Denver meetings of the Society for American Archaeology and subsequently sent out by the author to a number of readers for comment. The comments indicated that the approach taken, which enunciated schools of thought by place and members, was not the best approach. That essay was abandoned and the current one stressing basic assumptions was adopted.

I am very grateful to Russell G. Handsman and Robert W. Paynter for major suggestions over ideas and organization in both essays. David J. Meltzer provided the freedom and confidence to make the needed choices that led to both pieces.

Thoughtful, important opinions and observations were written to me by Barbara Bender, Ian Hodder, Alice B. Kehoe, Daniel Miller, Carmel Schrire, Christopher Tilley, and Gorden R. Willey. Conversations with Arthur S. Keene, Randall H. McGuire, and Alison Wylie were important sources of orientation.

Permission to quote unpublished material has been granted by John C. Barrett, James F. Deetz, and David A. Freidel.

Literature Cited

Althusser, Louis
  1971   Ideology and Ideological State Apparatuses. In *Lenin and Philosophy*, translated from the French by Ben Brewster, pages 127–186. Monthly Review Press, New York.

Barnett, Steve and Martin G. Silverman
  1979   *Ideology and Everyday Life*. University of Michigan Press, Ann Arbor.

Barrett, John C.
  n.d.   The Field of Discourse: A Methodology for Social Archaeology. Manuscript, Department of Archaeology, University of Glasgow.

Baudrillard, J.
1975 *The Mirror of Production.* Telos Press, St. Louis.

Bender, Barbara
1985 Emergent Tribal Formation in the American Midcontinent. *American Antiquity* 50(1):52–62.

Bloch, Maurice
1977 The Past and the Present in the Present. *Man* 12(2):278–292.

Clarke, David L.
1973 Archaeology: The Loss of Innocence. *Antiquity* 47(1):6–18.

Conkey, Margaret W.
1982 Boundedness in Art and Society. In *Symbolic and Structural Archaeology,* edited by Ian Hodder, pages 115–128. Cambridge University Press, Cambridge.

Deetz, James
1967 *Invitation to Archaeology.* The Natural History Press, Garden City, New York.
1977 *In Small Things Forgotten.* Anchor Books, Garden City, New York.
1981 Material Culture and World View in Colonial Anglo-America. Paper presented in Millersville, Pennsylvania.
1983 Scientific Humanism and Humanities Science: A Plea for Paradigmatic Pluralism in Historical Archaeology. *Geoscience and Man* 23 (April) 29:27–34.

Donley, Linda Wiley
1982 House Power: Swahili Space and Symbolic Markers. In *Symbolic and Structural Archaeology,* edited by Ian Hodder, pages 63–73. Cambridge University Press, Cambridge.

Freidel, David A.
1981 Civilization as a State of Mind. In *Transformations to Statehood,* edited by Gordon Jones and Robert Kautz, pages 188–227. Cambridge University Press, Cambridge.

Freidel, David A., and Linda Schele
In press Symbol and Power: A History of the Lowland Maya Cosmogram. In *Maya Iconography,* edited by Elizabeth P. Benson and Gillette Griffin. Princeton University Press, Princeton.

Freidman, J., and Michael Rowlands (editors)
1977 *The Evolution of Social Systems.* Duckworth, London:

Furst, Peter T.
1968 The Olmec Were-Jaguar Motif in the Light of Ethnographic Reality. In *Dumbarton Oaks Conference on the Olmec,* edited by Elizabeth P. Benson, pages 143–174. Dumbarton Oaks, Washington, D. C.

Gero, Joan M.
1983 Gender Bias in Archaeology: A Cross-Cultural Perspective. *In* The Socio-politics of Archaeology, edited by Joan M. Gero, David M. Lacy, and Michael L. Blakey. *University of Massachusetts, Department of Anthropology, Research Report* 23:51–57. Amherst.

Gero, Joan M., David M. Lacy, Michael L. Blakey (editors)
  1983 The Socio-politics of Archaeology. *University of Massachusetts, Department of Anthropology, Research Report* 23. Amherst.

Giddens, Anthony
  1979 *Central Problems in Social Theory.* Macmillan, London.
  1981 *A Contemporary Critique of Historical Materialism.* Macmillan, London.
  1982a *Profiles and Critiques in Social Theory.* Macmillan, London.
  1982b *Sociology: A Brief but Critical Introduction.* Macmillan, London.

Glassie, Henry
  1975 *Folk Housing in Middle Virginia.* University of Tennessee Press, Knoxville.

Gledhill, J.
  1981 Time's Arrow: Anthropology, History, Social Evolution, and Marxist Theory. *Critique of Anthropology* 16:3–30.

Godelier, Maurice
  1977 *Perspectives on Marxist Anthropology.* Cambridge University Press, Cambridge.
  1978 The Object and Method of Anthropology. In *Relations of Production: Marxist Approaches to Economic Anthropology,* edited by D. Seddon, pages 49–126. Frank Cass, London.

Habermas, Jurgen
  1971 *Knowledge and Human Interests.* Beacon Press, Boston.
  1981 *The Theory of Communicative Action, Volume 1: Reason and the Rationalization of Society.* Beacon Press, Boston.

Handsman, Russell G.
  1980 The Domains of Kinship and Settlement in Historic Goshen: Signs of a Past Cultural Order. *Artifacts* 9:2–7.
  1981 Early Capitalism and the Center Village of Canaan, Connecticut: A Study of Transformations and Separations. *Artifacts* 9:1–21.
  1982 The Hot and Cold of Goshen's History. *Artifacts* 3:11–20.

Hodder, Ian
  1982a [Editor.]*Symbolic and Structural Archaeology.* Cambridge University Press, Cambridge.
  1982b Sequences of Structural Change in the Dutch Neolithic. In *Symbolic and Structural Archaeology,* edited by Ian Hodder, pages 162–177. Cambridge University Press, Cambridge.
  1983 *The Present Past: An Introduction to Anthropology for Archaeologists.* New York: Pica Press.
  1984 Archaeology in 1984. *Antiquity* 58:25–32.
  1985 Postprocessual Archaeology. In *Advances in Archaeological Method and Theory,* edited by Michael B. Schiffer, 8:1–26. Academic Press, Orlando, Florida.

Kehoe, Alice B.
  1984 The Myth of the Given. Paper presented to the Society for American Archaeology, Portland, Oregon, April 1984.
  1984b The Ideological Paradigm in Traditional American Ethnology. Paper presented to the American Ethnological Society, Asilomar, California, April 1984.

Kristiansen, Kristian
    1984 Ideology and Material Culture: An Archaeological Perspective. In *Marxist Perspectives in Archaeology,* edited by Matthew Spriggs, pages 72–100. Cambridge University Press, Cambridge.

Kus, Susan
    1982 Matters Material and Ideal. In *Symbolic and Structural Archaeology,* edited by Ian Hodder, pages 47–62. Cambridge University Press, Cambridge.

Landau, Misia
    1983 The Anthropogenic: Paleoanthropological Writing as a Genre of Literature. University Microfilms, Ann Arbor, Michigan.
    1984 Human Evolutions as Narrative. *American Scientist* 72:262–268.

Leach, Edmund
    1973 [Concluding Address.] In *The Explanation of Culture Change,* edited by Colin Renfrew, pages 761–771. University of Pittsburgh Press, Pittsburgh.

Leone, Mark P.
    1981a Archaeology's Material Relationship to the Present and the Past. In *Modern Material Culture,* edited by Richard A. Gould and Michael B. Schiffer, pages 5–14. Academic Press, New York.
    1981b The Relationship between Artifacts and the Public in Outdoor History Museums. In *The Research Potential of Anthropological Museum Collections,* edited by A. M. Cantwell, Nan Rothschild, and James B. Griffin, pages 301–313. New York Academy of Sciences, New York.
    1983 Method as Message. *Museum News* 62(1):35–41.

Lukacs, Georg
    1971 Reification and the Consciousness of the Proletariat. In *History and Class Consciousness,* translated by Rodney Livingstone, pages 83–222. M.I.T. Press, Cambridge.

Meillassoux, C.
    1972 From Reproduction to Production. *Economy and Society* 1:93–105.

Meltzer, David
    1981 Ideology and Material Culture. In *Modern Material Culture,* edited by Richard A. Gould and Michael B. Schiffer, pages 113–125. Academic Press, New York.

Miller, Daniel
    1982a Artifacts as Products of Human Categorisation Processes. In *Symbolic and Structural Archaeology,* edited by Ian Hodder, pages 84–98. Cambridge University Press, Cambridge.
    1982b Explanation and Social Theory in Archaeological Practice. In *Theory and Explanation in Archaeology,* edited by Colin Renfrew, Michael J. Rowlands, Barbara Abbott Segraves. Academic Press, New York.
    1985 Ideology and the Harappan Civilization. *Journal of Anthropological Anthropology* 4:1–38.

Miller, Daniel, and Christopher Tilley (editors)
    1984 *Ideology, Power and Prehistory.* Cambridge University Press, Cambridge.

Moore, Henrietta
  1982 The Interpretation of Spatial Patterning in Settlement Residues. In *Symbolic and Structural Archaeology,* edited by Ian Hodder, pages 74–79. Cambridge University Press, Cambridge.

Moore, James A., and Arthur S. Keene (editors)
  1983 *Archaeological Hammers and Theories.* Academic Press, New York.

Parker Pearson, Michael
  1982 Mortuary Practices, Society and Ideology: An Ethnoarcheological Study. In *Symbolic and Structural Archaeology,* edited by Ian Hodder, pages 99–113. Cambridge University Press, Cambridge.
  1984 Economic and Ideological Change: Cyclical Growth in the Pre-state Societies of Jutland. In *Ideology, Power, and Prehistory,* edited by Daniel Miller and Christopher Tilley, pages 69–92. Cambridge University Press, Cambridge.

Patterson, Thomas C.
  1984 Exploitation and Class Formation in the Inca State. Paper presented at the May 1984 meeting of the Canadian Ethnological Society, Montreal.

Paynter, Robert
  1985 Models of Technological Change in Historical Archaeology. Paper read at the Council on Northeast Historical Archaeology, SUNY-Binghamton, October 19–21.

Perper, Timothy, and Carmel Schrire
  1977 The Nimrod Connection: Myth and Science in the Hunting Model. In *The Chemical Senses and Nutrition,* edited by Morley Kare and Owen Maller, pages 447–459. Academic Press, New York.

Potter, Parker B., Jr., and Mark P. Leone
  In press Archaeology in Public in Annapolis: The Four Seasons, Six Sites, Seven Tours, and 32,000 Visitors. *American Archaeologist.*

Schrire, Carmel
  1984 Wild Surmises on Savage Thoughts. In *Past and Present in Hunter Gatherer Societies,* edited by Carmel Schrire. Orlando: Academic Press.

Shanks, Michael, and Christopher Tilley
  1982 Ideology, Symbolic Power and Ritual Communication: A Reinterpretation of Neolithic Mortuary Practices. In *Symbolic and Structural Archaeology,* edited by Ian Hodder, pages 129–154. Cambridge University Press, Cambridge.
  In press *Studies in Archaeological Theory and Practice.* Cambridge University Press, Cambridge.

Shennan, Stephen
  1982 Ideology, Change, and the European Early Bronze Age. In *Symbolic and Structural Archaeology,* edited by Ian Hodder, pages 155–161. Cambridge University Press, Cambridge.

Spriggs, Matthew
  1984 *Marxist Perspective in Archaeology.* Cambridge University Press, Cambridge.

Thorpe, I. J.
  1981 Anthropological Orientations on Astronomy in Complex Societies. Pa-

per read at the third Theoretical Archaeology Group Conference, Reading, U.K.

Tilley, Christopher
  1982 Social Formation, Social Structures and Social Change. In *Symbolic and Structural Archaeology,* edited by Ian Hodder, pages 26–38. Cambridge University Press, Cambridge.
  1984 Ideology and the Legitimation of Power in the Middle Neolithic of Southern Sweden. In *Ideology, Power and Prehistory,* edited by Daniel Miller and Christopher Tilley, pages 111–146. Cambridge University Press, Cambridge.

Trigger, Bruce
  1984a Alternative Archaeologies: Nationalist, Colonialist, Imperialist. *Man* 19(3):335–370.
  1984b Archaeology at the Crossroads: What's New? *Annual Review of Anthropology* 13:275–300.

Wallerstein, I.
  1976 A World-System Perspective on the Social Sciences. *British Journal of Sociology* 27:343–352.

Wobst, H. Martin, and Arthur S. Keene
  1983 Archaeological Explanation as Political Economy. In *The Socio-politics of Archaeology,* edited by Joan M. Gero, David M. Lacy, Michael L. Blakey. *University of Massachusetts, Department of Anthropology, Research Report* 23:79–88. Amherst.

Wylie, Alison
  1981 Epistemological Issues Raised by a Structuralist Archaeology. In *Symbolic and Structural Archaeology,* edited by Ian Hodder, pages 39–46. Cambridge University Press, Cambridge.
  1985 The Reaction against Analogy. In *Advances in Archaeological Method and Theory,* edited by Michael B. Schiffer, 8:63–111. Academic Press, New York.
  In press Putting Shakertown Back Together: Critical Theory in Archaeology. *Journal of Anthropological Archaeology.*

Archaeological Interpretation, 1985

Introduction

To say something truthful and enlightening about current archaeological interpretation is a very challenging assignment. Nevertheless, two obvious alternatives present themselves: (1) to put together a summary account, or fact-sheet—topically organized, perhaps—indicating what categories of laboratory and field research are being conducted at present and with what results; or (2) to try to define significant current trends together with their implications for the future. The latter alternative is riskier but more interesting, and that is the path I have chosen to follow.

At any one time, interpretive goals in a discipline vary from one individual practitioner to another and from institution to institution (among universities, museums, and research institutes, for example). Interpretive goals also vary through time at the disciplinary level as scholarly schools rise, become prominent or dominant, decline, and fade away or are assimilated into other schools. In this paper I define what I mean by archaeological interpretation, describe and discuss what seem to be the currently dominant interpretive modes, and then relate these to past trends and possible future developments. Two other archaeologists have recently published relevant overviews (Robert Dunnell 1984, and Bruce Trigger 1984), so it seems appropriate that I make comparative reference to them in several places. Dunnell's is a relatively detailed account focused primarily on a single year (1983), whereas Trigger's is a more general assessment of the present situation and of the two to three decades antecedent to it.

Archaeological Interpretation

In this paper I take interpretation to mean what the archaeologist does to or with archaeological data to make sense of them, both particularistically (explaining a specific piece of a specific site) and generally (explaining the past). That part of an archaeological site report labelled "interpretation" is the crowning achievement of the project. It is the final chapter in which everything is tied together into one coherent—although always partly or largely conjectural—whole. Of course one's interpretive orientation is also present in everything one does as an archaeologist. The word conveys "what it all means" not just at the formal wrap-up level, but also at every other level of archaeological endeavor: from the initial conception of the research question through the design of field work and analysis to the presentation of specific results and of their theoretical and methodological significance.

One of the most wholesome emphases of new archaeology was on making explicit one's problem, the means chosen to solve it, and the degree of success in reaching a solution. Yet, as noted by David Clarke (1973), this is also a very threatening procedure, and indeed it induced a variety of skeptical crises among archaeologists. These emerged during the later 1970s and into the 1980s.

The more immediate result, however, in the 1960s and early 1970s, was a heady euphoria about the information potential of the archaeological record. For a while it seemed that with sufficient ingenuity, an emphasis on deductive inference, and use of new-fangled equipment and techniques (computers, magnetometers, trace-element analyses, flotation devices, pollen spectra) wielded by interdisciplinary teams (geoarchaeologists, zooarchaeologists, archaeobotanists), we could say something interesting, significant, and true about any part of the archaeological record to which we turned our attention. That situation is captured, with only very slight exaggeration, by Derek Roe's (1984) description of the Very Model of a Modern [Archaeologist]. I have taken some liberties with Roe's rendering—itself, of course, an adaptation of the original Gilbert and Sullivan libretto—as indicated by brackets:

> I am the very model of a modern
>   [Archaeologist]:
> A geoethnoarchaeoeconomobiologist.
> I've seventeen research degrees,
>   from fifteen different colleges,
> Mostly in America, where all the

latest knowledge is;
I can calibrate chronologies, with all
  the latest jargon,
Using isotopes of oxygen, uranium,
  or argon;
I can quantify regression lines, in
  terms of their obliquity,
And publish them in [*Science*] when
  rejected by [*American Antiquity*].
If you're into symbiosis at [Cahokia]
  or at [Chaco], I'm
The colleague to consult before you
  promulgate your paradigm.
I've hired a taphonomer and fired
  my typologist:
I am the very model of a modern
  [Archaeologist].

The 1960s phase of enthusiastic and widespread response to the urgings of revolutionaries led by Lewis Binford is even more faithfully reflected in our book (Watson et al. 1971) *Explanation in Archeology* written in 1969–1970. The book exemplifies what is often called a positivist approach to the past (primarily the prehistoric past), an approach that was modified in various ways by some and rejected by others in the ensuing decade and a half (see our own recent reassessment: Watson et al. 1984).

It is these varieties of response and reaction in the 1970s that have produced the interpretive trends of 1985. Both Dunnell (1984) and Trigger (1984) enumerate and treat these current interpretive strands in some detail, but neither remarks upon the two facts that seem most remarkable to me: (1) Before, during, and after the new archaeology, the onslaught of CRM and contract archaeology, and the siren songs of "postprocessualist" approaches, the vast majority of Americanist archaeologists representing the behavioral mainstream of the discipline, have gone right on pursuing what I shall call the real past, via some form of cultural materialist strategy. (2) But, for the first time in the history of Americanist archaeology, there are now a few practicing archaeologists (a) who do not believe the real past is accessible. In addition, there is a somewhat larger number of archaeologists whose primary concern is with or has become (b) something other than the real past. Thus, this second (though minority) category among practicing archaeologists includes several subgroups, of which I can distinguish at least four: those whose primary concern is with something other than the real past: (a) some material culture analysts, and (b) some critical theorists; and among those who do not believe the real past is accessible: (c) all very narrow empiricists, and (d) some practitioners of actualistic studies.

Hence, there are grounds for markedly divergent opinions in 1985 about whether the discipline is on the verge of serious factionalization, or whether it is on its way to synthesis and rebirth.

I discuss the archaeological majority first, and then turn to a consideration of the various minority positions including that of the extreme archaeological skeptics. Because my concern in this paper is with the minority positions and their possible significance, I give rather short shrift to the archaeological majority. Fortunately, the excellent yearly summaries by Dunnell in the *American Journal of Archaeology* (Dunnell 1984 being the seventh in the series), as well as Trigger's recent account (1984), and the yearly appearance of review articles in *Advances in Archaeological Method and Theory* (Michael Schiffer, editor) make access to the current literature relatively easy.

The Archaeological Majority

The archaeological majority comprises those who use the archaeological record to pursue time-space systematics (more or less the same as Taylor's "chronicle"; Taylor 1948), culture history ("historiography" in Taylor's terms, "reconstructing prehistoric lifeways" in Binford's terms; Binford 1962), and/or culture process (roughly corresponding to Taylor's "archaeology as cultural anthropology," and to other authors' "archaeology as social science"; Watson et al. 1971:159–163). Topics of consuming concern to this majority group include ecological-environmental approaches (Butzer 1982); enthnoarchaeological studies (Binford 1978; Gould 1980; Hayden and Cannon 1984; Kent 1984); interest in refined dating techniques and materials analysis (Browman 1981; Farquhar and Fletcher 1984); investigation of site formation processes (Binford 1981; Stein 1983; Stein and Farrand 1985); use of geographic, biological, and many other models (Jochim 1983; Johnson 1977; Runnels 1981; Sabloff 1981); and research on paleo-belief systems (Hall 1977).

The archaeological majority thus includes purveyors of optimal foraging theory, central place theory, information theory, spatial analysis, and site catchment analysis, as well as seekers after prehistoric ideological or cognitive systems. Prominently present are those tracking site formation processes of all descriptions from the effects of earthworms and other bioturbatory mechanisms to alluvial, colluvial, and eolian deposition; erosion; and remodeling.

Although the methods and techniques used are varied—indeed, they are often seen as conflicting—their practitioners are, nevertheless, united by a common interest in the real past, believed to be accessible, if not directly then indirectly, through fairly straightforward inference from the archaeological record. This characterization includes CRM and contract archaeologists, as well as those working on large or small cultural historical questions.

Other members of the behavioral mainstream are those archaeologists among whose primary concerns are debates about theory and method in a continuation of some of the activities that characterized early days in the new archaeology movement. Examples include most of Binford's publications and many of Dunnell's and Hodder's; Kelley and Hanen in press; Leone 1981b; Marquardt 1985; Renfrew 1982; Salmon 1982; Schiffer 1981; Watson et al. 1984; Wylie 1985a, 1985b. This group includes those whom Flannery (1982) pejoratively characterizes as critics and observers rather than doers of archaeology (I do not subscribe to Flannery's categorically negative view).

In an attempt to get a modicum of empirical information on research or professional interests that might illuminate my topic, I examined the *Programs and Abstracts* of papers presented at the 1974, 1982, 1983, and 1984 SAA meetings. The sessions at these meetings are devoted to the topics just referred to as characterizing the archaeological majority, with the minority subgroups (discussed below) barely discernible. Other than a few, lone papers here and there, there were only two sessions that might fit into the minority category: one 1982 symposium on critical approaches, and one on symbolic archaeology at the 1983 meetings. What then is the significance of these minority subgroups— virtually invisible in the programs of recent meetings—and who peoples them?

The Archaeological Minority

Antecedents

As already noted, the current majority grouping includes work stimulated by skeptical crises of the 1970s when the exuberant claims of 1960s new archaeology began coming home to roost. Binford (1983c) refers to this 1970s period as a generation gap; I recently called it a secondary loss of innocence (Watson 1982). I was harking back to David Clarke's 1973 discussion of the new archaeology which he viewed as representing the loss of innocence characteristic of traditional archaeology with its almost wholly intuitive goals. Clarke called for disciplinary self-consciousness among archaeologists, but predicted that this might be painful, or at least that confusion would be engendered by it (Clarkel 1973:8; see also Wylie 1982; Pinsky and Wylie in prep.). The prediction came true. Although much of the new archaeology was adopted and indeed is now central to the field, revisionist moves of various sorts soon emerged, chief among them a rapidly burgeoning concern with site formation processes approached via ethnoarchaeology, geoarchaeology, and experimental archaeology. Many archaeologists are happily and productively employed in these and related areas, but others have experienced still deeper skeptical crises, which have led some of them to (or toward) the minority positions now to be discussed.

Classification of the Archaeological Minority

As noted, I am aware of four minority subgroups: (a) some material culture analysts (Leone 1973:136–150, 1981a, 1981b; Rathje 1978:50, 1981), (b) some critical theorists (Leone 1973:128–136, 1981a, 1981b; Tilley in prep.; Conkey and Spector 1984; Gero 1985; Hall 1984; Kennedy 1979), (c) all very narrow empiricists (Dunnell 1978a, 1980), (d) some practitioners of actualistic studies (Binford 1981:21–30; Binford and Sabloff 1982; Hodder 1982b:212).

Subcategories (a) and (b) are rather readily comprehensible, and examples are easily available. Some of these archaeologists are not concerned with the past at all, but rather with the way material culture, viewed at least in part as archaeologists view it, can instruct us about our own society (Leone 1973; Rathje 1978, 1981). Others are concerned with the real past, but believe for very good and sufficient reasons that a focus on critical approaches is essential because the real past is inaccessible unless we can analyze adequately, and then neutralize or circumvent, the social and political ideologies that bias and shape our understanding of it (Conkey and Spector 1984; Gero 1985; Hall 1984; Kennedy 1979).

The third subgroup (very narrow empiricists) is the most interesting for the present analysis, and also the most disquieting. A central figure here is Robert Dunnell whose dogged and dogmatic empiricism is laid out in a number of publications (Dunnell 1971, 1978, 1980, 1984a, 1984b). He is near or at the "artifact physics" horn of the archaeologist's dilemma described by DeBoer and Lathrap (1979:103; see further discussion of this dilemma in Wylie in prep.):

> Either [the archaeologist] becomes a practitioner of an over-extended uniformitarianism in which past cultural behavior is "read" from our knowledge of present cultural behavior, or he [or she] must eschew his [or her] commitment to understanding behavior altogether and engage in a kind of "artifact physics" in which the form and distribution of behavioral by-products are measured in a behavioral vacuum. This is the familiar quandary of choosing between a significant pursuit based on faulty method or one which is methodologically sound but trivial in purpose [DeBoer and Lathrap 1979:103].

Dunnell apparently wishes to separate archaeology from its close relationship with cultural anthropology because that relationship has led to what he regards as a very seriously flawed or fallacious approach to archaeological interpretation: the reconstructionist school (Dunnell 1980:77–83, 87–88). This approach is the common one in which the past is inferentially constructed, or reconstructed as most archaeologists speak of it, on the basis of ethnographic information and ethnographic analogy. Dunnell insists on a direct use of the archaeological record on its own terms rather than this indirect use. He believes that evolutionary theory (not with reference to cultural evolution, but to evolution as it is understood in biology) should be applied to the archaeological record.

> The units in any theory that purport to be scientific whether evolutionary or not, must be empirically identifiable and measurable in the phenomenological record. This is the basic flaw in the "behavioral correlates" notion of the reconstructionist school . . . . If it [evolutionary theory] is to be used in archaeology, it must be rewritten in terms that have empirical representation in the archaeological record. Archaeological evolutionary theory will have to be constructed by deducing the consequences of evolutionary theory as employed in biology and as applicable to ethnographic data for artifacts, their frequencies and distributions. Even so, some aspects of the archaeological record, those not directly subject to selection, will require explanation in strictly cultural terms [Dunnell 1980:87–89].

Thus, although he allows for some aspects of the archaeological record (those that represent style rather than function) that cannot be encompassed by a scientific evolutionary approach, his concern is with the evolutionarily significant portion of the record that can, he believes, be so encompassed (Dunnell 1978a). Description and understanding of that portion will not come via reconstruction of the past, but via analysis of "the hard phenomena of the archaeological record" themselves (Dunnell 1978b:195).

There are a number of difficulties with Dunnell's argument (Watson et al. 1984:251–256). Perhaps the greatest for me is understanding how one can say anything about the archaeological record without covertly if not overtly employing a reconstructionist approach to some nontrivial degree.

What, exactly, are the hard phenomena of the archaeological record, "the empirical data themselves" (Dunnell 1980:78)? How can they even be comprehended in the absence of constructionist or reconstructionist inference based on knowledge of relevant contemporary phenomena?

Secondarily, how can the differential distribution (diachronic and synchronic) of stylistic vs. functional artifacts and attributes be detected and documented in the absence of reconstructionist reasoning? That is, how can one distinguish stylistic traits from functional ones without relying on reconstructionist inference?

It is, however, simply Dunnell's insistence on a totally empirical approach to the archaeological record that causes me to place him in the camp of extreme skepticism about access to the real past.

Dunnell's position is one node of an extreme skeptical syndrome, but there are at least two other nodes, defined by highly influential people: Lewis Binford and Ian Hodder. These two archaeologists are prominent exemplars of those who have temporarily undertaken full-time research in actualistic contexts to enable, eventually, more adequate and accurate understanding of archaeological site formation and of the nature and functioning of past societies. This is the endeavor Binford and others call "middle range theory." Middle range theory is widely regarded as the best—perhaps the only—means of achieving extensive, detailed, and accurate information about the real past. Binford's brilliant ethnoarchaeological forays into Nunamiut lifeways are internationally known, admired, and emulated. As Dunnell (1984:501) observes, Binford's work program is most comprehensively and comprehensibly displayed in his book *In Pursuit of the Past* (Binford 1983b), which is a clear, compelling account of how the basic position he represented twenty years ago has matured and evolved through many years of thought and effort. Yet in some of his recent publications (Binford

1981:21–30; Binford and Sabloff 1982; and see Wylie in prep.), Binford seems to take a skeptical position about access to the real past. He says:

> There is an important characteristic of all inferential arguments, simply that we can never reason in a valid manner from premises to a conclusion that contradicts the premises with which we start. This fact has important implications for archaeologists:
>
> 1. All our statements about the past are inferences relative to observations made on the contemporary archaeological record.
>
> 2. The accuracy of our inferential constructions of the past is directly dependent on the accuracy of the assumptions or premises serving as the basis of our inferential arguments.
>
> The conclusion we must draw is that we cannot use either the archaeological record or the inferred past to test our premises or assumptions . . . how do we develop reliable means for knowing the past? . . . we must engage in middle-range research, which consists of actualistic studies designed to control for the relationship between dynamic properties of the past about which one seeks knowledge and the static material properties common to the past and the present, Whitehead's "eternal objects"—in short, the characteristics about which uniformitarian assumptions may be made, those things which the present shares with the past. These common things provide the basis for a comparison of the events from different times in the past.
>
> The dependence of our knowledge of the past on inference rather than direct observation renders the relationship between paradigm (the conceptual tool of description) and theory (the conceptual tool of explanation) vague, it also renders the "independence" of observations from explanations frequently suspect and commonly standing in a built in relationship, thereby committing the fallacy of "confirming the consequent" [Binford 1981:29; see also Binford and Sabloff 1982:149].

There are two problems with this position. One is pointed out by Alison Wylie in the paper already cited (Wylie in prep.). She notes that actualistic studies are just as "paradigm-bound" and theory dependent as are interpretations of the archaeological record, so their results or conclusions are as vulnerable as are inferences from observations on the archaeological record.

The second problem is that even were we to obtain very well-confirmed laws and regularities about behavioral correlates in presently observed societies—what Trigger (1984) calls "absolute middle-level generalizations"—these cannot be used to explain past societies without making an inferential leap as great as the one Binford labels as affirming the consequent and hence as unacceptable procedure. How can one decide, with the certainty he apparently requires, which things "the present shares with the past" and which things are not so shared? We must always affirm the consequent if we are to do any meaningful interpretation at all, but we do it explicitly and as a calculated way, not of achieving dead certainty—even in the heyday of *Explanation in Archaeology* we denied that was possible (Watson et al. 1971:4, 22–23)—but rather of reducing uncertainty.

Hence, I think that Binford would be well advised not to tread this extreme skeptical ground but rather to continue refining approaches to archaeological inference as he has been doing in such papers as "The Archaeology of Place" (Binford 1982) and "Historical Archaeology" (Binford 1977), as well as other publications flowing from his Nunamiut research (Binford 1983a, 1983b; see also the analyses by Wylie 1985b, and in prep.).

Ian Hodder has taken a different path toward skepticism about access to the real past. His skeptical attitude is implicit in *Symbols in Action* (1982a) and rather clearly revealed in *The Present Past* (1982b). When he began his ethnoarchaeological research in Africa in the late 1960s, he apparently did so for the same reason that motivated Binford: to strengthen archaeological inference, or at any rate to improve certain types of inferences made from the archaeological record. However, unlike Binford who has—with a few exceptions such as those just discussed—steadfastly pursued that aim, Hodder seems to have lost, or perhaps deliberately abandoned, his way in the fascinatingly intricate world of cognitive, or symbolic/structuralist studies and critical approaches. In the introduction to *Symbols in Action* (1982a:1) he says:

> The initial aim of the research was to see what material "cultures" (geographical areas with recurring associations of artifacts) represented and were related to in a living context. The concern was to shed some light on the analysis and interpretation of cultures in prehistoric archaeology . . . . When do ethnic units identify themselves in material culture? What is the spatial patterning that results? What happens at material culture boundaries?

In *The Present Past* (1982b:212) he states "as much as the past informs the present, so the present informs the past," and indeed throughout the book he maintains this critical or skeptical stance toward archaeological interpretation so strongly that in one place he concludes that the proper purpose of archaeology may be to aid attainment of critical self-awareness by members of our modern industrialized society.

In our attempts to become aware of the preconceptions that we might impose on the past, we must "live" archaeology, not in the sense of Gould's . . ."living archaeology," but in the more radical sense of gaining knowledge and experience from the world in which we live our daily lives. There is a danger, though, that if we only look at ourselves we may be blind to the relativity of our own logic. Contrasts with other cultures and with the results obtained by social anthropologists encourage awareness of our own cultural bias. The proper purpose of archaeology may be to contribute to this critical self-awareness [Hodder 1982b:212].

Hodder does not attempt to assess the adequacy or validity of social anthropological data, so I do not know how he thinks social anthropologists have escaped the relativity of their logic and the preconceptions they may have imposed upon events or processes they observe in living but undeniably alien cultures.

To return to Hodder's skeptical stance with regard to the past, however, near the end of the last chapter of the book in a discussion of a science of material culture, he enumerates nine aspects of material culture each of which potentially introduces ambiguity and uncertainty into the interpretation of the archaeological record. This litany, together with the subsequent account of contemporary punk behavior and symbolism in Britain (Hodder 1982b:215–216) and with his stress throughout the book on the deep significance of unique historical contexts, leaves the archaeological reader (as I believe Hodder deliberately means to do) with a sense of bewilderment, confusion, or just plain dismay about the feasibility of adequate archaeological interpretation.

In other words, I think Hodder is toying with (although—at least in these publications—not outwardly advocating) a fundamental skepticism about knowledge of the past that would be quite counterproductive were it to become widespread among archaeologists. On the one hand, his analyses are fascinating and can play a useful role in making us more sensitive and more sophisticated in our interpretations; on the other hand, followed to their logical conclusion, they would seem to rule out hope of saying anything of substance or truth about the real past.

In sum, Hodder, much of the time, and Binford, at least part of the time, seem not only to have lost their innocence about what archaeology is and what archaeologists can do, but also they seem to have lost their faith in the archaeological record as a guide to the real past. Because both are vigorous, productive, and charismatic figures, this situation might seem alarming for the future well being of the discipline.

An even more alarming prospect is afforded the analyst who takes a developmental or evolutionary view of these recent events. One can conceive of the following sequence of phases or stages:

Phase I (Age of Innocence, pre-1960s). The archaeological record is viewed as a direct reflection of the past, limited in some ways because of obvious preservation problems, but otherwise comprising priceless relics of the human past.

Phase II (First Burst of the New Archaeology, 1962–1972). It is believed that with the application of sufficient ingenuity and the use of new techniques and methods, the archaeological record will yield a great wealth of information about prehistoric human social and cultural behavior.

Phase III (Loss of Innocence, Stage 1, 1972-mid/late 1970s). It is realized that interpreting the archaeological record is rather problematic because of interference by natural and cultural site formation processes. These must be studied mainly in the present and hence mainly by actualistic techniques (geoarchaeological, ethnoarchaeological, and replicative [experimental archaeological]) so that the distorting effects can be neutralized in interpretation.

Phase IV (Loss of Innocence, Stage 2, late 1970s-1980s). It is believed that neutralization of distorting influences is an inadequate and possibly even an erroneous way to arrive at interpretation of the archaeological record. The only hope for achieving genuine advances in archaeological theory (and hence in archaeological interpretation) is by means of actualistic studies.

Phase V (Terminal Skeptical Crisis, possibly late 1980s-1990?). Knowledge gained through ethnography is impossible to apply to the past. Human behavior is too complicated, too intricate, too intangible to be captured and preserved in material remains, and too idiosyncratic and particular to be understood even if it were somehow so preserved. Moreover, contemporary sociopolitical forces inevitably warp and distort our perceptions of all alien social processes, present or past. And, finally, the archaeological record—far from being static—is so dynamic a playground for all manner of bio- and geoturbatory factors, that there is no hope of retrieving past human behavior from it.

QED: Archaeology is impossible. There is no real past, or at any rate no access to it.

I am not unduly upset or pessimistic about all this, however, at least not as an abstract possibility. The first reason for my relative equanimity is that I know most field archaeologists have very solid intuitions very firmly directed at the real past. Even our most penetrating critics admit that when we get down in our trenches or up on our lab stools we generally know what we are doing even if we are not always highly articulate about why we are doing it (Salmon 1976, 1982:49, 77; Wylie 1981, 1985a, 1985b). For purposes of maximizing the archaeological record, however, we must strive to be explicitly thoughtful about goals, methods, and techniques, and we must justify our inferences about the past.

All practicing archaeologists behave in fundamentally the same way; they work back and forth in a continuous dialog between what they expect or think or hope is correct (i.e., hypotheses, theories, hunches about the correct interpretation of a portion of the archaeological record), and the archaeological record itself (Watson et al. 1971:12–16, 114–121; Wylie 1985b). While operating in this way, the most fruitful results are obtained by those who are most clearly aware of what they are doing and why, because they will explicitly choose significant rather than trivial questions to answer, and will select appropriate data recovery methods best calculated to produce abundant, relevant information. They will also be most clearly aware that today's knowledge is tomorrow's ignorance; i.e., that their understandings of the evidence are continually changing, necessitating new questions to ask the record and new techniques for getting answers. Thus, the process of understanding the archaeological record is thoroughly dynamic, and also thoroughly dependent upon intelligently devised research designs, intelligently applied to a piece of that record. No one's work exemplifies this more clearly than does that of Binford, who, most of the time, both practices and preaches the procedure just described (Binford 1983a:389–394, 1983b: chapters 4,5,8,9). It was his attempt to understand the well-documented variability in Mousterian assemblages that drove him from the ethnographic literature to ethnographic field work explicitly designed to answer specific archaeological questions. He then returned to that and other portions of the Paleolithic and early post-Pleistocene record armed with the results of actualistic research, and continues to work to and fro between the two realms in the best (and only) possible means to obtain relatively well-founded understanding of the real past.

Our knowledge of the past will never be perfect, but we can achieve significant control over the imperfections by clever, critical, and persistent coordination of observations on the archaeological record with those made actualistically. It is important that there be some degree of skepticism in carrying out this task, but it is even more important that the original goal of reliable access to the real past neither be mired in a slough of skeptical despond, nor abandoned altogether for seemingly greener actualistic fields.

The second reason for my relatively tranquil state of mind is that I know the pull of the archaeological heartland—the real past—to be extremely powerful, not just to the professionals who read the latest technical literature and hear the electrifying papers read at meetings, but also to avocational archaeologists and the general public who do not. These people—amateurs, avocationals, and the informed or just simply the interested lay public—are fascinated by all aspects of the real human past. A substantial number of professional archaeologists are, in fact, reformed pothunters or relic collectors, hence have entered the profession from the ranks of this same interested lay public. And, of course, most current funding for prehistoric archaeology in the United States is public money.

Therefore, in a certain fundamentally important sense, nearly all of us who call ourselves archaeologists as well as those who support our work are particularists: *We want to know what happened and why,* not only in history, but also in prehistory. Only archaeologists can attain historical and social scientific understanding of the real, human, prehistoric past, and they have the strongest possible mandate to do so. I find that in spite of skeptical skirmishes and many differences in specific goals, methods, and techniques, "Archaeological Interpretation, 1985" displays the same central tendency as "Archaeological Interpretation, 1935": describing and explaining the real past.

I cannot close, however, without interjecting a final and less optimistic comment about the real world of the present. I believe as strongly as ever that it is vitally important to think about what we are doing and why we are doing it, and to discuss these issues in a variety of different contexts. But, at least in the continental United States, we do not have the luxury of unlimited time for these discussions. At the present rate, by the year 2000, if not before, virtually all the prehistoric archaeological record here will be gone. In other words, contemporary Americanist archaeology is, in a very immediate sense, a gigantic conservation and salvage operation. This means that we simply cannot afford a major diversion in debates about archaeological theory from our first order of business: describing and explaining the human past. Hence, although I remain calm about the abstract possibility, for practical and logistical reasons, I do view with alarm contemporary moves toward denial of the real past or of access to it. Rather we must redouble our efforts to conserve wherever possible, and where not, to extract from the archaeological record the maximum amount of information about that real past. This commitment necessitates greater attention to significant archaeological problems and to research designs appropriate to solve them within all forms of field archaeology.

So I conclude with respect to "Archaeological Interpretation, 1985" that explicit attention to theory is more important than it has ever been in the 100 years since formalization of archaeology in America. Most critical of all is relentless attention to the conservation of the archaeological record, and to the integration of theory with the field work that is applied to that record. Archaeological sites are being destroyed so rapidly that in the very near future our access to the real prehistoric past will be even more attenuated than it is now. Soon we will have as data only excavation reports and museum specimens representing but a tiny fraction of the archaeological record. The best possible theory of recovery and recording is essential to assure that we do not make irretrievable more of the prehistoric past than has already been lost.

Acknowledgments

This paper was heavily influenced by many discussions with Alison Wylie over the past three years, and more recently with Mary Kennedy, neither of whom is to blame for the actual content. Without Mary's word-processing expertise, however, the manuscript would certainly not have been ready in final form by the deadline. I am grateful to her for that and for help in assembling the Literature Cited. Finally, I am thankful to Richard A. Watson and to David J. Meltzer for astute editorial suggestions that significantly improved the final manuscript.

Literature Cited

Binford, Lewis R.
  1962 Archaeology as Anthropology. *American Antiquity* 9:208–219.
  1977 Historical Archaeology: Is It Historical or Archaeological? *In* Historical Archaeology and the Importance of Material Things. *Society for Historical Archaeology, Special Publications* 2:13–77.
  1978 *Nunamiut Ethnoarchaeology.* Academic Press, New York.
  1981 *Bones: Ancient Men and Modern Myths.* Academic Press, New York.
  1982 The Archaeology of Place. *Journal of Anthropological Archaeology* 1:5–31.
  1983a *Working at Archaeology.* Academic Press, New York.
  1983b *In Pursuit of the Past: Decoding the Archaeological Record.* Thames and Hudson, London and New York.

1983c Working at Archaeology: The Generation Gap—Reactionary Arguments and Theory Building. In *Working at Archaeology* by Lewis R. Binford, pages 213–227. Academic Press, New York.

Binford, Lewis R., and Jeremy Sabloff
1982 Paradigms, Systematics, and Archaeology. *Journal of Anthropological Research* 38:137–153.

Browman, David L.
1981 Isotopic Discrimination and Correction Factors in Radiocarbon Dating. In *Advances in Archaeological Method and Theory*, edited by Michael B. Schiffer 4:241–295.

Butzer, Karl
1982 *Archaeology as Human Ecology*. Cambridge University Press, Cambridge, England.

Clarke, David
1973 Archaeology: The Loss of Innocence. *Antiquity* 47:6–18.

Conkey, Margaret, and Janet Spector
1984 Archaeology and the Study of Gender. In *Advances in Archaeological Method and Theory*, edited by Michael B. Schiffer, 7:1–38.

DeBoer, Warren R., and Donald W. Lathrap
1979 The Making and Breaking of Shipibo-Conibo Ceramics. In *Ethnoarchaeology: Implications of Ethnography for Archaeology*, edited by Carol Kramer, pages 102–138. Columbia University Press, New York.

Dunnell, Robert C.
1971 *Systematics in Prehistory*. The Free Press, New York.
1978a Archaeological Potential of Anthropological and Scientific Models of Function. In *Archaeological Essays in Honor of Irving B. Rouse*, edited by R. Dunnell and E. Hall, Jr., pages 41–73. Mouton, The Hague.
1978b Style and Function: A Fundamental Dichotomy. *American Antiquity* 43:192–202.
1980 Evolutionary Theory and Archaeology. In *Advances in Archaeological Method and Theory*, edited by Michael B. Schiffer, 3:35–99.
1984 The Americanist Literature for 1983: A Year of Contrasts and Challenges. *American Journal of Archaeology* 88:489–513.

Farquhar, Ronald M., and Ian R. Fletcher
1984 The Provenience of Galena from Archaic/Woodland Sites in Northeastern North America: Lead Isotope Evidence. *American Antiquity* 49:774–785.

Flannery, Kent
1982 The Golden Marshalltown: A Parable for the Archaeology of the 1980s. *American Anthropologist* 84:265–278.

Gero, Joan
1985 Socio-Politics and the Woman-at-Home Ideology. *American Antiquity* 50:342–350.

Gould, Richard A.
1980 *Living Archaeology*. Cambridge University Press, Cambridge, England.

Hall, Martin
  1984   The Burden of Tribalism: The Social Context of South African Iron Age
         Studies. *American Antiquity* 49:455–467.

Hall, Robert L.
  1977   An Anthropocentric Perspective for Eastern United States Prehistory.
         American Antiquity 42:499–518.

Hayden, Brian, and Aubrey Cannon
  1984   The Structure of Material Systems: Ethnoarchaeology in the Maya
         Highlands. *Society for American Archaeology Papers* 3. Washington,
         D.C.

Hodder, Ian
  1982a *Symbols in Action*. Cambridge University Press, London.
  1982b *The Present Past*. Pica Press, New York.

Jochim, Michael
  1983   Optimization Models in Context. In *Archaeological Hammers and
         Theories*, edited by J. Moore and A. Keene, pages 157–172. Academic
         Press, New York.

Johnson, Gregory
  1977   Aspects of Regional Analysis in Archaeology. *Annual Review of An-
         thropology* 6:479–503.

Kelley, Jane, and Marsha P. Hanen
  In press *Archaeology and the Methodology of Science*. Academic Press, To-
            ronto.

Kennedy, Mary C.
  1979   Status, Role, and Gender: Preconceptions in Archaeology. Manuscript
         on file, Department of Anthropology, University of Minnesota, Min-
         neapolis.

Kent, Susan
  1984   *Analyzing Activity Areas: An Ethnoarchaeological Study of the Use of
         Space*. University of New Mexico Press, Albuquerque.

Leone, Mark P.
  1973   Archaeology as the Science of Technology: Mormon Town Plans and
         Fences. In *Research and Theory in Current Archaeology*, edited by
         Charles L. Redman, pages 125–150. Wiley, New York.
  1981a The Relationship between Artifacts and the Public in Outdoor History
         Museums. *Annals of the New York Academy of Sciences* 376:301–314.
  1981b Archaeology's Relationship to the Present and the Past. In *Modern Ma-
         terial Culture: The Archaeology of Us*, edited by R. Gould and M.
         Schiffer, pages 5–14. Academic Press, New York.

Marquardt, William H.
  1985   Complexity and Scale in the Study of Fisher-Gatherer-Hunters: An Ex-
         ample from the Eastern United States. In *Prehistoric Hunter-Gatherers:
         The Emergence of Cultural Complexity*, edited by T. Douglas Price and
         James A. Brown, pages 59–98. Academic Press, New York.

Pinsky, Valerie, and M. Allison Wylie, (editors)
  In prep. Critical Traditions in Contemporary Archaeology.

Rathje, William L.
  1978   Archaeological Ethnography . . . Because Sometimes It Is Better to Give Than To Receive. In *Explorations in Ethnoarchaeology,* edited by Richard Gould, pages 49–75. University of New Mexico Press, Albuquerque.
  1981   A Manifesto for Modern Material Culture Studies. In *Modern Material Culture: The Archaeology of Us,* edited by R. Gould and M. Schiffer, pages 51–56. Academic Press, New York.

Renfrew, Colin
  1982   Explanation Revisited. In *Theory and Explanation in Archaeology,* edited by Colin Renfrew, Michael Rowlands, and Barbara Segraves, pages 5–23. Academic Press, New York.

Roe, Derek
  1984   Advancing the Study of Early Man in East Africa. *Quarterly Review of Archaeology* 5:3–4.

Runnels, Curtis N.
  1981   A Diachronic Study and Economic Analysis of Millstones from the Argolid, Greece. Doctoral dissertation, Indiana University, Bloomington.

Sabloff, Jeremy A. (editor)
  1981   *Simulations in Archaeology.* University of New Mexico Press, Albuquerque.

Salmon, Merrilee
  1976   "Deductive" versus "Inductive" Archaeology. *American Antiquity* 41:376–381.
  1982   *Philosophy and Archaeology.* Academic Press, New York.

Schiffer, Michael B.
  1981   Some Issues in the Philosophy of Archaeology. *American Antiquity* 46:899–908.

Society for American Archaeology
  1974   *Program and Abstracts, Thirty-ninth Annual Meeting of the Society for American Archaeology, Washington, D.C., May 2–4, 1974.* 62 pages.
  1982   *Program and Abstracts, Forty-seventh Annual Meeting of the Society for American Archaeology, Minneapolis, Minnesota, April 14–17, 1982.* 97 pages.
  1983   *Program and Abstracts, Forty-eighth Annual Meeting of the Society for American Archaeology, Pittsburgh, Pennsylvania, April 27–30, 1983.* 120 pages.
  1984   *Program and Abstracts, Forty-ninth Annual Meeting of the Society for American Archaeology, Portland, Oregon, April 11–14, 1984.* 110 pages.

Stein, Julie K.
  1983   Earthworm Activity: A Source of Potential Disturbance of Archaeological Sediments. *American Antiquity* 48:277–289.

Stein, Julie K., and William Farrand (editors)
  1985   *Archaeological Sediments in Contexts.* Center for the Study of Early Man, Institute for Quaternary Studies, University of Maine, Orono.

Taylor, Walter
  1948 A Study of Archaeology. *American Anthropological Association Memoir 69.*

Tilley, Christopher
  In prep. Archaeology as Socio-political Action in the Present. In Critical Traditions in Contemporary Archaeology, edited by Valerie Pinsky and M. Alison Wylie.

Trigger, Bruce
  1984 Archaeology at the Crossroads: What's New? *Annual Review of Anthropology, 1984* 13:275–300.

Watson, Patty Jo
  1982 EA to AE: Coming of Age in Americanist Archaeology. Paper read at the 48th Annual Meeting of the Society for American Archaeology, Pittsburgh.

Watson, Patty Jo, Steven A. LeBlanc, and Charles L. Redman
  1971 *Explanation in Archaeology: An Explicitly Scientific Approach.* Columbia University Press, New York.
  1984 *Archeological Explanation: The Scientific Method in Archeology.* Columbia University Press, New York.

Wylie, M. Alison
  1981 Positivism and the New Archaeology. Doctoral dissertation, State University of New York, Binghamton.
  1982 The Prospects for Philosophical Analysis in Archaeology. Paper read at the 48th Annual Meeting of the Society for American Archaeology, Pittsburgh.
  1985a Between Philosophy and Archaeology. *American Antiquity* 50:478–490.
  1985b The Reaction Against Analogy. In *Advances in Archaeological Method and Theory,* edited by Michael B. Schiffer, 8:63–111. Academic Press, New York.
  In prep. The Dilemma of Interpretation. In Critical Traditions in Contemporary Archaeology, edited by Valerie Pinsky and M. Alison Wylie.

In Pursuit of the Future

Background

In the late 1950s and early 1960s a number of us advocated some fundamental changes in the way archaeologists viewed the archaeological record and particularly in the conventions then current for assigning meaning to archaeological facts. Subsequently, there have been major changes in the ways archaeologists approach the archaeological record and, in turn, in the ways in which we seek to justify the meanings we assign to archaeological observations. What I wish to discuss is not what we have done—that is a matter of record and should perhaps more appropriately be discussed by others. Instead, I want to discuss what needs to be done.

Science is a field that is dedicated to addressing our ignorance and, as such, should have built-in tactics designed to guide us to the recognition of ignorance in need of investigation. For the generation of those who were my teachers, recognized ignorance consisted largely of the sites we had not dug or the places and time periods we had not investigated. Ignorance was recognized as primarily arising from a lack of observations or discoveries. I tried to challenge this view of ignorance by pointing out that ignorance must also be recognized in the character of the knowledge and belief base that we use when interpreting our observations.

This challenge arose directly from the implications that the findings of general anthropology have for archaeology. It was difficult to ignore the teachings of anthropology, especially the demonstration that culture, the received knowledge and beliefs that we use in viewing the world, (1) is different among diverse sociocultural systems, and (2) is characterized by different stages during the historical trajectory of a given cultural system. It had to be acknowledged that scientists are not exempt from culture; they, like all other humans, are participants in culture. This means that for science to be truly successful it not only has to acknowledge ignorance about the external world but also to view its task as recognizing ignorance of a particular type, ignorance relative to the culture, the received "knowledge" and beliefs, of the scientists themselves. This is a very different view of science than that which characterized the earlier phases in the development of scientific methods. Under early, strict empiricists' views it was thought that the dedicated scientist could clear his mind of cultural bias and see reality "objectively." Anyone familiar with anthropology cannot accept such a position. We cannot operate as humans outside our cultural milieu.

The task of science is not only to sharpen and hone our culturally conditioned ideas about the external world but, in addition, to investigate the limitations of our received knowledge and beliefs about the external world. In short, the task of science is not the objective approximation of "truth" but just the opposite: the investigation of our culturally guided ignorance about reality. If we accept this goal, and the view that culture is learned, then it is clear that the enhancement of knowledge could modify our culture. If as anthropologically informed scientists we are successful in approaching our goal, then our refinement of knowledge (and thus of culture itself) will enrich our ability for dealing with reality.

How well does our received knowledge allow us to deal with the world of experience? How accurate is our alleged knowledge of the world? If one adopts other perspectives or contrastive means of observation, how different does the world of experience appear? These are the questions and tactics I used in my early papers to question the utility of the traditional archaeological paradigm. I tried to demonstrate that using the normative culture concept as an exclusive explanation for archaeologically observed differences and similarities was inadequate and misleading. I tried to demonstrate that processes and forces other than the mental templates of the ancients conditioned the archaeological record as seen by archaeologists. Once this is recognized, it becomes clear that the archaeological record contains information of relevance to the interesting problem of understanding cultural differences themselves. This was an attempt to enrich our archaeological knowledge. At the same time it was a critical evaluation of the inadequacy of traditional archaeological concept of culture to guide us to an understanding of the past and, more importantly, of cultural processes themselves.

Two Responses to the New Archaeology

The shift from believing in culture as the exclusive explanation for the archaeological record to recognizing that the deposits contain information that will potentially enlighten us as to the very nature of culture itself is described by David Clarke (1973) as our loss of innocence. For many, the state of innocence was a secure one. With the loss of innocence and security, they found themselves in a sea of uncertainty. What do we do? How do we proceed? What is a productive strategy? In this situation many archaeologists began to seek guidance from other fields of investigation; in many cases, this has had enriching consequences. On the other hand, there has grown up within archaeology a number of misguided arguments that many claim are gaining converts among those who will replace the current generation. It is these arguments that I feel are in need of review. If they are not treated seriously, they could well lead archaeology into still another backward and nonproductive era. I will refer to these arguments as (1) reconstructionism and (2) contextual-structuralism. There are many points of disagreement between these two approaches, and while I treat them as intellectually unique, their proponents will surely be offended by my failure to acknowledge many of their detailed claims to distinctiveness.

I consider reconstructionism to be an intellectual legacy of archaic science or strict empiricism. It is an approach with which traditionalists would be quite comfortable. It advocates the position that the growth of knowledge and understanding is exclusively dependent upon building an accurate structure of knowledge about external reality brick by brick. While in a strict sense this is not completely wrong, it is tragically limiting. Its practitioners may acknowledge that we are the ones who think about the world of experience, yet it operationally assumes (as did the archaic scientists) that truth resides in the external world. It assumes that by gaining an accurate understanding of archaeological formation processes—processes that should be clear to the "objective" observer—we can, by force of will, see the archaeological record objectively. Thus, criticism from this point of view frequently takes the form of attempting to point out, by remonstration and cautionary tales, the biases of "this world" that keep the archaeologist from seeing the "true" nature of the archaeological record (see Binford 1983 for a previous statement on this issue).

In addition, reconstructionism tends to be anti-intellectual, in that advocates fail to appreciate the importance of both conceptual growth and change. New ideas that are not perceived as simple, self-evident extensions of "direct-empirical" experience are disparaged (e.g., Schiffer's [1985:192] concept of personal gear and Gould's [1985:640–641] discussion of the same issue). In such discussions the demand is made that the warrant for an idea of potentially great importance must rest with the empirical credentials out of which the reconstructionists expect it to have arisen. Here we see the old, discredited notion that theory and concepts *must* be directly generalized from experience! If one is evaluating and seeking a more useful set of intellectual tools and one demands that all new tools be justified with respect to experiences cognized in a manner consistent with the old tools, then one never changes the paradigm; one only elaborates the old one. New approaches come from new ideas. Their utility must be tested in the future, not by reference to old ideas or to the credentials of their origins.

Nevertheless, at the observational level reconstructionists admonish us to build brick by brick a solid structure of knowledge and understanding about the processes of archaeological formational dynamics, without addressing the important issue of evaluating our archaeological culture or seeking to understand what we want to know in new ways. We are only reminded of alleged biases that could prevent us from seeing "reality" clearly. According to reconstructionist literature, if we would only open our eyes to the lessons of nature through the use of more detailed and rigorous observational strategies, we could empirically understand archaeological formation processes and, therefore, archaeological truth.

I recently read a paper by two behavioral archaeologists who list all the "distorting" events that might stand between the archaeological record as observed and the systemic context as it might have existed in a past system. The paper is supposed to be an object lesson to archaeologists who would seek to make statements about past systems before they had recognized and correctively "transformed" all the behavioral events that intervened to render the organization of the archaeological record different from the organization of on-going life as it existed in the past. The old empiricists' argument regarding the limitations of the archaeological record is central to these positions. The distortions, and the reality that all events are not equally visible archaeologically, are boringly repeated to caution archaeologists not to think beyond their data (Gould 1980:1–28, 1985; Schiffer 1985:192). The message is clear. We must build up generalizations about past systemic contexts by the laborious "transformation" of contemporary data in its archaeological context into descriptive statements about past behavior. This reconstructionist process assumes that the inferential target is the on-going behavioral events of the once-living individuals who participated in the community responsible for the archaeological remains. Presumably, if we could accomplish this we could then participate as peers with ethnologists in their discussions of behavioral variability.

In the early days of the new archaeology a number of arguments were mounted to demonstrate that cultural systems were internally differentiated and, as such, could be expected to result in the differential spatial partitioning of distinctive cultural remains within and among sites. If true, this ontological assertion about the world would devastate the ways in which traditional archaeologists sampled the archaeological record and would successfully challenge the basic assumptions underlying their interpretive arguments. If these new arguments were accurate, it would no longer be possible to consider measured differences among casually collected archaeological samples as direct measures of cultural differentiation at the ethnic level of organization. These arguments called for a restudy of the nature of archaeological reality in order to demonstrate that the archaeological concept of culture was inadequate and thus had a distorting effect on our views of the past.

In this context, it became important to demonstrate that cultural systems were in fact internally differentiated organizationally so that a difference in cultural content could not necessarily be taken as a simple measure of ethnic difference. (This position has been sustained by every major piece of research designed to evaluate it [e.g., Binford 1976, 1978, 1979, 1980, 1982; Hodder 1982b; Longacre 1981; Weissner 1983].) The focus in this intellectual context was to demonstrate that organizational conditions within cultural systems could produce different forms of archaeological remains without implying different cultures at the pansystemic level. There was discussion of the meaning of interassemblage variability, study of the internal differentiation of sites into activity areas, and exploration of social differentiation from the standpoint of status and social groupings within societies that might affect variability in the archaeological record.

This was a testing period, an exploration of the external world for the purpose of evaluating the utility of the assumptions made about that world by traditional archaeologists. It exposed and criticized the degree to which certain conventional interpretive devices were unrealistic or simply wrong. It focused on the world of experience but was guided by new ideas about that world. Instead of viewing this situation as a tactical phase in the growth of a science, the reconstructionists seem to have tossed out the "testing of ideas" aspects and focused on the external world as the direct source of knowledge. They saw knowledge as flowing to us from "discoveries" in the world of experience (Gould 1985). Our ideas were tacitly seen as potential "distortions" of the true reality, a reality that could be known directly through insightful, observational "purification" and accurate measurement. This purification has been extended to include skepticism regarding the "borrowing" of ideas from other fields (Schiffer 1981:901–904), a failure to see value in concept and theory development (Schiffer 1981:905), and, recently, the open advocacy of a return to empiricism (Gould 1985).

The tactical research focus on behavior by new archaeologists, which occurred in the context of idea evaluation, has been strangely misinterpreted as a denial of the importance of culture itself. Some have even advocated the scrapping of the culture concept in favor of a focus on behavior (see Flannery 1982 for a reaction to this trend). For them, the goal of archaeology should be the accurate reconstruction of past dynamics in the proximate or behavioral sense, which will eventually lead to an "ethnographic" picture of the past. The final goal is seen as uncovering, in the empiricist's sense, laws of human behavior. The challenge offered by new archaeologists and the tactics appropriate to that challenge were proposed as an evaluation of the intellectual tools of archaeology and paradigmatic growth. Reconstructionists, however, were led to redirect the goals of archaeological inference (i.e., describing past behaviors particularistically rather than past cultures organizationally) and adopted a reactionary idea of science.

At the same time that reconstructionism was building in the literature, another important and very different reaction to the new archaeology was taking place. This response was guided not from an attempt to return to outdated methods of science, but from what was thought to be a "new" view that challenged the very utility of science itself. I refer to this reaction as contextual-structuralism.

The recognition that we cannot achieve "objectivity" in the manner conceived by archaic scientists became a popular point for endless reiteration. The recognition of the importance of culture, standing as a filter between us and "reality," was emphasized. During the era of the growth of the new archaeology the writings of Thomas Kuhn (1970) were read widely by the new generation of archaeologists. Kuhn makes important points regarding objectivity that are directed toward philosophers of science. When read from a nonscientific perspective, however, these arguments appear to cripple the approach to learning that many readers naively believe to be the scientific method: the archaic view of science. The result has been exactly the opposite of the response by the reconstructionists. Where the reconstructionists have adopted a "reactionary" view of science by returning to a strict empiricism, the contextual-structuralists have largely rejected all science. Where some reconstructionists essentially reject the concept of culture, the contextual-structuralists embrace it not only as the explanation for the archaeological record (Hodder 1982a) but the explanation for the behavior of scientists (Landau 1981: Perper and Schrier 1977). They espouse the view that science is incapable of producing knowledge; instead, it is thought to be capable only of projecting subjective, culture-bound views onto the external world. From this perspective the new archaeologists are labeled out-of-date archaic scientist/empiricists or "dirty" positivists, while at the same time the demand is made for a return to the traditional "cultural" approach for the interpretation of archaeological remains. This posture leads to crippling skepticism. It denies that we can evaluate the utility of our own ideas and that we can analytically understand culture; in short, it denies that science can help us to learn.

> We might be able to see the past more clearly if we could distinguish between our misinterpretations and what actually occurred. But realistically, there is no suitable method [Leone and Palkovich 1985:430].

What can we do? Advocates of this position have only nihilistic answers. We should abandon the "tyranny" of scientific methodology in favor of "important" issues of relevance in our own society, since "our research is a result of our social context" (Moore and Keene 1983:4–11). For those of us who are convinced that we can learn from our interaction with experience, these appear to be silly, chauvinistic suggestions. In contending with contextual-structuralism and reconstructionism, archaeology is clearly in an intellectual "double bind."

A Theoretical Response to the Issues

As in many conflicts there are nuggets of truth mixed with misguided thought. For instance, it is quite true that I cannot use knowledge I do not have. It is equally true that I cannot think with ideas I do not have. Thus, the contextual-structuralist argument that we are limited by received knowledge and by the conceptual tools available in our time is demonstrably correct. Demonstrating that the ideas with which we work are consistent with the culture of which we are a part is trivial. Do we really expect scientists to be "outside" their culture? That, of course, is impossible. Pointing such things out, however, does not mean that we are intellectually determined. Just because scientists are culture-bearing animals does not mean that they are intellectually shackled by culture and doomed to the ignorance and subjectivity of their time. Similarly, demonstrating a consistency between what we think at any one time and the broader cultural matrix in which we participate does not provide an evaluation of the utility and accuracy of those ideas, regardless of their origin.

The reconstructionist position contains equally limiting ideas. The most restricting, in my opinion, is the strict empiricist approach to learning. The reconstructionist tendency is to view empirical generalizations as the primary goal of research; to attempt the inductive elevation of such descriptive statements to "lawlike" status; and in turn to believe that this empirically grounded description of the world will somehow allow us to gain an understanding of the world (Raab and Goodyear 1984; Salmon 1982; Schiffer 1976:4; Smith 1982). The positive aspects of this "empirically grounded" posture are that a focus on description can lead to more accurate recording, to the recognition of complexity (such as many of the so-called distortions that may stand between the static record and the dynamics of the past), and to a greater appreciation for the character of the empirical domain that we study: the archaeological record. Accurate description and justified inference are crucial to science, but as Hugh Mellor (1982:60) has pointed out:

> Explanation is not a kind of inference. Just because the phenomenon to be explained would be more safely predictable if it were more probable doesn't mean it would therefore also be better explained.

When the strict empiricist approach to understanding is followed there is a disdain for the use of imagination and for inventive thought, and a cry for grounded empirical relevance for every idea introduced (Gould 1985:641). But the search for understanding—explanation—is an intellectual activity and not strictly a synthesis of observations. Thus, the empiricist approach ensures that understanding will not be forthcoming, only that we will have a more accurate description of the world as it appears when we are guided by our particular cognitive framework. If one accepts this damning criticism of empiricism, then the consequence will be that empiricists in fact only describe the world "subjectively," and the growth of knowledge will be tragically curtailed.

The defenders of empiricism could note with justification that "discoveries" are possible, that we can encounter experiences for which we have no prior cognitive devices for accommodation, and that we can thereby expose the limitations of our ideas. Although this is certainly correct, the presence of anomalies does not ensure their recognition. As most cultural anthropologists would be quick to point out, we have the remarkable capacity to accommodate the world of experience to what we already believe about that world. I would argue that discoveries are not simply the intrusion of the external world on our cognitive framework. Instead, they come about largely from a skeptical posture on the part of the scientists, who search for the inadequacies in their received wisdom and thereby prompt their most valuable asset (their imaginations) to develop and invent new and more appropriate cognitive devices and theories. Such things come from us, not from experience.

The empiricist approach seeks to ground empirically our experiences in conventionally made and synthesized observations. This ensures that we will never see challenges to our conventions. A strict empirical approach tends to reinforce the false view that our contemporary cognitive tools and knowledge are adequate and at the same time suppresses our most valuable asset, our imaginations. The important point here is to have a clear understanding of how we use our experiences. An approach that seeks empirical generalizations demands description in conventional terms. On the other hand, the correct approach to learning is dependent upon the use of experience to expose the limitations of our conventions. As a learning strategy, empiricism is clearly limited.

Although the contextual or structuralist approaches may appear to challenge science itself, many of these positions can be argued in ways that could well contribute to the growth of our science. For instance, strong dedication to the position that we cannot think thoughts that we do not have or use knowledge that is unavailable to us is crucial. Acceptance of this position validates the goals of science as I have presented them, namely, the skeptical mistrust of our own cognitive and theoretical tools and hence the scientists' dedication to the exposure of their limitations. The continuous demonstration of our own culture-bound perspectives clearly falsifies the old claim of "free will" and "objectivity" that plagued both archaic science and traditional attempts to explain human behavior. The limitations of the contextual-structuralist position appear when there is a failure to acknowledge that the enhancement of scientifically guided learning strategies can result in the growth of knowledge.

The anti-science posture derives not from recognizing the role of culture in our daily lives but from the acceptance of a "generative" model of culture change, which is characteristic of the contextual-structuralist position. A generative view assumes that an inner core serves as the organizing feature for surficial behavior or action. This organizing feature is manifest by the actions of participant/actors who are programmed to this core of belief, meaning, or symbolic structure (for a clear example of this view, see Glassie 1975 and Deetz 1982).

As Ernest Gellner (1982:116) has insightfully argued, however,

> the point about the symbol tokens used by systems such as language is that they are cheap. . . . Sounds, marks on the paper, symbolic gestures, all cost virtually nothing. . . . Because this is so, but only because this is so . . . we can expect symbolic systems to play out their full inner potential.

Unfortunately, as Gellner (1982:116) also points out, adherents to this "generative" view fail to appreciate a fundamental point, namely, that

> there are extensive aspects of human life, alas including those that seem essential to survival, whose actual sequence of events is determined not merely by the free play of some underlying core mechanism (if it indeed exists at all), but by the blind constraints and shortages and competitions and pressures of the real extraneous environment.

Generative approaches fail to explain cultural systems because of their stubborn denial that we are dealing with thermodynamic systems, not simply with cost-free symbolic codes. Cultural systems are organizations with essential dynamics that are dependent upon the flow of energy through them. Energy is captured by such systems in nature, not by human participants thinking or codifying costless symbolic dreams about this very concrete materialist process. In turn, the trajectory of a culturally organized thermodynamic system is not determined by what the bearers think about the process. Instead, it is determined by the behavioral and organizational ways in which the system articulates with energy sources and with internal and external competitors. Understanding patterning in the history of past cultural systems derives from an understanding of these processes, not from some imaginative character-ization of a stable and internally closed symbolic system capable only of "acceptable" rearrangement of its finite components. The structuralist position is inappropriate to sociocultural systems, and more importantly, it is wrong.

The falsity of this posture is demonstrable by the fact that a paradox is inherent in its arguments. For instance, we acknowledge, as contextual-structuralists have, that we cannot use ideas we do not have or reason with information we do not possess. The paradox arises when this proposition is linked with the false generative idea of sociocultural dynamics described above. When this is done, it is commonly suggested that we cannot know the past except by seeking to understand the par-ticular symbolic codes or systems of thought held by ancient peoples. We might reasonably ask, how would this aid us if those ancient peoples, like us, could neither think ideas they did not have nor accumulate knowledge relevant to questions they never asked? For example, from my retrospective viewpoint as an archaeologist I might reasonably ask, what caused the transition from Middle to Upper Paleolithic? If I could magically go back in time for an ethnographic interview with a popula-tion of late Neanderthals, I would most certainly find that (1) they would not know that they were living during such a transition, and (2) they would have little if any awareness that major processes both condition their lives and at the same time move the trajectory of their culture his-tory in the direction of a way of life unknown or unimaginable to them.

How can the thoughts, beliefs, or opinions of the participants in ancient cultural systems aid me in solving a problem that arises from a totally different perspective—a perspective that the ancients could nei-ther experience nor reason about with knowledge they did not have? No Neanderthal would or could provide realistic solutions to problems posed by me, problems arising in the context of my vastly different per-spective, knowledge base, and temporal viewpoint. As a modern archae-ologist I have the wonderful opportunity to know something of the past on a temporal scale virtually invisible to participants in any intellectually unspecialized cultural system. Similarly, from the perspective of past par-ticipants I can know something of their future in ways unimaginable to them. I can quite literally gain insights into an order of reality that was unknown to participants in ancient cultural systems. Demanding that I adopt a participant's perspective (see Binford and Sabloff 1982 for a dis-cussion of this issue) as the only reality makes about as much sense as demanding that we not look through microscopes, since the "true" reality is that which is available only to the naked eye! Archaeology is not served by acceptance of a false ontological assumption.

We cannot understand the past through the eyes of the ancients. Similarly, we cannot know the past or the present by simply accepting one form of subjective view as correct on the basis of asserted privileged insight (e.g., binary oppositions). We must seek to know the past accurately through, and not in spite of, the use of our perspective. It follows that we must accept responsibility for the character of the intellectual tools we use, and we must continuously seek to improve and modify them in terms of the knowledge available to us and the opportunities for learning open to us. At the same time we accept this responsibility, we must realize that both our knowledge base and the conceptual tools with which we approach the archaeological record may be limited and/or inappropriate. As suggested earlier, our job is quite literally the evaluation of our own cultural tools—the tools that we use in seeking to describe and understand the external world, which for us is simply the archaeological record.

Most contemporary archaeologists, except the strict empiricists, acknowledge that we cannot know reality in terms of itself, but only through the cognitive and explanatory devices that we use. We further acknowledge that these devices may be wrong and are part of a broader tradition of received "knowledge" within which we participate (in other words, our own culture). Many may reasonably ask, how can we know the past? Frequently, the answer is that we cannot. We should, therefore, abandon our self-deceiving exercises and address ourselves to a critical understanding of our own culture-bound ideas from the perspective of internal criticism, since the external world is thought to be denied us by virtue of our subjectivity (see Hodder 1984).

This position has been well stated by Mary Hesse. She concludes that we must adopt a position denying "that there is a fundamental distinction between theoretical and observation predicates and statements" (Hesse 1974:33). The nature of the external world is denied to us by virtue of the assumed fact that our cognitive system molds experience so that the external world is not permitted to intrude on its internal integrity. At first blush this sounds reasonable; it even appears consistent with many of the points I have advocated here. In addition, on one level it is good advice. Certainly, the more aware we are of the context of our ideas, the less likely we would be to accept such received ideas as "true" (Leone 1982). In denying a scientific method for evaluating ideas, however, the position moves so as to transform archaeology into moral philosophy.

We can accept the fact that we can neither reason with knowledge we do not have nor think with cognitive devices unknown to us, and we can also acknowledge the fact that we commonly accommodate the world of experience to our own belief system of the moment. We can support the view that an awareness of how our ideas of the moment came into being could constructively sharpen our skepticism. We can subscribe to the position that we should be both moral and ethical in our search for knowledge. We may subscribe to the view that our choices of research problems should be sensitive to the needs for knowledge within our own society. None of these positions, however, demands that we deny our ability to learn and in turn to modify the limiting effects that our culture places on our understanding of external reality.

A Practical Response to the Issues

Science is a strategy for learning. What scientists hope to accomplish is to perfect ways of seeking experiences in the external world so that they will implicate inadequacies in our alleged knowledge. Put another way, scientists study the accuracy and reliability of their alleged knowledge by seeking experiences designed to expose limitations in the body of ideas and beliefs with which they begin their quest. They seek to put their ideas in jeopardy, not to make them more secure, as a creationist might be prone to do. Science is not dedicated to the discovery of "truth" or to the demonstration that a given body of ideas is "right."

These ideas constituted the central thrust of the new archaeology. It advocated attention to the procedure that seeks to transform ignorance into knowledge. The important issues to be addressed are whether we can learn and, if we can, how we learn. We do not learn by falsely deceiving ourselves into thinking that we can purge ourselves of ignorance and "objectively" approach nature for instruction. Similarly, we do not learn by denying that learning is possible. Finally, we do not learn by editing an alleged past to serve as justification for adopting a particular value-laden political or moral posture in the present. We learn by exploring learning strategies, by experimenting with scientific methods that continuously place our ideas in jeopardy relative to the world of experience.

There was a past, and there is an archaeological record that was created in the past. Although we may be capable of fooling ourselves for a time about both of these realities, a learning procedure that continuously compares our ideas with our experiences cannot help but reveal situations in which our ideas are inadequate. In short, ambiguities deriving from inadequacies in our cognitive and intellectual tools will be exposed. I am suggesting that, like sociocultural systems, intellectual systems can also be open systems, although at times they may appear to be closed and internally "generative." This is particularly true for archaeologists, since the target of our search for knowledge no longer exists. The past cannot speak back or object; in short, there is little cost and hence little risk of being wrong that does not derive from our own competitive social matrix. The openness of our intellectual structure must be provided by our methods and procedures. We must ensure that the past "gets a say," that it can object and guide our growth toward understanding.

The opportunity that opens this important door, that gives the past a chance to object, occurs when ambiguity arises in our own thoughts relative to external experiences we have had. Ambiguity exists relative to some experience when two or more lines of reasoning would lead us to two or more incompatible conclusions. In this situation we are in a deductive posture aimed at evaluating our ideas. (This is quite different from Gould's [1985] demand for inductive justification for ideas.) In such a situation we can be sure that there are inadequacies in one or more of our lines of reasoning. This is the flag, the signal, that we must examine in detail. When this signal is given we must research both our intellectual tools and the cognitive tools with which we assimilate experiences (Binford in press). At the same time we must use our most powerful tool, our imagination, to generate new cognitive devices and intellectual tools that will resolve the ambiguity. This is how we learn and how we grow: by placing our intellectual tools in interaction with one another in the context of experience.

Given such a posture, what realities do we address? Where do we seek experience? I have already suggested that archaeology is the science of the archaeological record. Pessimists, and particularly empiricists, endlessly point to aspects of the past about which we cannot learn, even given our increasing ability to understand the archaeological record and the conditions in the past that brought it into being. This pessimistic attitude is incorrect; we will not know what these limitations on understanding the past might be until we completely understand all facets of the archaeological record, a condition that we have not yet achieved. On the other hand, optimists commonly identify goals for learning that do not derive from an understanding of the archaeological record but arise instead from their limited experiences and from the political/moral biases of our contemporary world.

Pessimists decry attempts to develop learning strategies regarding aspects of the past for which they see no concrete, "empirical" remnants in the archaeological record, but they fail to realize that all statements about the past are inferences. On the other hand, optimists seek to learn things for which there are no understood methods for knowing. The pessimistic situation results in dull description of the archaeological record in contemporary terms, while the overly optimistic situation results in wild, speculative, just-so stories. Archaeologists must face the fact that they do not study the past, they create it. What they study is the archaeological record. The created past is only as correct as the understanding of the properties of the archaeological record, and the processes that brought those properties into being. The development of theoretically guided middle-range research is the key to the inferential problem.

Another problem concerns the distinction between the aspects of the past we seek to know and the aspects of past reality that the archaeological record indicates. Some would say that the archaeological record is the simple result of human actions, that is, human behavior as we understand it, given our perspective as participants in a cultural system. Others, as discussed above, assert that the archaeological record is a manifestation of a core ideational structure insulated from the energetic world of life and changing only through the free, creative actions of individuals (Leaf 1979:336). Still others suggest that it is a distorted, fragmented, limited record of *the* past, as if there had been only one past reality. From an ontological standpoint I would like to suggest that all these views are inaccurate. I have already suggested that the archaeologist can know something of both the past and the future of a past cultural manifestation, knowledge that was denied the participants. Clearly, then, the archaeological record presents us with information vastly different from that which was available to the participants within past systems. In turn, the type of information that is available must guide what we seek to know of the past.

The archaeological record also demonstrates temporal durations or a tempo of chronological change that is very different from that perceived by persons who participated in it. The rates of culture change for most archaeologically known eras are much slower than the rates of generational replacement for participants in those systems. This fact must be appreciated in two ways. First, the beliefs and perceptions of the past participants could not have been germane to a reality of which they could not have been aware, the macrotemporal scale of systems change and the factors that were conditioning it. Second, the observations by ethnographers and historical figures, while perhaps documenting something of the internal dynamics of cultural systems, cannot be expected to be necessarily germane to an understanding of a much slower and larger-scale process of change and modification. Thus, the reality with which we deal is one that living, breathing persons have in fact never directly experienced. It is true that their cumulative participation provides the energy base upon which the macroforces of change operate; yet they never experienced such impersonal forces. The archaeologist, seated in the present, is outside history in the participant sense. We have a chance to understand humankind in a way that no participant, or no social scientist addressing the quick-time events of direct social experience, could ever imagine. To fail to recognize this potential, to fail to grasp a new understanding of humankind from this different perspective—the perspective of the macroforces that condition and modify lifeways in contexts unappreciated by the participants within complex thermodynamic systems—is quite literally to "abandon our birthright."

It is true that archaeology is anthropology in that it seeks to understand humankind. Yet it is simply wrong to attempt to force our unique data and our ability to appreciate dynamics on a macroscale, in the organizational sense of the term, into the limiting experiences and frameworks developed for treating the quick-time events of the human participants in history. We are not ethnographers of the past, we are not sociologists, we are not historians in the humanistic sense of the term; we are scientists dedicated to an understanding of the archaeological record. Its patterning and character strongly suggests that the common social science perspectives on humankind are inappropriate to our archaeological view of humanity. Although we may, in Pompeii-like situations, sometimes reconstruct quick-time events and situations, it is equally true that we have the opportunity to view these human-scale events simultaneously in terms of other observational properties indicative of the organizational contexts in which they were conducted. In this opportunity we can learn something of the properties of the systems within which past persons participated but did not necessarily cognize.

For a long time archaeologists have had an inferiority complex relative to ethnologists and cultural anthropologists. We were convinced that the participant perspective and its personalized scale of experience was the only reality. The archaeological record was viewed as a poor, distorted reflection of this assumed unitary reality. Surely we need to develop links between the varying scales of perception suggested above; but more importantly we must realize that we have the opportunity to study scales of reality that are experientially denied to the ethnographer. The appropriate action for us is not to lament the "limitations" of the archaeological record but to appreciate the limitations of the ethnographic experience and the records and ideas that arise in the ethnographer's brief touch with a circumscribed reality. The archaeological record documents a broader and potentially more fascinating reality.

Conclusion

My message in pursuit of the future has been made up of several components. First, I have argued that cultural systems are not closed ideological structures. They are thermodynamic systems open to influence and even determinancy from the broader thermodynamic forces with which they must articulate. Second, I have suggested that since there is an external world our scientific culture need not be viewed as a closed system that is subject only to internal generative types of change. We as scientists have the opportunity to learn by placing our received and subjective views of the world in jeopardy, by seeking experiences in the external world that are designed to expose the limitations of our ideas. Finally, I have suggested that the particular experiential domain that archaeologists study, the archaeological record, documents a scale and domain of process that was operative in the past and undoubtedly continues to operate today, but because of our limited life span and knowledge this process is generally not appreciated by participants.

Archaeologists are faced with the challenging task of seeking to understand at least two kinds of phenomena that none of us have ever experienced directly: the past itself and, more important, the long-term macroprocesses that the archaeological record documents. Archaeologists have the opportunity to gain an understanding of humankind and its transformations not previously appreciated by most social scientists.

I think it is fair to say that most practicing archaeologists see themselves as strict empiricists at the level of "dirt archaeology" and relegate the fundamental debates regarding methods for inference to an independent domain of theoretical discussion that is considered to be largely irrelevant to their day-to-day activities. This response stems from the fact that at least one of the messages central to the "new archaeology" has not been received: namely, the view that our ideas directly condition how we meaningfully organize and assimilate experience at the very point of observation. On the other hand, unquestioning acceptance of this same proposition has led to the belief that we cannot learn from experience; hence, nihilism and skepticism permeate many "theoretical discussions." In turn, the "dirt archaeologists," correctly convinced that they can learn from experience, relegate such discussions to the stratosphere of speculative, irrelevant side issues. Many return to the sterile posture of particularism, as exemplified by traditional culture-historical approaches, even though this posture has long since been demonstrated to be inadequate. Our success in the future depends upon our thoughtful attention to this impasse.

I suggest that there are solutions. I also believe that our future depends not only upon our successful response to the "dirt archaeologist's" view of the problem but upon a shift in the character of archaeological education as well. If the young persons entering our field are not educated to the character of the very real intellectual issues that archaeologists must solve, and if education continues to be in the hands of "dirt archaeologists" who largely do not understand the nature of our intellectual problems, archaeology will stagnate in the dead end of strict empiricism and particularism. On the other hand, if theoretical discussion remains in the hands of those who are skeptical about our abilities to learn, "dirt archaeologists" are correct in rejecting theory as being irrelevant.

In my opinion, many of our problems stem from adopting the arguments of ethnologists as if they somehow had a more "direct" understanding of reality. Similarly, the skeptical attitude of many "dirt archaeologists" regarding theory is probably rooted in a realistic appreciation of what the archaeological record is. It is not the same reality that ethnologists study. We need to devote our energies to the development of archaeological science, which means the building of theory appropriate to our world of experience as guided by scientifically rooted learning strategies.

In the future we must pursue increased sophistication in scientific learning strategies, increased dedication to understanding the archaeological record, and importantly, the development of knowledge regarding the operation of processes that transcend the quick-time events and experiences of participants in systems. Pursuit of these goals will realize for us a potential understanding of humankind that is uniquely offered to archaeologists.

Literature Cited

Binford, L. R.
  1976   Forty-seven Trips: A Case Study in the Character of Some Formation Processes of the Archaeological Record. *In* Contributions to Anthropology: the Interior Peoples of Northern Alaska, edited by Edwin S. Hall. *National Museum of Man, Mercury Series* 49:299–351. Ottawa.
  1978   *Nunamiut Ethnoarchaeology.* Academic Press, New York.
  1979   Organization and Formation Processes: Looking at Curated Technologies. *Journal of Anthropological Research* 35:255–273.
  1980   Willow Smoke and Dogs' Tails: Hunter-Gatherer Settlement Systems and Archaeological Site Formation. *American Antiquity* 45:4–20.
  1982   Objectivity-Explanation-Archaeology-1981. In *Theory and Explanation in Archaeology,* edited by C. Renfrew, M. J. Rowlands, and B. A. Seagraves, pages 125–138. Academic Press, London.
  1983   Reply to "More on the Mousterian: Flaked Bone from Cueva Morin" by L. Freeman. *Current Anthropology* 24:372–377.
  In press   Researching Ambiguity: Frames of Reference and Site Structure. In *Method and Theory for Activity Area Research,* edited by Sue Kent. Columbia University Press, New York.

Binford, L. R., and J. Sabloff
  1982   Paradigms, Systematics, and Archaeology. *Journal of Anthropological Research* 38:137–153.

Binford, S. R., and L. R. Binford (editors)
  1968   *New Perspectives in Archaeology.* Aldine Press, Chicago.

Clarke, D. I.
  1973   Archaeology: The Loss of Innocence. *Antiquity* 47(1):6–18.

Deetz, J. F.
  1982   Households: A Structural Key to Archaeological Explanation. *American Behavioral Scientist* 25(6):717–724.

Flannery, K. V.
  1982   The Golden Marshalltown: A Parable for the Archeology of the 1980s. *American Anthropologist* 84:265–278.

Gellner, E.
  1982   What is Structuralism? In *Theory and Explanation in Archaeology,* edited by C. Renfrew, M. J. Rowlands, and B. Abbott-Segraves, pages 97–123. Academic Press, London.

Glassie, H.
  1975   *Folk Housing in Middle Virginia.* University of Tennessee Press, Knoxville.

Gould, R. A.
  1980   *Living Archaeology.* Cambridge University Press, New York.
  1985   The Empiricist Strikes Back: A Reply to Binford. *American Antiquity* 50:638–644.

Hesse, M. B.
  1974   *The Structure of Scientific Inference.* MacMillan, London.

Hodder, I.
  1981   Towards a Mature Archaeology. In *Pattern of the Past,* edited by I.
         Hodder, G. Isaac, and N. Hammond, pages 1–13. Cambridge University Press, London.
  1982a *Symbols in Action: Ethnoarchaeological Studies of Material Culture.*
         Cambridge University Press, Cambridge.
  1982b *The Present Past—An Introduction to Anthropology for Archaeologists.* Pica Press, New York.
  1984   Archaeology in 1984. *Antiquity* 58(1):25–32.

Kuhn, T.
  1970   *The Structure of Scientific Revolutions.* 2nd edition. University of Chicago Press, Chicago.

Landau, M.
  1981   *The Anthropogenic: Paleoanthropological Writing as a Genre of Literature.* Doctoral dissertation, Department of Anthropology, Yale University, New Haven.

Leaf, M.
  1979   *Man, Mind, and Science.* Columbia University Press, New York.

Leone, M. P.
  1982   Some Opinions about Recovering Mind. *American Antiquity* 47:742–760.

Leone, M. P., and A. M. Palkovich
  1985   Ethnographic Inference and Analogy in Analyzing Prehistoric Diets. In
         The Analysis of Prehistoric Diets, edited by R. I. Gilbert and J. H.
         Mielke, pages 423–431. Academic Press, New York.

Longacre, W.
  1981   Kalinga Pottery: An Ethnoarchaeological Study. In *Pattern of the Past,*
         edited by I. Hodder, G. Isaac, and N. Hammond, pages 49–66. Cambridge University Press, London.

Mellor, D. H.
  1982   Probabilities for Explanation. In *Theory and Explanation in Archaeology,* edited by C. Renfrew, M. J. Rowlands, and B. Abbott-Segraves,
         pages 57–63. Academic Press, London.

Moore, J. A., and A. S. Keene
  1983   Archaeology and the Law of the Hammer. In *Archaeological Hammers
         and Theories,* edited by J. A. Moore and A. S. Keene, pages 3–13. Academic Press, New York.

Perper, T., and C. Schrier
  1977   The Nimrod Connection: Myth and Science in the Hunting Model. In
         The Chemical Senses and Nutrition, edited by M. Kare and O. Maller,
         pages 447–459. Academic Press, New York.

Raab, L. M., and A. C. Goodyear
  1984   Middle Range Theory in Archaeology: A Critical Review of Origins
         and Applications. *American Antiquity* 49:255–268.

Salmon, M. H.
  1982   Models of Explanation: Two Views. In *Theory and Explanation in Archaeology,* edited by C. Renfrew, M. J. Rowlands, and B. Abbott-
         Segraves, pages 35–44. Academic Press, London.

Schiffer, M. B.
  1976   *Behavioral Archaeology*. Academic Press, New York.
  1981   Some Issues in the Philosophy of Archaeology. *American Antiquity* 46:899–908.
  1985   Review of "Working at Archaeology" by L. R. Binford. *American Antiquity* 50:191–193.

Smith, B.
  1982   Explanation in Archaeology. In *Theory and Explanation in Archaeology*, edited by C. Renfrew, M. J. Rowlands, and B. Abbott-Segraves, pages 73–82. Academic Press, London.

Weissner, P.
  1983   Style and Social Information in Kalahari San Projectile Points. *American Antiquity* 48:253–276.

SCHOOLCRAFT
COLLEGE LIBRARY